HUMAN RIGHTS: A EUROPEAN PERSPECTIVE

Liz Heffernan, Editor

HUMAN RIGHTS
A European Perspective

LIZ HEFFERNAN, EDITOR

with

JAMES KINGSTON

with a foreword by

MARY ROBINSON

President of Ireland

THE ROUND HALL PRESS

in association with

IRISH CENTRE FOR EUROPEAN LAW

This book was typeset
in 11 on 13 Ehrhardt for
THE ROUND HALL PRESS
Kill Lane, Blackrock, Co. Dublin, Ireland,
and in North America
THE ROUND HALL PRESS
c/o International Specialized Book Services,
5804 NE Hassalo Street, Portland, OR 97213.

A catalogue record for this title
is available from the British Library.

ISBN 1–85800–033–5
ISBN 1–85800–023–8–pbk

The publication of this book has been
assisted by a Human Rights Grant
from the Council of Europe.

Printed in Ireland by
Colour Books Ltd, Dublin

FOREWORD

MARY ROBINSON

It gives me particular pleasure to be associated with this book since it gathers together, and puts at the disposal of its readers, a valuable and painstaking perspective on a vital issue. In providing this public service, in putting together a database and focus for future debate on human rights issues, the Irish Centre for European Law has lived up to the hopes of its founders.

I am proud to have been one of them. I remember the surprise I felt in 1988, when seeking to set up the Centre, at the immediate and positive response to its establishment. On reflection, it was quite obvious then that there was a real need to promote research and analysis of the legal issues arising from Ireland's membership of the Council of Europe and the European Community. There was a keen recognition of that fact in the University and, of course, particularly in the Law School.

Part of this recognition included a timely sense that what was required was an applied approach to these issues, and not just an academic one. There was a sense that practical consequences needed analysis. The legal issues involved in this initiative were ones which had a broad impact on the commercial, agricultural and social life of a vibrant and contemporary Ireland. And so the format which was devised—of a centre based on individual and corporate membership, with an independent Board and its own relationship with the University—allowed the close links to be formed with all the sectors concerned, including Government departments and other State bodies.

From the very start the Centre sought to develop and disseminate expert analysis on a broad range of European issues as they affected different areas of Irish life, and with a success which can justly be measured by this sourcebook. Because, of all the issues which the Centre was involved with, the most fundamental was certainly the theme of this book: human rights. And so it was appropriate that the ICEL would organize a series of public lectures in 1992, given by distinguished Irish and European contributors, which dealt with aspects of human rights in Europe and related them to the Irish context.

The result is this sourcebook. It fills a need, almost amounting to a hunger, for information about human rights. And just as the need for that knowledge is not confined to lawyers, so this book does not confine its style to a narrow legal one. It provides information and analysis across a wide range of legal and socio-political issues in a way which can be grasped by lawyers and non-lawyers alike. In this way it achieves what is both rare and necessary. It offers information and access at the same time, and on issues which concern every one of us.

CONTENTS

PREFACE

This book has its origins in an eight-week lecture series on Human Rights in Europe convened by the Irish Centre for European Law, Trinity College Dublin, in association with the Irish Centre for the Study of Human Rights, University College Galway, in 1992. The success of the series was due in no small measure to the efforts of the staff of the Irish Centre for European Law, and Jantien Findlater, in particular. The Centre is also grateful to Tom O'Malley of the Irish Centre for the Study of Human Rights for his assistance in the organisation of the lectures. In addition, I would like to acknowledge the generous contribution of the following individuals who acted as chairpersons or panellists during the lecture series and whose contributions greatly assisted the discussion contained in this book: Mr Joe Costello, TD; Ms Niamh Hyland (Jean Monet Lecture in Law at Trinity College Dublin); Mrs Jane Liddy (Member of the European Commission of Human Rights); Mrs Mary McAleese (Director, Institute of Professional Legal Studies, Queen's University Belfast); Ms Sylvia Meehan (formerly Chief Executive, Employment Equality Agency); and Mr Justice Brian Walsh (Justice of the European Court of Human Rights).

I would like to thank a number of individuals who have provided me with invaluable assistance in the various stages of the preparation of this book: Hilary Delany, Paul Coughlan, Bride Rosney, Caroline Hart and Karen O'Connor. Special thanks are due to Alex Schuster, Director of the Irish Centre for European Law, and Michael Adams of The Round Hall Press. I am very grateful for the generous support of President Mary Robinson in writing the foreword. Equally, I greatly appreciated the contribution, co-operation and encouragement of each of the individual authors. Finally, my thanks to James Kingston for his editorial assistance and to Nuala Jackson for both inspiring and realising idea of the lecture series and of this book.

The Irish Centre for European Law would like to acknowledge the generous contribution by the Council of Europe of a Human Rights Grant in respect of this publication.

Liz Heffernan

3 January 1994

CONTRIBUTORS

KEVIN BOYLE
is a Professor of Law and the Director of the Human Rights Centre at the University of Essex. He was the founding director of Article 19, International Centre Against Censorship.

ALPHA CONNELLY
is a Lecturer at the Faculty of Law and a Member of the Equality Studies Programme at University College Dublin.

TOM COONEY
is a Lecturer in Law at University College Dublin and a Member of the Executive Committee of the Irish Council for Civil Liberties.

KEVIN COSTELLO
is a Lecturer in Law at University College Dublin. He was formerly a Lecturer in Law at University College Galway.

PAUL COUGHLAN
is a practising barrister and a Lecturer in Law at Trinity College Dublin.

MEL COUSINS
is a Barrister-at-Law and a former Administrator of FLAC (Free Legal Advice Centres).

PATRICK DILLON-MALONE
was formerly a Lecturer in Law at University College Galway and is presently working for the Directorate of Legal Affairs of the Council of Europe attached to the Secretariat of the European Commission for Democracy Through Law (Venice Commission).

NOEL DORR
is Secretary of the Department of Foreign Affairs, Dublin. He was formerly Permanent Representative to the United Nations, New York.

WILLIAM DUNCAN
is Professor of Law and Jurisprudence at Trinity College Dublin and a member of the Law Reform Commission of Ireland.

SUSANNE EGAN
is a Lecturer in Law at University College Dublin.

LIZ HEFFERNAN
is a Lecturer in Law at Trinity College Dublin and co-Editor of the Irish Centre for European Law's Bulletin of European Legal Developments.

GERARD HOGAN
is a practising barrister and a Fellow of Trinity College, Dublin.

NUALA JACKSON

is a practising barrister and lecturer in law at University College Galway. She is co–Editor of the Irish Centre for European Law's Bulletin of European Legal Developments.

JAMES KINGSTON

is a Research Officer at the British Institute of International and Comparative Law and a part-time Lecturer in Law at the School of Oriental and African Studies, London.

BARBARA MAGUIRE

is a solicitor with the firm of McCann Fitzgerald and a part-time Lecturer in Law at Trinity College Dublin.

EOIN O'DELL

is a Lecturer in Law at Trinity College Dublin.

PAUL O'HIGGINS

is Vice–Master of Christ's College Cambridge and Honorary Professor of Law at Trinity College Dublin.

TOM O'MALLEY

is a Lecturer in Law at University College Galway. In 1992–93 he was a Visiting Fellow at the University of Oxford's Centre for Criminological Research.

VINCENT POWER

is a solicitor with the firm of A & L Goodbody.

GERARD QUINN

is a Lecturer in Law and the Director of the Irish Centre for the Study of Human Rights, University College Galway.

HENRY SCHERMERS

is Professor of Law at the University of Leiden and a Member of the European Commission of Human Rights.

BILL SHIPSEY

is a practising barrister and a founder of Refugee Legal Advisory Services (RELAS).

GERALDINE VAN BUEREN

is Director of the Programme on International Rights of the Child at the Department of Law, Queen Mary and Westfield College London.

ALAIN VAN HAMME

is a Legal Secretary at the Court of First Instance.

FERDINAND VON PRONDZYNSKI

is Professor of Law and Dean of the Law School, University of Hull. He was formerly a Fellow of Trinity College Dublin.

SEAMUS WOULFE

is a practising barrister and a former part-time Lecturer in Law at Trinity College Dublin.

ABBREVIATIONS

AC	Appeal Cases
ACHPR	African Convention on Human and Peoples' Rights
ACHR	American Convention on Human Rights
AJIL	American Journal of International Law
All ER	All England Law Reports
Am Bar Foundation Res J	American Bar Foundation Research Journal
BYIL	British Yearbook of International Law
Capital U L Rev	Capital University Law Review
CDE	Cahiers de droit éuropeen
CEDAW	Convention on the Elimination of All Forms of Discrimination Against Women
CERD	Convention on the Elimination of All Forms of Racial Discrimination
Ch	Chancery Division
CLJ	Cambridge Law Journal
CMLR	Common Market Law Reports
CML Rev	Common Market Law Review
Col L Rev	Columbia Law Review
CPT	Committee for the Prevention of Torture
CSCE	Conference on Security and Co-operation in Europe
Cyprus L R	Cyprus Law Reports
D & R	Decisions and Reports (European Commission of Human Rights)
DULJ	Dublin University Law Journal
ECJ	European Court of Justice
ECR	European Court Reports
ECHR	European Convention on Human Rights
EEA	European Economic Area
EEC	European Economic Community
EHRR	European Human Rights Reports
EJIL	European Journal of International Law
EPC	European Political Co-operation
ESC	European Social Charter
EU	European Union
Eur L Rev	European Law Review
FAO	Food and Agriculture Organisation of the United Nations
FSR	Fleet Street Reports of Patent Cases
GATT	General Agreement on Tariffs and Trade
HRC	Human Rights Committee
HRLJ	Human Rights Law Journal
HRQ	Human Rights Quarterly
HRR	Human Rights Review
ICCPR	International Covenant on Civil and Political Rights
ICEL	Irish Centre for European Law
ICESCR	International Covenant on Economic, Social and Cultural Rights

ICJ	International Court of Justice
ICJ Rev	International Commission of Jurists Review
ICLQ	International and Comparative Law Quarterly
ICR	Industrial Court Reports
ICRC	International Committee of the Red Cross
IJRL	International Journal of Refugee Law
ILA	International Law Association
ILO	International Labour Organisation
ILM	International Legal Materials
ILRM	Irish Law Reports Monthly
ILT	Irish Law Times
Ind JIL	Indian Journal of International Law
Int'l J Law & Fam	International Journal of Law and the Family
IPR	Intellectual Property Reports
IR	Irish Reports
ISLR	Irish Student Law Review
J Eur Soc Pol	Journal of European Social Policy
JIBFL	Journal of International Banking and Finance Law
JSPTL	Journal of the Society of Public Teachers of Law
JWTL	Journal of World Trade Law
LIEI	Legal Issues of European Integration
LQR	Law Quarterly Review
Mich YB IL Stud	Michigan Yearbook of International Law Studies
MLR	Modern Law Review
NGO	Non-Governmental Organization
NIEO	New International Economic Order
NIJB	Northern Ireland Judgment Bulletin
NLJ	New Law Journal
NZLR	New Zealand Law Reports
OECD	Organisation of Economic Co-operation and Development
PCIJ	Permanent Court of International Justice
QB	Law Reports, Queen's Bench
RPC	Reports of Patent Cases
SCR	Canada Law Reports, Supreme Court
SEA	Single European Act
SJ	Solicitors' Journal
TLR	Times Law Reports
Trocaire Dev Rev	Trocaire Development Review
UDHR	Universal Declaration of Human Rights
UN	United Nations
UNGA	United Nations General Assembly
UNHCR	United Nations High Commissioner for Refugees
U Pa L Rev	University of Pennsylvania Law Review
UNESCO	United Nations Educational, Scientific and Cultural Organisation
Vand JIL	Vanderbilt Journal of International Law
Vict Univ Well L Rev	Victoria University of Wellington Law Review
Virginia JIL	Virginia Journal of International Law
WLR	Weekly Law Reports
WHO	World Health Organisation
YB ECHR	Yearbook of the European Convention on Human Rights
YBEL	Yearbook of European Law

TABLES

CASES

EUROPEAN COURT OF JUSTICE

TREATIES

IRISH CONSTITUTION

LEGISLATION

EUROPEAN COMMUNITY

IRELAND

1 : INTRODUCTION

1.1   Developments since 1945

NOEL DORR

The focus of this paper is on the period since 1945. But to bring out fully the significance of what has happened since the end of the Second World War it is necessary to go back much earlier. At the outset, therefore, I want to look at the origin of our concept of human rights and how human rights came to be a matter of legitimate international concern; I will go on to consider the new international importance which human rights acquired when the United Nations was established at the close of the Second World War, and the network of declarations and conventions at world level which has grown up since then. I will conclude with a brief description of some important developments in the promotion of human rights at regional level in Europe—in particular in the Council of Europe and the Conference on Security and Co-operation in Europe (CSCE).

What are human rights? I do not know of any readily available, succinct and universally accepted, cross-cultural definition of human rights. But I am attracted by the terms in which the distinguished writer Isaiah Berlin describes the growth of the idea of liberty in the 19th century. On this view, he says, it is not enough that liberty "must not be violated unless someone or other—the absolute ruler or the popular Assembly or the King in Parliament or the judges or some combination of authorities or the laws themselves . . . authorises its violation." There must rather be "some frontiers of freedom which nobody should be permitted to cross." Different names or natures may be given to the rules which determine these frontiers: "they may be called natural rights, or the word of God, or Natural Law, or the demands of utility or of the permanent interests of man." But, he says—and it is this that I find particularly helpful:

> what these rules or commandments will have in common is that they are accepted so widely, and are grounded so deeply in the actual nature of men as they have developed through history, as to be, by now, an essential part of what we mean by being a normal human being. (See I. Berlin, *Four Essays on Liberty*, Oxford, 1969, at p. 165.)

1

This is a description rather than a precise definition. What I like about it is that, without denying the idea that certain rights are fundamentally grounded in human nature, it allows scope also for the idea that there has been a growth and development of human nature through history which allows us to speak of certain rights as being "by now, an essential part of what we mean by being a normal human being." This allows also for the possibility that there could be some further development in the future which would add to the range of rights regarded as essential to decent human living.

ORIGIN OF THE CONCEPT

It is, nevertheless, of interest to look at the diverse sources from which, historically, we have derived the belief that each individual human has an intrinsic dignity as a person and certain fundamental rights which may not be curtailed by any State or other authority.

Virtually every human society has had some concept of human worth, of justice, and of meeting obligations. But in most cases these things are seen primarily as part of a network of obligations which maintains a balance and harmony that transcends the individual and relates him or her to the family, the society or the cosmos. Our modern emphasis on the intrinsic fundamental rights of the individual as a person, rights which society must respect and uphold, is largely a western construct. For the Christian who believes in a personal God who created each human person in his or her own image and became incarnate to redeem humanity, it is obvious that each human individual must have a special worth and dignity. This has been indeed a powerful influence on the development of the notion of individual human rights. Other influences which helped to shape our modern concept were Stoic ideas about natural law; Roman law concepts of *ius gentium*; the system of obligations of European feudalism; the growth of European cities with their "liberties"; and, particularly, the strong re-affirmation in the Protestant Reformation of the responsibility of each individual before God. The concept of individual liberty and rights was further articulated by 17th- and 18th-century European philosophers; and it was asserted with powerful rhetoric in such political documents as the American Declaration of Independence and the French Declaration of the Rights of Man—ringing declarations which still echo strongly today.

But the primary focus in these cases was on the assertion of political rights *within* States against arbitrary authority and on the right of rebellion against a king. There was, as yet, no general acceptance of the concept of the rights of each and every human individual as such. Slavery continued in the United States of America; and even in the freest societies, women's rights were very limited indeed. Kant, indeed, was a strong advocate of the view that human persons must always be regarded as ends in themselves and not as means to some other end. But he saw rights within a State as a consequence of its form of government. He believed that the achievement of full rights for the individual would result once the proper form of domestic government—which he believed to be a liberal republic—was adopted.

18TH- AND 19TH-CENTURY VIEW OF INTERNATIONAL RELATIONS

It is of particular interest to note here that human rights as such were not seen at that time as a subject for legitimate international concern, at all—for other States or for international society as a whole. The State was sovereign in its own territory.

This concept of the State as a sovereign entity, established within territorial frontiers and claiming the full allegiance of all its citizens emerged in Europe in the 17th century. It has now become the universal, world-wide form of human social/political organization. In each such State, the government speaks for the State in its relations with other States; international law has evolved as a juridical framework of relations between States.

For theorists of international law, such as Vattel in the 18th century, it was for a government to interpret its obligations in relation to its own citizens or to those present within its territory. Other States had no standing to complain in the absence of some very specific agreement affording protection to aliens. Sometimes, great powers intervened to protect their citizens abroad; and so-called "capitulations" occasionally allowed special status to privileged aliens in weaker States. There were also isolated cases such as the Treaty of Berlin, 1878, under which the great powers of the day exacted a pledge from Bulgaria, Montenegro, Serbia, Romania and Turkey to grant freedom of worship to their nationals; and it is possible to find the beginnings of later international action on human rights in various anti-slavery treaties or treaty provisions of the 19th century. But human rights, as such, were not otherwise seen as a legitimate international concern—although some international lawyers by the end of the 19th century had begun to argue that they *ought* to be.

WORLD WAR I AND THE LEAGUE OF NATIONS

The collapse of the 19th-century European "balance of power system" into the carnage of the First World War gave rise to a great deal of new thinking in the post-war era. The Allies at the Peace Conference and in the Covenant of the League of Nations set themselves the task of developing what would nowadays be called "a new world order" to end conflict. There was a strong sense, on the part of some leaders at least, that the amoral and pragmatic "balance of power system" which had collapsed so disastrously in 1914 must yield to some more principled international system and code of behaviour. This idea was further influenced by memories of propaganda allegations by the Allies against Germany, of atrocities in Belgium, the emphasis on "the rights of small nations", and, above all, the high moral tone of the "Fourteen Points" which US President Woodrow Wilson adopted as US policy for the post-war era.

One consequence of this was that the League Covenant, in setting up the "mandate system" under which territories formerly held by Germany and Turkey were to be prepared for independence, spoke of "a sacred trust". Article 23 of the Covenant which spoke of "labour conditions" and what was called "the traffic of women and children" also showed some concern for human rights. The establishment of the International Labour Office (ILO), with its concern for working conditions, was also of some importance. In the drafting of the League Covenant at the Paris Peace Conference in 1919, however, Japan—the only "non-white" major power at the time—argued valiantly, but unsuccessfully, for the inclusion of a clause on racial equality.

Each of these developments contributed to a growing acceptance of the idea that certain human rights were a matter of legitimate international concern. But the concern at this stage was limited and partial and it related only to particular rights rather than to rights in general. There was still no general concept of an international codification of human rights as such—still less of internationally accepted mechanisms and structures for their implementation.

WORLD WAR II

The decisive event which changed this and led to the development over the past half century of a network of increasingly detailed international instruments, agreements and conventions to protect human rights, was the Second World War. That war quickly took on the form of a crusade against a regime which was not only bent on conquest and domination but which was arguably more intrinsically and objectively evil than any in human history. In reaction, various declarations of war aims by the Allies gave an emphasis to the specific term "human rights". These included US President Roosevelt's call to uphold the "Four Freedoms" in his message to Congress in January 1941, the Atlantic Charter of August 1941 (both before the US entered the War), and the declaration of what had now come to be called the "United Nations" at Washington on 1 January 1942.

It was, however, the revelation in the closing stages of the war of what the Nazis had done in the concentration camps that had the greatest impact. The horror of this gave a new and decisive impetus to the idea of human rights, as such, as a matter of legitimate international concern.

I feel it necessary to dwell for a moment on that horror. We think of the Holocaust—of Auschwitz, Birkenau, Dachau and the other concentration camps—as appalling in that they were places where millions were exterminated. But we need to keep in mind too, not just the general slaughter but the slave labour; the detailed, methodical, brutalization and dehumanization of each individual which those trains and gas ovens involved; and the careful collection of valuables, clothing, human hair and dental fillings which took place. This was more than efficient mass killing—it systematically degraded each individual human being and reduced him or her to the status of an object to be used and discarded.

Can there have been, at any point in history, such an explicit and direct antithesis of the individual dignity and worth of each human person—the concept on which human rights must rest? The Nazi policy was the precise opposite of Kant's injunction to treat every person as an end and not a means. And it came not from barbarism but from the heart of our western civilization; from a culture which had produced Kant himself—and Hegel, Goethe, Beethoven and Mozart.

We have not yet come to terms with this and it is hard to see how we ever will. It has shown us, not what Germans, but what human beings, as such, are capable of. We live now with this knowledge; and we must adjust the optimistic belief in civilization and progress which prevailed in the late 19th and early 20th centuries to take it into account.

THE ORIGINS OF THE UNITED NATIONS

An immediate concern of the victorious Allies was the establishment of a new international organization to replace the League of Nations and to provide a system of collective security for the post-War world. The new body which emerged from proposals worked out during the War years—the United Nations (UN)—was an organization of States. It was seen primarily as a structure to cope with potential conflict between States and to deal with "threats to international peace and security". But the rhetoric of the Allies during the War and the revelation in its full horror of what had been done in the concentration camps opened the way for some new and potentially very important provisions bearing on individual human rights to be afforded a place in the UN Charter. It is of interest to look in somewhat more detail at how these provisions came to be included.

Preliminary studies and proposals for the post-war world concluded in the US State Department early in the war had favoured the "international promulgation" of human rights provisions—though without any commitment to enforcement. There was, initially at least, a great reluctance on the part of the major Allies to accept the weakening of national sovereignty which effective international monitoring of human rights would involve. Some important countries were also worried that they themselves might be obliged to implement and accept internationally agreed provisions against racial discrimination. The US, for example, still had racial segregation laws in some states; and both Australia and the US had what could be seen as racially restrictive immigration laws and quota systems. Many European powers believed, too, that an international commitment to racial equality would cause problems in relation to their control of colonial territories.

Japan, which had argued unsuccessfully in the drafting of the League Covenant in 1919 for a clause on racial equality, was now "an enemy State." But another Asian country, China, had emerged, by courtesy at least, to great power status; and China took up this issue of racial equality in preliminary exchanges between the major allied powers in preparation for the Dumbarton Oaks Conference, 1944, where the major powers drew up proposals for the future UN organization. China submitted an official proposal setting out two basic principles for the new organization: (a) it should be "universal in character, to include eventually all States;" and (b) "the principle of equality of all States and all races should be upheld."

The Chinese proposal of 1944 was no more welcome to the "Big Three" then than Japan's proposal for a "racial equality" clause in the League Covenant had been to the major powers in 1919. The US delegation, headed by the Under- Secretary of State Edward Stettinius, was willing to include in the draft charter a statement of general principle about respecting "human rights and fundamental freedoms", but not so explicit a reference to race as that proposed by China. As one study of the origin of the human rights provisions in the Charter notes:

> The *Soviet* representative, Andrei Gromyko, initially opposed even this proposal, arguing that reference to human rights and basic freedoms was not germane to the main tasks of an international security organization. Sir Alexander Cadogan, leading the *British* delegation, also opposed even a general statement of principle in the belief that it would create the possibility that the organization would engage in criticism of the internal policies of Member States and thus violate the principle of sovereignty. (See P.G. Lauren, (1983) *HRQ* 1 at pp. 10–11.)

So the draft charter which emerged in late 1944 from the major powers' consultations at Dumbarton Oaks contained only one brief reference to the promotion of "respect for human rights and fundamental freedoms". For the rest, the approach in the draft was predicated on the traditional concept of "non-intervention in the internal affairs of States".

When this draft charter, as worked out by the major powers, was submitted for adoption to the fifty-nation San Francisco Conference in 1945, the question of human rights and racial equality was one of several issues which became the subject of a "tug-of-war". The original Chinese approach now had wider support; and many Latin American States, as well as States such as Egypt and India, argued strongly for clearer and more explicit provisions on human rights. Other "middle powers" such as Australia and Canada were dissatisfied for other reasons and were particularly dubious about the veto rights and the special status which the "Big Five" planned to retain for themselves in the new organization. These pressures from middle and smaller States did have some effect. The major powers were anxious to get agreement on the basic structure and, provided they got their way on that, were prepared to give something in other areas particularly in the language on human rights.

So the Charter which finally emerged after months of argument and discussion at San Francisco, and which came into force on 24 October 1945, was a compromise. It was still based mainly on the great power draft from Dumbarton Oaks. But this had been modified in several respects. In particular, it now included some additional general formulations on human rights and on economic and social issues. However, proposals to refer to the need to "safeguard," "guarantee" or "enforce" human rights principles were defeated. The new Charter instead used much weaker terms like "encourage" and "promote". Nevertheless, it was a matter of great significance that even these weaker provisions in regard to human rights should have been included for the first time in history in a major international document negotiated and agreed between the representatives of fifty sovereign States and in principle open for signature by all other "peace-loving" States.

THE UN CHARTER

It is clear, therefore, that there was an ambiguity built into the UN Charter from the outset. The UN was, and is, an organization set up by States to regulate relations and control conflict between them. The Charter includes a provision, Article 2(7), which specifically precludes the Organization, as such, from intervening in the internal affairs of any Member State:

Nothing contained in the present Charter shall authorize the United Nations
to intervene in matters which are essentially within the domestic jurisdiction
of any State . . .

On the other hand, because of the compromise at San Francisco, the Charter
also contains a good deal of general language about human rights which seems
to indicate that human rights should be a concern of the Organization. For
example, the preamble speaks of ". . . the Peoples of the United Nations" as
"determined . . . to reaffirm faith in fundamental human rights, in the dignity
and worth of the human person, in the equal rights of men and women, and of
nations large and small . . . "; Article 1 speaks of "promoting and encouraging
respect for human rights and for fundamental freedoms for all . . . "; Article 55
speaks of promoting "universal respect for, and observance of, human rights and
fundamental freedoms for all without distinction as to race, sex, language, or
religion"; Article 62 provides for recommendations to be made by the Economic
and Social Council in this area and Article 68 directs the Council to set up a
Commission for "the promotion of human rights".

Some commentators have spoken critically of this aspect of the Charter. I
would prefer to speak of a "creative tension" between the limiting provision of
Article 2(7) and the more general provisions elsewhere in the Charter which do
seem to envisage a role for the UN in the international promotion and protection
of human rights. These provisions—non-specific as they may have seemed at
the outset—were to acquire increasing importance over the following decades
as the UN expanded and acquired a Third World, anti-colonial, majority.

The very existence of the Charter as a basic document adopted initially by
some fifty States served an important function in setting a framework of
principles and procedures for international relations. For States emerging from
colonial rule, admission to the UN marked their accession to independence. As
part of this process they automatically accepted the Charter. Thus, from the
outset, they were "socialized" into a structured international society which had
adopted the Charter as its "constitution".

This influx, from 1960 onwards, of something over one hundred States who
had newly recovered their independence, helped greatly to erode the strict
construction of Article 2(7) initially adopted by some Western States who had
argued that their rule over their colonial territories was purely an internal matter
and, therefore, no business of the UN. As more and more former colonies joined
the UN, the balance in the General Assembly tipped decisively against the
concept of colonialism itself. Colonialism, which was seen as racist, was finally
"outlawed" formally by a General Assembly resolution of 1960 (UNGA Res.
1514(XV), 14 December 1960).

Even more explicitly racist was the apartheid system in South Africa. It aroused deep feelings in the rest of Africa and more generally in the Third World. This, together with the indefensible nature of that system in the eyes even of "strict constructionists" in the West, had a particularly important effect in eroding the impact of Article 2(7) as a barrier to UN concern about human rights violations within States. There was support, too, for the idea that, apart from its specific provisions, the "spirit and purpose" of the Charter created certain more general obligations which all States should take into account. (In some ways this resembles developments over the past two generations in both the US and the Irish legal systems. In each case the Supreme Court, moving away, somewhat, from "strict construction," has held that certain rights are implicit or "latent" in general provisions of the Constitution and that they can, and should, be given effect by the courts.)

I have described the UN Charter and its origins in some detail because it was the foundation for all that followed. As one writer puts it:

> Prior to this document the international community in its practices, insti-
> tutions and laws remained deathly silent on the subject of individual
> liberties. Since then, the world has experienced a virtual explosion of
> instruments, procedures, declarations and decisions designed to confront
> the global issue of basic human rights. The politics of this remarkable and
> dramatic movement have been filled with hopes and frustrations, careful
> calculations and emotions, harmony and tension, successes and failures.
> (See P.G. Lauren, (1983) *HRQ* 1 at p. 25.)

THE UNIVERSAL DECLARATION OF HUMAN RIGHTS

The elaboration of more detailed human rights provisions within the UN framework began at an early date. The work has proceeded in parallel with the expansion of the membership of the Organization which is now—with all its limitations—a universal world organization with some pretensions to be what Tennyson dreamt of, a "Parliament of Man", even if it is still in form simply an organization of States.

The most important single development since 1945 in the promotion and protection of human rights at global level was the adoption within the UN framework of the Universal Declaration of Human Rights in 1948. This docu-ment, taken together with the two international covenants—the International Covenant on Civil and Political Rights (ICCPR) and the International Covenant on Economic, Social and Cultural Rights (ICESCR) which were adopted in 1966 and came into force in 1976— are together sometimes described as the "International Bill of Human Rights".

The primary role in drafting the Universal Declaration was played by the UN Human Rights Commission. Article 68 of the UN Charter itself had envisaged the establishment of a commission for the promotion of human rights and the body was set up by the Economic and Social Council in early 1946. The UN General Assembly, at its very first session in London in January 1946, considered a draft declaration of fundamental human rights and freedoms and transmitted it to the Economic and Social Council for reference to the Commission on Human Rights.

In due course, the Commission set up a drafting committee which decided to prepare two documents. One was to be a declaration setting forth the general principles and standards of human rights. The other was to be a convention which would define specific rights and their limitations. It was decided in 1947 to apply the term "International Bill of Human Rights" to the whole series of documents then in preparation.

Meeting in Paris on 10 December 1948, the General Assembly itself adopted and proclaimed the Universal Declaration of Human Rights, with forty-eight votes in favour, none against and eight abstentions. The Assembly also requested the Human Rights Commission to prepare, as a priority, a draft covenant on human rights and draft measures of implementation. By 1951, the Assembly revised its request, somewhat, and asked the Commission "to draft two covenants on human rights, one to contain civil and political rights and the other to contain economic, social and cultural rights". The Assembly specified that both covenants should include an article providing that "all peoples shall have the right to self-determination". It also specified that the two covenants should contain as many similar provisions as possible.

Work on these covenants—first in the Commission and then in the Committees of the General Assembly on an article-by-article basis—continued through the 1950s and they were eventually completed in 1966. In addition, an optional protocol to the ICCPR established an international mechanism to deal with communications from individuals who claim to be victims of violations of any of the human rights in the Covenant. The two Covenants came into effect in 1976 and the Optional Protocol in March 1979. As of 31 July 1993, some one hundred and twenty-two States had become parties to the ICCPR, seventy-four States to the Optional Protocol to the ICCPR, and one hundred and twenty-two States to the ICESCR.

In adopting the Universal Declaration, from which the Covenants later developed, the UN General Assembly proclaimed it "as a common standard of achievement for all peoples and all nations". The Declaration was, legally speaking, just that, a declaration, unlike the Covenants which are legally binding instruments for those States which have ratified and accepted them. It would be hard, however, to exaggerate its importance. This lies not only in its content but also in the fact that, in adopting it, the community of nations had, for the first time, committed itself to a solemn declaration of rights and fundamental freedoms. As a pamphlet issued by the UN Centre for Human Rights puts it:

> Since 1948 it has been and rightly continues to be the most important and far reaching of all UN declarations and a fundamental source of inspiration for national and international efforts to promote and to protect human rights and fundamental freedoms. It has set the direction for all subsequent work in the field of human rights and has provided the basic philosophy for many legally binding international instruments designed to protect the rights and freedoms which it proclaims.

THE COVENANTS

The Covenants create binding obligations for the States which have ratified or acceded to them and are, thus, an elaboration in specific legal form of broad ideas proclaimed in the Declaration.

The preambles and some of the initial articles of the two Covenants are almost identical. There are, nevertheless, significant differences in the nature of the obligations imposed by each Covenant. The ICCPR imposes on the States who subscribe to it an obligation to guarantee those rights immediately. The ICESCR, on the other hand, requires States Parties to undertake the progressive safeguarding of the rights set out in its various articles. This difference of approach is inherent in the nature of the two kinds of rights: civil and political rights can be implemented immediately but economic and social rights go hand in hand with economic and social development. They may, therefore, to some extent, have to depend on the stage of development attained by a particular society.

Specific implementation procedures are provided for by each of the two Covenants. The ICCPR established a Human Rights Committee (Article 28) for the purpose; and States Parties undertake to submit reports to the Committee for examination on the measures they have adopted to give effect to the rights in the Covenant (Article 40). A State may also make an optional declaration accepting that the Committee may receive a complaint against it from any other State Party that it is not fulfilling its obligations (Article 41); and the Optional Protocol to the Covenant allows a State Party to accept that the Committee may receive individual complaints against that State.

The ICESCR makes provision for reports by State Parties on the measures they have taken to achieve observance of the rights in that Covenant (Article 16).

These reports are examined by the Committee on Economic, Social and Cultural Rights and, in certain cases, by the specialised agencies of the UN; the Economic and Social Council may transmit such reports to the Commission on Human Rights for study and recommendation or for information.

OTHER UN HUMAN RIGHTS CONVENTIONS

This corpus of fundamental human rights documents comprises, therefore: a non-legally binding declaration of universal authority; two treaties, along with an optional protocol, legally binding on the large number of States who have accepted them; as well as provision for implementation measures. This is the core of the structure developed by the UN since 1945 to codify and promote human rights at a global level. Around it, over the past half century, have developed many other human rights conventions and instruments which deal in greater detail with particular rights. There are five which I consider to be of particular importance:

- The Genocide Convention, 1948;

- The Convention on the Elimination of All Forms of Racial Discrimination,1969;

- The Convention on the Elimination of All Forms of Discrimination Against Women, 1979;

- The Convention Against Torture, 1984;

- The Convention on the Rights of the Child, 1989.

    There is by now a whole network of commissions, sub-commissions and committees in place in New York and in Geneva to work further on these issues and to monitor implementation.

UN COMMISSION ON HUMAN RIGHTS

The UN Commission on Human Rights is perhaps the most important of these. It comprises representatives of fifty-three Member States of the UN elected for three-year terms; and it meets each year for a period of six weeks in Geneva. The Commission on Human Rights has established a number of subsidiary bodies to assist in its work. These include, for example, a Sub-Commission on the Prevention of Discrimination and Protection of Minorities and special rapporteurs or representatives who are asked on occasion to undertake a fact-finding role in studying situations in specific States (e.g., Afghanistan, Chile, El Salvador, Guatemala and Iran). Such special rapporteurs or fact-finding missions usually report annually to the Commission and they may also submit interim reports to the UN General Assembly at its annual session. Other working groups of experts reporting to the Commission study various themes and issues which may, in time, become the subject of a new international declaration or convention. Topics studied include, for example, summary executions, disappearances, torture of detainees, and self determination.

The active investigatory role of the Commission is a new development. It began in 1967 when a group of experts was set up to investigate allegations of ill-treatment of persons in police custody in South Africa. Since then the practice has developed of scrutinizing human rights situations in many parts of the world—either in public or confidentially under what has become known as "the 1503 procedure".

This confidential procedure may begin, for example, with a complaint sent to the UN Centre for Human Rights in Geneva by individuals or by non-governmental organizations. The Centre of Human Rights invites the observations of the government concerned and refers the initial complaint, together with any response received, to the Commission on Human Rights or to a sub-Commission. The complaint then goes through various stages *in camera,* the aim of which is to resolve the situation and to end the human rights violations through dialogue with the government concerned. If the responses received continue to be unsatisfactory, the Commission may appoint a special rapporteur to investigate the situation and report back on it.

All of this puts pressure on the government concerned. It is true that the Commission does not, and cannot, exercise coercive authority. But it can, and does, generate very considerable pressure on any State against whom human rights violations are alleged—a pressure which comes not from a body of individuals but from a Commission, acting as representative of the global community.

OTHER UN MONITORING BODIES

Other UN bodies at work in the area of human rights are those established under the terms of various UN human rights instruments or conventions to monitor implementation. For example, there is the Committee on the Elimination of Racial Discrimination established in 1970 in accordance with Article 8 of the

Convention on the Elimination of Racial Discrimination. It consists of eighteen experts elected by the States Parties to the Convention for four-year terms. The Committee considers reports on the legislative, judicial, administrative or other measures which States Parties have adopted to give effect to the provisions of the Convention; and it may establish an *ad hoc* conciliation commission to make its good offices available to States Parties in any dispute about the application of the Convention.

Another such body is the Human Rights Committee which was established in 1977 in accordance with Article 28 of the ICCPR. It too consists of eighteen members elected by States Parties for four-year terms. One task of the Committee is to study reports on the measures States have adopted to give effect to the provisions of the Covenant. It too may establish a conciliation commission to use its good offices in a dispute. The Human Rights Committee also exercises a role arising from the Optional Protocol to the ICCPR, which I mentioned earlier. The States which are parties to this Optional Protocol have agreed that individuals who claim that their rights as set out in the Covenant have been violated and who have exhausted all available domestic remedies may submit written complaints to the Human Rights Committee for consideration.

The Committee holds three sessions every year and reports annually to the General Assembly through the Economic and Social Council. At each of its sessions it examines reports from States Parties to the Covenant on the measures taken by them to give effect to the rights recognized in the Covenant, on the progress made in the enjoyment of those rights and on any factors and difficulties affecting the implementation of the Covenant. These reports are considered in public in the presence of representatives of the reporting States.

I may also mention, in passing, the Committee on Economic, Social and Cultural Rights established by the Economic and Social Council in 1985; the Committee on the Elimination of All Forms of Discrimination Against Women established in 1982, in accordance with Article 17 of the Convention on the Elimination of All Forms of Discrimination Against Women; and the Committee Against Torture, established in 1987 in accordance with Article 17 of the Convention Against Torture.

The UN Secretariat has also a role in promoting human rights. The Centre for Human Rights in the UN Office in Geneva, which is under the direction of the UN Under-Secretary General for Human Rights, can play an important role in offering what might be called technical assistance to poorer developing States. This may take the form of advice and expert assistance in their efforts to bring their law and administrative practice into line with human rights requirements.

Finally, I should mention the UN General Assembly itself. Through the work of its Third Committee, which meets for several months in New York in the autumn of each year, the Assembly plays an important role in debating general issues in relation to human rights as well as specific instances of alleged human rights violations in particular countries.

EVALUATION

I have mentioned only some of what is now a very large network of human rights bodies operating at global level within the UN framework. How are we to evaluate the work they do and their effectiveness in actually ensuring that human rights are respected?

On the positive side, it is remarkable that the UN and its family of human rights bodies has built up a series of procedures which include: debates on violations in any part of the world; the examination in private of complaints from organizations and individuals about violations of human rights in particular countries; and the appointment of investigators in relation to specific States or specific types of violation. These procedures have engaged governments at global level and have subjected them to steadily increasing pressure for the fuller observance of human rights in a way that would have been unthinkable before 1945.

On the negative side, it is legitimate enough, perhaps, to criticize the work of these bodies and, in particular, of the UN Human Rights Commission on the grounds that it is sometimes ineffective or selective and politically motivated. But what is remarkable, especially in recent years, is not how little but how much has been achieved—granted that we still operate in a world of States each of which claims to be sovereign. In such a world, with no single overriding world authority, there is often no way to proceed other than by what has been called "the bargaining, arranging, calculating, negotiating, mediating, conciliating and arbitrating of interests which by the nature of things conflict and go on conflicting". A crusading approach might be more satisfying emotionally. But it would be less likely to achieve or secure full respect for human rights, as a crusade too often involves what Isaiah Berlin calls "the slaughter of individuals on the altars of the great historical ideals—justice or progress or the happiness of future generations or the sacred mission of emancipation of a nation or race or class or even liberty itself" (see I. Berlin, *Four Essays on Liberty*, Oxford, 1965).

A more serious criticism that is occasionally made of this whole global framework of human rights which has developed since 1945 is that in its origins it is culture-bound. Certainly the great trunk of the Universal Declaration, from which the Covenants grow as boughs and the other conventions and instruments as branches, is firmly rooted in western soil. It is always wise to cast what has been described as "a suspecting glance" at institutions and models which have developed out of our western tradition. We need to consider whether they ought to be re-evaluated by reference to other cultural, social and political traditions and experience—particularly the experience of peoples who unlike most European nations, were for centuries the objects rather than the subjects of history. It is also necessary to entertain the idea that there are new rights such as the right to development. I believe, however, that we should be wary of going back on the Declaration and careful in any re-evaluation not to diminish its status and importance as a "universal" declaration of human rights.

It is true that the Declaration was adopted in 1948 by a vote of only forty-eight States at a time when many of the present Member States of the UN were still under colonial rule. Ireland, indeed, was not a member of the UN at that time and we played no part in the working-out of the Universal Declaration of Human Rights. But the process of drafting the Covenants which followed was a long drawn-out one, extending over some eighteen years. This gave ample scope for different voices, speaking out of other traditions, to be heard and taken into account.

It is arguable, too, that if the world has accepted the sovereign, territorial State, which evolved in the West and made it the universal model of social and political organization for all of humanity, then it should equally accept the basic principles evolved in the West which protect the dignity and worth of the human person against the power of the State. There could still be scope for adding to those basic rights certain other rights drawn from the wider experience of the diverse human community.

In any case, the fact is that over the past two generations these rights and freedoms proclaimed in the Universal Declaration have been accepted as standards by the whole international community; and the elaboration of those principles in the Covenants and other instruments has been given binding effect for a large number of States by their own free choice and decision. It would be retrograde and sad if States which have freely committed themselves to these minimum principles as universally valid for decent human living were now to abridge or abrogate them.

That is not to say that the nations of a particular region or tradition should not, if they wish, go further between themselves in developing regional agreements on human rights. Indeed it is, in general, very desirable that they do so—provided that the result is to add to, or amplify, and not to detract from, the global "International Bill of Rights". In concluding this paper I will look briefly at two particular cases where this has been done at European level, to great effect.

REGIONAL LEVEL—
THE EUROPEAN CONVENTION ON HUMAN RIGHTS

One such case originated in Western Europe where the countries of the Council of Europe in the early 1950s adopted the European Convention on Human Rights. This Convention, concluded between the like-minded States of post-war Western Europe, is the most advanced and developed framework and structure for the international protection of human rights anywhere in the world. It is admirable that the continent and civilization which before 1945 saw a systematic degradation of human beings should have produced, a few short years later, the most advanced international instrument to ensure that human rights would be promoted and protected.

The Convention is a legally binding instrument under which sovereign States agree to accept positive duties and to recognize that individuals have rights under international law, described succinctly in a standard pamphlet published by the Council of Europe as:

> [a] collective guarantee at a European level of a number of principles set out in the Universal Declaration of Human Rights, supported by international judicial machinery making decisions which must be respected by Contracting States.

The right of individual petition is of crucial importance and it has been said that it lies at the very heart of the Convention-system of protection. A second distinctive feature is that, in addition to the procedures of the Commission and of the Committee of Ministers, the Convention established a court— the European Court of Human Rights. All Contracting States have now accepted both the right of individual petition and the compulsory jurisdiction of the Court; and there is a striking increase in the Court's activities in recent years as the Convention and its mechanisms become embedded in the life of Western Europe. The Court took twenty-six years to deliver its first hundred judgments whereas it reached its second hundred a little more than four years later.

THE CONFERENCE ON SECURITY AND
CO-OPERATION IN EUROPE

The European Convention on Human Rights shows how far a group of like-minded States, sharing a common culture, can go in building on and developing the basic rights of the Universal Declaration and providing better measures for their implementation. Another development at European level shows the remarkable effect which human rights provisions worked out by negotiation between States with very different social systems have had in bringing about change and promoting democratic freedom. This is the Conference on Security and Co-operation in Europe (CSCE), preliminary work for which began in the early 1970s and which was brought into effect by the Helsinki Final Act, 1975.

The CSCE had its origins in an attempt by the Soviet Union in the late 1960s to have the post-war frontiers in Europe accepted by the western powers. This was at first rejected by the West. But in the early 1970s a bargain was struck which eventually took shape as the Helsinki Final Act. Simply put, this document gave expression to a deal.

The Soviet Union and its allies got a statement of principles to govern relations between participating States, which were carefully negotiated by the West but which included the important commitment that frontiers in Europe could be changed only by agreement; the West got agreement on a series of human rights provisions which the socialist States would have been reluctant to subscribe to at the outset but which they committed themselves to as part of a deal. A third element in the Final Act was a series of agreed provisions governing economic co-operation between participating States.

The CSCE framework brings together all of the States of Europe and the US and Canada. It may have seemed unspectacular at the outset but its indirect consequences have been remarkable. Over the years, the human rights provisions of the Helsinki Final Act were elaborated and further developed in conferences and meetings on what came to be known as "the Human Dimension".

A document issued at the conclusion of a meeting of the participating States of the CSCE, held in Moscow in 1991, gives some sense of how far the international community has moved, at European level at least, from the strict interpretation of the principle of "non-intervention in internal affairs" which was set out in Article 2(7) of the UN Charter:

> The participating States emphasise that issues relating to human rights, fundamental freedoms, democracy and the rule of law are of international concern, as respect for these rights and freedoms constitutes one of the foundations of the international order. They categorically and irrevocably declare that the commitments undertaken in the field of the human dimension of the CSCE are matters of direct and legitimate concern to all participating States and do not belong exclusively to the internal affairs of the State concerned.

At a time of major change in Central and Eastern Europe, the CSCE offers a framework of principles governing relations between States and covering issues of security and co-operation. The most difficult issue, however, is to evolve a framework of new principles to govern questions of self-determination and the rights of minorities in areas such as the former Yugoslavia and the former Soviet Union. It is easy to affirm the "self-determination of peoples"; it is much more difficult to decide what should be the "self" or the "people" which determines. There is much to be done on these issues.

But future historians studying the sudden and remarkable collapse of the monolithic systems of Central and Eastern Europe and the Soviet Union will certainly attribute considerable importance to the eroding effect on those systems of the human rights commitments which the governments concerned accepted when they signed the Helsinki Final Act. The enormity of change since 1975 is reflected in an extract from the Charter of Paris adopted by all CSCE Member States (including the then Soviet Union) in November 1990:

> Democratic government is based on the will of the people, expressed regularly through free and fair elections. Democracy has as its foundation respect for the human person and the rule of law. Democracy is the best safeguard of freedom of expression, tolerance of all groups of society, and equality of opportunity for each person.
>
> Democracy, with its representative and pluralist character, entails accountability to the electorate, the obligation of public authorities to comply with the law and justice administered impartially. No one will be above the law.

CONCLUSION

In this paper I have traced the growing acceptance of the concept that human rights are a matter of legitimate international concern and looked at some of the instruments which have been developed for their promotion since the watershed year of 1945. I have had to omit, necessarily, some other important developments such as the work of the International Committee of the Red Cross; the adoption of the Geneva Conventions and Protocols on the Laws of War and Armed Conflict; and the very significant role of non-governmental organizations such as Amnesty International and the International Commission of Jurists.

I have spoken mainly of documents and of structures—of commissions, committees and sub-committees. But this is only part of the story. Since 1945 there have been some appalling abuses of human rights and much unnecessary human suffering. What we can say, however, is that over that same period, despite the limitations imposed by State sovereignty, the promotion of human rights and the ending of abuses have been formally acknowledged by the international society of States for the first time in history as a matter of legitimate, global concern; standards have been set; and structures and mechanisms have been developed which put pressure on individual States to conform to them. The pressures and the mechanisms are not always effective. But they are slowly becoming more so. Modern news media technology makes us in many ways a single world community; and massive abuses of human rights within States are no longer easily concealed from the rest of the "global village." It was said by Kant that "out of the crooked timber of humanity no straight thing was ever made." Man's inhumanity to man will no doubt continue. But since 1945, by instituting rules and procedures, the world is beginning to build barriers at international level against it.

1.2   A Look to the Future

TOM O'MALLEY

International human rights have been described as the world's first universal ideology. That description is probably justified to the extent that most States in the world claim to be committed to the promotion of human rights in one way or another. In many States, of course, there is a great difference between the reality and the official rhetoric. It might be more accurate, then, to describe human rights as the world's first *official* universal ideology. Be that as it may, the development of international human rights law since 1945 gives us cause to celebrate. The speed with which the concept of human rights has been embraced and promoted throughout the world during the past half-century or so must have few parallels, if any, in human history.

The phenomenal growth in human rights since 1945 is manifested by the number of international human rights treaties now in existence, the number of State and non-governmental organizations dealing with human rights activities and the impact which this body of law has had on the domestic law of many States. There is every reason to believe that this momentum will be maintained over the coming years and well into the next millennium. But it is well to remember that, in relative terms, international human rights law is still at an early stage of development. Compared with the many centuries over which the common law has developed, the fifty years or less of the UN's existence is a very short time indeed. It is appropriate, then, as we approach 1995, the fiftieth anniversary of the foundation of the UN, that we should reflect on what lies ahead.

The concept of the human right as we now know it was born in a time of war, the Second World War, and developed during another kind of war, the Cold War. While the world can scarcely be said to be at peace today, it is a radically different place from what it was in 1945 or, even 1985, in view of events in Eastern Europe during the past few years. As East-West tensions subside and as more States espouse democratic structures, we may wonder about the role of international human rights organizations in the new political order which seems to be developing in the Northern hemisphere. The break-up of the Soviet Union has meant the removal of one major pariah for many human rights activists, especially those belonging to US-based organizations. The argument I wish to advance in this paper is that much remains to be done, as human rights in their fullest sense are far from secure in many parts of the world, but the focus of our attention must shift from more traditional concerns to a different set of problems and realities. To be more specific, I would like to draw attention to four issues:

- the relationship between human rights and democracy;

- the cultivation of human rights awareness;

- the implementation of economic, social and cultural rights;

- the need for openness in developing concepts of human rights.

HUMAN RIGHTS AND DEMOCRACY

The tensions that can arise between human rights aspirations and the claims of nation States to self-determination in political and cultural terms is manifested in several contexts. It is most evident in those States which are governed by fundamentalist regimes and in which political authority is claimed from divine rather than human sources . But we can also find examples, less dramatic, closer to home, where the legitimate human rights claims of minorities may be repugnant to a large part of the population. These tensions pose a major challenge to those responsible for the implementation of human rights at both national and global levels. In States with democratic forms of government, the argument may be made that individual citizens are not truly free and able to participate in the democratic process unless they are accorded the maximum liberty compatible with public order and with their own dignity. With regard to those States which have non-democratic forms of government, the international community must remain vigilant. Even if we chose to remain agnostic as to the best form of government, we could not ignore activities which by universal standards amount to gross violations of human rights. This was one of the major functions which the UN was established to discharge. We must all remain vigilant to ensure that the UN and other major international organizations will not allow human rights concerns to be dislodged from the central role they have come to occupy in international relations.

THE CULTIVATION OF HUMAN RIGHTS AWARENESS

There are many individuals and organizations throughout the world working to increase public and official awareness of human rights issues. They have achieved a great deal, but it is necessary, at the same time, to cultivate an environment in which rights consciousness will become part of the culture in which people live and are educated. As it happens, we now have in the most recent major human rights treaty to be adopted, an ideal vehicle for bringing about this level of global awareness.

The Convention on the Rights of the Child, which was adopted by the UN General Assembly in November 1989, deserves special mention. This Convention is of great significance for a number of reasons. In the first place, it provides for the very first time, in treaty form, an exhaustive catalogue of the rights to which children are entitled. Secondly, the rights which it protects extend beyond the traditional rights to be found in other major human rights instruments. For example, it provides that children shall be free from abuse and exploitation of all kinds, including sexual abuse. Most importantly perhaps, it aims to set in motion a process which, if successful, will lead to the creation of a new international environment in which there will be a far greater awareness than at present of the importance of respecting the human rights of others. Among the more important provisions of this Convention are those dealing with education and the purposes of education in particular. It provides that education should have among its purposes: the development of all the child' s personality and talents; the development of respect for human rights; and the development of respect for the child's cultural identity and for civilizations different from the child's own. The Convention also makes special provision for physically and mentally handicapped children. Among its many other valuable provisions is one dealing with the role of the mass media catering for the needs of children, culturally, intellectually and socially.

The Convention on the Rights of the Child has the potential to create an entirely new world environment for the protection of human rights. If all the children of the world, or a substantial number of them, are brought up in a society in which they see their own rights honoured and in which they are taught to respect the rights of others, the world can only be a better place as a result.

Any State which ratifies this Convention is taking a very courageous step. The obligations which the Convention imposes, if they are to be taken seriously, are onerous. But given the plight of children and young people throughout the world—many in Ireland included—nothing less than a courageous step is required to give them a future worth looking forward to. Some have compared the Convention in terms of importance to the Universal Declaration of Human Rights itself. The comparison is not all that far-fetched; both documents provide a common standard of achievement which all States in the international community should seek to attain.

The challenges which adherence to this Convention will pose are many, but not, I think, insurmountable. Just by way of example, I will take the area of broadcasting. As already mentioned, the Convention requires that the organs of the mass media should be required to cater for the developmental and cultural needs of children. This is a fine aspiration of which everybody would approve in principle. But its implementation will call for some tough decisions. We live in an era when commercial competition is being proposed as the great economic saviour. We have recently enacted important competition legislation in Ireland. Irish government policy on broadcasting strongly favours competition as well, though not with a great deal of success at national level. If unrestrained competition is allowed to dominate broadcasting policy at both local and national levels, the prospect of fulfilling the mandate of the Convention on the Rights of the Child is not very good. Commercial broadcasting enterprises have, naturally enough, the object of making profit. The State must be willing to insist that local radio stations devote a reasonable proportion of their time and resources to broadcasting material conducive to the overall development of children and young people; it is unlikely that many of these stations will take the initiative themselves.

I would also mention here, in passing, the rights of children belonging to linguistic and cultural minorities. Again, the Convention specifically provides that broadcasting policy should be tailored to meet their needs. In an Irish context, this gives rise to the question of broadcasting in the Irish language. I do not propose to dwell on this because it is a long-running saga. But it is worth emphasizing that the absence of an Irish language television service, apart from being in blatant disregard of the spirit of the Constitution, means that children (and adults) in Irish-speaking communities and Irish-speaking families throughout the State, are being deprived of their rights to enjoy their own language and culture. Indeed, the failure of the mass media to cater for Irish-speaking persons and communities is not only counter to the Convention on the Rights of the child, but it also leaves the State in possible breach of Article 27 of the International Covenant on Civil and Political Rights which we have also ratified.

THE IMPLEMENTATION OF ECONOMIC, SOCIAL AND CULTURAL RIGHTS

Needless to say, for millions of children and adults around the world, broadcasting is the least of their worries. The greatest human rights problem with which we have to deal in the late 20th century is that of hunger and malnutrition (see T. O'Malley, (1991) *Trocaire Dev Rev* 91). Every year, millions of people throughout the world die from hunger and hunger-related diseases. This is a most uncomfortable fact and it raises a question which, in my view, should be central to discussions on human rights. Has the entire human rights "episode" of the past fifty years been an inglorious failure? I am not trying to be melodramatic about this, but there is a tragic irony in the fact that a system which grew out of a justified revulsion at the deaths of so many millions of innocent people during the Second World War has itself presided over many more millions of deaths of innocent people in the meantime. Surely we could have done better than that?

For many today human rights is a religion. But we may as well admit that it has become an industry as well. The number of organizations, institutes, conferences, colloquia, seminars, lecture series, guide-books, hand-books, textbooks, journals, magazines, data-bases and documentation centres devoted to human rights continues to grow each year. Human rights is a major source of employment, not to mention foreign travel. Yet, while all this is happening, millions are dying because of being denied the most basic human right of all, the right to the necessities for survival or, in short, the right to life.

It is not that the international human rights community is unconcerned about the right to life. The problem is that for many individuals and organizations the term "right to life" is given a very narrow and selective meaning. In fact, it is rather alarming that in many societies, including Irish society, the term "right to life" is understood to refer only to the right of the unborn child. For my part at least, I fully recognize the right to life of the unborn child, but I also support the right to life of the born person, no matter of what age. At other times, the term "right to life" is used in a more political context to refer to arbitrary executions. Surely, there is something warped about a society in which the arbitrary killing of one person by a political leader who happens to be out of favour with the industrialized States will cause more international outrage than the deaths of those millions who die annually for want of food, shelter or medicine.

Unless the international community is prepared to take steps which will result in the recognition of each human being as having an equal right to life, whether born or unborn, whether living in the Northern or the Southern hemisphere, it cannot be said that international human rights law has been successful. To achieve progress in this field, we do not need any new international convention or specialized organization. The two International Covenants on Civil and Political Rights (ICCPR) and Economic, Social and Cultural Rights (ICESCR) have very explicit provisions on the rights to life and survival.

Article 6 (1) of the ICCPR reads:

> Every human being has the inherent right to life. This right shall be protected by law. No one shall be arbitrarily deprived of his life.

Most States Parties to the Covenant have given a restricted definition to "life" in their reports, concentrating on capital punishment, arbitrary killings and enforced disappearances. On several occasions, the Human Rights Committee has commented on this narrow interpretation. In 1982, the Committee issued the comment that "the right to life cannot be understood in a restrictive manner, as the protection of this right requires States to adopt positive measures". The Committee went on to say that it would be particularly desirable for States "to reduce infant mortality and increase life expectancy, especially in stopping measures to eliminate malnutrition and epidemics". It has issued many similar comments in more recent years. It is important that all States Parties should develop a broader understanding of the right to life for the sake of their own populations and for that of the international community generally.

The ICESCR contains, as one might expect, very specific provisions on rights to food, shelter and health care. Article 11 which deals with the right to food is especially worthy of note. This Article states:

> (1) The States Parties to the present Covenant recognize the right of everyone to an adequate standard of living for himself and his family, including adequate food, clothing and housing, and to the continuous improvement of living conditions. The States Parties will take appropriate steps to ensure the realization of this right, recognizing to this effect the essential importance of international co-operation based on free consent.
>
> (2) The States Parties to the present Covenant, recognizing the fundamental right of everyone to be free from hunger, shall take, individually and through international co-operation, the measures, including specific programmes, which are needed:
>
> (a) To improve methods of production, conservation and distribution of food by making full use of technical and scientific knowledge, by

disseminating knowledge of the principles of nutrition and by developing or reforming agrarian systems in such a way as to achieve the most
efficient development and utilization of natural resources;

(b) Taking into account the problems of both food-importing and food-
exporting countries, to ensure an equitable distribution of world food
supplies in relation to need.

When first drafted, this Article had read simply: "States Parties to the
Covenant recognize the right of everyone to adequate food, clothing and
housing". But in 1963, at the 18th session of the UN General Assembly's Third
Committee, the Director General of the UN Food and Agriculture Organization
(FAO), Dr Sen, strongly advocated that the texts of Articles 11 and 12 (on the
right to health) should be extended in order to deal in a realistic way with the
problem of world hunger. The text of Article 11, as it now stands, provokes
mixed feelings. On the positive side, it designates as fundamental the right of
everyone to be free from hunger. Paragraph (1), however, confirms the programmatic nature of the right (like, of course, all others contained in the ICESCR).
The measures advocated in paragraph (2) deal with scientific methods of
improving food production and agrarian systems, and ensuring equitable distribution of world food supplies. It also says that regard must be had to the
problems of both importing and exporting States. Lack of foreign exchange is
often one of the major problems facing States needing to import food. But the
fact remains that the FAO, the UN specialized agency dealing with scientific
aspects of food production, has claimed that it is widely recognized that "by
adopting the measures indicated in Article 11 (2) . . . the international community
would be in a position to eliminate completely the present state of chronic
malnutrition and undernourishment and mitigate considerably the effects of
calamities".

Implementation mechanisms are clearly of central importance in realizing
the rights to food and other prerequisites for survival. This leads to three central
questions: what is meant by the "programmatic" nature of the ICESCR? what
obligations does the Covenant impose on States Parties in regard to their own
populations? what obligations does it impose on States Parties in relation to the
relief of hunger in other countries?

It is worth examining in some detail the obligations imposed by the Covenant
as set out in Article 2 (1). This paragraph has already been subjected to exhaustive scholarly analysis. Of particular interest in this regard are "the Limburg
Principles on the Implementation of the ICESCR". These were principles drawn
up by a group of distinguished experts in international law, convened by the
International Commission of Jurists and other bodies in 1986. This group drew

up a set of principles which it believed should govern the interpretation of the Covenant. With regard to States' obligations "to take steps", the group concluded that: "All States have an obligation to begin immediately to take steps towards full realization of the rights contained in the Covenant". It also concluded that the obligation to achieve progressively the full realization of the rights contained in the Covenant requires States "to move as expeditiously as possible towards the realization of the rights".

With regard to the most crucial element in Article 2(1), the obligation on States to achieve the rights "to the maximum of its available resources," the Limburg Principles hold that this term refers to both the resources within a State and those available from the international community through international co-operation and assistance. They also hold that "States Parties are obligated, regardless of the level of economic development, to ensure respect for minimum subsistence rights for all". It should be recalled that when the Covenant was being drafted, the US had suggested that the words "for this purpose" be added to the "to the maximum of its available resources". The suggestion was not adopted after many States rightly objected to the level of discretion which this form of wording would give to States in the allocation of their resources.

The Covenant, then, imposes definite, positive obligations on the Contracting States. The allowance which it makes for progressive implementation is not be interpreted as a licence for inertia. As to the obligations of States Parties *vis-à-vis* their own populations, it is clear that they must, in accordance with the above interpretation, begin to honour the terms of the Covenant immediately following ratification. Under the Vienna Convention on the Law of Treaties, Article 31(1) of which states that "a treaty shall be interpreted in good faith in accordance with the ordinary meaning to be given to the terms of the treaty in their context and in light of its object and purpose", States are obliged to give effect to the substance, and not merely to the form, of their treaty obligations. It follows that a State which has ratified the ICESCR should proceed to re-allocate its resources to ensure that all its people (citizens and others) have the means of survival to the greatest extent compatible with human dignity.

The final question, and the more awkward one, concerns the obligations which the ICESCR may impose on States Parties to ensure that the rights it protects are accorded to people outside their own borders or, for that matter, outside their own continents. To phrase the question in a more concrete fashion: does ratification of the Covenant by Ireland and other developed States impose any legal obligation on them to work towards the eradication of hunger and poverty in the developing world? An examination of the *travaux preparatoires* of the Covenant fails to yield any indication of a positive duty to give aid to poorer States.

On the other hand, Articles 55 and 56 of the UN Charter mandate joint and separate action by the Members, in co-operation with the UN itself, to further the aims of Article 55 which, as we have seen, includes the promotion of higher standards of living and universal respect for human rights and fundamental freedoms. The Limburg Principles hold that this co-operation "must be directed towards the establishment of a social and economic order in which the rights and freedoms set forth in the Covenant can be fully realized". This mandate is reflected in Article 2(1) of the ICESCR which requires States to take steps "individually and *through international co-operation and assistance*" to achieve the realization of the rights set out in the Covenant (emphasis added). Under this provision, States are certainly obliged to accept assistance necessary for the fulfilment of the Covenant's obligations. It follows that other States are envisaged as contributors. What may be said with some certainty, therefore, is that all States Parties to the Covenant are obliged to co-operate in good faith in international efforts to secure the rights of people everywhere. This co-operation will require material assistance from those States that can afford it as well as a commitment from all States to have regard, in the formulation of their domestic and foreign policies, to the needs of the people (as opposed to the governments) of developing States.

Ireland is now a full party to both Covenants and to the Optional Protocol to the ICCPR. This means that the Irish Government is answerable to the supervising body, the Committee on Economic, Social and Cultural Rights, in regard to the manner in which it is fulfilling the terms of the ICESCR within the State. It will have to provide reasonably detailed information on the steps it is taking to ensure that everyone has adequate nutrition, health care, social security rights and so forth. The Committee will be particularly anxious to ensure that those of minority status, like members of the travelling community, are being fully accorded these rights. But our concern here is with developing States. As suggested above, it is unlikely that the Covenant can, as yet, be interpreted as imposing a distinct obligation on any State to provide aid for other countries, but it does impose an obligation to co-operate in international efforts to secure the right of people everywhere to survival. If Ireland is to interpret the Covenant in good faith, as it must do, it will have to examine closely its present policies in regard to development aid, and, in particular, the amount of such aid which it can, in good faith, provide. But its obligations do not end there. It must also make use of its membership of the UN and of any specialized agencies of the UN in which it is represented, to press for the provision of greater development assistance to those countries in need of it. It should be remembered that, now that it has acceded to the Covenants, Ireland will be able to exercise increased influence in these matters. Hitherto, there was the danger that Irish diplomatic efforts would have been thwarted by our own failure to accede to the two major Covenants. Ireland could now show further good example by increasing its development aid to the level recommended by the UN.

THE NEED FOR OPENNESS IN DEVELOPING CONCEPTS OF HUMAN RIGHTS

The norms and standards found in our international human rights instruments are not, for the most part, the inventions of the founders of the UN or other international bodies. Most of the basic civil and political rights have their roots in legal traditions, including the common law, going back over several centuries. Many were to be found in State constitutions, including our own, which pre-date the foundation of the UN. These are rights founded in the liberal and natural law traditions which are widely shared in many parts of the world. It is important, however, that the bodies charged with interpreting these rights should recognize and welcome the contribution being made by newer movements and traditions in the legal and social field. I have in mind, in particular, the contribution being made by feminist jurisprudence and thought to our understanding of rights and liberties. We have to recognize that our traditional rights were developed from an entirely male perspective. Those who subscribe to the philosophy of John Stuart Mill that the only reason why the law should curtail individual liberty is to prevent harm to others must recognize that male conceptions of harm are often different from harms as perceived by women. This is illustrated, for example, by the very weak protection against sexual harassment to be found in many countries, including Ireland. What may be seen as freedom of expression by one gender is seen as victimization by another. It should be a fundamental tenet of public policy that all decision-making processes in the field of human rights should involve equal representation of women and men as well as including representation of all interested minorities.

POSTCRIPT

The above discussion is the text of a talk delivered in spring 1992. In the eighteen months or so since the above talk was given, much has occurred in the field of human rights, some of which gives us cause to celebrate and more of which, unfortunately, must almost lead us to despair. Here in Ireland, there have been many positive developments to applaud. The Government ratified the UN Convention on the Rights of the Child in autumn 1992 and about the same time presented its first report under the ICCPR to the UN Human Rights Committee. A copy of the Report, a handsome volume in itself, was made available to the public at the nominal charge of £1. Within the past few months, the Criminal Law (Sexual Offences) Act, 1993, was enacted giving effect to the judgment of the European Court of Human Rights in the case of *Norris v. Ireland*. The government also seems firmly committed to the introduction of an Irish-language television station.

As against all this, however, at international level, the tragedy of Bosnia has made it difficult to keep faith in human rights. It is not, of course, that such conflict and suffering has been unknown throughout the world since 1945. Civil strife has rarely been absent from our planet, or indeed, from our own island. What makes the Bosnian situation particularly frightening, though, is that it is occurring on the doorstep of Europe, a continent which, according to all indications, is one in which structures exist to ensure that never again would atrocities occur like those committed during the Second World War. But they have, and those great monoliths of progress and civilization, the European Community and the Council of Europe, have quite simply failed to stop them. We have seen tens of thousands of people (perhaps more when the full story is finally told) denied their most basic rights to life and to freedom from torture and inhuman treatment. Once more, we have seen that women and children are the victims of the more horrendous violations. When Susan Brownmiller published her classic work *Against Our Will: Men, Women and Rape* (1975), she was accused by some critics of exaggeration for her claims that rape was a common form of terrorism in time of war. Bosnia has proved that it was no exaggeration. The entire tragedy bears witness to the importance of the distinction now being emphasized by Stanley Cohen and others between knowledge and acknowledgement. Human rights activists have traditionally been preoccupied with "knowledge" in the sense of freedom of information and freedom of expression. We must now move beyond this and begin to think in terms of the obligation on both States and individuals to *acknowledge* gross human rights violations. This will not, in itself, prove to be a panacea for all ills, but it will be a good beginning.

2 : THE EUROPEAN CONVENTION ON HUMAN RIGHTS

2.1 Introduction

Gathering in Rome, on 4 November 1950, to sign a treaty for the protection of fundamental rights and freedoms in Europe, the Foreign Ministers of the Members States of the Council of Europe affirmed their resolve "to take the first steps for the collective enforcement of certain of the rights stated in the Universal Declaration".[1] Little could they have imagined the extent to which the European Convention on Human Rights (ECHR) would dominate European affairs in the years to follow. This regime for the regulation of inter-State relations and, more significantly, of relations between the individual and the State, was to flourish over the course of the next four decades, well beyond the ambitions of its founders.

Confirmation of the success of the ECHR is readily apparent in a number of guises. The level of State accession to the Convention is constantly on the rise. For example, the number of Contracting States currently stands at twenty-eight[2] and is expected to expand further with the impending admission of new members to the Council of Europe from among the ranks of the the emerging democracies in Eastern Europe. So central is the Convention to the affairs of the Council, that accession to the former is essentially a pre-requisite to membership of the latter. Secondly, contrary to the presumption of the Convention signatories that inter-State complaints would form the basis of the supervisory procedure, the so-called "option" of responding to individual petitions[3] has been exercised by all States, bar the most recent recruits, and, in fact, has become the backbone of activity in Strasbourg. The number of applications has spiralled, prompting certain modest attempts at procedural reform.[4] In addition, the substantive Convention guarantee has been extended to embrace new rights, not covered in the 1950 text.[5] Finally, and perhaps most importantly, the bulk of the Contracting States have taken strides to realize the full potential of the Convention at domestic level, by incorporating its provisions into national legal systems.

Yet, the ECHR is not without its ills and the observation is frequently made that the Convention has become "a victim of its own success".[6] There are misgivings concerning the operation of the current supervisory system; the respective roles, therein, of the European Commission of Human Rights, the

European Court of Human Rights and the Committee of Ministers of the Council of Europe; and the ability of the current or, indeed, of any reformed system, to cope with the quantitative challenges that lie ahead.[7] Concerns also lie with respect to the exercise of judicial power in Strasbourg; the development of the jurisprudence of the Commission and, more especially, the Court;[8] and the efficacy of the Convention process regarding the troublesome issue of enforcement:

> And yet, symptoms of a deep-seated crisis cannot be overlooked. As any mechanism for the protection of human rights, the Strasbourg system must be measured by the concrete results which it produces in favour of the aggrieved individual. It is not the legal perfection of its normative structure that matters in the last analysis, but its actual impact on the real enjoyment of human rights. In that respect, substantial reasons barring euphoria exist.[9]

One aspect of this crisis is particularly acute, namely the fate of the individual application. In his paper on individual remedies, Patrick Dillon-Malone documents the obstacles facing the Irish applicant on the lengthy and cumbersome trail to Strasbourg. The caseload of the Commission and Court is now such as to guarantee delays that would dissuade all but the most determined of applicants:

> The number of cases brought to Strasbourg has increased dramatically over the last decade. In 1980, the Commission registered 396 applications, 596 in 1985, and 1,657 in 1990. The number of cases referred to the Court was 8 in 1980, 12 in 1985, 61 in 1990, and 93 in 1991. The number of cases referred to the Court in 1991 is almost equal to the total number of cases referred during the first 24 years of its existence.[10]

The consequential level of delay in the supervisory process is particularly ironic, given the substantial attention which the Strasbourg organs devote to reviewing the compatibility of domestic civil and criminal process with the Article 6(1) guarantee of "a fair and public hearing *within a reasonable time* by an independent and impartial tribunal established by law" (emphasis added). The question has been aptly posed:

> How can a lawyer propose the seeking of redress in Strasbourg when it now takes over five years to get a decision from the European Court of Human Rights or the Committee of Ministers? And this five-year period does not even take into account domestic court proceedings which invariably precede a petition in Strasbourg.[11]

While there has been some tinkering within the current system, for example, through the reforms to the practice and procedure of the Commission introduced by the Eighth Protocol,[12] any tangible improvements have become subsumed in the ever-increasing workload of the Commission and Court. A radical overhaul to the Strasbourg system has become an imperative. On-going discussion on the subject of reform has tended to focus on three proposals: the elevation of the current status of the existing Commission and Court from part-time to full-time bodies; the maintenance of a two-tier system but transformed into the style of a court of first-instance and a court of appeal; and the establishment of a single permanent court.[13] The Committee of Ministers has now decided to pursue this last option.[14]

Regardless of the fate of the Strasbourg supervisory system, the role of national authorities in enforcing Convention standards remains a crucial issue. Ireland is now one of the few Convention States in which the substantive guarantee remains unincorporated. As Alpha Connelly's paper indicates, the relevance of the Convention in the domestic development of human rights law and practice should not be limited to those instances where Ireland is the respondent State to a particular complaint. The words of the General Rapporteur to the Strasbourg Conference in preparation for the Vienna World Human Rights Conference are apposite:

It is also an important reality that international mechanisms for protecting human rights are subsidiary to the national system. Human rights are better protected at home subject to the system of outer-protection afforded by international bodies. We should, however, be careful to ensure that the existence of international mechanisms is not used as a pretext for failure to take appropriate measures at national level.[15]

LIZ HEFFERNAN

2.2 Ireland and the European Convention on Human Rights: An Overview

ALPHA CONNELLY

The Convention for the Protection of Human Rights and Fundamental Freedoms, more commonly known as the European Convention on Human Rights, was signed on 4 November 1950, and entered into force on 3 September 1953. Over the years, the list of rights protected by the Convention has been extended and the procedures whereby alleged violations of these rights are heard have been improved. These developments have been achieved through the conclusion by States Parties of a number of protocols to the original text. As of 1 June 1993, ten protocols had been agreed and consideration was being given to the desirability of concluding a further protocol which would afford protection to members of certain minorities.[1]

The Convention required ten ratifications to enter into force and Ireland was one of the original ratifying States.[2] As of 1 January 1994, twenty-eight States were party to the Convention.[3] Subscription to the Convention is dependent upon membership of the Council of Europe and membership of the Council has grown substantially in recent years and is likely to grow further in the years ahead. Nowadays, it is expected that when a State joins this organization, it will sign the Convention, and several Baltic and East European States have done so. Other East European States send observers to meetings of the Council and may themselves become members in the near future.

It is only because of recent events that the possibility of accession by East European States to the Convention has arisen at all. Drafted in the late 1940s, the Convention reflects the political concerns of western governments at that time. It was intended to afford a bulwark in the Contracting States against two perceived threats to individual liberty: fascism and communism. As the former President of the European Court of Human Rights, Judge Pallieri, put it: "[i]t is unthinkable that a country with a totalitarian regime, whether of right or of left, would ever join our Convention".[4] The Convention laid down a set of standards by which the treatment by national authorities of persons within their jurisdiction would be judged as acceptable or unacceptable. These standards were designed to uphold liberal democratic values and institutions: values such as individual freedom, pluralism, tolerance and the rule of law, and institutions such as an independent judiciary, a representative parliament and a free press.[5] One of the recurrent themes in the case law of the European Court of Human Rights is that the Convention protects the individual against the arbitrary exercise of power by public authorities and that domestic law must contain safeguards for the individual in this regard.

Despite its title, which suggests that the Convention deals with the full spectrum of human rights, the Convention and its various Protocols afford protection only to certain rights. Indeed, the Preamble to the Convention explicitly states that the signatory governments are enforcing only certain of the rights proclaimed by the UN General Assembly in 1948 in the Universal Declaration of Human Rights. The rights guaranteed by the Convention are mainly civil and political rights: rights such as the right to life, to freedom from torture and from inhuman and degrading treatment or punishment, to personal liberty, to a fair trial, to respect for private and family life, to freedom of religion, freedom of expression, freedom of assembly and freedom of association. The right to vote, a right essential to representative democracy, is guaranteed not in the original text but in a protocol.[6] Economic and social rights, such as the right to work and the right to social welfare, are the subject of a separate treaty, the European Social Charter, 1961.[7] However, as we shall see later, the fact that the Convention essentially protects rights in the civil and political spheres has not prevented the European Court of Human Rights from interpreting these rights in a way which has implications of an economic and social nature for Contracting States.

This Convention blazed a trail in the international protection of human rights. It not only provided a commonly agreed catalogue of human rights for European States, it also established procedures whereby alleged violations of these rights could be heard and determined by independent bodies. Even today, it is only a minority of States in the world that are prepared to submit themselves to international adjudication of their human rights performance. The Convention established two bodies, a European Commission and a European Court of Human Rights. The procedure for the hearing of a complaint is long and involved. Despite amendment by protocol, it still bears the hallmark of the time when it was originally adopted. Only a small number of cases brought under this procedure ever end in a judgment of the European Court of Human Rights.

This paper will focus on judgments of the Court which directly concern Ireland. Some mention will also be made of judgments involving other States which have implications for Irish law and practice. It should not be forgotten, however, that many Irish cases have been held inadmissible by the European Commission of Human Rights and that a few have been amicably resolved with the conclusion of a friendly settlement between the applicant and the Irish authorities. A recent example of the former was the challenge brought by Betty Purcell and a number of other journalists and persons involved in broadcasting to the Ministerial Order made under section 31 of the Broadcasting Authority Act, 1960 (as amended, 1976).[8] It was argued that the Order, which prohibits, *inter alia*, the broadcasting of anything said by a representative of Sinn Fein or an interview with a spokesperson of that organization, infringed the applicants' right to freedom of expression. As interpreted by Radio Telefís Éireann, the prohibition applies to anything said by a member of Sinn Fein (e.g., comments on social affairs) and not merely to words advocating support for the IRA or paramilitary activities.[9] The application was rejected by the Commission which held that this interference with the applicants' freedom was justified in view of the overriding public interest in the defeat of terrorism. An example of an application which ended in a friendly settlement is one concerning the inferior succession rights of a child born outside wedlock compared to those of a child born within wedlock. In settling the case, the Irish Government paid the applicant IR£10,000 and informed the Commission that it had initiated legislation "the purpose of which is to equalise the rights under the law of all children, whether born within or outside marriage".[10]

There are two routes for the filing of a complaint under the Convention. One is by way of inter-State application; any State Party to the Convention may complain that another State Party is not complying with its obligations under the Convention. The other is by way of application either by an individual, by a group of individuals or by a non-governmental organization; complainants using this route must allege that their own rights have been violated by the State. Under the Convention, one person may not complain that another person's rights have been violated. Irrespective of route, an application is heard in the first instance by the European Commission of Human Rights. It may, at a later stage, but not necessarily, be referred to the European Court of Human Rights for a legally binding decision. I shall deal separately with these two avenues of complaint in relation to Ireland.

INTER-STATE APPLICATIONS

Article 24 of the Convention provides that any State Party may refer to the Commission any alleged breach of the Convention by another State Party.

Ireland has never been accused of a breach of the Convention by another State acting under this Article. However, on two occasions in the early 1970s, Ireland itself invoked Article 24 to bring applications against the United Kingdom with respect to events in Northern Ireland. The second of these applications was discontinued but the first was eventually referred to the European Court of Human Rights for a judicial decision. This is in fact the only inter-State dispute to date of which the Court has been seised. The Court gave its decision on 18 January 1978.[11]

The events in Northern Ireland which triggered this application were the introduction of internment without trial, on 9 August 1971, and the subsequent ill-treatment of detainees. Before the European Court of Human Rights, Ireland challenged internment without trial as a violation of the personal liberty and fair trial guarantees under Articles 5 and 6 of the Convention and the ill-treatment as contrary to the guarantee in Article 3 of freedom from torture and inhuman or degrading treatment or punishment. Ireland also alleged that the fact that the extra-judicial powers were used mainly against those suspected of involvement in IRA terrorism and less against suspected Loyalist terrorists constituted prohibited discrimination under the Convention.

The Court held that internment ran counter to the guarantee of personal liberty and also, assuming it to apply, to that of fair trial, but that, given the circumstances prevailing in Northern Ireland at the time, it was justified under Article 15 of the Convention, which allows a State to derogate from some of its human rights obligations in time of public emergency threatening the life of the nation, to the extent strictly required by the exigencies of the situation. Ireland did not contest the existence of such an emergency and the Court considered it "perfectly clear from the facts".[12] As to the need for resort to special powers of detention to deal with the situation, the Court found that, "being confronted with a massive wave of violence and intimidation", the British authorities

> were reasonably entitled to consider that normal legislation offered insufficient resources for the campaign against terrorism and that recourse to measures outside the scope of the ordinary law, in the shape of extra judicial deprivation of liberty, was called for.[13]

The ill-treatment complained of ranged from the required performance by detainees of irksome and painful exercises to the infliction of severe injury. Complaints were also made about the use of disorientation or sensory deprivation techniques in the questioning of some detainees. The Court found that, for a period, detainees at the Palace Barracks in Holywood, County Down, had been repeatedly subjected to violence constituting inhuman treatment. As to the interrogation techniques, the Court held that their combined use amounted to inhuman treatment because of the intense pain and suffering inflicted thereby on the persons subjected to them. The combined use of these techniques also constituted degrading treatment

> since they were such as to arouse in their victims feelings of fear, anguish and inferiority capable of humiliating and debasing them and possibly breaking their physical and moral resistance.[14]

It did not, however, in the Court's view, constitute torture since "it did not occasion suffering of the particular intensity and cruelty implied by [this] word".[15]

The difference in the use of the special powers against suspected IRA and Loyalist terrorists was found not to be discriminatory, *inter alia*, because the IRA was a far more structured and well-organized paramilitary group, because of the scale of the IRA's activities and because it was, in general, easier to institute criminal proceedings against suspected Loyalists than against IRA terrorists.

Inter-State applications are rare; and these applications against the United Kingdom are the only two occasions on which Ireland has invoked the Article 24 procedure. When gross violations of human rights have occurred, as in Greece under a military junta in the late 1960s and early 1970s, in Cyprus after the Turkish invasion of the island in 1974, and in Turkey under military rule in the early 1980s, the initiative has been left to other States Parties to institute proceedings. Ireland has not chosen to play a leading role in the "collective enforcement"[16] of the rights guaranteed by the Convention. This role has been played by Denmark, France, the Netherlands, Norway and Sweden.[17] Political and economic considerations, of course, affect a State's decision whether or not to take action against another State. The degree and extent of human rights violations will not be the only, or even necessarily the predominant, consideration. But one cannot help feeling that opportunities have been missed for Ireland to be seen at the European regional level as a champion of human rights.

INDIVIDUAL APPLICATIONS

Article 25 of the Convention allows individuals and non-governmental organizations to complain to the Commission that their rights have been infringed by a Contracting State. The competence of the Commission to hear such complaints is dependent upon a declaration having been made by the State concerned whereby it recognizes the competence of the Commission to receive such complaints. Ireland made this declaration, without any time limit, when it first became party to the Convention. As of 1 January 1994, the European Court of Human Rights has delivered six judgments on the merits of complaints against Ireland under Article 25 and a seventh case was before the Court.

The first case ever to go the European Court of Human Rights was, in fact, an Irish case, that of *Lawless*. Strictly speaking the Court rendered three judgments in this case, the first dealing with preliminary objections and questions of procedure, the second concerning the standing of the applicant before the Court, and the third on the merits.[18] Like the inter-State case, the merits concerned detention without trial, a measure used in the Republic in the mid-1950s in response to IRA violence. Complaints under Articles 6 (right to fair trial) and 7 (freedom from retroactive criminal offences and penalties) were rejected on the ground that these provisions were not applicable, Lawless not having been charged with, or found guilty of, any criminal offence. His detention, though not permitted by the personal liberty guarantee of Article 5, was found to be justified under Article 15 in view of the emergency situation in the Republic at the time. In this case, the Court gave a definition of the words "public emergency threatening the life of the nation". These words, it said, refer to "an exceptional situation of crisis or emergency which affects the whole population and constitutes a threat to the organized life of the community of which the State is composed".[19] The Court found that the existence of such a situation had reasonably been deduced by the Irish Government from the various activities of the IRA at the time and their effects. In accepting that Lawless's detention was necessary in the circumstances, the Court appears to have adopted a stricter standard of review of the need for such a measure than it did in the later case of *Ireland v. United Kingdom*. It considered whether other less serious measures would have sufficed and examined the various safeguards for individuals against abuse of the power to detain without trial. In the later inter-State case, the Court limited its review to deciding whether or not the view of the national authorities as to the need for the measure was reasonable.

It was another eighteen years before Ireland was to find itself again as a respondent State before the European Court of Human Rights. The 1979 case of *Airey* must be one of the better known Irish cases to be decided by the Court.[20] Indeed the Court's judgment in this case still carries reverberations as regards the compatibility of the present system of civil legal aid in Ireland with the Convention. The main allegations were of breaches of the fair trial guarantee of Article 6 and of respect for private and family life under Article 8. Mrs Airey argued that her rights under these provisions had been violated because, owing to a lack of financial means, she had been unable to get a lawyer to act for her in judicial separation proceedings. The Irish Government contended that Mrs Airey could have taken proceedings herself before the High Court without the assistance of a lawyer and that she, therefore, enjoyed a right of access to court. The reply of the European Court of Human Rights to this contention was that the Convention "is intended to guarantee not rights that are theoretical or illusory but rights that are practical and effective".[21] It had to ascertain, therefore, whether Mrs Airey would be able "to present her case properly and satisfactorily"[22] without legal assistance before the High Court. After examining the legal issues and procedure involved and noting "the degree of objectivity required by advocacy in court"[23] and that in all such proceedings in the previous seven years the petitioner had been represented by a lawyer, the Court thought it most improbable that Mrs Airey could effectively present her own case. This situation constituted a violation of her rights under Article 6 and Article 8 of the Convention. In dealing with her complaints under both of these provisions, the Court stated that fulfilment of a State's obligations under the Convention required not only that it refrain from unjustifiably interfering with individual liberty but also that, on occasion, it take some positive action to ensure respect for the guaranteed rights. In response to the Irish Government's argument that the Court should not interpret the Convention in such a way as to achieve any social or economic development in a Contracting State, the Court stated that, although the Convention essentially sets forth civil and political rights, many of these have implications of a social or economic nature, and that, therefore, the mere fact than an interpretation of the Convention might extend into these fields was not a decisive factor against such an interpretation. It also pointed out that the institution of a legal aid scheme was merely one way of ensuring an effective right of access to the courts, and that there are others, for example, a simplification of procedure.[24]

Seven years later, in the 1986 case of *Johnston and Others*, the Court had to consider the compatibility with Ireland's obligations under the Convention of the position under Irish law of an unmarried couple and their daughter.[25] The couple had been living in a stable relationship for years but, owing to the constitutional ban on divorce, could not marry, Mr Johnston still being in law the husband of a woman he had married over thirty years earlier. They alleged that the non-availability of divorce infringed their right to marry under Article 12 and their right to respect for family life under Article 8. Moreover, they argued that their lack of certain rights *vis-à-vis* one another under Irish law, such as maintenance and succession rights, also constituted a violation of Article 8. The Court found against them on all these points. On the other hand, the inferior position of their child under Irish law compared to that of a child born of a married couple was found to constitute a violation of all three applicants' right to respect for their family life under Article 8. In the Court's view, this provision required that a child born of an unmarried couple "be placed, legally and socially, in a position akin to that of a legitimate child".[26]

In 1988, in the *Norris* case, the Court had to consider the compatibility of the penalization of buggery and acts of gross indecency between men with the right to respect for the private life of an active male homosexual.[27] Reiterating what it had said in an earlier case, that the matter before it concerned "a most intimate aspect of private life",[28] the Court required that "there must exist particularly serious reasons before interferences on the part of public authorities" in this area of private life will be regarded as acceptable under the Convention. No such reasons were found to exist in the circumstances. In particular, the Irish Government had adduced no evidence to show that the lack of enforcement of the criminal provisions in recent years with respect to consensual conduct between adult men in private had been injurious to moral standards in Ireland or that there had been any public demand for stricter enforcement of the law.

While the last three cases concerned aspects of private and family life, the next Irish case to be decided by the European Court of Human Rights—*Pine Valley Developments Ltd and Others*—raised somewhat different issues.[29] This case involved the property interests of two companies, and the managing director of one of the companies, which had purchased land in reliance on outline planning permission for industrial warehouse and office development on the site. The outline planning permission was subsequently found by the Supreme Court to be invalid. One of the consequences of this decision was a substantial reduction in the value of the property. Legislation passed to validate such permission, given in material contravention of the relevant development plan, did not apply to the applicants. They alleged that they had suffered a violation of their property rights under Article 1 of the First Protocol and that the remedial legislation discriminated against them. The European Court of Human Rights found that Pine Valley itself enjoyed no property rights under the Protocol since it had parted with ownership of the land (to one of the other applicants) prior to the Supreme Court's decision. As regards the other two applicants, the Court held that there had been an interference with their right to the peaceful enjoyment of their possessions but that the interference was justified in order to protect the environment, that is, to preserve the green belt around Dublin. However, the Court found for these two applicants on the discrimination issue. In fact, the Irish Government had advanced no justification before the Court for the difference in legislative treatment between the applicants and other holders of outline planning permission.

In the sixth case, *Open Door Counselling* and *Dublin Well Woman Centre Ltd and Others*, the applicants complained that an injunction restraining counselling agencies from providing information to pregnant women about specific abortion services in Great Britain infringed their freedom to impart and to receive information as guaranteed by Article 10 of the Convention.[30] The Court upheld their complaints. It noted that it was not a criminal offence under Irish law for a pregnant woman to travel abroad in order to have an abortion and that abortion services are, in fact, lawful in other Convention States and may be crucial to a woman's health and well-being. It added that limitations on information concerning activities which had been and continued to be tolerated by national authorities call for "careful scrutiny by the Convention institutions as to their conformity with the tenets of a democratic society".[31] While accepting that the injunction pursued a legitimate aim under the Convention, the protection of morals, of which the protection in Ireland of the right to life of the unborn is one aspect, the Court found that it was overly broad and had a disproportionate impact on the applicants' freedom of expression. The Court criticized its "absolute nature".[32] It imposed a "perpetual restraint" on the provision of information to pregnant women concerning abortion facilities abroad, regardless of age or state of health or the reasons for seeking counselling on the termination of pregnancy.[33] On this ground alone, the Court thought the injunction disproportionate. This view was confirmed, however, by other factors. The counselling agencies had neither advocated nor encouraged abortion. They had merely explained the available options, of which abortion in Great Britain was one. Also, information about abortion facilities abroad could be obtained from other sources, such as magazines and telephone directories or persons with contacts in Great Britain. Furthermore, the injunction was largely ineffective since it did not prevent large numbers of women from continuing to obtain abortions in Great Britain. In addition, the available information suggested that the injunction had created a risk to the health of women who were seeking abortions at a later stage of pregnancy and who were not availing themselves of customary medical supervision after abortion. The injunction might also have had more adverse effects on women who were not sufficiently resourceful or had not the necessary level of education to have access to alternative sources of information. The Court made it clear that it was not called upon to examine, nor was it necessary for the purpose of the case to decide, "whether a right to abortion is guaranteed under the Convention or whether the foetus is encompassed by the right to life as contained in Article 2". [34]

A further case was referred to the Court in April, 1993, *Keegan v. Ireland*. The case concerns the placing for adoption of a child born out of wedlock by its mother without the knowledge or consent of its natural father. The latter is complaining about his lack of status under Irish law: that he did not enjoy even a defeasible right to be appointed guardian of his child and that he had no standing in the adoption proceedings. He alleges violations of his right to respect for family life (Article 8), his right to a fair hearing (Article 6(1)), and discrimination against him as a natural father (Article 14). In its Report on the case, the Commission concluded that he had suffered violations of his rights under Article 6(1) and Article 8 of the Convention and, in view of these findings, did not think it necessary also to examine the issue of discrimination.[35]

Ireland has been asked to justify its human rights performance before the European Court of Human Rights on only seven occasions in almost forty years. However, one should be careful not to draw facile conclusions from the paucity of cases. Many factors affect the decision of an individual whether or not to have recourse to this procedure, and likewise, once invoked, a number of factors will determine whether or not a grievance is ever referred to the Court for a judicial decision.

In five of the six cases decided by 1 January 1994, Ireland was found to be in violation of one or more of the applicants' rights under the Convention. The

Pine Valley case does not appear to have any wider implications beyond the situation of the particular applicants. The same cannot be said of the other four cases: *Airey, Johnston and Others, Norris,* and *Open Door Counselling and Dublin Well Woman Centre Ltd and Others.* Indeed the Court explicitly recognized in *Norris* that its decision would have effects extending beyond the confines of the particular case and stated that it was for Ireland to take the necessary measures in its domestic legal system to ensure the performance of its obligation to abide by the decision of the Court.[36] All four of these judgments had implications for Irish law and practice on the matters in question. Although it would not be accurate to speak in terms of sole cause and effect, it is clear that each of these applications has been promotional of change in the areas concerned. A scheme of civil legal aid and advice was introduced in Ireland post *Airey* ; and encouraged, by Airey's success, other applicants are, I believe, currently seeking to challenge aspects of the present scheme before the European Commission of Human Rights. A year after the decision of the European Court of Human Rights in *Johnston and Others,* the legal position of a child born of an unmarried couple was significantly improved by the Status of Children Act, 1987, and is now akin, but not identical, to the position of a child born of a married couple. It was, however, five years after the *Norris* judgment, that legislation was passed to decriminalize homosexual acts between consenting adult men in private: the Criminal Law (Sexual Offences) Act, 1993.[37] Change was somewhat quicker in relation to abortion information. As a result of a constitutional referendum in November 1992, a sentence was inserted into Article 40.3.3 of the Constitution which provides that this subsection

> shall not limit freedom to obtain or make available in the State, subject to such conditions as may be laid down by law, information relating to services lawfully available in another State.

Information about abortion services in Great Britain may now, therefore, be made available and may be obtained, but the availability and the obtaining of this information may be regulated by law. As of 1 January 1994, such legislation had yet to be enacted.[38]

Two of these cases, *Johnston and others* and *Norris,* raised issues comparable to ones which had already been considered and decided by the Court some years earlier, and are suggestive, therefore, of a certain reluctance and/or dilatoriness on the part of the Irish Government to change the law, where it may be said that the need for change, or at least for consideration of change, has been signalled by the European Court of Human Rights. The position under Belgian law of children born outside marriage had come before the Court in 1979, in the *Marckx* case;[39] in that case the Court had found that the inferior rights of a child born outside marriage compared to those of a child born of a married couple violated both the child's and its mother's right to respect for their family life and were discriminatory. As long ago as 1981, the Court held in the Northern Ireland case of *Dudgeon*,[40] that the same legislative provisions as were in issue in the *Norris* case, infringed the applicant's right to respect for his private life.

GENERAL SIGNIFICANCE OF JUDGMENTS OF THE EUROPEAN COURT OF HUMAN RIGHTS

The European Convention on Human Rights gives expression to standards in the field of human rights to which a group of European States subscribe and which they are anxious to uphold. In becoming parties to the Convention, these States have conferred upon the European Court of Human Rights the competence to interpret these standards and have accepted that the Court's interpretation is binding upon them in international law. Even cases in which a State is not directly involved may result in an interpretation of the Convention which casts doubt on the compatibility of that State's law or practice with its obligations under the Convention. Moreover, the Court has stated on several occasions that it regards the Convention as "a living instrument",[41] that is, that it does not regard the standards expressed therein as static, but will interpret them in the light of developments in the law and practice of Contracting States and of changes in social attitudes. This dynamic approach to the interpretation of the rights guaranteed by the Convention is manifest, *inter alia*, in the standards applicable to corporal punishment and the legal rights of transsexuals,[42] as well as to the understanding of concepts such as family life and mental illness.[43] Standards are evolving rather than fixed; and, in general, Contracting States are expected to adhere to these evolving standards. All of the case law of the Court is therefore of interest to Contracting States, not merely those cases in which they participate either as an applicant or a respondent State.

I shall give but two examples from the Court's case law of a series of cases which are of particular significance for Ireland, even though Ireland did not participate in the relevant proceedings. One series of cases concerns the detention of persons on grounds of mental illness, the other the tapping of telephones.

Starting with a landmark decision in 1979 involving the Netherlands, the Court of Human Rights has gradually posited a number of criteria which must be fulfilled if the detention of a person in a mental institution is to be regarded as legitimate.[44] Not only must the person be mentally ill as determined by what the Court terms "objective medical expertise",[45] but the mental illness must be of a kind and degree to warrant compulsory confinement, and the validity of continued confinement depends upon the persistence of this illness. It has also required that a person so detained should have access at reasonable intervals to a court or other independent body of a judicial kind to challenge the lawfulness of the detention, that this body should afford certain procedural safeguards to the individual concerned, and that it should itself examine the grounds for the person's detention, form its own view thereon, and have the power, if it is of the view that the person should not be detained, to order the release of that person. Irish law on the detention and treatment of the mentally ill is contained in the Mental Treatment Acts, 1935 and 1961. These statutes do not afford the safeguards required by the European Court of Human Rights in respect of detention of persons on grounds of mental illness. Such safeguards are contained on the Health (Mental Services) Act, 1981, but the Act requires an order of the Minister for Health to bring the Act or any of its provisions into effect, and no such order has been made to date.

It was earlier, in 1978, in a case against the Federal Republic of Germany, that the Court started to assess the compatibility of a system of secret surveillance with the Convention, in particular with the individual's right to respect for private life and correspondence.[46] The Court held that, given the threat to democratic institutions posed by terrorism and espionage, some degree of secret surveillance was acceptable. However, being aware of the danger which such surveillance presents of undermining or even destroying democracy on the ground of defending it, the Court required that "whatever system of surveillance is adopted, there must exist adequate and effective guarantees against abuse".[47] Invoking the rule of law, which it described as "one of the fundamental principles of a democratic society",[48] the Court stated that:

> an interference by the executive authorities with an individual's rights should be subject to an effective control which should normally be assured by the judiciary, at least in the last resort, judicial control offering the best guarantees of independence, impartiality and a proper procedure.[49]

In subsequent cases, the Court has made it clear that, even when the surveillance is initially authorized by a member of the judiciary, other independent checks must exist. The Court has also emphasized that surveillance must have a basis in domestic law and that this law must regulate such matters as who may authorize surveillance, on what grounds, and for how long, and must contain safeguards in respect of the transmission from one person to another of the information gleaned thereby, the use of the information and its retention. Until recently, Irish law did not satisfy these requirements. However, the

Interception of Postal Packets and Telecommunications Messages (Regulation) Act, 1993, now remedies the situation. It meets the Convention requirements with respect to the authorization of surveillance etc., and contains two safeguards of a judicial kind. First, a High Court judge will be entrusted with the task of keeping the operation of the Act under review and of ascertaining whether its provisions are being complied with. Secondly, persons who suspect that their post has been intercepted or telephone tapped may apply to a Complaints Referee, who shall be a judge of the Circuit or District Court or a practising barrister or solicitor of not less than ten years' standing, for an investigation of the matter. The Referee has the power, in appropriate cases, to quash the authorization, to order the destruction of any copy of the intercepted information, and to recommend the payment of compensation.

Both of the examples I have given suggest yet again a certain dilatoriness on the part of the Irish Government in implementing Convention standards. In the Government's defence, it might be argued that, since the standards are evolving, it is wise to wait until the standards are clear before taking action thereon. However, since the standards are *continually* evolving, this approach, if carried too far, endorses inaction. The "wait and see" attitude of the Irish Government, especially when the wait exceeds ten years, will do nothing to enhance Ireland's reputation as a champion of human rights.

CONCLUSION

The European Convention on Human Rights was, at the time of its adoption, extremely innovatory. In particular, the conferral of competence upon an international body to hear individual complaints of human rights violations was a new departure in international law. Although this procedure is now widely subscribed to by European States, it should be remembered that even today many States in the world are unwilling to submit their human rights performance to such scrutiny. And who would have envisaged in 1950, the year the text of the Convention was adopted, that forty years later the States of Eastern Europe would be queueing up to sign?

The inter-State complaints procedure has been little used and there is little likelihood of its increased use either by Ireland or by any other State. It is the individual complaints procedure which provides the lifeblood of the Commission and the Court. The Court has now decided well over two hundred cases and the ever-increasing number of complaints (as well as the number of parties to the Convention) has serious implications for its workload and its composition. Although resort to this procedure by individuals in Ireland has been somewhat restrained, a greater awareness in recent years, both among lawyers and among the public at large, of this avenue of redress for human rights violations will, in all likelihood, eventually be reflected in an increased number of applications to the European Commission of Human Rights. The applications to date, though small in number, have played a role in promoting legislative reform. Moreover, as we have seen, reform may be required by the interpretation afforded the Convention rights by the Court in cases involving other States.

Yet too much should not be expected of the Convention. As indicated at the beginning of this paper, it deals with a restricted number of human rights and there are rights even in the civil and political fields which its does not protect. Moreover, human rights are principally guaranteed by the domestic law of Contracting States and it is mainly by having recourse to procedures at the national level that individuals may gain redress for violations of these human rights. As the European Court of Human Rights has recognized, the protection afforded by the Convention is subsidiary to that afforded by national legal systems.

While, at times, Ireland may have displayed some hesitancy in implementing the Convention standards, no Irish Government has, as far as I am aware, ever seriously considered voluntarily withdrawing from the Convention. The question of denunciation (permitted by Article 65) has surfaced in recent years, however, in the context of a possible conflict between the provisions of the Irish Constitution and those of the Convention. When, in 1986, the European Court of Human Rights declined to read into either the right to marry, or the right to respect for private and family life, a right to divorce, it thereby avoided any conflict between Ireland's obligations under the Convention and the constitutional prohibition on the dissolution of marriage. A conflict did emerge, however, in the wake of the judgment of the Court in *Open Door* between the State's obligation to guarantee the right to freedom of expression under Article 10 of the Convention and the Supreme Court's interpretation of the constitutional right to life of the unborn as forbidding the dissemination in Ireland of information about specific abortion services abroad. The conflict was resolved in favour of freedom of expression by the adoption of a constitutional amendment in November 1992. If such a conflict were ever to occur again, it is to be hoped that the question would be resolved by the electorate in a referendum, in which the arguments both for and against any constitutional amendment, including consideration of Ireland's obligations under the Convention, would be fully debated.

2.3 Individual Remedies and the Strasbourg System in an Irish Context

PATRICK DILLON-MALONE

It is the purpose of this paper to consider the remedies available to an individual in respect of an alleged or anticipated breach of his or her rights as set forth in the European Convention on Human Rights. For reasons of space and clarity, the discussion is limited to the availability of such remedies in the existing supervisory system[1] and having regard to the existing status of the Convention in Irish law.[2] For similar reasons, it does not attempt to provide a detailed description of practice and procedure in the Strasbourg system.[3]

THE STATUS OF THE CONVENTION IN IRISH LAW

In common with other international instruments for the protection of human rights and with the primary concern of international human rights law in general, the central objective of the Convention is to ensure observance of the standards set down in the Convention in domestic law.[4] To this end, Article 1 provides that the Contracting Parties "shall secure to everyone within their jurisdiction the rights and freedoms" defined in the Convention and its substantive protocols. This obligation, however, does not mean that the Convention itself must be incorporated into domestic law.[5] Nor are national courts, as a matter of Convention law, under any obligation to examine its provisions with a view to ascertaining whether they are self-executing, and so enforceable, in the internal legal order.[6]

Instead, the question falls to be considered as a matter of domestic law,[7] and in Ireland the unequivocal answer is that the Convention forms no part of Irish law. Article 29.6 of the Constitution adopts an explicitly dualist approach to international agreements,[8] so that in the absence of legislation incorporating the provisions of the Convention, the Irish courts have consistently and quite correctly declined to apply any such provision against a conflicting provision of Irish law.[9] In consequence, and unlike the domestic courts in those European jurisdictions where it has been so incorporated,[10] the Irish courts will rarely listen to argument or offer any interpretation on the scope and meaning of the Convention's provisions.[11] The same is true of judgments of the European Court, even those directed to Ireland as the respondent State.[12] Irish courts are therefore also absent from what has been described as a dialogue between

European courts and the European Court of Human Rights which has gradually given to the Convention the status of a common constitutional instrument in the field of human rights.[13]

It is true that there has been some selective reliance upon the Convention by Irish courts. Among these sporadic judgments, however, few depart from the bare text of its provisions.[14] In some instances, the Convention is invoked to bolster the reasoning of the court with respect to Irish law.[15] In others, the existence of a Convention right is taken as evidence that a similar right is protected by the Irish Constitution.[16] In yet others, the courts have gone so far as to state that there is a presumption that Irish law is in conformity with the Convention[17] and, somewhat bizarrely, particularly with certain provisions thereof.[18] If this be the case,[19] it must be accepted that this is no more than one of many presumptions, no greater than a principle of statutory interpretation or a presumption at common law. Although it might operate to clarify[20] or even supplement[21] statutory words, it cannot prevail against them[22] nor provide a remedy when statutory provisions are lacking completely.[23] It might also be questioned whether such a presumption can operate in respect of laws enacted prior to Ireland's signature of the Convention in 1950, and subsequent ratification in 1953.[24]

The High Court has affirmed that a similar rule of presumption applies to the more amorphous body of the common law and, more particularly, to those rules of the common law which are openly based upon considerations of public policy.[25] In *Desmond v. Glackin*, O'Hanlon J had regard to the corresponding guarantees of freedom of expression in the Irish Constitution and the Convention in holding that the latter was a persuasive consideration in determining issues of public policy in the common law rules on contempt of court.[26] However, experience shows that public policy considerations in Irish law will not be capable of such a reading in all cases. In addition, and notwithstanding that courts are marginally more free in applying rules of common law or equity than in interpreting statutes,[27] this new presumption is subject to the same limitations as those affecting a statutory presumption in this context.

These rules of presumption should be distinguished from the question of whether the Convention can operate to delimit the scope of administrative powers and duties in public law.[28] If such an argument can be made out, and if Irish law enforcement agencies and other administrative officials are accordingly under a duty to have regard to the provisions of the Convention as a relevant consideration in the exercise of their powers and duties, all public law remedies in Irish law might, in theory,[29] be significantly affected. Yet, once again, no Irish court has accepted such a far-reaching proposition. In the United Kingdom, following some tentative resort to the Convention in order to determine the limits of certain discretionary powers,[30] it is now clear that any such judicial exercise will be regarded as an unwarranted attempt to introduce the Convention into domestic law by the back door.[31] Whereas Irish courts may not be so inhibited by deference to parliamentary intent in this regard,[32] the manner in which Irish law would allow the Convention to be used in the *ultra vires* control of administrative powers is not readily apparent. Even those recent decisions on asylum law which might at first sight be taken to support such a proposition are based upon considerations of legitimate expectation which have no parallel in a Convention context.[33]

These developments nevertheless raise the possibility of increased resort to the Convention in Irish law.[34] In this connection, it is of interest to note that a recent decision of the English Court of Appeal has provoked some discussion as to whether courts, in a context other than Community law,[35] must, or rather may, have regard to the Convention in the event of ambiguity.[36] The answer, on the authorities, is clearly in favour of discretionary reliance.[37] In particular, a court which fails to respond to a Convention-based argument can hardly be said to have erred outside its jurisdiction.

A RIGHT TO AN EFFECTIVE REMEDY IN DOMESTIC LAW?

Whatever may be the position in Irish law, it is in any case clear that neither Article 1, nor the Convention in general, lays down for the States Parties any given manner of ensuring, within their internal law, the effective implementation of any its provisions.[38] Instead, and in accordance with general principles of State responsibility in international law,[39] the finding of a violation gives rise only to "obligations of result" whereby the respondent State must see its own way towards discontinuing the wrongful act and providing reparations and guarantees against its repetition.[40] Yet, at the same time, Article 13 of the Convention provides, in part:

> Everyone whose rights and freedoms as set forth in this Convention are violated shall have an effective remedy before a national authority.

The European Court of Human Rights has confirmed that this means that where an individual has an arguable claim to be the victim of a violation of a Convention right, a State Party is obliged to provide a mechanism, judicial or otherwise, for determining whether the substance of such right has been violated and, if so, to provide a remedy for its breach.[41] Beyond this general statement of principle, however, the waters become muddied, and for present purposes, it is enough to point out that Article 13 is not what it appears to be, that it raises a number of complex questions concerning the nature of the procedural guarantees contained in the Convention, particularly in Articles 5 and 6, and that the question of what constitutes an effective remedy will vary according to the particular substantive right being invoked.[42] In practice, it is not something to be invoked before the Irish courts, but an independent question of substance to be argued before the Strasbourg authorities.[43]

Even then, an Article 13 complaint against Ireland is unlikely to succeed.[44] This is because its requirements are met if effective remedies exist in the domestic legal order for vindicating rights which in their nature and scope are substantially co-extensive with those protected under the Convention.[45] Furthermore, although Article 13 does not oblige States Parties to make available to individuals a method of challenging legislation as such,[46] the existence of such a jurisdiction in the Irish Superior Courts means that Article 13 will not be breached even where an established violation of a Convention right is directly attributable to the maintenance in force of legislation.[47]

NO GENERAL RIGHT TO COMPENSATION

The corollary of what has been said above is that once a domestic court or other national authority has established State responsibility for the unlawful[48] conduct at issue, the only question then remaining, under the Convention, is whether the redress obtained at the national level is so inadequate that the individual may still be regarded as a "victim" within the meaning of the Convention. In certain such very exceptional circumstances, a complaint may still lie to the Commission under Article 25, and the individual's redress will then depend upon the success or failure of his or her case in Strasbourg.[49] If not, as, for example, where a declaratory remedy plus costs will satisfy the grievance, the matter ends there.[50] In general, therefore, there is no right to compensation for an established breach of one's Convention rights.

The Convention itself, in Article 5(5), provides for one exception to this rule for everyone who has been the victim of arrest or detention in contravention of the provisions of Article 5. In such circumstances, there is an enforceable right to compensation which forms a separate substantive right under the Convention.[51] Having regard to the protection afforded to the right of liberty in Irish law, resort to this provision in an Irish context is unlikely.[52] Article 3 of the Seventh Protocol now adds a second such right for victims of miscarriages of justice within the meaning of that provision. Ireland has not yet ratified this Protocol, and the exact scope of the entitlement in Article 3 remains ambiguous.[53] It is probable, nevertheless, that the proposed Irish legislation on miscarriages of justice will meet its requirements.[54]

THE SYSTEM'S POWERS OF COMPULSION

The resulting simple conclusion is that it is necessary to look for practical remedies for alleged or anticipated breaches of the Convention to the international supervisory mechanism established thereunder. As a first question, it is worth asking, as a practitioner must, whether it is capable of compelling a delinquent State to do anything at all against its will.

Looking to the powers of the European Court of Human Rights, which represents the judicial apex of the three Strasbourg organs, the immediate response to this inquiry is not an encouraging one. On the positive side, the Court has the power to award damages and costs to the successful applicant.[55] In all other respects, however, its decisions have no dispositive effect; the Court has no power to reverse or declare void the measures or decisions found to be in breach of the Convention; it cannot repeal legislation, annul administrative acts, set aside judicial decisions or otherwise make consequential orders requiring the State to take a particular course of action.[56] This is because the Court's decisions are binding on the respondent State as a matter of international law alone and cannot, in the absence of incorporation or a new ratified international agreement to that effect, be enforced in domestic courts. Put in another way, the respondent State is under an obligation to abide by the judgment of the Court[57] but, except in the order for monetary compensation, the Convention leaves to the State every latitude as regards the consequences flowing from a violation. This conclusion is unaffected by the possibility that a fresh or even continuing violation of the Convention may result from the judicial enforcement of laws[58] maintained in force following an adverse finding in Strasbourg.[59]

The same reasoning applies to the case of a violation which results wholly or in part from a decision of a domestic court. The decision will continue to enjoy the force of *res judicata*, and States Parties are under no obligation to make possible the review or reopening of proceedings following an adverse finding in Strasbourg.[60] Although the Court has itself commented that such fresh proceedings might bring about a result as close to *restitutio in integrum* as is possible, in the nature of things,[61] no such possibility exists in Ireland. Even if it did, review proceedings need not always lead to a more favourable outcome for the individual. In these circumstances, and having regard also to the protracted nature of the proceedings as a whole, it has been argued that the most equitable reform would allow a successful applicant to choose between restitution and pecuniary compensation.[62] However, the policy implications of such a reform are enormous. In a criminal context, it would allow a fruit-of-the-poison-tree rule to be invoked by a defendant in respect of all breaches of Convention rights; and in the fields of civil and administrative law, an undesirable burden might be placed on the private litigant and the public decision-maker, respectively. For these reasons, it is perhaps better to grant a right of restitution only in respect of those decisions for which compensation is deemed an inadequate remedy.[63]

It follows that an individual who looks to the Convention for redress must recognize that it does not offer coercive remedies against the State similar to those available in either civil or public law at the domestic level. In the Strasbourg system, there are no international sheriffs; there is no provision for attachment of State taxes and nothing approaching a contempt jurisdiction in the Court.[64] Instead, it is the State itself which holds out the promise, within a framework of international co-operation, of complying with the standards set forth in the Convention. Although the overwhelming number of infractions are established at the instance of complainants pursuant to the individual complaints procedure, and although that procedure might be adapted to provide ever more facility in obtaining redress, the ultimate sanction will always rest in the political[65] or legal measures taken against a delinquent State by the other members of the Council of Europe.

Apart from lawful acts of reprisal in international law,[66] such legal measures are to be found in the supervisory role of the Council's principal political organ, the Committee of Ministers, under Articles 32 and 54 of the Convention.[67] Article 54 of the Convention provides that the "judgment of the Court shall be transmitted to the Committee of Ministers which shall supervise its execution". Clearly, this does not confer a power to take or recommend specific remedial measures to be applied in the State concerned, a conclusion which is confirmed by the Rules and practice of the Committee not only in relation to its supervision of Court judgments but also in the exercise of its quite distinct powers in ensuring compliance with Commission reports which it has adopted under Article 32 of the Convention.[68] Damages plus costs may also be "recommended" under the Article 32 procedure, and in both cases payment is an easy matter to supervise.[69] In other respects, the measures necessary to comply with the decision of the Court or the Commission will often be obvious to everyone concerned.[70] Otherwise, the inability to insist on particular remedial measures should not in itself cause alarm in a body whose quasi-judicial functions are governed by political considerations. In practice, the same result is achieved by adopting Article 54 resolutions only after the Committee has been satisfied that the respondent State has complied with the judgment of the Court.[71] Equally, it is the practice of the Committee to combine its functions under Article 32 in a single resolution encompassing both its finding of a violation and its satisfaction that remedial measures have been taken in consequence of that finding and concluding by a simple statement that the case is over.[72]

It would appear that it was the former practice of some governments to insist that the Committee could no longer question the execution of the Court's judgment once the Article 50 payment has been made.[73] This narrow interpretation of the Committee's powers has now been discredited as contrary to the very purpose of the international controls established by the Convention,[74] and it would certainly be surprising if the powers of the Strasbourg organs were more limited with respect to the execution of the Court's judgments than with respect to Commission findings and recommendations.

On the contrary, the sanction of the Committee under Article 32 is potentially more limited than its powers under Article 54 in at least one respect.[75] If it cannot adopt the report of the Commission or decide upon the measures necessary to give effect to such a decision by a majority of two-thirds of its members, a "non-decision" results whereby a successful complainant before the Commission is left without a formal finding of a violation and without any possibility of doing anything about it.[76] This has long been recognized as an anomaly, and a simple majority rule will come into operation upon the entry into force of the Tenth Protocol.[77]

PARTICULAR PROBLEMS OF COMPLIANCE

In an Irish context, the well-known failure of successive governments to comply with the decision of the Court in *Norris v. Ireland*, despite contrary declarations of intent made in both Strasbourg and Ireland, had the inevitable consequence of undermining the Convention. This was particularly unfortunate in that it eclipsed the otherwise remarkable success of judgments of the Court in prompting or accelerating legislative reforms in the respondent and sometimes even in third States.[78] Seemingly, Strasbourg could be ignored with impunity, although, as a matter of law, this is not true. The result was all the more insidious in that an Irish court was unlikely to be called upon to apply the provisions in question in circumstances which might call attention to the more obvious human consequences of maintaining them in force. Although this particular tale has drawn to a close, it holds no lessons for an understanding of the Convention other than that Irish governments may be slow to comply with Court decisions in matters of public morality.

Yet it might appear that even prompt compliance can result in a hollow victory. Experience of the Convention has shown that most violations occur just beyond the limits of a State's discretion, in circumstances where the measures at issue are not quite proportionate to the admittedly compelling social interests sought to be protected.[79] With some modifications to the practice or law so found to be in violation, the State may continue to regulate the matter within the legitimate bounds of the "margin of appreciation" allowed to it under the Convention.[80] Once the Committee has declared itself satisfied with the changes, the possibility that the measures may still breach the Convention is unlikely to be tested again in Strasbourg. Worse still, a respondent government might allow those measures to fall into abeyance, and few are likely to make a fresh application to Strasbourg when the first has so demonstrably failed. The acknowledged inadequacy of the existing scheme of civil legal aid, first introduced following the judgment of the Court in *Airey v. Ireland*, is a case in point.[81]

In response, however, it should be remembered that Strasbourg does not hold out the prospect of international government nor of international regulation in matters affecting the enjoyment of Convention rights. Instead, the "margin of appreciation" is the corollary of circumscribing legislative, administrative and judicial discretion throughout Europe by reference to the provisions of the Convention.[82] The "margin of appreciation" is accordingly an integral and necessary aspect of the system which, in an Irish context, has enabled the Government to accept the need to introduce changes in the law relating to private homosexual conduct, the legal relations of children born outside marriage, and civil legal aid.[83] The inadequacy or tardiness of the Irish Government's response to these matters does not affect this conclusion.

Yet further difficulties might be said to result not from the extent of the Court's finding, but from the scope of its inquiry. In particular, the finding of a breach may rest solely upon the absence of a sufficiently clear and accessible legal basis for the measures at issue, thus leaving open the question of whether such measures would otherwise be permissible. The decision of the majority of the Commission in *Open Door Counselling and Dublin Well Woman Centre v. Ireland* is a case in point: if the Court had confined itself to similar reasoning, it would in theory have been possible for the Government to introduce legislation prohibiting the provision of abortion information in terms similar to the present injunctions of the courts.[84] The compatibility of such legislation with the Convention would then have to be tested all over again in Strasbourg, with all the expense and time that this entails.

Even if the Court had taken this narrower approach to the resolution of the issue in the *Open Door* case, however, its insistence upon the rule of law in this or in any other context should not be underestimated. At the very least, it can provoke public debate and end legislative inertia in respect of matters which the public at large and politicians, in particular, may have chosen to ignore. In this manner too, it may be noted, the achievement of the Convention is realized in circumscribing discretion. Indeed, the reasoning of the Commission in *Open Door* is to be preferred in that it cannot be taken to support the wisdom of regulating complex areas of human behaviour by reference solely to constitutional provisions.

COSTS, DAMAGES AND LEGAL AID

An award of just satisfaction under Article 50 covers damages for material and non-material prejudice suffered,[85] together with all reasonable costs and expenses necessarily and actually incurred in the proceedings undertaken to prevent or redress the breach before both the national and Strasbourg authorities.[86] The precise manner in which the Court arrives at a lump sum figure is not at all clear from the cases, and the global formula of assessment favoured by the Court has been the subject of some criticism.[87] Just satisfaction will only be awarded in cases where the Court finds a violation, where adequate reparation under the internal law of the respondent State is not possible[88] and, crucially, only when a claim for just satisfaction has been specifically pleaded before it.[89] Furthermore, the award is discretionary, so that if the Court determines that its finding constitutes sufficient vindication of the applicant's rights in all the circumstances of the case, the successful applicant is not even entitled to nominal damages and must take his or her losses as he or she finds them.[90] It would appear that the particular circumstances most likely to give rise to such a refusal may be broadly divided into those where the claim for damages is unsubstantiated and those where the violation results wholly or substantially from procedural error.[91]

The harshness of this rule might be said to be mitigated somewhat by the absence of any provision in the Strasbourg system generally for an award of costs to be be made against an individual applicant. As against this, the summary procedure and the short-form decision procedure adopted by the Commission both operate to ensure that a respondent State is not put to undue expense in defending itself in Strasbourg,[92] and it can be argued that the time and energy invested in bringing a successful case to the Court should not go unrewarded in any circumstances.

On the other hand, it was always the intention that Article 50 should work as a subsidiary remedy to the relief available at the domestic level,[93] and the Court is concerned that the Strasbourg jurisdiction should not be used as a forum for damages.[94] These prevailing policy considerations are reflected also in the very low level of damages generally awarded in the guise of just satisfaction. It is true that in certain cases of peculiar economic loss, such as that arising in the case of *Pine Valley Developments Ltd v. Ireland*,[95] the award of damages can be expected to be higher. As a general rule, however, it is worth bearing in mind that awards of damages in Strasbourg are not as generous as those in Irish courts. Although the Court is also concerned not to encourage high costs of litigation in a human rights context and has consistently refused to accept municipal rules or practice as binding upon it in this context,[96] it appears that it has not had occasion to question the costs and expenses on this ground in any Irish case to date.[97]

Similar awards may be recommended by the Committee of Ministers for costs and expenses incurred in proceedings before the Commission and as just satisfaction for other damages suffered. For this purpose, it may request the Commission to estimate the appropriate measure of damages, yet the making of such a recommendation remains at the discretion of the Committee itself and, once again, will not follow in every case from the finding of a violation.[98] Unlike the award of the Court, the Committee's recommendation does not rest on any specific provision of the Convention, but has been recently adapted as part of its supervisory functions under Article 32(2). It is probable, nevertheless, that the Committee will be most likely to decline to make such a recommendation in similar circumstances as the Court.

Provision is also made in the Commission's Rules of Procedure and the Rules of Court for the granting of legal aid in appropriate cases, as well as for the discretionary payment of the expenses of witnesses, experts and other persons whom either body hears at the request of an individual applicant.[99] It should be noted, however, that legal aid will not be considered in respect of any complaint which fails to survive the earliest stages of Commission procedure by being declared inadmissible without communication to the respondent government.[100] Furthermore, the fees offered to legal representatives are usually lower than those available in the domestic system.[101]

INTERIM MEASURES

No specific provision is made in the Convention for injunctive remedies against a State in respect of anticipated or continuing violations of Convention rights, and the institution of proceedings before either the Commission or the Court does not have suspensive effect. At the same time, any failure on the part of national authorities to provide for appropriate injunctions and court orders at the national level falls to be considered under the Convention, *ex post facto*, only by reference to Articles 5, 6 and 13.[102] Yet it is well established that State responsibility under the Convention is activated by a continuing breach of one's Convention rights.[103] Equally, although such responsibility is not generally engaged by a threatened breach,[104] the Convention organs will also pronounce on the existence or otherwise of a potential violation where it is both serious and irreparable.[105] To this end, both the Commission and the Court have adapted their respective rules of procedure to expedite such cases.[106] More importantly, both bodies have sought to rely on their internal rules as a legal basis for interim and conservatory measures in the Convention system.[107]

This latter innovation, known as Rule 36, has been highly successful. Invoked in cases where there is a serious risk that irreparable damage may be caused to the applicant during the consideration of a case,[108] it has been met with almost universal compliance by respondent States and has enabled the Commission, in particular, to develop some of its most important jurisprudence in the most drastic cases of anticipated mistreatment or family separations.[109] However, the Court has recently confirmed by the narrowest of majorities that the application of Rule 36 cannot be equated with a true jurisdiction in the Strasbourg authorities to order interim measures.[110] In holding that a respondent State is not bound under the Convention to comply with a Rule 36 request, the Court declined to accept an argument which appeared to follow from its own previous insistence that the guarantees set forth in the Convention, including the guarantee of the right of individual petition in Article 25, are "practical and effective, not theoretical or illusory".[111] One curious but necessary consequence of this finding is that if a person does not in fact suffer although the State has by its conduct risked a serious and irreparable breach of that person's rights, no breach of the Convention arises. As a result, and although it is unlikely that respondent States will henceforth adopt a cavalier approach to Rule 36 requests, the need to create an explicit power in the Strasbourg authorities to order interim and conservatory measures must now be undisputed.[112]

FRIENDLY SETTLEMENT

The importance of friendly settlement in the Convention system cannot be overstated. It is firmly embedded in the practice and procedure of the Commission, the Court and the Committee of Ministers and, while it is not intended here to provide a detailed description of the procedures followed by each in the exercise of its inherent power or express duty to facilitate such agreements,[113] it is important that legal advisors be alert to the possibility of negotiating a settlement at every stage of the complaints procedure. Having regard, in particular, to the many frustrations in obtaining an adequate remedy at law as traditionally understood in the domestic legal order, it is often the most satisfactory outcome for the individual applicant. For governments, too, friendly settlement of a human rights complaint has obvious attractions.

For the Strasbourg organs, and in particular for the Commission,[114] the resolution of a dispute by agreement may provide the fastest and most effective way of ensuring that offending laws and practices are altered in accordance with the respondent State's obligations under the Convention. This is not merely because the State will be more likely to act upon the concrete terms of a negotiated agreement than on a general obligation to abide by a decision of the Court or Committee, but also because the Strasbourg organs are under a duty to ensure that those terms are consistent with a continued respect for human rights generally. If not, as for example when the agreement does not contemplate the amendment or removal of an offending law, the Commission or the Court may refuse to strike the case off its list.[115] Although this has never happened in practice, the threat of such a possibility evidently informs the conduct of negotiations.[116]

As regards the question as to how such agreements might be enforced by the Strasbourg authorities, it is only in the case of friendly settlements approved by the Court that the Committee of Ministers is charged with supervising, in accordance with Article 54 of the Convention, the execution of any undertakings given.[117] In the case of settlements approved by the Commission, the Committee is informed of its terms but has no role in supervising its execution;[118] and in the rare case of settlements approved by the Committee after transmission of the case from the Commission but before the adoption of the report, the super-vision of its terms may be regarded as an inherent aspect of the Committee's political functions.[119] In any such case, it appears that the question of supervising friendly settlements is a non-issue in practice because the respondent State will not have agreed to terms which it is unwilling to implement.

DELAY IN PROCEEDINGS

On average, it takes six years for an application to be decided upon by the Court or as many years to be decided upon by the Committee of Ministers from the date of its first registration with the Commission.[120] Together with the time spent exhausting domestic proceedings, this means that the delays in the Strasbourg system will often be intolerable and may in many cases operate to deny the applicant any real sense of justice other than moot satisfaction.[121] Although it is not perhaps fair to judge this burgeoning international system by the standards required of a modern domestic legal system, it is to be noted that the European Court itself has refused to accept that structural difficulties might excuse an otherwise intolerable delay in administering justice.[122] Proposed reform of the Strasbourg system will attempt to tackle this problem as a matter of priority. In the meantime, the status of the Convention in Irish law will continue to work together with these delays to deprive the Convention of any immediacy save in those cases of urgency where the Commission and Court choose to expedite matters.[123]

MISCELLANEOUS PITFALLS

It is crucial to an understanding of the Convention to remember that there are a number of procedural and substantive requirements, set out in Articles 26 and 27 of the Convention, which can and in most cases do operate to stop an Article 25 application dead in its tracks. These notorious hurdles have been well described elsewhere[124] and it is not my purpose here to describe them in detail. Most are properly regarded as common sense features of any system of international supervision which can be readily surmounted by a well drafted petition. Others require more attention and, in particular, a familiarity with the reasoning of the Commission and the Court in the decided cases.

AN OBVIOUS WARNING

This last admonition applies with particular force to the question of what types of complaint will fail by reason of their subject-matter alone as incompatible *rationae materiae* with the provisions of the Convention.[125] Although it is true that the Strasbourg authorities are limited to their attributed jurisdiction as set down in the plain text of the Convention and its substantive protocols,[126] a reading of that text alone may be unhelpful in many cases. There is no Convention right to asylum, for example, nor to a pension, yet the Convention may offer a remedy to a refugee or to a pensioner whose protected rights have been threatened or infringed. More generally, the wide notion of civil rights and obligations in Article 6 means that the procedural guarantees of that Article may be invoked in relation to almost every conceivable legal dispute.[127] As with any other area of the law, therefore, there is no substitute for a knowledge of the law itself.

DRITTWIRKUNG

The question also arises as to whether the Convention has any effect on the relations between private parties. The simple answer here is that the Convention has no horizontal effect in the sense of enforcement of Convention rights against private individuals, *a fortiori*, in States such as Ireland where such judicial innovation at the domestic level is foreclosed.[128] Nevertheless, the Convention's impact on private law should not be underestimated. Although a private suit may be lost, the fairness of the proceedings may be put in issue with a view to salvaging some money, at least, although not from the successful litigant but from the State itself.[129] In rare cases, the obligation deriving from Article 1 has been interpreted to extend also to a positive obligation on the State to take measures, legislative or otherwise, to ensure that Convention rights are not destroyed by other individuals.[130] However, neither such possibility should be mistaken for an active Convention *Drittwirkung*, nor be allowed to cloud the view of any legal advisor who has it properly in mind that human rights law is preoccupied with State responsibility.

MANIFESTLY ILL-FOUNDED

It is on this ground, in particular, that the Commission may be seen to control the docket of the Convention organs by pronouncing on the merits without engaging the full Strasbourg mechanism. Broadly speaking, a complaint will be dismissed as manifestly ill-founded where there is no *prima facie* disclosure of a case to answer. It is distinguished in principle from incompatibility *ratione materiae* by the notion of Commission competence to consider the complaint in the first place. In principle too, it should be confined to cases where the ill-founded character is evident at first sight from an informed knowledge of the Convention and the constant jurisprudence of the Commission and the Court. In practice, however, it is well known and has often been lamented that the reasoning of the Commission in rejecting complaints as manifestly ill-founded can be very complex.[131] Yet, on another view, and providing always that the decisions of the Commission are consistent and accessible, the complexity of its reasoning at the admissibility stage should not be regarded as so treacherous, but should rather serve to demonstrate the need in practice to make a full and reasoned argument in one's first communications with the Commission. In this connection, it may be remembered that oral hearings before the Commission are invariably concerned with both admissibility and merits so that the rejection of a complaint as inadmissible does not necessarily deprive the applicant of an adversarial procedure.[132]

EXHAUSTION OF DOMESTIC REMEDIES

As a general rule, it is advisable to pursue all available legal remedies, that is, all appellate procedures which can still substantially affect the decision on the merits.[133] It is also crucial to remember that the Commission will not be satisfied with the mere formalistic pursuit of remedies at the domestic level—the particular argument, the subject of your complaint to Strasbourg, should therefore be pleaded before the Irish courts by reference to Irish law.[134] Furthermore, all parallel remedies should be pursued.[135] At the same time, the Commission does not insist on formal exhaustion of domestic remedies in all circumstances, but only on such remedies as are "effective and sufficient" within the meaning of the decided cases.[136] For example, an appeal to the Supreme Court with leave at the discretion of the Attorney General need not be pursued.[137] Nor, more generally, need an applicant have lodged an appeal which had no prospect of success according to well-established case law.[138] Yet caution must once again be exercised in attempting to circumvent the otherwise very strict application of the domestic remedies rule. Even if it is thought that the case is on all fours with a previous Supreme Court decision, it may be advisable, pending the Commission's determination of the issue, to lodge one's domestic appeal within the prescribed period at the same time as submitting an Article 25 complaint to Strasbourg.[139]

THE SIX MONTHS RULE

Time starts running, for the purposes of the six months rule in Article 26, from the date of the final effective and adequate decision or, where such decision is not public, from the date of its notification to the applicant.[140] The rule is applied very strictly indeed, and until recently it appears to have been abandoned only in extreme cases of chronic ill-health.[141] Even now, the circumstances in which the rule is relaxed must be regarded as exceptional.[142] In circumstances where time is in imminent danger of running out, a simple letter or fax to the Commission, setting out the factual substance of one's complaint, will operate to stop time running from the date of its receipt.[143]

THE SCOPE OF THE COURT'S REVIEW

Although the establishment and verification of facts is primarily a matter for the Commission,[144] the Court is not bound by its findings of fact and remains free to substitute its own determinations in the light of all the evidence before it.[145] For this reason, it is worth remembering that fresh evidence may be introduced before the Court.[146] The Court has interpreted its jurisdiction under Article 45 as extending also to questions of admissibility which the Commission has already considered and, obviously, not rejected in the particular case before it.[147] The consequence for individual applicants, fairly or unfairly,[148] is that their cases may still be vulnerable to rejection by the Court as manifestly ill-founded, or for want of exhaustion, or for failure to observe the six months rule, or for any other ground of inadmissibility, even after protracted consideration of the matter by international lawyers over a period of six years (on average) and with the benefit of two oral hearings (usually) and extensive written submissions.[149]

PARTICIPATION OF THE APPLICANT

On a strictly formal analysis, there is a surprising degree of confidentiality and even secrecy surrounding certain aspects of the consideration of an individual application in Strasbourg, to the extent even of placing procedural handicaps on individual applicants *vis-à-vis* respondent States. In practice, however, these restrictions have been largely shed and, insofar as they survive, they are mainly attributable to the continuing participation of the Committee of Ministers in the adjudication process. The greatest remaining handicap is the incapacity of individuals to seise the Court directly following a Commission decision on the merits, and this objection will be well met by the procedure envisaged in the Ninth Protocol to the Convention.[150] Finally, it should be remembered that an application will proceed largely on the basis of written communications with professional lawyers in the respective Secretariats of the Commission and the Court.[151] Applicants will find that this correspondence is both easy and efficient and should not interpret any apparent coolness as indifference on the part of the Strasbourg authorities.

CONCLUSIONS

The international system of supervision established by the Convention has outgrown its present framework and is in urgent need of institutional reform.[152] Yet this should not colour the twofold conclusion which may be drawn from this survey. The first, clearly, is that by any measure there is a significant procedural burden on those who seek to compel Ireland to comply with its obligations under the Convention; the second, that many of the difficulties of availing oneself of the Convention in an Irish context are traceable to Ireland, not Strasbourg.

At the domestic level, incorporation cannot cure every imperfection. For example, provision is not made in all jurisdictions which have incorporated the Convention for the reopening of proceedings following an adverse finding of the Court. Some domestic courts, usually those with an analogous domestic jurisdiction, are empowered to declare laws and measures contrary to the Convention, whereas in others the offending measure is simply ignored. Yet these are minor difficulties because the full range of court orders can be invoked at the domestic level to uphold the rule of law in this context as in any other. In this connection too, it should be remembered that domestic courts when applying domestic laws are often constrained by considerations of severability and the separation of powers in the exercise of judicial review.

Historically, it is perhaps still arguable that the above catalogue of procedural obstacles and uncertainties may be no more than a *quid pro quo* for the acceptance of the right of individual petition in the first place. Legally, incorporation remains no more than "a particularly faithful reflection" of the intention of the Convention's drafters.[153] Yet it is now becoming increasingly clear that the future reform of the Strasbourg system may be predicated upon domestic applicability of the Convention in all States party thereto. This should not be mistaken for centralist zeal. On the contrary, it has forcefully been argued by a President of the Court that the creation of an advisory jurisdiction analogous to that enjoyed by the European Court of Justice under Article 177 EEC is inappropriate in a Convention context precisely because it does not require uniform application throughout Europe.[154] Instead, the principal responsibility for interpreting and applying the Convention will rest with the superior courts of each European jurisdiction, having regard to its own peculiar considerations of policy and subject to a more streamlined and accessible review procedure by an enlarged, but not staggered, European Court of Human Rights.[155]

In most European jurisdictions, the first part of this process is already well underway.[156] States with an established bill of rights have had little difficulty in accommodating the one beside the other, and in those countries which in addition have had a tradition of strong judicial independence, experience shows that there is no correlation between incorporation and established violations of the Convention. Of course, the argument goes the other way too: the absence of incorporation cannot be linked to a lesser respect for human rights. Instead, the virtue of incorporation is that, at least, it allows individuals to argue before domestic courts or other State authorities that the Convention applies in a particular context without forcing them to establish its relevance at considerable inconvenience and expense and with uncertain consequences. Furthermore, the case law of the Commission and Court can throw fresh light on the balance of interest between the individual and the State and serve as a source of constitutional ideas and concepts which can only be to the benefit of our own legal system.[157]

For the moment, the thrust of any advice given in practice, other than in emergency cases, can continue to do no more than almost stupidly echo the words of Lord Denning in one case that "in the long run—and I am afraid it may be a long run— . . . justice may be done. But not here".[158] As evidenced by the character of successful Irish cases to date, this is a hook only for the most stubborn and committed.

2.4 Select Bibliography

TEXTS AND MATERIALS

E.A. Alkema et al. eds., *The Domestic Implementation of the European Convention on Human Rights in Eastern and Western Europe* (Kehl am Rhein, 1992).

R. Beddard, *Human Rights in Europe*, 3rd ed., (London, 1993).

V. Berger, *Case Law of the European Court of Human Rights, volume I: 1960–1987 and volume II: 1988–1990* (Dublin, 1989 and 1992).

A.A. Cancado Trindade, *The Application of the Rule of Exhaustion of Local Remedies in International Law—Its Rationale in the International Protection of Individual Rights* (Cambridge, 1983).

J.P. Clarke, "The European Convention on Human Rights and Fundamental Freedoms and Irish Law" (unpublished paper, Centre for Human Rights, University College Galway, 1981).

M. Delmes-Marty, ed., *The European Convention for the Protection of Human Rights: International Protection versus National Restrictions* (Dordrecht, 1992)

A. Drzemczewski, *The European Human Rights Convention in Domestic Law: A Comparative Study* (Oxford, 1983).

J.E.S. Fawcett, *The Application of the European Convention on Human Rights*, 2nd ed., (Oxford, 1987).

F. Matscher and H. Petzold, eds., *Protecting Human Rights—The European Dimension: Essays in Honour of G.J. Wiarda*, 2nd ed., (Köln, 1990).

J.G. Merrills, *The Development of International Law by the European Court of Human Rights* (Manchester, 1988).

L. Mikaelsen, *European Protection of Human Rights: The Practice and Procedure of the European Commission of Human Rights on the Admissibility of Applications from Individuals and States* (Alphen aan den Rijn, 1983).

A.H. Robertson and J.G. Merrills, *Human Rights in Europe: A Study of the European Convention on Human Rights*, 3rd ed., (Manchester, 1993).

P. van Dijk and G.J.H. van Hoof, *Theory and Practice of the European Convention on Human Rights*, 2nd ed., (Deventer, 1990).

R.R. Wallace, *Human Rights in Europe* (12 Stair Memorial Encyclopedia) (London, 1992).

ARTICLES

T. Bingham, "The European Convention on Human Rights: Time to Incorporate" (1993) 109 *LQR* 66.

J. Bengoetxea and H. Jung, "Towards A European Criminal Jurisprudence? The Justification of Criminal Law By the Strasbourg Court" (1991) 11 *Legal Studies* 239.

B. Bix and A. Tompkins, "Unconventional Use of the Convention?" (1992) 55 *MLR* 721.

T. Blake, "The National Archives: New Perspectives on Ireland's Approach to the International Protection of Human Rights" (1992) 10 *ILT* (n.s.) 43.

K. Boyle, "Practice and Procedure on Individual Applications under the European Convention on Human Rights" in H. Hannum, ed., *Guide to Human Rights Practice* (London, 1983) 133.

R.R. Churchill and J.R. Young, "Compliance with the Judgment of the European Court of Human Rights and Decisions of the Committee of Ministers: The Experience of the United Kingdom, 1975–1987" (1991) 62 *BYIL* 283.

A. Drzemczewski, "The Sui Generis Nature of the European Convention on Human Rights" (1980) 29 *ICLQ* 57.

A. Drzemczewski, "The Need for a Radical Overhaul" (1993) January *NLJ* 126.

A. Drzemczewski, "A Full-Time European Court of Human Rights in Strasbourg" (1993) October *NLJ* 1488.

C. Gearty, "The European Court of Human Rights and the Protection of Civil Liberties: An Overview" (1993) 52 *CLJ* 89.

H. Golsong, "On the Reform of the Supervisory System of the European Convention on Human Rights" (1992) 13 *HRLJ* 265.

J. Jaconelli, "The European Convention on Human Rights as Irish Municipal Law" (1987) XXII *Irish Jurist* (n.s.) 13.

P. Mahony, "Judicial Activism and Judicial Self-Restraint in the European Court of Human Rights: Two Sides of the Same Coin" (1990) 11 *HRLJ* 57.

A.R. Mowbray, "Procedural Developments and the European Convention on Human Rights" [1991] *Public Law* 353.

P. Mulchinski, "The Status of the Individual under the European Convention on Human Rights and Contemporary International Law" (1985) 34 *ICLQ* 376.

M. O'Boyle, "Practice and Procedure under the European Convention on Human Rights" (1980) 20 *Santa Clara L Rev* 697.

M. O'Boyle, "The Reconstruction of the Strasbourg Human Rights System" (1992) 14 *DULJ* (n.s.) 41.

J. Polakiewicz and V. Jacob-Foltzer, "The European Convention on Human Rights in Domestic Law: The Impact of Strasbourg Case Law Where Direct Effect is Given to the Convention" (1991) 12 *HRLJ* 65.

J. Raymond, "A Contribution to the Intepretation of Article 13 of the European Convention on Human Rights" (1980) 5 *HRR* 161.

H.G. Schermers, "Has the European Commission of Human Rights Got Bogged Down?" (1988) 9 *HRLJ* 175.

C. Tomuschat, "Quo Vadis, Argentoratum? The Success Story of the European Convention on Human Rights—and a Few Dark Stains" (1992) 13 *HRLJ* 401.

G. Whyte, "Application of the European Convention on Human Rights Before the Irish Courts" (1982) 31 *ICLQ* 856.

3 : THE EUROPEAN COMMUNITY

3.1   Introduction

The idea that European Community law may control a breach of fundamental rights by a Member State should be an area of particular interest to practitioners. The issue may arise not only where a Member State is implementing Community legislation, for example, an Irish Act implementing a directive, but also where one finds a national measure touching an area "within the sphere of European Community law". The significance is that the European version of fundamental rights may be better than the Irish constitutional version, as interpreted by the Supreme Court. The last decade saw a higher level of protection of fundamental rights by the European Court of Human Rights, arising from a stricter scrutiny of any alleged State interest or public policy. One need only compare how much more "user-friendly" the European Court of Human Rights seemed towards the right of privacy in *Norris v. Ireland*[1] than our own High Court and Supreme Court had been in the domestic proceedings.[2] It seems likely that the European Court of Justice would also apply a high level of protection similar to the European Court of Human Rights and this "ups" the anticipation for Community law protection of human rights.

If an Irish person could invoke "European fundamental rights"[3] via European Community law, two advantages might arise. In the first place, the litigant could do so from the outset in the national court. Compare this with the usual situation where one can only rely on rights under the European Convention on Human Rights having first exhausted all domestic remedies. Secondly, if one wins in the Irish court, the result by definition is automatically part of Irish law. A rule, or consequence, of Community law will be supreme over any conflicting national law by virtue of Article 29.4.3. One might contrast this with the outcome of the *Norris* case in Europe, where the violation of human rights as found by the European Court of Human Rights has only recently found vindication in Irish law.[4]

There are of course certain disadvantages or problems with trying to achieve in Ireland a European version of fundamental rights via the back door of European Community law. The following problems spring to mind. In the first place, this approach involves asking the European Court of Justice to deal with matters not really within its main or natural competence. It may involve the

European Court of Justice in second-guessing an approach of the European Court of Human Rights as to what approach that latter Court would take regarding sensitive questions of national policy. For example, in the case of *SPUC v. Grogan*,[5] it was argued that the Irish ban on dissemination of abortion information was a breach of the defendant's freedom of expression as protected by European Community law. It was submitted that the Irish measure resulting in such a ban was one within the sphere of Community law as it bore upon the free movement of persons. Because another Irish case raising the freedom of expression arguments was pending before the European Court of Human Rights,[6] counsel for the defendants in *Grogan* suggested to the members of the ECJ that they might let the fundamental rights arguments stand over until the Strasbourg Court had dealt with the matter. One is mindful of the possibility for conflict between the Luxembourg Court and the Strasbourg Court if in a given case the Luxembourg Court were to find no breach of fundamental rights and then in a later case raising the same issues the Strasbourg Court were to determine a definite breach of fundamental rights. Judge Lenaerts has referred to a possible sense of shame if the European Court of Human Rights were to reject an ECJ interpretation of fundamental rights.[7] Indeed in the *Grogan* case itself, the Advocate General may have made an error in dealing with the fundamental rights argument. He spoke of the aim of the national measure being to preclude assistance in procuring an abortion. But the crucial feature of the national measure in question was to preclude assistance in procuring an abortion *in another Member State*. It is difficult to imagine the European Court of Human Rights finding this far-reaching aim a valid one. When it came to the ECJ judgment, the Court was able to avoid the fundamental rights issues (as well as the substantive Community law issues) by reliance on a narrow *locus standi* approach. So one can only speculate as to how the ECJ would have dealt with the fundamental rights arguments on their merits.

Secondly, there is a danger that the ECJ will not have all the proper evidence before it to reach a fully informed decision. On an Article 177 reference, the Court only deals with the legal points and no evidence is heard. In contrast the European Court of Human Rights considers a mass of factual material, including reports and studies, etc. In the *Grogan* case, the defendant's legal representatives appended a report from an English social scientist to the written submissions in an attempt to put certain facts before the Court of Justice. In the end, of course, the Court did not deal with the issues but the Advocate General reiterated the point that the Court is not entitled to take into consideration factual arguments which the national court did not bring to the Court's notice as being established facts.

A further difficulty arises from the fact that while the invocation of fundamental rights via Community law may shorten the road to a finding of a breach of "European fundamental rights", paradoxically it may also lengthen the road.

In order to leave open the possibility of an eventual journey to Strasbourg, one is probably obliged to raise all possible arguments in the national courts in order to exhaust domestic remedies. This may include seeking an Article 177 reference on the point of a possible breach of fundamental rights under Community law. For example, the *Grogan* case went from the interlocutory stage, High Court, to interlocutory stage, Supreme Court, to the ECJ, for the Article 177 reference, and then returned to the High Court, for the trial of the action. Potentially, it might have faced an appeal to the Supreme Court from the trial judge before finally facing a final lap around the international circuit to Strasbourg so as to meet the European Commission on Human Rights and the European Court of Human Rights, eventually and finally. By no stretch of the imagination could this be called an effective method for the protection of human rights. Part of the solution for avoiding future duplication or triplication might be to allow the European Court of Justice to state a case to the European Court of Human Rights on a fundamental rights issue and a proposal to move in this direction has already been made.[8]

Finally, as we move towards closer European integration, more and more national rules will be "within the scope of Community law" and thus the whole topic under discussion will become more important. If there is going to be a federal evolvement, it seems logical that the fundamental rights standards will have to converge across Europe. There will be less and less room for particular national sensitivities. Moreover, if we are going to have "European fundamental rights" available by Community law, there are procedural problems to be faced regarding effective enforcement of these rights. In particular, problems will arise at the interim and/or interlocutory stage. A national court may be disinclined to lean towards the "European fundamental rights" at the interlocutory stage in preference to national measures. In the *X* case,[9] for example, could the young defendant have applied to the ECJ for *interim* measures to protect her European rights, assuming for the moment that such rights existed? If Community law is really going to take on board the protection of fundamental rights, then one must remember that any right is of little use without an available remedy.

SEAMUS WOULFE

3.2 Human Rights and the Treaty of Rome

ALAIN VAN HAMME

The European Council of Maastricht has proven that the founding fathers of the Community were undoubtedly right when they anticipated that, through some spill-over effect, the process of European integration initially confined to coal and steel production (ECSC), atomic energy (EAEC) and general economic matters (EEC) would gradually call for even more integration between the Community's Member States.

As a consequence of this on-going process of European integration, no one can deny that the Treaty of Rome (hereinafter the Treaty) has grown to become more than a treaty designed for economic integration, now that the European Court of Justice itself has referred to this Treaty as the Community's basic constitutional charter.[1] In view of this development it is quite logical, on reflection, that the Community legal order should guarantee an adequate protection of fundamental human rights which are at the core of Europe's democratic society.

At the same time it should be stressed, however, that the evolution which actually permitted this result was not exempt from hurdles. Initially, fundamental human rights gained recognition in Community law in the case law of the ECJ which stressed that these rights were part of the general principles of law which the Court is bound to apply pursuant to Article 164 of the Treaty.

However, since 1987, with the Single European Act, protection of human rights has found its way into Community legislation. It is the purpose of this paper to outline this evolution.

THE SUPREMACY OF COMMUNITY LAW AND THE PROTECTION OF HUMAN RIGHTS

The Treaty does not list a catalogue of human rights and does not lay down any procedure specifically designed to ensure effective compliance with those rights. As mentioned, this can easily be explained by the fact that within the field of application of the Treaty (initially limited to general economic matters) the protection of human rights did not seem to have immediate practical signifi-cance, even though the Treaty imposes compliance with some basic principles inherent to the organization of an international free market economy, such as the prohibition of discrimination on the basis of nationality (Article 7), the freedom of movement of workers (Article 48), the freedom of establishment for undertakings (Article 52) and the prohibition of gender discrimination with respect to salary (Article 119). In contrast, the draft treaties on the European Defence Community[2] and on the European Political Community,[3] specifically provided for the protection of human rights, in the context of a general field of application going beyond economic matters.[4]

As regards the Treaty, the question of human rights first arose when economic operators tried to challenge the validity of secondary Community legislation before the European Court of Justice, on the basis that such legislation allegedly infringed fundamental rights expressed in their own national constitutions. The success of such proceedings would have meant that constitutional rules of one Member State could constitute a valid ground for the annulment of Community acts. Clearly, such claims threatened the primacy of Community law over national law, and hence the very foundations of Community law as an autonomous legal order.

Against such claims, the Court refused, in the *Stork, Praesident Ruhrkohlen-verkaufsgesellschaft* and *Sgarlata* cases, to consider whether Community acts, adopted by the competent Community institutions, complied with the constitutional provisions of a Member State, even if these provisions expressed fundamental rights,[5] because such review would be tantamount to recognizing the precedence of such rules over Community law. Hence, the aforementioned judgments should not be analysed so much as an express denial of the relevance of fundamental human rights within the realm of Community law, but rather as a confirmation of the Court's main concern until the end of the 1960s, namely, to uphold the primacy of the Community legal order over national legal orders and its direct effect within national jurisdictions.[6]

But, in Germany and Italy, where a constitutional court is specifically entrusted with the task of ensuring the compliance of all national legislation and regulations with the national constitution and the fundamental rights enshrined therein, the jurisprudence of the ECJ caused serious concern on the basis that the protection of fundamental rights in the Community context should not fall behind the protection afforded in the liberal democratic constitutions of the Member States concerned.[7]

More specifically, the German Constitutional Court held in the German *Handelsgesellschaft* case that the protection of fundamental rights was an essential element of the German Federal Constitution, an element which could not be automatically restricted by transferring sovereignty to a supranational organization. In the opinion of the Constitutional Court, the fundamental human rights of the German Constitution were insufficiently protected under Community law, as long as (*solange*) the Community lacked a democratically legitimated and directly elected Parliament and a codified catalogue of fundamental rights.

Moreover, the protection of fundamental rights by the Court of Justice was considered insufficient as the case law of courts cannot fully guarantee legal certainty.[8] The Italian *Corte Costituzionale* expressed a similar concern in its judgment of 27 December 1973.[9] It declared itself competent to ensure that the Treaty was compatible with the basic principles of the Italian Constitution at least in the case, albeit in its view unlikely, that an "unlawful power to infringe the basic principles of our Constitution or inviolable human rights" would be inferred from the sovereign powers assigned to the Community.

Both Constitutional Courts quite rightly highlighted the existence of a *lacuna* within the Community legal order but, at the same time, their reasoning threatened the very foundations of Community law.

In the absence of any legislation purporting to protect human rights at Community level, the European Court of Justice recognized that there was a need for an *aggiornamento* of its own case law so as to introduce these fundamental values within the ambit of the Community legal system. The Court took a first step in this direction in its judgment of 12 November 1969 in the *Stauder* case, where it held that the challenged provision of Article 4 of Decision no. 69/71 "contained nothing capable of prejudicing the fundamental human rights enshrined in the general principles of Community law and protected by the Court".[10] The Court thus accepted, albeit in an implicit way, that human rights were not alien to Community law.

In its judgment of 17 December 1970, in the *Internationale Handelsgesellschaft* case, the Court developed its implied reasoning in the *Stauder* case and stated very clearly the two elements which underpin recognition of human rights as part of the general principles of Community law. On the one hand, the Court stressed, in accordance with its previous case law that

> [r]ecourse to the legal rules or concepts of national law in order to judge the validity of measures adopted by the institutions of the Community would have an adverse effect on the uniformity and efficacy of Community law. The validity of such measures can only be judged in the light of Community law. In fact, the law stemming from the Treaty, an independent source of law, cannot because of its very nature be overridden by rules of national law, however framed, without being deprived of its character as Community law and without the legal basis of the Community itself being called in question. Therefore the validity of a Community measure or its effect within a Member State cannot be affected by allegations that it runs counter to either fundamental rights as formulated by the constitution of that State or the principles of a national constitutional structure.

But, on the other hand, the Court accepted that

> [a]n examination should be made as to whether or not any analogous guarantee inherent in Community law has been disregarded. In fact, respect for fundamental rights forms an integral part of the general principles of law protected by the Court of Justice. The protection of such rights, whilst inspired by the constitutional traditions common to the Member States, must be ensured within the framework of the structure and objectives of the Community.[11]

These passages show that the Court was in a position to introduce protection of fundamental human rights within Community law through their incorporation in the general principles of law. Indeed, under Article 164 of the Treaty, the Court is bound to ensure that, in the interpretation and application of the Treaty, the law—and not just the Treaty itself—is observed. In that respect, Article 164 of the Treaty can be compared to Article 38 (1)(c) of the Statute of the International Court of Justice, which explicitly refers to "the general principles of law recognized by civilized nations" as a source of law.

In its milestone judgment of 14 May 1974, in the *Nold* case, the Court repeated that fundamental rights form an integral part of the general principles of law, and clarified that in safeguarding these rights the Court is bound to draw inspiration from constitutional traditions common to the Member States, and cannot therefore uphold measures which are incompatible with fundamental rights recognized and protected by the constitutions of those States. But the Court added, quite significantly, that:

> [s]imilarly, international treaties for the protection of human rights on which the Member States have collaborated, or of which they are signatories, can supply guidelines which should be followed within the framework of Community law.[12]

But it was only in its judgment in the *Rutili* case that the Court referred *expressis verbis* to the European Convention on Human Rights and to the Fourth Protocol to the same Convention. This was a consequence of the fact that the last Member State, France, had finally ratified the Convention in 1974, although it was not until 1981 that France recognized the right of individual petition to the European Commission of Human Rights. Following the *Rutili* judgment, the ECJ's case law on the protection of human rights developed consistently on the basis of the following three elements.

In the first place, the Court recognizes fundamental human rights as an element of the general principles of law, which the Court upholds in accordance with Article 164 of the Treaty. Hence, fundamental human rights appear as an indirect source of Community law.

Secondly, the application of human rights must operate within the structures and objectives of the Treaty. This means that the provisions of the Convention cannot be applied, as such, but must be construed with specific reference to the relevant context of Community law. For instance, in the *Dow Benelux* case, the Court did not uphold the fundamental right to the inviolability of a person's home, recognized in Article 8(1) of the Convention, but rather, granted to the undertakings concerned, which were under scrutiny by the Commission pursuant to Regulation 17, an analogous protection derived from the rights of defence under Community law.[13]

Finally, within the realm of Community law, human rights cannot be defined with reference to purely national rules, but should be inferred from the common constitutional traditions or from relevant international treaties, with special reference to the European Convention on Human Rights.[14]

Given these developments, both the German and Italian Constitutional Courts gave up their initial reservations as to the protection of human rights at Community level.[15] For its part, the German Constitutional Court decided, in 1986, that it would not rule on the question whether secondary Community law was sufficiently in conformity with German constitutional requirements, "as long as the Community itself continued to protect fundamental rights at the present level".[16] This recognition ended the controversy concerning the absence of any protection of human rights at Community level but it did not stop further evolution which was to go beyond the realms of judicial innovation.

AN AFTERMATH OF POLITICAL INITIATIVES

Although this breakthrough in the jurisprudence of the ECJ was warmly welcomed, questions arose as to the strength or weakness of such a development as regards the definition and enforcement of fundamental rights which are, in essence, general and objective concepts. More especially, it is argued that judicial protection of human rights is not sufficient to achieve legal certainty or predictability. In other words, the existence of a formal legal remedy is often not enough. As was pointed out in a research paper prepared under the auspices of the European University Institute, individuals may not be aware of the remedy, indeed of the violation of human rights; they may not have the money or the knowledge to invoke the remedy and, in many cases, such as the violation of diffuse and fragmented rights, an individual remedy is simply not ideal.[17] It has been contended, therefore, that a systematic and comprehensive protection of fundamental rights can only be provided by representative institutions with democratic legitimacy. This concern has been at the basis of a series of initiatives at the political level[18] which can be listed as follows:

(1) The Resolution of the European Parliament of 4 April 1973 "concerning the protection of the fundamental rights of Member States' citizens when Community law is drafted".[19]

(2) The Joint Declaration by the European Parliament, the Council and the Commission of 5 April 1977, in which the political institutions of the Communities stress "the prime importance they attach to the protection of fundamental rights and declare that they respect and will continue to respect those rights in the exercise of their powers and in pursuance of the aims of the European Communities".[20]

(3) The Resolution of the European Parliament of 16 November 1977 "on the granting of special rights to the citizens of the European Community".[21]

(4) The "Declaration on Democracy" by the Heads of State and Government of the Member States meeting as the European Council in Copenhagen on 7 and 8 April 1978. In that declaration the Heads of State and Government pointed the way forward and confirmed their will "to ensure that the cherished values of their legal, political and moral order are respected and to safeguard the principles of representative democracy, of the rule of law, of social justice and of respect for human rights".

(5) The Memorandum of the Commission of 4 April 1979 on "the Communities becoming a signatory of the European Convention on Human Rights".[22] The memorandum is cautiously in favour of adhering to the European Convention on Human Rights as a first step towards the consolidation of the protection of fundamental rights in the EEC. In addition, it is proposed that the democratically representative Community institutions draw up an autonomous charter of fundamental rights.

The Commission has advanced two justifications for accession by the Community to the ECHR. In the first place, it would promote the protection of human rights in a uniform way throughout Europe and, secondly, it would emphasize that the Community legal order is a fully fledged legal order equivalent to those of the Member States. This second rationale caused some of the Member States to hesitate. They are not all strong supporters of the Community's legal order as a separate and comprehensive legal order. The proposal was not followed, owing to a lack of unanimity among the Member States. The Commission renewed it in 1990.[23]

It should be noted that a report by the British House of Lords Select Committee opposed accession, notably on the basis that it would undermine the strength of the Convention, given the fact that it would be applied by both the ECJ and the European Court of Human Rights.[24]

(6) The Resolution of the European Parliament of 27 April 1979, in which the accession of the European Communities to the European Convention on Human Rights is urged, and, as a parallel step, the establishment of a Committee of Experts with a view to drafting a European Charter of Civil Rights is envisaged.[25]

(7) The Resolutions of 14 September 1983 "concerning the substance of the preliminary draft Treaty establishing the European Union" and of 14 February 1984 "on the draft Treaty establishing the European Union" (the Spinelli Report).[26] The European Parliament has enlivened the perpetual discussion of fundamental rights. The resolutions emphasize the significance of embodying fundamental and human rights in a constitutional manner in the future European Union and they acknowledge the principles of pluralistic democracy, the rule of law and the exercise and protection of civil, economic, social and political rights. Respect for those principles is to be a precondition for the existence of the Union and for membership of the Union.

(8) The Resolution of the European Parliament of 12 April 1989 adopting the Declaration of Fundamental Rights and Freedoms where the Parliament considers that "the identity of the Community makes it essential to give expression to the shared values of the citizens in Europe".[27]

In one way or another, all these initiatives have kept alive the idea that the protection of human rights should be developed into a structural principle of the European Community. But none have resulted in a major breakthrough, mainly because they were not integrated in an overall restructuring of the Community, acceptable to all Member States. This would only become possible with the successful revival of European integration brought about by the European single market programme.

HUMAN RIGHTS AS A DIRECT SOURCE OF COMMUNITY LAW

With the Single European Act, the evolution was taken one step further. In its preamble, the Member States confirmed that

they were determined to work together to promote democracy on the basis of the fundamental rights recognized in the constitutions and laws of the

Member States, in the Convention for the Protection of Human Rights and Fundamental Freedoms and the European Social Charter, notably freedom, equality and social justice.

The ECJ recognized this development when it held in *Commission v. Germany*, that

> Regulation No. 1612/68 must also be interpreted in the light of the require-ment of respect for family life set out in Article 8 of the Convention for the Protection of Human Rights and Fundamental Freedoms. That require-ment is one of the fundamental rights which, according to the Court's settled case law, restated in the preamble to the Single European Act, are recognized by Community law.[28]

Article F of the Maastricht Treaty comes even closer to a direct recognition that fundamental rights are at the core of Community law when it states, in its second paragraph, that the

> Union shall respect fundamental rights as guaranteed by the European Convention for the Protection of Human Rights and Fundamental Free-doms and as they result from the constitutional traditions common to the Member States as general principles of Community law.

This provision will certainly make obsolete the discussion which arose in the 1970s when it was stated that further to Article 234 of the Treaty, the Community was, in fact, already bound by the Convention. According to Article 234, "rights and obligations arising from agreements concluded before the entry into force of this Treaty between one or more Member States on the one hand, and one or more third countries, on the other, shall not be affected by the provisions of this Treaty".

The proponents of this thesis also referred to the Court's judgment in the *International Fruit Company* in which the Court confirmed that the Community was itself bound by GATT, although the GATT Agreement had been signed by the Member States prior to the Treaty of Rome, on the basis that in the area governed by GATT, the Community assumed the powers previously exercised by the Member States.[29] They defended a similar line of reasoning as to the application of the Convention but, however attractive, their reasoning could not overcome difficulties inherent in procedural aspects of the Convention, such as possible reservation or even withdrawal by the signatory States and, above all, the absence of the Community institutions in the operation of the institutional machinery of the Convention.

In this respect, it should be recalled that, until now, the European Commission of Human Rights has always declined to examine complaints brought against Community institutions on the basis that the Community, as such, is not a party to the Convention.[30]

THE EUROPEAN CONVENTION ON HUMAN RIGHTS AND THE PROTECTION OF HUMAN RIGHTS UNDER COMMUNITY LAW

As far as the ECHR is concerned, it should be recalled that quite a substantial number of its provisions have direct effect and can be invoked before the courts of most of the States Parties to the Convention. Moreover, the European Commission and European Court of Human Rights supervise compliance with the Convention through procedures which are also designed to guarantee its uniform application and interpretation. Finally, it should be recalled that the Convention's substantive field of application is general and cannot be confined to one or more particular areas of Member State action.

Within the Community, the recognition that fundamental human rights are part of the general principles of Community law implies, quite logically, that Community institutions must act in accordance with these rights, whenever they actually exercise their competencies under the Treaty.

It also means that Member States must comply with fundamental human rights as part of Community law principles when acting in the field of application of Community law but, at the same time, the Member States must comply with the Convention in all circumstances irrespective of the subject matter involved. It is quite clear that this may cause confusion and may even endanger uniform application and interpretation of human rights by the Court of Justice on the one hand, and the Strasbourg institutions on the other. To dispel this confusion, the Court has started to clarify to what extent it is competent to appraise national rules in the light of the aforementioned general principles of Community law with regard to fundamental rights and freedoms.[31]

In its judgment in *Cinéthèque*, the Court declined to check French legislation for compliance with Article 10 of the European Convention on Human Rights, which is concerned with freedom of expression:

> Although it is true that it is the duty of this Court to ensure observance of fundamental rights in the field of Community law, it has no power to examine the compatibility with the European Convention of national legislation which concerns, as in this case, an area which falls within the jurisdiction of the national legislator.[32]

In a later judgment in *Demirel*, the Court confirmed this position but reformulated the last phrase quoted above as follows :

> [the Court] has no power to examine the compatibility with the European Convention on Human Rights of national legislation lying outside the scope of Community law.[33]

In the still more recent case of *Wachauf*, the Court examined whether Community legislation adopted by the Council was compatible with the requirements of the protection of fundamental rights but the Court added that "those requirements arc also binding on the Member States when they implement Community rules".[34]

It appears from the case law that a national rule adopted to implement a Community law provision will be reviewed by the Court from the point of view of its compatibility with fundamental rights and freedoms. But even within this area, the rulings of the Court should not diverge from the interpretation of the Convention given by the Strasbourg institutions. To that effect, it has been proposed that the Court should be allowed to request a preliminary ruling from the Strasbourg Court on any question relating to the interpretation of the Convention and its Protocols. This would allow it to build a limited procedural bridge between the judicial apparatuses of the two supranational European legal orders. It is worthwhile mentioning that this solution had already been advanced by Advocate General Warner in his opinion in the *Prais* case:

> Here I will say at once that I regret the absence from that Convention of any power for this Court, or for national Courts, to refer to the European Court of Human Rights for preliminary ruling questions of interpretation of the Convention that arise in cases before them. However, in the absence of such a power, we must do our best.[35]

Judge Lenaerts has advocated the same solution as part of a more general attempt to achieve consistency between the Convention and a specific Community system of human rights.[36] This proposal, as well as the above-mentioned development which led to the introduction of an explicit reference to fundamental human rights in the Maastricht Treaty, reduce the relevance of the Commission's proposal that the Community should adhere to the Convention. In this respect, it may be recalled that the House of Lords' Select Committee opposed this proposal notably on the basis that it might undermine the Convention's strength as *the* European charter for the protection of human rights since accession might result in divergent interpretations of the Convention by the ECJ and the European Court of Human Rights.

TOWARDS A COMMUNITY CATALOGUE
OF HUMAN RIGHTS

As mentioned, Community legislation, adopted to implement the Single Market programme, has pervaded almost every area of economic activity to an extent never imagined.[37] This expansion has taken place within a framework which is still deficient in terms of democratic control. For instance, even under the new co-operation procedure introduced by the Single European Act, the European Parliament's role is still much less important than that of the Council. Against that background, the protection of human rights represents an indispensable check on, rather than an extension of, Community powers. In other words, expanding Community competencies call for a corresponding up-grading of human rights protection insofar as this development, together with a proper application of the principle of subsidiarity, helps to achieve a balance of power within the Community framework.

On the other hand, recognition of the overriding importance of human rights at Community level could contribute to the fashioning of European integration. Is it enough, after all, to promise prosperity and economic vitality through the Single European market if the ultimate goal of European integration remains the development of a European Union? All of these factors call for the elucidation of a human rights action-plan or catalogue at Community level which extends beyond judicial activism.

A research project of the European University Institute in Florence yielded a number of very detailed proposals which were presented at a conference hosted by the European Parliament in Strasbourg in 1989.[38] Moreover, in his aforementioned article, Lenaerts has attempted to define the various constitutive elements of a Community catalogue of fundamental rights, which could be represented as a series of concentric and interactive layers. The fundamental rights provided for in the Convention and its present and future protocols would constitute the nucleus thereof. Without advocating adhesion by the Community to the Convention, Lenaerts rightly stresses that this recognition of the Convention at Community level could be regarded as one of the binding elements throughout the European continent as a whole.

The next layer would consist of the general principles of law which the ECJ enforces at present time on the basis of Article 164 of the Treaty. A further circle would contain the fundamental rights specifically related to the status of citizens of the European Community. These mainly encompass the right for Community citizens to move freely and the right to choose their residence within Community territory but also the right of all Community citizens to vote (and to be a candidate for elective office) in the election for the European Parliament and in the municipal elections at the place of their residence. A final circle may encompass social and economic rights, cultural and educational rights, environmental rights or consumer rights. All these rights share the characteristic that they cannot, as a matter of course, possess any real significance without an appropriate intervention by the public authorities.

Needless to say, the effective drafting of such catalogue would trigger fundamental questions as to the distribution of competencies between the Member States and the federal institutions at Community level. Even if these proposals *de lege ferenda* appear theoretical, they provide new and flexible work-hypotheses for the future development of human rights protection at Community level which may well be on the agenda of a future intergovernmental conference.

3.3 Human Rights and the EEC

VINCENT J. G. POWER

The purpose of this paper is to describe and discuss in very broad terms certain selected aspects of the human rights law of European Community. The aspects chosen for examination are:

- the institutional perspective on the formulation of EEC human rights law;

- gender discrimination;

- nationality;

- religious discrimination;

- human rights as they may arise in competition law;

- the death penalty;

- some Irish aspects of EEC human rights law; and

- the external dimensions of EEC human rights law.

Before examining these selected aspects, it is useful to make a few comments on EEC human rights law generally. None of the Foundation Treaties contain

82 *Vincent J.G. Power*

specific provisions promoting or protecting human rights.[1] This was a deliberate omission because these Treaties were charters of economic organisations rather than constitutions of civil and political entities. Nonetheless these Treaties contain provisions which are human rights-type provisions: Articles 7 (a general prohibition of discrimination on grounds of nationality); 36 (protection of industrial and commercial property); 48 (free movement of workers); 52 (freedom of establishment); 117–118 (promotion of improved working conditions, improved standards of living, vocational training, social security, right of association and collective bargaining); 119 (the principle of the equality of sexes); and 222 (protection for the protection of existing systems of property ownership).

THE INSTITUTIONAL PERSPECTIVE ON THE FORMULATION OF EEC HUMAN RIGHTS LAW

It is interesting to review the work of the EEC institutions[2] in the area of human rights. As a general rule, the cause of human rights in the EEC has been championed by the European Parliament and the European Court of Justice[3] as opposed to the Commission or the Council of Ministers.

It is widely (but not universally) accepted that it has been the ECJ which has developed the EEC law relating to human rights.[4] It was ECJ cases (such as *Nold*,[5] *Stauder v. City of Ulm*[6] and so on) which have developed the law rather than the actions of the Council of Ministers and the Commission or the aspirations of the European Parliament.[7] The ECJ was not always inclined to act in this area. Early cases such as *Stork v. High Authority*,[8] *Geitling v. High Authority*[9] and *Sgarlata v. Commission*[10] did not give much hope: the Court showed "a worryingly enigmatic stand against protecting individual rights".[11] It was only in *Stauder v. City of Ulm*[12] that the ECJ confirmed that human rights were enshrined in the general principles of EEC law and were enforceable by the ECJ.[13] The ECJ amplified this approach in *Internationale Handelsgesellschaft mbH v. Einfuhr-und Vorratsstelle fur Getreide und Futtermittel*,[14] *Hauer*[15] and *Keller*.[16] The ECJ has also *indirectly* improved the enforcement of human rights; Article 119 of the EEC Treaty enunciated the principle of equal pay for equal work but the principle was not always adhered to and Directive 75/117/EEC had to be adopted. Shortly after its adoption, however, the ECJ ruled that Article 119 was directly effective and thus the need for the Directive was greatly reduced.[17] The ECJ is now using human rights not only to defend the supremacy of Community law but also to extend the jurisdiction of the ECJ. In finding that Community law was superior to national law, the ECJ had to fill the gap of national protection of human rights by finding some means of Community-based protection.

Given the limitations on its powers, the European Parliament has done, in relative terms, a great deal in this area. On 4 April 1973, the European Parliament adopted a Declaration concerning the protection of the fundamental rights of Member States' citizens. On 16 November 1977, the European Parliament adopted a Resolution on the Granting of Special Rights to the Citizens of the European Community. On 27 April 1979, the European Parliament urged the Community to accede to the European Convention and Human Rights. The Parliament has also proposed the establishment of the Committee of Experts to draft a Charter of Civil Rights. A high point in the work of the European Parliament in the area of human rights came on 12 April 1989, when the Parliament adopted its Declaration of Fundamental Rights and Freedoms.[18] This Declaration which contains classical civil rights as well as administrative rights was the first real step in the process towards development of a Community Code of Rights. The Parliament has done much of its work through the Political Affairs Committee and the Sub-Committee on Human Rights. In retrospect, the European Parliament has probably done as much as could be expected from it given its limited powers.

The Commission might argue that it has been involved in this area due to, on the one hand, its initiation of measures such as Directive 75/117/EEC on equal pay[19] or Directive 76/2070/EEC[20] on equal treatment and, on the other hand, its proposal that the Community accede to the European Convention on Human Rights.[21] It may also argue that its relations with the UN (in accordance with Article 229 of the EEC Treaty) means that it is involved in human rights matters. The Commission might also argue that it has been involved in the promotion of greater freedom in South Africa, for example its condemnation of the imposition of the death penalty on the Sharpeville Six in 1988. There is a great deal the Commission can do in coming years to link EEC aid with respect for human rights.[22]

The European Council adopted at its April 1978 Copenhagen meeting a Declaration on Democracy.[23] Moreover, the Council has spoken on several human rights issues such as the formerYugoslavia, South Africa, the former USSR and Sri Lanka.

The Council of Ministers, Commission and Parliament have combined to make a Joint Declaration on Human Rights.[24] The operative clauses of this Declaration read:

1   The European Parliament, the Council and the Commission stress the prime importance they attach to the protection of fundamental rights, as derived in particular from the constitutions of the Member States and the European Convention for the Protection of Human Rights and Fundamental Freedoms.

2   In the exercise of their powers and in pursuance of the aims of the European Communities they respect and will continue to respect these rights.

This Declaration is not binding in itself but it is of political significance.

The Member States themselves have achieved some progress in this area through European Political Co-operation (EPC). There is a working group within the EPC on human rights. EPC human right initiatives have been taken in the confines of the UN and the Conference on Security and Co-operation in Europe (CSCE). It is also worth mentioning the EEC's human rights role in the Lome Conventions programme; for example, Article 5 of Lome IV allows for the expenditure of extra money for the promotion of human rights.

In conclusion, therefore, it has been the ECJ which has been the most active of the Community's institutions in the promotion and protection of human rights both regionally and globally.

GENDER DISCRIMINATION

Gender (or sexual) discrimination[25] is unfortunately commonplace. The existence of gender discrimination bankrupts society. Evelyn Ellis has written:

> Without the right to equality irrespective of sex, the individual remains unable to exploit his or her talents to the full and cannot make the most of what life has to offer: inequality is simply unfair. The community at large suffers too since valuable resources go untapped and potential gifts remain unutilized.[26]

It is a tribute to the Community that it has been particularly active in this area.[27] It was concerned with equal pay from the beginning; for example, the 1957 Treaty of Rome deals with the concept of equal pay in Article 119 which is the only explicit reference in the Treaty to gender discrimination.[28] The equal pay guarantee has been the springboard for all the subsequent developments in the area of gender discrimination.[29] Article 119 confers no secondary law-making power on the institutions and thus regard must be had on occasion to Articles 100[30] and 235[31] of the EEC Treaty.

Directive 75/117/EEC[32] (the "Equal Pay Directive")[33] was adopted on the basis of Article 100 of the EEC Treaty so as to harmonize the laws of the Member States relating to equal pay. Article 1 of the Equal Pay Directive provides that the guarantee of equal pay for men and women outlined in Article 119 of the Treaty, called the "principle of equal pay", means, for the same work, or for work to which equal value is attributed, the elimination of all discrimination on grounds of sex with regard to all aspects and conditions of remuneration. The Directive was necessary because while the principle of equal pay was embodied in Article 119, since 1957 there had been a failure to effectively enforce that provision; indeed, this failure was characterized as a "scandal of the stunted development of the social aspect of the Community".[34] Thus, the Directive was adopted. In fact, the ECJ soon after ruled[35] that Article 119 was directly effective and thus the need for the Directive was greatly reduced. Nonetheless, the Directive was in place. The Directive also helped to elucidate or clarify Article 119.[36]

Directive 76/207/EEC on equal treatment[37] is also interesting for present purposes. Its Preamble is instructive:

> Whereas Community action to achieve the principle of equal treatment for men and women in respect of access to employment and vocational training and promotion and in respect of other working conditions also appears to be necessary: whereas equal treatment for male and female workers constitutes one of the objectives of the Community . . .

With respect to social security, the scope of Directive 79/7/EEC[38] is set out in Article 2:

> This Directive shall apply to the working population including self-employed persons, workers and self-employed persons whose activity is interrupted by illness, accident or involuntary unemployment and persons seeking employment until retired and invalided workers and self-employed persons.

Article 3 provides that the Directive applies to:

(a) statutory schemes which provide protection against the following risks: sickness; invalidity; old age; accidents at work and occupational diseases; and unemployment;

(b) social assistance, in so far as it is intended to supplement or replace the schemes referred to in (a).

The Directive has proved to be very controversial, not least in Ireland in such cases as *McDermott and Cotter v. Minister for Social Welfare*.[39]

The subject of pregnancy discrimination has proved of significant interest over recent years. In two cases, *Dekker v. Stichtung Vormingscentrum voor Jong Volwassen Plus*[40] and *Habdels-og Kontorfunktionoeremes Forbund i Denmark*, acting for *Hertz v. Dansk Arbeijdsgiverforening*,[41] the ECJ has held that a dismissal or a refusal to employ a woman on a ground relating to her pregnancy will amount to unjustifiable direct discrimination irrespective of fault.[42] The two decisions are limited in that dismissal on grounds of repeated illness, albeit illness relating to pregnancy and birth, when the illness continues after maternity leave, is not discriminatory. The decisions also leave it for the Member States "to fix the period of maternity leave in such a way as to allow female workers to be absent during the period during which problems due to pregnancy and confinement may arise".[43] Nonetheless, these cases by going so far almost enacted the subsequent Pregnancy Directive! An interesting observation has been made on the two cases by Josephine Shaw:

> The decisions . . . take Community law further towards a major recapitulation of the notions of discrimination and equal treatment. It is now possible to argue that discrimination is not concerned so much with comparing the treatment of women with that of men, that is, setting up men as a norm against which women are to be tested as being the same as men, or different from men, but with examining the treatment of women which occurs because they are women.[44]

There is a great deal of unfinished business in the area of the EEC and gender discrimination. Areas such as contraception, abortion and pornography will become more controversial and there will be nettles to be grasped by the ECJ in the coming years. Non-legally binding measures such as the Council Recommendation of 13 December 1984 on the positive action programme for women will need to be converted into legally binding instruments.

NATIONALITY

The principle of non-discrimination on grounds of nationality is recognized generally as a basic human right. The EEC Treaty endorses this principle in the context of Treaty activities in Article 7:[45]

> Within the scope of application of this Treaty, and without prejudice to any special provisions contained therein, any discrimination on grounds of nationality shall be prohibited.
>   The Council may, on a proposal from the Commission and in co-operation with the European Parliament, adopt, by a qualified majority, rules designed to prohibit such discrimination.

Article 7 is one of the most helpful provisions to any "would-be" human rights litigant in the EEC. In *Walrave and Koch v. Association Union Cycliste*

Internationale[46] it was ruled that discrimination on the ground of nationality by private parties was prohibited by the provision. Similarly, Community institutions need to comply with it. Moreover, a Member State cannot discriminate against its own nationals because of the existence of Article 7.[47] The concept applies both ways: not only is it wrong to treat similar situations differently but it is also wrong for different situations to be treated similarly.[48]

RELIGIOUS DISCRIMINATION

It is difficult to imagine how EEC human rights law could be concerned with religious discrimination. Yet the operations of the Community and its institutions can infringe the right of someone to practice his or her religion. An example arose in a staff case, *Prais v. Council.*[49] In this case, an entrance examination to the Council of Minister's staff was held on a Saturday. The applicant examinee was a Jewess whose Sabbath was Saturday. She requested to be allowed sit the examination on a day other than a Saturday but her request was refused. The ECJ in the resultant litigation recognized the freedom of religion.

COMPETITION

In considering human rights law, one would not immediately consider competition law. Yet, considerations of human rights law have proved critical in such cases as *National Panasonic (UK) Ltd v. Commission*[50] as well as five cases (*Solvay/Orkem etc.*)[51] during autumn 1989 alone. These five cases turned on Articles 11 and 14 of Regulation 17/62/EEC.

The EEC institutions charged with the task of enforcing competition law (principally, the Commission[52]) do not pose any serious threat to the rights of either natural or legal persons: they are not the organs of some super-State; they are not treacherous tyrants. Nonetheless, these institutions occasionally breach procedures. Sometimes these breaches could violate the fundamental rights of various persons.

In *Orkem v. Commission*[53] the applicant sought to annul a Commission Decision taken under Article 11(5) of Regulation 17/62/EEC. The ECJ held that an undertaking under investigation need not be obliged to answer questions of the Commission where to do so would be to incriminate themselves. The ECJ thereby set a very high standard of protection for a legal person.

In *Solvay v. Commission*,[54] the applicant sought to annul a Commission Decision taken under Article 11(5) of Regulation 17/62/EEC. *Orkem v. Commission*[55] was a similar case. In *Orkem v. Commission*, the ECJ said:

29   In general, the laws of the Member-States grant the right not to give evidence against oneself only to a natural person charged with an offence in criminal proceedings. A comparative analysis of national law does not . . . indicate the existence of such a principle . . . which may be relied upon by legal persons in relation to infringements in the economic sphere, in particular infringements of competition law.

30   As far as Article 6 of the European Convention [on Human Rights] is concerned, although it may be relied upon by an undertaking subject to an investigation relating to competition law, it must be observed that neither the wording of that Article nor the decision of [the] European Court of Human Rights indicated that it upholds the right not to give evidence against itself.

31   Article 14 of the International Covenant [on Civil and Political Rights], which upholds, in addition to the presumption of innocence, the rights (in paragraph 3(g)) not to give evidence against oneself or to confess guilt, relates only to persons accused of a criminal offence in court proceedings and thus has no bearing on investigations in the field of competition law.

32   It is necessary, however, to consider whether certain limitations on the Commission's powers of investigation are implied by the need to safeguard the rights of the defence which the Court has held to be a fundamental principle of the Community legal order (Case 322/82 *Michelin v. Commission*[56]).

33   In that connection, the Court observed recently, in its judgment in Joined Cases 46/87 & 227/88 (*Hoechst v. Commission*[57]), that whilst it is true that the rights of the defence must be observed in administrative procedures which may lead to the imposition of penalties, it is necessary to prevent those rights from being irremediably impaired during preliminary inquiry procedures which may be decisive in providing evidence of the unlawful nature of conduct engaged in by undertakings and for which they may be liable. Consequently, although certain rights of the defence relate only to contentious proceedings which follow the delivery of the statement of objections, other rights must be respected even during the preliminary inquiry.

34   Accordingly, whilst the Commission is entitled, in order to preserve the useful effect of Article 11(2) and (5) of Regulation 17, to compel an undertaking to provide all necessary information concerning such facts as may be known to it and to disclosed to it, if necessary, such documents

relating thereto as are in its possession, even if the latter may be used to establish, against it or another undertaking, the existence of anti-competitive conduct, it may not, by means of a decision calling for information, undermine the rights of defence of the undertaking concerned.

35 Thus, the Commission may not compel an undertaking to provide it with answers which might involve an admission on its part of the existence of an infringement which it is incumbent upon the Commission to prove.

In *Hoescht v. Commission*[58] the applicant sought to annul Commission decisions taken under Article 14(3) of Regulation 17/62. The ECJ held that Article 8 of the European Convention on Human Rights, on privacy, did not afford any protection to Hoescht in respect of a search of its premises by the Commission's Directorate-General on Competition (DGIV). The Court however held that where an undertaking refuses to collaborate with DGIV investigators operating under an Article 14(3) order, such investigators cannot insist on entry unless they have complied with the national safeguards associated with searches.

In *Dow v. Commission*,[59] the applicant sought to annul Commission decisions taken under Article 14(3) of Regulation 17/62. The Court again held that where an undertaking refuses to collaborate with DGIV investigators operating under an Article 14(3) order, such investigators cannot insist on entry unless they have complied with the national safeguards associated with searches.

This is an area which will evolve in the coming years. It is an interesting point to remember that the Commission is the policeman, investigator, judge and jury in Community competition law matters but is always subject to the supervisory jurisdiction of the ECJ.

DEATH PENALTY

The European Parliament adopted a resolution on the death penalty. The Resolution stated:

The European Parliament,

— having regard to the motion for a resolution (Doc. 1–20/80),

— having regard to petition Nos 16/80 and 41/80,

— whereas the European Community is not simply a "common market", but also a common civilization,

— whereas any concept of human rights consonant with the principles of European civilization requires that the rights to live be respected and guaranteed for all, therefore the law must be both strong to defend potential victims and consistent by never ordering that human life be taken,

—— aware that the responsibilities deriving from universal suffrage give the European Parliament a political and moral duty to contribute to the formation, guidance and expression of the opinion of the peoples of Europe faithful to the principles of European civilization,

— whereas the application of the death penalty makes it impossible to correct judicial errors,

— whereas the death penalty may be replaced by long prison sentences that are just as powerful a deterrent (in cases where the assailant can be deterred) and whereas, as the statistics in countries which have abolished capital punishment have amply demonstrated, the incidence of those crimes for which the death penalty was formerly imposed has not varied significantly from the incidence of crime generally,

— whereas efforts must be directed towards preventive care and curative treatment to reintegrate the criminal into society wherever possible,

— whereas an implementing agreement to the European Convention on the Suppression of Terrorism was signed in Dublin in December 1979 and work has begun at the request of the Ministers for Justice of the Nine meeting in Dublin on the preparation of a draft Convention for cooperation in matters of criminal law between the Member States of the European Community,

— whereas co-operation in matters of criminal law should not consist solely of repressive measures, but must also help to strengthen existing humanitarian measures,

— voicing the hope that this initiative will provide inspiration for all countries in the world which still enforce the death penalty,

— having regard to Resolution 727 (1980) and Recommendation 891 (1980), in which on 22 April 1980, the Parliamentary Assembly of the Council of Europe declared itself in favour of the abolition of the death penalty for crimes committed in times of peace and asked that Article 2 of the European Convention on Human Rights be amended accordingly,

— having regard to the joint declaration by the European Parliament, the Council and the Commission on respect for fundamental rights,[60]

— drawing attention to its resolution of 21 November 1980 on the abolition of the death penalty in the Community,[61] in which it called upon Member States to abandon capital punishment,

— having regard to the report of the Legal Affairs Committee (Doc. 1–65/81),

1 Expresses its strong desire that the death penalty should be abolished throughout the Community;

2 Invites the Member States to amend their legal provisions, where necessary, and to take active steps within the Committee of Ministers of the Council of Europe to ensure that the European Convention on Human Rights is amended accordingly;

3 Hopes, with that end in view, that a wide-ranging debate on the abolition of the death penalty will take place within the competent national bodies and in the necessary spirit of calm consideration;

4 Instructs its President to forward this resolution to the parliaments and governments of the Member States and to the Council and Commission.

The death penalty is now of little practical relevance in the Community but the Member States may be able to bring pressure to bear on jurisdictions elsewhere in the world which maintain the penalty.

SOME ASPECTS OF THE IRISH PERSPECTIVE

This part examines the Irish perspective through the experience of one Irish case which is of particular interest and relevance in the contexts of human rights, group rights and employment. *Groener v. Minister for Education and the City of Dublin Vocational Education Committee (CDVEC)*[62] is an interesting case involving the interplay between culture, language and human rights. As Advocate General Darmon said in paragraph 1 of his Opinion, the case "relates to one of the most sensitive aspects of cultural identity" namely, "the power of a State to protect and foster the use of a national language".

Groener, a Dutch woman, had been working for two years as a part-time teacher at the College of Marketing and Design in Dublin. That College is supervised by a public body, namely, the Vocational Educational Committee (VEC). The VEC required candidates for permanent posts to have a proficiency in the Irish language. In 1984, she entered a competition for a permanent post. She was successful in the competition for the job generally but failed the examination on her competency[63] in the Irish language.

Groener complained that the linguistic requirement of the VEC embodied in a circular letter was incompatible with Article 48 of the EEC Treaty (the free movement of workers provision) as well as Article 3 of Regulation 1612/68.[64] The Regulation permitted a linguistic requirement when the nature of the post required a linguistic competence. She then sought judicial review in the Irish High Court of the Minister's refusal to exempt her. The High Court then made an Article 177 preliminary reference to the ECJ.

The ECJ opined that "the nature of the post" (*in casu*, an art teacher) did justify a linguistic requirement and thus Groener was not being discriminated against by the circular letter. The Court was motivated by two main factors. First, Article 8 of the Irish Constitution states that the Irish language is the first official language of the State. Secondly, the Irish Government has consistently attempted to promote the use of the Irish language through a variety of means, including education. As the ECJ said:

> The importance of education for the implementation of such a policy must be recognized. Teachers have an essential role to play, not only through the teaching which they provide but also by their participation in the daily life of the school and the privileged relationship which they have with their pupils. In those circumstances it is not unreasonable to require them to have some knowledge of the first national language.[65]

The ECJ opined that a Member State may have a policy to promote the use of its first language provided that the policy was neither disproportionate nor discriminatory. The fact that the Court's judgment is confined to the first[66] language of the State is important; the ECJ did not opine on regional or secondary languages (such as Welsh) and thus this case is perhaps the opening, but not the final, shot in this area.

Bryan McMahon has commented on *Groener* in the following terms:

> The *Groener* decision is to be welcomed as recognizing the desirability of having a multilingual society in Europe and in allowing Member States a reasonable measure of autonomy in these matters. Cynics might say that the Court recognized the political necessity for such a decision and realized the cultural backlash which would have been inevitable if it had refused to recognize the legality of the Irish measures. In this connection, such critics might point to the narrow approach of the Court in its decision as an indication of the Court's reluctance. A more gracious and generous view, however, might be that we are here witnessing a real recognition of the legitimacy of national concerns in relation to national cultural heritage and a tentative move by the Court towards Community elaborated demarcation

guidelines. The bureaucrats and the economists will have to recognize that cultural diversity cannot be indiscriminately swamped in the name of economic unity.[67]

EXTERNAL PERSPECTIVE

It is interesting to observe the role of the Community in human rights internationally. The EEC has been very active in the promotion and protection of human rights around the world. In particular, the European Parliament has monitored human rights internationally by way of receiving reports on human rights situations around the world[68] and has studied human rights violations in Central America. This section takes an outward-looking view of EEC human rights law.

There is an interesting angle to EEC human rights law which is rarely explored but which deserves consideration. It is the issue of to what extent is public international law a source of Community human rights law? It is submitted that the EEC is bound to comply with such human rights as are embodied in customary international law, the *jus cogens* of international law and certain treaties. Customary international law contains few specific human rights which would be directly relevant to the operations of the EEC. Similarly, the *jus cogens* would be of limited value but could be relevant in the context of right to life cases. The treaties may be more relevant: the point has been made that the EEC may be bound by treaties which preceded the Foundation Treaties (such as the European Convention on Human Rights, 1950, the Slavery Treaties, 1926 and 1956, as well as the Genocide Convention, 1948).

The European Convention on Human Rights[69] has proved to be a significant source of EEC human rights law. The ECJ first recognized it as a source of inspiration in the second *Nold* case.[70] Pescatore later described the Convention as being "the best possible combination of [the] constitutional traditions [of the Member States] to which the Court has referred".[71] By one judgment, the European Convention had weaved its way into Community law. It has appeared in many cases and in many contexts since. Article 7 of the ECHR arose in *R v. Kirk*,[72] and Article 8 in *National Panasonic (UK) Ltd. v. Commission*.[73] Article 9 was directly relevant in *Prais v. Council*.[74]

Is the EEC bound by the ECHR? At first sight, this seems an absurd question: how could the Community be bound by an agreement which it has not signed? The principle of substitution[75] implies that as the Convention is binding on all Member States then the Community itself is bound by the Convention, insofar as it exercises jurisdiction in substitution of the Member States.[76] While such an approach has the attraction of logic, does it have the approval of reality? It is submitted that if third States (including other parties to the Convention) would not see the EEC as itself bound then the notion of substitution is a matter only between the Member States and not on the international plane generally. Certainly the Convention provides "guidelines"[77] but perhaps not binding convention-based rules. If the EEC is not bound by the ECHR then should it accede to it? The Commission has proposed that the Community accede to the Convention.[78] The question is now answered by the Maastricht Treaty. The ECJ has reserved to itself the power to define the human rights which are protected under Community law. The problem is that the ECJ may differ from the European Court of Human Rights in relation to the interpretation of a particular provision in the ECHR.

The ECJ stated in *Cinéthèque SA v. Fédération Nationale des Cinémas Françaises*,[79] that the ECJ has no power to examine the compatibility with the ECHR of national laws which fall outside the scope of Community law. This approach has since been reiterated, for example, in *Neryen Demirel v. Town of Schwabisch Gmund*.[80] This classification of matters falling inside and outside Community law is a matter of complexity and controversy: notice the difference of opinion between the Supreme Court in *AG (SPUC) v. Open Door Counselling*[81] and Carroll J in *SPUC v. Grogan*.[82] There is another limitation. The actions of EEC institutions can only be reviewed by the ECJ and not by the European Commission on Human Rights or the European Court of Human Rights.[83]

In recent times, developments in Eastern Europe have dominated the field of external relations. The EEC commented on human rights violations in Eastern Europe and the former Soviet Union. For example, negotiations leading to a trade agreement between the EEC and Romania were suspended because of human rights violations by the Ceausescu regime and were only reopened after the December 1989 revolution.[84] The Commission's aid programme to Poland and Hungary (the PHARE Programme) as well as aid to Bulgaria, the former Czechoslovakia, the former East Germany, Romania and the former Yugoslavia, has involved consideration of whether or not these States adequately respect human rights.

The economic strength of the EEC would allow it to take a stance in international negotiations and diplomacy on human rights. The 1976–1980 Carter Administration in the US often linked aid with the recipient having a satisfactory human rights record. In the context of Eastern Europe, it is worth remembering that the EEC has extended some of the rights guaranteed in its law to non-EEC nationals. For example, under the EEC–Morocco Co-operation Agreement[85] certain non-nationals have EEC rights.

CONCLUSION

The ECHR is the primary regional international treaty on human rights. All of the EEC Member States have ratified the Convention. The ECJ first specifically referred to the Convention in 1975 in the *Rutili* case.[86] The Single European Act specifically mentioned the ECHR in the preamble as a source of the fundamental rights recognized by the EEC. It is the most important document in Community human rights law and has been cited in all of the important human rights cases since. The relationship between the Convention and Community law is a very complex question which goes beyond the scope of this chapter.[87]

The EEC Treaty does not contain any explicit catalogue of human rights. It is submitted that a catalogue of human rights unique to the EEC should be drafted and adopted by the Community. The use of another organization's catalogue (with different aims and wider membership) does not make sense. The Community has a unique agenda of its own and this should be catered for in a catalogue of its own. It is recognized that the enumeration and description of such rights could be a painful process but it would be worthwhile to do it now. Such a catalogue need not be exhaustive because the ECJ could be relied upon to fill in the gaps at a later stage.

The Community as a whole must take up the challenge. The Stuttgart Administrative Court in its decision in the *Stauder v. City of Ulm* case said:

> . . . the Community institutions were called upon to assume, in their fields of jurisdiction, a responsibility for the protection of fundamental rights that had previously been guaranteed by the national courts of West Germany; for if the Court of Justice of the European Communities would not constructively fulfil its duties, then the national courts of the Federal Republic of Germany would, in spite of disruption of such a result, feel compelled to reserve for themselves the ultimate power of examining the constitutionality of Community Acts . . . according to the fundamental rights laid down in the Federal Republic's Constitution . . .

A word must also be said with respect to the use of human rights law in business. There is a temptation on the part of many commercial lawyers to ignore human rights. To a large extent, their instinct is correct. Nonetheless, human rights law can occasionally come to the aid of a commercial client.[88] The early German cases demonstrate in part this use of human rights.

Employees have been able to use the rights vested in Directive 75/129/EEC on collective redundancies,[89] Directive 77/187/EEC on transfer of undertakings and Directive 80/987/EEC on protection of employees' rights in the event of the insolvency of the employer.[90] Some businesses have used EEC human rights in their defence of claims by the Commission of breaches of competition law.[91] It is suggested that Irish businesses (and their legal advisors) should think a little more creatively in regard to the use of EEC human rights law as a management strategy. It was obviously used successfully in *Orkem v. Commission*[92] in which the ECJ held that an undertaking under investigation need not be obliged to answer questions of the Commission where to do so would be to incriminate themselves. EEC human rights law recognizes the right to carry on an economic activity,[93] to own property and to practice a trade or profession so it should not be too surprising that there is a link between human rights and business.[94]

The Community will expand by both accession and association. What will be the impact of this expansion on human rights policy? On the one hand, this is very positive in that the existing high standards of EEC human rights law (including the European Convention) can reach an even larger group (particularly in the context of Eastern European states which have denied these rights for too long). There is the converse argument however that to broaden the base would be to dilute its strength.

The EEC is the world's largest trading bloc. It has a special responsibility for the enforcement of human rights. The Commission outlined in the PHARE programme that adherence to human rights is a necessary pre-requisite to aid. The European Bank for Reconstruction and Development has a special role to play in this regard. The EEC is able to underpin its moral stance with economic power and should not be afraid to use its power provided it does so fairly, evenly and constructively.[95]

There is a practical logistical problem facing any "would-be" human rights litigant in Europe: the multiple fora of proceedings. The same case may start, for example, in some part of Ireland, move to Dublin, on to Luxembourg, back to Dublin, and perhaps, may move on to Strasbourg. There are three systems of law and three systems of courts. This may be a call in the dark but would it not be more helpful if there was a more streamlined system? Would it not be at least more convenient if the European Commission on Human Rights held hearings in the Contracting States—as it did in the *Greek Case*? Or would it not be better still if the ECJ went on Circuit?

Written Community law contains no specific provisions dealing with respect for fundamental rights in the Community authorities' dealings with Community citizens. This gap in Community law gave rise to particular difficulties in France and Germany. It is not unreasonable to propose that the Community should fashion a co-ordinated and coherent human rights policy on its own. A strong legal basis should be put in place. This may seem an almost forlorn hope in the light of the views of some Member States (especially the UK) but it is not impossible (witness the great advances made in the internal market programme).

There are many outstanding issues which will cause difficulties in this area in the future: asylum; voting rights for foreign nationals; technological changes (such as those relating to data protection and databases); group rights; health rights—both in terms of treatment and illness-prevention; cultural rights; and environmental rights. The Community is and will become more concerned with human rights in the broader sense and not just fundamental human rights.[96]

The Community will have to be careful that progress on unification at other levels is not hampered by the diversity of the philosophy of its peoples on human rights issues. Debates over abortion, divorce, euthanasia, can and will cause problems. The Community must act decisively. The protection of human rights will help the Community to gain respect from its citizens. The European Parliament

[b]elieves that while there is still no clearly defined Community human rights policy as such, a basis for such a policy has begun to emerge and that there is an increasing awareness that concern for human rights is one of the elements which binds the Community together and gives it its particular identity *vis-à-vis* third countries or groups of countries.[97]

In the drive towards becoming a richer and more respected society, one hopes that we do not become poorer by not respecting one another's human rights.

3.4   Select Bibliography

TEXTS AND MATERIALS

L. Betten, *The Right to Strike in Community Law: The Incorporation of Fundamental Rights in the Legal Order of the European Communities* (Deventer, 1985).
R. Blanpain, *Labour Law and Industrial Relations of the European Community* (Deventer, 1991).
J.W. Bridge, *Fundamental Rights* (London, 1973).
A. Byre, *Leading Cases and Materials on the Social Policy of the EEC* (Deventer, 1989).
A. Cassese, A. Clapham and J.H.H. Weiler, *1992, What Are Our Rights?* (Florence, 1989).
A. Cassese, A. Clapham, and J.H.H. Weiler, *Human Rights and the European Community: The Substantive Law* (Baden-Baden, 1992).
A. Clapham, *Human Rights and the European Community: A Critical Overview* (Florence, 1991).
E. Ellis, *European Community Sex Equality Law* (Oxford, 1991).
T.C. Hartley, *The Foundations of European Community Law* (Oxford, 1981).
F.G. Jacobs, ed., *European Law and the Individual* (Amsterdam, 1976).

P.J.G. Kapteyn and P. Van Themaat, *Introduction to the Law of the European Communities*, 2nd ed. (Deventer, 1989).
R. Rasmussen, *On Law and Policy in the European Court of Justice: A Comparative Study in Judicial Policymaking* (London, 1986).
M. Reid, *The Impact of Community Law on the Irish Constitution (I.C.E.L. No.13) (Dublin,* 1990).
M. Spencer, *1992 and All That: Civil Liberties in the Balance* (London, 1990).
P. Watson, *Social Security Law of the European Communities*, (London, 1980).

ARTICLES

N. Burrows, "The Promotion of Women's Rights by the European Economic Community" (1980) 17 *CML Rev* 191.
R.R. Churchill and N.G. Foster, "Double Standards in Human Rights? The Treatment of Spanish Fishermen by the European Community" (1987) 12 *EL Rev* 430.
A. Clapham, "A Human Rights Policy for the European Community" (1990) 10 *YEL* 309.
J. Coppel and A. O'Neill, "The European Court of Justice: Taking Rights Seriously?" (1992) 29 *CML Rev* 669.
R.M. Dallen, "An Overview of European Community Protection of Human Rights, With Special Reference to the UK" (1990) 27 *CML Rev* 761.
M. Dauses, "The Protection of Fundamental Rights in the Community Legal Order" (1985) 10 *EL Rev* 398.
A. Drzemczewski, "The Domestic Application of the European Human Rights Convention as European Community Law" (1981) 30 *ICLQ* 118.
K. Economides and J.H.H. Weiler, "Accession of the Communities to the European Convention on Human Rights: Commission Memorandum" (1979) 42 *MLR* 683.
W.R. Edeson and F. Wooldridge, "European Community Law and Fundamental Human Rights: Some Recent Decisions of the European Court and National Courts" (1976) 1 *LIEI* 1.
W. Finnie, "The Location of Fundamental Rights in the Community Treaty Structure" (1982) 1 *LIEI* 89.
J. Forman, "The Joint Declaration on Fundamental Rights" (1977) 2 *EL Rev* 214.
J. Forman, "The Equal Pay Principle under Community Law—A Commentary On Article 119 EEC" (1982) 1 *LIEI* 17.
N. Foster, "The European Court of Justice and the European Convention on Human Rights" (1987) 8 *HRLJ* 245.
N. Grief, "The Domestic Impact of the European Convention on Human Rights as Mediated Through Community Law" [1991] *Public Law* 555.
R. Hartley, "Federalism, Courts and Legal Systems: The Emerging Constitution of the European Community" (1985) 34 *AJCL* 229.
F.G. Jacobs, "The Protection of Human Rights in the Member States of the European Community: The Impact of the Case Law of the Courts" in J. O'Reilly, ed., *Human Rights and Constitutional Law: Essays in Honour of Brian Walsh* (Dublin, 1992) at pp. 243–61.
K. Lenaerts, "Fundamental Rights to be Included in a Community Catalogue" (1991) 16 *EL Rev* 367.
J.W. McBride & L. Neville Brown, "The United Kingdom, the European Community and the European Convention on Human Rights" (1981) 1 *YEL* 167.
M.H. Mendelson, "The European Court of Justice and Human Rights" (1981) 1 *YEL* 121.
M.H. Mendelson, "The Impact of European Community law on the Implementation of the European Convention on Human Rights" (1983) 3 *YEL* 99.
E.U. Petersman, "The Protection of Fundamental Rights in the European Communities" (1975) 23 *Annuaire Européen* 179.

P. Pescatore, "The Protection of Human Rights in the European Communities" (1972) 9 *CML Rev* 73.

H.G. Schermers, "The European Court of First Instance" (1988) 25 *CML Rev* 341.

H.G. Schermers, "The European Communities Bound by Fundamental Human Rights" (1990) 27 *CML Rev* 225.

U. Scheuner, "Fundamental Rights in European Community Law and in National Constitutional Law" (1975) 12 *CML Rev* 171.

J.H.H. Weiler, "Thou Shalt Not Oppress a Stranger: On the Judicial Protection of the Human Rights of Non-EC Nationals—A Critique" (1992) 3 *EJIL* 65.

4 : SECURITY OF THE PERSON

4.1 Introduction

The papers in this chapter deal with but a small sample of issues affecting the security of the person, as they arise both within and outside the operation of the European Convention on Human Rights. The subject is a vast one and in the context of the Convention alone, draws upon several substantive guarantees, such as the right to life (Article 2), the right to freedom from torture and inhuman or degrading treatment or punishment (Article 3), the right to liberty (Article 5) and the right to fair trial (Article 6). Together, these provisions represent the bulk of the case-load examined annually by the European Commission and the European Court of Human Rights.

As Gerard Hogan's discussion indicates, the European Court of Human Rights has yet to determine the precise parameters of the Convention guarantee of the right to life and, in particular, to decide whether Article 2 embraces the unborn. The abortion question has been entertained by the Commission, albeit without a definitive conclusion on the substantive issue, while both the Commission and the Court have addressed the implications of a ban on abortion information as it arose in the recent Irish case of *Open Door Counselling Ltd and Others v. Ireland.*[1] There is, as yet, no case law specifically dealing with the subject of euthanasia.

The issue of killings by security forces has proved one of the more vibrant sources of discussion in Strasbourg under the rubric of the right to life. Article 2(2) provides:

> Deprivation of life shall not be regarded as inflicted in contravention of this Article when it results from the use of force which is no more than absolutely necessary:
>
> (a) in defence of any person from unlawful violence;
>
> (b) in order to effect a lawful arrest or to prevent the escape of a person lawfully detained;
>
> (c) in action lawfully taken for the purpose of quelling a riot or insurrection.

101

Some confusion surfaced in response to the initial case law of the Commission which seemed to suggest that paragraph (2), above, should be read in conjunction with the statement in paragraph (1) that "no one shall be deprived of his life *intentionally* . . . " (emphasis added).[2] Such an interpretation would operate to legitimize all negligent or accidental acts on the part of security forces which result in civilian deaths.[3] In *Stewart v. United Kingdom*,[4] a Northern Irish case arising out of the death of a thirteen-year-old boy who was shot in the head with a plastic bullet fired by a soldier, the Commission revised this approach and confirmed that the use of disproportionate force resulting in death falls foul of Article 2(2), irrespective of any question of intention.[5] It is significant also that this provision constituted one of the grounds on which more widespread abuse was alleged in the inter-State cases of *Cyprus v. Turkey*,[6] and *Ireland v. United Kingdom*,[7] although, in the latter instance, it did not survive the admissibility stage.

The text of Article 2 permits the intentional deprivation of life "in the execution of a sentence of a court" following a conviction for a crime for which the death penalty is provided by law. A gradual shift in European attitudes to the death penalty found expression in the extension, in 1983, of the Convention's substantive guarantee in order to provide for the abolition of the penalty. The Sixth Protocol to the Convention entered into force in 1985[8] and, as of 1 January 1994, twenty States had accepted its terms. Ireland has not yet chosen to do so, despite the removal of the death penalty from the Irish statute books in 1990.[9]

The death penalty was challenged before the European Court of Human Rights in the landmark case of *Soering v. United Kingdom*.[10] Here the Court held that Article 2 could not operate to prevent a State from extraditing an individual to face the death penalty *per se*. Nevertheless, extradition would violate the Convention where it exposed the individual to a significant risk of treatment running counter to the Article 3 guarantee of freedom from torture or inhuman or degrading treatment or punishment. In the particular circumstances of this applicant, the Court found that the death-row syndrome, as practised in the US state of Virginia, involved such a risk.

The importance of the non-derogable status of Article 3 was illustrated by the *Ireland v. United Kingdom*. Despite the findings of the Court that the imposition of internment without trial in Northern Ireland in the 1970s constituted a breach of the guarantees of liberty (Article 5) and fair trial (Article 6), the right of the United Kingdom to suspend compliance with Convention standards was confirmed on the basis of the state of emergency deemed to be in existence in Northern Ireland at the time. Accordingly, the Article 3 challenge to the interrogation techniques practised upon republican prisoners provided the only ground on which a violation of the Convention was ultimately sustained.

These are just two among a number of significant Strasbourg decisions upholding the fundamental tenet of freedom from ill-treatment.[11] Nevertheless, the case law is equally, if not more, replete with unsuccessful challenges to State practice on the basis of Article 3.[12] The initial jurisprudence of the Commission and Court was somewhat inconsistent and unclear. Moreover, there has been a good deal of critical debate concerning the Court's determination of the threshold of "torture" for the purposes of Article 3. The Strasbourg organs recognize three categories of ill-treatment—torture, inhuman treatment and degrading treatment—distinguishable, one from another, on a sliding scale of suffering. Although the offending interrogative techniques challenged in *Ireland v. United Kingdom* amounted to inhuman treatment, in the view of the Court, they had not produced "suffering of the particular intensity and cruelty implied by the word torture".[13] A recent confirmation of this approach is the Court's decision in *Tomasi v. France*,[14] which concerned ill-treatment in police custody. The need for greater emphasis on supervision and enforcement of the guarantee of freedom from torture and inhuman and degrading treatment and punishment was one of motivations behind the conclusion of the European Convention for the Prevention of Torture, discussed below.

The decision of the European Court of Human Rights in *Tomasi* also embodies significant consideration of the rights of liberty and fair trial. Aside from acknowledging that the applicant had been a victim of inhuman and degrading treatment at the hands of the French authorities in contravention of Article 3, the Court had little difficulty in concluding that his detention on remand for a period exceeding five years involved violations of Article 5(3) and 6(1). The circumstances which led to this application serve as an austere reminder of the continuing relevance of Strasbourg supervision of State compliance with basic human rights guarantees. Indeed the volume and diversity of case law on liberty serves as a constant reminder of this fact.[15] From an Irish perspective, mental health law and practice, the subject of Tom Cooney's paper, stands out as an area in need of reform.

There are similarities between Articles 5 and 6 in terms of the length and detail of the provisions, the volume of case law generated and the importance of the specified rights in the overall Convention context. Most applications to Strasbourg will invite the Commission and Court to engage in some measure of review of domestic legal and administrative process on the basis of the fair trial guarantee. Mel Cousins examines an aspect of the right to fair trial which is particularly pertinent in the Irish context, namely access to the court.[16] As his paper suggests, the subject raises far more general issues, for example, relating to information and advice, than the jurisprudence of the European Court of Human Rights might suggest.

LIZ HEFFERNAN

4.2   The Right to Life and the Abortion Question Under The European Convention on Human Rights

GERARD HOGAN

As we in this jurisdiction know only too well, the entire abortion question raises profound medical, ethical, social and religious dilemmas. It is now proposed in this article to examine briefly the jurisprudence of the European Commission of Human Rights and that of the European Court of Human Rights on this very question, with particular emphasis on the Court's recent judgment in the *Open Door Counselling* case.[1] The picture which emerges is one characterized by a marked judicial reluctance to interfere with the legal regime prevailing in each Contracting State, with both the Commission and Court endeavouring genuinely to respect the divergent views on this issue throughout Europe, while at the same time ensuring that the degree of judicial deference is not so marked that it allows a departure from minimum Convention standards.[2]

Article 2 of the Convention provides in part:

> Everyone's right to life shall be protected by law. No one shall be deprived of his life intentionally save in execution of a sentence of a court following his conviction for a crime for which this penalty is provided by law.

There are a number of curious features to this provision. First, the right to life is not, as such, expressly granted or conferred on individual persons—rather the duty is placed on the State to protect that right. This, of course, presupposes that the State will adequately vindicate that right by every means available to it. This suggests, in turn, that the armoury of the criminal law will be employed to protect the right to life and also, perhaps, that adequate security measures will be taken to defend that right.[3] Thus, for example, a failure to make the intentional deprivation of life punishable by law would constitute a breach of Article 2, as would a deliberate failure to enforce those laws. In this context, a manifestly unreasonable failure to prosecute might well constitute a breach of Article 2. Nevertheless, the Commission has hinted that this is an area which calls for judicial restraint.[4]

ARTICLE 2 AND THE ABORTION QUESTION

To date, the approach of the Commission in cases presenting it with abortion issues
has been largely hesitant. The Commission, conscious, perhaps, of the wide divergences in views among and within the Contracting States, has seemed anxious
to leave as many issues open as possible. This hesitancy has been characterized
by a reluctance to pronounce definitively on the key question of whether unborn
life comes within the scope of Article 2.[5] In effect, therefore, the Commission's
view appears to be that while a Contracting State is entitled to take all necessary
measures to protect unborn life, some limitations on that right must be recognized in order to safeguard the right to life of the mother. At the same time, there
is a marked reluctance on the part of the Commission to intervene in this area
and this is evidenced by the fact that it is neither willing to condemn States with
liberal abortion regimes nor to intervene at the behest of applicants who claim
that the abortion regime in their own State is too restrictive.

It will be instructive, perhaps, if we now turn to consider the case law on
this subject.

THE COMMISSION'S JURISPRUDENCE

Bruggemann and Scheuten v. Federal Republic of Germany[6] was the first substantial application raising these issues to come before the Commission. Here two
German women alleged that, in the wake of a decision of the German Constitutional Court,[7] the legal rules governing abortion in Germany violated Article
8 of the Convention (the respect for private and family life provision) in that
they were not free "to have an abortion carried out in case of an unwanted
pregnancy". The Constitutional Court had decided that unborn life was in
principle protected by Article 2(2) of the German Basic Law,[8] but had allowed
for exceptions based on a danger to the life of the mother or of serious injury to
her health.

The Commission concluded that these circumstances did not give rise to a
breach of Article 8. It reasoned:

> Pregnancy cannot be said to pertain uniquely to the sphere of private life.
> Whenever a woman is pregnant, her private life becomes closely connected
> with the developing foetus. The Commission does not find it necessary to
> decide, in this context, whether the unborn child is to be considered as 'life'
> in the sense of Article 2 . . . or whether it could be regarded as an entity
> which under Article 8(2) could justify an interference "for the protection of
> others". There can be no doubt that certain interests in pregnancy are legally

protected, e.g. as shown by a survey of the legal order in 13 High Contracting Parties. This survey reveals that, without exception, certain rights are attributed to the conceived but unborn child, in particular the right to inherit. . . .The Commission therefore finds that not every regulation of the termination of unwanted pregnancies constitutes an interference with the right to respect for the private life of the mother. Article 8(1) cannot be interpreted as meaning that pregnancy and its termination are, as a principle, solely a matter of the private life of the mother. In this respect the Commission notes that there is not one member state of the Convention which does not, in way or another, set up legal rules in this matter.[9]

The Commission concluded by indicating that there was no suggestion that the parties to the Convention had ever intended "to bind themselves in favour of any particular solution under discussion". This latter remark can only be interpreted as implying that the States Parties will enjoy an especially wide margin of appreciation with regard to this particular issue.

There the matter rested until *Paton v. United Kingdom*,[10] where the complainant was a husband who had unsuccessfully attempted to seek an injunction restraining his wife from having an abortion.[11] Here it was claimed that the legislation which permitted this to occur (the Abortion Act, 1967) violated the unborn child's right to life (under Article 2) and that it constituted an unjustified interference with respect for family life (under Article 8).

The Commission first examined the term "everyone" as it appeared in Article 2 and elsewhere in the Convention and it observed:

> In nearly all these instances the use of the word is such that it can apply only postnatally. None indicates clearly that it has any possible prenatal application, although such application in a rare case . . . cannot be entirely excluded. . . . All of [the] limitations [contained in Article 2] by their nature concern persons already born and cannot be applied to the foetus. Thus, both the general usage of the term "everyone" ("toute personne") of the Convention and the context in which this term is employed in Article 2 tend to support the view that it does not include the unborn.[12]

The Commission then examined the question of whether the word "life" could include unborn life. It had been argued that Article 2 recognized an absolute right to life on the part of foetus, but this the Commission would not accept:

> The "life" of the foetus is intimately connected with, and cannot be regarded in isolation from, the life of the pregnant woman. If Article 2 were held to

cover the foetus and its protection under this Article were, in the absence of any express limitation, seen as absolute, an abortion would have to be considered as prohibited even where the continuance of the pregnancy would involve a serious risk to the life of the pregnant woman. This would mean that the "unborn life" of the foetus would be regarded as being of a higher value than the life of the pregnant woman. The "right to life" of a person already born would thus be considered as subject not only to the express limitations [contained in Article 2(1)] but also to a further, implied limitation.

The Commission finds that such an interpretation would be contrary to the object and purpose of the Convention. It notes that, already at the time of the signature of the Convention (4 November 1950), all High Contracting Parties, with one possible exception,[13] permitted abortion when necessary to save the life of the mother and that, in the meanwhile, the national law on termination of pregnancy has shown a tendency towards further liberalization.[14]

The Commission therefore concluded that even if Article 2 applied to unborn life, the authorization by the United Kingdom authorities of the abortion complained of was compatible with Article 2(1):

Because if one assumes that this provision applies at the initial stage of pregnancy, the abortion is covered by an implied limitation, protecting the life and health of the woman at that stage, of the "right to life" of the foetus.[15]

Since this was the background to the termination of pregnancy in the present case, the Commission concluded by observing that the husband's right to respect for family life under Article 8 had not been violated:

In the present case the Commission, having regard to right of the pregnant woman, does not find that the husband's and potential father's right to respect for his private and family life can be interpreted so widely as to embrace such procedural rights as can be claimed by the applicant, i.e. a right to be consulted, or a right to make applications, about an abortion which his wife intends to have performed on her.[16]

Again, this must be seen as a decision which allows a Member State the widest possible margin of discretion in relation to this issue.

OPEN DOOR COUNSELLING LTD AND OTHERS
V. IRELAND

One of the curious ironies of both *Bruggeman and Scheuten* and *Paton* was that neither case had come before the European Court of Human Rights. The abortion issue eventually came before the Court in *Open-Door Counselling Ltd. v. Ireland*,[17] where the applicants challenged the abortion information ban which had been imposed by the Supreme Court in *Attorney General (Society for the Protection of Unborn Children (Ireland) Ltd) v. Open Door Counselling Ltd.*[18] This latter case involved relator proceedings brought at the instance of the Society of the Protection of Unborn Children (Ireland) Ltd (SPUC) to restrain the activities of two womens' clinics, Open Door and Dublin Well Woman. The clinics provided what they described as "non-directive counselling" for pregnant women, i.e. that abortion would be one the options discussed in the course of that counselling session. If at such a session a pregnant woman wanted to consider the abortion option further, the clinics would arrange to refer her to a medical clinic in the UK. SPUC claimed that this contravened the provisions of Article 40.3.3 of the Constitution:

> The State acknowledges the right to life of the unborn and, with due regard to the equal right to life of the mother, guarantees in its laws to respect, and, as far as practicable, by its laws to defend and vindicate that right.

As far as the Supreme Court was concerned, the issue was quite a straightforward one:

> . . . [T]he issue and the question of fact to be determined is: were they thus assisting in the destruction of the life of the unborn? I am satisfied beyond doubt that having regard to the admitted facts the defendants were assisting in the ultimate destruction of the life of the unborn by abortion in that they were helping the pregnant woman who had decided upon that option to get in touch with a clinic in Great Britain which would provide the service of abortion. It seems to me to be an inescapable conclusion that if a woman was anxious to obtain an abortion and if she was able by availing of the counselling services of one or other of the defendants to obtain the precise location, address and telephone number of, and method of communication with, a clinic in Great Britain which provided that service, put in plain language, that was knowingly helping her to attain her objective.[19]

The Chief Justice added that there could not be a constitutional right to information "about the availability of a service of abortion outside the State which, if availed of, would have the direct consequence of destroying the expressly guaranteed right to life of that unborn child".[20]

The absolutist nature of this interpretation of Article 40.3.3 was underscored by the Supreme Court's judgment in *Society for the Protection of Unborn Children (Ireland) Ltd v. Grogan*.[21] Here student union groups sought to distribute and disseminate information about the location, identity and method of communication with abortion clinics in the United Kingdom. It had been suggested that the activities in question—such as the publication in student manuals of the names, addresses and telephone numbers of such clinics—could be distinguished from the *Open Door* case, but this contention was trenchantly rejected by Finlay C J:

> It is clearly the fact that such information is conveyed to pregnant women, and not the method of communication which creates the unconstitutional illegality, and the judgment of this Court in the *Open Door Counselling* case is not open to any other interpretation.[22]

It was against this background that the *Open Door* case first came before the Commission in March 1991. The majority opinion of the Commission—characteristically, it might be thought—avoided the more difficult issues and simply concluded that the restrictions imposed by the Supreme Court violated Article 10 of the Convention, inasmuch as they were not "prescribed by law":

> In the Commission's view [Article 40.3.3] primarily imposes obligations upon the State, including an obligation to legislate for the protection of the right to life of the unborn. It does not provide a clear basis for the individual to foresee that providing information about lawful services abroad, albeit affecting the right to life of the unborn, would be unlawful.[23]

But, as some of the other members of the Commission observed,[24] this analysis is rather weak. It is plain that, as a matter of Irish constitutional law, a provision such as Article 40.3.3 can apply to third parties, even if only addressed in terms to the State.[25] In addition, with appropriate legal advice, it should have been reasonably foreseeable

> [b]y any Irish citizen of voting age and ordinary intelligence that any activity which might at some stage have led to the procurement of an abortion, even if it occurred abroad, would sooner or later have been open to challenge in the Irish courts since the effects of such an abortion would ultimately have been felt in Ireland.[26]

The other opinions—both concurring and dissenting—are full of interest, but since they bear principally on the question of whether the injunction granted was "necessary in a democratic society" within the meaning of Article 10, they fall outside the ambit of this paper. However, the concurring opinion of Mr Schermers is especially worth noting, since it contains the following passage:

> As regards the Government's reliance on the protection of the rights of others, the Commission refers to its consistent case law under Article 2 of the Convention which guarantees the right to life, but which right does not confer absolute protection on the foetus (*Paton v. United Kingdom*). However, I am of the view that wider considerations may apply to the scope of the rights of others envisaged by Article 10(2) of the Convention. I note that in the thinking in the Member States of the Council of Europe, there is a wide divergence of thinking as to the stage at which unborn life requires legal protection, whether it be from conception onwards, as under Irish law, or whether some notion of the viability of the foetus is required, as under English law. In such a controversial area I consider that a High Contracting Party is entitled to confer the protective status of "other", within the meaning of Article 10(2) of the Convention, upon the life of the unborn. I am also of the view that the issues in the present cases fall within the notion of the protection of morals.[27]

There is much to be said for this approach, recognizing as it does the divergent moral views on the sensitive question throughout Europe, while at the same time not eschewing the duty to examine whether actions on the part of States Parties infringe the Convention's provisions.

Before the matter came before the European Court of Human Rights, there was one further important domestic devlopment. In the celebrated case of *Attorney General v. X*,[28] the Attorney General sought an injunction restraining a fourteen year old rape victim (who wished to obtain an abortion in England) from leaving the State. The victim was apparently suicidal, but in the High Court, Costello J granted an injunction, as he considered that this step was necessary to give effect to Article 40.3.3.[29] A majority of the Supreme Court allowed an appeal, on the ground that the victim's suicidal state was such that it presented a "real and substantial risk to her life." This being the case, it followed that "such a termination is possible [within the State] having regard to the true interpretation of Article 40.3.3 of the Constitution.[30] The reasons for this decision were somewhat surprising, especially in view of the earlier judgments in *Open Door* and *Grogan*. There is a clear discordance between the judgment in *X* case, on the one hand, and the earlier authorities, on the other, inasmuch as it would seem to follow that if there exists within the State a category of lawful abortion then there must exist a correlative right on the part of the pregnant woman herself to receive information about abortion.

The European Court of Human Rights heard argument in the *Open Door* case in March 1992, some three weeks after the judgment in the *X* case. It gave judgment in late October 1992, some four weeks before the Amendment of the Constitution Act, 1992, was enacted by the People.

What it interesting is that the Court first rejected the principal feature of the Commission's decision, since in its view the restrictions imposed were "prescribed by law":

> Taking into consideration the high threshold of protection of the unborn provided under Irish law generally and the manner in which the Irish courts have interpreted their role as the guarantors of constitutional rights, the possibility that action might have been taken against the corporate applicants, must have been, with appropriate legal advice reasonably foreseeable.[31]

The Court then went on to hold that the injunction served a legitimate aim, and thereby avoided deciding whether the term "others" as it appears in Article 10(2) extended to the unborn:

> It is evident that the protection afforded under Irish law to the right to life of the unborn is based on profound moral values concerning the nature of the right to life which were reflected in the stance of the majority of the Irish people against abortion as expressed in the 1983 referendum. The restriction thus pursued the legitimate aim of the protection of morals of which the protection in Ireland of the right to life of the unborn is but one aspect. It is not necessary in the light of this conclusion to decide whether the term "others" under Article 10(2) extends to the unborn.[32]

And since the present dispute concerned only the compatibility of the injunction with Article 10, the Court saw no need to address the question of whether the right to life of the foetus was embraced by Article 2. The Court then proceeded to examine whether the injunction was a proportionate restriction on the right to provide information in view of the State's admittedly legitimate aim of protecting moral values. It first observed that that it was not a criminal offence under Irish law for a pregnant woman to travel abroad in order to have an abortion:

> Furthermore, the injunction limited the freedom to receive and impart information with respect to services which are lawful in other Convention

countries and may be crucial to a woman's health and well-being. Limitations on information concerning activities which, notwithstanding their moral implications, have been and continue to be tolerated by national authorities, call for careful scrutiny by the Convention institutions as to their conformity with the tenets of a democratic society.[33]

This is, undoubtedly, a powerful argument which draws attention to the principal weakness in the Government's case, namely, that if the vindication of Article 40.3.3 was such a moral imperative as to call for a complete ban on the provision of abortion information, consistency and logic would suggest that a travel ban would also be necessary to give effect to that moral standpoint.[34]

The Court then continued by saying:

The Court is first struck by the absolute nature of the Supreme Court injunction which imposed a "perpetual" restraint on the provision of information to pregnant woman concerning abortion facilities abroad, regardless of their age or state of health or their reasons for seeking counselling on the termination of the pregnancy. The sweeping nature of this restriction has since been highlighted by the case of *Attorney General v. X* and by the concession made by the Government at the oral hearing that the injunction no longer applied to women who, in the circumstances as defined in the Supreme Court's judgment in that case, were now free to have an abortion in Ireland. On that ground alone the restriction appears over broad and disproportionate.[35]

But there were other factors which confirmed the correctness of this assessment.

First, the Court emphasized that the clinics merely engaged in "non-directive counselling" and thereby confined themselves to "an explanation of the available options". In turn, this meant that

[t]he decision as to whether or not to act on the information so provided was that of the woman concerned. There can be little doubt that following such counselling there were women who decided against a termination of pregnancy. Accordingly, the link between the provision of information and the destruction of unborn life is not as definitive as contended.[36]

Secondly, the Court stressed that the information in question could be readily obtained through a variety of other sources, such as magazines, telephone directories or by persons with contacts in Great Britain:

Accordingly, information that the injunction sought to restrict was already available elsewhere, although in a manner which was not supervised by qualified personnel and thus less protective of womens' health. Furthermore, the injunction appears to have been largely ineffective in protecting the right to life of the unborn since it did not prevent large numbers of Irish women from continuing to to obtain abortions in Great Britain.[37]

There was also the fact that the available evidence suggested that the lack of proper counselling created a risk to the health of women who were now seeking abortions at a later stage of their pregnancy "due to lack of proper counselling and who are not availing of customary medical supervision after the abortion has taken place". In addition:

> The injunction may have had more adverse effects on women who are not sufficiently resourceful or had not the necessary level of education to have access to alternative sources of information. These are certainly legitimate factors to take into consideration in assessing the proportionality of the restriction.[38]

Not surprisingly, therefore, the Court concluded that the restrictions imposed by the Supreme Court judgment were disproportionate to the aim sought to be achieved, although the Court stressed that this judgment should not be interpreted as "calling into question under the Convention the regime of protection of unborn life that exists under Irish law." Nevertheless, there appears to be a strong hint underlying much of this analysis that had Irish law been even more rigorous in its defence of Article 40.3.3, the restrictions on the distribution of information might have been upheld, especially when the Court, in its recapitulation of the problem, recalled that

> the injunction did not prevent Irish women from having abortions abroad and [that] the information it sought to restrain was available from other sources. Accordingly, it is not the interpretation of Article 10 but the position in Ireland as regards the implementation of the law that makes possible the continuance of the current level of abortions obtained by Irish women abroad.[39]

As has already been stated, this is undoubtedly a powerful argument; yet, for those who insist that the life of the law has been experience rather than strict logic, the dissent of Judge Pettiti will have a strong appeal:

> The fact that Ireland cannot *effectively* prevent the circulation of reviews or of English telephone directories containing information on clinics in the

United Kingdom, so that anyone can obtain information on abortion clinics in that country and the possibility of having an abortion in such clinics, can only . . . confirm the *necessity* of a specific measure such as that taken by the Irish courts. Such reviews, the directories and the persons possessing information on abortion clinics in the United Kingdom are "passive" factors, which require a personal and spontaneous attitude on the part of the person seeking advice. The activity of agencies which organize trips and provide special services for their clients, thereby influencing the decisions of those clients, is something entirely different. The *partial* ineffectiveness of a law or a principle of case law is not a reason for deciding not to take specific measures designed to prevent the activities of organizations committed to seeking means of obtaining results which do not conform to the interests and values of the legal system.[40]

Nevertheless, it would have to be conceded that the subsequent decision in the *X* case rather undermined the logic of the earlier *Open Door* case and, for that reason alone, it would have been surprising had the absolute information ban survived the European Court's scrutiny. What was surprising, however, was the European Court's willingness to examine the nexus between the provision of information and the ultimate termination of pregnancy and thereby to arrive at a different conclusion on that issue to that of the Supreme Court.

IMPLICATIONS OF THE OPEN DOOR CASE FOR ARTICLE 40.3.3.

It would seem that the European Court is, understandably, seeking a *via media* on the abortion issue. It is plain that Ireland may adopt a strict anti-abortion regime without infringing the Convention, since the State's interest in the enforcement of Article 40.3.3 is embraced in the protection of morals clauses contained in Article 8 (respect for private and family life); Article 10 (freedom of information) and, indeed, even in Article 2 of the Fourth Protocol (freedom to travel). As we have seen, part of the reason why the information ban was held to be disproportionate in *Open Door* was the rather erratic nature of its application, in that, it did not, for example, prohibit the distribution of English telephone directories. Had Article 40.3.3 been applied with rigorous consistency to the point where a travel ban was imposed, then both the Commission and the Court would have been faced with a dilemma, since the logic of their respective positions suggests that this is but a proportionate response to the public morality underlying Article 40.3.3.

In this connection, it is interesting to speculate as to the possible reaction of both bodies to an application had the *X* case been decided differently by the Supreme Court and the travel injunction, which had been granted by Costello J in the High Court, upheld. The response would probably have been to focus on the isolated and haphazard manner in which an application of this nature had been made by the Attorney General in a case of this kind, while no attempt had been made by the State to enforce Article 40.3.3 in this manner with respect to thousands of other Irish women who are seeking to travel to England for the purpose of seeking an abortion. Analysed in this way, such a travel injunction would also seem to be a disproportionate interference with a woman's right to travel. In the event, of course, it was not necessary for the matter to come before the Strasbourg authorities and the matter is now beyond doubt by the enactment of the Twelfth and Thirteenth Amendments of the Constitution Acts, 1992, which secure the right to travel and information, respectively. But—to pursue this speculation further—there is equally no doubt that a rigorous enforcement of Article 40.3.3 by the imposition of both a travel and information ban would have presented the Strasbourg authorities with genuine difficulties. This would surely have been a proportionate response[41] which was necessary for the protection of morals, yet one which would surely have been tinged with oppressive overtones. Unless, therefore, the Commission and Court would have been prepared to branch off into new directions, it would seem that, consistently with the approach taken in *Open Door*, neither body could have interfered with such a strict approach unless it could have been demonstrated that the rigours of such a law jeopardized the lives of women.

CONCLUSION

In conclusion, therefore, it may be said that the following principles emerge from the case law of the European Commission and European Court of Human Rights.

In the first place, Article 2 of the Convention probably does not, as such, protect the right to life of the unborn. Even if it does, that right to life is subject to certain implied restrictions which favour the protection of the mother's right to life. To the extent that these rights may conflict, the Convention would—contrary to the equality principle enshrined in Article 40.3.3 of the Constitution—seem to favour the right to life of the mother.

Secondly, this fact notwithstanding, the Convention does not preclude a Contracting State from adopting a strict anti-abortion regime, since it may legitimately pursue such an aim under the rubric of the protection of morals.

Thirdly, the limits of such an approach remain somewhat unclear. In principle, it might be thought that there is no Convention objection to a strict ban on information and even travel, provided they are applied evenly and proportionately. In *Open Door*, the ban was found to be disproportionate, partly by reason of its rather uneven application and partly as a result of the subsequent decision in the *X* case.

Finally, now that the issues of information and travel have been disposed of by the Twelfth and Thirteenth Amendments of the Constitution Acts, 1992, it seems likely that Irish abortion laws will not further trouble the European Commission and Court, unless, as seems unlikely, Article 40.3.3 is judicially re-interpreted in such a manner as will deny an abortion to a woman whose life is otherwise in jeopardy by the continuation of pregnancy, or a further constitutional amendment which will have this effect is enacted by the People at a future referendum.

4.3 The European Convention for the Prevention of Torture: A Euro-Window on the Plight of Detainees

LIZ HEFFERNAN

Freedom from torture and other forms of ill-treatment is recognized at national, regional and international levels as a fundamental human right. Yet even as among the rights which we commonly categorize as fundamental, this freedom holds a particularly special place. Two immediate and obvious ways in which this unique character is registered relate to the frequency and to the vehemence with which the right is affirmed. It finds expression in an extraordinarily broad range of international legal sources. For example, it features high on any catalogue of civil and political rights such as that found in the European Convention on Human Rights.[1] In addition, it has been the subject of resolutions of international and regional organizations,[2] has attracted judicial recognition as a fundamental rule of customary international law,[3] and, most recently, has been the subject of specialist treaties such as the UN Convention Against Torture[4] and the European Convention for the Prevention of Torture.[5]

As to the force or potency of the right, freedom from torture and other forms of ill-treatment creates an immediate and unqualified State obligation. In international agreements it is framed in absolute terms. The succinct provision in Article 3 of the ECHR that "no one shall be subjected to torture or to inhuman or degrading treatment or punishment" contrasts with other guarantees such the right to life, or to freedom of expression, which are subject to immediate limitations and qualifications within the respective terms of Articles 2 and 10 of the Convention. Moreover, while a State Party to the ECHR may derogate from its obligations in time of war or other public emergency, no such derogation is permitted in respect of Article 3.

The challenge, therefore, lies not in establishing the normative character of the guarantee against ill-treatment but rather in coercing State practice into rigorous compliance. Too often, standard-setting in international instruments is not matched by adequate procedures to identify and tackle violations and to ensure future conformity:

> The existing mechanisms for enforcing compliance with international standards on the treatment of detainees simply cannot stop violations; they do not appear to have a sufficiently strong and deterrent effect. Plainly, in a sphere such as human rights, where violations are in large measure irremediable, in the sense that nothing can ever efface the victim's memory of suffering—and, in many cases, its scars, physical or psychological—the key is prevention.[6]

Increasingly, international endeavour is being redirected toward monitoring the practical implementation of human rights standards and with devising more effective ways and means by which State adherence can be verified and strengthened. The European Convention for the Prevention of Torture and Inhuman or Degrading Treatment or Punishment (the Convention)[7] embodies one such experiment, its basic rationale of supervision and control rendering it virtually unique in European, and indeed international, terms. The Convention established an independent committee—the European Committee for the Prevention of Torture and Inhuman or Degrading Treatment or Punishment (CPT)— entrusted with responsibility for visiting places of detention in the Contracting States and drawing up reports on the basis of its findings, with a view to protecting detainees from torture and other forms of ill-treatment. The Committee comprises independent experts, nominated by the Contracting States but sitting in an individual capacity.[8] The signatories to the Convention declared themselves

> [c]onvinced that the protection of persons deprived of their liberty against torture and inhuman or degrading treatment or punishment could be strengthened by non-judicial means of a preventive character based on visits.[9]

The primary aim is consistent periodic visiting and reporting, forming a basis for sustained communication between the CPT and each of the Contracting States. The theme of co-operation infuses the exercise. As the Explanatory Report on the Convention indicates:

> In the application of the Convention, the Committee and the State are obliged to co-operate. The purpose of the Committee is not to condemn states, but, in a spirit of co-operation and through advice, to seek improvements, if necessary, in the protection of persons deprived of their liberty.[10]

Nevertheless, the possibility of more aggressive, condemnatory action on the part of the CPT is not entirely negated. In particular, provision is made for supplementary visits of an *ad hoc* nature, principally to investigate allegations of consistent abuse. Furthermore, irrespective of a general requirement of State consent to the publication of reports, the CPT has the authority to issue a public statement where a State fails to co-operate or refuses to take steps to improve protections afforded to detainees.

The Convention has now been in operation for almost five years, during which time visits have been conducted to virtually all of the current membership of twenty-four Contracting States.[11] Clearly it would be premature to draw watertight conclusions as to the success of the CPT. The level of State response, for example, will grow readily more apparent with the repetition of visits and the conclusion of follow-up reports. Nevertheless, the Convention has attracted a remarkably rapid rate of accessions during its short lifetime, such as to engage the CPT in a flurry of activity. It is apposite, therefore, to take stock of the progress of the CPT, not least in light of the fact that Ireland was one of the last States to receive a visit. In autumn 1993, public institutions in Ireland came under the scrutiny of the Committee for the first time.[12]

BACKGROUND

The actual idea of providing in treaty-form for a system of periodic visits to places of detention is attributed to Jean-Jacques Gautier, the founder of the Swiss Committee Against Torture. He was inspired, in turn, by the activities of the International Committee of the Red Cross (ICRC) in conducting visits to places where prisoners of war are detained. The legal mandate for ICRC visits is found in the Geneva Red Cross Conventions, 1949, and the Additional Protocols, 1977,[13] although the Red Cross also conducts visits on the basis of voluntary bilateral agreements with State authorities. A proposal to incorporate a similar arrangement in a European treaty was taken up by the Legal Affairs Committee of the Council of Europe in the early 1980s and led to the completion of a draft convention in 1983. The Convention was opened for signature in 1987, entered into force in 1989 and currently commands the participation of the vast majority of the members of the Council of Europe.

At first brush, the respective spheres of competence of the ICRC and the CPT would seem to preclude the eventuality of a conflicting overlap. While the ICRC directs its efforts towards scenarios of international and non-international armed conflict, the CPT is a essentially a peacetime mechanism, concerned with the habitual circumstances of detainees.[14] Nevertheless, Article 17(3) specifically addresses the relationship between the two by stipulating that the CPT shall not visit places which are the subject of regular visits by the ICRC by virtue of the Geneva Conventions.[15] Initial concerns that this provision might import a significant limitation in the potential exclusion of the CPT from those very circumstances where international condemnation may be needed most, have proved unfounded, to date. In particular, it has not prevented the Committee from examining places and conditions of detention in Northern Ireland.[16]

The Convention was designed to build upon existing arrangements for the protection of detainees exercised under the auspices of the Council of Europe. These measures include the European Prison Rules and, most notably, the European Convention on Human Rights. At several junctures, the Convention emphasizes the complimentary nature of its role to the operation of the ECHR. In many respects, the contrasting ambitions of the two arrangements minimize the dangers of conflict or competition. The Convention does not purport to establish new norms, nor to engage the CPT in *post facto* legal analysis; the CPT is not a judicial body and has no mandate to act on the basis of specific complaints nor to adjudicate on individual cases. It is left to the European Commission of Human Rights to guide the aggrieved individual down the lengthy path toward the specific remedies of judgment and just satisfaction at the direction of the European Court of Human Rights.

Nevertheless, a caveat must be entered, since practice to date is suggestive of further complexity in the relationship between the two regimes than the text of the Convention might indicate. Despite theoretical differences, the existence of a common field of practice in terms of fact-finding and investigation poses some threat of overlap:

> . . . problems arise from both the dual nature of the Torture Committee's work and from the way in which it has set about it. Whilst periodic visits are clearly intended to create an ongoing relationship between the Committee and the State party in question and are not intended to focus upon particular

instances of alleged mistreatment, *ad hoc* visits do have such a role and run the risk of straying into the area mapped out for petitions under the ECHR; that is, determining whether a violation of Article 3 has occurred. To this must be added the fact that the bulk of ECHR visits have concerned applications by prisoners relating to prison conditions.[17]

The CPT is guided by the legal standards set by the European Court of Human Rights in determining the ambit of the Article 3 imperative that "no one shall be subjected to torture or to inhuman or degrading treatment or punishment". In practice, the mandate of the CPT has not been constrained by the technicalities of the Court's jurisprudence. Applying the yardstick of a basic threshold of degradation, the CPT does not concern itself with the distinct categories of ill-treatment laid down by the Court in cases such as *Ireland v. United Kingdom*,[18] and, furthermore, scrutinizes a far broader range of treatment and diversity of conditions than the Commission or Court could be realistically expected to consider.

Condemnation by the CPT and the formulation of recommendations for reform constitute clear and grave indications of unacceptable State behaviour. In certain of the reports which have been published,[19] references to individual cases, even in the context of general discussion, "do carry an implication that there have been breaches of Article 3 in these particular cases".[20] Irrespective of its non-judicial character, the CPT's findings inevitably impact upon the operation of Article 3 of the ECHR. Even at a general level, the existence and practice of the CPT has implications for the participants—applicants, States and Strasbourg organs, alike—in the ECHR process.

THE VISIT

A typical visit is carried out by a delegation which is made up of four to five members of the Committee (none of whom are nationals or representatives of the State concerned), assisted by experts, interpreters and members of the CPT's secretariat.

Article 2 provides that each State Party shall permit visits "to any place within its jurisdiction where persons are deprived of their liberty by a public authority". The Explanatory Report on the Convention adds that "[i]t is immaterial whether the deprivation is based on a formal decision or not".[21] Investigation of police stations and prisons have dominated the visits conducted to date, although psychiatric hospitals,[22] a refugee centre,[23] and a military detention centre,[24] have also been the subject of scrutiny. The mandate of the CPT is sufficiently broad to embrace other institutions, such as those in which the elderly or minors are housed,[25] although the ever-increasing workload of the CPT may prevent any practical extension of its activities in the immediate term. The facility or institution may be private provided that the deprivation is carried out by a public authority. This would seem to cover scenarios such as the privatization of prisons and hospitals but difficulties may arise, for example, with respect to specific concerns involving hospital patients admitted on a voluntary basis.

The CPT must notify the government of its intention to carry out a visit,[26] although specification of the length of notice was deliberately omitted from the text of the Convention in order to allow for the possibility of an immediate, unexpected visit.[27] A three-stage notification procedure is applied in practice to the conduct of periodic visits. States are selected by lot and informed of their inclusion on a provisional programme of periodic visits at the close of the preceding year. This selection is also the subject of a public press release. Formal notification is transmitted some two weeks in advance of the visit and, finally, a matter of days before the arrival of the delegation, the national authorities are presented with a list of the institutions which will be the subject of investigation, on average about ten in number, located in two or three geographical areas.[28] This list is not exhaustive and may be extended, unexpectedly perhaps, during the course of the visit. Article 8 stipulates that the government is obliged to guarantee the unrestricted right of the CPT to travel within the jurisdiction and to facilitate unlimited access to any place where persons are deprived of their liberty. This includes the right to move inside such places without restriction. Article 15 provides for the appointment of a liaison–officer to communicate with the CPT generally on the subject of visits.

In order to make effective decisions concerning the institutions which should be visited and the facilities and conditions which warrant particular inspection, the CPT must be well informed as to the circumstances of persons detained by public authorities in the Contracting States. The effective functioning of the Convention depends upon the active participation of individuals and non–governmental organizations in the supervisory process. National authorities are obliged to furnish the CPT with full information on the places where persons deprived of their liberty are being held. Moreover, following the receipt of such information, details of remedial action taken by national authorities may be requested.[29] Nevertheless, the information-gathering function of the CPT secretariat is also fuelled by the licence given to the CPT, by virtue of Article 8(4), to communicate freely with any person whom it believes can supply relevant information. Independently, and in correspondence with non-governmental organizations (NGOs), the Committee assembles information regarding State practice, while delegations engage in consultation with national interest-groups immediately prior to the commencement of their investigations.[30] There is also specific provision, in Article 8(3), for the conduct of private interviews with individual detainees, their families, doctors, lawyers, etc.

Central to the efficacy of the entire procedure is the cloak of confidentiality which envelopes several aspects of CPT activity. Included among these is a guarantee that the information gathered in relation to a visit shall remain confidential.[31] The CPT must exercise caution, *inter alia*, to ensure that information concerning pending investigations or proceedings is not revealed.

There are inherent limitations in the theory and practice of conducting visits to places of detention. Clearly, the CPT cannot coerce individuals to communicate with it,[32] nor can it "organize formal hearings in the legal sense with all the procedural conditions that this would imply".[33] While a government may not be in a position to prevent a visit taking place, there remains a sufficient measure of State discretion to enable national authorities to impede, significantly, the task of the delegation. For example, there have been blatant instances of bad faith, such as the movement of detainees immediately prior to a visit.[34] Nevertheless, the CPT reports that "[c]o-operation between national authorities at ministerial level and visiting delegations have invariably been very good. Further, visiting delegations have generally speaking been received in a satisfactory manner by the authorities in charge of the places visited".[35]

THE REPORT

After the visit, the delegation submits its conclusions to the CPT which draws up a report for submission to the State concerned.[36] The report is based on the facts gathered during the visit and takes account of any observations which the State concerned might wish to make.[37] Generally, it will comprise the following:

(i)   An opening statement (setting out the legal framework within the particular State);

(ii) A description of the CPT's findings;

(iii) Recommendations;

(iv) Requests for further information (if required);

(v)   A request for an interim report (in the form of a reply).

The Explanatory Report on the Convention indicates that where the facts found during a visit are unclear, the CPT may inform the State concerned, suggest that further investigations be conducted at national level and issue a request to be kept informed.[38] In order to pursue the matter further, the CPT may arrange for fresh investigations of sites which have already been the subject of a visit. There is also an important provision which enables the CPT to make certain observations during the visit itself.[39] This is seen as an exceptional measure to be used, for example, in cases where there is an urgent need to modify the treatment of persons deprived of their liberty. Nor is it intended to detract from the formulation of a full report in accordance with Article 10.

Article 12 brings the CPT back to its original point of reference. Subject to the rules of confidentiality, it must submit a general report to the Committee of Ministers which will be transmitted to the Consultative Assembly of the Council of Europe and made public.

The completed report may be published but only at the request of the State concerned. In all other respects, the information gathered remains confidential. In particular, Article 11(3) provides that "no personal data shall be published without the express consent of the person concerned", as a means of protecting the confidentiality of private interviews with detainees and others. Surprisingly, perhaps, a number of States, including Austria, Denmark and the United Kingdom, have consented to the publication of reports, even where the findings of the Committee have been particularly unfavourable.

SUBSTANTIVE ISSUES

An impressive range of issues have been investigated by the various delegations, with particular themes of concern surfacing in the reports which have been published to date.

In the context of detention in police custody, the CPT attaches particular importance, *inter alia*, to the right of the detainee to notify a third party of the fact of his or her detention, the right of access to a lawyer and the right to request a medical examination by a doctor of his or her own choosing.[40] The CPT has also given consideration to various aspects of the interrogation process and to general matters such as the physical conditions of detention in police custody; the length such detention; the maintenance of a single, comprehensive custody record; and the existence of an independent mechanism, at local level, for examining complaints about treatment whilst in police custody.[41]

With respect to imprisonment, the CPT has stated:

> . . . all aspects of the conditions of detention in a prison are of relevance
> to the CPT's mandate. Ill-treatment can take numerous forms, many
> of which may not be deliberate but rather the result of organizational
> failings or inadequate resources. The overall quality of life in an estab-
> lishment is therefore of considerable importance to the CPT. That quality
> of life will depend to a very large extent upon the activities offered to
> prisoners and the general state of relations between prisoners and staff.[42]

It follows, for example, that overcrowding is an issue of particular concern to the
CPT and a matter which was highlighted in the report to the UK Government[43]
following a visit in 1990.[44] The delegation found that the conditions of detention
in the three male local prisons visited were "very poor":[45]

> Overcrowding, a significant problem at Wandsworth, worse at Brixton,
> reached at outrageous level at Leeds prison. At the outset of the delegation's
> visit the establishment was holding 1,205 prisoners, in other words almost
> twice its CNA [certified normal accommodation] figure of 627 . . .

> The cells in Brixton, Leeds and Wandsworth Prisons were of an acceptable
> size for one person. However, they were cramped accommodation for two
> persons . . . and excessively cramped accommodation for three. . . . [46]

Other aspects of imprisonment addressed by the CPT included isolated
allegations of ill-treatment, the role and training of prison staff, health–care
services, regime activities (work, education and sport) and the lack of integral
sanitation in the prisons visited.

A visit to Malta in 1990, provided the first opportunity for the CPT to
examine a mental health institution. The visit was a brief one, preventing "a
thorough examination of conditions at the hospital". Although impressed with
the general level of maintenance, the delegation was critical of the lack of
professional training among the nursing staff:

> . . . of the 120 male nurses only 5 were qualified as professional psychiatric
> nurses and the 80 female nurses were generally trained but not qualified
> in psychiatric nursing. The delegation felt that more professional
> training would enable a less restrictive environment within the hospital.[47]

THE PUBLIC STATEMENT

In the case of a repeated failure to co-operate, the Committee may resort to an exceptional measure—the issuing of a public statement in accordance with Article 10. In contrast to other decisions which need no more than a simple majority, this measure must be sanctioned by a two-thirds majority of the Committee. Essentially, it provides an alternative means of publishing the contents of the Committee's findings. But it is perceived to be a measure of last resort[48] and has only been invoked on one recent occasion, namely in December 1992, in respect of Turkey.[49]

Turkey is also the only Contracting State which has been the recipient of *ad hoc* visits by the CPT. These visits followed a considerable number of reports received by the CPT from a variety of sources, containing allegations of ill-treatment, particularly in relation to persons held in police custody. The investigations of the CPT led it to the damning conclusion that police authorities frequently resorted to torture and other forms of physical and psychological ill-treatment when holding and questioning suspects.[50] Subsequent on-going dialogue between the CPT and the Turkish authorities, as well as further communication following a periodic visit, did not result in any measure of satisfactory State response:

> In short, more than two years after the CPT's first visit, very little had been achieved as regards the strengthening of legal safeguards against torture and ill-treatment and no concrete steps capable of remedying the situation . . . had been taken.[51]

In response, the CPT decided to utilize its power to issue a public statement, setting out in graphic detail the findings of its delegations, and its recommendations for required action. The statement closes:

> The CPT is convinced that it would have been counterproductive from the standpoint of the protection of human rights for it to have refrained—as it was requested to do by the Turkish authorities—from making this public statement. *The statement is issued in a constructive spirit. Far from creating an obstacle, it should facilitate the efforts of both parties—acting in co-operation—to strengthen the protection of persons deprived of their liberty from torture and inhuman or degrading treatment or punishment.*[52]

CONCLUSION

Without doubt, the CPT has travelled a significant distance in a relatively short lifetime and the initial response to its creation and operation should be a positive one. Certainly, the Convention has its limitations, not least among them some-times modest impact at local level of internationally-inspired endeavour. More specifically, misgivings may appear with respect to a number of matters (some of which are beyond the scope of the present discussion) such as: the composi-tion of the CPT, the level of dependency on State co-operation; forms of ill-treatment beyond the practical reach of the CPT; the withholding of State consent to the publication of reports; the relationship with other regimes (not merely the ECHR and the ICRC but also the UN Convention Against Torture and the UN Special Rapporteur on Torture[53]); and the forthright provision for enforcement (for example, in the form of a role for the Committee of Ministers) in extreme cases of repeated non-compliance.

The observation is sometimes made that the speed with which the Conven-tion was drafted and accepted is attributable to the fact that States did not perceive it as a threat. Nevertheless, that the Convention provides for a signifi-cant intrusion into an area which was previously considered solely within the realm of State sovereignty is now a reality. It remains to be seen, however, to what extent States will be prepared to modify domestic practice in response to this measure of external influence.

4.4   Psychiatric Detainees and the Human Rights Challenge to Psychiatry and Law: Where Do We Go From Here?

TOM COONEY

Eugene Brody observes that the disparity of power between psychiatrist and patient is no longer obscure but has been exposed by the "increasing self-aware-ness and assertiveness of previously powerless minorities, including the mentally ill".[1] He adds that this change "has forced our attention to the ethical dilemmas of a social tradition of care for impaired persons that— on clinical grounds— has been able to suspend attention to the values of justice, autonomy, and benefi-cence considered important to the culture at large". Pointedly, he says: "This suspension allows the clinical encounter itself to threaten a personhood already impaired by illness". He calls for renewed recognition of the claims of the mentally ill to respect and just treatment based on their common humanity with others. From a civil liberties perspective, I welcome this observation because if there is a single moral imperative to which we must respond in the context of mental health law it is the human rights obligation to translate the core ethical principles of respect for personal autonomy, justice, and paternalistic caring into the legal code. Here I will focus on one important facet of mental health law and practice: the question of how we should reform the law and procedure governing the admission and treatment of involuntary patients (or "psychiatric detainees") under the Mental Treatment Act, 1945, as amended.

In so doing, I am not suggesting that law is the most vital element in the provision of psychiatric services, nor do I intend to devalue important issues concerning the proper organization and delivery of such services (such as funding, and the training and legal protection of health carers). At the same time I would like to stress—against the ruling professional psychiatric view—that law has an essential role to play in this area. My root assumption is that law should be used as follows: first, to ensure that access to health and social services is not based upon charitable or professional discretion, but upon enforceable legal rights; second, to shield consumers or patients from arbitrariness, irrational decisions, or malice in the distribution of those services; third, in the interests of personal autonomy and liberty, to set limits on coercive or intrusive psychiatric powers and measures in relation to, for example, involuntary admission to hospital and treatment and hazardous treatments given with the consent of the patient; and, finally, to guarantee the civil status of those who become enmeshed in the psychiatric services.

At the outset I will set down the gist of my response to the question, "Where should we go from here". Law reform should, at least, do the following: (1) define the criteria for involuntary hospitalization; (2) create a more stringent involuntary admission procedure, involving mental health review tribunals; (3) guarantee the right of competent involuntary patients to refuse treatment, and provide checks in respect of the administration of hazardous and suspect treatments; (4) stitch in a legally enforceable bill of rights; (5) establish an independent panel of patients' advocates and a legal aid scheme; and (6) retrench the various discriminations burdening involuntary patients.

WHERE ARE WE NOW?

To answer the question, "Where do we go from here?", we must first squarely recognize where we are now. To answer this question I will note the classes of psychiatric patient created by our mental health law. Then I will make some observations about these classes.

Under the 1945 Act, two main classes of patients are admitted to psychiatric institutions, namely voluntary patients and non-voluntary (or involuntary) patients. Voluntary patients are those who freely decide for themselves to apply for admission to and treatment in a psychiatric institution.

Non-voluntary patients are those who have been compulsorily admitted and detained, a procedure which is sometimes called civil commitment. There are two categories of non-voluntary patient, namely temporary patients and persons of unsound mind. Both voluntary and non-voluntary patients are further classified into eligible patients and private patients. An eligible patient is a person with full eligibility or a person with limited eligibility for health services.[2] A private patient is a person who enters a psychiatric hospital and pays full charge for maintenance and treatment, though normally he or she will be covered by private health care insurance. The legal procedures governing admission to psychiatric hospitals vary depending upon the category to which the patient belongs.

A temporary patient is a person who is thought to need detention but is believed to require for his or her recovery not more than six months suitable treatment, or an addict who by reason of his or her addiction to drugs or intoxicants needs compulsory detention.[3] A person of unsound mind is a person who is certified to need detention and to be unlikely to recover within six months.[4]

A person not less than sixteen years may submit himself or herself voluntarily for psychiatric treatment in an approved psychiatric institution. From the legal point of view admission of a voluntary patient is governed by Sections 190 to 196 of the Mental Treatment Act, 1945.[5]

Where it is desired to admit the person "as a voluntary patient and as an eligible patient", the person shall apply "in the prescribed form" to the person in charge of the institution concerned. The Acts do not make it a prior condition of admission that the person concerned produce a medical report or recommendation, though usually a person will seek admission to a psychiatric institution on medical advice. In the case of an eligible patient a form similar to that provided in Form 8 of the Mental Treatment Regulations, 1961, should be signed by the applicant for admission. There is no statutory form of application in the case of a voluntary private patient.

If the person is less than sixteen years the application for admission will have to be made by his or her parent or guardian.[6] It will be necessary to produce a recommendation from a registered medical practitioner stating that he or she has examined the person, on a specified date not more than seven days before the date of the application, and that in his or her opinion the patient will benefit by the proposed reception. There is no statutory form on which this recommendation has to be given.

At this point, some comments seem appropriate. In the first place, it may be said that voluntary patients are admitted to hospital of their own free will and freely and competently consent to treatment. Consent— explicit or implicit— to treatment is essential because without it treatment may be an assault or an act of negligence, depending on the circumstances of the case. If the person in charge of the hospital, or a doctor to whom this task has been properly delegated, decides that treatment is required, the patient completes a simple written application. The procedure varies slightly in the case of a person under sixteen years. Here, application must be made by a parent or guardian and must be accompanied by a recommendation from a registered medical practitioner stating that he or she has examined the patient on the specified date not more than seven days before the date of the application and that, in his or her opinion, the patient will benefit by the proposed reception.

For discharge, a voluntary patient may give notice that he or she wishes to leave the hospital. He or she must then be allowed to do so on or after the expiration of seventy-two hours. If the patient is under sixteen years, the notice must be given by the parent or guardian, who is then entitled to remove the patient immediately. It would appear that in practice the seventy-two-hour notice requirement is not commonly observed. It may reasonably be questioned whether seventy-two hours is excessive on the basis that if there is need to hold on to a voluntary patient to have him or her detained as an involuntary patient a lesser time would suffice, say, six hours.

On the issue of reform, it may be said that a less formal admission procedure — such as applies in the case of general hospitals— might encourage people who need psychiatric care to come to hospital at an early stage. However, an important concern is how do you safeguard people against being pressured to admit themselves as voluntary patients in name only? At present, an adult patient may not be admitted as a voluntary patient unless his or her mental condition is such that, at the time, he or she is able to express a wish to avail himself or herself of hospital treatment. Even with the statutory form of application there are no real safeguards against the practice of coercing individuals into admitting themselves as voluntary patients. Severe family pressure or the threat of involuntary detention is sometimes used to force people to admit themselves "voluntarily" into psychiatric hospital.

Secondly, it should be pointed out that the 1945 Act does not define in any detail what constitutes a sufficiently severe mental disorder for the purposes of justifying involuntary detention. The Act would seem to formalize the exercise of medical discretion. The Act does not in strict terms require that the person be a danger to himself or herself or to others because of some form of psychosis (or gross breakdown of rationality), that he or she be incompetent, that the disorder be treatable, and that the detention be the least intrusive way of dealing with the situation. Moreover, there is no mental health tribunal system in which a detained patient could have the detention reviewed. The Health (Mental

Services) Act, 1981, provides for the creation of a system of psychiatric review boards (comprising three people, a psychiatrist, a lawyer, and a lay person) to do just this. The Act ossified in the Department of Health. Psychiatrists complained that they were not adequately consulted so they intimated that they would not be prepared to work it. Moreover, the recession and the monetarist policy behind dismantling the health services gave the review concept the appearance of a luxury. Most important of all, Fine Gael and Labour Ministers (particularly Mr Dick Spring and Mr Patrick Cooney) opposed the idea of mental health tribunals.

Thirdly, application for admission is made by a near relative, or, in certain circumstances, any interested person. In the case of a public patient, the application must be accompanied by a medical certificate signed by one doctor to the effect that the person is suffering from mental illness, or is an addict, and requires treatment. In the case of private patients, this certificate must be signed by two doctors. There is no reasonable basis for this distinction; it simply reflects the 19th-century idea (surely antithetical to Article 40.1 of the Constitution) that a person owning property has more reason than a property-less person to fear arbitrary detention.

Fourthly, the generally observed psychiatric practice has been to merge involuntary admission and incompetency to decide upon treatment. That is to say, many psychiatrists simply assume that once a person has been committed to a psychiatric hospital against his or her will that entails that he or she lacks the capacity to make a free and informed decision about treatment even where the proposed form of treatment creates the risk of serious adverse side-effects.

CRITIQUE

The issue of involuntary hospitalization of the psychiatrically ill cannot be adequately considered until our legislators (and our judges) decide whether respect for individual autonomy or utilitarian State paternalism takes precedence. The preamble to the Constitution enunciates that respect for individual dignity and freedom is constitutionally inviolate in the sense that no person should be treated simply as a means to satisfy the preferences or interests of others. Article 40.1 makes it clear that individuals are entitled to equal concern and respect before the law. Articles 40.3 and 40.4.1 guarantee that no one's liberty shall be taken away save in accordance with principles of fundamental fairness. Every competent person enjoys a right of self-determination in relation to medical treatment. Although the Supreme Court blandly upheld the constitutionality of the 1945 Act in *In re Philip Clarke*,[7] it seems more convincing to state that the law trenches upon basic constitutional principles.

(1) The current grounds for involuntary commitment are hopelessly vague. In reality an individual can be committed just because the required number of doctors consider that he or she is in need of psychiatric treatment. The 1945 Act fails to provide fair and adequate notice of what circumstances or conditions will justify detention, and furnishes doctors with excessive discretion about who should be committed and for what. The elasticity of the concept of mental disorder lies in the fact that its interpretation in the particular circumstances of a case is left entirely to the doctor and is dependent on the norms he or she employs. This position contrasts with that of the criminal suspect who has a constitutional right not to be deprived of his or her liberty save in accordance with a statutory provision framed in clear and specific terms. It also flies in the face of the decision of the European Court of Human Rights in *Winterwerp v. The Netherlands.*[8]

This flaw compounds a deeper flaw. There is no requirement that a person be irrational and dangerous to himself or herself or to others. The point is the 1945 Act reveals a lack of legislative concern about the justifications for taking away a psychiatrically ill person's freedom.

(2) The procedures for detention are lax, unfair and unreliable. The courts have shown a disquieting unwillingness to require the medical profession to observe stringently the detention procedures under present law.[9] For this reason the law fails to ensure procedural fairness and regularity.

Many studies show that the validity and reliability of psychiatric diagnoses or formulations are poor. Reliability refers to the degree to which two or more psychiatrists will agree about a conclusion given a certain set of facts. Validity is the degree to which psychiatrists' conclusions match reality. Psychiatrists often disagree on broad diagnostic judgments and even on specific diagnoses. Women are often diagnosed as mentally ill on the basis of different standards from that used for men. Women tend to receive psychiatric treatment when describing symptoms identical to those for which men receive a physical diagnosis.

There is simply no basis for the conventional view that psychiatrists can reliably predict whether a person is likely to engage in violent behaviour. "Dangerousness" is a question of social perception and not a clinical concept. Psychiatrists are more likely than others to over-predict dangerousness, perhaps out of a fear that a mistaken prediction of non-dangerousness will anger the community or lead to litigation. In 1966, in *Baxstrom v. Herold,*[10] the US Supreme Court struck down a New York statute that permitted the detention of convicted prisoners in a high security mental hospital after their prison sentence had elapsed. As a result about one thousand patients were transferred to civil hospitals. Less than fifty-percent of them turned out to be dangerous. There are studies that suggest that over-prediction may be over seventy-percent under the stress of the admission ward in a hospital.

It is offensive to justice that detained psychiatric patients have no automatic right to an independent review of the need for detention. Arguably, independent review is a requirement of the European Convention of Human Rights.[11]

(3) The current law confers on psychiatrists the power to decide whether a detained person is competent or not to decide upon treatment. It is assumed, generally, that a detained patient is by definition incompetent to decide about treatment. The reality is that competence is not a clinical matter although a doctor's evidence may be relevant to a decision on the issue. There is no basis for claiming that involuntary patients are inherently incapable of making treatment decisions. Although a particular person might lack competence to decide about hospitalization, he or she might be competent about treatment matters. The present law allows an assault upon the autonomy of patients who have the capacity to make a rational decision about treatment. The rational competence of individuals must be respected even when they are adjudged foolish in their treatment decisions so long as they are able to understand the nature, purpose and risks of the treatment, and the implications of taking or refusing the treatment, and to articulate their will coherently.

Forcible methods of treatment may encompass psychotherapy, behaviour therapy, drug treatment, and electric shock treatment. It is a violation of human rights that our law does not guarantee the right of detained competent patients to refuse treatment especially since there are harmful psychiatric treatments. For example, patients who have been treated with neuroleptic drugs (euphemistically called "major tranquillisers") commonly develop adverse side effects including irreversible brain damage (*tardive dyskinesia*) characterized by involuntary sucking and smacking of the lips, lateral jaw movements and darting of the tongue. So much for the constitutional right of bodily integrity.[12]

There is still the question of what controls should be placed upon medical discretion in relation to the administration of treatments which are intrusive, irreversible in their effects, or unpredictable. The problem is that a patient might consent to a course of treatment which is hazardous because he or she feels vulnerable and finds the atmosphere of the hospital inherently compelling. It is important therefore that doctors be required by law to obtain a second opinion before administering such a treatment. The core question is the character of the patient's consent and his or her ability to weigh up the factors involved. These are not exclusively medical matters and, for this reason, an independent tribunal with lay participation should be provided to make the second independent judgment.

(4) Irish mental health law provides little in the area of patients' rights. It is crucial that reform include the concept of a legally enforceable bill of rights for

psychiatric patients. The list of rights should include rights to refuse treatment, to be treated in the least restrictive alternative conditions, to be free from physical assault, to be protected against the arbitrary imposition of solitary confinement, to have privacy, expression, correspondence, visitors and so on. To make such rights more practically realizable it would be essential ensure that patients have understandable information and advice about their rights. A system of independent patients' advocates would serve this purpose. Moreover, it is necessary that our legislators repeal Section 260 of the 1945 Act because it is, despite what the Supreme Court says in *O'Dowd*, a naked piece of prejudicial discrimination against detained patients who wish to sue on the grounds that their rights have been violated.

REFORM

The pressure for reforming our mental health law comes from international legal commitments (both the Council of Europe and the UN have created minimum standards in relation to detained psychiatric patients) and from groups (e.g. Irish Council for Civil Liberties and a former patients' group known as Wrongfully Institutionalized Persons) in Ireland who are concerned about the injustice of our current law. I indicated at the start of this paper what reforms appear necessary. Here I would like to focus upon two items in the context of reform, namely, what should the grounds of detention or civil commitment be, and what might a statutory bill of rights contain.

GROUNDS OF DETENTION

The grounds of civil commitment should be as clear and specific as possible so as to guard against arbitrary deprivations of liberty. I would propose five cumulative grounds justifying compulsory hospitalization.

(1) A new law should use the term "severe mental disorder" so as to limit the application of commitment to people suffering from major mental or emotional impairments. The definition of severe mental disorder should cover the three elements of mental functioning—emotion, choice and understanding —in language intelligible to lay people, including lawyers. It might then be defined as a severe impairment of emotional capacity, capacity for conscious control of one's behaviour or capacity to understand reality or to reason, which impairment is evidenced by proven recent instances of grossly disturbed behaviour or perceptions. Shaping the definition in this way would require a doctor or

psychiatrist to specify disordered mental capacity in functional terms and make an explicit quantitative assessment about severity. He or she would also have to describe exact manifestations of such disorder. The value of this approach would be that a doctor would have to furnish clear and convincing evidence in the form of specific, factual testimony about disordered behaviour rather than make conclusory or theoretical assertions. It would remain for a mental health tribunal to decide whether the disorder is severe and whether the instances of impaired behaviour or perception are gross. The definition should exclude epilepsy, mental handicap, old age, unconventional sexual practices, sexual orientation, intoxication and addiction as grounds in themselves justifying detention. If abuse of alcohol or other substances has produced a severe continuing mental disorder, then the definition should accommodate this as a ground of detention.

(2) The next criterion should involve a requirement that the individual be shown on the basis of clear and convincing evidence to lack the capacity to make free and informed decisions about his or her need for hospitalization. This requirement is essential from a human rights point of view. Detention in a psychiatric hospital allows the state through its agents, the doctors, to substitute its judgment about what is in the committed patient's best interests. This raises the basic question: when is forcible hospitalization in an individual's best interests?

There is no knockdown answer to this question because there is no metric to measure the variables involved. The detained individual loses personal liberty, control over his or her mind and behaviour, autonomy regarding treatment, and possibly other social goods as well (e.g. his or her job). Other variables include possible improvement after treatment, possible adverse side effects of treatment, prevention of possible harm to self or others, and the stigma of committal. In general, if we respect an individual as a morally independent agent who is, to use Kant's evocative phrase, "sovereign in the kingdom of ends", then we will assure him or her the right to weigh the various factors relating to his or her health concerns and decisions with reference to his or her own values and preferences. The most respectful way to serve any competent person's interest is to give him or her the relevant information and leave him or her to his or her own values to decide upon what he or she judges to be a worthwhile course of action. Against this moral background state intrusion on paternalistic grounds is defensible only when the individual is unable to make these decisions for himself or herself, that is, when he or she is incompetent.

With regard to severely mentally disordered individuals who lack the capacity to decide about the need for hospitalization, civil commitment is a proper substitute decision making process. However, it should be remembered that many individuals diagnosed as mentally disordered are capable of making their own competent decisions about health care. Their decisions should be respected even where doctors (or anyone else) considers that their decisions are foolish. Physically injured or ill individuals may suffer severe health impairment, even death, as a result of decisions to forego medical treatment. For example, doctors may disagree strenuously about a particular competent individual's decision not to have a coronary by-pass operation. Nonetheless the law does not coerce such a person to submit to an involuntary operation. Equal respect demands that we similarly not interfere with a psychiatrically ill person's decision to refuse hospitalization or treatment unless he or she is incompetent to make a decision about the need for hospitalization.

In defining "incompetency" we should focus upon the person's capacity to understand. Therefore, the fact that a person is mentally disordered or the fact that he or she has a foolish preference should not in themselves be treated as evidence of incompetency. The concept may be understood to refer to the person's incapacity to achieve a rudimentary understanding, by reason of mental condition, after conscientious efforts at simple explanation of the purpose, nature, and possible significant benefits of hospitalization.

(3) The grounds for detention should also include a reference to the principle of the least restrictive means. This would require that before a person is detained in a psychiatric hospital health carers should ensure—and satisfy a mental health tribunal—that all available less restrictive alternatives to commitment have been investigated and found unsuitable.

(4) A new Act should also require those who wish to commit another person to show that there is substantial cause to believe, based upon a recent act, attempt, or threat to do serious harm, that the person is in imminent danger of inflicting serious physical harm upon himself or herself or others, or that there is substantial cause to believe that the person is in imminent danger of death from grave disablement.

(5) Finally, a treatability clause should be included in reforming legislation. This would require the state to show that the person's condition is amenable to treatment and care and that adequate treatment resources are available.

These should, I think, be grounds for civil commitment. Reform should require the recommendation of two general practitioners and a social worker before a person could be committed. Once in a hospital the person would be assessed by an interdisciplinary team. This team should have twenty-four hours to decide whether the person should be discharged or detained. If they decide upon detention then they should be required to apply to an independent mental health tribunal (comprising a psychiatrist, a lawyer, and a lay person) and to prove on the basis of clear and convincing evidence that the person satisfies the grounds for commitment. The tribunal should adjudicate upon the application not later than seventy-two hours from the time of detention or later provided the person concerned agrees to a delay. A person who is the object of committal proceedings should have the right to a lawyer or advocate. He or she should have whatever adversarial safeguards are necessary to prevent improper detention. If an individual is committed by a tribunal then the commitment should be for not more than twenty-eight days in the first instance. Provision should be made for extending the period of commitment but only after a hearing before the tribunal.

A STATUTORY BILL OF RIGHTS

A reforming statute should embody an enforceable bill of rights dealing with the rights of psychiatric patients but especially with the rights of detained patients. A bill of rights should cover such subjects as the right to wear one's own clothes, to have one's own money, to express oneself, to be free from arbitrary restraint or seclusion, to adequate treatment, and the right of a competent patient to refuse treatment. It would be essential that patients be informed of their rights by an independent person. The creation of a patient's advocacy service would advance this requirement. At the very least a bill of rights should include the provisions contained in the addendum to this paper.

CONCLUSION

It is important that reform of admissions procedures to psychiatric hospitals must go hand-in-hand with the development of comprehensive community health care services. Otherwise, our system of mental health care will become a system of mental health neglect. In this contribution I have commented upon civil commitment but there are other aspects of mental health law calling for reform. These include the position of individuals who are found guilty but insane or unfit to make a plea in the criminal process as well as the position of children or incompetent voluntary patients. It is so true that we live in and by the law. It defines in fundamental ways what we are. We should be concerned about how our law defines people who become enmeshed in the psychiatric process. Current law too easily allows people to be forcibly hospitalized for benevolent or other motives, and too easily forgets them once they are in hospital.

ADDENDUM: BILL OF RIGHTS

1   All patients shall have a right to equal concern and respect in the design and administration of mental health facilities, in the delivery of mental health care services, and from the health carers who treat them.

   A person shall not lose his or her rights merely because he or she is currently receiving treatment for a mental disorder.

   The rights specified in this bill of rights shall be additions to, and not replacements for, the rights of patients as autonomous human beings.

2   All patients shall have a right to suitable treatment in the least restrictive setting.

3   All patients shall have the right—

   • to wear their own clothes;

   • to keep and use their own possessions, including their own toilet articles;

   • to keep and be free to spend a reasonable sum of their own money;

   • to have access to individual locked storage space for their own private use;

   • to see visitors at any time during each day;

   • to have reasonable access to telephones both to make and receive confidential telephone calls;

   • to have ready access to letter writing materials, including stamps, and to send and receive unopened letters;

   • to consult at any time with their lawyer (or patient's advocate) in privacy;

   • to go out of doors each day, and to make visits outside the hospital;

   • to have use of facilities and equipment for physical exercise, recreation, and relaxation;

   • to have access to programmes providing experience in skills involving self-care, leisure, and occupation;

   • to communicate and interact with persons of their own choice, including members of the opposite sex, upon the consent of such persons.

   The rights specified in this section shall not be restricted or taken away without a written statement in the patient's treatment plan which shows a compelling justification in terms of the patient's medical welfare for the restriction or justification.

Such statements in the patient's treatment plan shall be made only by an authorized doctor in the hospital or facility and a social worker who are involved in treating the patient, and shall explain, in factual terms, why the restriction or deprivation is strictly necessary for the medical welfare of the patient.

The patient (and his or her advocate) shall be furnished with written notice of each restriction or deprivation, and shall be given a copy of the relevant statement.

A written restriction or deprivation shall be in force for a period not to exceed twenty-one days, and shall be renewed only by a written statement by an authorized doctor and a social worker in the patient's treatment plan which shows in factual terms the compelling justification for the renewal of the restriction or deprivation.

In each case of the renewal of a restriction or deprivation, the patient (and his or her advocate) shall be given written notice of the renewal and a copy of the relevant statement.

4 Physical restraint or involuntary seclusion of a patient shall not be used except when it is strictly necessary as the only means available to prevent serious physical harm to the patient or to others, and it shall not be prolonged beyond the period which is strictly necessary for this purpose.

All instances of restraint or involuntary seclusion, the reasons for them and their nature and extent, shall be recorded in the patient's treatment plan (and notice shall be given to the patient's advocate).

A patient who is restrained or secluded shall be kept under humane and comfortable conditions and be under the care and constant supervision and attention of hospital staff approved for this purpose.

5 Each patient shall have a right to religious freedom and freedom of conscience.

6 Each patient shall have a right to express his or her convictions and opinions, and shall, in particular, have a right to express criticism of treatment policies and practices in the hospital or facility.

7 No patient shall be compelled, either directly or indirectly, to perform work which contributes to the operations or maintenance of the hospital or facility for which the hospital or facility would otherwise employ a person who is not a patient.

A patient who freely and knowingly engages in such work shall be entitled to fair pay.

Under no circumstances shall less restrictive conditions, discharge or privileges be conditional upon the performance of such work.

8 No patient shall be compelled to queue in a line on a ward or at an office in the hospital for the purposes of obtaining medication.

9 Corporal punishment shall not be inflicted on any patient.

10 The confidentiality of a patient's medical record shall be guaranteed. A patient's medical record shall not be open to inspection by persons other than those who are directly responsible for providing mental health care to the patient, without the free and informed consent of the patient prior to each instance of disclosure.

Every patient shall have full access to his or her medical record, unless a specific adjudication is made by the mental health review tribunal that there is genuine and compelling evidence that the receipt of such information would be inimical to the patient's mental health.

11 The media, the public and public representatives shall have access to the hospital or facility with the consent of the person or persons to be visited.

12 All patients shall have the right to treatment, including medical and dental care, rehabilitation or habilitation.

All patients shall have the right to prompt and adequate treatment in the least restrictive conditions necessary to fulfil the purpose of treatment.

To the fullest extent possible, all treatment proposed to be administered shall be planned in consultation and co-operation with the patient and he or she shall be kept informed as to the nature, purpose and possible consequences of his or her treatment.

Every patient shall have a right to a programme of treatment tailored to his or her individual needs and which is designed to optimise his or her abilities and improve his or her ability to live an autonomous life in the community.

13 Every patient shall have the right to an individual written treatment plan formulated by the responsible interdisciplinary team of health carers in the hospital or facility.

A treatment plan for every patient shall be implemented no later than seven days after the patient's admission or, in the case of out-patient care and treatment, no later than seven days after the patient has been accepted for such care and treatment.

The patient (and his or her advocate) shall be given a copy of the treatment plan.

14 Each individualized treatment plan shall contain:

- a statement designating the person in charge of implementing the plan of treatment, care and services;

- a statement of the patient's history, the results of examination following admission or acceptance for out-patient care and treatment, and of the diagnosis or formulation;

- a statement of the nature of the specific problems and needs of the patient;

- a statement of the prognosis and a description of the intermediate and long-term treatment goals, with a projected timetable for their attainment;

- a statement and rationale for the treatment plan designed to achieve these intermediate and long-term goals;

- a specification of staff responsibility and a description of proposed staff involvement with the patient in order to attain these treatment goals;

- a statement of the least restrictive treatment conditions necessary to achieve the purposes of admission;

- a statement of the criteria for release to less restrictive treatment conditions, and of the criteria for discharge;

- a detailed notation of any therapeutic tasks, including occupational therapy under the guidance of occupational therapists, to be performed by the patient;

- an estimated date for release or discharge of the patient;

- a description of the services to be provided for the patient after release from the hospital;

- upon review, an evaluation of the reasons that any goals or estimated dates contained in a preceding plan were not met.

Each individual treatment shall be regularly reviewed by the persons responsible for its formulation, at least every twenty-one days.

A copy of the individual treatment plan shall be given to the patient (and his or her advocate).

15 No treatment shall be given to a voluntary patient or to a competent involuntary patient without his or her free and informed consent and, in particular, where a competent involuntary patient refuses to give a consent to treatment, he or she shall not be treated against his or her wishes.

Where an involuntary patient is unable to give an informed consent, the interdisciplinary team responsible for his or her care and treatment may give the patient the proposed treatment provided the treatment is appropriate and a written report of the rationale, nature, and course of the treatment is made every twenty-one days to the mental health tribunal.

In the case of urgent necessity, treatment which is not usually hazardous or irreversible, and is treatment which has been fully established according to generally accepted and reasonable standards, may be given to the patient without his or her consent on the authority of the medical director of the hospital or facility, but the decision and the reasons for it shall be recorded immediately in detail in all relevant records in relation to the patient.

Treatment which is unusually hazardous, intrusive, irreversible, unpredictable, or not fully established according to generally accepted and reasonable scientific standards shall not be given without the patient having given his or her informed consent and the decision to give the treatment having been reviewed and approved by the mental health tribunal.

Electroshock treatment, psychosurgery, behaviour therapy involving aversive stimuli or substantial deprivations, and medication having potential risks of adverse side effects constitutes hazardous treatment.

All persons shall have a right to be free from unnecessary or excessive medication.

The administration of experimental treatment that would subject the patient to any mental risks or physical risks shall be prohibited.

16 Any patient, advocate, or legal adviser, or health carer may apply to the mental health tribunal for clarification or directions in individual cases as to whether a particular treatment is or is not hazardous.

17 Any patient, advocate, or legal adviser, or health carer shall have *locus standi* to proceed with an application to the mental health tribunal on the grounds that the provision of this bill of rights have been violated.

4.5 Access to the Courts—The Limitations of a Human Rights Approach

MEL COUSINS

Access to the courts has been recognized as a human right under the European Convention on Human Rights. However, this article argues that the concept of access to the courts has been interpreted in quite a limited way under the Convention and that attempting to guarantee a right of access to the courts by way of the Convention is likely to have limited success, unless it is combined with effective political and social campaigning.[1]

The article first outlines a working definition of access to the courts and some of the barriers which impede such access. It goes on to look briefly at the manner in which access to the courts is protected both under the European Convention on Human Rights and under European Community law. Finally the limitations of a human rights approach in guaranteeing adequate access to the courts are considered.

ACCESS TO THE COURTS

The concepts of "access to the courts" and "access to justice" can be quite nebulous ones with a meaning which varies according to the user.[2] In this article, the term "access to the courts" is used to mean the right of access for an individual to an effective determination of his or her entitlements by a court or tribunal. Although, for brevity, the term "access to the courts" is used, the courts may include the general judicial courts, quasi-judicial tribunals or other independent adjudicative bodies. The important point is the extent to which the body concerned provides an effective and independent determination of the rights of the individual rather than the description of the body involved.

Access to the courts does not simply involve the existence of an independent adjudicative body. It is also necessary that:

(i)   the individual should be aware of his or her entitlements in the first place;

(ii) that he or she should be aware of how to enforce these rights if necessary;

(iii) that he or she should decide to make use of the court to have a determination of his or her rights; and

(iv) that he or she should be able to put forward his or her case fairly before the court.

These can be summarized as *knowledge* of entitlements, *knowledge* of the courts, *willingness* to use the courts, and a *fair hearing* in the courts. The first depends on the level of information and advice available generally, the second on advice (and specifically legal advice) services, the third depends on a complex range of factors including the general perception of the courts, the educational and social class of the individual, the perceived utility of the remedy, the stigma or nuisance value involved, etc. The fourth aspect depends on the actual procedures of the courts and on the assistance provided to individuals in presenting their claims, whether by way of legal aid or otherwise.[3] These requirements are criteria against which a system can be evaluated but they are not prescriptive, i.e. they do not require any particular type of court composition, advice provision, etc.

BARRIERS TO ACCESS TO THE COURTS

Some of the barriers which can arguably impede access to justice are set out below. These are looked at, first, from the point of view of the individual and, second, from the point of view of the institutions.

INDIVIDUAL BARRIERS

Lack of information: If a person is not aware that he or she has, or may have, an entitlement, then there is little likelihood that he or she will attempt to enforce it. Studies suggest that this may be one of the greatest barriers to access to the courts. Secondly, if a person is aware of the existence of the right but does not know how to go about enforcing it, this is also likely to act as a barrier to access to the courts.

Unwillingness to go to court or seek advice: Even where an individual knows of the existence of a possible entitlement and of how to enforce it, many persons decide not to attempt to enforce their rights.[4] This may be because of the nuisance value of going to court (the disruption of their daily activity, etc.). It may be because of a stigma associated with seeking advice or appearing in court or because the individual is nervous or worried about having to appear in court. It may be that the person does not see such remedies as being appropriate for him or her or does not see the remedy as appropriate in relation to the specific problem.

People may feel that the courts or the legal system or lawyers are not for their use. In Ireland, lawyers and judges come from a very different background to many of the individuals who might wish to use their services. The average individual has very little day to day involvement in the judicial system. It may be that the individual feels alienated from the political and legal system generally. All these factors may give rise to a psychological barrier between the individual and effective access to the courts.

However, the willingness of individuals to use the services of a lawyer or to go to court varies greatly according to the *type* of case involved. Some studies have suggested that persons from all social classes will almost always seek legal advice in relation to the sale of a house but that very many people will not seek advice about other problems for example, consumer complaints or social security problems.[5]

Inability to present a case fairly: A person may not be able to put his or her case fairly before the court. At the most basic level, many people may be somewhat inarticulate or have writing difficulties, and may not be able to present their case properly either in writing or orally. Many lay persons will not be aware of the relevant legal issues before the court and will thus not be able to address themselves properly to these issues. They may not realize what evidence is relevant and thus may not have brought relevant witnesses or documents. They may not be able to argue about relatively complex legal points. These disadvantages are heightened where the individual is opposed by an experienced representative in an adversarial situation.

Many people are not able to afford the costs of a private lawyer. In some cases, the losing party may be ordered to pay the costs of the winning party and this may allow persons to avail of legal services even though they have few resources. In Ireland, many personal injury claims are taken by lawyers for impecunious clients on the basis that they will only be paid if costs are recovered. However, this can only apply in cases such as personal injuries where large damages may be recovered. It does not apply to many small claims or in situations where costs are not normally awarded, such as family law, employment or social welfare. A litigant who is in a better financial position also has the advantage of being able to afford long delays and of being able to produce more (and more expensive) expert witnesses.

Most individuals going before the courts may only do so once or twice in their lives. In contrast, large employers, social security authorities and immigration authorities appear before the courts on a regular basis and have all the advantages in terms of of experience and training and the ability to develop a litigation strategy.

INSTITUTIONAL BARRIERS[6]

Lack of advice and information services: Many of the institutional measures create the barriers which prevent individuals from enforcing their rights. Thus, if the State legislates to establish rights but then fails to provide information and advice about those rights, it effectively creates a barrier to the enforcement of rights by the individuals for whom they are (presumably) intended.

Many persons will not be able to afford to pay for legal services and will thus be dependent on government subsidized services. Persons may be deterred from seeking such advice or assistance, possibly because no services are readily available or because they would involve long delays, long journeys or other inconveniences.

Lack of consumer-orientated services: The courts are, to a large extent, public adjudication services. They provide a forum to adjudicate on disputes between citizens or between an individual and the State. They provide a service to individuals in the much same way that a hospital or a school provides medical or education services. Yet, unlike the trend in relation to medical and education services, there is little consumer involvement in the delivery of the service.[7] There exist few (if any) complaint mechanisms for persons who feel dissatisfied with the courts (except by way of an appeal to another court). There appear to be few (if any) mechanisms for allowing the courts to respond to consumer demand (or even to find out what consumer demand is).

In fact, there is little evidence of any acceptance that the courts should respond to consumer demands. The courts are one of the few services where many of those providing the service openly argue that it is useful if the users are somewhat in awe of those providing the service. Given this background, it is hardly surprizing that psychological barriers are created with many individuals feeling that the courts do not belong to them and not making use of the courts to a greater extent. Apart from the psychological barriers this creates, the lack of any consumer-orientated approach often leads to practical barriers such as excessive legalism in court, courts in poor condition, in awkward locations, at the wrong times, etc.

These criticisms also apply in many cases to the providers of legal advice. The legal profession aims to make its service attractive to those who are able to pay most for the services it provides. Thus it does not generally try to provide a service for the many people who cannot afford legal services and who therefore rely on legal aid. Such persons must generally depend on the legal aid scheme, yet the Irish legal aid scheme has no consumer involvement in the overall control or day to day management of its services. Again, it can hardly be surprising if many barriers arise to the effective use of its services by the supposed consumers.

Lack of effective judicial procedures: Many courts do not have any effective investigation procedures. Litigants are, particularly under the adversarial approach, expected to produce their own evidence and argue their own case. The court is simply there to make a decision.

Yet this ignores the fact that many persons are unable to present their own case effectively. If such an adversarial model is to be followed, legal aid will be required in many cases. Alternatively (and this will often be required in addition to, rather than instead of, legal aid) courts must be provided with proper methods of establishing the facts and of resolving disputed questions of law. This may require the establishment of appropriate investigative powers for the courts and additional training for the decision-maker.

Lack of collective procedures: In the case of the individual, the claim may involve a relatively small amount of money or it may involve opposition to a particular government decision or the resolution of a complex issue of law. This will increase the difficulty for any one individual to bring the issue before the courts. However, the same issue or point of law may affect very many individuals, for example in social security claims. The lack of any collective procedures will effectively bar such persons from obtaining effective access to the courts.

This section has outlined various issues which may act as a barrier to access to the courts. These barriers have been demonstrated by some research, primarily in the UK and the US (although similar research also exists in Canada and Australia). However, little (if any) research exists in Ireland. Research on take-up of social security benefits has suggested that before a person decides to claim a benefit a series of thresholds, relating to need, knowledge, eligibility, etc. must be passed, or that a series of trigger events must occur before a claim is made.[8] It is likely that a similar range of issues are relevant in relation to a decision to go to court. Unfortunately, in Ireland, there is no research on the factors which are relevant in such decisions (and which may well vary from one country to another). Thus one has little way of knowing to what extent the factors listed above affect access to the courts in Ireland nor the relative weight which should be given to each factor.

ACCESS TO THE COURTS AS A HUMAN RIGHT[9]

The European Convention on Human Rights: Article 6(1) of the European Convention on Human Rights provides that

> [I]n the determination of his civil rights and obligations . . . , everyone is entitled to a fair and public hearing within a reasonable time by an independent and impartial tribunal established by law . . .

In the *Golder* case,[10] the Court held that Article 6(1) embodied the right of access to a court for the determination of civil rights and obligations and that, therefore, the denial of access to a solicitor, in order to obtain advice about Golder's legal situation, which effectively denied access to a court, was in breach of the Convention.

Article 6(1) was again considered by the European Court of Human Rights in the case of *Airey v. Ireland*.[11] Mrs Airey wished to obtain a judicial separation from her husband. However, because of her low income, she could not afford to retain a solicitor and she was not in a position to proceed with such a case without legal advice and assistance. At that time there was no provision for civil legal aid in Ireland.

In *Airey* the Court rejected the Irish Government's argument that Mrs Airey did enjoy access to the High Court since she was free to appear before that court without a lawyer. The Court stated that

> The Convention is intended to guarantee not rights that are theoretical or illusory but rights that are practical and effective. This is particularly so of the right of access to the courts in view of the prominent place held in a democratic society by the right to a fair trial.[12]

The Court identified several factors which led to the conclusion that the applicant, although able to present her case in person, in theory, was denied the guarantee of access to court and a fair hearing contained in Article 6(1), in practice. In particular, the case involved complex procedures and complicated points of law; it involved the proof of facts such as adultery or cruelty which might require that expert evidence be found and witnesses called and examined; and the case involved an emotional involvement incompatible with the objectivity required for advocacy in court.[13]

The Court went on to hold that

> Article 6(1) may sometimes compel the State to provide for the assistance of a lawyer when such assistance proved indispensable for an effective access to court . . . by reason of the complexity of the procedure or of the case.[14]

The Court also held that the failure to provide access to the courts was in breach of Article 8 of the Convention which provided for the protection of family life.

The Court has also relied on Article 6 in relation to other aspects of access to the courts including excessive delays,[15] unfair procedures,[16] or the absence of any "independent and impartial tribunal".[17] Broader aspects of the right to a fair hearing guaranteed by Article 6, such as the the composition and impartiality of the courts, which have been considered by the Court of Human Rights,[18] are beyond the scope of this article.

EEC Law: There is no express reference in the Treaty of Rome to access to the courts. However in a series of cases the European Court of Justice has held that respect for fundamental rights, particularly those set out in the European Convention on Human Rights, forms an integral part of the general principles of law protected by the Court.[19] The specific provisions of the European Convention on Human Rights have been considered in several cases before the Court of Justice. Therefore, in areas of Community competence, the rights set out in the European Convention on Human Rights and, in particular, the right of access to the courts set out in Article 6 of the Convention, must be considered in interpreting Community law.

In accordance with Article 5 of the Treaty of Rome, the Member States are obliged to "take all appropriate measures . . . to ensure fulfilment of the obligations arising out of this Treaty or resulting from action taken by the institutions of the Community". There are several specific references in secondary legislation to access to the courts. Thus several of the the directives on equal treatment of men and women refer to a duty resting on Member States to bring the particular provision to the attention of those affected by it. There are also several references to the obligation to introduce into the national legal systems such measures as are necessary to enable all persons who consider themselves wronged by failure to apply the particular provision to pursue their claims by judicial process. The legislation on free movement of workers also provides for access to legal remedies.[20]

It can be argued that the particular provisions regarding information and access to a judicial remedy referred to above are simply declaratory of a general rule of Community law, arising from Article 5 of the Treaty and the case law of the European Court of Justice, requiring Member States to provide such information and to provide access to the courts where necessary in order to ensure the effective implementation of Community law. Clearly it will be impossible in practice for Community provisions to have any effect unless adequate information and advice is provided about the particular provisions and unless persons are able to obtain legal assistance where necessary to enforce their rights.

In *Johnston v. RUC*, the ECJ stated that the requirement of judicial control, contained in the equal treatment directives, reflected

> a general principle of law which underlines the constitutional traditions common to the member States. That principle is also laid down in Article 6 and 13 of the European Convention for the Protection of Human Rights and Fundamental Freedoms . . .

The Court stated that "the principles on which that Convention is based must be taken into consideration in Community law" and went on to hold that

> all persons have the right to obtain an effective remedy in a competent court against measures which they consider contrary to the principle laid down in [EEC law]. It is for the member States to ensure effective judicial control as regards compliance with the applicable provisions of community law intended to give effect to the rights for which [EEC law] provides.[21]

Thus Community law recognizes the importance of access to the courts. Although there is no express reference in EEC legislation to legal aid or advice, it is arguable that where the absence of legal representation would deny the right to effective judicial control, Community law may also establish a right to legal aid and advice in such cases.

THE EFFECT OF THE EUROPEAN CONVENTION AND EUROPEAN COMMUNITY LAW

The protection of the right of access to the courts under the European Convention on Human Rights outlined above, can be described as a minimum guarantee of standards and is confined largely to procedures closely linked to the courts rather than involving any general right to information and advice. Nonetheless, even at this level these provisions do provide a valuable safeguard. The Irish legal aid scheme was introduced in response to the decision of the European Court of Human Rights in the *Airey* case.[22] Similarly, procedures under the Netherlands social security system have been revised in the light of the decision of the court in *Feldbrugge*.[23]

However, there are several limitations to the usefulness of the existing measures. First is the content of the protection. Neither the European Convention on Human Rights nor EEC law generally contain any explicit protection of the right of access to the courts (except the specific provisions in the case of free movement of workers and equal treatment under EEC law). Such rights have been derived by the courts. Thus the courts have responded to the particular difficulty before them. The *Airey* case is a perfect example of this. Mrs Airey's case was argued on the basis that her lack of access to the courts in relation to a family law matter arose from her financial inability to obtain a lawyer. The judgment of the Court of Human Rights responded to this particular set of facts. In turn, as Whyte points out, the Irish Government introduced a legal aid scheme which concentrated on the area of family law and which responded only to the financial difficulty encountered by persons in obtaining access to the courts.[24] No effort was made to deal with those who are denied access to the courts due to lack of information or an unwillingness to go to court.

In addition, the judgments of the Court are given at a high level of generality and do not specify any particular actions to be taken by the Member State. In the *Airey* case, the Court said that "it is not the Court's function to indicate, let alone dictate, which measures should be taken".[25] Thus, a very wide margin of discretion is left to the States in complying with the principle of access to the courts.

Second, the judgments under the European Convention of Human Rights have no direct effect in Irish law.[26] Thus if a dispute arises as to whether the present provisions concerning access to the courts are compatible with the Convention, it will be necessary to bring a case before the European Commission of Human Rights or, ultimately, the European Court of Human Rights in order to have a definitive decision on the particular issue. For example, the Free Legal Advice Centres have argued that the current Irish legal advice scheme is so inadequate that Ireland is currently in breach of the Convention. The Government would doubtless deny this. Only by once again bringing an individual case before the European Court of Human Rights can a definitive decision be obtained.

This leads to the third point. It is extremely difficult to establish rights solely by bringing a series of cases before the courts. This can be seen in almost any study of test-case actions. There must first be an organization, or group of organizations, sufficiently organized and funded to adopt a test-case strategy. Suitable plaintiffs must also be found. This can be particularly difficult when one is attempting to establish the right of access to the courts. Individuals may want to establish a right to social welfare benefits, a right not to be dismissed, or to win custody of their children. Very few want to have to engage in long drawn out proceedings in order to establish a right of access to the courts. So the people who are most denied access to the courts are the very people who are never going to go to court to establish that they are denied that very right.

The difficulties in building a right of access to the courts are perhaps demonstrated by the fact that there has been no further civil legal aid case before the European Court of Human Rights since *Airey* and that the decisions in relation to access which went to the European Commission on Human Rights have been largely negative. The same difficulties may well apply to any effort to give effect to a right of access to the courts under European Community law. This leaves to one side the fact that States may simply ignore a judgment of the European Court of Human Rights or the ECJ for a considerable period of time (as in the *Norris* case)[27] or respond to the judgment in a minimal fashion (*Airey*).

However, the main problem with the human rights approach is arguably that it sees access to the courts from a legal point of view only and thus it can only seek to respond to recognized legal difficulties, e.g. the lack of legal representation, long delays in proceedings, unfair procedures, etc. It ignores the sociological barriers, such as the disinclination of many persons to make use of the courts, and the fact that people need basic advice and information if they are going to have adequate access. Thus, even if the practical difficulties outlined above could be overcome, the existing concept of access to the courts as a human right does not enable many of the most important barriers to access to be removed.

CONCLUSION

In its submission to the European Court of Human Rights in *Airey*, the Irish Government argued that access to the courts is ultimately dependent on social and economic developments in the State concerned. In the long run, this is correct. The human rights approach may provide a useful minimum guarantee and may form a important part of an overall campaign for access to the courts. Ultimately however, real improvements in access to the courts can only be gained from politicians and administrators not lawyers and judges.

4.6 Select Bibliography

TEXTS AND MATERIALS

S.H. Bailey, D.J. Harris and B.L. Jones, *Civil Liberties: Cases and Materials*, 3rd ed. (London, 1991) chs.2–4.
A. Cassese, ed., *The International Fight Against Torture* (Baden-Baden, 1991).
Irish Commission for Justice and Peace, *A New Safeguard for People Deprived of Their Liberty: The European Convention for the Prevention of Torture and Inhuman or Degrading Treatment or Punishment* (Human Rights Note No.5) (Dublin, 1993).
S. Livingstone & T. Owen, *Prison Law: Text and Materials* (Oxford, 1993).
L.J. Macfarlane, *Human Rights: Realities and Possibilities* (London, 1990) ch. 2 at pp.89–100.
B.G. Ramcharan, ed., *The Right to Life in International Law* (London, 1985).
G. Robertson, *Freedom, the Individual and the Law*, 6th ed. (London, 1991) chs. 1 & 8.

N.S. Rodley, *The Treatment of Prisoners under International Law* (Oxford, 1987).
M. Roth and R Bluglass, eds. *Psychiatry, Human Rights and the Law* (Cambridge, 1985).
A. Whelan, ed., *Law and Liberty in Ireland* (Dublin, 1993).

ARTICLES

T. Campbell, "The Rights of the Mentally Ill" in T. Campbell, ed., *Human Rights: From Rhetoric to Reality* (Oxford, 1986) 123.
A. Cassese, "A New Approach to Human Rights: The European Convention for the Prevention of Torture" (1989) 83 *AJIL* 128.
P. Charleton, "Judicial Discretion in Abortion: The Irish Perspective" (1992) 6 *I J Fam L* 349
M. Cousins, "Access to the Courts" (1992) 14 *DULJ* (n.s.) 51.
M. Cousins, "Neither Flesh Nor Fowl: The Status of the Scheme of Civil Legal Aid and Advice" (1992) 10 *ILT* (n.s.) 41.
D. Curtin, "Constitutionalism in the European Community: The Right to Fair Procedures in Administrative Law" in J. O'Reilly, ed., *Human Rights and Constitutional Law: Essays in Honour of Brian Walsh* (Dublin, 1992) 293.
P.J. Duffy, "Article 3 of the European Convention on Human Rights" (1983) 32 *ICLQ* 316.
M. Evans and R. Morgan, "The European Convention for the Prevention of Torture: Operational Practice" (1992) 41 *ICLQ* 590.
J. Freidman, "On the Dangers of Moral Certainty and Sacred Trusts: The Judgments in the *SPUC* Case and the Issue of Free Speech" (1988) 10 *DULJ* (n.s.) 71.
F.J. Hampson, "Restrictions on Rights of Access and the European Convention on Human Rights: The Case of Powell and Rayner" (1990) 61 *BYIL* 279.
D.J. Harris, "The Right to Fair Trial in Criminal Proceedings as a Human Right" (1967) 16 ICLQ 352.
I. Kennedy, "Patients, Doctors and Human Rights" in R. Blackburn and J. Taylor, eds., *Human Rights in the 1990s: Legal, Political and Ethical Issues* (London, 1991) 81.
J. Kingston and A. Whelan, "The Protection of the Unborn in Three Legal Orders" (1992) 10 *ILT* (n.s.) pp. 93, 104, 166 and 279.
P.T. Muchlinski, "Mental Health Patients' Rights and the European Human Rights Convention" (1980) 5 *HRR* 90.
M. O'Boyle, "Torture and Emergency Powers under the European Convention on Human Rights: *Ireland v. The United Kingdom*" (1977) 71 *AJIL* 674.
T. O'Malley, "A Ray of Hope for Prisoners—The New European Convention Against Torture" (1990) 8 *ILT* (n.s.) 216.
E. Palm, "Access to Court—Strasbourg and Stockholm: in J. O'Reilly, ed., *Human Rights and Constitutional Law: Essays in Honour of Brian Walsh* (Dublin, 1992) 61.
W. Peukert, "Human Rights in International Law and the Protection of Unborn Human Beings" in F. Matscher and H. Petzold, eds., *Protecting Human Rights—The European Dimension: Essays in Honour of G. J. Wiarda*, 2nd ed. (Köln, 1990) 511.
G. Quinn, "Civil Commitment and the Right to Treatment under the European Convention on Human Rights" (1992) 5 *Harvard HRJ* 1.
H.G. Schermers, "The Right to Fair Trial Under the European Convention on Human Rights" in R. Blackburn and J. Taylor, eds., *Human Rights for the 1990s: Legal, Political and Ethical Issues* (London, 1991) 59.
S. Trechsel, "The Right to Liberty and Security of the Person: Article 5 of the Europan Convention on Human Rights in the Strasbourg Case Law" (1980) 1 *HRLJ* 88.
P. van Dijk, "Universal Legal Principles of Fair Trial in Criminal Proceedings" in A. Rosas and J. Helgesen, eds., *Human Rights in a Changing East-West Perspective* (London, 1990) 89.
G. Whyte, "Abortion and the Law" (1992) 42 *Doctrine and Life* 352.
B. Wilkinson, "Abortion, the Irish Constitution and the EEC" [1992] *Public Law* 20.

5 : PRIVACY

5.1 Introduction

Privacy is dealt with in Article 8 of the European Convention on Human Rights and Fundamental Freedoms which provides that:

1 Everyone has the right to respect for his private life and family life, his home and his correspondence.

2 There shall be no interference by a public authority with this right except such as is in accordance with the law and is necessary in a democratic society in the interests of national security, public safety or the economic well-being of the country, for the prevention of disorder or crime, for the protection of morals, or for the protection of the rights and freedoms of others.

From the outset, it should be noted that Article 8 does not protect the right to privacy *per se*; it provides that various elements of the individual's personal (and perhaps business) life should be respected.[1] Therefore, it is possible that certain encroachments on an individual's privacy may be deemed not to constitute an interference with respect for private life and, accordingly, not protected by the provisions of Article 8. On the other hand, because respect is mentioned, there is a strong case for arguing that Article 8 involves positive obligations, as well as negative ones: that is, that the State must, through its laws and practices, ensure that third parties do not interfere with the private life of individuals.[2]

One can also see that the Convention protects not only private life, as such, but also family life, home and correspondence. This may mean that aspects of commercial life may also be protected by Article 8, as will be discussed below.

When looking at a case under Article 8, the Commission or Court will generally go through a four-tier test in examining alleged State interference with privacy rights. First, it will see whether or not there has been an interference with the right to respect for private life (or any of the other rights protected by Article 8). In many case the respondent State will accept that an interference has occurred, but argue that it was justified. For example, in the *Ludi* case,[3] the Court held the use of a police agent, who had set up a drugs deal and recorded telephone conversations with the applicant concerning the deal did not constitute

153

an infringement of Article 8, as engaging in criminal activity does not come within the scope of private life. The Court also held that the recording of telephone conversations in this context did not constitute a breach of respect for correspondence, although the applicant's correspondence had clearly been interfered with.

Secondly, once an interference has been established, the Commission or Court will consider whether or not it is in accordance with law. Clearly, if the interference is not permitted by domestic law this issue can be disposed of fairly simply. However, if the domestic law is not so clear and foreseeable as to allow an individual (with appropriate legal advice) to ascertain whether or not his or her conduct is within the law, the requirements of the Convention will not be met.[4]

Thirdly, if it is established that an interference has occurred and that it is in accordance with law, the Commission or Court will look at the legitimacy of the State's aim; that is, the State will have to show that the interference took place in order to fulfil one of the aims laid down in paragraph 2 of Article 8. Generally, the good faith of the respondent government is accepted in this matter.

Finally, the issue of the necessity of the interference will be looked at. In this regard, the Convention requires that the level of interference be proportionate to the aim being pursued. "Necessity" is looked at in the light of the requirements of a democratic society; however, States do have a margin of appreciation in this area, although it is ultimately subject to review by the Commission or Court.[5]

It should be noted that if a breach of positive obligations is involved, the provisions of paragraph 2 do not come into play and the issue will be dealt with from the perspective of respect alone. This is particularly significant in light of the fact that the Court has rejected the notion of inherent limitations on rights contained in the Convention.[6]

The concept of private life is quite far-reaching. It includes the right to keep information about one's personal life outside the public sphere in certain circumstances. This can raise problems where a conflict arises with other rights guaranteed by the Convention. One example of this is the tension between free speech and private life. To an extent this is dealt with by laws relating to defamation, but wider issues are involved. In some States, such as France, the whole area has been dealt with by the domestic legal system for years. However, in other States, such as Ireland and the UK, the law is in a state of flux. Modern technology means that it has become increasingly easy to both collect and disseminate information about individuals. The issue has been examined in great detail in the UK, particularly in the *Calcutt* reports and responses thereto. Another area where technology has touched upon privacy is that of data protection. As can be seen from Paul Coughlan's paper, the provisions of Article 8 alone are not sufficient to deal with the problem and measures have been taken at both Council of Europe and European Community level to deal with the matter in a more comprehensive way. Private life also covers the whole area of sexuality (discussed later in this chapter). A particularly controversial area is that of abortion. The Court has not yet dealt with this matter; it was raised in the *Open Door* case, but the Court dealt with the case under Article 10. The Commission has, however, dealt with the issue in a limited number of cases.[7]

As well as the general area of private life, Article 8 specifically mentions respect for the home. There has been little case law in this area. The positive element of the State's obligation seems to be minimal, given that Article 8 has been held not to entitle one to have a home.[8] To date, the only a few cases have come before the Court.[9]

The right to respect for correspondence is also protected by Article 8. There seem to be two levels of protection afforded by the Convention in this area: one for persons at liberty[10] and the other for prisoners.[11] This is despite the Court's rejection of inherent limitations in *Golder*. Another interesting element of the right to respect for correspondence is the fact that commercial correspondence is covered.[12] The position under European Community law may be different.[13]

A short introduction, such as this, cannot hope to deal with the issue of privacy in any depth. However, the foregoing may indicate how the Convention's jurisprudence in this area may be analysed[14] and identify some of the more important areas coming within the scope of Article 8.

JAMES KINGSTON

5.2 Personal Information and Privacy

PAUL COUGHLAN

Article 8 of the European Convention on Human Rights espouses various rights which together may be regarded as constituting the "right to privacy". In the United Kingdom, the *Report of the Committee on Privacy*, which had been chaired by the Rt. Hon. Kenneth Younger, identified freedom from intrusion and privacy of information as the two main aspects of the law of privacy.[1] Empirical research revealed greater public awareness and concern in respect of the latter. The holding and disclosure of information regarding an individual can impinge upon the right to privacy in two distinct ways. On the one hand, if the information is false or inaccurate, its dissemination can adversely affect one's reputation, good name and financial interests. Generally speaking, the amelioration of such harm is a matter for the law of tort, in particular defamation,[2] malicious falsehood[3] and, to a lesser extent, passing off.[4] However, information which is correct but irrelevant can cause embarrassment, injury or damage if it is revealed either to the world at large or to a class of persons which is wider than is strictly necessary. The latter type of information, which for present purposes will be referred to as personal information, can be divided into:

1 Information held by the individual in question, the use and disclosure of which he or she wishes to control.

2 Information regarding the individual which is held by others, the nature of which may or may not be known to the individual.

In the latter situation the individual may not actually object to the holding of the information, but may seek to ensure that it is accurate and used for the limited purposes for which it is kept. However, countervailing policy considerations, such as the protection of national security, the public interest in the prevention and detection of crime, and the effective performance of public functions, may act as substantial obstacles to attempts by individuals to ascertain the nature of information held in respect of them. While such matters are expressly enumerated in Article 8(2), the European Court of Human Rights has made it clear that they cannot be invoked in an arbitrary or unregulated manner.

In *Leander v. Sweden*,[5] the applicant was refused employment at a museum located within a naval base after a security check, which included an examination of a secret police register, was carried out. The applicant claimed that he should have been permitted access to the information contained in the register so that he could make representations in respect of it. The European Court of Human Rights held that the holding and dissemination of the personal information, and the refusal to allow the applicant access to it, constituted an interference with his right to respect for his private life and was contrary to Article 8. However, given that this system of personnel control contained effective safeguards and monitoring mechanisms, it was justified on the grounds of national security within the terms of Article 8(2).

In *Gaskin v. United Kingdom*,[6] the applicant had spent most of his childhood in local authority care and, on attaining his majority, sued the local authority for negligence. In the context of these proceedings he sought access to social services files pertaining to his period in care. Access was refused on the grounds of public interest. The European Court of Human Rights conceded that the confidentiality of public records was important in so far as it ensured the receipt of reliable information and protected third parties. Nevertheless, it held that making access to records dependent on the consent of the contributor did not vindicate the interests of an individual when access to information pertaining to the latter's private or family life was denied as a result of the contributor either improperly refusing consent or being unavailable. It was essential that there should be some means by which the refusal could be subjected to impartial scrutiny and, as no such mechanism existed in the instant case, there had been a failure to respect the applicant's private and family life.

At the level of domestic law, the Constitution, as the ultimate source of privacy rights, has undoubtedly engendered an appreciation of the concerns expressed above.[7] But the absence of specific provisions and a relatively small amount of case law precludes the formulation of a precise framework.[8] Common law protection in respect of personal information is, at best, sporadic and ill-defined. Recent statutory initiatives also fall short of constituting a comprehensive scheme for safeguarding privacy in this context.

CONFIDENTIALITY AND PERSONAL INFORMATION[9]

A person who has received information of a confidential nature may be prevented from disclosing it by means of an injunction.[10] While it is well established that the duty to respect a confidence may arise independently of an express or implied contractual term to this effect, the exact basis of the court's jurisdiction remains unclear. In *Fraser v. Evans*, Lord Denning MR observed that it was based ". . . not so much on property or on contract as on the duty to be of good faith".[11] In *House of Spring Gardens Ltd v. Point Blank Ltd*, Costello J was of the opinion that in such cases the court was " . . . being asked to enforce what is essentially a moral obligation".[12] In the Supreme Court, McCarthy J disagreed with this rationalization and identified "commercial necessity" as the basis of the jurisdiction.[13] Another possible explanation is that the information remains the property of the confider who is thus entitled to control its use.[14] In any event the essential features of a successful action for breach of confidence were summarized by Megarry J in *Coco v. A N Clark (Engineers) Ltd.* as follows:

> First, the information itself, in the words of Lord Greene MR in the *Saltman* case,[15] must "have the necessary quality of confidence about it". Secondly, that information must have been imparted in circumstances importing an obligation of confidence. Thirdly, there must be an unauthorized use of that information to the detriment of the party communicating it.[16]

Litigation involving the law of confidence is usually concerned with information of a commercially sensitive nature such as secret processes[17] and customer lists[18] which the confider is attempting to keep out of the reach of competitors. However, in *Argyll v. Argyll*[19] Ungoed-Thomas J made it clear that the doctrine was not solely concerned with business matters. Here the plaintiff succeeded in preventing her former husband and a newspaper from publishing details of private and intimate matters which she had discussed with her husband during their married life together. In his Lordship's view, the policy of the law had always been in favour of protecting communications between husband and wife, and the fact that the plaintiff had breached confidence herself and committed adultery was not a defence. Conversely, in *Lennon v. News Group Ltd*[20] the plaintiff was refused an injunction to restrain the publication of revelations concerning his married life because prior disclosures by both him and his first wife had placed details of their relationship in the public domain.

In the final analysis, the law of confidence is an exclusively judge-made principle which has evolved on an *ad hoc* basis. At present it would appear to be more concerned with the circumstances in which information has been imparted rather than its quality. Furthermore, as will be seen below, it is inhibited by various limitations which hinder its ability to prevent unauthorised revelations and redress injury and damage suffered as a consequence. Nevertheless, it has been suggested[21] recently that the law of confidence has assumed greater significance in the light of the judicial reluctance to regard invasion of privacy as a tort.[22] Of course this impetus may not be of such importance in Ireland where there is constitutional protection,[23] but its potential utility should not be underestimated. In *Kennedy v. Ireland*[24] the State was held liable to pay exemplary damages because its deliberate and unjustified tapping of two journalists' telephones constituted an infringement of the constitutional right to privacy. Notwithstanding the fact that the Constitution made no express reference to such a right and it fell upon the plaintiffs to argue that it was protected as one of the unenumerated personal rights guaranteed by Article 40.3,[25] it would appear that breach of confidence was not pleaded as an alternative ground of claim.

PERSONAL INFORMATION AS PROPERTY

Generally speaking, as far as the criminal law is concerned, there would appear to be no property in confidential information apart from the material on which it is physically recorded. In *Director of Public Prosecutions v. Withers*[26] the appellants ran an investigation agency. In the course of inquiries carried out on behalf of third parties, they obtained information from banks and building

societies regarding their customers' accounts by falsely represent
were officers of another bank. They were convicted of conspir
public mischief by unlawfully obtaining private and confidenti
The House of Lords upheld their appeals against conviction on the grou
a conspiracy to effect a public mischief, in the sense of an agreement to
perpetrate an act which, while not being unlawful in itself, was injurious, did
not amount to a criminal offence. In the words of Lord Simon of Glaisdale, there
had been nothing more than a conspiracy to invade privacy.[27]

A more direct attempt to use the criminal law to protect information failed
in *Oxford v. Moss*.[28] Here it was alleged that a student had, in securing unauthorised prior access to an examination paper, stolen the university's intangible
property. It was conceded that the defendant had not intended to steal the
examination paper in so far as it constituted tangible property. The Divisional
Court held that the right to confidential information was not intangible property
within the meaning of section 4(1) of the Theft Act, 1968.

Limited statutory inroads have been made in respect of this approach in
Ireland recently. Section 1(1) of the Criminal Damage Act, 1991, includes "data"
within its definition of "property" and defines the former term as "information
in a form in which it can be accessed by means of a computer and includes a
program". The same provision defines the phrase "to damage", in relation to
data, as "to add to, alter, corrupt, erase or move to another medium or to a
different location in the storage medium in which they are kept (whether or not
property other than data is damaged thereby)" or "to do any act that contributes
towards causing such addition, alteration, corruption, erasure or movement".

In civil litigation the term "property" is generally used in this context as
nothing more than a convenient shorthand to describe the confider's right to
restrain unauthorised revelations and, usually in the area of trade secrets, the
ability to sell, assign and dispose of the information by will. But there have been
occasions when judges have referred to the defendant as having "appropriated"
or "stolen" the plaintiff's "property". This has happened where the defendant
obtained confidential information, but it was impossible to identify which of a
finite number of confidants had acted in breach of confidence.[29] Some have
argued that the proprietary analysis may help to resolve the problematic situation where it is clear that no confidant is guilty of such a breach and the
information has been obtained surreptitiously (e.g. as a result of being overheard
by means of telephone tapping or scanning devices).[30] However, it must be
conceded that the recognition of rights of property in confidential information
is by no means well-established.[31]

The widely accepted formulation of the principle by Megarry J in *Coco v.
A N Clark (Engineers) Ltd* requires that the information should have been
imparted in circumstances importing a confidence. In other words, to be bound

y an obligation of confidence one must have received the information on the understanding that it should not be divulged. Having said this, it would appear that the confider may secure an injunction against not only the confidant but also any third party to whom the confidant has disclosed the information. As pointed out by the same judge in *Malone v. Metropolitan Police Commissioner*,[32] this may be explained in terms of the equitable nature of the jurisdiction by reference to the third party's conscience being affected by the knowledge that the information is of a confidential nature. But it was also held that " . . . a person who utters confidential information must accept the risk of any unknown over-hearing that is inherent in the circumstances of the communication".[33] In the view of Megarry VC, there was no reason why someone who overheard a secret communication should be prevented from divulging what he or she had heard. In any event, the law of confidence could not provide a remedy where phone tapping sanctioned by the Home Secretary had taken place.

However, some judges are beginning to dispense with the requirement that there should be a confider. In *Francome v. Mirror Group Newspapers Ltd*[35] an interlocutory injunction was granted to restrain the publication of details pertaining to the plaintiffs' telephone conversations. *Malone* was distinguished on the basis that different considerations might apply where confidential infor-mation was obtained by private citizens through illegal phone tapping. Whilst a telephone user could be regarded as accepting the risk of having confidential communications overheard due to a crossed line or some other defect in the telephone system, it was doubtful whether a similar conclusion could be drawn in respect of the criminal acts of others.

Courts in other parts of the common law world have demonstrated greater flexibility without reference to the legality or otherwise of the defendant's conduct. In *Concrete Industries (Monier) Ltd v. Garner Bros. & Perrott (WA) Pty Ltd*,[36] Fullagar J, speaking in the Supreme Court of Victoria, observed that it was immaterial whether the information was secured through industrious eavesdropping instead of being imparted by the plaintiff to the defendant. The Hong Kong case of *Koo v. Lam*[37] goes even further. Here Bokhary J observed:

A man's confidential information is his property. The courts have jurisdic-tion to protect such property from misuse. Such jurisdiction is not confined to cases in which such information has been imparted in confidence or to cases in which an obligation to keep the same confidential arises under contract. Any use, including self-use by the wrong doer, following any misappropriation—whether by force, menaces, trickery or stealth—is, in general, misuse which is liable to be restrained or made the subject of an order for damages or an account.[38]

Bokhary J went on to hold that the plaintiffs had never allowed the defendant access to their confidential questionnaires and that he had obtained them surreptitiously with a view to incorporating their contents into his research projects. Accordingly, the defendant was liable for copyright infringement and "misuse of confidential information".[39] It could be argued that the latter is a novel head of liability distinct from breach of confidence and that instead of being an equitable wrong it is tortious in nature. This development certainly has the support of Scott L J writing extra-judicially.[40] On the other hand, if it is to be regarded as an extension of the law of confidence, the fact that decisions critical of the proprietary analysis were not considered undoubtedly weakens this approach.

THE BALANCING OF INTERESTS

The protection of privacy does not automatically take priority and in some cases the operation of the law of confidence must be examined in the light of other fundamental rights. In *Attorney General for England and Wales v. Brandon Book Publishers Ltd*[41] the plaintiff sought to restrain publication of the book "One Girl's War" which had been written by a member of the British intelligence service. Carroll J pointed out that an application to prohibit the publication of material of public interest had to be considered in the light of Article 40.6.1 of the Constitution which guaranteed the right to express freely one's convictions and opinions subject to public order and morality. Publication of this book was not contrary to the public interest in Ireland and an interlocutory injunction was refused because the plaintiff had failed to discharge the onus of establishing that that constitutional rights of the defendant should not be exercised.

Without mentioning the Carroll J's decision, Keane J has cast doubt upon the relevance of Article 40.6.1 in resisting the enforcement of an obligation of confidence. In *Oblique Financial Services Ltd v. The Promise Production Co Ltd* his Lordship observed:

> Article 40.6.1 is concerned, not with the dissemination of factual informa-
> tion, but the rights of the citizen, in formulating or publishing convictions
> or opinions, or conveying an opinion; and the rights of all citizens, arise, in
> our law, not under Article 40.6.1, but from Article 40.3.1.[42]

The defendants' constitutional right to communicate information was subject to other rights, and in particular the right of confidentiality enjoyed by the plaintiff. Accordingly an interlocutory injunction was granted so as to restrain them from publishing details as to the identity of an investor in a film project.

Questions of public interest can sometimes affect the extent to which an obligation of confidence will be recognized. Thus in *Lion Laboratories Ltd* v. *Evans*[43] Stephenson L J observed:

> The duty of confidence, the public interest in maintaining it, is a restriction on the freedom of the press which is recognized by our law, as well as Article 10(2) of the European Convention for the Protection of Human Rights and Fundamental Freedoms . . . ; the duty to publish, the countervailing interest of the public in being kept informed of matters which are of real public concern, is an inroad on the privacy of confidential matters.[44]

It has been consistently held that "there is no confidence as to the disclosure of iniquity".[45] In *Initial Services Ltd v. Putterill*, Lord Denning MR pointed out that this meant that not only could an obligation of confidence not be invoked to conceal crime or fraud,[46] but it would also be ineffective in an attempt to restrain the disclosure of " . . . any misconduct of such a nature that it ought in the public interest to be disclosed to others".[47] Here the defendant had given information to a newspaper relating to activities of the plaintiff, his former employer, which suggested a breach of the statutory duties imposed on the plaintiff by the Restrictive Trade Practices Act, 1956. Given that this legislation had been enacted in the public interest, the Court of Appeal held that an employee's duty of confidence could not be used to conceal conduct which was inimical to that interest. Lord Denning MR was careful to add:

> I say nothing as to what the position would be if he disclosed it out of malice or spite or sold it to a newspaper for money or for reward. That indeed would be a different matter. It is a great evil when people purvey scandalous information for reward.[48]

But in *Woodward v. Hutchins*[49] the Court of Appeal refused to grant an injunction to prevent the former employee of various celebrities from selling information to a newspaper regarding their private activities which, while not unlawful in any sense, cast some of them in an unfavourable light. The case was regarded as being somewhat unusual in that the defendant had been employed to secure a favourable image for the plaintiffs in respect of their public and private lives. Lord Denning MR added that:

> If a group of this kind seek publicity which is to their advantage, it seems to me that they cannot complain if a servant or employee of theirs afterwards discloses the truth about them. If the image which they fostered was not a true image, it is in the public interest that it should be corrected. In these

cases of confidential information it is a question of balancing the public interest in maintaining the confidence against the public interest in knowing the truth.[50]

The move from the public interest in ensuring compliance with the law, articulated in *Initial Services Ltd v. Putterill*, to the almost "consumer protection" approach to self-publicity applied by the Court of Appeal in *Woodward v. Hutchins*, is far from convincing. The revelations in the latter indicated that the plaintiffs were guilty of nothing more than behaving badly or conducting their personal lives in a manner inconsistent with accepted social norms. It suggests that sometimes the court's willingness to countenance a breach of confidence can be inspired by value judgments made in respect of supposed moral short-comings of an undoubtedly trivial nature which are manifested in private. Fortunately, a more principled approach to the issue of whether the disclosure of confidential information is in the public interest has been adopted in recent years. For example, in *Lion Laboratories Ltd v. Evans*,[51] whilst the Court of Appeal emphasized that it was not a prerequisite of the public interest defence that there should be wrongdoing or iniquity on the part of the person seeking to restrain a breach of confidence, their Lordships also echoed the observation of Lord Wilberforce in *British Steel Corporation v. Granada Television Ltd* that "there is a wide difference between what is interesting to the public and what is in the public interest to make known".[52]

In *Stephens v. Avery*[53] the plaintiff claimed that information pertaining to a lesbian relationship which she had imparted to the defendant, her former friend, had been disclosed by the latter in breach of confidence to a newspaper which had published it. Whilst accepting that the court would not enforce a duty of confidence relating to matters of a grossly immoral nature, Sir Nicolas Browne-Wilkinson VC pointed out it was difficult to so categorize the conduct of the plaintiff here because the newspaper had no objection to giving it widespread coverage. In any event, in this context it was difficult to isolate an objective standard of morality by which to judge the plaintiff's conduct. His Lordship added:

> If it is right that there is now no generally accepted code of sexual morality applying to this case, it would be quite wrong in my judgment for any judge to apply his own personal moral views, however strongly held, in deciding the legal rights of the parties. The court's function is to apply the law, not personal prejudice. Only in a case where there is a generally accepted moral code can the court refuse to enforce rights in such a way as to offend that generally accepted code.[54]

Finally, his Lordship pointed out that there was no reason in principle " . . . why information relating to that most private sector of everybody's life, namely sexual conduct, cannot be the subject matter of a legally enforceable duty of confidentiality".[55]

In *X v. Y*[56] the plaintiff health authority was granted an injunction against a newspaper preventing it from publishing information taken from medical files pertaining to two doctors who were being treated for AIDS at a certain hospital. Employees of the plaintiff had divulged the information to the newspaper in breach of confidence. Rose J rejected an argument that disclosure would be in the public interest and that the defendants should be permitted to publish the information in a way which identified neither the hospital nor these patients. His Lordship identified the competing interests as follows:

> On the one hand, there are the public interests in having a free press and an informed public debate; on the other, it is in the public interest that actual or potential AIDS sufferers should be able to resort to hospitals without fear of being revealed, that those owing duties of confidence in their employment should be loyal and should not disclose confidential matters and that, prima facie, no one should be allowed to use information extracted in breach of confidence from hospital records even if disclosure of the particular information may not give rise to immediately apparent harm.[57]

Notwithstanding the need for freedom of the press and the public interest in knowing that which the defendants sought to publish, the fact remained that the plaintiffs were not guilty of misconduct of any kind and the records of AIDS sufferers should be kept as confidential as possible. Permitting publication in the restricted form suggested by the defendants would have enabled them to procure breaches of confidence and rendered nugatory the law's protection of confidential information when no countervailing public interest had been shown.

INADEQUATE REMEDIES

Leaving aside situations where the duty of confidence arises by virtue of an express or implied contract, it is beyond dispute that this branch of the law originated in equity's exclusive jurisdiction, with an injunction restraining disclosure being the principal means by which the confider's rights were protected. Because equitable remedies are discretionary, it is possible that a plaintiff may not be able to restrain a blatant breach of confidence if the court takes the view that his or her conduct was sufficiently reprehensible to constitute a disentitlement to relief. As *Hubbard v. Vosper*[58] demonstrates, this is quite distinct from questions relating to the public interest. Here the defendant was a former member of the Church of Scientology who had written a book recounting many of the Church's practices, some of which he had learned about in circumstances giving rise to an obligation of confidence. Lord Denning MR took the attitude that, given the dangerous nature of some of the material taught by the Church during its courses, it was in the public interest that it should be made known. On the other hand, after referring to some of the Church's precepts which effectively endorsed the perpetration of criminal acts in respect of those persons whose activities were regarded as being against its interests, Megaw L J observed:

> ... there is here evidence that the plaintiffs are or have been protecting their secrets by deplorable means such as is evidenced by this code of ethics; and, that being so, they do not come with clean hands to this court in asking the court to protect those secrets by the equitable remedy of an injunction.[59]

Somewhat surprisingly, it is still unclear to what extent a plaintiff may be entitled to monetary compensation in respect of a breach of confidence. Although an account of profits may prove to be of value where the information has enabled the defendant to realise a financial gain through exploiting it himself or selling it to a third party,[60] it is not difficult to envisage situations where personal information with little or no commercial value has been disclosed to the detriment or embarrassment of the confider. Here the equitable nature of the wrong precludes the award of common law damages.[61] In *Seager v. Copydex Ltd*,[62] the Court of Appeal awarded damages for a breach of confidence which arose out of the defendants making use of information supplied by the plaintiff regarding the design of a carpet grip.[63] However, the court did not advert to the exact basis for this award and the decision has been explained as an instance of damages being awarded in lieu of an injunction, under section 2 of the Chancery Amendment Act, 1858 (Lord Cairns' Act).[64] As the availability of an injunction is an essential prerequisite to the court's jurisdiction to award such "equitable damages", it would appear that monetary compensation will not be available to a plaintiff when distress or injury has resulted from an unauthorised disclosure, but an injunction is unnecessary because repetition of the breach of confidence is unlikely.[65] Thus in the Northern Irish case of *O'Neill v. DHSS*,[66] the plaintiff was a single woman who had disclosed the fact that she was pregnant to a clerk of the defendant when applying for a maternity clothing grant. The clerk informed the plaintiff's brother of her pregnancy. Carswell J held that because there was no need for an injunction, damages under Lord Cairns' Act were likewise unavailable.

COMPUTERS AND PERSONAL INFORMATION[67]

On its own, the collection of information relating to individuals by both State agencies and private concerns, such as credit rating organizations, poses an obvious threat to an individual's privacy. But when this activity is performed by means of data processing equipment, and in particular the computer, considerable unease is engendered. After all, such technology has the ability to select, collate and cross-reference vast quantities of personal information from many sources in an extremely short space of time so as to compile an overall profile of an individual. This disquiet is exacerbated by the apparent potential for abuse. Access to such data is regarded as being open to many, easy to obtain and difficult to regulate. The information placed in the system may have been inaccurate to start with, or may be intentionally or inadvertently corrupted after being input. Leaving aside what actually happens in practice, the widespread use of data banks creates the impression that many important decisions are taken about people, for example in the area of employment or in respect of financial matters, without personal contact and solely on the basis of information which is held regarding them.[68]

As the inability of the individual to establish the existence and accuracy of this information could give rise to serious prejudice, many countries have enacted so-called "data protection" legislation. The term would appear to be a misnomer because these laws regulate not only the keeping of data which are processed automatically and the uses to which they may be put, but also the extent to which the individual may have access to the data in order to ensure that his or her rights are being respected (sometimes referred to as the principle of transparency). Essentially there are two basic models of data protection legislation. The sectoral approach, which has been favoured by some United States jurisdictions, focuses attention on specific fields of activity, such as banking, where the processing of data is perceived as presenting particular risks.[69] This may be contrasted with the omnibus approach, which has been adopted in the domestic laws of most European countries, whereby the individual is generally afforded protection in respect of the automatic processing of personal data, irrespective of the identity or activities of the particular person performing such processing. In any event, it is arguable that the function and operation of data protection law is quite different to that of privacy law. Instead of merely establishing rights in favour of the individual, it seeks to provide a means of balancing the interests of the individual, the person who wishes to use the data and the community at large.[70] The operation of the system is usually monitored by an independent supervisory authority. In Ireland this is the function of the Data Protection Commissioner whose office was established under section 9 of the Data Protection Act, 1988.

A significant number of the domestic schemes currently in operation were enacted as a result of various international initiatives, which have contributed to the emergence of a set of basic data protection principles. In 1980 the Organization for Economic Co-operation and Development issued *Guidelines on the Protection of Privacy and Transborder Flows of Personal Data*. It was recommended that States should take these non-binding policy recommendations into account in framing domestic legislation and strive to remove and avoid barriers to transborder data flows which might impede international trade and co-operation. On 18 December 1986, Ireland endorsed the Guidelines and also signed the Council of Europe Convention for the Protection of Individuals with Regard to Automatic Processing of Personal Data.[71] Whilst the data protection principles articulated by this Convention are very similar to the OECD Guidelines, it concentrates on the individual's right to privacy rather than the economic aspects of transborder data flows. Signatories were obliged to enact legislation giving effect to the Convention's provisions and in response the Data Protection Act, 1988, was passed by the Oireachtas. Finally, in 1990, the UN issued non-binding Guidelines Concerning Computerized Personal Data Files.[72]

Action at European Community level was prompted by the increasing incidence of personal data processing in the various spheres of economic and social activity. The Commission took the view that the free movement of goods, persons, services and capital within the internal market required the unimpeded flow of personal data, regardless of the Member States in which they are processed or requested. But it also accepted that the purpose of national data protection laws was to protect fundamental rights, and in particular the right to privacy guaranteed by Article 8 of the ECHR. Notwithstanding greater international co-operation and technological advances, there was the danger that disparities in the protection of privacy in domestic legal systems might prevent cross-border transmissions of data between Member States and thereby interfere with the operation of the internal market, distort competition and impede the administration of Community law. Accordingly, in an effort to remove obstacles to the flow of personal data and achieve a degree of harmonization in domestic data protection legislation, the Commission recommended that Member States should ratify the Council of Europe Convention.[73]

Not all Member States took this step and in 1990 the Commission produced a draft Directive with a view to approximating national laws so that each State would have an equivalent level of privacy protection in relation to data processing.[74] In doing so it was acknowledged that the principles articulated in the draft Directive were largely founded upon those contained in the Convention.[75] But many aspects of this proposal were greeted with widespread criticism. For instance, it drew a line of demarcation between the public and private sectors with disparate criteria governing the processing of personal data in each sector.

Although this dichotomy was discarded in a drastically amended proposal which appeared in November 1992,[76] the main objectives of the draft Directive were unchanged.[77] Thus Article 1(1) obliges the Member States to protect the rights and freedoms of natural persons with respect to the processing of personal data and Article 1(2) precludes restrictions or prohibitions on the free flow of personal data between Member States justified by reference to such protection. With a view to striking a balance between privacy and freedom of expression (as recognised by Article 10 of the ECHR), Article 9 of the draft Directive requires the Member States to prescribe exemptions from the Directive in respect of the processing of personal data solely for journalistic purposes by the press, the audio-visual media and journalists. By virtue of Article 3(2), the Directive does not apply to the processing of data in the course of an activity which falls outside the scope of Community law.

Having said all this, it should also be borne in mind that the enactment of data protection laws is frequently motivated not by a regard for the rights of the individual, but the need to protect commercial interests. It is obvious that such a perspective can affect the scope and quality of the system eventually adopted. Generally speaking, the aim of the various international initiatives is to secure a degree of uniformity among the data protection laws of individual States. Without such consistency, there is the danger that certain States might refuse or fail to pass appropriate legislation and thereby achieve the status of "data havens" where personal data could be kept and processed without any regulation. Because this could frustrate the operation of domestic data protection laws, in accordance with Article 12 of the Council of Europe Convention it has become commonplace for domestic laws to preclude the export of data to States which do not provide "equivalent protection". The enactment of the Data Protection Act, 1988, was due in no small measure to the fear that Irish businesses, particularly those involved in areas such as banking and insurance, would suffer unless appropriate legislation was introduced.

SCOPE OF THE LEGISLATION

All too often in this debate concerning privacy, the technology, and not the manner in which it is used, is regarded as the problem.[78] Thus when attempts are made to regulate the holding and use of information, attention is generally directed to situations in which it is kept in a form which can be processed automatically, to the neglect of information kept in manual filing systems which, despite their limitations, still present considerable potential for abuse. Although Article 3(2)(c) of the Council of Europe Convention provides that States may also apply the Convention to personal data files which are not processed automatically, the Oireachtas declined to do so. Section 1(1) of the 1988 Act defines "data"[79] as "information in a form in which it can be processed" and "processing" as "performing automatically logical or arithmetical operations on data." The scope of the EEC Commission's draft Directive on the protection of personal data is also broader than the 1988 Act in so far as it covers structured manual files.[80] According to Article 3(1), it applies

> . . . to the processing of personal data wholly or partly by automatic means, and to the processing otherwise than by automatic means of personal data which forms part of a file or is intended to form part of a file.

According to Article 2 "personal data" means any information relating to an identified or identifiable natural person. It also defines a "personal data file" as

> . . . any structured set of personal data, whether centralized or geographically dispersed, which is accessible according to specific criteria and whose object or effect is to facilitate the use or alignment of data relating to the data subject or subjects

and "processing of personal data" as:

> . . . any operation or set of operations which is performed upon personal data, whether or not by automatic means, such as collection, recording, organization, storage, adaptation or alteration, retrieval, consultation, use, disclosure by transmission, dissemination or otherwise making available, alignment or combination, blocking, erasure or destruction.

Nevertheless, the draft Directive does not prescribe uniform treatment for all types of data. For instance, subject to certain exceptions where there are adequate safeguards, Article 16(1) provides for

> . . . the right of every person not to be subjected to an administrative or private decision adversely affecting him which is based solely on automatic processing defining a personality profile.

DATA PROTECTION PRINCIPLES

The data protection principles articulated by Article 5 of the Council of Europe Convention are reflected in the duties imposed on data controllers by section 2(1) of the 1988 Act. They may be summarized as follows:

1   The data, or the information constituting the data, must have been obtained fairly and the data must be processed fairly.

2   The data must be accurate and, where necessary, kept up to date.

3   The data must be kept only for one or more specified and lawful purposes.

4   The data must not be used or disclosed in any manner which is incompatible with that purpose or those purposes.

5   The data must be adequate, relevant and not excessive in relation to that purpose or those purposes.

6   The data must not be kept for longer than is necessary for that purpose or those purposes.

7   Appropriate security measures must be taken to prevent unauthorized access to, or alteration, disclosure or destruction of, the data and to prevent their accidental loss or destruction.[81]

These rules are supplemented and amplified by other provisions of the 1988 Act, so as to bring Irish law into conformity with the principles articulated in the various international instruments. Similar principles are set out in Articles 6 and 17 of the EEC draft Directive. Article 7 provides that personal data may be processed only in a limited number of situations. These include:

1   Where the data subject has given informed consent.

2   Where the processing is necessary for the performance of a contract with the data subject.

3   Where the processing is necessitated by an obligation imposed by law.

4   Where the processing is necessary in order to protect the vital interests of the data subject.

5   Where the processing is necessary for the performance of a task in the public interest.

6   Where the processing is in the interests of the data controller or a third party save where these interests are overridden by the interests of the data subject.

Furthermore, subject to public interest constraints, under Article 11 when data is being collected, the data controller is obliged to give the data subject information regarding matters such as the purposes of the processing for which the data are intended, the recipients of the data and the existence of the latter's rights of access and rectification.

REGISTRATION REQUIREMENTS

Under section 16 the Commissioner is obliged to maintain a register in respect of those persons who fall within the ambit of the section. The register is open to public inspection. Whilst the Garda Síochána and the Defence Forces are expressly excluded, this provision covers, *inter alia*, data controllers who are public authorities (including the Government, Government ministers, local authorities and health boards), certain financial institutions and those who keep what could be described as sensitive data (i.e. personal information relating to race, political or religious beliefs, physical or mental health, sexual life and criminal convictions).[82] In respect of those who fall within the latter category, under section 17(3), the Commissioner may not accept an application for registration unless he or she is of the opinion that appropriate safeguards for the protection of the privacy of the data subjects are being provided. Under section 19(1), a data controller to whom section 16 applies must not keep personal data unless there is a current entry in respect of him or her in the register. Furthermore, under section 19(2), a registered data controller may not keep personal data other than that specified in his or her entry on the register or use personal data for any purpose other than that described in the entry.

In a similar vein, Article 30 of the draft Directive contemplates the establishment by the individual Member States of supervisory authorities which will be independent public authorities with investigative and enforcement powers designed to secure compliance with national laws enacted pursuant to the Directive. Article 21 obliges the supervisory authority to maintain a public register in respect of notified processing operations. Article 18 imposes a duty on controllers to deliver detailed notifications to the supervisory authority prior to performing processing operations. Before processing material which poses specific risks to the rights and freedoms of individuals can commence, the supervisory authority must examine the processing within a period of fifteen days from the date of notification. However, national law may provide that such processing operations may be authorized beforehand by law or by a decision of the supervisory authority. Under Article 19, processing operations which do not affect the rights and freedoms of data subjects may be exempted from the notification procedure or made subject to simplified procedures.

KNOWLEDGE AND ACCESS

These rules can be regarded as manifestations of the openness and individual participation principles.[83] Under section 3, an individual who believes that a person keeps personal data regarding him or her is entitled, on making a written request, to be informed by the latter as soon as may be and in any event within 21 days as to whether he or she keeps any such data and, if data are kept, to be given a description of the data and the purposes for which they are kept. Under section 4(1), on making a written request to a data controller, an individual must be informed by the former as soon as may be, and in any event within 40 days, as to whether data kept by him or her include personal data relating to the individual, and be supplied by him or her with a copy of the information constituting any such data. It is further provided that where information is expressed in terms that are not intelligible to the average person without explanation, the information must be accompanied by an explanation of those terms. While the data controller may require the payment of a fee in respect of such a request, such a fee may not exceed such amounts as may be prescribed or an amount which the Commissioner regards as reasonable having regard to the estimated cost of complying with the request. Such fees must be returned where the individual's request is not complied with or the data controller rectifies, supplements or erases part of or the whole of the relevant data. Under section 4(3) the data controller may reasonably require the individual to produce information in order to establish his or her identity and to locate any relevant personal information or data. These latter provisions clearly have the potential to impede the exercise of the right to access. Any refusal to comply with a request made by an individual under section 4 must be in writing, must state the reasons for the refusal and must indicate that the individual may complain to Commissioner about the refusal.

ENFORCEMENT

The 1988 Act provides data subjects and the Commissioner with various means of redress to ensure that data controllers comply with the data protection principles. In respect of personal data kept for the purpose of direct marketing, section 2(7) entitles the data subject to make a written request to the data controller to cease using the data for this purpose. If the data is kept for no other purpose it must be erased within 40 days of the request, and if it is used for other purposes its use for the purpose of direct marketing must cease.[84]

In the event of a contravention by the data controller of the data protection principles enshrined in section 2(1), section 6 entitles the relevant data subject to make a written request to him or her requiring either the rectification or erasure of the data in question.[85] The data controller is obliged to comply with this request as soon as possible and in any event within 40 days of its receipt.[86]

Section 10(1) makes provision for the investigation by the Commissioner, either at the instigation of an individual or of his or her own volition, as to whether there has been a contravention of the provisions of the Act. The Commissioner is obliged to investigate complaints unless he is satisfied that they are frivolous or vexatious. If satisfied that there has been a contravention of the Act, under section 10(2) the Commissioner may serve an enforcement notice on the data controller or the data processor specifying what steps should be taken to comply with the Act. The addressee of an enforcement notice may appeal to the Circuit Court against an enforcement notice. In any event, failure to comply with a requirement specified in an enforcement notice without reasonable cause or excuse is a criminal offence by virtue of section 10(9). Under section 31(2), in the event of a person being convicted of an offence under the Act, the court may order any data material which appears to be connected with the commission of the offence to be forfeited or destroyed and the erasure of any relevant data.

Finally, under section 12, the Commissioner may serve a written notice on any person requiring him or her to furnish in writing such information in relation to specified matters as is necessary or expedient for the performance by the Commissioner of his or her functions. An appeal lies to the Circuit Court[87] and it is a criminal offence to fail or refuse to comply with an information notice without reasonable excuse, or to supply false or misleading information which one knows to be false or misleading. Under section 24 information may also be secured on behalf of the Commissioner by authorized officers who may enter and inspect premises, examine data equipment and inspect data and information.

UNAUTHORIZED DISCLOSURE AND ACCESS

Under section 21 of the 1988 Act, a criminal offence is committed if a data processor, his or her employee or agent discloses personal data without the prior authority of the data controller on whose behalf they are processed. It is likewise a criminal offence, under section 22, for a person who obtains access to personal data, or obtains any information constituting such data, to disclose that data or information to another person without the prior authority of the data controller or data processor by whom the data are kept.

In this context it is also worth referring to section 5(1) of the Criminal Damage Act, 1991, which makes it an offence for a person, without lawful excuse, to operate a computer within the State with intent to access any data kept either within or outside the State, or to operate a computer outside the State with intent to access any data kept within the State, irrespective of whether or not that person actually obtains access to any data. Where it is alleged that such an offence was committed by a person outside the State, section 7(1) of the 1991 Act provides that proceedings may be taken, and for all incidental purposes the offence may be regarded as having been committed, in any place in the State.

COMPENSATION

Article 10 of the Council of Europe Convention obliges signatory States to " . . . establish appropriate sanctions and remedies for violations of provisions of domestic law giving effect to the basic principles for data protection . . . ". However, instead of creating a complete scheme entitling an individual to compensation in the event of his or her suffering loss or damage as a result of a breach of the statutory duties imposed by the 1988 Act, section 7 adopts the somewhat indirect and unsatisfactory expedient of declaring that:

> For the purposes of the law of torts and to the extent that that law does not so provide, a person, being a data controller or a data processor, shall, so far as regards the collection by him of personal data or information intended for inclusion in such data or his dealing with such data, owe a duty of care to the data subject concerned.

One commentator has expressed the view that it is doubtful whether section 7 constitutes much of an extension to ordinary negligence principles.[88] The decision of Tudor Evans J in *Lawton v. BOC Transhield*,[89] holding that an employer owed a duty of care to a former employee when supplying a character reference, suggested that even in the absence of section 7 there would be sufficient proximity between the data controller or processor and the data subject. But the fact that the Court of Appeal recently overruled *Lawton* in *Spring v. Guardian Assurance plc*[90] has the converse effect of casting section 7 in a more favourable light.

Nevertheless, the section does have some obvious shortcomings. For instance, it fails to address situations in which a person is prejudiced by the transmission of inaccurate information relating to a third party (e.g. a relative).[91] The harmonization envisaged by the EEC Commission's draft Directive may not take matters much further. Article 23(1) provides that any person whose personal data are undergoing processing and who suffers damage as a result of an unlawful processing operation or of any act incompatible with the national provisions adopted pursuant to the Directive is entitled to compensation from the controller. Article 23(2) permits the Member States to provide that the controller may be wholly or partially exempted from liability for damage resulting from the loss or destruction of data or from unauthorized access if he or she proves that he or she has taken appropriate measures in relation to data security.

DEROGATIONS

Whilst establishing valuable rights in favour of the data subject, the 1988 Act simultaneously delimits these rights by restricting access in some cases and permitting disclosure in others. Even though many of these derogations can be grouped under the general heading of the public interest, the net result would appear to be that the application of the Act to some parts of public sector is frequently more apparent than real. Indeed, it has been observed that while secret information-gathering is sometimes required in the interests of a democratic society in order to protect national security or for the prevention and detection of crime, exempting the bodies responsible for such intelligence-gathering from most or all of the data protection rules " . . . is to negate the effectiveness of such laws in the very areas where they are most needed—which could contravene Article 8 of the ECHR".[92] In the light of the decision in *Leander v. Sweden* it could be argued that exemption from data protection rules is not objectionable *per se* as long as the agency is subject to sufficient scrutiny and is accountable. The Data Protection Commissioner clearly has no such function.

The wording of the European Community draft Directive is far from satisfactory on this point. Article 14(1) of the permits the Member States to restrict the data subject's rights to know of and have access to data on grounds of, *inter alia*, national security, defence, criminal justice and public safety. But Article 14(2) goes on to provide that the supervisory authority shall be empowered, at the data subject's request, to carry out necessary checks so as to verify the lawfulness of the processing within the Directive "respecting the interests to be protected in accordance with paragraph 1". Whether the supervisory authority can determine the legitimacy of using these public interest grounds in the particular context or must simply defer to their invocation is unclear.

EXEMPTED DATA

Section 1(4) provides that the 1988 Act does not apply to:

1 Personal data which in the opinion of the Minister for Justice or the Minister for Defence are, or at any time were, kept for the purpose of safeguarding the security of the State.

2 Personal data consisting of information which the person keeping the data is required by law to make available to the public.

3   Personal data kept by an individual and concerned only with the manage-
    ment of his or her personal, family or household affairs, or kept by an
    individual only for recreational purposes.

    Under section 23(1), the Act does not apply to a data controller in respect
of data kept, or to a data processor in respect of data processed, outside the State.
Furthermore, under section 23(4), the Act does not apply to data processed wholly
outside the State, unless the data are used or intended to be used in the State.

EXEMPTION FROM DATA PROTECTION PRINCIPLES

1   By virtue of section 2(3), the requirement that data, or the information
    constituting the data, should be obtained fairly and that the data should be
    processed fairly does not apply to data kept for the purpose of preventing,
    detecting or investigating offences, apprehending or prosecuting offenders,
    or assessing or collecting taxes, duties or moneys due to the State or local
    authorities, in any case where the application of these principles would be
    likely to prejudice any of the aforementioned activities.

2   By virtue of section 2(4), the requirement that data should be accurate and,
    where necessary, kept up to date does not apply to back-up data (i.e. data
    kept only for the purpose of replacing other data in the event of their being
    lost, destroyed or damaged).

3   By virtue of section 2(5), the requirement that data should not be kept for
    longer than is necessary does not apply to personal data kept for historical,
    statistical or research purposes. Furthermore, such data cannot be regarded
    as having been obtained unfairly solely because its use for any of these
    purposes was not disclosed when it was obtained, provided that the data are
    not used in such a way that damage or distress is, or is likely to be, caused to
    any data subject.

RESTRICTIONS ON THE RIGHT OF ACCESS

Section 5(1) provides that section 4 shall not apply to data:

1   Kept for the purpose of preventing, detecting or investigating offences,
    apprehending or prosecuting offenders, or assessing or collecting taxes,
    ˙ duties or moneys due to the State or local authorities.

2 To which section 4 does not apply by virtue of 1 above, and which are kept for the purpose of discharging a function imposed by any enactment and consisting of information obtained for such a purpose from a person who had it in his or her possession for any of the purposes mentioned under 1 above.

3 In respect of which the application of section 4 would prejudice security, discipline or order in a prison or place of detention.

4 Kept for the purpose of performing functions imposed under any enactment which are deemed to be designed to protect the public against financial malpractice in the banking, insurance and financial services sectors, and the conduct of persons who have been adjudicated bankrupt.[93]

5 Where the application of section 4 would be contrary to the interests of protecting the international relations of the State.

6 Which is kept by the data controller for the purposes of estimating the amount of his liability in respect of a claim for damages or compensation, where the application of section 4 would prejudice the interests of the data controller in relation to the claim.

7 Where legal professional privilege could be claimed.

8 Kept only for statistical or research purposes.

9 That are back-up data.

PERMITTED DISCLOSURES

Under section 8, the Act's restrictions on the disclosure of personal data do not apply where the disclosure is:

1 Required for the purpose of safeguarding the security of the State.

2 Required for the purpose of preventing, detecting or investigating offences, apprehending or prosecuting offenders, or assessing or collecting taxes, duties or moneys due to the State or local authorities.

3 Required in the interests of protecting the international relations of the State.

4 Required to prevent injury or damage to the health of a person, or damage to property.

5 Required under any enactment, rule of law or order of a court.

6   Required for the purpose of obtaining legal advice, or in the course of legal proceedings where the party making the disclosure is a party or a witness.

7   Made to the data subject or to a person acting on his or her behalf.

8   Made at the request or with the consent of the data subject or a person acting on his or her behalf.

TRANSBORDER DATA FLOWS

The preamble of the Council of Europe Convention makes it clear that safeguards for privacy were necessitated, at least in part, by "the increasing flow across frontiers of personal data undergoing automatic processing". Thus under section 19(2)(d) of the 1988 Act a registered data controller may not directly or indirectly transfer personal data to a place outside the State other than one named or described in the register entry. Section 11 entitles the Data Protection Commissioner to prevent the transfer of personal data from the State to a place outside the State by serving a prohibition notice on the person proposing to transfer the data concerned. An appeal lies to the Circuit Court and non-compliance with the notice without reasonable cause or excuse is a criminal offence. In considering whether to prohibit such transfers, the Commissioner is obliged to have regard to Article 12 of the Convention. Furthermore, under section 11(3) the Commissioner may not prohibit a proposed transfer of personal data unless he or she is of the opinion that the transfer would, if the place were in a state bound by the Convention, be likely to lead to a contravention of the basic principles of data protection set out in Chapter II of the Convention. The Commissioner must also consider whether the transfer would be likely to cause damage or distress to any person, and have regard to the desirability of facilitating international transfers of data. Section 11 does not apply where the transfer of data, or the information constituting the data, is required or authorized by or under any enactment, or required by any convention or other instrument imposing an international obligation on the State.

   In relation to transborder data flows to places outside the European Community, Article 26(1) of the EEC Commission's draft Directive permits Member States to provide for the temporary or permanent transfer of personal data to third countries only where the latter ensure an "adequate level of protection". But this proviso is immediately qualified in respect of contractual situations in which the data subject has consented or been informed of the implications of the transfer, or where the transfer is required by important public interest considerations or in order to protect the vital interests of the data subject. Similarly, Article 27(1) permits a Member State to authorize the transfer of personal data to a third country which does not provide an adequate level of protection if the controller can justify its transfer. Appropriate contractual provisions guaranteeing the effective exercise of data subjects' rights may provide sufficient justification. The Commission and the other Member States must be informed of the proposal to grant authorization and may object.

5.3 Sex and Sexuality under the European Convention on Human Rights

JAMES KINGSTON

The right to privacy is one of the rights protected by Article 8 of the European Convention on Human Rights. The concept of privacy is extremely wide, covering issues as diverse as telephone tapping and intellectual property. This paper, however, will deal with the issues of sex and sexuality, and how privacy in this area is protected by Article 8 (and, to a lesser extent, by other articles in the Convention). The main focus will be the legal regime applying to transsexuals and to male homosexuals. First, however, I wish to briefly consider the issue of the age of consent.

THE AGE OF CONSENT

In its report on *X v. FRG*,[1] the Commission, in a statement which sums up the approach taken by the Strasbourg organs in this area, held that:

> A person's sexual life is undoubtedly part of his private life ... Some of its aspects however may be the subject of state interference and in particular that of the national legislature in accordance with the provisions of paragraph 2 of Article 8.[2]

It went on to say that the relevant legislation, which criminalized homosexual activity by males over the age of eighteen with persons under the age of twenty-one, was enacted to protect the rights of young persons and to enable them to achieve "true autonomy" in sexual matters. This was a lawful purpose within the terms of Article 8(2), as it restricted the rights of the applicant, who was over the age of twenty-one, in the interests of "protecting the rights of others". The Commission recognized that opinions varied considerably regarding the age of consent and that such opinions were changing very rapidly. Therefore, States had a considerable margin of appreciation[3] in the area and such limits could vary depending on the attitude of society. In the instant case before it, the Commission was of the opinion that while an age limit of twenty-one was relatively high it was permissible.

The Commission does not seem to have looked at the practical effect of the legislation before it. For example, if two males, under the age of eighteen, commenced a sexual relationship the criminal law would not punish them. However, it would intervene while there were between the ages of eighteen and twenty-one, although it would be lawful for them to recommence the relationship when they were both over twenty-one. It seems extraordinary that such arbitrary and capricious interference with a right guaranteed under Article 8(1) has been permitted by a Convention organ.

The age of consent for male homosexuals in the UK is also twenty-one and has also been accepted as permissible by both the Court and the Commission.[4] However, it could be argued that such a high age limit would be regarded as unacceptable now, because of changes in attitudes towards sexual activity, including male homosexual activity, in the past decade or so. It should also be noted that the Commission, in *X v. UK*,[5] was of the opinion that, bearing in mind the high level at which the age of consent was set, the onus was on the UK government to justify it. Presumably some limits must be placed on States' margin of discretion in this area. Bearing in mind the considerable difference regarding the age of consent for various types of sexual activity throughout the Council of Europe, it is possible that at least some States have overstepped their margin of appreciation, even though the Convention's organs recognize that opinions on matters of morality and sexuality can vary between States.[6] As just mentioned, States such as the UK may be in breach of Article 8 because of their high age of consent for male homosexuals; however, it should also be noted, *pace* the Commission in *X v. FRG*, that legislation imposing age limits on sexual activity is aimed at protecting the rights of young people. It could be argued that States, such as the Netherlands, which, in 1991, formulated legislative proposals which would have reduced the age of consent to twelve years, could be charged with not adequately protecting the right of their young citizens to privacy: the right to develop their sexuality free from abuse by older persons arising out of too early an exposure to sexual relations.[7] *A fortiori*, States such as Cyprus,[8] which do not have an age of consent for male heterosexual conduct, could be in breach of Article 8. It is important to note that Article 8 gives rise to positive obligations to Member States in this area and may also impose obligations on individuals.[9]

Linked to this argument, is the point that the age of consent must be considered, not only from the point of view of persons over the relevant limit, but also from the point of view of those below it. Osphal, in his separate opinion in *X v. UK*,[10] accepted the majority view that the interference with the right to privacy of persons over the age of consent by confining their sexual activity to contact with other such persons was so minor as to be justified as being proportionate and, therefore, justified in a democratic society. However, he felt that if the age limit was looked at from the point of view of persons under that age it might be difficult to justify a total ban on their sexual activity. A recent challenge to UK legislation has been taken by three applicants, two of whom are under twenty-one; therefore, the Commission and Court may now have to address the issue raised by Osphal.[11]

DISCRIMINATION

Various states have different ages of consent applying to persons of different sexes and sexualities. In this regard the anti-discrimination provisions of Article 14 arise. To date, case law before the Convention organs has concentrated on the different age limits applicable to male homosexual and heterosexual activity and to male and female homosexuals within a particular State. In relation to the latter, the Commission, in *X v. FRG*,[12] accepted that there was no breach of Article 14 in conjunction with Article 8, arising out of the differing ages of consent applicable to lesbians and gay men (the latter being higher),[13] as it was of the view that there was less danger of young women being "led into" a homosexual lifestyle by older women than of young men being introduced to homosexual activity by older men. Discrimination between heterosexuals and (male) homosexuals has also been justified on similar grounds.[14] The justifiability of discrimination between male and female heterosexuals has not to date arisen in the jurisprudence of the Court or the Commission. However, some States, such as Ireland, impose different ages of limit for female and male heterosexual conduct.[15]

It may well be that the Convention would permit this type of different treatment, if the line of thinking in the cases previously mentioned was to be followed. Such an approach to different treatment is questionable; based as it is on assumptions and prejudices about men and women, homosexuals and heterosexuals, rather than on a rigorous analysis of the arguments put forward to justify different treatment. One would assume that sex or sexuality based discrimination is *prima facie* unlawful and that differentiation would be presumed to be contrary to the Convention, until cogent and compelling reasons were put forward to justify it.

To date, discussion of discrimination has taken place within the broader framework of restrictions on male homosexuality and it is to this issue that we now turn.

MALE HOMOSEXUALITY

The parameters of the discussion by the Convention organs in relation to male homosexuality seem to be as follows. Both the Commission[16] and the Court[17] regard sexual life as coming within the right to privacy protected by Article 8(1). However, regulation of the rights of male homosexuals, and, indeed, persons of other sexes and sexual orientations, may be regulated.[18] The majority of the Court in *Dudgeon* seem to be of the opinion that any interference with the individual's sex life must be justified with regard to the provisions of Article 8(2). However, Walsh J in his partly dissenting judgment, indicates that not all sexual activity enjoys the protection of Article 8 (1).

The question to be considered at this stage is the extent to which Article 8(2) can justify intervention by the State into the sexual activities of its citizens when they are carried out consensually and in private. Originally, the Commission accepted that an outright ban on homosexual activity could be justified, under Article 8(2), on grounds of health and morality, and that as the ban was justified under Article 8 there could be no discrimination contrary to Article 14 at issue.

The decision was subsequently reversed. In *Dudgeon*, the Commission and the Court both held that Northern Ireland's outright ban on consensual sexual activity between adult males in private constituted an unjustified interference with the applicant's right to privacy. There was a clear interference with the rights guaranteed under Article 8(1). Regarding the terms of Article 8(2), it was held that while the interference was prescribed by law and its aims were legitimate (to protect the rights of others and the moral order), it could not be regarded as being necessary in a democratic society. The requirement of necessity laid down in the Convention was a strict one and must constitute a "pressing social need", as opposed to a convenient or reasonable means of dealing with a perceived problem.[20] In the area of public morality States have a particularly wide margin of appreciation, wider than in other fields; however, it is "not only the nature of the aim of the restriction but also the nature of the activities involved [which] will affect the scope of the margin of appreciation". In this case the activities involved were of a very private nature; therefore, there was a very high onus on the government to justify the interference. This it failed to do.

The Court regarded as relevant the fact that many Member States of the Council of Europe, including the Federal Republic of Germany and the UK (in relation to England and Wales), had lifted their total ban on male homosexual activity. In many instances, including corporal punishment,[21] the status of children born outside marriage,[22] transsexuality[23] and differential ages of consent in relation to homosexual activity,[24] the Court will have regard to changing mores in interpreting the provisions of the Convention. This approach allows the Strasbourg organs to disregard or refuse to follow earlier decisions.

The Court held that it could not impose "Euro-morals". The religious and moral climate prevailing in Northern Ireland was a factor to be taken into account;[25] it could justify a different regime applying there than in the rest of the Council of Europe, but, in fact, the mores of Northern Ireland were not such as to justify its total ban on male homosexual acts. The non-enforcement of the relevant legislation against consenting adults who carried out their sexual activity in private was evidence that there was not a pressing social need for the ban in Northern Ireland. This is somewhat ironic as the Government had sought to use this fact to show that the applicant's private life had not been interfered with! The Government had also failed to show that the positive effects of the law, the protection of the moral fibre of Northern Irish society, outweighed the negative effects the legislation had on persons such as the applicant.

Walsh J, in his partly dissenting judgment, also makes the point that homosexuality, as such, was not banned under the legal regime in force in Northern Ireland and that not all sexual activity between males was banned, only buggery and such "indecent" acts as constitute "gross indecency". This view is contrary to that of the majority who were of the opinion that all sexual acts between men constituted "gross indecency". Furthermore, there is an implicit assumption that, whether legally permissible or not, all sexual activity between men is, by definition, "indecent".

The rationale of the *Dudgeon* decision is largely followed in the case of *Norris v. Ireland*.[26] The operation in Ireland of the same legislation, sections 61 and 62 of the Offences Against the Person Act, 1861, and section 11 of the Criminal Law (Amendment) Act, 1885, was implicated and many of the arguments adduced by the Irish Government were similar to those raised (unsuccessfully) by the UK Government in *Dudgeon*. One new point raised by Ireland was that morality was a matter peculiarly within the competence of the Member States of the Council of Europe and, therefore, the tests of social necessity and proportionality should not be used in this field. This was rejected by the Court, which affirmed its earlier case law, holding that although States have a particularly wide margin of appreciation in this area, it is subject to review by the Court by reference to Article 8(2).[27] The Irish legislation in this area has recently been amended.[28]

It should be noted that both these judgments deal with the 1885 Act, rather than the 1861 legislation, as the former applies to male homosexuals only, whereas the latter applies equally to both men and women. The 1861 Act has not yet been challenged by married persons, but it is interesting to note that in the UK the prohibition of buggery remains in force in relation to heterosexuals.

In the recent case of *Modinus v. Cyprus*,[30] the Court, by an eight-to-one majority, held that Cypriot law contravened Article 8, as the Criminal Code prohibited carnal knowledge between men. Although prosecutions were not allowed by the Attorney General in the case of private consensual sexual activities between adult males since the Court's judgment in *Dudgeon,* the Court was not satisfied that the applicant's private life was not being interfered with. The Court pointed out that a future Attorney General could reverse this policy; furthermore, the applicant could be subjected to police investigation or to private prosecution.[31]

The Cypriot Government had also stated that the relevant criminal provisions could not be enforced as the Constitution provided that municipal law was subject to international law and also contained a privacy guarantee similar to that laid down in Article 8 of the Convention. The Court, however, referred to the fact that the Cypriot Supreme Court had held[32] that while it would follow judgments of international bodies, such as the European Court of Human Rights, in the case of homosexuality, it would follow the reasoning of Zeika J in his dissenting judgment in *Dudgeon.* This judgment had stated that because of differing attitudes to sexual morality in different Member States of the Council of Europe, Article 8 could not be said to prohibit a blanket ban on sexual activities between men. The Court rejected arguments that the decision was handed down prior to *Norris* and before *Dudgeon* was fully understood and that the Supreme Court's remarks could be ignored, as they were *obiter.*[33]

The Cypriot judge, Pikis J, however, dissented. He was of the opinion that the Cypriot Constitution did, in fact, provide protection similar to that given by Article 8. In this regard, he referred to recent (*post Costa*) jurisprudence of the Cypriot Supreme Court and to the fact that it's comments in relation to the Convention in that *Costa* were *obiter.* He also referred to the fact that the Attorney General had a policy of not prosecuting where consensual sexual activity was carried out in private between adult males (although he accepted that this was not a cast iron guarantee). He also pointed out, that unlike the situation in *Norris* where anyone could initiate a private prosecution, Cypriot law only allowed for private prosecutions to be initiated by the victim of a crime. He did not feel that the applicant's private life had, in fact, been interfered with and pointed out that he had not been prosecuted, despite being openly involved in a homosexual relationship and in gay rights organizations.

From the case law mentioned above, it can be concluded that a total ban on male homosexual activity is not permissible, but that discriminatory age limits, even above the age of majority, may be countenanced in the moral climate of western liberal democracies in the late twentieth century. Other forms of discrimination may also be allowed. In *B v. UK,*[34] the Commission upheld section 66 of the Army Act, 1955, which empowered courts martial to impose penal sanctions on male persons subject to military law who engage in sexual activity with other men, even if their sexual partner is a civilian and the activity takes place when the soldier is off duty and outside military property.[35] The

Commission accepted the Ministry for Defence's position that the nature of military life[36] was such that homosexual activity by soldiers had greater negative consequences than similar activities by civilians; due to the intimate nature of military life the presence of homosexuals (even in the absence of a sexual relationship between military personnel) could lead to disorder. It also accepted arguments that there was a need to protect younger soldiers and those of lower rank from the sexual attentions of their elders and betters. The Commission also implicitly accepts the UK Government's argument that homosexual soldiers could pose a security risk in that they could be blackmailed. It also seems to accept the Ministry of Defence's policy of not recruiting or retaining soldiers known or suspected to be homosexuals. This gives a very wide licence to States as it is homosexuality, rather than homosexual activity, which is at issue. It should also be noted that the "security risk" argument could be easily applied to many other government positions and that while Article 8 protects privacy it does not give rise to a right to equal treatment.[37] The approach of the Commission can be further criticized on the basis that discriminatory treatment of male homosexuals by the State is justified on the grounds that private individuals may blackmail such people or threaten them in other ways. Thus the law is allowed to reinforce, rather than counteract, prejudice. The approach of the Court may be compared to that of the judge in Limerick, in the early part of this century, who is reputed to have acquitted two men who assaulted a Jewish resident of that city and instead convicted the latter of causing a breach of the peace by walking the streets in clothing which identified him as being Jewish.

The Convention does not recognize the concept of a homosexual family. While heterosexuals couples cohabiting on a long term basis can constitute a family, homosexual couples in a similar position cannot, although they may be entitled to protection if their private life is interfered with.[38] Homosexual couples are also not entitled to marry, as Article 12 confers a right to marry solely on couples of the opposite biological sex.[39]

Article 14 does not seem to prohibit, in any significant way, different treatment of homosexuals, although it contains an implicit ban on discrimination based on sexual orientation.[40] The scope of this article is limited and has been very strictly construed by the Convention organs.[41] It is not an equality provision equivalent to Article 40(1) of the Irish Constitution or Article 26 of the International Covenant on Civil and Political Rights (ICCPR). They are, in essence, free-standing and guarantee equality before the law; in contrast, Article 14 merely guarantees equality in relation to those rights protected by the Convention, that is, a very limited number of (largely) civil and political rights. The lack of such protection in the Convention is a serious flaw which should be remedied at the earliest possible opportunity.

From the foregoing, it can be seen that while the Convention does limit a State's freedom to completely ban male homosexual activity, it does not offer anything like a full guarantee of equal treatment to homosexual men.[42] The position in Ireland must be looked at in the light of these factors.

THE IRISH POSITION

As previously mentioned, Irish law criminalized all (or, *pace* Walsh J, nearly all) sexual activity between men until very recently. This position was held to be in accordance with the Irish Constitution.[43] It is not clear whether or not the Constitution requires such a ban as, to date, there has not been a constitutional challenge to the recently introduced legislation repealing the offending portions of the 1861 and 1885 legislation. Despite the recent changes, it should be noted that not only did the Government fail to act for five years after the judgment in *Norris*, it had had advance warning of the likelihood of Ireland's being in breach of the Convention since the *Dudgeon* decision in 1981.[44] The fact that the Irish government, in effect, ignored this clear indication of the Court's thinking in this matter shows that it is prepared to take, at best, a reactive approach to human rights, rather than seeking to remedy its legislation pro-actively.

This highlights the limited role of the Convention in preventing human rights breaches; perhaps a system of periodic State and general reports, similar to that in operation under the ICCPR, under which States' obligations are dealt with in a broader context, would give rise to a political climate in which human rights abuses are dealt with at the earliest, rather than the latest possible, opportunity.

On the 10 November 1992, the Irish Government was given six months to bring its laws into conformity with its obligations under the Convention by the Council of Europe.[45] It finally complied with its obligation with the introduction of the Criminal Law (Sexual Offences) Act, 1993.

The Act broadly implements the recommendations of the Law Reform Commission Report on Child Sexual Offences,[46] which, in turn, broadly recommended that homosexuals be treated the same as heterosexuals in the area of sexual offences. The British position, which merely creates limited exceptions to what is otherwise a crime (in much the same way that British abortion law merely creates exceptions to *prima facie* criminal conduct), was rejected by the government, which decided to opt for an "equality" type regime. It also rejected moves to define "in private" or to exempt the Defence Forces from the ambit of the legislation, as is the case in the UK.

Section 2 of the Act repeals sections 61 and 62 (which prohibited buggery and attempted buggery) of the 1861 Act, insofar as they relate to persons.[47]

Section 4 of the Act penalises buggery and attempted buggery with boys under the age of 17. Section 5 (1) prohibits buggery and attempted buggery, as well as actual and attempted sexual intercourse, with mentally impaired persons (subject to certain defences).

The Act is also repeals section 11 of the 1885 Act which prohibits "gross indecency" between males and replaces it with a provision which provides that:

> A male person who commits or attempts to commit an act of gross indecency with another male person under the age of 17 years shall be guilty of an offence and shall be liable on conviction on indictment to imprisonment for a term not exceeding 5 years.

Although section 4 does not specifically refer to section 11, the Schedule to the Act provides that it is repealed. Section 5 (2) also prohibits gross indecency with a mentally impaired man.

It can be seen from the foregoing, that the Act attempts to treat homosexual men in a fashion that is broadly similar to the way that heterosexuals are treated. The "age of consent" is seventeen, that is, the age at which women may lawfully consent to sexual intercourse. However, the position of heterosexual men continues to be different, in that they can consent to intercourse with women from the age of fifteen. Furthermore, whilst girls above the age of fifteen may consent to non penetrative sexual activity (with either males or females), boys between the ages of fifteen and seventeen cannot consent to such activity with another male. Section 4 was specifically designed to ensure that this was the case; the provision also maintains the concept of "gross indecency", which does not apply to sexual conduct other than between men. The Law Reform Commission had recommended, as a general rule,[48] that non-penetrative sex between males should not be an offence once both parties were over fifteen. Accordingly, while the 1993 Act is largely positive in its treatment of male homosexuals, it fails to provide completely equal treatment.[49]

Irish law provides some further protection for homosexuals: the Prohibition of Incitement to Hatred Act, 1989, prohibits a wide range of activity, including public speech, broadcasting and publishing, where the aim or effect of such activity would be to incite hatred directed at individuals or groups on the basis of a number of grounds, including their sexual orientation.[50] Similarly, the Video Recording Act, 1989, permits the banning of videos on the ground that they may stir up hatred based on, *inter alia*, sexuality. The Civil Service Code also provides protection in that it prohibits discrimination in the civil service based on sexual orientation. The Unfair Dismissals Act, 1993, also protects homosexuals, in that it prohibits dismissal from employment based on the sexual orientation of the employee.

While Irish law has developed considerably in this area in the past few years, it cannot be said that homosexuals are yet legally regarded as being equal to heterosexuals.

TRANSSEXUALITY

The case law of the Convention on male homosexuality deals with the State's obligation not to interfere with the private lives of its citizens. In its case law on transsexuality the Convention organs also deal with the State's negative obligation of no interference with private life.[51] However, they also consider the positive obligations of States in this area.

In the first case involving transsexuals to proceed to a hearing before both Commission and Court, *van Oosterwijk v. Belgium*,[52] the Commission stated that the applicant's problems arose because the State had brought into existence a legal system whereby his sex was mentioned in a variety of official documents, including national identity cards and birth certificates. Although the Belgian authorities had recognised his need to change his outward appearance, by permitting his sex change surgery, it had refused to allow him to change his birth certificate and its legislation did not permit any other means changing civil status. In Belgium the birth certificate is not a historical record of the individual's status at birth, but can be changed upon marriage, change of name, etc. Although Belgian law allowed certain measures whereby the applicant could reduce the difficulties arising from the difference between his outward appearance and his official sex, such as permitting him to change his forenames (a more formalised process than in common law jurisdictions), and enabled him to reduce the incidences whereby he had to reveal this to other persons, it did not officially recognise him as a man. This failure, in the Commission's opinion, amounted to a failure to respect the applicant's right to privacy under Article 8.

The Court found that the applicant had failed to exhaust local remedies and, therefore, could not appear before the Convention organs; accordingly, it did not examine the merits of the case. However, it indicated that measures such as allowing the applicant to change his forenames would not rectify his situation as the cause of his difficulty was: "the respondent State's non-recognition of his sexual identity . . . or its social consequences".

The next case to be heard on its merits[53] was *Rees v. UK.*[54] The Commission, in accordance with its reasoning in *van Oosterwijk*, took a strongly pro-applicant line. It stated that sexual identity was made up of both biological and psychological factors and that the latter could be a determining factor. This, coupled with the its opinion that sex is one of the essential elements of human personality, led it to interpret Article 8 as prohibiting the non-recognition of an individual's changed sex as part of his or her personality, following a lawful sex change operation. The fact that the Government, through the National Health Service, had recognized the need for the operation, and had paid for it implied that it was obliged to recognize the applicant's new sex. Article 8 does not require that the legal recognition of the applicant's psychological sex be extended to cover the period prior to the gender reassignment surgery; however, it must be possible for an individual to confirm his or her normal appearance by official documentation. The UK does not have a national identity card system, but passports and drivers' licences are often used as a means of identification. However, although these documents could be altered, to an extent, to better reflect the individual's changed appearance, frequently an individual had to produce his or her birth certificate, e.g., to passport officials when applying for a first passport. In the UK the birth certificate mentions the holder's official sex, such sex being the same as that entered in the Register of Births. The Register is a historical document, it records the individual's status at birth. It is not amended following change of name, etc. With the exception of amendments made following adoption or legitimation the Register can only be changed in case of error. The Commission was of the opinion that the government's failure to consider an amendment to the Register and to allow him a new birth certificate reflecting his new sex amounted to a breach of Article 8.

It was noted that for the legal purposes, such as marriage[55] and legislation relating to sexual offences,[56] only biological criteria were used in determining sex. Sex, when recorded on a birth certificate, was also based solely on biological grounds, and, for many areas of the law, including social welfare and labour legislation, post-operative transsexuals were treated as being of the sex recorded therein.

The Court, however, took a different approach. It was of the opinion that the refusal of the Government to alter official documents did not amount to an interference with the applicant's private life. The scope of a State's positive obligations under Article 8 depended on the context; in the present case legislation in the various States was widely divergent; therefore, States had a wide margin of appreciation. This approach is similar to the approach taken by the Strasbourg organs in relation to the criminalisation of male homosexuality, regarding the age of consent,[57] but is in contrast to its reasoning in many other areas.[58] In the present case, the Court was of the opinion that a balance had to be drawn between the interest of the applicant and that of the public. It could not force the UK to adopt a system of civil status documentation similar to that in other Member States of the Council of Europe whereby changes in sex could be more easily incorporated. The Court accepted the Government's reasoning that annotation of the Register and the issuing of new birth certificates to legitimated and adopted persons was not analogous to such changes in relation to transsexuals; to adopt such measures in relation to transsexuals would amount to "falsification"[59] of the facts and would deny information to third parties, such as the armed forces and insurance companies, with a "legitimate" interest in "being informed of the true [*sic*] situation". The Court does not make it clear why anyone would have a legitimate interest in finding out a person's biological sex; for example, the only reason the army would need to know an individual's sex would be to discriminate against them on the grounds of sex. One reason for differentiating between transsexuals and persons such as adoptees, in the Court's view, was that adoption had legal consequences, whereas sex changes did not. This would seem to be a somewhat circular argument and, as was pointed out by the dissenting judges,[60] if the UK recognized the change in status, the change in the birth certificate would be required for legal purposes. Similarly, the minority refuse to follow the majority line of reasoning that the changes would not fully (although they would largely) satisfy the applicant's wishes and, therefore, should not be required of the Government.

In the next case to come before the Court, *Cossey v. UK*,[61] it reiterated its judgment in *Rees*. Despite its reference in the latter case to the rapidly changing views in society on the issue, and despite the fact since that case the number of states in the Council of Europe who recognized, to a greater or lesser extent, had increased dramatically, from five to fourteen, the Court was not of the opinion that it was necessary to change its interpretation of the Convention to reflect societal change and remain in line with present day conditions.[62]

However, the decision was reached by a smaller (ten-to-eight) majority than in *Rees* and a particularly trenchant dissent was delivered by Martens J. He thought that *Rees* was wrongly decided and that, in any event, societal changes which had taken place since the Court had delivered its judgment in that case, warranted a change in its jurisprudence. To deal with the last point first, he said that the Court should overturn a previous judgment if, and only if, it was convinced "the new judgment is clearly the better law".[63] Martens J was of this opinion. He also pointed out that the Court would be overruling a single judgment, not a long line of case law; to confirm that judgment would limit its ability to change its jurisprudence at a later stage.[64] Furthermore, the fact that the respondent in both the cases was the UK would mean that Mr Rees, as well as Ms Cossey, would benefit and, therefore, it could not be said that any disparity between the applicants would arise. He was also of the opinion that societal development, including the changes in legislation in many States and relevant resolutions of the European Parliament and the Parliamentary Assembly of the Council of Europe, justified a change in approach on the part of the Court. While the national legal systems varied, even in States which recognised transsexuality, he was of the opinion that the majority assertion that there was little common ground was unwarranted. He pointed out that while harmonization of laws was not suggested by either of the aforementioned parliamentary bodies, they were of the opinion that legal recognition of changed sex was required as a minimum.

In relation to the substantive issue, he made the point, similar to that raised by the Commission in *van Oosterwijk*, that not only the positive obligations of governments were at stake. The fact that the UK Government had a legal system whereby the incongruence between her psychological and biological sex was revealed was the source of the applicant's problem, rather than its refusal to alter the Register of Births and to issue new birth certificates to post-operative transsexuals. The fact that only (certain) biological factors were deemed relevant amounted to a refusal to recognise the "important societal fact"[65] of transsexuals' sexual identity and could not be justified as being "necessary in a democratic society". (In this regard the fact that other states had accommodated transsexuals was regarded as relevant.) Even if positive obligations alone were involved Martens J was of the opinion that the UK was in breach of its obligations. He stated that the margin of appreciation was not enjoyed as of right by the States, but was simply an example of judicial self-restraint in areas where national legal systems diverged. In the present context, the margin only came into play in relation to how States recognize the change in status of a post-operative trans-sexual; they have no margin of appreciation as to whether or not to recognize this change. Therefore, the highly technical approach of the Court in looking at the intricacies of the various and varying European legal systems, was not valid. He stated: "It is my firm opinion that the Court, by . . . exercising judicial self-restraint, sadly failed its vocation of being the last-resort protector of oppressed individuals".[66]

Despite this strong dissent, Martens J did not address the issue as to why it is ever valid for the State to know, or record and make public and official, the sex of the individual. In a non-sexist society the sex of the individual should, in general, not be a matter of concern for the State. It may be that traditionally the State has concerned itself with such matters, just as racist States, such as South Africa at the height of apartheid, concerned themselves with the colour of their citizens. However, in a truly egalitarian society, or one which wishes to attain that status, sex, colour or other personal attributes should not be taken note of by the legal system, save to ensure that neither public nor private bodies discriminate against the individual on these grounds.

The most recent case to come before the Court is that of *B v. France*.[67] In this case, while the Court found that a violation of Article 8 had occurred, it was careful to restrict the case to its facts. It declined to hold that ongoing changes in societal attitudes to transsexuality and increased scientific research into its causes were such as to warrant the overturning of its decisions in *Rees* and *Cossey*. It distinguished them on the basis of differences between French and UK legislation. It was noted that the function of the Registry of Births and the birth certificate in France, as in Belgium, was not to act as a historical record, as in the UK, but rather served as a record of current status and were regularly updated, following changes in marital status, etc. The Court noted that fore-names could only be changed in limited circumstances. French case law in relation to both changes of forename and changes in civil status following gender reassignment surgery was unsettled and in a state of change. However, the applicant had been refused permission to change either her sex as recorded on her birth certificate or her forenames. These refusals led to a situation whereby in her daily life the applicant suffered inconvenience to "a sufficient degree of seriousness"[68] to lead the Court to conclude that her right to privacy had been violated.[69] The Court went on to point out that it was up to France to take whatever means it saw fit to ameliorate this situation; it would not tell the French Government to undertake any particular course of action.

From the foregoing, it can be seen that while societal attitudes and national legislation have become increasingly sympathetic to transsexuals since the 1970s, the Court seems to have moved in the opposite direction. While it will protect the individual from particularly embarrassing situations arising in day to day life, it does not require the State to recognize the individual's right to be recognized, in law, as being of the sex they regard themselves as belonging to. Neither does it take the position, which it can be argued most strongly affirms the right to privacy, that a person's sex is nobody's business but his or her own.

THE POSITION IN IRELAND[70]

The position in Ireland must be looked at in the light of the foregoing cases. To date, the issue of the legal recognition of a person's sex following a sex change operation has not been raised before the Irish courts. There is no legislation governing the legality or otherwise of sex change operations or recognising the right to change one's sexual identity in law; neither does the Department of Justice have an overall position on the matter. However, a number of government departments and bodies have dealt with transsexuals. It should be noted that all decisions taken are made on an *ad hoc* basis and should not be regarded as constituting legal recognition of changed sexual status. In any event, the Con-vention does not seem to require such recognition.

In Ireland, as in the UK, there is, at present, no system of national identity cards.[71] The State does, nonetheless, provide and require official documentation in which the sex of the holder of the document is mentioned. In Ireland all persons are registered at birth and the sex of the baby is recorded. The Register is available to the public. It is a historical record, as in the UK. As a general rule, it cannot be amended. Therefore, changes in either surnames or forenames, while permitted by Irish law, cannot be recorded on the birth certificate, even if the purpose of the name change is to reflect a new sexual identity. Similarly, changes in sex cannot be recorded on the birth certificate. However, it is possible to have errors on a birth certificate rectified. While the Registrar of Births, Marriages and Deaths is aware that transsexuals may regard their new sexual identity as the correct one, and their initial gender designation as mistaken, to date it has not acceded to a request by a transsexual to change the record of their sex.

In relation to passports, the Department of Foreign Affairs has taken a sympathetic approach to transsexuals. A post-operative transsexual may apply to have certain changes made to his or her passport. Each application is dealt with on an individual basis, the applicant will have to present to the passport office all relevant surgical, medical and psychological reports; he or she will also have to show evidence of a change of name, including change of name by deed poll (if applicable) and other indicia of the name change (for example, bank statements, etc). Once the information is provided the passport office will decide on the application. The practice appears to be that the new name will be put on the passport and where the sex of the holder is normally designated by a "F"of "M" an "X" is substituted. As titles, such as "Mr" or "Ms", are not recorded on Irish passports, no problem arises in this regard.

A number of other departments, including the Department of Social Welfare, have dealt with transsexuals. The approach of the latter department is to accommodate such persons as far as possible. Any difficulties which may have arisen in the past, due to sexually discriminatory social welfare legislation have largely, although not completely, been done away with.

In practice, the sex change operation is not made available in Irish hospitals. However, the Department of Health has stated that in certain circumstances the holder of a medical card could be entitled to such an operation under the free health care scheme. The holder of a medical card is entitled to any "necessary" medical care and the Department would look at any relevant medical or psychological evidence indicative of the necessity of a sex change operation in the case of a particular applicant. It would not be possible, however, to fund an operation which the Department was of the opinion was being sought for "cosmetic" reasons, falling short of "necessity".

As can be seen from the foregoing, Irish law in this area is in an embryonic state. Insofar as the State's negative obligation, not to interfere with private life, is concerned, it could be argued that Ireland is in breach of its obligation under Article 8(2) to clearly regulate the position of transsexuals by law. However, the Court's reluctance to look at this area from the point of view of negative obligations may render this a somewhat unlikely prospect. With regard to positive obligations, we have seen that the Convention's requirements are somewhat limited. In the absence of any domestic case law or legislation it is impossible to say whether or not Ireland is conforming with its obligations. However, it is desirable that legislative moves are taken to ensure that we in this country treat transsexuals in a compassionate way and that our standards are at least as high as those imposed on us by the Convention.

CONCLUSION

As mentioned above, neither the Commission nor the Court has adverted to the possibility that the requirement that an individual reveal his or her sex to the State and to the public at large could constitute a breach of Article 8. One example of the absurdity of applying legal definitions to individuals is illustrated by the case of *Eriksson and Goldschmidt v. Sweden*.[72] The applicants' claim, which was found to inadmissible, was based on Article 12 of the Convention. The first applicant was registered at birth as a male, but following an application to the relevant authorities, had been recognized as a female under Swedish law. However, he had decided not to undergo gender reassignment surgery and had entered into a relationship with the second (female) applicant. Under Swedish law persons of the same sex are not permitted to marry and as the applicants were both, for legal purposes, female, they fell within this prohibition. The Commission held that the ban was permissible on the grounds that Article 12 only covers the right to marry someone of the "opposite" sex.[73] The result of this case is as absurd as the Commission's findings in on discriminatory age limits imposed against male homosexuals, which were discussed earlier in this paper.[74]

As can be seen from the jurisprudence discussed in this article, Article 8 allows widespread intervention by national legislatures in the area of sex and sexuality. However, in this most intimate area of human life it may be hoped that lawmakers will act in such a way as to foster pride rather than prejudice.

5.4   Select Bibliography

TEXTS AND MATERIALS

S.H. Bailey, D.J. Harris and B.L. Jones, *Civil Liberties: Cases and Materials*, 3rd ed. (London, 1991) Ch.8.
R. Clark, *Data Protection Law in Ireland* (Dublin, 1990).
A. Coleman, *The Legal Protection of Trade Secrets* (London, 1992).

F. Gurry, *Breach of Confidence* (Oxford, 1984).
A.H. Robertson, ed., *Privacy and Human Rights* (1973).
G. Robertson, *Freedom, the Individual and the Law*, 6th ed. (London, 1989), Ch. 3.
C. Tapper, *Computer Law*, 4th ed. (London, 1989).

ARTICLES

A. Connelly, "Irish law and the Judgment of the European Court of Human Rights in the Dudgeon Case" (1982) 4 *DULJ* (n.s.) 25.
A. Connelly, "Problems of Interpretation of Article 8 of the European Convention on Human Rights" (1986) 35 *ICLQ* 567.
L. Doswald Beck, "The Meaning of the Right to Respect for Private Life under the European Convention on Human Rights" (1983) 4 *HRLJ* 283.
P. Duffy, "The Protection of Privacy, Family Life and other Rights under Article 8 of the European Convention on Human Rights" (1982) 2 *YBK Eur L* 191.
R. Ermanski, "A Right to Privacy for Gay People Under International Law" (1992) *Boston College Int & Comp L Rev* 141.
O. Estadelle-Yuste, "The Draft Directive of the European Communities Regarding the Protection of Personal Data" (1992) 41 *ICLQ* 170.
K. Golden, "Transborder Data Flows and the Possibility of Guidance in Personal Data Protection by the International Telegraphic Union" (1984) 6 *Houston JIL* 215.
B.D. Goldstein, "Confidentiality and Dissemination of Personal Information: An Examination of State Laws Governing Data Protection" (1992) 41 *Emory L J* 1185.
D. Korff, "International Data Protection" (1991) 6.4 *Inter Rights Bul.* 59.
L.G. Loucaides, "Personality and Privacy under the European Convention on Human Rights" (1990) 61 *BYIL* 175.
B. Markesinis, "The Calcutt Report Must Not be Forgotten" (1992) 55 *LQR* 118.
A. Michel, "Abortion and International Law: The Status and Possible Extension of Women's Right to Privacy" (1982) 20 *J Fam L* 241.
G. Naldi, "No Hope for Transsexuals?" (1987) 137 *NLJ* 129.
P.M. North, "Breach of Confidence, Is There a New Tort?" (1972) 12 *JSPTL* 149.
R. Omrod, "Sex Determination" (1972) 40 *Medico-Legal J* 78.
R. Redmond-Cooper, "The Press and the Law of Privacy" (1985) *ICLQ* 769.
C. Reid, "Press Censorship into the 1990s: The Calcutt Report and the Protection of Individual Privacy" (1992) 43 *NILQ* 99.
M. Schauss, "The Amended Proposal for an EC Directive on Data Protection; Progress on the Face of It, Disillusion After Scrutiny" (1993) *JIBFL* 80.
R. Scott, "Developments in the Law of Confidentiality" [1990] *Denning LJ* 77.
N. Savage and C. Edwards, "Transborder Data Flow: The European Convention on Human Rights and UK Legislation" (1986) 35 *ICLQ* 710.
I. Walden and R. Savage, "Data Protection and Privacy Law: Should Organisations be Protected?" (1988) 37 *ICLQ* 337.

6 : FREEDOM OF EXPRESSION

6.1   Introduction

The principle of freedom of expression is one which is widely recognized and accepted in all western democracies as a basic human right. However, despite widespread recognition of the principle, it is generally accepted that some restraints on its exercise are necessary and desirable where it conflicts with other fundamental human rights. Examples of the areas in which such conflicts arise are the protection of a person's good name, protection of public morality and where matters of national security are at issue.

It is at this point that divergences arise on the extent of these prior restraints. This divergence is most obvious in the area of permissible prior restraints on freedom of expression in the interests of national security. A comparison of American and English case law in this area provides an interesting insight into the difference of interpretation.

In the US, freedom of expression is expressly protected by the First Amendment to the Constitution. This right is absolute and no reference is made to any exceptions or limitations, unlike Article 40.6.1.(i) of the Irish Constitution which guarantees "the right of the citizens to express freely their convictions and opinions", but the exercise of this right is "subject to public order and morality". The American courts have given the First Amendment an absolutist interpretation and, as a rule, are very reluctant to allow any prior restraints on communications.

A good example of the approach of the American courts is the decision of the US Supreme Court in the case of *New York Times v. United States*.[1] That case involved an application by the US Attorney General for an injunction to prevent the publication by the *New York Times* of top secret documents relating to the Vietnam war which was being fought at the time. The Supreme Court by a six-to-three majority refused to grant the injunction as the Attorney General could not prove that publication would definitely cause direct, immediate and irreparable harm to the nation. The fact that it might do so was not sufficient. Indeed, Black and Brennan J J went so far as to say that the First Amendment prohibited any judicial restraint on speech and Black J added that the *New York Times* should be commended for publishing the documents.

This extremely strict interpretation of the principle of freedom of expression,

197

which allows very few restrictions on its exercise, is in complete contrast to the way in which the principle has been interpreted in other jurisdictions. The best example of this contrast is probably the well-known volume of litigation which arose when Peter Wright, a former officer in MI5, decided to publish his memoirs.

These proceedings were first initiated in Australia in December 1985 when the English Attorney General obtained an *ex parte* injunction in a court in New South Wales preventing the publication of Peter Wright's book, *Spycatcher*, on the grounds of breach of Wright's duty of secrecy and of his duty of confidence. However, this injunction was later lifted by the High Court of New South Wales[2] and this decision was affirmed by the New South Wales Court of Appeal,[3] as the information was by then in the public domain. The High Court of Australia unanimously rejected the Attorney General's appeal against the lifting of the injunction on the ground that it was an attempt to enforce a foreign law.[4] It is interesting to note that in coming to its decision, the Court relied on the decision of Kingsmill Moore J in the Irish case of *Buchanan v. McVey*.[5]

In June 1986, the *Guardian* and *Observer* newspapers published an outline of the allegations made by Wright in his book. The Attorney General got further *ex parte* injunctions, this time preventing the publication by the *Guardian* and the Observer of information obtained by Wright in his capacity as a member of the British secret service. The injunctions were subject to certain limited exceptions. For example, information disclosed in open court in Australia or already revealed by Wright on television could be published. In July 1986, the *Sunday Times* published extracts from *Spycatcher* and the Attorney General promptly brought proceedings against it for contempt of court. He argued that the publication by the *Sunday Times* was in breach of the injunctions obtained against the *Guardian* and *Observer*. The action was consolidated with the *Guardian* and *Observer* proceedings.

When three other English newspapers, namely the *Independent*, the *Daily News* and the *Evening Standard*, later published extracts from *Spycatcher*, proceedings were also commenced against them for criminal contempt of court. The Attorney General accepted that publication of the *Spycatcher* extracts by the three newspapers did not constitute a breach of the injunction against the *Guardian* and *Observer* because the three newspapers in question were not restrained from publication by the earlier injunctions. He argued, however, that publication of the extracts constituted a criminal contempt of court because it would frustrate or impede the due administration of justice.

Browne-Wilkinson VC, at first instance, rejected the Attorney General's arguments. He said that to hold the three newspapers in contempt would be contrary to natural justice and it would be an unacceptable extension of the law of contempt to hold a third party in breach of a court order made in his or her absence to which he or she had no opportunity to raise a defence.[6]

The Court of Appeal, however, reversed the decision of Browne-Wilkinson VC and held that the defendants would be guilty of contempt if they published the extracts knowing of the existence of the injunctions against the *Guardian* and the *Observer* because by doing so they would be damaging or destroying the confidentiality which the Court in granting the original injunctions was trying to protect.[7]

This decision represents a large restriction on freedom of expression as it extends the scope of an injunction preventing publication of information to third parties who were not originally envisaged at the time of the granting of the injunction as being within its scope.

The next important date in this calendar of events is July 1987 when *Spycatcher* was published in the US and so became widely available. By this stage the appeals against the granting of the interlocutory injunctions against the *Guardian* and the *Observer* had reached the House of Lords which upheld their continuation pending full trial of the action.[8]

The newspapers in their appeal argued that as *Spycatcher* was by then widely available in the UK there was no longer any confidential information to be preserved by the continuation of the injunctions. Lord Bridge, in his dissenting judgment, agreed.[9] He said that the maintenance of the injunctions in such circumstances would be ridiculous as they related to matters of undoubted public interest which the rest of the world now knew about and could discuss freely. He added that freedom of speech is always the first casualty under a totalitarian regime and the attempt by the Attorney General to insulate the British public from information which was freely available elsewhere would be a significant step down that road.

Lord Oliver also agreed with the newspapers' argument. He said that while the decision to grant the injunctions was correct at the time, the circumstances were now different as the information which the injunctions had sought to protect was now in the public domain. He added that the liberty of the press is essential to the nature of a free State and, although it must be restricted in cases of national security, national emergency and to preserve confidentiality, in this case the Court was being asked to restrict the liberty of the press to protect a confidentiality which had already been lost.[10]

The majority of the House of Lords, however, held that the injunctions should continue pending a full trial of the matter despite the fact that much of the information in the book was widely available. The three judges, namely Lords Brandon, Ackner and Templeman, took the view that if the injunctions were lifted before a full trial, the newspapers would immediately publish extracts from the book, thereby rendering a full trial futile and damages in such circumstances would not be an adequate remedy for the Attorney General. If, however, the injunctions were kept in place and the newspapers won the final trial and then published the extracts they would not have suffered any loss but would have merely been delayed in their publication. As Lord Ackner said, "the cause of free speech will not have suffered".[11]

In coming to their decision, the majority referred to Article 10 of the European Convention on Human Rights which upholds the right of free speech. However, the reference to Article 10 was not to emphasize the importance of that freedom but to show that Article 10(2) expressly recognizes that there may be exceptions to it.

This reference to the Convention to justify restrictions on free speech epitomises the approach of the English courts to freedom of expression. In contrast to the US approach which begins with the basic principle of freedom of expression and is very reluctant to allow any exceptions to that principle, the English courts are extremely willing to allow exceptions, especially in the area of national security.

When the full trial of the case eventually reached the House of Lords in November 1987, their Lordships finally recognized that the injunctions against the newspapers should be lifted.[12] The decision was based, however, not on any considerations of free speech, but on the ground that because *Spycatcher* was by then widely available in the UK, there was no justification for keeping the injunctions in force. Yet again this highlights the extremely low priority which is given by the English courts to the principle of freedom of expression.

The final chapter in this volume of litigation was the decision of the European Court of Human Rights in November 1991. Following the decision of the House of Lords upholding the continuation of the injunctions pending a full trial, the newspapers had brought an application to Strasbourg on the basis of Article 10 of the Convention. The Attorney General argued that the injunctions came within the permissible exceptions specified in Article 10(2) as being "necessary in the interests of national security".

The European Court held that the injunctions had been justifiable when they were first imposed in July 1986 because *Spycatcher* was not generally available at that time, but following its publication in the US in July 1987, the book became widely available. Therefore, the confidentiality which the injunctions were supposed to preserve was destroyed and their subsequent interference with the right of the press to publish was unjustifiable.[13]

The six-year-long saga of litigation which arose from Peter Wright's decision to publish his memoirs provides an interesting insight into the order of importance which the UK authorities place on the fundamental civil liberty of freedom of expression, especially where it comes into conflict with any aspect of national security. It also highlights the contrasting approach adopted by the

European Court of Human Rights, which is extremely reluctant to allow any restrictions on what it regards as a very important fundamental principle but recognizes that some restrictions on that freedom must be permitted, but only in very limited circumstances, for example, to protect national security.

In Ireland, unfortunately, despite the explicit protection of freedom of speech in the Irish Constitution, the approach of the Irish authorities would appear to favour that of the English courts, rather than that of the European Court or the US courts. This similarity of approach is, no doubt, influenced by the fact that the principal Irish statute on matters of national security is the Official Secrets Act, 1963, which is broadly based on the UK Official Secrets Act, 1911, the statute which was at issue in *Spycatcher*. However, there has been little litigation in Ireland for many years in this area and it is to be hoped that if a case does arise in the future, the Irish courts will prefer the more reasonable approach of the US courts and of the European Court and will be extremely reluctant to interfere with the right of freedom of expression to which every individual is entitled.

BARBARA MAGUIRE

6.2 Freedom of Expression

HENRY G. SCHERMERS

One of the most fundamental human rights is the freedom of thought and conscience. For living one's own life and for developing one's own personality one must be free to think whatever one wants to think. In practice, interference with the freedom of thought is extremely difficult. As one can never know for sure what other people think one cannot control their freedom to do so. Nevertheless, history contains numerous examples of efforts to influence the thinking of people. Indoctrination and brain-washing are just a few examples. Efforts to try to influence other people's thinking are a normal part of inter-human relations. They become objectionable only when persons are compelled to undergo indoctrination. Such compulsion is prohibited by Article 9 of the European Convention of Human Rights (ECHR), of 4 November 1950, which begins with the words: "Everyone has the right to freedom of thought, conscience and religion" and by Article 19(1) of the International Covenant on Civil and Political Rights (ICCPR), of 19 December 1966, which provides: "Everyone shall have the right to hold opinions without interference". Both treaties devote an entire article to the freedom of thought. Article 9 of the ECHR also regulates the freedom to manifest one's religion or beliefs and Article 19 of the ICCPR covers freedom of expression. Both articles permit exceptions when they are necessary and provided for by law, but these exceptions do not cover the freedom of thought and conscience. These freedoms may not be interfered with under any circumstances. Fortunately, brain-washing and compulsory subjection to indoctrination do not occur in present day Europe. Complaints of serious violations of the freedom of thought or conscience have not been brought before the European Commission of Human Rights.

Next to the right to hold opinions is the right to express these opinions and to communicate them to others. These rights are incorporated in Article 10 of the ECHR which provides:

> 1   Everyone has the right to freedom of expression. This right shall include freedom to hold opinions and to receive and impart information and ideas without interference by public authority and regardless of frontiers. This article shall not prevent States from requiring the licensing of broadcasting, television or cinema enterprises.

> 2   The exercise of these freedoms, since it carries with it duties and responsibilities, may be subject to such formalities, conditions, restrictions or penalties as are prescribed by law and are necessary in a democratic society, in the interests of national security, territorial integrity or public safety, for the prevention of disorder or crime, for the protection of health or morals, for the protection of the reputation or rights of others, for preventing the disclosure of information received in confidence, or for maintaining the authority and impartiality of the judiciary.

Article 19 (2) and (3) of the ICCPR provides:

> 2   Everyone shall have the right to freedom of expression; this right shall include freedom to seek, receive and impart information and ideas of all kinds, regardless of frontiers, either orally, in writing or in print, in the form of art, or through any other media of his choice.

> 3   The exercise of the rights provided for in paragraph 2 of this article carries with it special duties and responsibilities. It may therefore be subject to certain restrictions, but these shall only be such as are provided by law and are necessary:

> (a) for respect of the rights or reputations of others;

> (b) for the protection of national security or of public order (*ordre publique*), or for the public health or morals.

The possibility of exceptions, of course, raises the risk of undermining the human right. Exceptions, therefore, should be restrictively interpreted. The European Court of Human Rights has accepted that the words "prescribed by law" are not necessarily restricted to statute law. The expression also covers unwritten law provided that this law is adequately accessible and formulated with sufficient precision to enable the citizen to regulate his or her conduct.[1] Next, the measures restricting the freedom of expression must be taken for one of the purposes enumerated in Article 10(2). It is not enough, however, that they serve one of these purposes; they must also be "necessary in a democratic society". The European Court has held that "necessary" is not synonymous with "indispensable"; neither has it the flexibility of such expressions as "admissible", "ordinary", "useful", "reasonable", or "desirable". According to the Court it requires a "pressing social need".[2] According to the Court Article 10(2) leaves to the Contracting States a considerable margin of appreciation. National authorities are best equipped to decide what would be necessary in their societies. Nonetheless, the Court will give the final ruling on the question whether a restriction is reconcilable with the freedom of expression as protected by Article 10.

The question arises whether the extent of the margin of appreciation should be relative to the kind of expression involved. Roughly we may distinguish five different methods of expression:

(a) Sometimes people want to get things off their minds by telling them to others, or by seeking advice from others. It is not their wish to spread their opinion widely but they feel a need to express it to one or more other people. One could call this "private expression".

(b) Sometimes people have ideas which they want to disseminate to as large a public as possible because they consider that other people may have benefit from these ideas. This could be called "public expression".

(c) The imparting of information and ideas may be one's business, in which case it could be called "professional expression". Two sorts of occupation immediately come to mind: the journalist and the advertiser. The aims of the two are different, but the borderline between them is not always stark. Freedom of the press has been recognized as one of the most fundamental achievements of European society; the freedom to advertise is more limited.

(d) Freedom of expression should also include a freedom not to express oneself, the freedom to keep silent (non-expression).

(e) Apart from words one can also use acts to express ideas. In particular, demonstrations may clearly indicate the opinion of people.

PRIVATE EXPRESSION

Freedom to express oneself in private is virtually unlimited. Of the restrictions enumerated in Article 10(2) of the ECHR and in Article 19(3) of the ICCPR only the interests of national security (the keeping of State secrets) and the rights and reputations of others are of practical importance. An action for libel in respect of an expression in a private conversation is rather unlikely as it would cause more damage to the insulted person than it would help him or her. To my knowledge, no complaints in respect of this kind of private expression have ever been brought. Mr Muller had created paintings which reflected a conception of sexuality that was at odds with the currently prevailing social morality. He was convicted by the Swiss courts and his conviction was upheld by the European Court of Human Rights,[3] but in neither case by reason of the fact that he had expressed himself in this way but rather for the reason that he had exhibited his paintings in public. The drawing of dirty pictures for one's own satisfaction cannot been seen as endangering existing morals.

One may submit that private expression needs the highest degree of protection. Only in cases of extreme necessity should governments be permitted to interfere.

PUBLIC EXPRESSION

Sometimes individuals hold opinions which they consider of importance to others and which they want to spread to other people either in writing or by audio, or audio-visual, means. Provided the information or opinion concerned is not libellous or does not betray State secrets, governments will normally not object to the spread of such information. In other cases, the main problem will be to find a means of communication for their opinions. Written articles require a publisher. Commercial publishers will normally only spread information when they expect sufficient interest for selling the information with profit. Journals will use their own criteria for selecting the opinions which they publish. Authors with extreme ideas may find it difficult to find an opportunity for publication. The question then arises to what extent the freedom of information entails obligations for others to incorporate the information offered in newspapers or journals. As a rule such an obligation does not exist. The only exception to this rule is that newspapers can be compelled to publish rectifications to previous articles which proved to be wrong and to publish replies of affected persons to previously published articles.

The best means to spread one's opinions is via broadcasting. When the ECHR was drafted, channels for broadcasting were scarce. In Article 10, a sentence has been added providing that "this Article shall not prevent States from requiring the licensing of broadcasting, television or cinema enterprises". This sentence was intended to allow for the possibility of a fair distribution of available frequencies, but it also reflected a political concern on the part of several States.[4]

Since 1950, possibilities for radio communication have increased considerably so as to diminish the necessity of invoking this additional sentence. The question remains, however, as to whether States may require licensing in order to ban undesirable opinions from the media.

In the *Groppera Radio* case, the European Court of Human Rights held that the object and purpose of the above quoted sentence and the scope of its application must be considered in the context of the Article as a whole and in particular in relation to the requirements of paragraph 2. The quoted sentence amounts to an exception to the principle set forth in the first and second sentences of the Article and is of a limited scope. Its purpose is mainly technical, aiming at an orderly control of broadcasting.[5] If governments consider it necessary to ban undesirable opinions from the media, they should resort to paragraph 2 of the Article, and the conditions of that paragraph should be fulfilled.

The ICCPR, which was drafted some fifteen years later does not contain a corresponding provision to the above-quoted sentence of Article 10 of the ECHR. A similar sentence was proposed but rejected for fear of abuse and on the ground that generally a licence could be required for the protection of public order which permits exceptions to the freedom of information under Article 19(3) of the Covenant.

In the *Groppera Radio* case the question was also raised to what extent light music and commercials are covered by the notion "information" of which the imparting should be protected. The Court held that both broadcasting of programmes over the air and cable re-transmission of such programmes are covered by the right enshrined in the first two sentences of Article 10(1) without there being any need to make distinctions according to the content of the programmes. It follows that light music should be seen as a means of expression, protected under the Convention.

PROFESSIONAL EXPRESSION

The free press: The most important institution entrusted with the task of imparting information and ideas is the press. In neither the ECHR nor the ICCPR is the freedom of the press expressly mentioned, but under both treaties it forms part of the freedom of information. In particular, under the ECHR the freedom of the press has been developed as the most important element of the freedom of expression. The European Court of Human Rights considered in its *Lingens* judgment[6] that the fact that freedom of expression constitutes one of the essential foundations of a democratic society is of particular importance as far as the press is concerned:

> Whilst the press must not overstep the bounds set, *inter alia*, for the "protection of the reputation of others", it is nevertheless incumbent on it to impart information and ideas on political issues just as on those in other areas of public interest. Not only does the press have the task of imparting such information and ideas: the public also has a right to receive them.[7]

The Vienna Court of Appeal had expressed the opinion that the task of the press was to impart factual information and that the conclusion whether the facts imparted constituted reprehensible conduct or not had to be left primarily to the reader. The European Court expressly rejected this view.

In the same *Lingens Case*, the European Court held that

> freedom of the press furthermore affords the public one of the best means of discovering and forming an opinion of the ideas and attitudes of political leaders. More generally, freedom of political debate is at the very core of the concept of a democratic society which prevails throughout the Convention.[8]

Normally, a free press acts as a watchdog against the authorities. It can bring mistakes and failures into the open and thus stimulate public debate on them. Until recently, the newspapers were the important voices of the press. Increasingly, television has taken over this role and, with it, a new problem with respect to the freedom of the press comes to the foreground. Modern techniques for imparting information are expensive and, therefore, available to a limited number of rather large companies. To compete with television, press agencies merge and the number of newspapers is reduced. Few television companies are able to collect reliable information from all over the world. Yet they attract the viewers. Increasingly, the spread of information comes into the hands of a relatively small number of people. Gradually, these people obtain a position which enables them to steer public opinion and thus to influence government policy. Undoubtedly, the free press can also manipulate public opinion. By selecting issues, reporting, or not reporting, on particular facts, criticism or support for a government can be provoked. That is why totalitarian regimes always try to control the press. If a news agency, or a conglomerate of news agencies, abuses a position of power by spreading false information or by instigating hatred against particular people, the question arises whether governments should have a right, or even an obligation, to intervene. The obnoxious effect of press campaigns was demonstrated in Nazi Germany where a systematic press campaign incited the population against the Jewish minority to an extent which provoked "the Crystal Night". In that case, the press campaign was instigated by a government. But one could imagine that a powerful independent press could obtain the same result. In such a case international law may oblige a government to intervene. Article 4(a) of the International Convention of the Elimination of All Forms of Racial Discrimination, 1965, obliges the States parties to declare as offences punishable by law, all dissemination of ideas based on racial superiority or hatred, incitement to racial discrimination, as well as all acts of violence or incitement to such acts against any race or group of persons of another colour or ethnic origin, and also the provision of any assistance to racist activities, including the financing thereof. Under public international law incitement to aggression is a criminal act which governments must prosecute and punish.

Article 10 of the ECHR enables governments to interfere with the freedom of the press, on the condition that such interference is provided for by law and necessary in a democratic society. It would go too far, therefore, to state that any State interference with the press is prohibited. One should be extremely careful, however. Only specific activities of the press which have been previously prohibited by law should be censured by the government. For example, in autumn 1991, the democratically elected Government of Lithuania replaced the general editors of some newspapers who were connected to the previous regime. It was considered vital for the democratic development of the country that the main newspapers be placed in the charge of people loyal to the majority of the electorate. However understandable such a position may be, it infringes the principle of the free press. That principle entails that anybody, however objectionable his or her ideas may be, should have the right to edit a newspaper and that it is the responsibility of the reader to decide which newspaper he or she wants to buy. Is this correct? Are the readers always able to identify hidden propaganda, false statements, or unjustifiable influence? Indeed, a real risk exists of the press manipulating the population. The remedy against this risk should not be found in government control, however, but in the possibility of competing press. Should a newspaper unjustifiably influence its readership, then other newspapers should denounce this. Still, this may not work if the public is insufficiently critical. It may be doubted whether the Western European system of free press and press control can also function in regions with considerably lower level of education. A good functioning of the free press requires a sufficiently educated and sufficiently critical readership.

In practice, not everybody holding ideas can start a free press in order to express them. Normally, one would have to try to find members of the existing press willing to publish one's ideas. For the purpose of offering persons sufficient room to get their ideas published, as well as for the purpose of limiting the risk of indoctrination by a particular newspaper, it is of great importance that in each linguistic community a sufficient number of newspapers is available. Merging newspapers will reduce costs. The costs involved will usually prevent easy establishment of a new newspaper. Therefore, readers are not always able to change to another journal whenever they disagree with the approach of a newspaper. It is a general responsibility of society to ensure that the number of newspapers is not so reduced as to leave insufficient choice to the readership. The problem of limited choice is even worse with respect to expression via television. Generally speaking, broadcasting requires a government licence which can enable governments to restrict possibilities for opposition parties. Modern developments which increasingly permit broadcasting from foreign countries decreases the risk, but, at the same time, demonstrate the influence of large television companies (such as CNN). Again, there is a public responsibility to guarantee sufficient diversity in television.

As good press offices are expensive, most developing countries have little means of promoting their own press. The news about most developing countries is made and spread by news agencies from the developed world. Some developing countries complain that the news about them, based on Western standards, is unnecessarily negative. They feel victim to some kind of propaganda against which they have no defence. In reality, objective information is difficult to obtain. Internationally, as well as within some national communities, there is pressure for some kind of control over the press. In principle, control other than control by the readership itself should be considered wrong, however. Nevertheless, it may be worthwhile to consider offering financial support to the large readership which is unable to express its preference by buying particular newspapers or by contributing to particular television companies.

Some English newspapers expressed concern about the high damages awarded against newspapers following the dissemination of misleading information. The risk of being condemned to pay extremely high damages in case of mistakes might make newspapers reluctant to spread any information of which the sources are not one hundred percent reliable. This might lead to a serious restriction on the freedom of information. It is difficult to establish whether their concern has moved British judges to restrict this kind of damages.

Advertisements: Any information can be spread through advertisements in newspapers or on radio or television. Through such advertisements one can impart information or ideas of a political or religious character and one can also try to persuade readers to buy a particular product. It has sometimes been contended that commercial advertizing is of a character different from the spreading of information but both the European Commission of Human Rights[9] and the European Court of Human Rights[10] have accepted that commercial advertizing cannot be excluded from the scope of Article 10. As advertizing may be a useful means of spreading ideas the exclusion of advertizing from the freedom of information would indeed be wrong. One cannot prohibit a person to hold the opinion that, for example, smoking is good for your health and that a particular kind of cigarette is particularly wholesome. The fact that information is untrue cannot in itself be a sufficient ground to prohibit its imparting. Article 10(2) of the Convention permits a limitation or prohibition on the dissemination of information if this is prescribed by law and necessary in a democratic society *inter alia*, in the interest of public safety, for the protection of health or morals or for the protection of the reputation or rights of others. Article 19 of the Covenant contains a similar provision. This opens sufficient possibility for government intervention against illegal advertizing.

NON-EXPRESSION

The European Court of Human Rights decided that the right to form and to join trade unions, guaranteed in Article 11 of the Convention, includes the right not to be compelled to join a trade union.[11] The question arises whether Article 10 would imply, on the same grounds, a right to refuse to impart information. The European Court of Human Rights has held, *obiter*, that the refusal to give evidence does not come within the ambit of Article 10.[12] Apparently, the Court considered that the obligation to give evidence is covered either by Article 8 or by Article 6. It may be doubted, however, whether this is correct. Giving evidence in a court case is also a way of expressing one's opinion and it should therefore, like all expression of opinion, be covered by Article 10. An obligation to impart information could also exist elsewhere. Police officers may require people to explain or to reveal things, tax and customs authorities may require all sorts of information, etc. I see no reason why the right to withhold information should not be protected equally as the right to impart information. In both cases the government may intervene only if the requirements of Article 10(2) are fulfilled. The obligation to testify in court will usually be necessary in a democratic society for the prevention of disorder or crime, for the protection of the rights of others or for maintaining the authority and impartiality of the judiciary. In case of doubt, however, it should be verified whether the obligation can indeed be supported by one of these grounds.

A special problem arises in States where not merely the sale but, in addition, the purchase of narcotics is a criminal offence. In order to convict drug dealers the testimony of their buyers may be required. Such testimony can be relatively easily obtained when the buyer himself or herself runs no risk, but where it might lead to self-incrimination, a refusal to testify seems likely. Whether such refusal can be justified will then depend on the question whether the obligation to testify is "necessary in a democratic society". In its interpretation of these words, the European Court of Human Rights evaluates whether interference with the freedom of information is proportionate to the interest of the individual in the protection of his rights. Considering the great interest of an individual against self-incrimination, a requirement that an individual testify to the purchase of drugs from a dealer may be disproportionate where such purchase is a criminal offence.

OTHER MEANS OF EXPRESSION

One can express feelings of love to another person in many different ways. According to the European Commission of Human Rights the concept of "expression" in Article 10 does not encompass any notion of the physical expression of feelings in the sense of sexual contact. This will be covered by Article 8.[13]

One can also express sympathy with particular ideas by demonstrating. The European Court of Human Rights has held that the freedom of demonstration is covered by Article 11 of the Convention which is a *lex specialis* in relation to Article 10 (a *lex generalis* in this respect). One can also express an opinion by manifesting one's religion or belief. As such manifestation is expressly mentioned in Article 9, that Article should also be seen as a *lex specialis* in this respect. Article 10 remains applicable, however, for any expression for which no *lex specialis* is available.

CONCLUSION

From the above we may conclude that the freedom of expression is an essential human right in the developed societies of Western Europe. It may be of lesser importance in communities where daily life is a struggle to acquire the basic needs of food and lodging, but it is essential in a community where people feel involved with events taking place outside their own homes. Apart from its important role in informing the general public, the free press has also task in controlling government. By mobilizing public opinion, abuse of power may be curtailed. However, the power to mobilize public opinion may also be subject to abuse. In principle, such abuses should be controlled by the readership, but in extreme cases government interference may be necessary. Such interference must be provided for and carefully defined by law.

6.3 Freedom of Expression and Democracy

KEVIN BOYLE

Freedom of expression is a broad canvas. To sketch in all of it would be an impossibility in the space available and perhaps even if space was unlimited. An alternative is to concentrate on one corner of the canvas and consider a concrete issue, perhaps civil defamation, given the publication of the Law Reform Commission's important report on that subject.[1] I will make mention of that report but I also want to raise some broader concerns and, in particular, the theme of democracy and freedom of expression.

The tendency of most popular and legal discussion of freedom of expression, is to focus on issues of restriction such as defamation, or contempt of court. We perhaps ask too infrequently, what is this right for?

In one sense, of course, the story of freedom of expression has always concerned questions of restriction. In the struggle for the recognition of freedom of speech and of the press in Europe, from the 17th century on, the object was to remove the interference of church and State with what might be said or written. Resistance to the democratic potential of the printing press, and later the popular newspaper, by established authority, was pursued through the use of laws on sedition, obscenity, libel and blasphemy. Once the freedom to speak and to publish was secured, the right came to be seen as a negative liberty, the freedom from arbitrary governmental interference. The legal focus came to rest on the justifiable limits to the right in a democratic society. Although the same grounds of restriction such as defamation, obscenity, and contempt of court are invoked today as in the past, the crucial difference is, or ought to be, that restriction is exercised on the basis of law which has a democratic mandate and within principles that recognize the role of freedom of expression in sustaining a democracy.

The historical background to the emergence of the right to freedom of expression and freedom of press and publication remain important for our understanding of the contemporary case for these rights as special democratic freedoms. So also does an appreciation of the historical circumstances in which the philosophical justifications for the abolition of censorship were first espoused in western thought.[2] Public and professional education including that of journalists and lawyers may be faulted in so far as it has neglected that history. The lawyer's emphasis on the study of limitation, when combined with the particular empirical legal culture we have inherited from the common law, has served to cut off this historical background and to obscure the purposes of a freedom which was not achieved easily.

It is true that in Ireland we have a formal written guarantee of freedom of expression in the Constitution, and although one might like to see a more embracing and less tentative statement of the right, it does at least provide us with the opportunity for reflection on freedom of expression and the press in positive and more theoretical terms.[3] We also have the European Convention on Human Rights (ECHR) and its jurisprudence which is teleological in its approach and has, with some lapses such as the *Purcell* case,[4] examined questions of limitation against a theory of the purposes of freedom of expression in a democratic society.[5]

In work that Marie McGonagle and I have undertaken over the last number of years on press freedom in Ireland we have attempted to widen debate by first calling for a greater "constitutionalizing" of freedom of expression issues. We have argued that media owners and journalists, lawyers and the public should place concerns, such as the law of defamation, within that normative context.[6]

The report from the Law Reform Commission on the civil law of defamation acknowledges that the Commission has been influenced by such calls for a wider approach.[7] It contains an extended critique of the constitutional norms on freedom of expression and the protection of the right to a good name along with a commentary on the relevant jurisprudence of the ECHR. Its key proposals on reform of the law of defamation, such as the removal of the presumption of falsehood, the new defence of reasonable care to a defamation action and new remedies for plaintiffs in addition to damages, represent an important effort to rethink the balance between the constitutional interests involved.

But for a contemporary understanding of freedom of expression as a whole we need to do more. We need to take the constitutional and the international standards to which we are committed and shape a more positive theory of the nature and purpose of freedom of expression, in particular its status as a democratic freedom. We need to revitalize and build on the classic justifications of freedom of expression and freedom of the media to help us interpret their role in the rapidly changing society in which we live.

DEMOCRATIZATION AND THE EUROPEAN CONTEXT

Since the fall of the Berlin Wall in 1989, we have seen the collapse of censorship and a wave of democratization in Eastern Europe and across the south of the world. Western States have longer experience with democracy. That does not mean however, that they have not the possibility of achieving greater democratization or do not need to think through what place freedom of expression and free media have to play in deepening democracy. The definition of democracy which I have in mind here consists of the elements of popular control over collective decision-making, equality for citizens in the exercise of that control and the right of each citizen to participate at all levels of civil society.[8] Such a definition could be said to underpin the Irish Constitution. However, the extent to which democratic forms ensure democratic substance is something we need to address in Ireland. It is equally something which requires attention in the new European possibilities we are entering now that the Treaty on European Union, the Maastricht Treaty, has been adopted by the European Community Member States.[9] In the context of a rising sense of crisis within Western Europe reflected in unemployment and in the growth of intolerance and xenophobia we need to deepen democratic commitment. Freedom of information, the right to freedom of expression and freedom for the greatest diversity of all media, both as values and as institutions, have a crucial role to play in such a strengthening of democratic order in Ireland and throughout the Community.

The impact of Europe is well demonstrated in the current debate in Ireland over the legal regulation of abortion. One of the many important aspects of that controversy has been just how dramatically the European dimension has featured and continues to feature. The intermeshing of the national and European levels of law, politics and public opinion which the controversy has engendered is striking. The Protocol to the Maastricht Treaty, and the involvement of both the European Court of Human Rights and the ECJ over issues concerning information and abortion, vividly reflect the very different environment in cultural, political, legal economic and social terms that Irish people will live in for the future.

GLOBALIZATION

But there is an even wider context of economy, law, politics and opinion which we are coming to appreciate, the global context. The responses to the controversy over the 14-year-old rape victim in *AG v. X and Others*, was for a time a world issue and brought world responses.[10] The extraordinary advances in communication technology are a significant cause of the shrinking of the world and of our understanding of the phenomenon of globalization, or the existence of international society. In the economic and environmental spheres for example, the traditional concept of the nation state, its assumptions of independence and of sovereign control over all aspects of its destiny is largely a thing of the past. We have entered a new reality in which States are interdependent, a new world in which the capacity of the State to control its destiny in an independent way is increasingly limited. To understand that world will require us to think of freedom of expression and information and the processes of global communication in new ways. It will also require us to think about democracy alongside the much discussed concept of a new world order for this new international society. It seems unlikely that we can sustain democracy in the long term in the countries of a European Union or elsewhere without a new international democratic order. From the perspective of freedom of information, that order will require us to address many complex questions about global communications, such as the reality of the concentration of global media power in the developed world. The question of inequalities between North and South in communications is of course a reflection of the larger picture of the economic gulf between the developing and developed world which should be the central concern of any new world order based on human rights and democratic principles.

PLURALISM, TOLERANCE AND DEMOCRACY

In an often quoted phrase from the *Handyside* case which concerned freedom of expression, the European Court of Human Rights spoke of the underlying conditions of democratic society as being characterized by the values of "pluralism, tolerance and broad-mindedness".[11] The Court here reminds us that the struggle for democracy was a struggle against absolutisms. A democratic society based on the consent of all its members cannot be reconciled with an enforced single ideology or single truth whether religious or secular. The history of the struggle for freedom of expression at least four centuries old began with the struggle for freedom of thought and conscience. Freedom of speech is the child of freedom of religion. It is only when it is possible to hold and express religious convictions and opinions, which established religious powers see as heresy or unorthodox, that differences of political and other opinion can emerge without fear of persecution. The struggle for toleration of religious difference is intimately linked to the freedom of the press and expression. Indeed a major historical and contemporary justification for freedom of expression is that it encourages tolerance by revealing the existence of diversity of opinion and overcoming ignorance of each other as citizens and as individuals in a common world.

To ensure that tolerance and pluralism are respected requires both the separation of State and government from civil society and the separation of church from State. The experience of an enforced single vision of truth by secular or religious ideology is not a thing of the past. Censorship and repression in the interests of the Party remain the experience of one fifth of the world's population who are Chinese. And the efforts to implement the Islamic vision of the fusion of State and religious power in such countries as Pakistan, Iran and

Saudi Arabia remind us that denial of freedom of conscience and freedom of opinion and expression on religious grounds is equally a reality for millions of people.

PLURALISM AND TOLERANCE IN IRELAND

In re-examining our own democracy in Ireland the test of acceptance of the values of pluralism, tolerance and broad-mindedness in Ireland should be applied by reference to a European gauge or standard. This important point is something which Professor Schermers identified in his dissenting opinion in the *Open Door* case before the European Commission of Human Rights.[12] In that case, brought by two women's clinics, Open Door Counselling and the Dublin Well Woman Centre, the applicants complained of an injunction imposed by the High Court and upheld by the Supreme Court which prevented them from offering information and non-directive counselling on abortion. The majority of the Commission held that Article 10 of the Convention had been violated but on a technical ground. Professor Schermers, however, held that the denial of the right to impart or to receive information violated Article 10 on substantive grounds, because the injunction did not conform with the European standard of democracy required by that Article:

> Since the second half of the twentieth century the nation States are no longer the only societies in Western Europe. Increasingly States have transferred sovereign powers to common institutions. Next to (or above) the national societies a European society is developing. For deciding whether a specific restriction on freedom of expression is necessary in Europe the European society as a whole should also be taken into account.[13]

In the *Johnston* case,[14] in which the European Court of Human Rights found the Irish constitutional prohibition on divorce compatible with the Convention on the finding that the Convention did not include a right to terminate a marriage, another dissenting opinion was based on the same concern with democratic principle. Judge De Meyer concluded that the prohibition on divorce in Ireland violated the right to freedom of conscience or belief under Article 9 (as well as being a violation of Article 8 and 12). He noted with respect to the constitutional barrier on divorce:

> For so draconian a system to be legitimate it does not suffice that it corresponds to the desire or will of a substantial majority of the population . . . democracy does not simply mean that the views of a majority must

always prevail: a balance must be achieved which ensures the fair and proper treatment of minorities and avoids any abuse of a dominant position.[15]

The challenge that such opinions represent should be placed against the following formulation of the contrary and arguably pervasive view in this country:

A Catholic Country and its government where there is a very considerable Catholic ethos and consensus shouldn't feel it necessary to apologize that its legal system constitutional or statutory reflects Catholic values. Such a legal system may sometimes be represented as offensive to minorities but the rights of a minority are not more sacred than the rights of a majority.[16]

There is little opportunity here to critique that statement made by the Irish Bishops to the New Ireland Forum in 1983. But its assumptions need to be confronted in any debate over democratization in this country. Many would worry about the description of a country as catholic and the compatibility of such a description with a European norm of pluralism. The assumptions implicit in the statement on the rights of religious or other minorities are highly questionable under international and even national standards of human rights. Majoritarianism is not democracy. Majority decision making in a democracy is a compromise where full consensus cannot be reached. Majority opinion or position should not be a vehicle for the expression of power or the insistence on the single truth in the matter of values; the democratic path is to seek where possible the consensus that reflects acknowledgment of diversity of belief or opinion and which recognizes that there are limits on the field of majority decision making in the liberal democratic state.

FREEDOM OF EXPRESSION AND INFORMATION AS A DEMOCRATIC RIGHT

Democracy as a means of government is in part designed to ensure popular control of governmental and collective decision making on an on-going basis. The ideal democracy might be direct decision-making by all citizens but the Greek city state experience is not replicable in modern political systems by reason of their size and by reason of time. Therefore we have evolved the idea of representatives to carry out the democratic wishes of the people. The role of a democratic system is to ensure that such representatives are accountable not only at election times but on a permanent basis to those they represent. At the same time a democratic society can encourage greater participation by its members over a wide field of social and communal activity.

Freedom of expression is clearly a central freedom within such a model. It enables the people to be informed about and to debate ideas. It enables the political parties who in practice emerge to represent the popular will to persuade people about their policies and to oppose each other's policies. The media, newspapers and electronic media, are a critical means to ensure that citizens are informed and in a position to ensure that governmental activity is accountable to them at all times. Greater participation by citizens at all levels of decision-making requires that they be informed or able to inform themselves about public issues.

The major justification for granting freedom of expression a special status is precisely that it performs these democratic functions. It is true that it performs other functions, from education to entertainment, but it is the role in linking citizen to representative and ensuring accountability of administration and government on an on-going basis, which justifies its special character. In this connection media are a partner in the democratic process. Media freedom is not something that belongs or is of concern only to the press; it is a public freedom in which all have an interest. In examining the national and international regulation within which freedom of expression operates these considerations should inform the critique. In particular the public function of media in sustaining and deepening democracy needs to be highlighted.[17] As I have already noted, the beginnings of this kind of thinking is to be found in the Law Reform Commission's Report on Civil Defamation. However the Report still reflects a tendency to consider the media as wholly a private and commercial special interest. Undoubtedly it is the case that newspapers, publishers and broadcasters have to make profits otherwise they would fail. But there is more to the media than simply a business and it is that public function which needs to be fostered and recognized in a society concerned to strengthen democracy.

One subject on which the Law Reform Commission disappoints, in its treatment of the democratic role of the press, concerns its failure to go some way to acknowledging the importance of the role of journalists. The Commission in particular rejects the proposal that journalists can claim a privilege except in clearly exceptional circumstances not to disclose the sources on which their stories are based. Yet it is difficult to see how the media's function as watch dog can be fulfilled in practice without the explicit recognition of this privilege.[18]

The corollary of the acceptance of the role of journalists and the media in a democracy is that the media in turn should be accountable as regards their functions. Arguing for a robust and free media does not mean that one should not also argue for an accountable and responsible media. The two principles are fully compatible in a democratic society, the difficulties lie in the precise models which should be implemented. The challenge is to find principles and procedures of accountability which do not involve the discredited path of enforcing responsibility by censorship. There are possibilities to offer the greatest freedom and independence to the media while ensuring that they account for the exercise of the freedom to the law and to their readerships and audiences. The policy needed is one that which will ensure both locally and internationally a diversity of publicly owned as well as private media and the establishment of a model of regulation that provides for both independence and accountability of all media. Work on such a policy for European conditions in which this country participates is being pursued by the Council of Europe.[19]

CONSTITUTIONAL REFORM

If we are to discuss new models for freedom of expression and media freedom in a democratic context, a beginning could be made in thinking about the recasting of the Irish constitutional protection offered to the right to freedom of expression. While the rights of media are recognized indirectly in the Constitution, it would be an advance if the concept of the freedom and accountability of all media was enshrined in the Constitution, including an acknowledgement of the democratic mission of free media. Alongside such a reformulation the need to guarantee, at the level of the Constitution, the general freedom of information could be considered. The Law Reform Commission in its recent series of studies on freedom of expression identified the topic of official secrecy as requiring review. This is a welcome proposal, but the legal scrutiny of the Official Secrets Act, 1963, should take place alongside a government commitment to legislate for the public's right to have access to official information and the government acceptance of the duty to promote openness in public administration. No other single policy would contribute more to the enhancing of democracy in Ireland. The concept of official secrecy is a pre-democratic notion we have picked up from our neighbours in Britain. It should be abolished. The unauthorized release of information held by government should be a specific and narrowly drawn offence of breach of trust and subject to a defence of public interest.

The Law Reform Commission has also been considering the subject of contempt of court.[20] While we must await the publication of its proposals it can perhaps be predicted that it will not propose that the concept should be abolished. Yet there is a strong case to be made that this body of common law rules should be consigned to the pre-democratic history which formed it. The alternative approach as far as citizens and the media are concerned is one which might legislate for specific offences of impeding justice in particular circumstances. The concept of contempt of judges and justice sits uneasily with the democratic principles of this state.

Alongside these suggestions for reform might be added the explicit protection in the Constitution of a right to privacy or private life. Privacy is vulnerable in a society with free media although it requires protection equally from other sources of private power and from government. As the Law Reform Commission noted, however, it is inadequate to consider the right to protection of privacy as an aspect of the law of defamation.[21] It requires independent treatment and, as suggested here, in the longer term explicit constitutional and thereafter legislative protection.

CONCLUSION

In conclusion I can repeat my opening remark that the subject of freedom of expression is a broad canvass. I can repeat too, my belief that in the extraordinary phase of change we are going through with the changing significance of territorial boundaries and the need to rethink the conceptual systems we have built on them, a process signified most obviously by the nature of global communications, there is a need to attempt to paint on the whole canvas.

If the trend towards global democratization is to have its effects here, we need to begin to examine our own democracy and its institutions, including media, afresh. In particular and with reference to current controversies we need to debate the extent to which those preconditions of a healthy democracy, pluralism, and tolerance as defined by European standards are present in this Republic.

6.4 Speech in a Cold Climate: The "Chilling Effect" of the Contempt Jurisdiction

EOIN O'DELL

The essays in this volume illustrate the importance of the mechanisms at a European level for the protection of human rights. However, very often, in this type of context, "Europe" is regarded as a "brooding omni-presence in the sky",[1] a vague external presence of little importance. As a result, the direct relevance of the principles contained in documents such as the European Convention on Human Rights is often missed in Irish domestic matters. To illustrate the practical interface between the Convention and Irish law, this paper will examine a now almost forgotten aspect of a recent controversy, and in analysing the implications for the right to freedom of expression, seek to illustrate the direct relevance of the Convention, and especially of Article 10, for Irish law.

THE CONTROVERSY

Elsewhere in this chapter, Kevin Boyle proposes a definition of democracy as popular control and suggested that there is room for debate on democracy in Ireland.[2] Perhaps such debate has already begun as a result of the controversy which began on Monday and Tuesday, 10 and 11 February 1992, when the High Court heard an action *in camera* in which the Attorney General sought injunctions the effect of which would have been to prevent the respondent from leaving the jurisdiction to obtain an abortion. On 11 February, Costello J reserved judgment. The first rumours of this action had begun to circulate the previous weekend, and on the morning of Tuesday 11 February, the *Irish Times* printed a short article on the front page, recording the existence of the action. Public interest quickened, and it became a matter of public and political comment. Against this background, on Thursday, 13 February 1992, the Attorney General issued a statement in which he stated that "it would be in contempt of court and contrary to the intention of the court that *any public discussion of the facts or issues* should take place. The publicity and public controversy so far given to the matter must be a source of great distress to the parties and should cease *forthwith*" (emphasis added). Of course, the statement had little effect, and the case dominated the media for a month, whilst the issues led to three referenda the following November. Judgment was given by the High Court on 17 February 1992, granting the injunctions, but the appeal was allowed by the Supreme Court on 26 February 1992, and the injunctions were discharged.[3] It is intended to concentrate here, not on the judgments in the case itself,[4] but on the effect of the Attorney General's statement. The enquiry is as to whether such a draconian prohibition not only on discussion of the facts of the case but also of the issues it raised is justified on any interpretation of the common law of contempt.

The full text of his statement, which may now safely be consigned to a footnote in history, is as follows:

> The Attorney General is concerned by the fact that publicity is being given to a case which was heard in the High Court earlier this week and in which judgment is pending.

The judge in the case ruled that the proceedings be held *in camera*. Such an order would only be made in order to protect the interests of the parties and to ensure that the highest standards of justice were adhered to.

Because of the existence of such an order, it would be in contempt of court and contrary to the intention of the court that any public discussion of the facts or issues should take place.

The publicity and public controversy so far given to the matter must be a source of great distress to the parties and should cease forthwith.

No doubt when the Judge is delivering judgment he will (while protecting the identity of the parties) set out the essential facts and issues in the case and the principles of law which will govern his decision.

What is needed now pending judgment is respect for the order of the court and consideration for the those who are personally affected by these proceedings.

In this matter, the Attorney General is acting in the discharge of his independent and non-governmental duties under the Constitution in accordance with the principle laid down by the Supreme Court in cases of this kind.[5]

The width of this statement goes to the very heart of the fundamental position of the "the free press" in a democratic society analysed by Henry Schermers in his contribution to this chapter.[6] As all three of the other papers in this chapter make clear, the right to free speech is inextricably bound up with the democratic process. This truth, recognized early in this century in the US in *Whitney v. California*,[7] formed a central plank in the reasoning both of the US Supreme Court in the seminal defamation case of *New York Times v. Sullivan*[8] and of the European Court of Human Rights in the analogous[9] *Lingens v. Austria*.[10] In *Sullivan*, the Court was concerned that the common law defamation rule at issue would have the effect of chilling political debate. The Court has also condemned the equivalent chilling effect on political speech of prior restraint contempt applications.[11] Undoubtedly, the Attorney General's statement was intended to have a similar chilling effect. The aim of this paper is to consider the legal justifications for this position.

LEGAL JUSTIFICATION FOR THE PROHIBITION?

The tone of this statement is not a little worrying. It must be recognized that the Attorney General does have the competence to issue statements of this kind. The Supreme Court in the case in question accepted that there are circumstances in which the Attorney General feels under a duty to act where consequently he has no discretion and must therefore act. The issuing of this statement seemed to the Attorney General to be such a case. The real worry lies in the assumptions it reflects as to the content of the rules of common law on contempt. The most disturbing aspect is the breath-taking width of the ambit of disallowed comment. He said: "Because of the existence of such an order, [that is an *in camera* order] it would be in contempt of court and contrary to the intention of the court that any public discussion of the facts or issues should take place".

This discloses two issues, one in respect of the special considerations which arise because the case was heard *in camera*, the second in respect of the law of contempt by publications in general, that is, the *sub judice* rule.

IN CAMERA

It would seem that the existence of an order directing the hearing of a case *in camera* does not *ispso facto* render *all* discussion of the case in question a contempt of court. Certainly, the fact that the hearing is *in camera does* impose *some* reporting restrictions. However, it does not drape a blanket of silence over the entire proceedings. The Constitution, which in Article 34.1 requires, in general, that "justice shall be administered in public" does recognize in the same Article that there may be "special and limited circumstances" in which this will not necessarily occur. But the Constitution also guarantees the right to freedom of expression in Article 40.6.1.(i). Where two Constitutional rights come into conflict, the Supreme Court has held that the doctrine of harmonious interpretation requires that this conflict be resolved in the manner which least restricts both rights.[12] Thus, given that the circumstances in which an *in camera* order may be made are "special and limited", it is only to the extent that these special and limited circumstances justify the *in camera* order that the right to freedom of expression will legitimately be curtailed. As a result, it is legitimate to curb publication of information which would breach the necessary privacy of the *in camera* proceedings. For example, the publication of the identity of the parties would constitute contempt of a lawful order of the Court, (in much the same way as an action contravening the terms of, for example, an injunction would constitute contempt). Such restrictions on comment are justified on the basis of the need to preserve the privacy and the secrecy of identity of the parties involved. But any further restrictions which are not necessary to subserve the rationale behind the *in camera* order will not be justified. Consequently, the existence of an *in camera* order does not of itself render it "in contempt of court . . . that any public discussion of the facts or issues should take place".

SUB JUDICE

The fact that the hearing is *in camera* means that certain comment is curtailed. However, the fact that there is a hearing at all means that the rules of *sub judice* contempt apply here as they do to any case. The strictest version of the *sub judice* test at common law is to be found in the House of Lords decision in *AG. v. Times Newspapers*.[13] Traditionally, publication which tends to create a substantial risk of prejudice to a pending trial is a *sub judice* contempt. In *Times*, the publication at issue was a discussion in the *Sunday Times* of the merits of a negligence action pending, though dormant, against Distillers, the makers of Thalidomide, a drug which had caused birth deformities in children whose mothers had taken it during pregnancy. Three law lords, Lords Cross, Morris and Reid, held that the article would lead to public prejudgment of the ultimate issues involved, since it would lead to disrespect for the law and to trial by newspaper, thus usurping the authority of the judiciary: the "prejudgment principle". The two other law lords, Lords Diplock and Simon, held that such a risk of prejudice is made out where the publication tends to put pressure on the parties to the action, and in so far as the article would pressure Distillers to settle the action to the advantage of the plaintiffs, it constituted contempt: "the pressure principle". Thus the House of Lords, unanimously, but for different reasons, were of the opinion that the article constituted contempt, and thus granted the Attorney General an injunction restraining its publication. This "prior restraint" stands in stark contrast to the US position in the *Pentagon Papers* case[14] where the Supreme Court proceeded from a "strong presumption" against the constitutionality of a prior restraint.

Leaving aside the subsequent developments in the law which will be dealt with later in this paper, if the Attorney General's view of contempt is accurate, then his prohibition on "any public discussion of the facts or issues" would have to be justified on at least one of the two tests in *Times*. However, if even this, the strictest common law statement of the *sub judice* principle, would not prevent such publication, then the Attorney General's opinion must have been overbroad. Thus, the question is whether either the "pressure principle" or the "prejudgment principle" would prevent such discussion.

Taking the "pressure principle" first, it is very difficult to see how discussion is going to influence a judge sitting alone, as in this case. It has been held that "professional judges are sufficiently well equipped by their professional training to be on their guard against allowing any such matter as this to influence them in deciding the case".[15] Indeed this was accepted by the House of Lords in *Times*.[16] Carroll J in *Weeland v. RTE*[17] was of the same opinion, as was Denham J in *Wong v. Minister for Defence*.[18] Thus, O'Higgins CJ in *Cullen v. Tobin*,[19] citing the importance of the right to freedom of expression, declined to hold in contempt an article which had appeared between conviction and appeal of an accused, arguing that it could "not be suggested that, in considering such questions, publication of this or any number of articles in any number of periodicals would have the slightest effect on the objective consideration of legal arguments". There, it was a case in which the facts were not in issue, and, as here, at the time the statement was issued the Court was considering the legal arguments. Analogically with O'Higgins C J in *Cullen v. Tobin*, it may be said that here, the pressure principle is not satisfied. Indeed, were it otherwise, the *Irish Times*, the pages of which became a forum for informed legal debate between the High Court decision and the Supreme Court appeal, would have been in contempt every day for a month, as would those lawyers, journalists and others who actually wrote the articles.

As to the "prejudgment" principle, it is even more difficult to see how it is satisfied. There were no facts to prejudge. Thus, the principle is not apt in this case.

As a result it will be seen that the Attorney General's prohibition on the "discussion of the facts or issues" arising out of *Attorney General v. X* is much too broad even on the strictest interpretation of the law (*Times*). Certainly, publication of some facts may be restrained by virtue of the *in camera* order. However, on neither the pressure nor the prejudgment principle is there a risk of prejudice to the trial sufficient to justify a restriction on the discussion of the facts and issues beyond that made necessary by the *in camera* order. Neither principle justifies the complete prohibition on "any public discussion of the facts or issues" sought by the Attorney General.

However, it must be noted that *Times* is probably not good law in Ireland anyway. Having lost in the House of Lords, *The Sunday Times* took the by now familiar long road to Strasbourg, where the European Court of Human Rights held that the restriction which the Attorney General's injunction imposed on the right to freedom of expression protected by Article 10(1) of the European Convention was disproportionate and thus not necessary in a democratic society for the protection of the authority of the judiciary: *Sunday Times v. UK (No. 1)*.[20] This decision has recently been followed in the Irish High Court by O'Hanlon J in *Desmond v. Glackin*.[21] As a result, the influence of the European Convention on the above analysis must be considered.

THE EUROPEAN CONVENTION ON HUMAN RIGHTS

In *Desmond*, the first defendant, Mr Glackin, was conducting a public inquiry into the business affairs of the plaintiff, Mr Desmond. Mr Desmond had taken legal action to restrain this inquiry, and the Minister for Industry and Commerce, the second defendant, made certain comments about this action in the course of a radio interview. In considering whether these comments consti-tuted contempt, O'Hanlon J recognized the importance of the decisions in *Times* both in the House of Lords and in the European Court of Human Rights.[22] However, he felt that the speeches in the House of Lords "tend to suggest that a new rule is being formulated rather than a statement of the existing law", so he looked to the ECHR for guidance. Drawing a parallel between the guarantee of freedom of expression in the Irish Constitution (Article 40.6.1) and the Convention (Article 10), he was of the opinion that since "the law of contempt of court is based . . . on public policy I think it is legitimate to assume that our public policy is in accord with the Convention or at least that the provision of the Convention can be considered when determining issues of public policy".[23] In the event, therefore, he held that the comments, although "ill advised" and "injudicious and indiscreet",[24] did not constitute contempt.

As a result of *Desmond* it will be seen that *Times* is almost certainly not good law in Ireland and instead that the approach under the ECHR is to be preferred. If the Attorney General's statement, which is the focus of the analysis here, does not satisfy the terms of the very broad test of contempt in *Times*, it is unlikely to satisfy any narrower test required by the European Convention. As Schermers has already outlined, a restriction on speech must be proportionate to the legitimate end pursued if it is to be necessary in a democratic society and thus be a justified restriction.[25] These legitimate ends are itemized in Article 10(2) of the Convention, the relevant one here being the maintenance "of the authority and impartiality of the judiciary". In *Sunday Times (No. 1)*, as we have already seen, the restriction on balanced reporting of the Thalidomide tragedy was dispropor-tionate. This formula was also considered in three later cases *Weber v. Switzer-land*,[26] *Barfod v. Denmark*,[27] and *Oberschlick v. Austria*.[28] This formulation was added at the drafting stage at the instigation of the United Kingdom expressly to cover the common law concept of contempt. It is therefore strange, to say the least, to observe its use in an attempt to justify restrictions on speech in non-common law countries such as Switzerland, Denmark and Austria.

Of the post-*Sunday Times* cases, the most directly relevant here is *Weber*. Mr Weber had instituted proceedings in (criminal) defamation against a news-paper which had criticized his nature-conservation operation, and held a press conference to announce this. As is the continental fashion, the criminal investi-gation was conducted by an investigating judge, who repeatedly requested certain information and documents from Weber. The criminal proceedings, which were confidential, failed. Weber lodged a complaint against the investi-gating judge, and held another press conference where he discussed both the failed defamation proceedings and his action against the judge, during which he denounced "the plot hatched against [him] by the [Canton of] Vaud authorities in order to intimidate him". For these comments he was committed for trial.

The European Court of Human Rights held that the penalty on this speech was not "necessary" since the information was largely already public (in this regard prefiguring its later *Spycatcher*[29] judgment). Furthermore, the statements did not constitute "an attempt to bring pressure to bear on the investigating judge and [thereby be] prejudicial to the proper conduct of the investigation [since] by that time the investigation was practically complete . . . It was accordingly not necessary to impose a penalty on the applicant from this point of view".

If restrictions on speech in a case such as this such are not justifiable, how much more unjustifiable would be the restrictions which the Attorney General sought to impose? The facts had become public before he issued the statement. From *Spycatcher* in general, and *Weber* in the particular context of contempt, it is clear that it is not justified in a democratic society to restrict speech on a matter which has already reached the public domain. The facts and issues were public when the Attorney General sought to restrain comment. Furthermore, the Court was distinctly sceptical of the possibilities of successfully putting pressure on a judge in this fashion. This echoes the common law's similar scepticism which we have already addressed, and suggests that under the Convention, prohibition of discussion of the issues in *AG v. X* is not necessary to maintain the authority and impartiality of the judiciary. In the event, most such comment was balanced, and there was a substantial legitimate public interest in a matter which so fundamentally affects notions of civil liberty in our society. These factors weighed in favour of speech in *Sunday Times (No. 1)*,[30] and *mutatis mutandis*, also do so here. Consequently, a consideration of the issues under the European Convention suggests that the prohibition on speech in the Attorney General's statement is disproportionate and over-broad.

Indeed, the trend of the Article 10 case law suggests that this prohibition would have been over-broad had it been issued to prevent discussion even *before* it had begun. Measures which prohibit or discourage open discussion on matters of public concern are very likely to be held in breach of Article 10. Thus, prosecutions for criminal defamation of journalists or politicians who comment on matters of serious public concern such as the character of a former Chancellor,[31] police brutality[32] and government complicity in the murder of dissidents,[33] have been held to be in breach. On the other hand, Article 10 will not justify a serious personal attack on the competence on lay judges.[34] Of course, predictably, free speech may also legitimately be restricted on the basis of national security.[35] Although it is clear from *Spycatcher* that the Court is not as ready to condemn the prior restraint contemplated here as the US Supreme Court has been, nevertheless, the Court has in the past found such measures to be in breach, as in *Sunday Times (No. 1)*. All of this reflects the importance of the right to free speech in the democratic process. Thus, given that *AG v. X* implicated serious matters of public concern going to the very heart of Irish society and of the legal process and democratic discourse, a blanket prior restraint would have been very difficult indeed to sustain. Comment which strayed beyond the range of protected speech, as in *Barfod*, would of course, be liable to subsequent punishment.

As a result of *Desmond*, such considerations are directly relevant to the common law.[36] Although in *In re O'Laighleis*[37] it was held that the Convention is not directly part of Irish law, Henchy J in *The State (DPP) v. Walsh*[38] held that there was a presumption that the common law, especially the common law in relation to contempt, was in conformity with the Convention. Thus, O'Hanlon J in *Desmond* held that judgments of the European Court of Human Rights have "persuasive" force,[39] and Costello J at first instance in *AG. v. X* (the case in respect of which the Attorney General issued this statement) accepted that there are circumstances in which it would be "relevant to consider the jurisprudence of the European Court of Human Rights".[40]

Furthermore, such considerations have recently also been successful in the English Courts in *Derbyshire County Council v. Times Newspapers*.[41] The question was whether a local authority could sue for libel in respect of criticism of its political activities. Guided by dicta of Lord Donaldson MR in the Court of Appeal and of Lord Goff in the House of Lords in *Spycatcher (No. 2)*[42] to the effect that "Article 10 of the European Convention is in effect the same as the . . . common law", and referring to the judgement of Lord Ackner in *Brind*,[43] the Court of Appeal held that the Convention may thus be used to "resolve some uncertainty or ambiguity in municipal law".[44] Concerned at the "chilling effect"[45] which a rule allowing a local authority to sue in such circumstances would have on political speech, the Court held that Article 10 considerations required that such a rule not form part of the common law.[46]

For a unanimous House of Lords, Lord Keith affirmed the Court of Appeal's decision. He was alive to the reality that a "civil action for defamation must inevitably have an inhibiting effect on freedom of speech".[47] He went on to refer to US authority,[48] in which context he acknowledged that "what is called the 'chilling effect' induced by the threat of civil actions for libel is very important".[49] By analogy with these premises, it is arguable that the "chilling effect" of the common law contempt rules is also over-restrictive of speech. Although he could conclude that there was no ambiguity in the common law, and thus no need to proceed with the issue under the Convention, Lord Keith approved the approach of the Court of Appeal in this regard. He concluded, with Lord Goff in *Spycatcher*,[50] that in the field of freedom of expression, there is no difference in principle between English law and Article 10 of the Convention.[51]

The Convention was relied upon, in both *Desmond* and *Derbyshire* (especially in the Court of Appeal), neither in a dissent nor as window-dressing on a *ratio*, but as the *ratio* in each case! It is therefore clear that the European Convention in general and Article 10 in particular will be relevant in any case which implicates rights in general and the right to freedom of expression in particular. As a result, the argument that the Attorney General's prohibition is unjustified under the ECHR is one of which an Irish court must take cognisance in the light of *Desmond*. Indeed, this point gains greater force from the rejection in *Derbyshire* of a common law rule which would have the effect of chilling political speech.

CONCLUSION

The aim of this paper was to analyse the justifications for the prohibition on speech in the Attorney General's statement. Certainly the fact that the hearing was *in camera* justified restrictions on speech in "special and limited circumstances" (Article 34.1). However the mere fact that it was *in camera* would not seem to have justified the extreme width of the prohibition on "*any public discussion of the facts or issues*"; nor would the rules of *sub judice* contempt, even in their extreme form in *AG v. Times Newspapers*. Furthermore, an analysis of the prohibition in the statement in the light of the European Convention suggests that it is disproportionate (*Sunday Times*; *Weber*), and whether the influence on this document is at the level of the common law (*Walsh*; *Derbyshire*) or of the Constitution (*Desmond*), it is an influence which Irish law cannot now ignore. As a result, it will be seen that the extreme nature of the Attorney General's prohibition is quite without foundation. It reflects the type of thinking which the common law engenders, and misses the influence of norms protecting free speech, in this case both Article 40.6.1.(i) of the Constitution and Article 10 of the European Convention on Human Rights. It is clear the they do not justify restrictions on speech which would have the chilling effect which the Attorney General's statement sought to achieve.

6.5   Comparative Commercial Speech

GERARD QUINN

The term "commercial speech" refers generally to any non-political or personal speech that is essentially economic in character. A good example is a newspaper advertisement to sell a car. The dividing line between political and pure economic speech can, however, be quite blurred. An advertisement for an abortion service in another State, for example, is part political and part commercial speech. It can be considered political in as much as it is related to the delivery of a civil or political right in another State. It is commercial in the sense that it conveys the existence of a commercial service upon certain conditions.

In this paper, I explore the extent to which traditional protections of freedom of expression can be and have been judicially extended to afford some protection to commercial speech whether connected with civil rights or not. I also explore the extent to which specific economic liberties such as the liberty to provide a service generate additional informational rights in their afterglow.

Two preliminary points seem in order. First, there appears to be a lack of reflectiveness in popular and legal culture in general as to the nature of the often conflicting human values honoured by the human rights movement. This factor impacts somewhat adversely on the quality of the available human rights literature which has a distinctively wooden and self-referencing feel to it. Likewise it has a bearing on the quality of advocacy before domestic and international courts which in turn influences both the content and transparency of judicial craftsmanship.

Secondly, this relative lack of even the most elementary philosophical sophistication is damaging and nowhere more so than in the field of freedom of expression. It is noteworthy that there is little deep and sustained enquiry in popular discourse into the value(s) of freedom of expression. Judicial outcomes are critiqued, if at all, almost exclusively in terms of results. That is, such decisions are lauded or attacked in terms of whether the values honoured in them happen to coincide with those of the critic. They are examined less in terms of consistency with some articulate theory of what freedom of expression stands for and even less in terms of the propriety of the assertion of raw judicial power.

To understand how and why courts are creating space for commercial speech it is necessary to stand back momentarily from the fray in order to come to terms with underlying theoretical commitments of freedom of expression. It is the leeway within these underlying theories that accounts for the extension of doctrinal coverage to embrace non–political areas of human endeavour.

TWO JUSTIFICATORY THEORIES OF FREE SPEECH CONTRASTED: LIBERAL AND DEMOCRATIC THEORIES

It will prove useful to recall that freedom of expression emanates historically from two different and related political philosophies; liberal theory and democratic theory.[1]

Liberal rights theory reflects a general liberal preference for the "right" over the "good"; that is, it reflects a preference for allowing individuals conceive and implement their own peculiar conception of the "good".[2] The liberal continuum commences with a commitment to "existence". Familiar rights such as the right to life, freedom from torture, right to bodily and psychic integrity advance this commitment. Concomitant to "existence" rights is the right to act on one's conception of the "good"; hence the emphasis in liberal theory on liberty and also on property as a liberty-enhancing device.[3] Hence also the emphasis on due process as an added insurance against arbitrary deprivation of rights. Since individual goals can seldom be achieved in isolation there must exist a further band of rights along the continuum dealing with rights of voluntaristic association.

Freedom of expression fits into this liberal schema in the sense that it enables individuals to form and constantly re-form their own self-realizations.[4] It enables individuals to vent their self-understandings and communicate freely their sentiments, feelings and concrete interests (economic and otherwise) to others. It is also vital, and justified as such within liberal thought, as an indispensable tool in the progressive but never ending pursuit of truth.[5]

Implicit in the above liberal vision is some conception of the economic market. However, human rights generally, and freedom of speech in particular, were not seen as having any direct bearing on the structuring of market relations. This was because rights flowed traditionally and exclusively between the individual and the State.[6] Such rights are, however, capable of having a bearing in the way that the State regulates (or allows private bodies to self-regulate) sectors of the market economy. Indeed, recent developments in the area of commercial speech bear this out.

The democratic justificatory theory to freedom of expression has a different focus. Viewed from this perspective, the right deserves protection since a fully functioning representative democracy is unworkable without it.[7] It is crucial to bear in mind that the while the right, when viewed from the perspective of democratic theory, inures to the benefit of specific individuals, it also performs more openly structural or utilitarian political tasks. Its chief structural task is the creation and maintenance of a fair and free political marketplace of ideas and information.[8] It is in this sense that theorists make the claim that the right should be viewed as a "system" of collection of related concerns or rights.[9] Included within the system, for example, is a concern for freedom of information as against State secrecy; a concern for open government as against closed government ("government in the sunshine"); a concern that private law such as the law of defamation be structured so as maximize the amount of relevant information in the public sphere; a concern for the drowning out effect of so-called "government speech".

It must be said at the outset that the democratic justificatory theory to freedom of expression (maintenance of a political market place) tends to be the one that is most visible in many textual expressions of the right and to be uppermost in the priorities of courts when interpreting its outer parameters. Recognizing that it has applicability to the economic marketplace brings out much that is implicit in liberal rights theory and it takes seriously our culture's democratic commitment to the market as a fair and efficient allocational mechanism.

I want to examine this trend of judicial recognition of "commercial speech" under US Constitutional law, under the European Convention of Human Rights and under European Community law.

EVOLUTION OF "COMMERCIAL SPEECH" IN THE US

There are two ways in which human rights generally can be used to generate informational rights of an economic character in a market economy.

First, it is at least logically plausible to argue that the related rights to liberty and property entail some vision of fair and free market relations. As perfect or near-perfect information is necessary to engender rationality in a market then it follows that informational rights must be seen as a corollary to liberty in general or to specified economic liberties such as the "liberty" to provide services etc. This avenue for the development of "commercial speech" is blocked off under US constitutional law for historical reasons.[10] It features prominently however in European Community law. This is not surprizing given the EEC's commitment to the creation of a single rational market throughout Europe.

Secondly, it is also possible to argue that the traditional formal right of freedom of expression has economic as well as personal and political applications. Such a move towards creeping expansion of the coverage of the right is no doubt hindered by the fact that most textual expressions of it owe their existence to the democratic or political rationale mentioned above. But the extension does make sound historical and intellectual sense.

The US Supreme Court fashioned the doctrine of "commercial speech" out of the First Amendment which reads in the relevant part as follows:

Congress shall make no law . . . abridging . . . freedom of speech.

It bears stressing that the US Supreme Court had for a long time taken the view that whereas the First Amendment on its face inures to the benefit of specific individuals that it also served much broader structural political purposes. Indeed, one of the main "systems" values lying back of the right is the concern to maximize relevant information in the public sphere.

The first "commercial speech" decision in the US, *Bigelow v. Virginia*,[11] which was decided in 1975, pivoted in essence on a consideration of what was necessary to give efficacy to a newly established (or extended) civil right. It was not therefore a pure "commercial speech" case although it set the stage for the development of the pure doctrine. Recall that the landmark *Roe v. Wade*[12] decision of 1973 expanded the right of privacy to encompass a woman's decision regarding abortion within certain bounds. It therefore rendered the procuring of an abortion legal within certain limits. Prior to *Roe*, some US states had more permissive abortion laws than others. Those states that had restrictive laws sometimes forbade the circulation of information regarding the availability of the service in other, more lenient, states. This patchwork quilt of informational rights persisted long after the *Roe* decision itself and put in jeopardy the efficacy of *Roe*. The persistence of this patchwork quilt of informational rights was at issue in *Bigelow*. There the Supreme Court reversed conviction under a Virginia statute that criminalized the circulation of any publication in Virginia to encourage or promote the processing of an abortion. The defendant was convicted of advertizing information in Virginia concerning the availability of abortion in New York. The Supreme Court stated:

> the Virginia courts erred in their assumption that advertizing, as as such, was entitled to no First Amendment protection

and added, significantly, that the

> relationship of speech in the marketplace of products or of services does not make it valueless in the marketplace of ideas.

Hence, the granting or extension of a civil liberty (privacy encompassing abortion) to enable individuals to procure a service which was generally provided through the market must have and did have an effect on the structuring of the market and on restrictive informational regulation. Similarly the extension of the privacy concept to encompass contraception (*Griswold v. Connecticut*[13] and *Eisenstadt v. Baird*[14]) led to corollary decisions dealing with information regarding the availability of the same (*Carey v. Population Services Int'l*[15]). Interestingly this linkage between the contraceptives decisions (*Griswold* and *Eisenstadt*) and informational decisions (*Carey*) is tracked in Irish law in *McGee v. Attorney General*[16] and *Irish Family Planning Association v. Ryan.*[17]

The first major US case to touch squarely on pure commercial speech, *Virginia State Board of Pharmacy v. Virginia Citizen's Consumer Council*,[18] involved a State statute that made the advertizing of the prices of prescription drugs "unprofessional conduct". The "speech" at issue was the communication through advertisement of the price of prescription drugs by the retailer to the consumer. The specifically economic character of the "speech" did not deny it of any judicial solicitude. However, due to the fact that it was economic rather than political in character, it did not enjoy full First Amendment protection.

The chief reason given by the Court for this extension of the coverage of First Amendment protection was simple and powerful and blends both liberal and democratic rights theory:

> So long as we preserve a predominantly free enterprise economy, the allocation of our resources in large measure will be made through numerous private economic decisions. It is a matter of public interest that those decisions, in the aggregate, be intelligent and well informed. To this end the free flow of commercial information is indispensable.[19]

The speech at issue was therefore seen as crucial to the rationality of the economic market. Hence its liberal foundation. It was also important because of the democratic commitment to the market. The Court took the opportunity to emphasise again that advertisement which is entirely commercial in its character may be of general public interest especially where it implicates the availability of a civil right.

The "commercial speech" doctrine is now well established with a host of applications dealing with the supply of various services and products to the consumer.[20] One area of particular application is the supply of legal services and informational rights pertaining thereto. Rendering the flow of relevant information more "perfect" as between the supplier of legal services and the consumer–client makes for greater rationality in two related markets. It ensures fairer competition as between new market entrants (recently qualified attorneys) and more established market actors (large law firms). It also ensures greater rationality from the point of view of the consumer who has more market information on which to base his or her decision of attorney.

The Supreme Court formally endorsed the application of the doctrine in the field of legal services in *Bates v. Arizona*.[21] It held that blanket bans on all lawyer advertizing automatically fall foul of the First Amendment. Lawyers frequently use the *Bates* ruling to challenge restrictive advertizing rules. As a result of *Virginia* and *Bates* combined, lawyers now have the right to advertise as to pricing (so long as it is for "routine" services that lend themselves to flat-rate advertizing), specialization listings[22] as well as the use of diagrams in advertizing.[23] In-person solicitation is excluded from coverage because, unlike advertizing, it may "encourage speedy and perhaps uninformed (consumer) decision-making" which can only detract from rationality in the market.[24] Writing a letter offering to take carriage of a legal case does not count as in-person solicitation.[25]

The Supreme Court enunciated a general four-pronged test to be applied

in colourable commercial speech cases in *Central Hudson Gas & Electric Corp.
v. Public Service Comm'n*. It stated:

> At the outset, we must determine whether the expression is protected by
> by the First Amendment. For commercial speech to come within that
> provision, it at least must concern lawful activity and not be misleading.
> Next, we ask whether the asserted governmental interest [in curbing it] is
> substantial. If both enquiries yield positive answers, we must determine
> whether the regulation directly advances the governmental interest asserted,
> and whether it is not more than is necessary to serve that interest.[26]

The particular regulation at stake in the instant case was in fact found to be
over-broad. Concurring members of the Court voiced objection to one premise
in the decision of the Court that seemed to leave open to the government the
option of regulating the flow of commercial information regarding a legal service
as a way of indirectly influencing consumer behaviour and levels of demand; the
so-called "social engineering" option.

This question of the application of the doctrine to the provision of "legal"
products or services in the market was broached in *Posadas De Puerto Rico
Associates v. Tourism Company of Puerto Rico*.[27] Such speech enjoys no added
protection because it lacks a clear connection to civil rights and must therefore
stand on its own. Many more or less harmful products (for example, cigarettes)
or services are quite legally offered to the consuming public and are in demand.
How much latitude is given to states to regulate information (and by implication,
demand) concerning such products or services? The state of Puerto Rico had
legalized casino gambling principally to attract out-of-state visitors. But it
curbed casino advertizing targeted at Puerto Rico residents. The Court upheld
the restriction by a narrow majority (5–4) on the basis that since the state had
the legal power to ban the activity altogether (unlike the situation in *Carey* and
Bigelow), that the greater power (to ban) necessarily included the lesser power
to regulate demand through advertizing restrictions. Justice Brennan (joined by
Marshall and Blackmun J J) entered a strong dissenting judgment as did Justice
Stevens. The essence of Brennan J's dissent was an objection to allowing First
Amendment principles to yield to "social engineering" objectives. Illegal
economic activity cannot by definition enjoy any commercial speech coverage.[28]

The fourth prong of the *Hudson* test was diluted somewhat in *Board of
Trustees of State University of New York (SUNY) v. Fox*.[29] At issue was a SUNY
restriction of commercial enterprises on College campuses. This challenge to
the constitutionality of the regulation turned on the means used rather than
the substantiality of the governmental interests asserted. The Court held that

what our [previous] decisions require is a "fit" between the legislature's ends and the means chosen to accomplish those ends . . . a fit that is not necessarily perfect, but reasonable.

In sum, pure commercial speech attracts some protective coverage under the First Amendment. Only partial coverage of the First Amendment is afforded. This is no doubt due in part to a fear that traditional First Amendment concerns in the political arena might be diluted by association with "commercial speech" principles. Certain limiting principles apply. Deceptive, misleading or untruthful speech is excluded. Time, place and manner restrictions apply and have special relevancy given consumer tastes and sensibilities. Even commercial speech relating to legal activities may be curbed if the state reasonably takes the view that harm might ensue.

COMMERCIAL SPEECH UNDER THE EUROPEAN CONVENTION ON HUMAN RIGHTS[30]

It is of course entirely possible to argue that the rights to liberty (Article 5) and to private property (Article 1 of Protocol 1) under the ECHR entail additional informational rights in the economic sphere. The argument for implication is that such extra rights are necessary to give full efficacy to the core rights of liberty and property in a market economy. This route has not been travelled. Given that the accent is on political and civil liberty rather than economic liberty the Commission and Court would probably prove hostile to such logical arguments.

The Commission and Court have, however, recognized as a matter of general principle that the coverage of Article 10 dealing with the formal right of freedom of expression extends somewhat to encompass "commercial speech" although the term itself is seldom used. The very text of Article 10, which specifically mentions "information" without tying it to political ideas, is quite amenable to such a broad interpretation. It reads in the relevant part:

Every one shall have the right to freedom of expression. This right shall include freedom to hold opinions and to receive and impart information and ideas without interference by public authority and regardless of frontiers.

The Court and Commission recognize that a right whose primary rationale it is to honour individuals and maintain a political marketplace of ideas has some applicability to economic market relations. Doubtless the cogency of the arguments crafted by the US Supreme Court in favour of such extension of coverage played on the minds of the judges to an incalculable extent. This intellectual debt to the US Supreme Court also shows through in the adoption of rules similar to those in *New York Times v. Sullivan*, in *Lingens v. Austria* and in its progeny.[31]

Early hints of doctrinal flexibility in the coverage of Article 10 were dropped by the Commission in 1979 in *X and the Church of Scientology v. Sweden*.[32] The case itself was ruled technically inadmissible as "manifestly unfounded". The Court had an opportunity to review the coverage of Article 10 in its 1985 decision of *Barthold v. Germany*.[33] On the facts the Court choose to characterize the speech at issue as squarely political instead of colourably economic or commercial in character and then proceeded to the next step of considering the application of Article 10(2) limiting principles. In the upshot the regulation imposed was found wanting under Article 10(2). However, one of the more influential members of the Court, Judge Pettiti, voiced strong approval for the inclusion of a doctrine "commercial speech" within the rubric of Article 10. In his concurring judgment he took judicial notice of a strong international trend against blanket bans on advertizing and adverted approvingly to American developments.

More tangible evidence of a trend in favour of extending Article 10 coverage beyond purely personal or political speech could be found in the Court's 1988 decision of *Muller & Others v. Switzerland*.[34] There the Court formally extended coverage to include artistic expression. On a purely textual point the Court declined to draw any negative inferences from the silence of Article 10(1) as to the extent of its coverage. In *Muller*, however, like *Barthold*, the applicant lost on the basis of Article 10(2) limiting principles.

The Court finally endorsed the extension of Article 10(1) coverage to encompass pure "commercial speech" in its 1989 decision of *Markt Intern Verlag v. Germany*.[35] Most disappointingly, however, the Court supplied no detailed reasoning why it thought the extended coverage warranted in theory or under the text. It simply announced that the speech in question was of a commercial nature and that "such information cannot be excluded from the scope of Article 10(1)".[36] Since the reasons are not articulated one cannot be sure of the outer boundaries to the right.

At least one interesting case dealing effectively with the overlap of political and commercial speech has made its way to the Commission in 1990 and is presently pending before the Court: *Open Door Counselling and Dublin Well Woman Centre & Others v. Ireland*.[37] The case joined three applications. One applicant was a registered Irish company and certain of its employees (Ms Maher and Ms Downes): Open Door Counselling Co. Another applicant was a registered Irish charity: Dublin Well Woman Centre. The third application came from two Irish women of child-bearing age: X and Ms Geraghty. The background to the application concerns the judicial gloss put on the Eighth Amendment to the Irish Constitution by the Irish Courts. The Eighth Amendment reads as follows:

> The State acknowledges the right to life of the unborn and, with due regard to the equal right to life of the mother, guarantees in its laws to respect, and, in so far as practicable, by its laws to defend and vindicate that right.

In purely mechanical terms the enactment by popular referendum of the Eighth Amendment in 1983 was designed to forestall one possible (though improbable) line of judicial development; the steady extension of the right of privacy to encompass a woman's decision regarding abortion. It thus signalled that one civil right (privacy) could not be stretched by the courts (or indeed by the legislature) to encompass abortion. The Irish courts interpreted the terms of the Eighth Amendment to be self-executing and to have negative implications for corollary informational rights; that is, right to impart or receive information regarding the availability of abortion in third jurisdictions. One objective of post-1983 litigation was to dry up the well of remaining sources of information concerning the availability of abortion in other jurisdictions.

These corollary informational issues were ventilated before the Irish courts in a series of celebrated cases.[38] The clear impression given by the Supreme Court was that the conveying of this form of speech was implicitly proscribed by the ambit and spirit of the Eighth Amendment. At play beneath the language of the various judgments was a balancing act[39] between the right to life on the one hand, and "lesser" rights such as privacy and freedom of expression on the other. Injunctions were successfully applied in the Irish courts against the first two applicants above who were admittedly engaged, *inter alia*, in non-directive counselling for abortion services in the UK.

The parallel between the Irish cases and the US Supreme Court's decisions in *Carey* and *Bigelow* described above is interesting. In *Carey* and *Bigelow* it was the expansion of a civil right (privacy) that impelled the Supreme Court to follow-through with expanded informational rights relating to relevant commercial services. In the *Open Door* litigation it was the effective curtailment of a civil right (privacy encompassing abortion) by the Eighth Amendment that impelled the Irish courts to follow-through by denying informational rights relating to the availability of relevant commercial services in the UK. In that sense the American and Irish informational decisions represent the reverse side of the same coin.

The essence of the joint application was that the injunctions were incompatible with Ireland's obligations under Article 10 (1) of the ECHR.[40] The speech at issue was colourably commercial in the sense that a charge was usually levied by the

Dublin clinics (depending on ability to pay) and also in the sense that it pertained to a commercial service available in the UK. The speech was colourably political in the sense that it related to services available in another jurisdiction required to implement an asserted civil right which was unavailable in Ireland.

The Commission did not, unlike the US Supreme Court in *Bigelow*, characterize the speech at issue as commercial. Instead it seems to have proceeded on the unstated assumption that it was essentially political speech. It found that the injunctions awarded by the Irish courts amounted to an "interference" that begged justification under Article 10 (2). It went on to hold for the applicants on the basis that the "interference" in question failed to exhibit sufficient preciseness and clarity as required under traditional Article 10 (2) jurisprudence.[41] The Commission's decision pivots therefore on quite a narrow ground; namely, the modalities of the "interference" as against the substantiality of the aims or object of the "interference". If the Court had followed the reasoning and conclusions of the Commission it would have been a relatively easy matter (technically, if not politically) for the Irish Government to inject the required "preciseness" into the "interference" through legislation.

Doubtless the characterization of the speech at issue in the *Open Door* case as commercial or as a hybrid between commercial and political would not have helped the applicants. After all, commercial speech usually attracts less protection than political speech. But it is surely a puzzle why the Commission did not address the pedigree of the speech (hybrid or otherwise) in question.

The European Court of Human Rights delivered its judgment in the *Open Door* case on 29 October 1992.[42] Like the Commission, the Court proceeded on the unstated assumption that the information in question was political rather than commercial in its nature. The Court found against Ireland on a different basis than the Commission. Unlike the Commission, the Court held that the "interference" in question possessed sufficient precision, transparency and predictability as required by the phrase "as prescribed by law" under Article 10 (2). This view certainly seems contestable. Instead, the Court climbed down the usual ladder of Article 10 analysis to investigate whether the "interference" had a "legitimate aim" and whether it was "necessary in a democratic society" as per Article 10 (2). The Court held that it did indeed serve a "legitimate aim" since it concerned the "protection . . . of morals" under Article 10 (2). It thus nicely avoided having to make a ruling on whether the interference in question fell to be scrutinized under the heading of protecting the "rights of others". To travel down such a route of enquiry would have forced the Court to decide whether a foetus was another human being.

The Court ruled against Ireland on the basis that the interference was disproportionate to the "legitimate aim" being pursued and thus not "necessary in a democratic society". Disproportionality was assessed as arising in several ways. The chief way in which the Court felt it arose concerned the linkage between the speech in question and the ultimate destruction of the unborn. The Court felt that insufficient evidence was forthcoming on that account. It is interesting to speculate as to what might be considered to count as good evidence of a firm linkage and whether, if such linkage could be proven, the Court would have taken the next logical step of declaring the "interference" to be within Ireland's margin of appreciation. Again, what is remarkable about the Court's judgment for our purposes is the fact that it avoids any characterization of the speech in question as political or commercial or a hybrid between the two.

EEC LAW AND "COMMERCIAL SPEECH"

Economic liberty and specific economic liberties lie at the very heart of the European Community legal order. Creating and maintaining a rational Pan-European market for goods, services, labour and capital is central to the mission of the EEC. Hence it is logical to expect that some of the more traditional liberties such as the liberty to provides services across borders would entail ancillary informational rights. The absence of such corollary informational rights or the prevalence of state-by-state regulation of commercial information would undermine the very rationality of the Pan-European market itself.

Not surprizingly the ECJ has recognized that informational rights do indeed flow from the inner logic of more traditional economic liberties. In the case of *GB-INNO-BM v. Confederation du Commerce Luxembourgeois (CCL)*,[43] for example, the ECJ held that free movement of goods:

> . . . implies . . . that consumers residing in one Member State must be able to enter freely into another Member State and make purchases under the same conditions as the local population. That right was curtailed [on the facts of the instant case] when consumers were denied access to advertizing material available in the country of purchase. A ban on the distribution of such [advertizing] material fell, therefore, within the scope of Articles 30, 31 and 36 of the [EC] Treaty.

It is therefore beyond doubt that, in as much as commercial speech is required to add rationality to the market, it receives protection in the shade of the penumbras to the various economic liberties of the EEC Treaty. Political speech is not of course directly protected in Community law.

What of commercial speech that is part political? What of commercial speech informing consumers in one Member State about the availability of a commercial service in another Member State implementing a civil right in the second that is denied in the first? A case on point arose before the ECJ in connection yet again with the Eighth Amendment to the Irish Constitution. A series of post-*Open Door* cases was brought by a private body against student unions and student union leaders in an effort to further dry up the well of information pertaining to foreign abortion in Ireland. In one such application before the Irish High Court, *Society for the Protection of Unborn Child v. Stephen Grogan & Others*, one judge took the view that not all Community legal issues pertaining to freedom of expression had been put fully before the Irish courts, much less resolved by them.[44] This set the stage for an Article 177 reference to the ECJ.

The ECJ handed down its judgment in the *Grogan* referral on 4 October 1991. It held that an abortion service amounted to a "service" within the terms of Article 60 of the EEC Treaty. That is, this "service" was essentially commercial in its nature. It went on to hold, however, that the Irish Constitutional prohibition in question (and the gloss put on it by the Irish courts) against the dissemination by Irish student union officials of information concerning the availability of such "services" in the UK did not amount to a "prohibition" requiring justification under Article 59 et seq. of the Treaty.

The Court reasoned that the student union officials in question were not in sufficient proximity to the economic actors actually providing the "service" and could not therefore plead the *jus tertii* of the rights afforded such actors under the Treaty. This situation was distinguished from the one obtaining in *GB-INNO-BM* where the speech in question was uttered by or on behalf of the provider of the goods. In sum therefore, the speech uttered by the student union officials was categorized as non-economic in nature and therefore civil or political in character. It followed, according to the ECJ, that the appropriate remedy (if any) lay in the civil and political rights field (for example, the ECHR) and not in the economic rights field.

The *Grogan* judgment of the ECJ effectively creates a line between persons who have sufficient proximity to the providers of goods and services and who can therefore stand on the informational rights of such entities and those who do not. To an economist at least, this line may make little sense since a rational market depends on perfect information emanating from whatever source. The basis to the *Grogan* decision is therefore extremely narrow. An agonizing analysis of the compatibility of the "prohibition" with general limiting principles in Article 59 et seq. is avoided by denying the technical existence of a "prohibition". Hence the parameters to commercial speech in general and commercial speech that overlaps with political speech must await further litigation in the ECJ.

CONCLUSION

Several conclusions seem to follow from the above analysis.

In the first place, it is clear that the decision in principle to extend the coverage of freedom of expression provisions to encompass commercial speech makes sense from the perspective of both liberal and democratic rights theory. It also makes sense not to award commercial speech as much protection as is afforded traditional political and personal speech.

Secondly, it is interesting to note the way in which the doctrine of commercial speech evolved. In the US it grew as a spin-off from certain civil rights decisions of the US Supreme Court. Creating and expanding civil rights must be accompanied by a judicial concern for the structural integrity of the marketplace. This is so since the reality in many western countries is that the actual availability of such rights depends on making relevant commercial services accessible to the consumer. The doctrine has now evolved in both the US and in Europe to the point that it encompasses pure commercial speech. But much of the litigation, especially under the European Community law and the ECHR, still concerns the overlap between civil rights and commercial speech. This is no doubt due to the fact that there continues to exist a patchwork quilt in Europe as to the levels of protection of some civil rights (privacy encompassing abortion) which is accompanied by a corresponding patchwork quilt of informational rights.[45]

Thirdly, speech about illegal activities is not covered by the doctrine though this begs a prior question about a country's legal power to make certain economic activities illegal. Nor, it seems, is economic speech necessarily covered simply because it relates to activity that is quite legal. A state may still take the view that consumer demand for legal but dangerous products or services needs to be regulated, *inter alia*, by advertizing restrictions. At least this is the net result of a divided US Supreme Court in *Posadas*. On this reasoning the European Commission ought to have no difficulty defending the proposed Council Directive on advertizing for tobacco products under Article 59 et seq. of the EEC Treaty.[45]

Finally, the American courts have been more forthcoming than either the European Court of Human Rights or the ECJ in providing an underlying intellectual rationale for the adoption of a doctrine of "commercial speech" and in teasing out its outer boundaries. This may be a function of the differing volume of relevant cases that come before these forums or it may reveal something deeper about differing American and European approaches to rights and, equally important, to judicial craftsmanship. The net result is that while both European Courts have embraced commercial speech (albeit from different angles) they have yet to come to terms with the limits of the doctrine.

6.6   Select Bibliography

TEXTS AND MATERIALS

S. Bailey, D.J. Harris and B.L. Jones, *Civil Liberties: Cases and Materials*, 3rd ed. (London, 1991) Chs. 5 & 6.

E. Barendt, *Freedom of Expression* (Oxford, 1985).

K. Boyle and M. McGonagle, *Press Freedom and Libel: A Report Prepared for the National Newspapers of Ireland* (Dublin, 1988).

A. Cassese and A. Clapham, eds., *Transfrontier Television in Europe: The Human Rights Dimension* (Baden-Baden, 1990).

S. Coliver, ed., *Striking a Balance: Hate Speech, Freedom of Expression and Non-Discrimination* (London, 1992).

S. Curry Jensen, *Censorship: The Knot that Binds Power to Knowledge* (Oxford, 1988).

T. Emerson, *The System of Freedom of Expression* (New York, 1970).

Law Reform Commission, *Consultation Paper on the Civil Law of Defamation* (Dublin, 1991).

Law Reform Commission, *Report on the Civil Law of Defamation* (LRC 31–1991) (Dublin, 1991).

A. Lester and D. Pannick, *Advertizing and Freedom of Expression in Europe* (Paris, 1984).

P. O'Higgins, *Censorship in Britain* (London, 1972).

G. Robertson, *Freedom, the Individual and the Law*, 6th ed., (London, 1989) Ch.7.

G. Robertson and A. Nichol, *Media Law*, 3rd ed., (London, 1992).

F. Schauer, *Free Speech: A Philosophical Enquiry* (Cambridge, 1981).

ARTICLES

E. Barendt, "Spycatcher and Freedom of Speech" [1989] *Public Law* 202.

E. Barendt, "Libel and Freedom of Speech in English Law" [1993] *Public Law* 449.

B. Bix and A. Tomkins, "Unconventional Use of the Convention?" (1992) 55 *MLR* 721.

M. Bullinger, "Freedom of Information: An Essential Element of Democracy" (1985) 6 *HRLJ*.

A.M. Collins, "Commercial Free Speech and the Free Movement of Goods and Services at Community Law" in J. O'Reilly, ed., *Human Rights and Constitutional Law: Essays in Honour of Brian Walsh* (Dublin, 1992) 319.

D. Conlon, "Contempt of Court—An Issue for Reform" (1992) 2 *ISLR* 53.

V. Dimitrijevic, "Freedom of Opinion and Expression" in A. Rosas and J. Helgesen, eds., *Human Rights in a Changing East-West Perspective* (London, 1990) 58.

P. Duffy, "The Sunday Times Case: Freedom of Expression, Contempt of Court and the European Convention on Human Rights" (1980) 5 *HRR* 17.

D. Elder, "Freedom of Expression and the Law of Defamation: The American Approach to Problems Raised by the *Lingens* Case" (1986) 35 *ICLQ* 891.

J. Fleming, "Defamation: Political Speech" (1993) *LQR* 12.

J. Freidman, "On the Dangers of Moral Certainty and Sacred Trusts" (1988) 10 *DULJ* (n.s) 71.

T. Gibbons, "Freedom of the Press: Ownership and Editorial Values" [1992] *Public Law* 279.

K. Greenawalt, "Free Speech Justifications" (1989) 89 *Col L Rev*. 119.

E. Hall and P. McGovern, "Regulation of the Media: Irish and EC Developments" (1986) 8 *DULJ* (n.s.) 1.

S. Henchy, "Contempt of Court and Freedom of Expression" (1982) 33 *NILQ* 326.

I. Leigh, "Spycatcher in Strasbourg" [1992] *Public Law* 200.

E. O'Dell, "Does Defamation Devalue Free Speech?" (1990) 12 *DULJ* (n.s.)50.

E. O'Dell, "Reflections on a Revolution in Libel" (1991) 10 *ILT* (n.s.) 181.

G. Malinverni, "Freedom of Information in the European Convention on Human Rights and in the International Covenant on Civil and Political Rights" (1983) 4 *HRLJ* 443.

F.A. Mann, "Contempt of Court in the House of Lords and the European Court of Human Rights" (1979) *LQR* 348.

G. Marshall, "Taking Rights for an Overide: Free Speech and Commercial Expression" [1989] *Public Law* 4.

G. Quinn: "The Right of Lawyers to Advertise in the Market for Legal Services: A Comparative Irish, American and European Perspective" (1922) 20 *Anglo-American L Rev.* 1.

U. Ní Raifeartaigh, "Defences in Irish Defamation Law" (1991) 13 *DULJ* (n.s.) 76.

U. Ní Raifeartaigh, "Fault Issues and libel Law—A Comparison Between Irish, English and US Laws" (1991) 40 *ICLQ* 763.

E. Spalin, "Abortion, Speech and the European Community" [1992] *J Soc Wel & Fam L* 17.

S. Walker, " Freedom of Speech and Contempt of Court: The English and Australian Approaches Compared" (1991) 40 *ICLQ* 583.

7 : ECONOMIC AND SOCIAL RIGHTS

7.1 Introduction

Where would an Irish person look for inspiration when invited to talk about equality? George Bernard Shaw, I thought to myself, had something provocative, if not worthwhile, to say about most topics. Right enough, in his *Everybody's Political What's What,*[1] Chapter 7 is devoted to Equality. There Shaw says two things: "Democracy means Equality". He is not so brief when it comes to defining "equality", but for Shaw "equality" means primarily the absence of any wide, socially unbridgeable, gap between the incomes of the poor and the incomes of the rich. Poverty, for Shaw, is seen as the single greatest threat to equality.

One may be surprised by this, but on closer inquiry we find that the problem of poverty is a problem which has obsessed many of the greatest thinkers. Indeed, it is an area where Irish thinkers have made a major contribution. For a variety of reasons—the absence of a Poor Law system, Irish land law including rackrenting, absentee landlords—meant that poverty in Ireland was deeper than in England. This led Dean Swift in 1729 to publish his *A Modest Proposal for Preventing the Children of the Poor People of Ireland from being a Burden to their Parents or Country; and for Making them Beneficial to the Publick.* In this work he suggested the salvation for the poor of Ireland lay in their fattening their children for dinner tables of the rich. Dean Swift had also much to say about that everlasting phenomenon, the beggars of Dublin.

Subsequently, innumerable Irish people, lawyers and clergymen alike, developed schemes or proposals for the improvement of the condition of the poor. Outstanding amongst these were Richard Woodward, Samuel Crump and James Butler Bryan.

Richard Woodward, an Englishman but a Trinity College Dublin graduate and Anglican Bishop of Cloyne, published in 1768, *An argument in support of the right of the poor in the Kingdom of Ireland, to a national provision; in the appendix to which an attempt is made to settle a measure of the contribution due from each man to the poor, on the footing of justice.* There were at least three other editions in 1772, 1775 and 1778. His second major work published in 1775 was *An address*

245

to the public, on the expediency of a regular plan for the maintenance and government of the poor. With some general observations on the English system of poor laws . . . To which is added an argument in support of the right of the poor in the Kingdom of Ireland to a national provision.

The main thrust of Bishop Woodward's argument can be seen in the titles of these two works, which combine the notion of a tax-based system of support for the poor coupled with a legal right to that support for each individual suffering from poverty. In that idea lies the germ of modern state-financed welfare systems.

One of the great problems of intellectual history is the source from which Tom Paine, in the second part of *The Rights of Man*[2] derived what Simon Schama, in the great work, *Citizens*,[3] called an "astonishing demand for the introduction of a welfare State". It is difficult, in my opinion, to avoid the conclusion that Thomas Paine derived his ideas from Richard Woodward.

Many other Irish thinkers contributed their solutions to the problem of poverty. Not the least significant of these was William Thompson who published, in 1824, his book *An inquiry into the Principles of the distribution of Wealth most conducive to Human Happiness, applied to the newly proposed System of Voluntary Equality of Wealth.* William Thompson also made a fundamental contribution on behalf of that other major group denied equality of treatment, women. In 1825, he published his book, *Appeal on one Half of the Human Race, Women, Against the Pretensions of the Other Half, Men, To Retain Them in Political, and Thence in Civil and Domestic Slavery.*

The very same name under which the Beveridge Welfare State was embodied in legislation, i.e. the National Insurance Act, 1946, derives from the work of another Irish social reformer, William Lewery Blackley, who, in 1878, published an essay advocating a system of compulsory national insurance to combat poverty. The New Zealand colonial Government ordered a thousand copies of Blackley's pamphlet which led in turn to the adoption in New Zealand of one of the first State welfare systems. Bismarck, too, in his social welfare reforms was influenced by Blackley. In the then United Kingdom of Great Britain and Ireland, Blackley's work led directly to the enactment of a scheme for old age pensions (1908).

It fell to yet another Irishman to recognize that providing a minimum income for the *unemployed* poor did not solve the problem of poverty, if workers continued to be paid starvation wages when in full-time employment. This was John Kells Ingram, most popularly renowned as the author of that great poem, *The Memory of the Dead*, the first lines of which are:

Who fears to speak of Ninety Eight?
Who blushes at the name?
When cowards mock the patriots fate,
Who hangs his head for shame?
He's all a knave or half a slave
Who slights his country thus;
But a true man, like you, man,
Will fill your glass with us.

It was John Kells Ingram who made one of the most lasting and significant contributions to modern social policy and to international labour law. In 1880, Professor Ingram delivered an address to the British Trade Union Congress meeting in Dublin. It was entitled: "On Work and the Workman". He saw clearly that poverty is not simply a problem of those without work but also was a problem for those in employment. Discussing the problem of wages paid to the worker, he said:

> Our views of the office of the workman must also be transformed and elevated. The way in which his position is habitually contemplated by the economists, and indeed by the public, is a very narrow, and therefore a false, one. Labour is spoken of as if it were an independent entity, separable from the personality of the workman. It is treated as a commodity, like corn or cotton—the human agent, his human needs, human nature, and human feelings, being kept almost completely out of view. Now there are, no doubt, if we carry our abstractions far enough certain resemblances between the contract of employer and employed and the sale of a commodity. But by fixing exclusive, or even predominant, attention on these, we miss the deepest and truly characteristic features of the relation of master and workman—a relation with which moral conditions are inseparably associated . . . By viewing labour as a commodity, we at once get rid of the moral basis on which the relation of employer and employed should stand, and make the so-called law of the market the sole regulator of that relation.

His view could not have been clearer. Labour was far too important for its price to be left to the operation of the market. "Labour", he said, "is not a commodity".

Some years later on the other side of the globe, Henry Bournes Higgins, in my opinion the greatest Irish judge in the 20th century, sitting as President of the Australian Arbitration Court in 1908 in the *Harvester* judgment,[4] had to decide what was meant by the statutory phrase "fair and reasonable wages". He said:

The provision for fair and reasonable remuneration is obviously designed for the benefit of the employees in the industry; and it must be meant to secure to them something which they cannot get by the ordinary system of individual bargaining with employers. If Parliament meant that the conditions shall be such as they can get by individual bargaining—if it meant that those conditions are to be fair and reasonable, which employees will accept and employers will give, in contracts of service—there would have been no need for this provision. The remuneration could safely have been left to the usual, but unequal, contest, the "higgling of the market" for labour, with the pressure for bread on one side, and the pressure for profits on the other. The standard of 'fair and reasonable' must, therefore, be something else; and I cannot think of any other standard appropriate than the normal needs of the average employee, regarded as a human being living in a civilized community. I have invited counsel and all concerned to suggest any other standard; and they have been unable to do so. If, instead of individual bargaining, one can conceive of a collective agreement—an agreement between all the employers in a given trade on the one side, and all the employees on the other—it seems to me that the framers of the agreement would have to take, as the first and dominant factor, the cost of living as a civilized being. If A lets B have the use of his horses, on the terms that he give them fair and reasonable treatment, I have no doubt that it is B's duty to give them proper food and water and such shelter and rest as they need; and, as wages are the means of obtaining commodities, surely the State, in stipulating for fair and reasonable remuneration for the employees, means that the wages shall be sufficient to provide these things, and clothing, and a condition of frugal comfort estimated by current human standards. This, then is the primary test, the test which I shall apply in ascertaining the minimum wage that can be treated as 'fair and reasonable' in the case of unskilled labourers.

The phrase "Labour is not a Commodity" appealed immediately to trade unionists and on the initiative of the American trade union leader, Samuel Gompers, was embodied in the US Sherman Anti-Trust Law, 1913. But its most significant embodiment was, in part due to the influence of Samuel Gompers, in the labour articles of the Versailles Treaty, 1919, where it is declared to be a fundamental principle of the International Labour Organization (ILO). Amongst those involved in the drafting of the labour articles was the Irishman E.J. Phelan. During the Second World War, when the ILO briefly became dormant, its Director-General on its revival at the International Labour Conference meeting in Philadelphia in 1944 was the same E.J. Phelan. At the Philadelphia meeting, the Organization adopted the Declaration of Philadelphia which re-defined the aims and purposes of the organization. First amongst the principles laid down in that Declaration was that "Labour is not a Commodity". Few may now remember the work of this great Irishman but to the end of his life he regarded as his most important contribution to human social progress the fact that he persuaded the Philadelphia Conference to re-affirm as one of its basic principles that "Labour is not a Commodity". From that great principle can be derived many of the principles of the ILO's Constitution such as the need for adequate wages to be paid, the right to freedom of association, the right to collective bargaining. Many of the ILO conventions are directly inspired by this principle, e.g. the Convention's outlawing the charging of fees by employment agencies. In turn, the ILO Constitution has been a source of inspiration for the provision of the European Social Charter, Article 4(2), guaranteeing proper remuneration for labour. This is repeated again in the EEC's Charter of Fundamental Social Rights for Workers (1990). The same principle lies at the basis of the EEC's Declaration on Multi-National Companies in South Africa, 1970, which requires such companies to ignore the market price at which they could obtain African labour and instead to pay them a proper wage. It is strange to think, but a matter for pride to us in Ireland, that John Kells Ingram should have first established the principle which of all principles represents the most fundamental rule in international labour law.

Most social policy is at a crisis point. We have to decide whether to follow Professor Hayek in leaving the pricing of labour exclusively to the market and in seeing human altruism, the foundation of modern social welfare legislation, as being the root of all evil, or to reassert those values which Irish thinkers have done so much to elevate, namely that "Labour is not a Commodity" and that society as a whole has a moral and legal obligation to ensure that the unemployed, the poor, the disabled and the old should enjoy an income sufficient to provide a reasonable standard of living.

PAUL O'HIGGINS

7.2 The Development of EEC Social and Employment Law

FERDINAND VON PRONDZYNSKI

In recent years, and in particular since 1989, the European Community has devoted increasing attention to what has become known as the "social dimension". This arises out of the view of the Commission, in particular, that there is a "need to ensure that economic growth and improved social conditions go hand in hand".[1] This has been an important point of emphasis in the development of the Single Market, achieved in 1993, and in that context the European Council, meeting in December 1990, declared that "the establishment of the single market must result in a genuine improvement in employment and in the living and working conditions of all Community citizens".[2]

It must be said immediately that rhetoric in support of an active social dimension is not a particularly new aspect of EEC policy and can be traced right back to the Treaty of Rome itself, but implementation of such rhetoric in Community law has not been a traditional feature. In this sense then there has been real movement in recent years, with some tangible results.

It is the purpose of this article to review the origins of the developing framework of the EEC's social law, and to consider the extent to which this framework is calling into question the traditional model of Irish labour law in particular. It is my contention that we may be witnessing the emergence of a new European model of both labour law and industrial relations, which may not entirely replace the various domestic systems, but may nevertheless change many of their traditional features.

THE ORIGINAL FRAMEWORK OF THE COMMUNITY'S SOCIAL POLICY

Although, as we have just noted, social policy was not initially an active ingredient of Community law, the EEC Treaty, nevertheless, contained within it the provisions which were later to drive this area. Articles 117 to 122 were included under the heading of "social policy", and they mapped out an agenda which, while vague and rather aspirational in parts, indicated a definite direction. Article 117 provided for "improved working conditions and an improved standard of living for workers", and envisaged harmonization of these throughout the Community. Article 118 charged the Commission with the task of promoting co-operation between Member States in the social field, with particular reference to aspects such as employment, labour law and working conditions, health and safety, and social security. Article 119 provided for an entitlement of equal pay for equal work as between men and women. Finally, Articles 120 to 122 dealt with various minor matters.

Until the late 1980s, the main area of activity in the social policy area was, at any rate in volume terms, that of sex discrimination, which received its impetus from Article 119; we shall return to this presently. But other areas also received at least some attention, and these were the following:

Collective dismissals and redundancies: EEC Directive 75/129 provided for procedures to be observed where an employer dismisses workers "for one or more reasons not related to the individual workers concerned",[3] that is, the concept of "redundancy" as already known in Irish law under the Redundancy Payments Acts. Under the Directive, Member States were to introduce measures to create an obligation on employers to inform the public authorities before such dismissals take place and to consult the employees' representative organizations in relation to them. An amending directive was passed by the Council of Ministers in June 1992, specifying more closely the nature and performance of the obligation to consult the employees' representatives.[4] In Ireland Directive 75/129 was implemented through the Protection of Employment Act, 1977.

Transfer of employment: EEC Directive 77/187—the Directive "relating to the safeguarding of employees' rights in the event of transfers of undertaking", usually known as the "Acquired Rights Directive"—required Member States to introduce measures under which the "old" and "new" employers, in the event of a transfer of the undertaking, have an obligation to consult the employees affected by the transfer, and to recognize the acquired rights of the employees arising out of the employment by the "old" employer. This was implemented in Ireland in the form of a statutory instrument, the European Communities (Safeguarding of Employees' Rights on Transfer of Undertakings) Regulations, 1980.

Employer insolvency: EEC Directive 80/987 required Member States to introduce measures to protect employees' rights in the event of employer insolvency, in relation to such matters as arrears of pay, pay related benefits, pension entitlements, and so forth. This was implemented in Ireland through the Protection of Employees (Employers' Insolvency) Act, 1984.

Apart from the above Directives, various draft measures were introduced by the Commission, particularly in the area of worker participation, but these were not adopted by the Council of Ministers. In general terms, by the early 1980s there was an appearance of stagnation of initiatives in this area. However, as we shall see presently, the development of the Single Market reinvigorated the social policy agenda.

SEX DISCRIMINATION

As we have already noted, the one area in which fairly rapid progress was made prior to the late 1980s was sex discrimination. The main basis of the legal framework in this area is Article 119 of the EEC treaty, the relevant parts of which read as follows:

> Each Member State shall . . . ensure and subsequently maintain the application of the principle that men and women should receive equal pay for equal work.

The original inclusion of the Article was connected with the desire of the French Government not to suffer economic and commercial handicaps as a result of its own equal pay legislation. However, the Article was largely ignored in practice until the 1970s.[5] The changes which then did occur were largely prompted by the case brought by a Belgian national, Gabrielle Defrenne, against the Belgian national airline, Sabena. Ms Defrenne had been employed as an airline hostess from 1951 until 1968, during which year she reached the age of forty and was, in line with the airline's normal practice for woman cabin attendants, compulsorily retired. She brought legal proceedings against the company based on a number of complaints, including:

(i)   the application of different retirement ages for men and women;
(ii) the fact that, as "principal cabin attendant", she had received lower pay than male cabin attendants working with her; and
(iii) her exclusion from the pension scheme enjoyed by male cabin attendants.

Ms Defrenne's action in the Belgian courts led to a number of references to the European Court of Justice under Article 177. In one of these the ECJ held that Article 119 was "one of the foundations of the Community", and could be relied upon directly in legal proceedings before national courts.[6] The Court held that direct pay discrimination could be challenged under Article 119, although the ability to claim back pay prior to the date of the Defrenne judgment was heavily qualified.

The *Defrenne* litigation prompted the Community's institutions to take urgent action and, as a result, a number of measures were passed in the ensuing period:

• Directive 75/117/EEC (the "Equal Pay Directive");

• Directive 76/207/EEC (the "Equal Treatment Directive");

• Directive 79/7/EEC (the "Social Security Directive");

• Directive 86/378/EEC (Directive on Equal Treatment in Occupational Social Security Schemes);

• Directive 86/613/EEC (Directive on Equal Treatment in Self Employed Occupations, including Agriculture . . .);

• Resolution on Sexual Harassment.

It may be worthwhile to focus briefly on the first two of these measures.

Directive 75/117 requires Member States to apply in law the principle of equal pay for equal work, or for work "to which equal value is attributed".[7] The Directive further provides for remedies where there are "provisions appearing in collective agreements, wage scales, wage agreements or individual contracts of employment" which discriminate in relation to pay,[8] and for remedies in cases of "victimization", that is, reprisals against employees who have brought or taken part in proceedings to enforce the equal pay entitlement. The concept of equal pay for work to which equal value is attributed is of particular importance, since it allows the comparison of jobs which are not identical but which have, to use the American terminology, "comparable worth". Overall, the Directive has been implemented in Ireland in the Anti-Discrimination (Pay) Act, 1974.

Directive 76/207 deals with employment-related discrimination in matters other than pay, in particular access to employment, vocational training, promotion, and conditions of work. The Directive introduces a "principle of equal treatment", which is defined as the principle that "there shall be no discrimination whatsoever on grounds of sex, either directly or indirectly, by reference in particular to marital or family status".[9] The only exception to the principle may apply where sex is a "determining factor", that is, where the gender of a person may be an objectively necessary criterion for the job (for example, actors and models). In Ireland the Directive has been implemented in the Employment Equality Act, 1977.

If the central aspect of Directive 75/117 is the concept of equal value, in the case of Directive 76/207 it is the concept of indirect discrimination, which the Directive itself does not define. However, the ECJ has laid down a set of guidelines, which could be summarized as follows: indirect discrimination exists where an employer applies a term or condition of employment, which is on the face of it apparently neutral; a substantially greater proportion of one sex is able to comply with it than of the other; the failure to comply is to the person's detriment; and the term or condition is not based on objectively justified factors, that is, "it does not correspond to a real need on the part of the undertaking", or is not "appropriate" and "necessary" for achieving that need.[10] This concept, therefore, allows applicants in appropriate cases to seek redress for unequal labour market conditions as well as overt discrimination.

In Ireland, therefore, a range of measures can be used before the courts to address sex discrimination problems:

• Article 119 of the EEC Treaty itself, since, as we have seen, it has direct effect; it has moreover been held that the Article covers not just pay, but benefits in kind, redundancy payments, occupational pensions and occupational social welfare benefits.[11]

- The Directives themselves, depend on the context of the cases in which they might be pleaded. The ECJ has held that they have vertical direct effect (that is, in actions taken against the State or bodies under the control of the State),[12] and in the *Francovich* case[13] the Court mapped out the consequences of a State's failure to legislate in response to a Directive, which might give an opening to litigants without a domestic remedy even where the actual discriminator is not the State or its agencies.

- The Irish domestic legislation, to be interpreted in the light of Article 119/EEC, the Directives and the case law of the ECJ.

Irish discrimination law is by and large recognized as progressive and advanced, and, in particular, it has addressed the need to define difficult concepts so that their application by the courts, the Labour Court and (where appropriate) the Employment Appeals Tribunal can be effective. However, the case law of the ECJ has demonstrated, on occasion, that there are problems in Ireland with the interpretation of the statutory provisions in the light of Community law, and that the common law tradition, in particular, may not always help to realize the social objectives of the legal framework.[14]

At the EC level, action to combat sex discrimination is an aspect of social policy which has, since the early 1970s, been fairly effectively pursued, and more recent developments (which we discuss below) tend to show that the Commission in particular is still committed to an active agenda in this area.

THE SOCIAL CHARTER AND THE MAASTRICHT PROTOCOL

In the period since the late 1970s, the main driving force behind the development of social policy has been the completion of the Single Market. In the discussions which preceded this, concern was expressed by some Member States (generally the "Northern" States such as Germany, the Benelux countries and France) that the Single Market could lead to what is sometimes described as "social dumping". This concept describes a process by which inward investment is influenced by labour costs, which in turn are deemed to be affected by the levels of statutory or other legal intervention in terms and conditions of employment, social security entitlements, and so forth. It was argued, therefore, by some that the Community should develop a framework of employment and social law which would, in many of its essentials, be common to all Member States. The European Commission took up this theme in a working paper in 1988, entitled *The Social*

Dimension of the Internal Market, in which it proposed to take certain initiatives to reduce the risk of social dumping (although it regarded the risk to be generally small). This process resulted in two initiatives: (a) the amendment of the Treaty provisions in the Single European Act, and (b) the drafting of the Community Charter of Fundamental Social Rights for Workers.

The main Treaty amendment introduced through the Single European Act was the new Article 118A, which provides for majority voting on the Council of Ministers where the subject-matter relates to "improvements, especially in the working environment, as regards the health and safety of workers". This now allows the Council to override the veto of a minority of Member States where a measure is to be adopted in this general area. There is some evidence of a creative interpretation by the Commission of the term "health and safety", which may at some point result in litigation. But in any event, it has been possible to proceed with some initiatives on the basis of unanimity.

The so-called "Social Charter" was adopted by eleven Member States at the European Council in Strasbourg in December 1989. The Charter does not have legal effect, but rather sets out a number of policy objectives of the Community in the social area. These objectives include the following: a right to freedom of movement;[15] the concept of employment which is "fairly remunerated" and an "equitable wage";[16] the aim of an "improvement in the living and working conditions of workers";[17] the "right of association", the right to "negotiate and conclude collective agreements", and the "right to resort to collective action";[18] the development of "information, consultation and participation for workers";[19] and the further development of "satisfactory health and safety conditions in [the] working environment".[20]

The adoption of the Charter was accompanied by a Commission Action Programme,[21] which indicated various initiatives which the Commission would seek to undertake in the implementation of the provisions of the Social Charter. The initiatives announced there included:

- a Directive on Working Time (first introduced by the Commission in September 1990);

- a Directive to establish written proof of the contract of employment (adopted by the Council in October 1991);[22]

- a Directive on maternity rights (adopted by the Council in October 1992);[23]

- legislation on information, consultation and participation of workers;

- Directives on health and safety; and

- Directives to protect "atypical" employees.

It is worth pausing briefly to pay particular attention to the Directives on atypical employment. The concept of atypical employment is based on the idea that there is a "typical" model of employment, based on a full-time, permanent (that is, open-ended) employment relationship with a clearly identified employer. There have always been employment relationships which do not reflect that model, but since the 1980s the incidence of "atypical" employment has greatly increased, leading to larger numbers of part-time, temporary, contract, home-working and other similar employees. This led the Commission to take the view that regulation of atypical employment was desirable, and it put forward the following argument in its Action Programme:

> Faced with the considerable development of very varied forms of employment contracts other then those of an open-ended type, there should be a Community framework ensuring a minimum of consistency between these various forms of contract in order to avoid the danger of distortions of competition and to increase the transparency of the labour market at Community level.[24]

In implementing its intentions the Commission introduced three draft Directives on atypical employment in August 1990, with the aim of giving equal rights to all employed persons who work an average working week of not less than eight hours in relation to a number of contexts, including health and safety, training, benefits, holidays, and so forth. Only the Directive on health and safety has been adopted to date,[25] but the general framework visible in the measures has already had a wider impact: for example, one outcome has been the Irish legislation on part-time employment enacted in 1991.[26] Whether there will be a more general re-drawing of the labour market remains to be seen, but other influences are also at work. The ECJ, for example, has held that discrimination against part-time workers (including the refusal to give them the same pro rata pay and conditions as full-time workers) may amount to indirect sex discrimination and may thus be unlawful.[27]

It is clear from the above that the Social Charter, with its accompanying documents and initiatives, has had a significant impact on the development of EEC social and employment law, an impact which moreover is set to continue. To this must now perhaps also be added the "Agreement on Social Policy" adopted by eleven Member States (excluding the United Kingdom) as a Protocol to the Maastricht Treaty in 1991. This sets out further areas in which the Community is to adopt measures, but in view of the UKs refusal to participate, it is not yet clear to what extent the Commission will continue to use the existing legal provisions in developing further initiatives.

CONCLUSION

The European Community consists of a variety of countries with very varied traditions of employment and industrial relations regulation, and very different concepts of what kind of social framework should be encouraged through legal intervention. Ireland has traditionally followed the British model, which, for all sorts of reasons, has tended to have a less developed system of labour law. It is hard to know whether the EEC will be able to "harmonize" a Community-wide model of social and employment law into existence, but if it does, that model will probably look more like the existing German framework than the British one. It will impose stricter controls on collective action, but in return offer greater rights for workers, both in relation to terms and conditions, and in relation to information, consultation and participation. There are at any rate some signs that this process has begun.

7.3 Procedural Aspects of the European Social Charter

LIZ HEFFERNAN

Debate over the classification of rights has long been a feature of international human rights law. From the outset, it seems, the development of international rules to regulate the relationship between the individual and the State was dominated by considerations of the character of the rights deemed worthy of protection. Although, in the present day, a web of international provisions, which combine to constitute an international code of legal protection, embraces rights across a broad spectrum of social, political, ideological and cultural divides, the status of individual rights varies considerably. Most graphic is the broad distinction between so-called "civil and political" rights and "economic, social and cultural" rights, a distinction which is sustained through the conclusion of separate instruments and cemented by the endorsement of differing standards in substance and procedure.

It is not proposed here to examine or evaluate common perceptions concerning the nature of rights nor to assess the aptness of this distinction.[1] With the acceptance of instruments such as the European Social Charter[2] and the International Covenant on Economic, Social and Cultural Rights (ICESCR),[3] the position of economic, social and cultural rights in the international legal code was firmly established.[4] However, a significant question remains concerning the efficacy of international protection in respect of these rights, as opposed to civil and political rights. Nowhere is this more apparent than in the European arena, where the success of the European Convention on Human Rights is in stark contrast to the modest claims of the European Social Charter. Despite the rhetoric of the Council of Europe to the effect that both the civil and political rights guaranteed by the ECHR as well as the economic and social rights protected by the Charter "are interdependent and together form an indivisible set of principles on which the democracies of Europe are founded",[5] it has been aptly observed that "[w]hereas the Convention is firmly established as the jewel in the Council of Europe crown, the Charter has led a twilight existence".[6]

An initial attempt at redressing this imbalance was embodied in an Additional Protocol to the European Social Charter which was opened for signature in May 1988.[7] This measure addresses the substance of the Charter and seeks to extend and supplement the catalogue of guaranteed rights.

The Charter itself contains four parts, the first of which comprises a series of economic and social policy aims which the Contracting States agree to pursue by all appropriate national and international means. For example, the first two principles are that "[E]veryone shall have the opportunity to earn his living in an occupation freely entered upon"; and that "[a]ll workers have the right to just conditions of work"; while the twelfth principle is to the effect that "[a]ll workers and their dependents have the right to social security". Part II of the Charter translates each of these basic principles into specific, detailed, legal obligations[8] but, moreover, introduces an approach unique to human rights treaties, namely, the selective assumption of State obligations. Article 20 provides that each Contracting State must guarantee the rights comprised in a minimum of ten articles,[9] five of which, at least, must be drawn from among seven core provisions.[10] The remaining obligations may be selected at the discretion of the State, with the ultimate objective of a gradual strengthening of State endeavour in the field of economic and social rights. The Additional Protocol incorporates its reforms into the existing framework of the Charter by extending certain general rights, for example, with respect to women and employment,[11] and by introducing new guarantees, such as the right of workers to information and consultation.[12]

This paper seeks to focus on a further more recent campaign of reform which targets procedural aspects of the Charter.[13] An informal Council of Europe Ministerial Conference on Human Rights held in Rome in November 1990 launched a drive to give fresh impetus to the Charter by inviting the Committee of Ministers of the Council of Europe "to take the necessary measures so that a detailed study of the role, contents and operation of the European Social Charter may be undertaken as soon as possible".[14] This led to the appointment of an *ad hoc* Committee[15] with a mandate to formulate proposals for reform, having particular regard to the functioning of the system of supervision contained in Part IV of the Charter. Its efforts resulted in the opening for signature of an Amending Protocol to the European Social Charter at the Ministerial Conference of October 1991 in Turin, on the occasion of the thirtieth anniversary of the conclusion of the Charter.

THE NEED FOR REFORM

Aside from predictable contrasts between the ECHR and the European Social Charter, borne of differing international approaches to civil and political as opposed to economic and social rights, an examination of the two instruments reveals that there there are, in fact, few parallels between these supposed counterparts. Certainly, the degree of similarity, both in substance and supervision, enjoyed by the two International Covenants (ICCPR and ICESCR) is lacking as between the ECHR and the Charter.[16] Moreover, even within their own regimes, the vibrancy of the ECHR has tended to accentuate the sluggish performance of the Charter. The contrast is most apparent, perhaps, with respect to State response, as exemplified by the levels of accession and adherence and the presence of political will. An initial signatory to the Charter, Ireland was one of the States which had deposited instruments of ratification upon entry into force of the Charter in 1965.[17] As of 1 January 1994, twenty Member States of the Council of Europe had become parties to the Charter,[18] while three States had ratified the Additional Protocol, thereby facilitating its entry into force in November 1992.[19] Although the number of Contracting States has increased considerably in recent years, it should be recalled that the level of adherence to the particular Charter provisions varies enormously, so that not merely in terms of the number, but also of the degree, of State participation, the Charter trails behind the ECHR.

The Charter's state of ill-health and, in particular, the imperfections of the existing supervisory system, had been apparent for some time and constituted, in itself, just cause for reform. Nevertheless, the revival of interest which surfaced at the close of the 1980s and resulted in the conclusion of the Amending Protocol can be traced to a number of external factors.[20] The first is the emergence of the new democracies in Central and Eastern Europe and the consequent swelling of membership of the Council of Europe. As Harris explains:

> The understanding is that the protection of economic and social rights is of the utmost importance in the operation of the free market economies that the former Eastern European States are seeking to establish and that the

European Social Charter provides the necessary benchmarks in this regard. Accordingly, it is important to the Council that the Charter is working efficiently if new member States and candidates for membership are to be measured by its standards.[21]

The emergence of workers' rights within the European Community including the adoption of an EEC Social Charter constitutes a second factor. This development has raised the spectre of the two regimes exercising competence, simultaneously, with respect to the actions of the EEC Member States in the field of economic and social rights. At a general level, therefore, EEC developments have had the indirect effect of focusing attention on the achievements of the Council of Europe in the field of economic and social rights. More specifically, however, given the integrated nature of the European Community and the potentially far-reaching impact of Community law on domestic legal systems, EEC action served as a spur for a reformist agenda with respect to the European Social Charter.

Finally, a further injection of concern with respect to the fortunes of the Charter, was administered following a measure of internal re-structuring within the Council of Europe. It is only since 1989 that the Charter has fallen within the competence of the Council's Directorate of Human Rights which also oversees the operation of the ECHR. Having found a place within this new home, the Charter was immediately subjected to close scrutiny with a view to the improvement of its condition.[22]

THE CURRENT SUPERVISORY PROCEDURE

As yet, the overhaul to the supervisory machinery of the European Social Charter incorporated into the Amending Protocol has not taken effect. Article 8 of the Protocol provides for its entry into force thirty days after all of the Contracting States to the Charter have expressed their consent to be bound. As of 1 January 1994, only three States had done so.[23] It follows that a review of the existing system of supervision remains a relevant exercise in respect of current practice as well as impending reform.

The essence of enforcement under the Charter is the operation of a State reporting mechanism. Unlike the ECHR, there is no provision for a right of individual or collective petition, nor is there a facility for inter-State complaints. Although no less than four bodies are involved in the supervisory process, the Charter lacks any provision for reference to a court of law.[24] In addition, the scope of the independent review is limited to obligations assumed under Part II of the Charter and does not extend to the general policy aims which all Contracting States are required to pursue in accordance with Part I.

Provision is made for two types of report. The mainstay of Charter activity is the bi-annual, Article 21, report, in which each Contracting State must detail the manner in which it has applied those provisions of the Charter which it has specifically accepted. Submitted to the Secretary-General of the Council of Europe, this report is examined by the "Committee of Independent Experts", in the first instance. Appointed by the Committee of Ministers of the Council of Europe from among a list of individuals nominated by the Contracting States, this body is comprised of experts "of the highest integrity and of recognized competence in international social questions".[25] The task of these experts is to formulate legally non-binding "conclusions" as to State compliance with Charter obligations, on the basis of the report and of any comments of approved national non-governmental organizations (NGOs) which have been forwarded to the Secretary-General by the State in question.[26] These "conclusions", together with the report, are examined by the "Governmental Committee of the Social Charter", a body composed of representatives of each of the Contracting States, which compiles a "report" of its own which is transmitted, in turn, to the Committee of Ministers.[27] A further review of the "conclusions" and the "report" is then conducted by the Parliamentary Assembly which adopts an "opinion".[28] Armed with these three documents, the Committee of Ministers adopts a resolution in which it may, at its discretion, issue non-binding recommendations for action to the Contracting State in question.[29]

The second, more occasional, form of report is required in respect of those Charter obligations which the Contracting State has not accepted. Article 22 limits the duty to report to instances where the Committee of Ministers has issued a specific request. Once submitted to the Secretary-General, this report follows the same route of supervision as its Article 21 counterpart.

The shortcomings of the supervisory system have been well documented both within and outside the Council of Europe.[30] Obvious criticisms relate to the excessive number of supervisory organs and the corresponding duplication of function. The Charter is by no means precise as to the respective roles of the Committee of Independent Experts, the Governmental Committee, the Parliamentary Assembly and the Committee of Ministers. A notable concern relates to the absence of any indication as to which body should have the final say on the interpretation of the Charter. In particular, the conclusions of the Committee of Independent Experts may be side-stepped or subsumed into the subsequent stages of review. Moreover, it is not unusual for the Committee of Independent Experts and the Governmental Committee to reach differing verdicts as to State compliance in a particular case.

The bureaucracy of the present system has produced a further undesirable side-effect, namely, considerable extensions to the length of the procedure. Current estimates suggest that the supervision cycle for Article 21 reports stretches over three years. This has led to the ludicrous result of Contracting States submitting new bi-annual reports in advance of the adoption of Committee of Ministers resolutions in respect of their previous reports.[31]

The apparent lack of independent pressure exerted by the Charter system on Contracting States represents an additional cause for concern. Certainly, the limits of State reporting must be recognized, particularly with respect to enforcement, where a consultative atmosphere may deny it the penetrative legal and psychological impact of the binding decision of a court of law handed down against a State in response to a specific complaint. Nevertheless, the advantages of State reporting are manifold and should not be underestimated. Much depends upon the structure of the reporting mechanism and the willingness of the institutional organs to maximize the supervisory powers provided. In both respects, the European Social Charter falls short of the mark. Clearly, there are misgivings about the absence of authority on the part of the Charter organs to deliver legally binding directions to the Contracting States. More alarming, however, is the fact that the Committee of Ministers has never utilized its power to issue a non-binding recommendation to a Contracting State, even where infringements of Charter standards have been acknowledged.

Finally, it must be conceded that the effectiveness of the State reporting in the Charter system has been severely undermined by a failure to take adequate steps to secure the contribution of NGOs. In contrast to the International Labour Organization (ILO),[32] the institutional framework of the Charter limits the potential input of NGOs, including employers' and trade unions' organizations, to a mere nominal involvement in the review of State compliance.

THE AMENDING PROTOCOL

The Protocol attempts to address, either directly or indirectly, the bulk of issues raised above, such as the respective functions of the supervisory bodies, the adoption of recommendations by the Committee of Ministers, and the role of NGOs in the supervisory process.

Perhaps the most significant advance relates to the roles of the Committee of Independent Experts and the Governmental Committee. By clarifying the respective competences of these bodies, the Protocol seeks to remedy the ills of functional overlap and interpretational uncertainty, thereby re-aligning the Charter with the intentions of the original signatories thereto. The amended Article 24(2) provides:

> With regard to the reports referred to in Article 21, the Committee of Independent Experts shall assess from a legal standpoint the compliance of

national law and practice with the obligations arising from the Charter for the Contracting Parties concerned.

Regarding a corresponding adjustment to the role of Governmental Committee, amended Article 27(3) states:

The Governmental Committee shall prepare the decisions of the Committee of Ministers. In particular, in the light of the reports of the Committee of Independent Experts and of the Contracting Parties, it shall select, giving reasons for its choice, on the basis of social, economic and other policy considerations the situations which should, in its view, be the subject of recommendations to each Contracting Party concerned, in accordance with Article 28 of the Charter. It shall present to the Committee of Ministers a report which shall be made public.

Thus, provision is made for a firm division of labour between the Committee of Independent Experts and the Governmental Committee with respect to the reporting procedure, albeit in language which is unhelpfully inexplicit. That the interpretation of the Charter and adjudication as to State compliance should fall within the exclusive purview of the Committee of Independent Experts is a predictable and welcome advance, although the Protocol does not go so far as to expressly bestow upon that Committee the exclusive power to issue binding interpretations of the Charter. Moreover, the rationale for the resulting role which has been carved for the Governmental Committee may prove somewhat difficult to sustain. As has been observed elsewhere, "it would have made sense to abolish the Governmental Committee altogether".[33] The efficacy of its new advisory function of must await its test and one can only speculate as to the "social, economic and other policy considerations" which it might bring to bear on the decision of the Committee of Ministers whether or not to issue a recommendation in a particular case. One inescapable implication is the exclusion, from the Governmental Committee's ambit of consideration, of an interpretation of the Charter or an adjudication on compliance which is inconsistent with the findings of the Committee of Independent Experts.[34] Any infraction of this division of powers would seem to render the purported change something of a nonsense.

In order to compliment the modified roles of the Committee of Independent Experts and the Governmental Committee, further changes with respect to the mechanics of these bodies are envisaged.

The Amending Protocol introduces a number of changes in respect of the composition of the Committee of Independent Experts,[35] and two very significant provisions dealing with procedure. Article 24(3) contains an important addition to the armoury of the Committee in the form of a power to address requests for additional information directly to the Contracting States. Previously, such requests were contained in the Committee's "conclusions" and would not receive a response until the next reporting cycle. In addition, it is envisaged that the Committee "may also hold, if necessary, a meeting with the representatives of a Contracting Party, either on its own initiative or at the request of the Contracting Party concerned". Given the decisive role of oral hearings in supervision of the ICESCR, the absence, to date, of any avenue for direct dialogue between the Committee and Contracting States is particularly lamentable. Hence Article 24(3) may prove to be one of the more significant contributions of the Protocol to the operation of the Charter.

Aside from, but consistent with, its specific advisory function with respect to the issuing of recommendations to individual Contracting States, the Governmental Committee has been entrusted with an additional power to submit proposals to the Committee of Ministers for studies to be carried out on social issues and on the possible updating of Charter provisions. Arguably, the Governmental Committee has always had this power at its disposal on the basis of Article 27. If so, the Committee has never chosen to exercise it and this express inclusion in the Protocol may prove useful, not least because "[a]s far as the updating of the Charter guarantee is concerned, there are several provisions in respect of which such studies would be timely".[36]

The Protocol also addresses the function of the Parliamentary Assembly, effectively opting to remove its current practice of issuing an "opinion" on the conclusions of the Committee of Independent Experts with respect to State reports. Instead, the Assembly is to be endowed with a general supervisory capacity, exercised through a review of the documentation produced by the other supervisory organs (the conclusions of the Committee of Independent Experts, the report of the Governmental Committee and the resolutions adopted by the Committee of Ministers). This review may lead to the holding of periodical plenary debates when the Assembly deems it appropriate. Thus an additional and, arguably superfluous, layer of supervision is conveniently removed without displacing the involvement of the Assembly altogether. Again, it remains to be seen whether its alternative role will prove a useful one. In any event, the combined effect of this amendment and those relating to the respective roles of the other supervisory organs in the State reporting process should serve to reduce considerably the time-period currently required for completion of the reporting cycle.

On the question of enforcement of the Charter, the Protocol takes steps to coax the Committee of Ministers into utilizing its authority to recommend State action on the basis of the findings of the other supervisory organs. As we have seen, more specific directions to the Committee on the subject of recommendations should be forthcoming from the streamlined analyses of the Committee of Independent Experts and the Governmental Committee, respectively. In addition, the wording of the provision has been tightened, so that for example, the current statement that the Committee of Ministers "may. . . make" recommendations will be replaced by the dictate that the Committee "shall adopt" such measures. Finally, a new Article 28 liberates the voting rules by which a resolution containing such recommendations may be adopted. At the present time, affirmative votes on the part of two-thirds of the members of the Committee (that is, two-thirds of the members of the Council of Europe) are required. Under the amended provision, a vote of two-thirds of the Contracting Parties to the Charter will suffice.[37] However, as Harris reminds us, the ultimate success of the Committee of Ministers' powers of enforcement will depend, not on the laxity of voting rules, but rather on the presence or absence of a requisite degree of political will.

The other significant area of reform tackled by the Amending Protocol concerns the role of NGOs in the supervisory process. Certain changes—by no means radical—should serve to enhance the limited opportunities currently open to employers' and trade unions' organizations to voice their responses to a State report. In the first place, while responsibility for the transmission to Strasbourg of NGO comments currently rests with the State, the Amending Protocol provides for direct communication between NGOs and the Secretary-General. Governments will have an opportunity to respond to these comments, but again, through the official channel of correspondence with the Secretary-General. Secondly, any such NGO comments will be forwarded not only to the Committee of Independent Experts but also to the Governmental Committee. Thirdly, provision is made for the dissemination of State reports by the Secretary-General to "the international non-governmental organizations which have consultative status with the Council of Europe and have particular competence in the matters governed by the present Charter".[38] Moreover, the category of organizations which may participate in the supervisory process has been extended, somewhat. Limitations remain, however, with respect to the status of eligible organizations and the extent to which they can insist that their views be entertained.[39]

To date, one of the greatest shortcomings of the Charter has been a failure to attract the input of NGOs. Very few organizations have been in a position to participate and fewer still have chosen to actively pursue that role. This must suggest that the Charter, at least in its current guise, holds little promise for such organizations of an effective advancement of their interests. While the Amending Protocol provides for some improvement in this regard, the changes are relatively modest and insufficient grounds for excessive optimism as to the practical benefits that may ensue.

Finally, brief mention should be made of a general development in the character of the Charter which will be ushered in by the Amending Protocol. The current practice of confidentiality with respect to State reports is to be replaced with a new atmosphere of openness. The conclusions of the Committee of Independent Experts as well as the reports of the Governmental Committee are to be made public, while State reports and any NGO comments shall be made available to the public upon request. This amendment seems eminently sensible and is long overdue. Indeed, there appears to be no good reason for retaining limitations on the circulation of State reports and NGO comments. The experience of the International Covenants suggests that State reporting can be an effective catalyst for change nationally, as well as internationally, provided that the national forum has the requisite information at its disposal.

CONCLUSION

It has been observed, elsewhere, that the Amending Protocol to the European Social Charter "bears the traces of compromise".[40] In many respects, the changes embodied in the Protocol do not go far enough. Nevertheless, while by no means radical, these changes are significant. When translated into practice, the Amending Protocol could herald a real revitalization of the Charter. Significant political will has been exerted to usher the current campaign of overhaul thus far—the fate of this progression now lies in the hands of the Contracting States. The requirements for entry into force of the Amending Protocol are such that its effective implementation may be several years away. Hence the Final Resolution of the Turin Conference urged the Contracting States and the Strasbourg organs to envisage the immediate application of certain of the measures provided for in the Protocol, insofar as the Charter will allow.

To date, the process of reform, although encouraging, has been ambling along at a modest pace. Efforts must now be made to apply and render effective existing amendments and to incorporate further reforms. In this latter respect, the drafting of an optional protocol providing for a system of collective complaints is a particularly welcome advance. The possibility of NGOs petitioning Strasbourg on specific issues of State compliance holds the promise of an entirely new relevance for the European Social Charter as an instrument for the protection of economic and social rights at international and national level. Finally, as the Final Resolution of the Turin Conference suggests, the time is also ripe to give further consideration to a revision of the Charter's substantive guarantees.[41]

7.4   Gender as a Human Rights Issue in Strasbourg

ALPHA CONNELLY

" . . . the advancement of the equality of the sexes is today a major goal in the Member States of the Council of Europe." (European Court of Human Rights in *Abdulaziz, Cabales and Balkandali*, 1985)

Equality is a core value in the endeavour to promote and ensure respect for human dignity and worth. In the words of the Universal Declaration of Human rights: "All human beings are born free and equal in dignity and rights."[1] Together with liberty and what today we might describe as solidarity rather than fraternity, equality infuses human rights norms which are gradually gaining global acceptance.

Equality is a measure of how society treats difference. At first sight simple and appealing, on further examination it is revealed as multi-faceted and problematic in its application to specific cases. I do not propose to explore here this complex idea. Rather I shall identify some of its aspects in order to afford a conceptual framework for a review of the legal record of one regional organization in advancing the equality of the sexes. That organization is the Council of Europe.

First, equality requires that if a difference between persons is not relevant for a specific purpose, it should be ignored. It is always possible to distinguish one persons from another on some basis. One person has red hair, another black. One person has blue eyes, another brown. For most social purposes such differences are irrelevant. For example, the colour of a person's hair or eyes has no relevance to how well, or how poorly, that person plays football. It should therefore be ignored in the selection of members of a football team since it is not relevant for this purpose. If an irrelevant difference has been taken into account so that one person has been advantaged or disadvantaged in comparison to another by reason of this difference, then unjust discrimination has occurred and the principle of equality has been infringed. This aspect of equality further requires that if a difference is only partially relevant, then to the extent that it is irrelevant, it should be ignored. With specific reference to gender, this means, for example, that if a man is refused permission to adopt a child merely because he is a man, without any reference to how well or how badly he might care for the child, when a woman would be allowed to adopt merely because she is a woman, without any consideration of how well she would care for the child, the man has been unjustly discriminated against. Even if it could be shown that women as a group are more caring and child-oriented than men, this would not of itself justify the automatic refusal of permission to a particular man to adopt a child. It would merely be one factor to be taken into account in assessing the man's suitability as an adoptive parent. If greater weight were to be afforded the man's sex in the adoption decision than was warranted in the circumstance, he would be unjustly disadvantaged. A law promotive of equality will prohibit such discrimination. This aspect of equality operates to ensure that a difference between persons, if irrelevant or to the extent that it is irrelevant, will not be taken into account. Rather they will be treated the same.

Secondly, equality endorses the recognition of pertinent differences and requires that the law treat persons differently to the extent that there is a relevant difference between them. In other words, equality does not always mean treating people the same. To treat people the same when there is a pertinent difference between them is to offend against the principle of equality. This aspect of equality operates to ensure that a difference between persons, if relevant and to the extent that it is relevant, will be taken into account, and that they will be treated differently.

Pertinent differences in the field of gender take a variety of forms. One form is differences which are gender-specific in that they pertain uniquely to one sex. A rather obvious example is pregnancy. A woman may become pregnant, a man may not. Thus actual or potential pregnancy may, in certain circumstances, constitute a pertinent difference between a man and a woman requiring different legislative treatment. Protection of women against dismissal from employment by reason of pregnancy is an example.

Another form of pertinent difference concerns the differential impact of a facially-neutral law on different groups. An example in the field of gender would be the use of an upper age limit for job applications, say thirty, which in practice would exclude many more women than men since, prior to that age, many women will have remained at home to rear children and will seek employment later in life than men. This latter fact is a pertinent difference, and unless the age limit can be shown to be directly relevant to the job or is permissible for some other reason, it is discriminatory. The ignoring of such a differential impact is usually described as indirect discrimination.

A third form of pertinent difference arises as a result of historical inequity. Where members of a particular group have been historically disadvantaged, equality suggests that it may not be sufficient to treat members of this group and other persons who have been advantaged historically in the same way, since such a policy can be expected to perpetuate the relative advantage/disadvantage of the different groups. Rather equality seeks to bring about an equilibrium in the position of all concerned by affording preferential treatment to the disadvantaged for as long as is necessary to achieve this goal. This positive or reverse discrimination aspect of equality is most controversial and problematic because, in advantaging a member of a disadvantaged group, other individuals not belonging to this group may be disadvantaged, and it arguably offends against the equal worth of each individual human being. Should the State reserve a number of top posts in the civil service for women because they have been excluded therefrom in the past? If it should, how many places should be reserved, and for how many years should such preferential treatment be continued?

All the aspects of equality which I have identified, with the exception of positive discrimination, have been endorsed by western liberal democracies and are promoted to varying degrees by the laws of these States. Positive discrimination has been adopted in some, for example, the Scandinavian States, but has not been universally accepted. Whether the liberal democratic model of social organization and government can in fact deliver equality in dignity and rights for all human beings is a question which I do not propose to address within the confines of this short paper. The Council of Europe is premised upon the subscription by its Member States to liberal democratic values, and it is by reference to the aspects of equality endorsed by these States that the record of the Council with respect to the advancement of the equality of the sexes will be examined here.

THE COUNCIL OF EUROPE AND HUMAN RIGHTS

Arising out of a concern for peace, order and security in the wake of the Second World War, the Council of Europe was established to promote closer co-operation among States in Europe on a range of matters. Its aim is the achievement of greater unity among its Member States for the purpose of safeguarding and realizing the ideals and principles which are their common heritage and facilitating their economic and social progress.[2] This aim it pursues, through its constituent organs, by discussions of questions of common concern, common action and the conclusion of international agreements.[3] Among the matters specifically assigned to it is the maintenance and further realization of human rights and fundamental freedoms. The seat of the Council is at Strasbourg.[4]

Since its inception in 1949, the Council has drafted many international agreements on human rights matters for adoption by Member States. Two major texts dominate the field and, together with the subsequent Protocols amending and extending the original texts, may collectively be described as the European

Bill of Rights. The two texts are the European Convention on Human Rights, 1950 and the European Social Charter, 1961.

The adoption of two texts reflects the belief that human rights are roughly classifiable into two categories: rights in relation to civil and political matters on the one hand, and rights in relation to economic and social matters on the other. According to this view, civil and political rights require little, if anything, by way of State action for their realization; and, in case of dispute as to whether or not a State has complied with its human rights obligations in these matters, the dispute is best settled by an independent tribunal which will, if necessary, afford a remedy to any individual whose rights it finds to have been violated. In contrast, economic and social rights require State action for their realization. Unlike civil and political rights, they are not justiciable, and a State's obligations with respect to economic and social rights are best monitored at the international level by bodies which advise and encourage States to adopt and implement appropriate policies rather than adjudicate on whether a State has in fact complied with its obligations or not.

The European Convention on Human Rights and its various Protocols guarantee rights in civil and political matters, rights such as personal liberty, freedom of expression, freedom of assembly and association, privacy and a fair trial. Two independent bodies were established by the Convention with the competence to hear complaints of alleged violations of the rights guaranteed by the Convention: the European Commission and the European Court of Human Rights. The Court has in fact only rarely been seised of gender issues. Most such issues have been considered and decided by the Commission at the admissibility stage of the proceedings.

The European Social Charter regulates States' obligations in relation to economic and social rights. It is concerned mainly with employment, but encompasses also rights such as the right to protection of health and the right to benefit from social welfare services. It entrusts international supervision of whether or not a State is complying with its obligations largely to political organs of the Council of Europe. Provision is however made for one independent element in the system of international supervision. This element is afforded by a Committee of Independent Experts which considers reports from States Parties on how they are implementing their obligations under the Charter. The conclusions of this Committee are then considered together with the State reports by the political organs of the Council.[5] It is the examination of this Committee of State reports which throws some light on the interpretation to be afforded the substantive provisions of the Charter, including those dealing with matters of gender.

THE EUROPEAN CONVENTION ON HUMAN RIGHTS

Unlike other civil and political rights treaties, the European Convention does not guarantee the right to equality before the law or to equal protection of the law.[6] Rather the Convention adopts a non-discrimination approach to the protection of the rights it guarantees. In other words, it contains a general provision that these rights shall be enjoyed without discrimination on any ground: Article 14. This is an ancillary rather than a separate substantive provision. Complaints relating to gender typically invoke Article 14 together with one of the substantive provisions of the Convention. Occasionally, however, such complaints are considered under one of the substantive provisions alone. The provision in respect of which this most frequently occurs is Article 8, which guarantees respect for private and family life.

Although the Convention itself does not contain any general equality guarantee, provision has been made in a Protocol for equality between men and women in a particular field. This is in the relationship between spouses and the relationship of each with their children. Article 5 of the Seventh Protocol provides that spouses "shall enjoy equality of rights and responsibilities of a private law character between them, and in their relations with their children, as to marriage, during the marriage and in the event of its dissolution."[7] This guarantee is subject to the rider that it "shall not prevent States from taking such measures as are necessary in the interests of the children". This Article has yet to be interpreted by the European Commission and European Court of Human Rights, but a likely reading is that, within the context of a legally recognized marriage, the spouses are to have the same rights and duties as one another in their mutual relations, for example with respect to maintenance, and in their relations with their children, for example with respect to custody, except where the interests of the child or children require that preference be given to one parent over the other. Leading commentators on the Convention have suggested that these rights are already largely guaranteed by the right to respect for private and family life, read either on its own or in conjunction with the non-discrimination provision of Article 14.[8] It remains to be seen exactly what further guarantee is afforded by the Protocol; but it is clear that it is of a limited kind. It applies only to the private law aspects of the relations mentioned, and does not apply, for example, to the taxation by a State of the individuals concerned or to situations where one spouse is the employee of the other.

There have been few complaints under the Convention of gender discrimination in the political field. Article 3 of the First Protocol whereby States undertake to hold free elections has been interpreted as guaranteeing the right to vote and to stand for election to the legislature. A Dutch woman invoked this provision, together with Article 14 of the Convention, because she wished to be listed in the electoral register under her maiden name only, but her request to be so registered was refused.[9] She was in fact registered under the name of her husband followed by her maiden name. She alleged that this was discriminatory since the marital status of men was not indicated on the list. The Commission disagreed. In its view, the different treatment of married men and married women in this regard pursued a legitimate aim and was not a disproportionate means of achieving this aim. The electoral register had merely an administrative function and did not directly affect the population. Furthermore, since the majority of married women in the Netherlands bear their husband's name, recording the latter in the electoral register reflected "a reality of the contemporary Netherlands society". Apparently the impugned legislation also did not prevent the municipal authorities, in drawing up the convocation sheets for elections, from taking into account the desire of some married women to be identified by their maiden name.

In an earlier case, a Swiss woman complained that she was not allowed to stand for election to the parliament of a canton under her maiden name, even though this was the name she had used since her marriage and by which she was known to the electorate.[10] She had to stand either under her husband's name or his name in combination with her maiden name. She was unable to plead Article 3 of the First Protocol since Switzerland was not party to this treaty, and sought to rely instead on Article 8 of the convention, both on its own and in combination with Article 14. She argued that respect for private life encompassed the protection of personality and that, by not allowing her to stand for election in her maiden name, the Swiss authorities had not respected her private life. The Commission was not convinced. Even if private life did encompass the protection of personality, the fact that she could stand under her maiden name in conjunction with the name of her husband meant that she was sufficiently identifiable by the electorate. On the discrimination issue, the Commission stated:

> In common with that of many European States, Swiss law considers it necessary for a family, that is to say the spouses and their children (at least when they are minor) to be easily identifiable *vis-à-vis* third parties. By reason of the many specific legal effects of marriage, both with respect to the spouses themselves and with respect to third parties, this aim must be considered reasonable . . . the obligation placed on spouses to bear the same name (in this case, that of the husband) constitutes a suitable measure, proportionate to the aim it is sought to realize.

This reasoning may be questioned. It implies that, because it is necessary to identify people for certain purposes, the same method of identification is appropriate for all purposes. Moreover, it is saying that a particular method of identification (by reference to the husband's name) is the right method without considering alternatives and stating why this particular method is the most appropriate—except perhaps because it is a method commonly adopted by European States.

In my opinion, the Commission's decisions on these cases smack of an "Adam's rib" mentality. They do not address the real issue which concerns the autonomy and identity of a woman. Why should a married woman always be identified through her husband, either by having her preferred name completely subsumed by that of her husband, or by having her husband's name attached to her preferred option? Administrative convenience or habitual practice do not seem to me to afford adequate reasons. A discriminatory practice is no less discriminatory because it is common.

Most complaints of gender discrimination have related to family law matters, and have hence raised issues of respect for private and family life under Article 8. Many of these cases have been brought by men, complaining about their legal position *vis-à-vis* their children. The complaints have concerned matters such as paternal affiliation, care and custody, access and adoption.

A Belgian case concerned the legal position of the natural father of a child, the mother being at the time married to someone else.[11] When a woman's husband disclaimed paternity, the child became, under Belgian law, the child of an adulterous relationship and, although maternal affiliation was recognized, it was impossible, owing to the particular terms of the applicable Belgian law, for the natural father to have his paternity recognized in law. The application was admitted by the Commission, but a friendly settlement was subsequently concluded in view of the introduction of new legislation in Belgium, in 1987, dealing *inter alia*, with the maternal and paternal descent of children born out of wedlock.

One paternity case has been decided by the Court. It was brought by a husband who sought to challenge his paternity after his divorce from the mother.[12] Under Danish law, if a wife wished to challenge the paternity of her child, she could do so at any time, and the matter would be decided by the courts on a case by case basis. However, Danish law imposed time-limits on such a challenge by the husband, and the applicant's paternity suit in this case was time-barred. In the Court's view, this was not discriminatory. Time-limits for the institution of paternity proceedings were designed to secure legal certainty and to protect the interests of the child, and although the law treated husbands and wives differently in this regard, it did not transgress the principle of proportionality. The Court noted that the law in question did not differ substantially from that of most other Contracting States, and endorsed the view of the national authorities that "such time-limits were less necessary for wives than for husbands since the mother's interests usually coincided with those of the child, she being awarded custody in most cases of divorce or separation". Two points need to be made about this approach. In the first place, the fact that other States regulate a matter in the same or a similar way does not necessarily mean that this way of dealing with the situation is not discriminatory. Secondly, even if a wife is usually awarded custody in cases of divorce or separation, what has this got to do with paternity? Custody is about who will best look after the child. Paternity is about much else besides—maintenance, succession rights, etc.

The extent to which the Strasbourg organs are prepared to accept the treatment in law of the situation of a particular individual by reference to the general situation, rather than requiring a more finely honed law which will cater for individual circumstances, is further illustrated by a case concerning the care and custody of a child born to unmarried parents. An unmarried couple, living together with their son, complained that, under German law, the mother of a child born out of wedlock enjoyed the right to care and custody of the child, whereas the father could only obtain this right if the couple married or in other limited circumstances.[13] In essence they were arguing for joint custody as a matter of legal right. The Commission noted that, in the particular case before it, the applicants were living together, that the mother was in fact sharing care and custody of the child with its father, and that custody would only become problematic if there was a rupture of the relations between the mother and the father. In its view:

> . . . the situation of the children born out of wedlock necessitates a distinct legislative regulation which has to take into account the general aspects of the problems involved. The . . . legislator has opted for a regulation which is considered to be in the best interests of the child born out of wedlock. . . . Between a child and his mother a first and strong family relation is already established by the very event of the birth itself and usually also the unmarried mother maintains the family tie while the father of a child born out of wedlock may often not be willing to assume any family obligations. Thus, a general regulation conveying the right to care and custody to the mother in general responds to the circumstances which prevail in cases of children born out of wedlock.

The difference in treatment between the mother and father as regards care and custody of a child born out of wedlock therefore had a basis in the fact that it is usually in the child's best interests that custody be afforded the mother; and the disadvantages for a father in such a situation were outweighed by the need to safeguard the child's well-being. If the father wished to improve his situation, there was the option of marriage to the mother, in which case he would gain a right to joint care and custody of the child. The view taken in this case of the typical father of a child born out of wedlock was regarded as justifying not only the differential treatment in law of the natural mother and father but also of an unmarried father as compared to a married father. It might be queried whether such an approach does not overly rely on stereotypes and is insufficiently sensitive to the circumstances of particular cases.

To whom the law accords custody and guardianship of a child will often be of crucial importance for the future relations of the child with its parents. For example, if custody is awarded to one parent with access for the other, and if subsequently the relations between the parents deteriorate significantly, it may be in the best interests of the child to terminate access, irrespective of any fault on the part of the parent without care and custody. It is therefore of great importance that the way in which the law treats questions of custody and guardianship and any decision thereon not be infused with a gender bias, based on stereotypical views of the role of men and women in society.

Two cases further illustrate this point. One concerns a British law according to which parental rights were awarded the unmarried mother of a child, but not the unmarried father.[14] When a local authority took proceedings to have the couple's child placed in care, the applicant, the father, was present at the hearing, but had no right to participate in the proceedings, being neither the recognized parent nor guardian of the child. The child was placed with foster parents, and the applicant was at first refused but then given limited access to it. He instituted wardship proceedings seeking, *inter alia*, care and control of the child. However, the national court decided that, in view of the stable and secure environment provided for the child in the foster home, it was in the child's best interests that it remain under the care and control of the foster parents. It granted the applicant access to his son twice a month at the foster parent's home. The second concerns the situation under Irish law according to which an unmarried mother is by virtue of the birth alone guardian of her child, whereas an unmarried father has no such automatic right to guardianship but may apply to the courts to be appointed guardian. In a case which was recently referred by the Commission to the Court, the applicant is an unmarried father whose child was given up for adoption by its mother without his knowledge or consent shortly after its birth.[15] He applied to the Irish courts to be appointed guardian and to be given custody of his child, but his application was eventually refused. The Supreme Court found that although the child would be well looked after by its natural father, with the passage of time it had grown attached to the prospective adoptive parents, and it was in its best interests that it be left with them. The applicant is alleging violation of his right to respect for family life contrary to Article 8, in that his child was placed for adoption without his knowledge or consent and that Irish law did not afford him even a defeasible right to be appointed guardian of his child. He is also alleging violation of his right of access to court under Article 6(1) in that he had no *locus standi* in the proceedings before the Adoption Board. He is further alleging discrimination against him as a natural father in the exercise of both these rights. In its report on the case, the Commission expressed the opinion that Ireland had violated his rights under Articles 8 and 6(1), and that it was not necessary also to examine the allegations of discrimination under Article 14.

I do not mean to question the validity of determining such cases of disputed custody and guardianship by reference to the best interests of the child concerned. Rather I wish to point out that the decision in such cases is to some extent determined, and may even be largely predetermined, by the original legal position with respect to the guardianship and custody of the child. If this is to be afforded one parent rather than the other at the outset, it is important that this allocation of rights and responsibilities be taken on objective grounds and not on assumptions about appropriate gender roles. Equality requires that the sex of a parent should not in and of itself be determinative of the legal relationship between a parent and child.

The European Court of Human Rights found British immigration rules in the 1980s to be discriminatory on the basis of sex.[16] Three women settled in the United Kingdom were refused permission for their husbands to remain with or to join them in the UK, and they complained, *inter alia*, of violations of Articles 8 and 14 in that it was much easier for a man settled in the UK than for a woman so settled to obtain permission for a foreign spouse to enter or to remain in the UK. Given the importance attached to the equality of the sexes in the Member States of the Council of Europe, the Court said it would require "very weighty reasons" before it would accept a difference of treatment on the ground of sex as compatible with the Convention. The British Government advanced two justifications. First, it argued that the greater restriction of the entry of foreign husbands was designed to protect the domestic labour market at a time of high unemployment, since men were more likely to seek work than women. The Court was not convinced that the relative impact of immigrant wives and husbands was as great as the British Government suggested, and thought that any difference of impact was anyway not sufficiently important to justify the differential treatment of spouses under the immigration rules. The other ground advanced by the Government was the advancement of tranquillity. It argued that, since immigration causes strains on society, it was necessary to maintain effective immigration control with a view to securing good relations between the different communities in the UK. The Court failed to see how the distinction drawn in the immigration rules between husbands and wives would secure this objective.[17]

At first sight matters of taxation and social security might appear to belong to the economic and social fields, and so not to come within the scope of a treaty intended to protect civil and political rights. However, the right to the peaceful enjoyment of one's possession is guaranteed by Article 1 of the First Protocol, and it has been argued that taxation and social security involve possessions within the meaning of this Article. Most cases of social security have been found by the Commission not to be covered by this Article,[18] but taxation does come within it. In fact, the Article specifically refers to the right of a State to enforce laws relating to the payment of taxes or other contributions.

In April 1993, the Commission referred to the Court a case in which the application is complaining of a law which requires all men aged between18 and 50 years old to serve for a period as firemen or, instead, to pay a special firemen's contribution/tax, whereas women are under no such legal obligation.[19] He is contending that the requirement to pay the firemen's contribution infringes his rights under both Article 1 of the First Protocol and Article 4(3)(d) of the Convention (the performance of a civic obligation) when read together with the non-discrimination provision, Article 14. The respondent Government has pleaded that there is an objective and reasonable justification for the difference in treatment between men and women. In particular, it has sought to rely on the fact that the fire service has traditionally been reserved for men and that the fire service in the country concerned (Germany) has recently been opened to women, and has argued that the legislation in question is designed to protect women from the dangers of the job. In its Report on the case, the Commission concluded that there had been a violation of Article 14 in conjunction with both Article 1 of the First Protocol and Article 4(3)(d) of the Convention.

Moreover, proceedings in relation to a dispute over social security benefits may fall within the ambit of Article 6(1) which guarantees a right to a fair hearing in the determination of one's civil rights.[20] In a recent case, the European Court of Human Rights found that a Swiss court had based its decision concerning a woman's entitlement to an invalidity pension solely on the basis of her sex.[21] The woman had been dismissed from her job when she contracted tuberculosis, and had consequently been granted an invalidity pension. Several years later she gave birth to a child, and her pension was subsequently cancelled on the grounds that her family circumstances has changed appreciably after the birth of her child, that a medical examination showed her health had improved, and that she was 60–70% able to look after her home and her child. When she appealed the cancellation of her pension, the Swiss court held that she was entitled to a half-pension if she was in financial difficulties. In so holding, the court considered the extent to which she was restricted in her activities as a housewife, but not her ability to work in her previous job, since it proceeded on the assumption that, having a young child, she would have given up gainful employment even if she had not had health problems. No such assumption was made in the case of men, and was decisive in the case. Recalling that the advancement of the equality of the sexes is today a major goal in the Member States of the Council of Europe, and reaffirming its view that very weighty reasons must exist before such a difference of treatment can be regarded as compatible with the Convention, the European Court of Human Rights could discern no such reason for the difference of treatment in the instant case, and found that the applicant had suffered a violation of her rights under Article 6(1) taken together with Article 14.

There has also been a gender dimension to some of the cases in which homosexuals have complained about the intrusion upon their privacy of laws penalizing homosexual acts. Typically such acts between men, even consenting adult men in private, have been penalized whereas such acts between women have not. The Commission has accepted, as justification for the penalization of acts involving teenage men, sociological and psychological data to the effect that homosexual acts between men present a social danger because male homosexuals often constitute a distinct socio-cultural group with a tendency to proselytize adolescents and this involves the latter in social isolation, whereas lesbians present no such threat to adolescent women.[22] Apparently the young men particularly at risk from the sexual attention of older men are those in the sixteen to eighteen year old bracket, and there is no comparable attraction of older women to younger women of this age. There appear to be certain assumptions underlying such a view. Why is it that young men subject to the sexual attention of older men are socially isolated? Is it being accepted not only that heterosexuality is the norm, but that it is the preferred form, or even the only acceptable form, of sexual expression; and that deviation from this norm by men is more threatening to society than deviation therefrom by women? One wonders whether there may not be other assumptions at work here too. Are gender stereotypes in operation? Are women being seen as passive, men as active? Is this another example of the invisibility of women compared to men—in this instance, as regards their sexuality?

Complaints under the European Convention with a gender dimension have typically been complaints about discrimination. They have concerned the first aspect of equality which I identified above. The applicant has alleged that he or she was treated differently to a person of the other sex when the sex of a person was irrelevant or was afforded more weight than it should have been in the circumstances. In other words, a person of one sex has claimed that he or she should have been treated the same in the circumstances as a person of the other sex. The Convention has rarely been involved to complain that a State has treated persons of both sexes the same when they should have been treated differently because there was a pertinent difference between them.

Few gender-specific issues have been raised in Strasbourg and have not involved claims to special treatment. Rather women have complained that a law which placed restrictions on the termination of pregnancy offended against their right to respect for their private life under Article 8. Applicants who sought to get recognition of the right of a woman to freedom of choice were unsuccessful. The Commission found that a German law which limited the termination of pregnancy to certain specific circumstances was consistent with women applicants' right to respect for their private lives.[23] The Commission has also found that the British law which permits abortion where the danger to the physical or mental health of the prospective mother is greater if the pregnancy is continued than if it is terminated is compatible with the Convention.[24] It has moreover stated that a husband may not derive from the Convention any right to be informed or consulted about his wife's proposed abortion.[25]

Gender specific issues can be expected to arise only infrequently under the Convention. It is unlikely that special allowance need be made for the pregnancy in the case of a woman or the growing of a beard in the case of a man in order that a person may enjoy such rights as the right of personal liberty, freedom of religion, or freedom of association.

A recent complaint of indirect discrimination was not examined as such but was subsumed into other issues in the case.[26] The Court found that the prohibition in Ireland on dissemination of and access to specific information about abortion clinics in England was contrary to the applicants' right to freedom or expression under Article 10. The argument that such a prohibition impacted adversely on women in a way which it did not on men had not been raised before the Commission and, in view of this fact and of its finding on Article 10, the Court declined to pronounce on the issue under Article 14 of the allegedly discriminatory effect of the prohibition.

Claims that a State should take measures of positive or reverse discrimination have not been brought under the Convention. Both the Commission and the Court have, however, allowed that in certain circumstances compliance by a State with its obligations under the Convention may require it to take some action on behalf of the individual. It is only in recent years that the Convention organs have started to develop a jurisprudence on this aspect of the operation of the Convention, and they have done so cautiously. Most of the case law in which they have done so relates to complaints under Article 9.[27] It may therefore be possible to argue, for example, that in some aspect of family relationships women have generally lost out in the past in comparison to men or vice versa, and that the applicant is now entitled to preferential treatment in order to remedy the injustices of the past; that to afford her or him merely the same rights as a persons of the opposite sex is not sufficient.

While the Convention, at least as interpreted to date, has not required positive discrimination, it does not prohibit it. Positive discrimination is controlled by the Convention, but is not completely forbidden. Thus a State may legitimately take such measures provided they meet certain criteria such as the pursuit of an acceptable purpose and proportionality. A Commission decision illustrates this point in relation to gender. It concerned allegedly discriminatory tax laws in the United Kingdom.[28] The applicants were married couple, the husband being the sole breadwinner, and they complained that they were more heavily taxed than married couples in which the wife was the sole breadwinner. The Government argued that the extra allowance in the latter case was introduced during the Second World War to encourage married women to go out to work, and that, in so doing, it advanced the equality of the sexes. One of the principal causes of discrimination against women, it contended, is "the prejudice in the minds of men as to the capability of women to take up work". The giving of an extra allowance to "working" wives helped to break down such prejudice by encouraging more women to work and thereby demonstrate that they were no less capable than men. The Commission agreed. The difference in treatment had "an objective and reasonable justification in the aim of providing positive discrimination in favour of married women who work".

One last point on the Convention case law. Although the Convention contains no general guarantee of equality between the sexes, there is a provision in the Convention which could be interpreted to catch, if not all, at least the most egregious cases of gender discrimination. This is the right not to be subjected to degrading treatment guaranteed by Article 3. The Commission opened the door to this possibility in 1973 when it found that British immigration legislation which discriminated against persons on the basis of their race or colour was degrading of the applicants.[29] The women who complained of the UK's discriminatory immigration rules with respect to the entry into the UK of foreign spouses sought to go through this door. The European Court of Human Rights barred their entry on the facts of the case. In its view:

> . . . the difference of treatment . . . did not denote any contempt or lack of respect for the personality of the applicants and . . . was not designed to, and did not, humiliate or debase.[30]

It could not therefore be regarded as "degrading". Other facts may however reveal the requisite degree of humiliation and lead to a different result.

THE EUROPEAN SOCIAL CHARTER

The European Social Charter affords some recognition to the principle of non-discrimination on the basis of gender. It is stated in the Preamble that "the enjoyment of social rights should be secured without discrimination on grounds", *inter alia*, of sex. Strangely this basic guarantee is not repeated in the operative provision of the text. A specific guarantee is however contained in the text of "the right of men and women workers to equal pay for work of equal value".[31] It is also stated in relation to vocational graining that there should be "a system of apprenticeship and other systematic arrangements for training young boys and girls in their various employments".[32] It should be noted however that the term is "various employments", not "same employment".

There is also some recognition of the special needs of women in the workplace. There is provision for at least twelve weeks' maternity leave,[33] and protection against dismissal from paid employment during the period of maternity leave.[34] There is also provision that mothers are entitled to sufficient time off to nurse their children.[35] The Charter does therefore address gender-specific differences and seeks to ensure that women are not disadvantaged in employment by reason of these differences.

Despite these enlightened provisions, a gender bias has however been written into the provision of the Charter. When children are mentioned in relation to their parents, it is in tandem with their mothers, not with their fathers. For example, a special provision is devoted to the right of mothers and children to social and economic protection.[36] There is no mention here of fathers, nor as one might have expected in a human rights text, to the right of everyone, irrespective of sex, to such protection. In the provisions dealing with migrant labour, the foreign worker is seen as a man with a dependent wife and children.[37] Moreover, even the provision on maternity leave, although it recognizes the special needs of women arising from childbirth, is not balanced with a comparable provision in relation to paternity leave. In other words, the birth and rearing of a child in its early days are seen as exclusively women's concerns. There is no recognition of a role for the father in these matters. The Charter also incorporates a paternalistic view of women in relation to certain types of work. Thus, States Parties are required "to regulate the employment of women workers on night work in industrial employment"[38] and to prohibit their employment "in underground mining, and, as appropriate, on all other work which is unsuitable for them by reason of its dangerous, unhealthy, or arduous nature".[39]

An international body entrusted with the interpretation of States' obligations under a treaty is limited by the text of that treaty. The Committee of Independent Experts has recognized the paternalistic bent of some of the Charter's provisions and has sought, in the light of changed attitudes to the equality of the sexes, to minimise their gender bias. So, with respect to the requirement that States Parties regulate the employment of women workers on night work in industrial employment, the Committee has developed a case law to the effect that, to comply with this provision, a State is not obliged to enact specific regulations for women if it can demonstrate the existence of regulations applying without distinction to workers of both sexes. Such regulations should specify the conditions governing night work, and be designed to limit the adverse effects of night work on workers' health and family lives.[40] As to the obligation to prohibit women from working in underground mining, the Committee has decided that this applies only to the employment of women on underground extraction work in mines. It does not apply to other work in mines such as a management job, a job as an inspector, or work of a social or medical nature.[41] As to the obligation to prohibit the employment of women, as appropriate, on other work which is unsuitable for them by reason of its dangerous, unhealthy or arduous nature, the Committee has taken the view that it applies only to cases where this is necessary, in particular to protect motherhood and future children.[42]

Finally, mention should be made of a provision in the Additional Protocol to the Charter which was opened for signature on 5 May 1988. Article 1 of Part II of the Protocol imposes a number of obligations on States Parties with respect to the realization of the right of all workers to equal opportunities and equal treatment in matters of employment and occupation without discrimination on the grounds of sex. Included are such matters as vocational training, access to employment, conditions of employment, promotion and protection against dismissal.[43] The obligations do not extend to the taking of special measures in recognition of the special needs of men or women; but the Article does specifically provide that national measures which are designed to protect women, particularly as regards pregnancy, confinement and the post-natal period,[44] and measures aimed at removing *de facto* inequalities[45] are not to be regarded as discrimination infringing the principle of equal treatment. More insidiously in view of the paternalistic interpretation and segregationist tendency of such provisions in the past, the Article allows States to exclude from its scope occupational activities which, by reason of their nature or the context in which they are carried out, can be entrusted only to persons of a particular sex.[46]

CONCLUDING REMARKS

The vast majority of cases taken under the European Convention on Human Rights have concerned the first aspect of equality to which I referred at the beginning of this paper. In other words, the complaint has been that a law or decision affecting the applicant treated gender as a relevant consideration where it was either irrelevant or less relevant than assumed. Pertinent differences between the sexes have featured much less often in the case law, whether in the form of a gender-specific difference, indirect discrimination or a claim for positive discrimination. Perhaps such differences are of more significance as regards the enjoyment of rights in the economic and social fields than in the civil and political. Certainly, some recognition of pertinent differences is explicitly afforded in the provisions for the European Social Charter, particularly in relation to childbirth and employment, but even this text does not appear to address issues of either indirect or positive discrimination. Indeed, some of its provisions display a paternalistic attitude to women, inhibitive of their access to certain forms of employment, and adopt a traditional view of the respective roles of men and women in family matters. The additional Protocol also adopts a predominantly non-discrimination approach to equality, requiring that men and women be treated the same in relation to employment. It permits but does not require differential treatment in recognition of pertinent differences between the sexes.

It is interesting that many of the complaints under the Convention have been brought by men challenging assumptions about the traditional roles of men and women in relation to children. They have concerned the private sphere of human relations, the sphere to which women have often historically been confined. Complaints from women about their rights in the public sphere have been less common, though there have been a few relating to elections. Such complaints about the public world of employment cannot be brought under the European Social Charter, since this treaty was not intended to afford individuals a remedy for violations of their rights. In this area therefore European Community law assumes prime importance. For those States Members of the Council of Europe which are also members of the European Communities, the provisions of Community law on equal pay for work of equal value and on equal treatment express standards which are enforceable by individuals, both at the national level and at the European level by the ECJ.[47] Moreover, these standards have evolved from requiring only that gender, with limited exceptions, be treated as irrelevant for purposes of employment to requiring also that allowance be made for gender differences particularly in relation to pregnancy.[48]

7.5 Rich People Have Rights Too?
The Status of Property as a
Fundamental Human Right

JAMES KINGSTON

The right to private property is often regarded as one of the mainstays of a liberal democracy. In fact, it is protected in not one, but two, provisions of the Irish Constitution, Articles 40.3 and 43. Indeed, section 1(1) of the latter, in the absolutist terminology frequently used in the Constitution in relation to quite debatable propositions, declares that:

> The State acknowledges that man, in virtue of his rational being, has the natural right, antecedent to all positive law, to the private ownership of external goods.

In fact, the status of the right to own private property *as a fundamental human right* has been the subject of much debate. Undoubtedly, it is one of the most fundamental rights in a philosophy based on the moral correctness of a *laissez-faire* economy. However, it would be hard to find a country run on this basis in Western Europe, or indeed anywhere else. The EEC, for example, is far from being a free market economy on the basis envisaged by *laissez-faire* philosophers. Rather, it is premised on the concept of a mixed and regulated market: free movement of goods, services and persons; continued "freedom" being guaranteed by comprehensive competition regulations[1] and a social policy dealing with, *inter alia*, sex equality, labour law and social welfare entitlements. A truly "free" market would have no time for such controls being placed on private business. The concept of a mixed economy which is incorporated in the EEC's constitutional order is mirrored by the provisions of Article 1 of the First Protocol to the European Convention on Human Rights and Fundamental Freedoms (ECHR). However, it should be noted, from the outset, that the philosophy underlying such an economic model is far from providing a clear framework within which to discuss state/individual relations in the field of private property.

The problem, in liberal democratic terms, lies not so much in providing for private property in the legal system,[2] to prevent theft and to allow for commercial transactions, but with the extent and nature of that right and the permissibility of its abrogation by the State. In fact, dispute as to the scope of the right to property was such that it was not included in the European Convention on Human Rights and Fundamental Freedoms, but was only recognized in the First Protocol to the Convention two years later.[3]

Of course, a number of theorists, including many socialists and feminists, would reject the notion of private property as a human right and may reject the concept of "rights" in its entirety. On the international sphere, while the right was included in Article 17 of the (formally) non-binding Universal Declaration on Human Rights, it was not incorporated into treaty law in either the International Covenant on Civil and Political Rights (ICCPR) or the International Covenant on Economic, Social and Cultural Rights (ICESCR).[4] This reflects the fact that between the 1940s and the 1960s many newly independent and/or socialist states became actors on the international scene, thereby challenging the liberal democratic hegemony of international law in the colonial era.

Before analysing the protection given to private property, as a civil right, in the ECHR, this paper will briefly deal with a number of issues: the development of human rights since the Second World War; civil and political rights versus social, cultural and economic rights; the scope of "property"; and protection of property in public international law. Against this background it will discuss the drafting history and intention behind Article 1 of the First Protocol to the ECHR and how that provision has, in fact, been interpreted by the European Court of Human Rights. Finally, it will suggest some tentative conclusions as to the desirability of dealing with property rights in a system such as the ECHR.

THE DEVELOPMENT OF HUMAN RIGHTS

It is not proposed, in this paper, to deal in any depth with the philosophical and political schools of thought from which the concept arose.[5] Briefly stated, the emergence of human rights in the international/transnational legal sphere arose largely as a reaction to the regime under which Nazi government operated prior to and during the Second World War. A wholly positivist jurisprudence could not cope with the notion of declaring acts committed by a government in relation to its own nationals to be illegal; the international political community could not cope with the notion of acts of severe brutality being legal; the concept of "human rights" was utilized to bridge the gap.

Human rights can thus be seen as the immediate response of the international community to unacceptable governmental behaviour. Attention was initially focused on the most extreme acts: torture, genocide, etc., but, by the time the UDHR was drafted in 1948, a whole range of "justice" related issues were addressed. While the concept of rights is espoused by many philosophers, especially of the "natural law" variety,[6] its theoretical bases in the international legal system remain confused. International law, even in the human rights sphere, does not fully recognize individuals as actors on the legal plane.[7] There is an uneasy relationship between positivist and natural law concepts. Many political groups utilize the language of human rights, even if they emphasize one "school" of rights over the other, and even if their ideological foundations are hostile to the rights concept.

The content of "human rights", rather than being universal and immutable, changes with time and according to the socio–political environment in which we live. Perhaps human rights discourse may best be seen as the pragmatic expression of those political goals the speaker sees as most important in the environment in which he or she lives.[8]

CIVIL AND POLITICAL VERSUS ECONOMIC, SOCIAL AND CULTURAL RIGHTS

Human rights are often divided into two main "schools"; civil and political rights, and economic, social and cultural rights. Again, due to considerations of space, this paper will not analyse the conceptual bases behind this classification, or, indeed, the desirability of such a division.[9]

While the UDHR contains both types of right, treaties tend to separate them. On the international plane, we have the ICCPR and the ICESCR. At European level there is the ECHR and the European Social Charter. The Irish Constitution contains "Fundamental Rights", largely of a civil and political nature, as well as "Directive Principles of Social Policy", which deal with what are often classified as economic, social and cultural rights.

Western liberal democracies tend to emphasize civil and political rights and may even question the validity of dealing with economic, social and cultural rights under the human rights rubric. On the other hand, second and third world countries have often given priority to rights of an economic, social or cultural nature.

At present, international law recognizes both categories of right. However, the treatment of the different types of right varies. Civil and political rights are regarded as justiciable: capable of being protected in the judicial and quasi-judicial sphere. Economic, social and cultural rights, while legal rights, are non-justiciable. This is because it is felt that these rights, as a general rule, involve broader policy considerations. Therefore, the logic runs, the limited focus of the judicial arena is not a suitable place to determine such issues; enforcement and protection of these rights is best left in the hands of the legislature, at national level, and to actors exerting political pressure (other governments, treaty organs supervising state reporting systems), on the international plane.

It is against this background that we must consider the desirability of classifying property as a human right, and more particularly, as one coming within the civil and political sphere. First, however, we shall look at what the concept of property encompasses.

THE CONCEPT OF PROPERTY

Schermers[10] points out that, at present, human rights law simply protects the right of an individual to hold onto whatever property he or she manages to acquire.[11] There is no right to possess property. He thinks that this is illogical: "If there is a human right to enjoy property then there must also be a human right to have property."[12] It is also in sharp contrast to other human rights, such as the right to respect for privacy or to freedom from torture, which must be afforded to every individual.

While the concept of property includes many benefits, such as land, goods and intellectual property, Schermers[13] prefers to utilize a hierarchy of categories based on need. The most fundamental of these is the "private property which an individual needs for developing his personal life". He believes that such needs may vary according to the economic wealth of the State in which the individual lives, but that there is, within each State, a core of private property with which the government may not interfere. The second category is that of earned income; however, earnings surplus to "needs" may be appropriated by the State and the extent to which the State provides for its citizens, by giving them pensions, etc., may determine the amount of private property they are entitled to as of right. The other two categories used are property acquired by inheritance and un-earned income, which he does not believe should be regarded as fundamental rights.

Schermers employs a relativist yardstick in deciding what rights should be regarded as fundamental, thereby allowing for regional variations in the protection of property as a human right. However, he believes that it detracts from the universality of human rights if what is classified as a right in one country is regarded as criminal or unlawful in others.

While this analysis is useful, it may be open to a number of criticisms. In relation to the last point, if such an analysis were employed more generally it would reduce the scope of many rights. For example, homosexual activity between males was (until very recently) regarded as a criminal offence in Ireland whereas it is protected by the privacy guarantee in Article 8 of the ECHR. The categorization of basic human needs as coming within the rubric of property may also be questioned. As Schermers himself points out, state benefits may obviate the need for private property.

Perhaps an alternative way of looking at this problem may be suggested. Human beings may be regarded as having a fundamental right to have their basic needs satisfied; such a right is incorporated in Article 11 of the ICESCR. These needs may be regarded as encompassing the rights to adequate food, clothing shelter and education. They may be satisfied by a number of mechanisms: the welfare State, society run on the basis of communal, State or private property, or other means so long as these basic needs are met.

Such an analysis would reduce the scope of benefits coming within any discrete right to property. The right to property, as such, would only relate to that surplus of resources available once the basic needs of all have been met. In theory one could develop an individual right to possess an equitable share of that surplus. In fact, Schermers, perhaps questionably, categorizes minimum income legislation as guaranteeing such a right. However, it would be far removed from the traditional "right" to private property, the essence of which is the right to enjoy whatever property one has managed to acquire, subject to whatever right the State may have to appropriate that property in the public interest. In other words, it is the right to own and utilize whatever (unequal) share of the world's resources one has come to possess by reason of one's parentage, physical or mental skills, educational advantages, hard work or good luck.

Before looking at the protection of this right at European level we must first look at how property was protected in traditional public international law.

THE PROTECTION OF PROPERTY IN PUBLIC INTERNATIONAL LAW

Traditionally international law was solely concerned with the rights and duties of states *inter se*. Individuals were not actors on the international legal plane. As already mentioned, even today they are not regarded as such, this is illustrated most clearly by the fact that individuals do not have *locus standi* before the European Court of Human Rights.

Under public international law, as generally understood at the time the Protocol was enacted, a State could not expropriate the property of aliens unless it awarded them "prompt, adequate and effective" compensation and the taking was not due to discriminatory political motives. If these conditions were complied with the taking was lawful, there was no breach of international law. If the requirements were not met the breach of international law could be remedied by payment of compensation. It is important to note that public international law never sought to interfere with the State's ability to deprive its own citizens of their property.

The traditional rules came under considerable pressure following the break up of direct (as opposed to neo–) colonial rule throughout Africa and Asia. Newly independent states began to realize that formal political independence was not a sufficient solution to their problems. They sought, through the development of concepts such as permanent sovereignty over natural resources, to bring about a "New International Economic Order". They articulated their goals through (the identically worded Articles 1 of) the ICCPR and the ICESCR and a number of important resolutions in the General Assembly of the United Nations.[14] Higgins[15] has pointed out that the concept of the New International Economic Order (NIEO) runs directly counter to traditional western notions of private property. The success of this strategy was limited and (due perhaps to increasing vulnerability to neo–colonial pressure following on from an ever increasing debt burden, and the collapse in world demand for many of the resources owned by these countries) by the early 1990s international law seems to have largely reverted to its traditional position.[16]

In public international law if rules relating to property are not complied with, the individual, as such, has no remedy. This is because it does not regard him or her as having any rights. The illegality arises because the expropriating State has wronged the individual's State of nationality. Harm is done to the possessions of the subject (possession) of the State. This reasoning is directly at odds with the rationale of human rights. Article 1 of the first Protocol to the ECHR, however, co- mingles the two concepts; this tends to weaken the status of property as a human right.

So, how then did this reference to international law come to be incorporated into Article 1? The possibility was canvassed before the European Court of Human Rights, in *Lithgow v. UK*,[17] that the purpose of this clause was to guarantee to all persons a right equivalent to the benefit enjoyed under public international law by citizens of one State against other States, by virtue of the obligations owed by the latter States to the former. However, the Court rejected this argument, stating that the purpose of the provision was to relieve any fears that the article could be used to expropriate the property of aliens with greater ease than theretofore. However, it may be argued that the actual effect of the clause has been to grant greater rights to aliens than to nationals; while this is a principle of international law, the general scheme of which the Convention does not wish to disturb, it is difficult to see why this desire had to be expressed in terms of *human rights*. It should also be noted that the effect of the article goes beyond simply not interfering with the protection (indirectly) given to aliens by international law; in fact, it considerably *improves* their position by allowing them to avail of legal remedies on their own initiative, rather than relying on support from their State of nationality.

The entitlement to private property should only be defined as a human right if it is one of the basic foundations on which we seek to build the international community. If it is, the next question must be whether we should define it as a civil or an economic right. While this paper does not purport to come up with a definitive answer to these questions it will examine how the right has been dealt with in the ECHR system.

THE EUROPEAN CONVENTION ON HUMAN RIGHTS —THE THEORY

Article 1 of Protocol 1 to the Convention states that:

> Every natural or legal person is entitled to the peaceful enjoyment of his possessions. No one shall be deprived of his possessions except in the public interest and subject to the conditions provided for by law and by the general principles of international law.
>
> The preceding provisions shall not, however, in any way impair the right of a state to enforce such laws as it deems necessary to control the use of property in accordance with the general interest or to secure the payment of taxes or other contributions or penalties.

While the wording of the text is complex and somewhat laboured some immediate issues spring to mind. First, this article is the only one that specifically states that *legal* entities have *human* rights. This seems a somewhat unusual concept! Another interesting point, which has already been dealt with, is the reference to general principles of international law.

It may be useful, at this stage, to look at the history of Article 1. Originally, it was sought to include a property clause in the Convention. But, as Higgins[18] points out, a perusal of the *travaux preparatoires* of the Convention throw considerable light on the difficulties that even western democracies find themselves in when trying to formulate such a right. Some States were of the view that property is an economic, rather than a civil, right. Others were of the opinion that while property could be regarded as a civil right, the machinery of the Convention was not an appropriate means of protecting and enforcing it. Therefore, it was not possible to include a property clause in the Convention.

Even when the principle of including the guarantee was accepted, at the time of drafting of the Protocol, further problems arose in relation to any reference to compensation, especially as it related to a State's own nationals. It was felt that a reference, such as that in Article 17 of the UDHR, which merely recognized the existence of the right to own property and that there should be no *arbitrary* deprivation of same, did not imply a right to compensation. The UK was strongly opposed to any reference to compensation as, *inter alia*, it felt that it was not appropriate for decisions taken by domestic authorities to nationalize property to be subject to review by international organs. Higgins points out that while the parties to the ECHR accept an international obligation to pay compensation to aliens, the deliberate non-inclusion of a reference to compensation in Article 1:

> entails through the use of language the result that as a matter of *practice* [emphasis added] all persons whose property is nationalized or taken is [sic] likely to be compensated and that there is an *obligation* [author's emphasis] to make such payment in the case of foreigners ... the compensation obligation [was] to be applied, as a legal requirement, only to non-nationals.[19]

A logical interpretation of Article 1 thus runs as follows:

(1) Everyone is entitled to own whatever property they have (lawfully?) acquired; but

(2) The State may interfere with the individual's right in certain circumstances, by:

  (i) extinguishing ownership rights, if this is in the public interest, provided the taking is within the terms of national law; or

  (ii) limiting ownership rights, by law, if this is necessary in the general interest, or if the purpose is to enforce taxation law, legal sanctions, etc.

(3) Compensation is mandatory only where the property is owned by aliens, and only if property is taken, rather than subjected to controls.

It seems hard to see how any taking of property by a State could violate the provisions of the Article, at least insofar as they relate to a state's own nationals. However, this is not the Court's interpretation of the article.

THE EUROPEAN CONVENTION ON HUMAN RIGHTS — IN PRACTICE

A detailed analysis of the Convention's jurisprudence is not within the limited scope of this paper. However, at the outset, it can be stated that Article 1 contains three rules. Leaving aside the question of compensation, the first two we shall deal with are apparent from the text of the provision; however, the third, first identified in *Sporrong and Lonnroth v. Sweden*,[20] is rather more controversial.

Article 1(1), second sentence, requires that any taking be in accordance with "conditions provided for by law"; in effect, this means that the national law must be sufficiently clear and precise to allow individuals to ascertain whether a particular course of action is lawful or not. The Convention organs will not look at the legality, under domestic law, of a State's actions; this being a matter for the national courts. The clause also requires that the taking be in the public interest; however, as van Dijk and van Hoof[21] point out, review of this requirement is "very marginal". There is no requirement of necessity: "Clearly the public or general interest encompasses measures which would be preferable or advisable, and not only essential, in a democratic society."[22] Questions of preferability and advisability are within the domain of national legislatures and unless they act in a manifestly unreasonable manner the Convention organs will not interfere.

Article 1(2) allows the state to impose such control of property as "it deems necessary" in the "general interest"; while this may seem to be a stricter test than that relating to expropriation it should be noted that, unlike other articles in the Convention, this requirement states that it is the States themselves which are the adjudicators of necessity. Initially the Court applied this provision literally, but subsequently, in *Marckx v. Belgium*,[23] the Court retreated from this position and stated that it could supervise the purposes of domestic legislation controlling the exercise of property rights. Such review is, however, also likely to be marginal. In relation to control of the use of property to secure the payment of taxes or other contributions or requirements the Convention does not specify any requirement of a public or general interest.

However, in *Sporrong and Lonnroth v. Sweden*, the Court identified another rule. In this case the applicants were the owners of property which had been subject to expropriation permits for twenty-three and eight years, respectively, (at which time the permits were cancelled) and to building prohibitions, which had lapsed after 25 and twelve years, respectively. The Commission had held that there had been no expropriation of the applicants' property (see Article 1(1)); there had been significant controls placed on their property (see Article 1(2)), but they were justified as being necessary in the general interest. The Court, by a bare ten-to-nine majority, took a different, novel, and some would say incorrect, approach. It was of the view that the applicants' property had not been either directly or indirectly expropriated, despite that fact that their ownership rights had become "precarious and defeasible" following the issue of the expropriation permits and despite the fact that they recognized that only substantive, as opposed to formal, expropriation was necessary to bring Article 1 into play. It was also of the view that the permits did not constitute "control" of the properties, as the aim of these measures was to, ultimately, expropriate, rather than simply control, them![24]

This would seem to indicate that no violation of Article 1 took place, however, the Court went on to reformulate the Article by saying that the right to peaceful enjoyment of possessions could be interfered with in other ways. These interferences, surely less severe than those specifically outlined, would have been permitted only if a balance was struck between the public and the private interests involved. This balance could only have been reached if the applicants had had "the possibility of seeking a reduction of the time limits or [emphasis added] *of claiming compensation*".[25] Swedish law, at the relevant time, had excluded both these possibilities, therefore, Article 1 had been violated.

It should be noted that *Sporrong and Lonnroth* did not, in terms, establish a general right to compensation. This requirement was read into the Convention in the cases of *James v. UK*[26] and *Lithgow v. UK*. Both these cases involved large scale expropriation of property, in pursuance of the social and economic policies of the governments of the day. The latter case dealt with the nationalization of the ship-building industry; the former with compulsory (*vis-à-vis* the landlord, and, in some cases, *vis-à-vis* the tenant) transfer of ownership of property held under long leases from the lessor to the lessee. Following rejection of the applicants' arguments that the reference to international law in Article 1 related to a State's own nationals, the Court went on to say that the requirement of balance inherent in the clause, as a general rule, requires the payment of compensation, the quantum of which has to be "fair". As the Court in *Lithgow* points out, fairness may not require the payment of full market price for the expropriated property.

The requirement of compensation is based solely on the notion of balance between public and private interests, rather than from any notion that the public or general interest, of itself, requires payment; a clear recognition that it may not do so! It seems, from the decisions of the Court in *James* and *Lithgow* (and the Commission's report in the follow-on case of *Scotts' of Greenock (Est'd 1711) Ltd and Lithgows Ltd v. UK*),[27] that while the Convention organs require payment of some compensation it will be largely left up to national legislatures to formulate what they regard as "fair" methods of valuation of property and what percentage of the value should actually be given to persons whose property has been expropriated. (While these matters are conceptually different, in practice, they are considered together.) The above cases give a brief, but reasonably representative, overview of the Court's attitude to the scope of Article 1; it is not proposed to discuss its other jurisprudence in any detail; however, a number of cases, involving Austria, deserve brief consideration, as they are among the few in which a violation of Article 1 has been found.

In the cases of *Erkner and Hofauer v. Austria*[28] and *Poiss v. Austria*,[29] the applicants had been forced to swap their lands with other persons in pursuance of their government's policy of land consolidation. The procedure took sixteen years (in the first case) and nineteen years (in the second case); the blame for the delay was largely due to the conduct of the State and, thus, constituted a violation of the requirement of Article 6 of the Convention that disputes relating to legal rights be dealt with within a reasonable time. This delay, in conjunction with the impossibility under Austrian law of reconsidering the transfers following successful appeals by the applicants and the lack of any compensation, constituted a breach of Article 1. The Court held that the applicants' property had not been expropriated nor had it been subject to control measures; however, their right to peaceful enjoyment of property had been interfered with in a manner out of line with the inherent balance which has to be struck between public and private interests.

One further case worth mentioning is that of *Pine Valley and Others v. Ireland*.[30] In this case the owner of lands had been granted outline planning permission for a scheme of development. The outline planning permission was granted, on appeal, by the Minister for Local Government, following a refusal by the relevant local authority of full planning permission on the ground that the development would have materially contravened the applicable Development Plan. The owner of the land then sold it to the first applicant. The local authority, however, refused its application for full planning permission. The first applicant then sought, and obtained, an order from the High Court directing the local authority to grant the permission.[31] The first applicant then sold the lands to the other applicants; subsequently the local authority appealed the High Court ruling to the Supreme Court, which allowed the appeal on the ground that the Minister had acted outside his statutory powers in granting the outline planning permission. Subsequently, the Local Government (Planning and Development) Act, 1982, was passed. Section 6 of that Act retrospectively validated planning permissions of the type granted in relation to the lands in question. However, it was subsequently found by the Supreme Court that the applicants were not entitled to the benefit of the 1982 Act, because it would be contrary to the constitutional doctrine of separation of powers for Parliament to pass legislation which would have the effect of overturning the judicial decision that the applicants were not entitled to planning permission for their proposed development. It was also held that the applicants were not entitled to compensation for loss caused by the Minister's *ultra vires* actions.[32]

The applicants' case eventually came before the European Court of Human Rights. The Court held that there had been an interference with the property rights of the second and third applicants.[33] The interference in question came within the scope of the second paragraph of Article 1 (control of property). The interference was in accordance with law and had a legitimate aim (protection of the environment, which is "in accordance with the general interest"). The measure was also proportionate: the planning permission had been nullified to ensure that the relevant planning legislation was complied with, the Supreme Court's decision was a proper, if not the sole, means of enforcing it; the decision effected a wide range of persons other than the applicants (hence the need for the 1982 Act); the applicants were business people involved in what they knew was a risky venture, they knew that the proposed development would have contravened the relevant Development Plan and that the local authority were opposed to any such contravention. Therefore, the annulment of the permission, even in the absence of retrospective validation or compensation did not contravene Article 1.

Thus far the case seems to be a classic example of the limited scope of Article 1 and the near impossibility of its being breached, at any rate where the Court does not invoke the general rule contained in the first sentence of Article 1(1), first identified in *Sporrong and Lonnroth*. However, the Court went on to look at the case in the light of Article 14 (in conjunction with Article 1). In this regard the Court noted that the second and third applicants had been treated differently than other owners of property subject to void planning permissions granted by the Minister for Local Government, that is, they did not receive the benefit of the 1982 Act. The Court was aware of the reasons why they could not receive the benefit of that legislation, the doctrine of separation of powers mentioned above; however, as the government had not relied on this reason for the different treatment accorded to the applicants the Court disregarded it and held that as no grounds had been advanced for the differentiation it was in breach of Article 14, in conjunction with Article 1! Even though, on the facts of the particular case, the Court's finding in relation to Article 14 is somewhat unusual, to say the least,[34] the decision does show that a freestanding guarantee of equality before the law may be of considerably more benefit to an individual than the sort of property protection afforded under the Convention.[35]

As of the end of 1992, over thirty cases have come before the Court in which a breach of Article 1 of the Convention has been alleged at some stage of the proceedings. Of these the Court has found as follows: no jurisdiction (2); inadmissible (5); not necessary to consider because of breaches of other (stricter) requirements of the Convention (4); no violation (15); no violation except in conjunction with Article 14 (4); violation (2).[35a]

It can thus be seen that of the six cases where a violation of the Convention has been found, four could have been dealt with in the absence of a property guarantee had the Convention contained a freestanding non discrimination clause, similar to that in the ICCPR or the Irish Constitution. Of the two cases where a violation of Article 1 has been found, the following points may be made: they involved a violation of peaceful enjoyment of possessions falling short of expropriation or control; the imputation of such a right (the rule identified in *Sporrong*) into Article 1 has been severely criticized; they involved considerable procedural delays and obstacles which were, in any event, contrary to the requirements of Article 6; these obstacles were added to by the lack of any compensation—it is unclear whether either the procedural faults or the lack of compensation taken individually would necessarily have constituted a violation of Article 1; the requirement to pay compensation to a State's own nationals does not seem to have been intended by the framers of Article 1.

It would, therefore, seem that if the provision had been interpreted as originally intended there would not, to date, have been any findings of violation. Where breaches have been found they have been based on very dubious interpretations of the clause. Even on these interpretations, once a State has paid any monetary compensation at all, the Court, to date, has found it to be fair. In those cases where a violation of Article 1 has been found, either alone or in conjunction with Article 14, the applicants would probably have been equally protected, and for reasons coming better within the general concepts of human rights, by a free standing guarantee of equality before the law.[36]

CONCLUSION

This paper has attempted, albeit briefly, to raise some of the issues concerning the desirability of regarding the right to property as a fundamental human right. Some tentative conclusions may, perhaps, be drawn from this discussion. Human rights may be regarded as political, rather than philosophical, constructs. The kernel of the right to property is the right to hold unto (and deal with as one pleases) possessions in excess of one's basic needs. In essence, the right is based on the perpetuation of inequality. Traditionally, international law protected property in very limited circumstances; the rationale behind this protection was not based on notions of human rights. There is considerable debate as to the desirability of regarding property as a human right at global level. In Europe, the right has been recognized as a human right, of the civil variety, in Article 1 of the First Protocol to the ECHR. The right is highly qualified; even though it has been interpreted in a more pro–individual manner than intended by the framers of the provision, it has failed to provide any notable protection to individuals. Such protection as has been given could equally well have been provided by rights falling more easily within the framework of human rights; such as a general right to freedom from discrimination and arbitrary treatment at the hands of the law.

In short, regarding property as a fundamental right gives rise to many difficulties, both conceptually and in practical terms. Perhaps if property was regarded as an economic, rather than a civil, right some of these difficulties would be resolved, although the fact that the right is premised on inequality could still give rise to conflict with directly countervailing values, such as the right to equality. The question posed in the title to this paper may, perhaps, be answered as follows: of course, rich people have rights, those rights shared by all human beings, such as freedom from torture, freedom to express themselves, freedom from hunger and from negative discrimination; however, it is not at all clear that they have the right to be rich too.

7.6   Select Bibliography

TEXTS AND MATERIALS

R.Blanpain, *Labour Law and Industrial Relations of the European Community* (Deventer, 1991).

A. Byre, *Leading Cases and Materials on the Social Policy of the EEC* (Deventer, 1989).

A. Connelly, ed., *Gender and the Law* (Dublin, 1993).

D. Curtin, *Irish Employment Equality Law* (Dublin, 1989).

E. Ellis, *European Community Sex Equality Law* (Oxford, 1991).

D.J. Harris, *The European Social Charter* (Charlottesville, 1984).

A. Jaspers and L. Betten, *25 Years European Social Charter* (Deventer, 1988).

W. McKean, *Equality and Discrimination under International Law* (Oxford, 1983).

D. Pannick, *Sex Discrimination Law* (Oxford, 1985).

M. Spencer, *1992 And All That: Civil Liberties in the Balance* (London, 1990) ch. 5.

G. Whyte, ed., *Sex Equality, Community Rights and Irish Social Welfare Law: the Impact of the Third Directive* (ICEL No. 2) (Dublin, 1988).

ARTICLES

A.F. Bayefsky, "The Principle of Non-Discrimination in International Law" (1990) 11 *HRLJ* 1.

D. Beck, "Equal Pay and the Implementation of Article 119 of the Treaty of Rome" (1978) XIII *Irish Jurist* (n.s.) 1.

B. Bercusson, "The European Community's Charter of Fundamental Social Rights for Workers" (1990) 53 *MLR* 624.

I. Boerofijn et al., "Towards a New System of Supervision for the European Social Charter" (1991) 46 *Int'l Com Jur Rev* 42.

N. Burrows, "International Law and Human Rights: The Case of Women's Rights" in T. Campbell, ed., *Human Rights: From Rhetoric to Reality* (Oxford, 1986) 80.

R.J. Cook, "Women's International Human Rights Law: The Way Forward" (1993) 15 *HRQ* 230.

M. Cousins, "Why Can't a Women be More Like a Man? Indirect Discrimination in Social Welfare" (1993) 11 *ILT* (n.s.) 147.

A. Eide, "Realisation of Social and Economic Rights and the Minimum Threshold Approach" (1989) 10 *HRLJ* 35.

M. Forde, "The Applicable Social Security Law in the European Court" (1979) XIV *Irish Jurist* (n.s.).

M. Gould, "The European Social Charter and Community Law—A Comment" (1989) 14 *Eur L Rev* 223.

D.J. Harris, "A Fresh Impetus for the European Social Charter" (1992) 41 *ICLQ* 659.

B. Hepple, "The Implementation of the Community Charter of Fundamental Social Rights" (1990) 53 *MLR* 643.

R. Higgins, "The Taking of Property by the State" (1982) III 176 *Hague Receuil* , ch. 1.

N. Hyland, "What Price Freedom? The Pregnant Woman in the Workplace" in A. Whelan, ed., *Law and Liberty in Ireland* (Dublin, 1993) 10.

S. Mullally, "Taking Women's Rights Seriously: The Convention on the Elimination of All Forms of Discrimination Against Women" (1992) 10 *ILT* (n.s.) 6.

R. Nielsen, "The Contract of Employment in the Member States of the European Communities and in Community Law" (1990) 33 *Germ Ybk IL* 258.

P. O'Higgins, "International Social Policy: Its Impact on Irish Legal Practice" in W. Duncan, ed., *Law and Social Policy* (Dublin, 1987) 9.

P. O'Higgins, "The European Social Charter" in R. Blackburn and J. Taylor, eds., *Human Rights in the 1990s: Legal, Political and Ethical Issues* (London, 1991) 121.

D. O'Keefe, "The Scope and Content of Social Security Regulation in European Community Law" in D. O'Keefe and H.G. Schermers, *Essays in European Law and Integration* (Deventer, 1992) 105.

A.J. Riley, "The European Social Charter and Community Law" (1989) 14 *Eur L Rev* 80.

H.G. Schermers, "The International Protection of the Right to Property" in F. Matscher and H. Petzold, eds., *Protecting Human Rights—The European Dimension: Essays in Honour of G.J. Wiarda*, 2nd ed. (Köln, 1990) 565.

J. Shaw, "Social Policy After Maastricht: A Brief Comment" (1991) *J Soc Wel & Fam L* 255.

V. Shrubsall, "The Additional Protocol to the European Social Charter—Employment Rights" (1989) *Ind LJ* 39.

C. Tomuschat, "The Right to Work" in A. Rosas and J. Helgesen, eds., *Human Rights in a Changing East-West Perspective* (London, 1990) 174.

P. Watson, "Social Policy After Maastricht" (1993) 30 *CML Rev* 481.

Lord Wedderburn, "European Community Law and Workers' Rights: Fact or Fake in 1992?" (1991) 13 *DULJ* (n.s.) 1.

8 : CHILDREN

8.1 Introduction

The protection afforded to family life by the European Convention on Human Rights is comprehensive and derives from a combination of a number of articles in the Convention, as interpreted by the case law of the Court. Such protections are not, however, stated as absolutes in the Convention but rather are limited by considerations such as democratic necessity and public order. It is interesting to note that the challenges which have been brought against Ireland before the Court, a substantial number of these have concerned alleged infringments of the guarantees in respect of family rights. The relevant articles are Article 8 which deals with a right to privacy and respect for family life; Article 12 which sets out the right to marry and found a family; and the equality of spouses guarantee set out in Article 5 of Protocol No. 7 (to which Ireland is not a party).

Although on its face, arguably, imposing only a negative obligation of non-interference, Article 8 has been afforded a broader interpretation by the European Court of Human Rights and it would now appear clear that, not only must the Contracting States refrain from interfering with the guarantees of privacy and protection for family life but, additionally, Contracting States are obliged to take positive steps to ensure that these rights are sufficiently protected. In *Airey v. Ireland*[1], the Court held that:

> . . . the object of Article 8 is essentially that of protecting the individual against arbitrary interference by public authorities, it does not merely compel the State to abstain from such interference: in addition to this primarily negative undertaking, there may be positive obligations inherent in an effective respect for private and family life.

Hence, in the instant case, it was inherent in Ireland's obligiations to introduce a civil legal aid which would enable the applicant to properly protect the rights being asserted by her.[2]

As to the substantive rights emerging from Article 8, under the privacy provisions, the Court has had to consider the permissibility of domestic criminalization of homosexual acts between consenting adult males in private. Such domestic provisions have been the subject of many applications before the

Court[3] and Ireland has been no stranger to such applications.[4] It has now been firmly established that such restrictions infringe the provisions of the Convention. In the case of *Norris v. Ireland*, the Court held Ireland to be in breach of the terms of Article 8 by maintaining in force legislative provisions which penalized buggery and acts of gross indecency between adult males. It is interesting to note that one of the arguments put forward by the Irish Government was that State interference in relation to the protection of morals when "necessary in a democratic society" was to be broadly interpreted and that the requirements and extent of such interference was largely a matter for the State itself to decide with a subjective rather than uniform approach to be taken to such measures. While acknowledging the wide margin of appreciation to be given to Contracting States in relation to moral issues, the Court held that this did not amount to an unfettered discretion and the evidence tendered did not indicate that the retention of such laws was required for the protection of moral standards. This case additionally shows that a ruling by the Court that an infringement of the terms of the Convention has taken place is merely a step along the road to reform and compliance and that such a ruling is not necessarily an end in itself. The judgment was delivered in this matter on the 26th day of October 1988, and despite protests in the interim in relation to Ireland's failure to act in response thereto,[5] the abolition of the challenged offences did not in fact come about until the enactment of the Criminal Law (Sexual Offences) Act, 1993.

The right to private and family life has also come up for consideration before the Court on several occasions in the context of gender alterations and transsexuality. This aspect of the respect due to private life was considered by the Court as far back as 1979 in the case of *Van Oosterwijk v. Belgium*. Although delineating the extent of the right to private life under the Convention,[6] the challenge made by the applicant was ultimately unsuccessful on procedural grounds on the basis that domestic remedies had not been exhausted. The applicant was a transsexual who sought to have his birth certificate altered to accurately reflect external and psychological, as opposed to biological, gender. The extent of the right to respect for private life was further considered in the context of transsexuality in *Rees v. United Kingdom*[7] and *Cossey v. United Kingdom*[8]. In both cases alleged breaches of Articles 8 and 12 were made in relation to the failure to recognize the changed gender of the applicants and also, in the latter case, to the failure to permit such persons to enter into valid marriages with persons of the gender opposite to that which they had assumed. These arguments were unsuccessful. The court held in the latter case that

> . . . refusal to alter the register of births or to issue birth certificates whose contents and nature differ from those of the original entries cannot be considered as an interference. What the applicant is arguing is not that the

State should abstain from acting but rather that it should take steps to modify its existing system. The question is, therefore, whether an effective respect for Miss Cossey's private life imposes a positive obligation on the United Kingdom in this regard.[9]

No such positive obligation was found to be imposed on the United Kingdom as this was an area in which Contracting States enjoyed a large margin of appreciation and this was not a topic upon which there was common ground.[10]

In relation to Article 12, no violation of the right to marry was found. In this regard, the Court approved of the adoption of a biological test of gender in determining a right to marry. The applicant argued that the right to marry had been totally denied her as "as a woman, she could realistically marry another woman and English law prevented her from marrying a man". Such a total prohibition on marriage by the applicant was, however, rejected with the Court somewhat unrealistically taking the view that the applicant's inability to marry a woman was due not to any legal prohibition. The extent of these rights were further disucssed in *B. v. France*,[11] a decision which indicates that the existence of different practices in different Contracting States may tilt the balance. Unlike the English practices which were scrutinized in the cases mentioned above, in the present case evidence was presented to the Court that France had previously caused the alteration of birth certificates in such cases to more accurately reflect gender choices. A change of forename, notwithstanding the non-recognition of a change of sex, had also been found to be previously permissible in France. Thus, having regard to the margin of appreciation, a violation of Article 8 was established. Thus, the subjective application of the Convention in the case of different Contracting States must be appreciated with the consequent result that uniformity of rights is not necessarily achieved.

The right to marry which is guaranteed by Article 12 must be compared with the right to a family life and a home. This distinction has arisen in a domestic context in Ireland also and, in conformity with the European interpretation, the single right to marry would appear to be of broader application than the right of the family to reside together as such. The latter is a continous right and is subject to the exceptions set out in Article 8(2) of the Convention. Nevertheless, although the latter appears to be more restrictive than the former, it is clearly essential, in order to avoid violation of Article 8, to ensure that the interference proposed is justifiable under Article 8(2) and that the exception is being legitimately and proportionately invoked.

The extent of the right to marry has been held by the Commission in *Draper v. United Kingdom* and *Hamer v. United Kingdom*[12] to include the right of prisoners to marry. The right to marry and to found a family has also been recogized as an unspecified right under the Irish Constitution although restrictions consequent upon the exercise of the common good have been acknowledged. In *Murray v. Ireland*[13], Finlay C J stated that:

> ... the Consititution implicity recognized and protected the right of each spouse in marriage to beget children. This right, protected by Article 40, is one to which each spouse to a lawful marraige was entitled and would be restricted by the imprisonment of either spouse.

Furthermore, the common good has, in an Irish domestic context, been found to justify interference with the right of the family to live together and to enjoy the society of each other.[14] To what extent is interference with the right of the family to live together and to enjoy the society of each other permissible under Articles 8 and/or 12 of the Convention? The first point which must be noted is that the right to respect for family life under Article 8 is not unlimited but is subject to such interference as is "in accordance with the law and is necessary in a democratic society in the interests of national security, public safety or the economic well-being of the country, for the prevention of disorder or crime, for the protection of health or morals, or for the protection of the rights and freedoms of others". Arguably, substantial interference might therefore occur before an infringement of Article 8 would necessarily result. Howver, the court has held that the right to found a family under Article 12 will usually encompass the right to live together. Thus, the deportation of a family member, where this will interfere with family relations, has been held to infringe the provisions of the Convention (*Berrehab v. Netherlands*[15]). However, the extent of the right contained in Article 8 is evident from the case of *Beldjoudi v. France*.[16] Here the applicants, an Algerian national and his French wife, successfully invoked Article 8 to prevent his deportation. Mr Beldjoudi had a lengthy criminal record in France which both preceded and followed the issuing of a deportation order against him. Such order was issued on the ground that he was a threat to public order. In view of the substantial connection between the applicants and France and their rights under Article 8, the Court determined that the deportation of Mr Beldjoudi was not proportionate to the legitimate aim pursued. This result is remarkably similar to the approach taken by the Irish courts in the most recent determination upon this point wherein it was held that division of the family by deportation would only be justified if, after due and proper consideration, the Minister for Justice was satisfied that the common good requires it and the common good must be predominantly and overwhelmingly demanding in order to justify interference with constitutional family law rights.[17]

The right to marry which is guaranteed does not encompass a right to re-marry. Article 12 states that the right to marry is to be exercised "according to national laws" applicable. In *Johnston v. Ireland*[18] the Court ruled that Article 12 is concerned with the formation and not the dissolution of marital relationships. However, even if Contracting States cannot be obliged to provide for re-marriage if domestic public policy disfavours divorce, it should be noted that (a) once such a right to re-marry is granted, restrictions thereon will not be entertained[19] and (b) the absence of divorce/re-marriage facilities, albeit justified, will not support interference with the right to family life. The *Johnston* case indicates that domestic laws which discriminate against the children of co-habitees where such persons are exercising their right to form a family will conflict with Article 8. However, the right to respect for family life extends not only to the protection of existing family life but is broad enough to extend to intended family life also. It is in this regard that the most recent challenge under Article 8 involving Ireland is of relevance. The case of *Keegan v. Ireland*[20] has been declared admissible before the Commission and this case will serve to indicate if Ireland's legislative response to the protection of family life in the case of the unmarried family, introduced in the aftermath of the *Johnston* case,[21] has been sufficient for compliance with the obligations imposed by the Convention.

Interference in family relations by the State through the taking of children into care has also been considered on several occasions by the Court. In the main, the violations found by the Court have focused on procedural irregularities such as the exclusion of parents from the proceedings in question and the absence of a fair hearing.[22] The Court has also considered Article 8 violations in the context of the substantive decision to take the child into care and also in relation to the implementation of the decision.[23]

N. JACKSON

8.2 Juvenile Justice

TOM O'MALLEY

It is widely accepted that the Irish juvenile justice system is in need of reform.[1] Critics of the present system point to the antiquity of the legislation on which it based (the Children Act, 1908), the number of young persons committed to adult prisons, and the lack of co-ordination between the Government departments responsible for the administration of the system. These are all valid criticisms, but many of the reform strategies proposed during the past twenty years or so have failed to recognize certain realities about youth and crime, or to identify the tension that almost inevitably exists between welfare and justice approaches to juvenile offending.

That juvenile delinquency has existed throughout much of recorded history should hardly cause surprise given that juveniles have always constituted a significant proportion of the population, and Ireland is certainly no exception in this regard. But history discloses another recurrent theme as well, the tendency of older generations to decry what they perceive as the unparalleled propensity of their younger contemporaries towards crime and other misbehaviour.[2] According to Donovan, "every generation since the dawn of time has denounced the rising generation as being inferior in terms of manners and morals, ethics and honesty".[3] We find Socrates lamenting over two thousand years ago that:

> Children now love luxury. They have bad manners, contempt for authority, they show disrespect for elders and love chatter in place of exercise. They no longer rise when their elders enter the room. They contradict their parents, chatter before company, gobble up dainties at the table and tyrannize over their teachers.[4]

Apart possibly from the reference to gobbling up dainties, a weakness now shared by all age-groups, this statement reflects many of the complaints made about children and young people in our own time. Furthermore, older generations tend to assume that the crimes committed by the young are now more serious and vicious than ever before, and they usually hark back to an earlier, supposedly golden age when youth crime was of less harmful nature.[5] Today, for example, some express alarm at the number of young female offenders and the seriousness of their crimes. Yet, in the 1830s, we find Elizabeth Fry, setting up the Chelsea Reform School for thirty "vicious little girls, aged between eight and thirteen".[6]

Expressions of disquiet about juvenile crime sometimes convey the impression that it is unnatural—an aberration from what should normally be expected from young people. It is true that juveniles commit a higher proportion of recorded offences than older age-groups, but to suggest that those under a certain age, say eighteen or twenty-one years, should be naturally indisposed towards crime and delinquency is to present a vision of childhood and youth more in keeping with the idealized world of Enid Blyton than with the hard, and sometimes harsh, realities of our times. Childhood and adolescence, like race and gender, are social constructions of reality and fairly recent ones at that. Historians of childhood have shown that the early stages of life were not always vested with the attributes of innocence, happiness and privilege now universally associated with them in Western society.[7] It has been claimed that, until the middle ages, children were treated as "little adults" as soon as they ceased to be dependent on their mothers. Adolescence, as a distinct phase, was to emerge even later; it gradually gained acceptance from the early 19th century onwards and firmly established itself with the explosion of youth culture in the middle of this century.[8]

Concepts of childhood and adolescence are now well established, but our expectations of those going through these phases are often contradictory. We expect them to learn and gain experience at a more rapid and concentrated pace than at any other time in their lives; we give them leisure and freedom from responsibility, attributes now inevitably linked with childhood and youth. But somehow, as we push them along the road towards adulthood, we expect them to learn only the good habits, never the bad, of those they are being trained to emulate and eventually replace. Understanding juvenile crime requires a re-examination of our collective vision of childhood and youth, and of what we expect from those going through these life-phases. We must ask if our concepts of legal responsibility for wrongdoing are compatible with the other attributes of our social construction of childhood which are mainly associated with lack of responsibility and dependency.

Another reality to be confronted is the frequent disparity in attitudes towards juvenile crime in general and towards particular juvenile offenders. Just as penal reformers have sometimes been accused of "hating the criminal but loving the inmate", so juvenile justice reformers must come to terms with their occasional outrage at the behaviour of individual young offenders while at the same time seeking to improve facilities for such offenders in general. Many a strong proponent of welfare for "young people in trouble" has been shaken in his or her beliefs by experiencing or witnessing victimization at the hands of those who would have been the beneficiaries of his or her concern. The danger inherent in this (entirely natural) reaction to individual acts is what Cohen and others have identified as "moral panic", which results in general policies being adopted on the basis of few well-publicized incidents.[9] This phenomenon is exemplified by the recent decision of the British Government to establish secure detention units for young offenders, largely as a result of certain incidents which, though serious in nature, were few in number.

Finally, we must accept that our concepts of crime (adult as well as juvenile) and the strategies proposed to prevent and punish it are inevitably linked to certain social and political ideologies. Statistically, juveniles commit relatively few violent crimes; most of their wrongdoing is directed against property. To a great extent, therefore, public concern about juvenile crime stems from the social and moral values attached to property and ownership. Not that there is anything wrong with these values which, apart from anything else, are enshrined in the Constitution.[10] But it is important that any reform exercise in the area of juvenile justice should be preceded by an honest appraisal of the values which society is seeking to protect.

A major transition, of the kind Ireland has witnessed in recent decades, from a largely rural to a largely urban society leads inevitably to an increased preoccupation with personal property. The property owned by urban and suburban dwellers may well be more valuable than that of their rural counterparts, but it is far less extensive; hence the preoccupation with preserving it. Traditionally, for example, a child living in the countryside who carved his initials on a tree in neighbouring lands was seen as engaging in the natural pursuits of a healthy youngster. Today, a suburban child who brands a prize tree in a neighbour's garden will probably be seen as perpetrating malicious damage and thereby stigmatized, formally or otherwise, as delinquent. If the group of illustrious Anglo-Irish writers who carved their initials, still to be seen, on that famous tree in Coole Park in County Galway did the same today on a tree in Merrion Square, they would be branded as criminal.

It is not being suggested that all juvenile crime or even a significant portion of it is as innocent as carving initials on a tree. Much of it involves theft, burglary and robbery. Some involves the infliction of serious personal injury. One of the problems about juvenile crime is that it tends to be characterized as either largely trivial or predominantly vicious. The fact is that it varies as much as adult crime and therefore demands different kinds of response. As West has written, '[t]he totality of youthful crime includes occasional offences by a vast number of different individuals and repeated offences by a small number of versatile and persistent delinquents'.[11] Consequently, any attempt at reforming the juvenile justice system must be preceded by careful analyses of crime patterns among the young and of the personal and social characteristics of those committing it.

THE EXTENT OF JUVENILE CRIME

There is no one source of information on the Irish juvenile justice system, nor on the criminal justice system as a whole. Information on the number of offences coming to the attention of the Gardaí are found in the annual reports of the Garda Commissioner, which also give some statistics on convictions and the age groups of those convicted. The annual Report on Prisons and Places of Detention, usually published several years in arrears, give statistics on admissions to prisons and St. Patrick's Institution. The Probation and Welfare Service publishes a separate annual report on the numbers admitted to probation supervision and community service. And finally, the Department of Education publishes an annual statistical report which includes some figures on the numbers in special schools, though it is difficult to derive any worthwhile information from these figures. One can only applaud the recommendation of the Dáil Committee on Crime that the Minister for Justice should be under an obligation to publish an annual report on the operation of the juvenile justice system.[12]

The numbers of juveniles convicted of indictable offences since 1985 are as follows:[13]

Year	*Under 14 Years*	*14 Years and under 17*
1985	386	1,679
1986	551	2,092
1987	519	2,331
1988	598	3,407
1989	541	3,119
1990	601	3,110
1991	392	2,806

Juveniles have generally accounted for nineteen or twenty percent of the total convicted. It will be noted that there was a remarkably steep increase for both age-groups between 1985 and 1988, but that there has been a moderate decline since then, with the most notable decrease in 1991. There could be several explanations for this: fewer people in those age-groups in the population at large, a lower level of detection, an increased use of cautioning, or simply less crime. The real explanation is probably some complex combination of all these factors.

The Garda statistics also reveal a relatively low number of offences against the person by juveniles convicted of indictable offences. The following tables show the number of offences against the person, offences against property with violence and offences against property without violence which came to the attention of the Gardai during 1989, 1990 and 1991 and in respect of which convictions were obtained in those years.

TABLE 1

OFFENCES AGAINST THE PERSON

Year	*Offender Age-groups*			
	Under 14	*14>17*	*17>21*	*21+*
1989	2	37	148	312
1990	–	42	136	339
1991	–	32	71	177[14]

TABLE 2

OFFENCES AGAINST PROPERTY
WITH VIOLENCE

Year	Offender Age-groups			
	Under 14	*14>17*	*17>21*	*21+*
1989	153	1,090	1,449	1,931
1990	156	980	1,565	1,533
1991	57	755	1,257	1,410

TABLE 3

OFFENCES AGAINST PROPERTY
WITHOUT VIOLENCE

Year	Offender Age-groups			
	Under 14	*14>17*	*17>21*	*21+*
1989	161	698	1,671	3,346
1990	168	632	1,568	3,221
1991	103	554	1,328	2,783

Again, a general downward trend is evident, despite steady increases in the total numbers of offences against property with violence and larcenies recorded in those years.[15] But it is clear that the number of juveniles convicted of offences against the person is very small.

A similar trend has been evident in England in recent years. The total number of juveniles proceeded against in the juvenile courts, *c*. 55,000 in 1991–2, is about half the 1983 figure.[16] There has also been a significant reduction in the numbers of ten to sixteen year olds convicted or cautioned. The general decline in the number of juveniles in the population is only part of the explanation for this decrease. The total number of juveniles found guilty or cautioned declined by thirty-seven per cent between 1980 and 1990 compared with a twenty-five per cent drop in the population of juveniles.[17] Contrary to what is often believed, most young people grow out of crime and the peak age of offending is usually in the late teens.

WELFARE AND JUSTICE MODELS OF
JUVENILE JUSTICE

Throughout the past hundred years or so, two competing models of juvenile justice have vied for superiority. These are usually designated as the "welfare" and "justice" models.[18] The former is predicated on the notion that the delinquent child is deprived rather than depraved. The deprivation need not be of a material nature; it could arise from inadequate supervision or from a lack of moral or ethical guidance. In jurisdictions guided by this model, the function of juvenile justice agencies is to further the best interests of the child. A court or tribunal dealing with a young delinquent is concerned, not so much with due process requirements, but with the measures necessary to cater for the perceived needs of the offender. The gravity of the crime will not necessarily be a deciding factor; a minor infraction may bring to light circumstances which, in the opinion of the court, warrant considerable State intervention in the life of the child.

Dissatisfaction with the welfare approach has led to a resurgence of the "justice model" in recent decades. In many countries, including England and the United States, critics of the welfare model began to protest at the number of children who were being incarcerated for long periods, supposedly in their own interests. As Naffine writes of the Australian system "[t]he idea of 'the child's best interests' as an overriding goal for criminal justice has come to be associated with the removal of rights for children rather than their augmentation".[19] This excessive paternalism led some liberals in the early seventies to argue for the child's "right to punishment".[20] The welfare model was carried to its furthest extreme in the United States where the juvenile courts, through being vested with a *parens patriae* jurisdiction, functioned essentially as chancery rather than criminal courts.[21] As Curtis has pointed out, *parens patriae* theory, in keeping with its equitable origin, was concerned principally with caring for and controlling children, not necessarily with rehabilitating them.[22] The theory was perhaps best summed by Mack when he wrote that the purpose of the juvenile court was not to ascertain the guilt or innocence of the offender, but to ask "what is he, how has he become what he is, and what had best be done in his interests and in the interests of the state to save him from a downward path".[23]

In fact, most States including Ireland try to strike a balance between due process and welfare. The general policy in Ireland is that the child or young person, once arrested or prosecuted, is afforded a range of procedural protections (described below) but, on conviction, is to be subject to a sentencing regime different from that applicable to adults. For children, however, there still remains the possibility of what Hudson has described as "repressive welfarism"[24] in that they can be committed to reformatories or industrial schools (now called residential homes or special schools, respectively) for several years depending on their age, though the offence committed might not objectively warrant such a long period of custody.[25] In the final analysis, it is very difficult to harmonize welfare and due process philosophies. One could adopt the "justice welfare" approach recommended by Harris[26] in which the court's concern for the welfare of the offender is acknowledged, but subject to the limiting principle of proportionality. This is easier said than done. Proponents of welfare will argue that if the needs of the child are the overriding consideration, a proportionality principle based on the offence might serve to weaken welfare-inspired measures.

In view of our international human rights commitments,[27] any reform of the juvenile justice system must continue to include a mix of justice and welfare principles, though there will have to be an improvement in the implementation of welfare at the post-conviction stage. In order to analyse our present system in the light of these obligations, it will be convenient to examine the "four Ds" —Decriminalization, Diversion, Due Process and Decarceration—advocated by reformers in other countries in recent years.

DECRIMINALIZATION

The obvious function of decriminalization is to remove the stigma and consequences of criminality from certain kinds of behaviour or from certain classes of person. It may be motivated by a desire to bring the law into harmony with contemporary social mores as exemplified by the general tendency to legalize consensual sexual acts between adults or by a recognition of the futility of using criminal law to deal with certain problems such as prostitution or vagrancy. In the context of young offenders decriminalization generally involves removing criminal liability from all offenders under a certain age. In countries like the US which have traditionally had "status offences" such as truancy and incorrigibility which can be committed only by persons under a certain age (hence the reference to "status"), decriminalization has even greater importance.[28]

In Ireland, decriminalization arises solely in relation to the age of criminal responsibility which is currently set at seven years. A child under this age is conclusively presumed to be *doli incapax* and cannot be held guilty of any crime. A child between the ages of seven and fourteen years is entitled to a rebuttable presumption of *doli incapax* which means that he or she cannot be convicted of a crime unless the prosecution proves to the satisfaction of the court that he or she had the necessary capacity. There are few precise rules on how this presumption may be rebutted. Essentially it must be proved that in addition to committing the offence with the necessary mental element, the child knew that what he or she was doing was seriously wrong.[29] If the act showed evidence of careful planning, or if the child took steps to conceal the harm or his or her involvement in it, the court is likely to hold that the presumption has been rebutted. It has also been held that the strength of the presumption varies with the age of the child and weakens as the age of fourteen is approached.[30]

Until recently, there was also a conclusive presumption that a boy under the age of fourteen was incapable of committing an act involving vaginal or, apparently, anal intercourse. This rendered boys under fourteen immune from conviction on counts of rape, incest, unlawful carnal knowledge, intercourse with a mentally defective person or buggery.[31] This has now been abolished by section 6 of the Criminal Law (Rape) (Amendment) Act, 1990. Consequently, the test of incapacity is now the same for all offences, sexual and otherwise. But a boy under fourteen charged with a sexual offence can still escape conviction if the prosecution fails to rebut the general presumption of *doli incapax*.

Seven years was the age of criminal responsibility at common law, having been borrowed directly from Roman law.[32] It was endorsed in Section 4(5) of the Summary Jurisdiction over Children (Ireland) Act, 1884, which provides that it shall not render punishable for an offence "any child who is not, in the opinion of the Court . . . above the age of seven years and of sufficient capacity to commit crime". By now, most other European countries have adopted substantially higher ages. In England and Wales, criminal responsibility begins on the child's tenth birthday;[33] in other countries it is set as high as fourteen or fifteen years.[34] There have been several recommendations for an increase in the age of responsibility here. The Kennedy report[35] recommended that it be raised to twelve years. The Task Force on Child Care Services[36] split on the matter, a majority favouring the retention of present age of seven years, a minority believing that the age should be increased to fifteen years with the possibility of what was termed "restraint proceedings" for those below that age. In 1992, the Dáil Select Committee on Crime recommended that the age be increased to twelve years,[37] but stressed that:

> those under 12 who get into trouble would not be left to their own devices. The Committee would envisage that they would be dealt with under the Garda Juvenile Liaison Officer Scheme or under the Child Care Act, 1991 as "children in need of care and protection".

This would require an amendment to the present Juvenile Liaison Scheme under which a caution can only be administered when an offence is admitted, a factor to which the Committee did not refer.

Debate about the appropriate age of criminal responsibility, like that about the age of consent for sexual acts, must necessarily be inconclusive. There is no scientific means of identifying a "right" age in either case. Maturity, as Jones has remarked, is not merely a matter of chronological age.[38] To a great extent, the resolution of the problem depends on the nature of the legal proceedings to which juveniles are subject. Having the age of responsibility raised to ten, twelve, or fifteen years would be a hollow victory if those under that age were to be subject to welfare or restraint proceedings which might deprived them of legal representation, the right to a fair trial and a disposition proportionate to the gravity of their wrongdoing. The advantage of leaving the age of responsibility as low as seven years, as the majority of the Task Force recommended, is that those over that age charged with offences are entitled to the full range of due process protections, though this does not preclude a modern and enlightened range of dispositions being available for those found guilty.

Having said that, seven years is a very low age of responsibility and the idea of children of eight, nine or even ten years being branded as criminals is repugnant to most modern thinking. One important matter deserving attention, especially if the age of criminal responsibility remains low, is the criminal record of children. There is a provision in the Children Act, 1908, that "the conviction of a child or young person shall not be regarded as a conviction of felony for the purposes of any disqualification attaching to felony".[39] There should be a statutory provision removing from record all criminal convictions entered against persons below a certain age. Such a policy would have many advantages not the least of which being the encouragement it would give to young offenders, once their slate was wiped clean, to refrain from further crime.

DIVERSION

Many countries, including Ireland, have developed diversionary strategies to keep young offenders out of the criminal justice system.[40] This is, in many ways, an enlightened approach as it prevents youngsters being "labelled" as criminals (the inevitable consequence of a formal conviction) and decreases the likelihood of institutional confinement which in many cases will be more criminogenic than rehabilitative. In Ireland, the Garda Juvenile Liaison Scheme was established on a non-statutory basis in 1963 and had developed considerably since then.[41] It provides for the cautioning and supervision of juveniles committing minor crimes. The requirements are that the juvenile admits the offence, that the victim (where identifiable) raises no objection and that the parents or guardian agree to co-operate with the supervising Garda. Juveniles who are cautioned are placed under the supervision of a Juvenile Liaison Officer for twelve months. In July 1991, the programme was extended to offenders up to the age of eighteen years (until then the upper age-limit was seventeen years) and at the same time a National Juvenile Office was established to co-ordinate the entire scheme. A procedure for informal cautioning was introduced at the same time. There are currently eighty-three Juvenile Liaison Officers assigned to thirty-seven major centres of population, with thirty-eight officers in Dublin alone.

By the end of 1990, a total of forty-one thousand, six hundred and fifty-three juveniles had been admitted to the scheme since its inception, of whom four thousand, four hundred and seventy-four, are known to have become involved in further crime. Four thousand, five hundred and eight juveniles were admitted in 1991 alone. After the possibility of informal caution became available in July 1991, about half those admitted to the scheme for the remainder of the year came by this means. Overall, the scheme has all the appearances of being very successful; the known recidivist rate (about ten percent) is encouraging, given the age group involved, and the number of juveniles convicted as a proportion of total convictions dropped from forty-seven percent in the early 1960s to twenty percent in 1988.[42]

Furthermore, the Juvenile Liaison Scheme is but part of a broader programme developed by the Garda Síochána over the years to increase community involvement. It also has a community relations section and a schools programme. The new two-year training course for Garda cadets, introduced in response to the recommendations of a Committee on Garda Training and Education chaired by the late Dr Tom Walsh, involves cadet placement with an emphasis on community participation. Many cadets, like their more senior counterparts, have become involved in organizing sporting and recreational activities for young people in the areas to which they are assigned.[43]

But diversionary programmes, like most other aspects of juvenile justice, have had their critics. The main criticism has centred on their potential for "net widening", a concept of which we have heard little in Ireland. It refers to the tendency of innovations like diversion and community-based sentences to draw into the net of social control (which includes the criminal justice system) persons who might otherwise have been free from restrictions.[44] The fear has been expressed that, while cautioning was intended as an alternative to prosecution, it may be applied to many juveniles who would not have been prosecuted anyway. Consequently, the argument goes, diversion has an inflationary effect on recorded levels of juvenile offending.[45] The other criticism is that a caution operates without the elements of due process which would have to proceed a valid conviction.

This argument against diversionary programmes must be treated with some scepticism. Opponents of such measures often fail to explain their opposition to social control or to prove that there is less need for it. Certainly, there should be structures in place to ensure that diversionary programmes are not abused by those administering them. But this is far from saying that less restrictive measures of control, such as cautioning schemes, should not be available to contribute to the maintenance of order within society. Ultimately, the question is one of social values. The liberal concern with protecting individual freedom at all costs must be balanced against the more communitarian interest in maintaining an ordered society. The availability of measures of low to medium intrusiveness, provided they are reasonably used, is probably the best means of reconciling these competing values.

DUE PROCESS

The rights of juveniles are most vulnerable during police questioning and court trial. Under the Criminal Justice Act, 1984, the Gardaí may detain suspects age twelve years or more[46] for up to a total of twenty hours for questioning in respect of a wide range of offences. A detainee under seventeen years must be informed, without delay, of his or her right to consult a solicitor, and his or her parents must be informed both of the detention and the right to consult a solicitor. Regulations made under the Act provide that a parent or guardian must be present when a juvenile is being questioned save in specified circumstances. The first Annual Report of the Garda Síochána Complaints Board drew specific attention to these rules and indicated that it would be keeping a close watch on the extent to which they were being honoured.[47] This approach is to be welcomed.

Under the Summary Jurisdiction (Ireland) Act, 1884, the District Court has jurisdiction to deal summarily with a child or young person charged with any indictable offence other than homicide. One of the major innovations of the Children Act, 1908, was the introduction of special children's courts which would sit at a different time and in a different place from the ordinary courts. This has been honoured only in part. After the foundation of the State, the Courts of Justice Act, 1924, provided for special children's courts in Dublin, Cork, Limerick and Waterford. In fact, only one of these, the Dublin Metropolitan District Court, was formally established. It used to sit in Dublin Castle, but moved in 1988 to a new building in Smithfield. In other towns and cities, the general practice is for District Courts to deal with children and young persons accused of offences at times different from those at which they deal with other offenders. With a few exceptions, the general squalor of Irish courthouses makes them unsuitable for dealing with any offenders, let alone children. This is clearly one area in which the spirit of the 1908 Act has not been honoured.

A child or young person accused of a serious offence is entitled to free legal aid and must be informed of that right under the same circumstances and conditions that apply to adults. This right was given the force of a constitutional guarantee by the Supreme Court in *State (Healy) v. Donoghue*.[48] The burden and standard of proof remain the same irrespective of the age of the offender.

The constitutional entitlement of juveniles to the essentials of due process has been strongly endorsed by the United States Supreme Court. In 1948, Justice Douglas had declared that "[n]either man nor child can be allowed to stand condemned by methods which flout constitutional requirements of due process".[49] The case of fifteen year-old Gerald Gault finally settled the matter.

Gault was charged with an offence which, if committed by an adult, would have attracted a maximum of $50 or a jail sentence of not more than two months. But he, being under eighteen years, was committed to custody for a maximum of six years (in his own best interests). Writing for the Supreme Court, to which the case was ultimately appealed, Justice Fortas stated that under the US constitution, "the condition of being a boy does not justify a kangaroo court".[50] Citing among other authorities, *State (Sheerin) v. Kennedy*[51] which had been decided the previous year by the Irish Supreme Court, the Court held that a juvenile is entitled to the essentials of due process and fair treatment, notably the rights to notice of charges, to counsel, to confrontation and cross-examination of witnesses, and to privilege against self-incrimination. A few years later, the Court had to return to the trial rights of juveniles in the context of the standard of proof. In *Re Winship*,[52] Justice Brennan emphasized that juveniles like adults are entitled to proof beyond reasonable doubt:

> ... intervention [in the child's best interests] cannot take the form of subjecting the child to the stigma of a finding that he has violated a criminal law and to the possibility of institutional confinement on proof insufficient to convict him were he an adult.[53]

Due process should not, however, be regarded as the panacea to all ills. The canonization of freedom before the law and procedural fairness may sometimes serve to obscure underlying social inequalities. A procedurally fair response to crime should not deflect us from seeking to discover the circumstances which led the person to offend in the first place.

DECARCERATION

Before describing the custodial regime for young offenders, it is necessary to clarify certain terminology. For the purposes of sentencing, a child is a person under fifteen years, a young person is one who is fifteen years or upwards and under seventeen years, and a juvenile offender is one who is not less than seventeen years, and not more than twenty-one years. Outside of the sentencing context, however, the term "juvenile justice" is often used, as in this paper, to describe the criminal law as it applies to all persons under the age of seventeen or twenty-one.

The dispositional options available to the courts when dealing with children and young persons are basically set out in section 107 of the Children Act, 1908:

(a) by dismissing the charge; or
(b) by discharging the offender on his or her entering a recognizance;
(c) by so discharging the offender and placing him or her under the supervision of a probation officer;
(d) by committing him or her to the care of a fit relative or other fit person; or
(e) by sending him or her to an industrial school; or
(f) by sending the offender to a reformatory school; or
(g) by ordering the offender to be whipped; or
(h) or by ordering the offender to pay a fine, damages or costs;
(i) or by ordering the parent or guardian of the offender to give security for his or her good behaviour; or
(j) by committing the offender to custody in a place of detention provided under this part of the Act; or
(k) where the offender is a young person, sentencing him or her to imprisonment; or
(l) by dealing with the case in any other manner in which it may legally be dealt with.

There is certainly no shortage of choice! Community service has since been added as a further option though this can only be imposed on a person aged sixteen years or over convicted of an offence which, in the opinion of the court, would be one of imprisonment, penal servitude or detention in St. Patrick's Institution.[54] It has been widely used for young and juvenile offenders. In 1988, fifty-four percent of those sentenced to community service were aged between sixteen and twenty-one years.

The levels of fine, costs and damages that may be imposed on a child or young person are very low: £2 or, at most, £10. The failure to increase levels of fine has been criticized by many commentators, and one assumes that the forthcoming Juvenile Justice Bill will correct the imbalance. The custodial measures available for children and young persons are something of a quagmire.[55] Essentially, children under twelve cannot be sent to special schools (formerly reformatory schools). They must be sent, if anywhere, to residential homes (formerly industrial schools). A child between the ages of twelve and fifteen may be sent to a residential home if he is of previous good character and has no previous offences. A child of twelve or over with a previous offence or a child of fifteen or over, if being detained, must be sent to a special school. A child sent to a special school cannot be kept there after reaching his or her sixteenth birthday unless the Minister for Education consents to his or her remaining there for another year for the purpose of completing his or her education.

One of the main problems in this context is the scarcity of places of detention, especially for girl offenders. At present, there is one centre for girls in Dublin which provides seven places for remand on assessment and four to eight long-term places. A larger centre with up to twenty places is due to open later this year. In 1990, a total of one hundred and thirty-eight boys and six girls were detained in special schools.[56] A male between seventeen and twenty-one years (and in certain cases sixteen year-olds) may be sentenced to St. Patrick's Institution (in the grounds of Mountjoy Prison) in lieu of prison. There is no equivalent place for females.

THE IMPRISONMENT OF YOUNG PERSONS

Children cannot be imprisoned under any circumstances, but young persons, although they cannot be sentenced to penal servitude, may in certain circumstances be committed to prison.[57] The Supreme Court has recently confirmed that under section 5(1) of the Summary Jurisdiction over Children (Ireland) Act, 1884, a District Judge cannot sentence a young person to more than three months' imprisonment for an indictable offence.[58] Section 102 (3) of the Children Act, 1908, provides:

> A young person shall not be sentenced to imprisonment for an offence or committed to prison in default of payment of a fine, damages, or costs, unless the court certifies that the young person is so unruly a character that he cannot be detained in a place of detention under this part of the Act, or that he is so depraved a character that he is not a fit person to be so detained.

Consequently, a court may commit a person between the ages of fifteen and seventeen years to imprisonment if satisfied that he or she is either (a) unruly or (b) depraved to the extent specified by the Act. A young person may be remanded in prison pending trial if the same conditions are fulfilled. Needless to say, the fewer the secure detention facilities available, the more this imprisonment provision is likely to be invoked.

In fairness, the Superior Courts have shown themselves willing to exercise vigilance over the use of this power by the District Court. In *State (Holland) v. Kennedy*,[59] the High Court held that a certificate of unruliness must not be lightly given. The District Court must be satisfied of the unruliness or depravity of the defendant and that he or she cannot (as opposed to ought not) be held in a place of detention. In *State (O'Donoghue) v. Kennedy*,[60] Finlay P emphasized the procedural requirements to be followed before arriving at a decision on unruliness or depravity:

> . . . the decision to certify a young offender as an unruly character is of the same status as any other decision in a criminal proceeding and as such can only be reached by a court upon sworn evidence properly admissible before it, the accused having the opportunity through his solicitor to cross-examine the witnesses deposing to the facts concerned.[61]

This general policy was recently endorsed by the Court of Criminal Appeal in *People v. DE*.[62] The trial judge had ordered the defendant who was fifteen years old and convicted of several offences, mainly larcenies from cars, to be imprisoned on the grounds of being unruly or depraved. The Court of Criminal Appeal found, however, that the applicant had changed his ways before trial and had completed a training course without being disruptive. Accordingly, an order could not have validly been made under section 102 (3) of the 1908 Act. The order was therefore quashed although there was no suitable place of detention for the offender in question, which meant that he had to be allowed go free. Thus, the decision as to unruliness or depravity must be made by reference to the offender's disposition at the time of trial, and not at some time in the past.

In another recent case, the High Court had the opportunity to consider a number of aspect of section 102(3), including its constitutionality and the meaning of "depravity". In *J.G. and D. McD v. Governor of Mountjoy Prison*,[63] G. had been sentenced in the District Court to a cumulative term of 18 months' imprisonment for breach of a recognizance and for assaulting a Garda, while D. had been sentenced to concurrent terms of six months and three months for assault and larceny. The District Justice had duly certified that each applicant was so depraved a character that she could not be detained in a place of detention under the 1908 Act. In the High Court, Blayney J rejected the argument that section 102(3) failed to vindicate the personal rights of the applicants under Article 40.3 of the Constitution:

> . . . in my opinion this sub-section does not in any way represent an unjust attack on the applicants' constitutional rights. If anything, the sub-section defends their rights since it prohibits the imprisonment of young persons except in certain specified circumstances . . . this is a perfectly fair provision as the other young persons in the place of detention must be protected against anyone who is of so depraved a character as to be not fit to be detained there . . .[64]

The second objection was to the term "depravity" which, the applicants submitted, was a vague and ill-defined term. In this connection, several affidavits were submitted from persons experienced in dealing with young offenders and from a professor of moral theology. The Court noted that, according to a dictionary definition cited in one affidavit, "depraved" meant "immoral", "vicious", "unprincipled", "wicked". Applying these definitions, Blayney J said:

> . . . I am quite satisfied that the learned District Justice's finding in regard to the applicants' character could not be disturbed. There was ample evidence on which he could find that objectively they were of so immoral and vicious a character that they were not fit to be detained in a place of detention provided under the Children Act.[65]

The applicants were not seeking release from prison; they were, in effect, seeking to compel the government to move them to an appropriate place of detention (though such a place did not, by all accounts, exist). Blayney J did find, however, that the applicants (who were imprisoned in Mountjoy) were being detained in breach of rules 223 and 224 of the Prison Rules[66] which required that they should have been located in a prison in which accommodation is set apart for juvenile offenders and that such offenders should not come into contact with adult prisoners. He left over for argument the relief to which they were entitled by virtue of this deficiency.

A month later, the matter was re-entered for further argument and Blayney J, having been informed that special arrangements had been made in Mountjoy for the applicants in the interim, held that their detention now complied with the Prison Rules.[67] In fact, although this is not recorded in the judgment, the "special arrangements" consisted of holding the applicants in complete segregation from other prisoners. They were given separate cells and allowed to exercise when the exercise area was not being used by other prisoners. Such an arrangement for fifteen year old girls must surely be in violation of every human rights instrument known to the human race, including the European Convention for the Prevention of Torture and Inhuman or Degrading Treatment or Punishment, and the UN Convention on the Rights of the Child, to name but two of the major treaties which Ireland has ratified.[68]

This case, more than any other, shows up the primitive and unreflective nature of our criminal justice system. There may have been little the judge could have done in this case, but the end result was a sad indictment of the executive branch of government. One can only hope that the forthcoming Juvenile Justice Bill will adopt the recommendation of the Dáil Committee on Crime that there be "a complete ban on the use of adult prisons to accommodate young people under 17 years".[69] According to the Annual Report on Prisons and Places of

Detention for 1988 (the last year for which it is available), there were twenty-six males and two females between fifteen and seventeen years in adult prisons on 1 January 1988.

INTERNATIONAL HUMAN RIGHTS LAW

All the major human rights instruments adopted by the UN and the Council of Europe aim to protect children as well as adults. The European Convention on Human Rights, for example, requires the Contracting States to secure the rights and freedoms it contains to everyone within their jurisdiction (Article 1). But in recent years, a number of instruments related specifically to juveniles have been adopted by the UN. In November 1985, the General Assembly adopted the Standard Minimum Rules for the Administration of Juvenile Justice[70] (known as the Beijing Rules, so called because they were agreed upon at a inter-regional preparatory meeting in Beijing in 1984). The Rules provide a thoughtful and comprehensive set of norms to govern the operation of juvenile justice systems. They provide (5.1) that such systems shall "emphasize the well-being of the juvenile and shall ensure that any reaction to juvenile offenders shall always be in proportion to the circumstances of both the offenders and the offence". A juvenile charged with an offence must be dealt with "according to the principles of a fair and just trial" (Article 14.1). Institutional confinement is to be a last resort and for the minimum period necessary (Article 19) and a large variety of dispositional measures shall be available "so as to avoid institutionalization to the greatest extent possible" (Article 18).

In December 1990, the General Assembly adopted two other important documents, United Nations Guidelines for the Prevention of Juvenile Delinquency (known as the Riyadh Guidelines)[71] and UN Rules for the Protection of Juveniles Deprived of their Liberty.[72] The first of these provides (1.2) that "the successful prevention of juvenile delinquency requires efforts on the part of the entire society to ensure the harmonious development of adolescents, with respect for and promotion of their personality from early childhood". It proceeds to outline in detail the contribution of family, education, the mass media, the community and social policy towards the attainment of that objective and the state policies to be adopted to enable those contributions to be made. The second document deals only with juveniles detained or imprisoned, a juvenile for this purpose being a person under the age of eighteen. They provide that imprisonment should only be used as a last resort (Article 1) and that those deprived of their liberty "have a right to facilities and services that meet all the requirements of health and human dignity" (Article 31).

But the most important international human rights instrument in this entire area is, of course, the UN Convention on the Rights of the Child.[73] It was adopted by the General Assembly in November 1989 and entered into force, with remarkable speed, in September 1990. It has since been ratified by about one hundred and ten States and provides a comprehensive catalogue of the rights, civil, political, economic, social and cultural, to which children are entitled. It contains two key articles on juvenile justice. Article 40 sets out the due process entitlements of a child accused of having infringed the law. (A child is defined as a person under eighteen years unless, by law, majority is attained earlier.) It provides that a variety of dispositions shall be available, such as care, guidance and supervision orders, counselling, probation, foster care, educational and vocational programmes and other alternatives to institutional care shall be available to ensure that children are dealt with in a manner appropriate to their well-being. Article 37 sets out the standards to be applied when children are deprived of their liberty. They must be treated with humanity and respect and "separated from adults unless it is considered in the child's best interest not to do so". They shall also have the right to challenge the legality of their detention before a properly constituted court.

AGENDA FOR REFORM

Juvenile crime will never be eliminated but it can, one hopes, be reduced. There are no instant solutions; a significant reduction in crime requires careful long-term planning, and public patience with the setbacks that will inevitably occur from time to time. Above all else, it calls for the development and articulation of a set of core social values to inform policies and practices. Law, as Cox has written, "is a human instrument designed for human needs and aspirations".[74] Responses to crime, whether committed by adults or juveniles, are always politically charged. This phenomenon is exemplified by the return to just deserts and incapacitative policies of punishment by conservative governments in Britain and the United States during the past ten years or so. Preferences as to outcome tend to determine how crime is explained. Those favouring a punitive response will portray the young offender as an autonomous human being who has chosen to do wrong and must now pay the price. Their appeal for concern for the victim usually ignores the fundamental reality that the main purpose of the criminal law is to prevent victimization and punish or rehabilitate those who cause it. The liberal view of crime as the outcome of disadvantage demanding help and rehabilitation rather than punishment may no longer be popular. Granted, it provided a full explanation of crime, some of which is carefully calculated for selfish ends. But many of the premises on which the liberal vision was based are still valid, at least in the case of juvenile crime. It is not that the poor commit more crime than the rich, it is just that crimes committed by the poor are more likely to be reported or detected. A youngster who steals £5 worth of goods from a city-centre shop will become a crime statistic. A public servant who uses the office franking machine to stamp his personal Christmas cards for posting will not, unless he is very unlucky.

In a state which has as one of its founding political documents the ringing promise to "cherish the children of the nation equally",[75] it is only right that the genuine needs of individual young people should take precedence over vague notions of the good of society. These young people are members of society, but the more they are labelled as outcasts, the less they will be able to contribute to it. It is vital, therefore, that when they come into contact with the law, they should be treated as individuals who are members of three fundamental unit groups of society, the family, the community and the State. It is with this recognition that policy-making should begin.

PARENTS AND FAMILY

Within the past two years or so, successive Ministers for Justice have indicated that new juvenile justice legislation, currently in preparation, will place more responsibility on parents for the wrongdoing of their children. This is very much a case of history repeating itself. When Herbert Samuel was introducing the Children Bill in 1908, he said it was based on three main principles one of which was that parents should be made to feel more responsible for the wrongdoing of their children.[76] This idea has enjoyed something of a renaissance under recent Conservative policy in Britain which one cannot but suspect as being the inspirational source of the policy now favoured by the Irish Government. The British Government's White Paper, Crime, Justice and Protecting the Public[77] proposed greater responsibilities for parents to pay fines and compensation orders imposed on their children and recommended binding over parents to exercise proper care and control of their children. These proposals have, in large measure, been implemented in the Criminal Justice Act, 1991, (sections 56–58) though a proposal made earlier by a Home Office Minister[78] that it should be a criminal offence for parents to fail to take reasonable care to prevent their children from committing crime was dropped.

That parents should have responsibility for their children's behaviour is beyond doubt, so long as children are amenable to the control of their parents. But this general principle must be subject to realistic exceptions. As children grow older, they will often be less amenable to control and not all parents will have the ability or resources to exercise the necessary control over even young children. Responsibility should not be placed on parents unless the State is satisfied that the parents are capable of discharging it. This, in turn, points to the need for family involvement in criminal proceedings brought against children. There is little point in inviting or compelling parents to attend hurried hearings in crowded courtrooms where the dispute is essentially handled by others— police, social workers, lawyers and judges. Instead, there is much to be said for the kind of children's hearings now favoured in France,[79] New Zealand[80] and elsewhere. The defining characteristic of those proceedings is that the tribunal concentrates on the problems of the children and the parents as a family. Both sides may talk to each other in an informal setting. The victim may also take part in the deliberations and the judge or members of the tribunal will follow up the progress being made by the child after the case has been disposed of.

Translating this approach into a jurisdiction like Ireland with constitutionally-mandated due process procedures (also required by the international instruments already described) should not be an insuperable obstacle. A Family Court presided over by one or more judges appointed in accordance with the Constitution should be able to exercise a similar jurisdiction without undue formality. The essentials of due process need not be sacrificed; legal representation and the rules of evidence can still be maintained. But there should be no difficulty, especially in a jurisdiction which sets the family on a constitutional pedestal,[81] in readjusting court procedures so as to deal with the delinquency problem as a family problem.

A procedure of this nature would enable the court to assess the justice and viability of imposing liability on parents. In many cases, it may be unrealistic to do so because of their circumstances; in others it may be quite just. Careful records should be maintained of all such proceedings and research should be encouraged. One of the major problems confronting Irish policy-makers right now is that they have little hard evidence about the nature or background of juvenile offending.

THE COMMUNITY

The status of the child as a member of a family, which conservative policy-makers have been so keen to emphasize in recent years, has served to obscure the strong impact of community on personality and character-formation. Children, unlike adults, cannot choose their social companions or environment. They must live, learn and play wherever their parents happen to live. It would, in many ways, be more realistic for the Government to talk of placing responsibility on communities for the behaviour of its younger members, rather than on parents. Community development is central to a reduction of juvenile crime. But it would be foolish to suppose that such development can be achieved by

sending in armies of social workers, probation officers, youth workers and Gardaí
to selected "trouble spots". Such persons can, of course, offer counselling, help
and guidance. But they cannot offer employment, education or accommodation.
The disastrous planning decisions made in many urban areas, notably Dublin,
during the past fifty years mean that little can be done about juvenile crime in
some suburban areas in the immediate future except to contain it. Hopefully,
the next generation will grow up in restructured communities with adequate
support mechanisms and access to employment. Otherwise, the cycle of crime
will continue.

THE STATE

State intervention is required at several levels. In organizational terms it is no
longer satisfactory to have responsibility for juvenile justice fragmented between
the Departments of Justice and Education, with some involvement from the
Department of Health. It is disappointing that the present Government, when
creating new ministerial portfolios, did not see fit to create a full ministry with
special responsibility for youth affairs. Co-ordinated structures must be put in
place both at cabinet and administrative levels. There should also be a body
equivalent to the Commission for the Status of Women which would report
periodically to the Government on all aspects of child care, including juvenile
justice.

Secondly, the Government must decide on its priorities in responding to
juvenile crime. It can take the easy option of bowing to pressure from those
expressing concern for the community and the victim, which is generally a
euphemistic demand for locking up as many offenders as possible. Alternatively,
it can recognize that offenders are also members of the community and, in many
cases, victims of community and political policies. That some young offenders
must be detained for some time in a secure environment is unfortunately true,
though the time spent in custody should be devoted to helping offenders
overcome their problems. Most young offenders can be dealt with in the
community if adequate professional and material resources are made available.

CONCLUSION

The barrage of criticism directed at the juvenile justice system in recent years
might lead one to believe that it remains fossilized in the thinking and practice
of the late nineteenth century. This would be an unfair assessment; much has
been achieved in the meantime. The greatest achievement of the past thirty years

has been the de-institutionalization of both delinquent and deprived children. In the late nineteenth century, there were ten reformatory schools in Ireland, five for boys and five for girls. In 1898, there were seventy-one industrial schools caring for eight thousand children.[82] By the time the Kennedy Report[83] was published in 1970, the number of reformatories had declined to three and there were twenty-nine industrial schools some of which were quite small, catering for 2,000 children.[84] These numbers have now declined drastically due to the development of foster care for deprived children and more community-based support for young offenders.

The Probation and Welfare service has also expanded greatly. Although the Probation Act, 1907, applied to Ireland and is still, with one or two amendments, in force here, few probation officers were appointed until the 1970s. In fact, the first probation officer was not recruited by the Department of Justice until 1942.[85] During the past twenty years, the service has expanded greatly, as has the network of social support provided by the Health Boards established in 1970.

Furthermore, the juvenile justice system has been subject to thoughtful examination in a number of reports. A Staff-Student Working Party at the Department of Social Studies in University College, Dublin published a detailed study in 1981[86] and the Task Force appointed by the Government in the 1970s examined child care law in general with some care. The basic law was set out in a report commissioned by the Director of Public Prosecutions[87] and the recent report of the Dáil Committee on Crime sets out the main aspects of the system in need of reform.

The Children Act, 1908, was a very enlightened piece of legislation in its day and, apart from certain anachronisms such as the provision for whipping male offenders which is in all probability in violation of the European Convention on Human Rights,[88] could still provide the basis for an enlightened juvenile justice system if implemented in accordance with present-day values. The main deficiency lies, not so much in the law, but in the lack of resources committed to its positive implementation. If there is one advantage to be gained from our legislative inertia since 1908, it is that we have the opportunity to learn from the experience and mistakes of some of our more adventurous neighbouring countries. But our main concern now must be to fulfil in good faith our international obligations under the UN Convention on the Rights of the Child. There are few better guides to an enlightened juvenile justice system.

8.3 The Protection of Children's Rights in Inter-Country Adoption

WILLIAM DUNCAN

About twenty thousand children are the subject of inter-country adoption each year. There can be few more poignant reminders of the complexity which characterizes the human order, or disorder, than that this radical form of intervention should so often appear necessary to achieve the simple end of securing a home for a child. Yet the number of inter-country adoptions appears to be on the increase, and there has, since the Second World War, been a progression of sad countries, the subjects of war, political turmoil or natural disaster, appearing as the latest providers of adoptable children—Korea, Vietnam,[1] Bangladesh, Romania,[2] Albania[3] and Bosnia. Add to them the many countries, notably in South America and Asia (Africa has never been a popular source), with crippling poverty and sometimes staggering levels of child abandonment,[4] and the product is a multitude of homeless children which reduces the twenty thousand to a drop in the ocean. It is not the purpose of this paper to explore or berate the global economic and political failures which have led to this pass and to a world divided, in the anodyne language of inter-country adoption, into countries of "origin" and "receiving" countries. It is, however, a context which cannot be ignored when discussing, as this paper attempts to do, the protection of children's rights in the inter-country adoption process.

The vulnerability of children provides the basic reason for conferring on them legal protections. But there are special reasons why the legal regulation of inter-country adoption is important. Adoption is essentially a means whereby a child who is without a natural family may be found an alternative family which meets his or her needs. There is always the risk of the process being viewed more as a means of supplying the needs of the adoptive parents.[5] Keeping the interests of the child uppermost in the adoption process must therefore be a primary concern, as much in international as in domestic adoption. In the international context, given that the number of homeless children in some countries is so great, the laws of "supply" and "demand" create a "buyers market"[6] in which the primacy of the child's interests may very easily be subverted. The child needs to be protected from the dangers of inappropriate placement. Inter-country adoption has, unfortunately, been associated with other more serious forms of abuse,[7] including the sale of and trafficking in children, the falsification and forgery of documents, the acceptance of bribes by officials, pressurising and offering inducements to natural parents to secure their consent, the exploitation of the system especially by lawyers, and generally the danger that lower standards and safeguards will be applied in the international than in the domestic context. It would be wrong to exaggerate the abuses that occur, or to fail to recognize the many occasions on which inter-country adoptions are conducted properly and in the best interests of the child. However, it is necessary to understand that, in the international context, in which sending countries may often be experiencing civil disruption or economic problems, the opportunities for exploitation and abuse are rife. Hence the pressing need for international co-operation in regulating the process of inter-country adoption.

INTERNATIONAL PRINCIPLES AND CO-OPERATION

The purpose of this paper is to examine some of the basic principles accepted internationally for the protection of children who are the subjects of inter-country adoption, as expressed in particular in the UN Convention on the Rights of the Child, 1989 (hereinafter the UN Convention).[8] It is proposed also to examine the way in which these principles are being given practical effect in the work being carried out at the Hague Conference on Private International Law towards the conclusion, in 1993, of a Convention on International Co-operation and Protection of Children in Respect of Inter-country Adoption[9] (the present draft of this Convention is referred to, hereinafter, as the Draft Convention).

Before 1989, much work had already been accomplished internationally in the form of bilateral[10] and regional[11] agreements or conventions to regulate inter-country adoption. The General Assembly of the UN had also adopted the UN Declaration on Social and Legal Principles Relating to the Protection and Welfare of Children with Special Reference to Foster Placement and Adoption Nationally and Internationally, on 3 December 1986. But it is Article 21 of the UN Convention on the Rights of the Child which may now be taken as expressing the most fundamental principles, namely:

States Parties that recognize and/or permit the system of adoption shall ensure that the best interests of the child shall be the paramount consideration and they shall:

(a) Ensure that the adoption of a child is authorized only by competent authorities who determine, in accordance with the applicable law and procedures and on the basis of all pertinent and reliable information, that the adoption is permissible in view of the child's status concerning parents, relatives and legal guardians and that, if required, the persons concerned have given their informed consent to the adoption on the basis of such counselling as may be necessary;

(b)   Recognize that inter-country adoption may be considered as an alternative means of child's care, if the child cannot in any suitable manner be cared for in the child's country of origin;

(c)   Ensure that the child concerned by inter-country adoption enjoys safeguards and standards equivalent to those existing in the case of national adoption;

(d)   Take all appropriate measures to ensure that, in inter-country adoption, the placement does not result in improper financial gain for those involved in it;

(e)   Promote, where appropriate, the objectives of the present article by concluding bilateral or multilateral arrangements or agreements, and endeavour, within this framework, to ensure that the placement of the child in another country is carried out by competent authorities or organs.

THE HAGUE DRAFT CONVENTION[12]

It was in January 1988, that the subject of international co-operation in respect of inter-country adoption was first submitted by the Permanent Bureau to a Special Commission on General Affairs and Policy of the Hague Conference on Private International Law, and in June 1990, that the first Special Commission on Inter-country Adoption met. Two further sessions of the Commission were held in April/May 1991 and February 1992, and the final diplomatic session in May 1993. So far a total of sixty-three States, six intergovernmental and eleven non-governmental organizations have participated in the Special Commissions. Considerable efforts were made by the Permanent Bureau to ensure the participation of States of origin, especially in Asia and South America, many of whom are not permanent members of the Hague Conference.[13]

The approach at the Hague has been based on a recognition that unilateral action, on the part of either receiving States or States of origin, is in itself insufficient to safeguard the interests of children in inter-country adoption.[14] Proper regulation requires the exercise of controls by, and co-operation between, the two States concerned. The Draft Convention seeks to accomplish this on a multilateral basis. The objects of the Draft Convention are:[15]

(a)   to establish safeguards to ensure that inter-country adoptions take place in the bests interests of the child and with respect for his or her fundamental rights;

(b)   to establish a system of co-operation among Contracting States to ensure that those safeguards are respected and thereby prevent the abduction, the sale of, or traffic in children;

(c)   to secure the recognition in Contracting States of adoptions made in accordance with the Convention.

The second Chapter of the Draft Convention sets out a number of substantive conditions which must be met before an adoption order may be made, whether in the receiving State or the State of origin , and divides responsibilities between those two States for ensuring compliance with those conditions.[16] The State of origin must, *inter alia*, establish the child's adoptability, ensure that due consideration has been given to the possibilities for placement of the child in that State and that an inter-country adoption is in the child's best interests, and ensure that the relevant consents have been freely given, including where appropriate the consent of the child.[17] The receiving State is responsible for determining that the prospective adopters are eligible and suited to adopt and that the child will be authorized to enter and reside permanently in that State.[18] There is also a provision[19] controlling unsupervised contact between prospective adopters and biological parents, and a further provision[20] designed to prevent the transfer of a child from one State to the other in circumstances where an adoption may not be possible, both of which seem likely to undergo modification in the final session.

Drawing inspiration from the very successful Hague Convention on the Civil Aspects of International Child Abduction, 1980,[21] the Draft Convention adopts a system of State Central Authorities whose functions will include co-operation with one another through the exchange of general information concerning inter-country adoption, as well as duties in respect of particular adoptions.[22] These latter duties may be delegated to accredited bodies[23] who are likely normally to be approved adoption agencies, though there is also provision for the continued involvement of individuals, such as lawyers, but subject to supervision and only where the States concerned permit them so to act.[24]

A chapter on Procedures[25] sets out the principal steps to be taken by the respective Central Authorities (or accredited bodies) in relation to the preparation of reports on the child and the prospective adopters, the placement process, the obtaining of consents, securing permission for the child to enter the receiving State, the making of arrangements for the transfer of the child, and the measures to be taken to safeguard the child in the rare event of a breakdown in the placement.[26]

Finally, apart from general provisions, the Draft Convention deals, as yet in an unfinished manner, with the recognition and effects of an adoption made under the Convention.[27] Recognition is by operation of law, with very limited grounds of refusal. The effects are likely to be that, as a minimum, the child will enjoy rights equivalent to those of other adopted children in the receiving State. It is possible that a provision will be included providing for a form of conditional recognition of an adoption granted in the State of origin where the receiving State insists on the successful completion of a period of probation.[28]

With this general description of the Draft Convention, we may now proceed to discuss the broad principles contained in the UN Convention and the problems of their practical application in the Draft Convention.

THE RIGHT TO A FAMILY LIFE

The preamble to the UN Convention recognizes

> that the child, for the full and harmonious development of his or her personality, should grow up in a family environment, in an atmosphere of happiness, love and understanding . . .

The importance of family life for the child gives rise to two obligations on the State. The first is to provide support for the family in carrying out its obligations. This is recognized in the preamble.[29] More specifically, Article 18(2) provides:

> For the purpose of guaranteeing and promoting the rights set forth in the present Convention, States Parties shall render appropriate assistance to parents and legal guardians in the performance of their child-rearing responsibilities and shall ensure the development of institutions, facilities and services for the care of children.

The second obligation is to take action in circumstances where the child's existing family no longer functions to meet the child's needs. Article 20 requires the State to provide special protection and assistance to a child who is temporarily or permanently deprived of his or her family environment, or to one who, in his or her own best interests, cannot be allowed to remain in that environment. The State is obliged, in accordance with its national law, "to ensure alternative care for such a child".[30] Such alternative care may include adoption.[31]

The child's right to a family life clearly offers the fundamental justification for the institution of adoption, including inter-country adoption. But the same right presupposes that, before adoption is resorted to, the State should make all reasonable efforts to assist the child's existing family in functioning to meet the child's needs. Within inter-country adoption this gives rise to a number of concerns.

The first is that activities should be suppressed which are directed towards encouraging or persuading parents to release their children for inter-country adoption. Poor parents, who may have a number of children to care for, are vulnerable to such pressure. An offer of money may be presented as a means of providing other children in the family with opportunities, and their feelings of guilt at depriving a child of the material advantages of adoption abroad may too easily be exploited. It is to prevent the possibility of such pressures being brought to bear by prospective adopters that Article 4 of the Draft Convention forbids unauthorized contact between them and the child's parents in the initial stages of the adoption process; though it should be cautioned that child placement agencies may not always themselves be immune from such pressures.[32] The provisions of Article 5(c) of the Draft Convention, relating to the counselling of persons whose consent to adoption is required and requiring that consents be free, are also relevant here.

The second concern has to do with the development of family support services in the poorer States. It is easy enough to articulate a principle that States should support families before resort is made to inter-country adoption; it is a different matter to secure that principle in practice. The ability of a State to develop its family support services depends in large part on its economic situation. Many States of origin do not have the capacity alone to tackle the appalling problems of poverty which numerous of their families face. It is hardly surprising that, at a recent meeting of experts on inter-country adoption in Manila, the first recommendations for international measures were directed towards the reduction of poverty in the many countries in Asia, Africa and South America where this has become the major cause of child abandonment.[33]

THE PARAMOUNTCY OF THE CHILD'S INTERESTS

Article 21 of the UN Convention requires States Parties who recognize or permit adoption to ensure that "the best interests of the child shall be the paramount consideration". In inter-country adoption, the most important consequence of this principle is that regulation should be based on a model which regards adoption as a means of satisfying first and foremost the child's need for a family, and only secondly the adoptive parents' desire for a child. It is a matter of finding suitable parents for children in need, rather than suitable children for adults in need. This is not to suggest that the feelings and desires of the prospective adopters are of no concern; of course, they are of great importance.

But the process itself, the order and manner in which events occur within matching and placement, should reflect the child-centred model.

This is not the easiest thing to achieve within inter-country adoption. The main reason is that a child-centred approach requires the exercise, in the country of origin, of careful control over the procedures for locating, assessing and matching children who are to be the subjects of adoption. Many foreign adoptions occur within countries where, for reasons including civil disorder and poverty, controls of any sort are difficult to apply. This may in the end prove to be one of the biggest problems in the implementation of the Hague Draft Convention. It is based on a child-centred model, and it does place upon countries of origin considerable responsibilities, not only in relation to assessment and matching of children, but also in ensuring that alternatives to intercountry adoption have been properly considered and that the rights of the biological family, as well as the child, have been protected within the adoption process. One can envisage the Convention working well as between States which have a settled practice of inter-country adoption, where the country of origin has had the time and the resources to develop its administrative controls, including its Central Authority. It is much more difficult to see it operating effectively in emergency situations where war or civil disruption lead to a sudden increase in homeless children, or indeed in countries where for reasons of scale the exercise of effective controls in outlying areas is difficult.

There is one other rather different point that should be made about the paramountcy principle, one which I have already expressed elsewhere[34] as follows:

[T]he principle that the child's interests should always be paramount in adoption is not reflected in every aspect of adoption law, even in those countries which accept the general principle. For example, in several countries[35] rules which provide for dispensing with the consent of biological parents do not allow this to occur simply on proof that adoption would appear on balance more likely to improve the child's prospects. In other words, some weighting is given to parental rights. Also, in inter-country adoption, the principle that priority should be given to placement of the child in his or her country of origin, though based principally on considerations of the child's interests, is sometimes given broader political and economic justifications. In short, both in national and in inter-country adoptions, there is concern lest the principle of giving priority to the child's interests be used as an excuse for social engineering, that is, to justify a more generalized transfer of children from poor to wealthy parents, or from developing to rich economies.[36]

THE SUBSIDIARITY PRINCIPLE

Article 21(b) of the UN Convention contains a principle which is regarded as crucial, especially by many countries of origin. It is the principle of last resort— that inter-country adoption may only be considered if there is no suitable alternative for the child in his or her country of origin. The principle derives in large part from considerations of the child's welfare, and it is reinforced by Article 20(3) which requires States, when considering alternative forms of care for a child, to pay due regard to the desirability of continuity in a child's upbringing and to the child's ethnic, religious, cultural and linguistic background.

In the Draft Convention the principle finds expression in the requirement that the competent authority in the State of origin must, before an adoption order may be made, have determined, after possibilities for placement of the child within the State of origin have been given due consideration, that an inter-country adoption is in the child's best interests.[37]

The principle of subsidiarity, while of central importance, is not one which should be applied in an inflexible manner. There will sometimes occur cases where, in the interests of the child, a placement with parents from abroad may be more appropriate than with prospective adopters in the country where the child is resident, as for example where the child's roots are in fact in that foreign country. Also it would be unfortunate if the principle were operated in a way which led to excessive delay in the placement of a child, as for example by the adoption of rigid administrative practices such as the imposition of quotas for foreign adoptions on placing agencies.[38] It is important that the idea of subsidiarity be always interpreted and applied in the context of the "best interests" principle.

It is also well to stress that the successful operation of the subsidiarity principle requires that the placing agency in the country of origin should have the capacity to explore the alternatives to inter-country adoption. This implies a placement system which in some way is integrated into, or at least has ready access to and information about, the child-care services generally within the country of origin.[39] It also implies a level and range of services which many countries of origin will find hard to achieve. Hopefully, the Convention will provide further impetus for the development of such services, and may indirectly thereby reduce the need for inter-country adoption.

SAFEGUARDS AND STANDARDS EQUIVALENT TO THOSE EXISTING IN NATIONAL ADOPTION

States Parties are required, under Article 21(c) of the UN Convention, to "[e]nsure that the child concerned by inter-country adoption enjoys safeguards

and standards equivalent to those existing in the case of national adoption."
The "safeguards and standards" may be interpreted as applying both to
procedures before an adoption order is made, and to the status of the child
following the making of an order. The principle is best understood in the
context of the more general rule against discrimination set out in Article
2 (1).[40]

One of the motivations in the drawing up the Draft Convention has been
the concern that the strict standards that are a feature of the domestic adoption
process in many jurisdictions have not been replicated in inter-country
adoption. Both the substantive requirements and the procedures set out in the
Convention are an attempt to rectify this. However, difficulties can arise, and
have arisen, over the measures which different countries regard as essential to
secure the interests of the child. The necessity or otherwise of a probation, or
waiting, period following placement of the child with prospective adopters has
been one of these.

Countries such as England and Switzerland regard the existence of a
probation period, to ensure that the placement is successful before a final
adoption order is made, as an essential means of securing the interests of the
child. They take the view that it would be contrary both to the letter and spirit
of the UN Convention to dispense with it in cases where their own residents are
adopting from abroad. Other countries, such as Ireland, who regard the
probation period as essential within domestic adoption, accept that, where the
adoption is made abroad, the different context justifies waiver of the requirement.[41] In a number of Latin American countries[42] the requirement of a probation period, in the case of children leaving their borders, is viewed, not as a
safeguard for the child, but as presenting serious risks for the child. Their
concern is that a child should not be transferred until his or her status as an
adopted child has been secured; yet a probation period implies the transfer of
the child and placement with the prospective adopters in the receiving country
before an order is made.[43]

The Draft Convention's solution to this problem is to provide, in Article
23, for a form of conditional recognition. A receiving country which insists on
the probationary period will be able to refuse full recognition to an adoption
made in the country of origin until the probationary period is satisfactorily
completed. Until such time, recognition extends only to the transfer of legal
responsibility of the child to the adopters. The country of origin will be aware
of which receiving countries wish to follow this procedure, and may of course
decide that they should not make adoption orders in favour of residents of such
countries. It might seem natural that a court (or other body) in a country of
origin would refuse to make an adoption in favour of residents of a country which
it knows will not fully recognize it. In fact, as the Irish experience shows, the

prospect of non-recognition in the receiving country has not always in the past inhibited the making of orders in countries of origin. Whether Article 23 will survive to be enacted in its present form remains a matter of some doubt. The anomalies which it creates may prove to be too indigestible.[44]

Another difficult problem, which may be considered under the rubric of equality of treatment, is to define the effects of an adoption recognized under the Draft Convention. The simplest formula might appear to be one which accords to the child adopted abroad rights at least equivalent to those of a domestically adopted child in the receiving State. This is the principle which appears in the tentative Article 24.

The problem lies in the fact that in several States of origin (especially Latin American), and in some receiving States, a form of incomplete or "simple" adoption is accepted either exclusively or as an alternative to full adoption. "Simple" adoption, which varies in its detailed effects from country to country, implies that in some respect(s) the severance of legal ties with the family of origin is incomplete. Where a receiving State accepts both forms of adoption in its domestic law, the problem of the effects of a foreign order may be avoided by a rule that the foreign adoption, whether it be full or simple, should have the effects of an equivalent domestic adoption. The more difficult case is one where a simple adoption is made in a State of origin in favour of adopters who reside in a State which knows only full adoption. The principle of equal treatment might suggest that the adoption should be recognized as a full adoption. On the other hand, it would seem wrong to treat an adoption as having severed all ties with the family of origin in a case where a natural parent has consented only to simple adoption. One way to avoid this problem would be to confine the Draft Convention to full adoption.[45] This would not be a happy solution, because it would result in a large number of adoptions being left outside the regulatory provisions of the Draft Convention. The ideal solution would be one which takes account of three considerations:

(a) The need to keep within the scope of the Convention both full and simple adoptions.

(b) The need to avoid giving to an adoption effects which go beyond those in contemplation when consent was being given.

(c) Subject to (a), the need to avoid, so far as is possible, discrimination between the rights of different classes of adopted children within the receiving State.

INFORMED CONSENT

Article 21(a) of the UN Convention requires States Parties to ensure that any required consent to adoption has been given, that the consent is informed and that it has been given on the basis of such counselling as may be necessary. These principles have been given effect in Article 5(c) of the Draft Convention, which requires further that the consent is in writing, that it has not been induced by payment or compensation of any kind, and that in the case of a mother's consent, it has given after the birth of the child.[46] The inevitable weakness in these provisions is that it is left to the State of origin to determine whose consent is required and in what circumstances a consent may be dispensed with. It was felt that the draft Convention was not the appropriate place in which to spell out in detail a uniform code on these matters. It is also noteworthy that the question of choice of law is ignored. It may be assumed that in most cases the State of origin will wish to apply its own domestic rules. Some difficulties may be anticipated in cases where the adoption is to be made in the receiving State and where that State's consent requirements are stricter than those operating in the State of origin.[47] In Ireland constitutional rights may be involved which cannot be ignored by the Adoption Board.[48]

Article 12(1) of the UN Convention contains a principle which is obviously relevant to adoption:

> States Parties shall assure to the child who is capable of forming his or her own views the right to express those views freely in all matters affecting the child, the views of the child being given due weight in accordance with the age and maturity of the child.

The Draft Convention requires, as a condition of the grant of an adoption, that the competent authorities of the State of origin ensure, having regard to the age and degree of maturity of the child, that:

> (i)   he or she has been counselled and duly informed of the effects of the adoption and of his or her consent to the adoption, where such consent is required,

> (ii) consideration has been given to the child's wishes and opinions,

> (iii) the child's consent to the adoption, where such consent is required, has been given freely and unconditionally, in the required legal form and in writing, and such consent has not been induced by payment or compensation of any kind.

Again the Draft Convention avoids laying down uniform rules prescribing the circumstances in which the child's consent will be required. The matter is left to be determined by the State of the child's residence, which may be expected to apply its domestic rules. However, where the adoption is to be made in the receiving State, the question may arise of whether mandatory (for example, constitutionally required) rules of that jurisdiction concerning the child's consent should also be applied.

COMPETENT AUTHORITIES

Article 21(a) of the UN Convention requires States Parties to ensure that the adoption of a child is authorized only by "competent authorities". It may be that this refers only to the body which grants the adoption, which in some countries is a judicial, and in others an administrative, body. The Draft Convention is neutral on this matter. It is also neutral on the question of jurisdiction; it matters not, under the draft Convention, whether the adoption is finally made in the State of origin or the receiving State, provided that the competent authorities in the two States have carried out their respective functions prior to the making of the adoption.

Article 22(c) of the UN Convention requires States Parties to ensure "that the placement of the child in another country is carried out by competent authorities or organs". A vexed question in the discussions leading to the Hague draft Convention has been the role of independent persons, such as lawyers or doctors, within the adoption process. Should they be allowed to become involved in the making of arrangements for inter-country adoption other than in a capacity directly related to their professional competences? At present such involvement is permitted in States such as the US, but is prohibited or strictly limited in other States such as the UK or Ireland, where it is felt that only non-profit authorized agencies can provide the range of expertise and the necessary objectivity to protect the interests of children within the adoption process. In particular, it has been argued that certain abuses (for example, pressure on natural parents or inappropriate placements) may be more effectively combated where only authorized agencies are allowed to operate.[49] The compromise struck within the draft Convention is that a Contracting State may permit the involvement of non-accredited persons or bodies in making arrangements for inter-country adoption within its territory, subject to supervision, and provided those persons or bodies "meet the requirements of integrity, professional competence, experience and accountability of that State".[50]

CONCLUSION

Article 21(e) of the UN Convention places States Parties under an obligation to promote the objectives of Article 21 generally by concluding bilateral or multi-lateral arrangements or agreements. The Hague Draft Convention represents an attempt to achieve those objectives on a multilateral footing. It is based on a model which requires close co-operation at administrative level between States of origin and receiving States. It sets out minimum standards, both substantive and procedural, that must be satisfied before an inter-country adoption is made. It does not prevent the application of stricter standards by individual States, nor does it inhibit the making of more detailed arrangements between States, for example, on a bilateral or a regional basis.

The problems which the Draft Convention will encounter in practice are likely to be many. Its successful operation will require the development in each contracting State of an efficient administrative machinery to ensure that the Convention standards are adhered to, and this in States many of which are experiencing extreme poverty and competition for scarce resources. Clearly in some of these States there will be other important priorities in child welfare and protection, including the important task of developing domestic adoption. Indeed the hope is that the Convention may serve indirectly as a stimulus to such developments.

Finally, two of the Draft Convention's limitations may be noted. It does not embrace long term fostering arrangements falling short of adoption, such as the Islamic institution of "kafalah". Because of the general view in the Islamic world that adoption is forbidden in Islam, the Convention is unlikely to be of interest to Islamic countries.[51] A second limitation arises from the fact that some of the worst abuses of inter-country adoption have occurred in countries suffering from war, internal strife or natural disaster. These are usually emergency situations in which normal administrative controls tend to break down. They are situations in which it may be very difficult for the Convention safeguards to operate effectively; indeed the country concerned may not be a Contracting party. In such cases, the main burden, and moral responsibility, of exercising control over inter-country adoption will necessarily fall on the receiving State.

8.4   Education: Whose Right is it Anyway?

GERALDINE VAN BUEREN

THE RIGHT OF THE CHILD TO EDUCATION

Ironically, the concept of the rights of the child is more commonly associated with the right to education than any other right. International law, however, has never been exclusively concerned with the child's right to education. This is made clear by Article 26(1) of the Universal Declaration of Human Rights, 1948, which declares that "[e]veryone has the right to education".[1] Although children are the principal beneficiaries of education, the focus of international law has been not on the rights of the child but on the rights of parents to exert a degree of control over the State in relation to children's education.[2] In this respect, international law reflected western social attitudes exemplified in an extreme and earlier form by the approach of Thomas Jefferson. Although Jefferson highlighted education as necessary to protect a free people against tyranny, he was reluctant to support the compulsory education of children over "the will of the parent".[3]

The traditional international legal approach to education, however, is slowly changing. Children now possess both the right to education as well as specific rights whilst they are in educational institutions:

Surprisingly, the earlier Declaration on the Rights of the Child, 1924, omitted any express reference to the educational rights of the child. The first specific global reference to the right of a child to education was enshrined in Principle 7 of the Declaration on the Rights of the Child, 1959, to the effect that "[t]he child is entitled to receive education . . . ".

Any reference to education in its broadest sense implies:

the entire process of social life by means of which individuals and social groups learn to develop consciously within and for the benefit of the national and international communities, the whole of their personal capacities, attitudes, aptitudes and knowledge. This process is not limited to any specific activities.[4]

International law, however, is not concerned with the enforcement of State duties in relation to such a broad definition of education. An examination of the justiciability of the right to education reveals that there is a difference between schooling, *droit a l'instruction*, and education, *droit a l'education*. According to the Hungarian jurist, Szabo, the use of the word "education" in international instruments indicates the more formal types of instruction given in institutions.[5] This is evidenced both by the case law and by its use in international and regional treaties.[6] Hence the European Court of Human Rights has distinguished education from instruction, the former being:

> the whole process whereby in any society adults endeavour to transmit their beliefs, culture and other values to the young, whereas teaching or instruction refers in particular to the transmission of knowledge and to intellectual development.[7]

International law refers to a right to education rather than a right to access to education. This formulation implies that states are under a corresponding duty to provide education at specific levels even where schools do not exist.[8] However, there is no such obligation as far as pre-school education is concerned. Aspects of the right to education in the majority of international and regional legislation only refer to elementary or primary, secondary or higher education, omitting any reference to pre-school education. This is an unfortunate omission as the opportunity to participate in pre-school education has been recognized as important because children's attitudes "for example on race" are often formed in the pre-school years.[9] The United Nations Educational, Scientific and Cultural Organization (UNESCO) attempted to fill this lacuna by seeking to amend the Convention on the Rights of the Child during its second reading and incorporating a binding duty on States parties to "facilitate the provision of early childhood care and education using all possible means, in particular for the disadvantaged child".[10] UNESCO's amendment failed, as many States were opposed to increasing their expenditure on education. Hence international law does not enshrine any duty on States to provide even minimal pre-school education. Nevertheless, reference to the value of pre-school education can be found in non-binding UNESCO recommendations. The UNESCO Recommendation Concerning Education for International Understanding Human Rights and Fundamental Freedoms provides that "as pre-school education develops" State schools should encourage pre-schools to use activities consistent with human rights and fundamental freedoms. Reference to pre-school education is also found in the International Charter of Physical Education and Sport which includes the right of children of pre-school age to develop their personalities to the full through physical education and sport programmes suited to their requirements.[11]

The right to education illustrates the artificiality of the traditional distinctions between economic, social and cultural rights on the one hand and civil and political rights on the other. Different facets of the right to education are found in the International Covenant on Economic, Social and Cultural Rights (ICESCR) and in the International Covenant on Civil and Political Rights (ICCPR). The ICESCR establishes the duty on State Parties to provide different levels and types of education and sets out the time frame for the provision of free education.[12] Implementation of these aspects of the right to education is progressive and States Parties are under a duty to improve the existing conditions relating to education to the maximum of their available resources, bearing in mind the best interests of the child when allocating scarce resources. In contrast, the ICCPR enshrines the immediate entitlement of parents to ensure that the religious and moral education of children is in conformity with their own convictions. The common approach of both Covenants is that they regard the right to education as so fundamental that it is non-derogable.

Aspects of the right to education are also to be found in regional human rights treaties and declarations. Article 2 of the first Protocol to the European Convention on Human Rights (ECHR) is the only regional or international human rights instrument to adopt a negative formulation of the right to education: "No person shall be denied the right to education". This negative formulation was adopted because at the time all the Member States of the Council of Europe had a general education system and it was regarded as unnecessary to require Member States to establish such a system. In addition, some States did not wish to adopt a positive formulation, in case it implied an obligation to bind States Parties to undertake effective action to enable every person to have access to instruction. Subsequently, in the *Belgian Linguistics* case, the European Court of Human Rights held that the right to education does not imply a duty on States Parties to provide free or subsidized education of a specific type or at a specific level.[13] Nor, according to the European Commission of Human Rights, does the right to education extend to imposing an obligation on a State Party to recognize or continue to recognize any particular institution as an educational establishment.[14] However, it is necessary that there should be official recognition of any completed educational studies.[15]

Although the right to education extends to both adults and children, the principle of compulsory education is only applicable to children. It is a principle which implies that it is in the best interests of the child that children are not entitled to refuse education below a specified level. The principle, however, can only be taken so far. Although there is a duty on the State to provide education up to a specific level, there is not any corresponding enforceable international duty on the child to receive an education. Indeed the UN Guidelines for the Prevention of Juvenile Delinquency recommend that status offences such as truancy should not be penalized.[16]

THE RIGHT OF CHILDREN TO BE EDUCATED IN
ACCORDANCE WITH THEIR CONVICTIONS

Traditionally the interrelationship between the right to education and the right to freedom of conscience has been perceived as a balance between the duties on a State and the rights of the parents. The child, as the beneficiary of education, was regarded by international law as a valuable but silent receptacle of knowledge. This approach even applied to choice of language and was stretched to its limit in a case before the Permanent Court of International Justice concerning the *Rights of Minorities in Upper Silesia*, when the German Government which originally referred the case of the Court, argued that the decision as to which school a child attends "depends solely upon its parents wishes" irrespective even of the language spoken by the child.[17] The approach established under the League of Nations and its Minorities Treaties has been continued in the United Nations. Article 13 of the ICESCR illustrates this approach, placing State Parties only under a duty to:

> have respect for the liberty of parents and when applicable, legal guardians to choose for their children schools other than those established by the public authorities, which conform to such minimum educational standards as may be laid down or approved by the State and to ensure the religious and moral education of their children in conformity with their own convictions.

The issue of respect for parental rights in education also arose during the drafting of the ICCPR. The *travaux preparatoires* reveal that international law provides parents with this right not only to protect their religious beliefs but also so that parents would be able to protect children from any possible risk of indoctrination by the State in State schools. During the drafting, many of the States recalled the abuses of the educational system by the Nazis.[18]

In the UN Human Rights Commission, during the drafting of the ICCPR, a number of States proposed that parents should have the right to determine the type of children's religious education. Other States wished to protect the right of parents to give children a secular education.[19] Consequently Article 18(4) places a duty on States Parties to:

> undertake to have respect for the liberty of parents and when applicable, legal guardians to ensure the religious and moral education of their children is in conformity with their own convictions.

This was based upon a Greek amendment submitted to the Third Committee, which some States initially hesitated to support because they believed that the Covenant should protect the rights of individuals and not third parties.[20]

The duty on States Parties is only to permit parents to choose from among different types of education, if such schools exist. The State Party is not under any obligation to ensure such schools exist by establishing favourable conditions for their creation. This is evidenced by the Greek response to the question "whether under the amendment States would be obliged to provide instruction in the religion of the parents' choice".[21] Greece explained that a State would only be under a duty to respect the wishes of the parents that their children be brought up in their own religion and would not be under a duty to provide such instruction.[22] There is, therefore, no duty under the Covenant to subsidize education according to parental preference. This has implications for private schools: States Parties are not under any duty to subsidize private schools either directly or indirectly. Consequently, in *Lindgren and Others v. Sweden*, the UN Human Rights Committee held that Sweden was not in breach of Article 26 of the Covenant in refusing municipal subsidies for school meals and textbooks.[23]

The duty on States to respect parental preferences in the matter of religious and moral education does not extend to other aspects of the curriculum. During the debate on the same issue but in relation to the ICESCR, a proposal was submitted that parents should have the freedom to choose the "programme" of instruction, but this was rejected as an exaggerated demand.[24]

The duty on the State to respect the rights of parents is also enshrined in two of the three regional human rights treaties: the American and the European Conventions on Human Rights. The second sentence of Article 2 of the First Protocol to the ECHR provides that:

> In the exercise of any functions which it assumes in relation to education and to teaching, the State shall respect the right of parents to ensure such education and teaching in conformity with their own religious and philo-sophical convictions.

In the course of drafting Article 2, the phrase "having regard to" was replaced by the word "respect" to convey a more positive obligation on the part of the State in an article which is primarily negative in tone.[25] Both the European Commission and the European Court of Human Rights have examined this provision in the cases of *Kjeldsen, Busk Madsen and Pedersen v. Denmark*[26] and *Campbell and Cosans v. United Kingdom*.[27] In *Kjeldsen*, the Court stated:

> The State in fulfilling the functions assumed by it in regard to education and teaching, must take care that information or knowledge included in the

curriculum is conveyed in an objective, critical and pluralistic manner. The State is forbidden to pursue an aim of indoctrination which might be considered as not respecting parent's religious and philosophical convictions. That is the limit that must not be exceeded.[28]

The same approach has been taken by the Human Rights Committee in interpreting a similar provision of the ICCPR in *Hartikainen and Others v. Finland*.[29] The Committee stated that where parents or guardians object to religious instruction for their children at school, it is compatible with Article 18(4) of the ICCPR for domestic legislation to require that instruction should instead be given in the history of religion and ethics, provided this is done in a neutral and objective way and respects the convictions of parents and guardians who do not believe in any religion.

Kjeldsen arose from the introduction of compulsory sex education in Denmark which resulted in a number of parents complaining of a breach of their rights as parents to have their children educated in conformity with their religious and philosophical convictions, in accordance with the second sentence of Article 2 of the First Protocol. According to the European Commission of Human Rights, respect implies the need to balance the rights of the State Party to regulate education according to the needs and resources of the community and of individuals and the State Party's obligations to respect the rights of the parents. The Commission concluded that the State had shown respect for the conditions in the way sex education was taught.

The European Court of Human Rights held that the setting and planning of school curricula was within the competence of a State Party. The second sentence of Article 2 did not have the effect of preventing States Parties from providing information of a religious or philosophical kind on the condition that this information was conveyed in an objective, critical and pluralistic manner and did not pursue an aim of indoctrination. The Court supported the Commission's opinion that Denmark had met this criteria, as the main purpose of the education was to inform pupils and not to indoctrinate them into following a certain path of sexual behaviour. The Court admitted that abuses were possible and stated that the authorities should take care that the parents' religious and philosophical convictions were not flouted through carelessness and proselytization but concluded that as this had not occurred the Convention had not been violated.

The European Commission adopted a similar approach regarding the required neutrality of religious instruction in *Angelleni v. Sweden*.[30] Nor did the European Commission find a violation when applicants complained that compulsory school education in mathematics and natural sciences imposed on the applicant's son a "technologically oriented ideology". Applying the principles of *Kjeldsen*, the Commission did not find that the teaching of mathematics and natural sciences amounted to indoctrination.[31]

Curiously, as the right to education is at least as much the child's right as the vicarious right of the parents, two fundamental questions appear to have been ignored by international human rights tribunals. The first question is whether children have the right to participate in decisions concerning the type of education, so that education is in conformity with the child's religious and philosophical convictions. Secondly, which rights, if any, have children under international law, if they disagree with their parents' choice of education.

It is obviously important that parents are given the legal capacity to intervene between the State and the child in order to be able to protect the best interests of the child, but merely because the wishes of the child and the parents frequently coincide does not necessarily imply that the child can never have an independent interest. In the light of the UN Convention on the Rights of the Child and with the snail-slow emerging awareness in human rights fora of the rights of children to participate in decisions affecting their own lives, this bipartite relationship between the parent and the State has to be re-examined to determine whether the State is under any form of international legal duty to consider the wishes of the child in being educated in accordance with the child's convictions.

The view which originally prevailed is reflected in Article 26(3) of the Universal Declaration of Human Rights which provides that "[p]arents have a prior right to choose the kind of education that shall be given to their children". Parents are given this prior right because it was assumed that the interests of the child and of the parents would coincide, so that there was no need to consider the separate wishes of the child. Although the word "prior" is not reiterated in the two Covenants, both instruments appear to have overlooked the rights of the consumer of education, the child.

The point was initially raised in *Kjeldsen* in the separate concurring opinion of Kellberg who stated that insufficient stress had been put on the rights of the child.[32] According to Kellberg, children "of a certain age" can demand that their views are respected. He cogently argued:

> It is hardly conceivable that the drafters would have intended to give parents something like dictatorial powers over the education of their children.[33]

He concluded that it would be "wrong" for children who hold different philosophical convictions from their parents to abide by their decision concerning educational matters in this field.

The same issue was also raised in the Supreme Court of the United States in a partially dissenting judgment of Douglas J. In *Wisconsin v. Jonas Yoder*,[34] it was held that a State's interest in universal compulsory education to the age of sixteen was not absolute and was not so compelling that it should override the established religious practices of Amish parents who wished to withdraw fourteen and fifteen year old children from the State system to be trained in the traditional Amish agrarian way of life. One of the children, Frieda Yoder, had testified as to her own religious views but had she not so testified, Douglas J clearly stated that if an Amish child wished to attend high school and was sufficiently mature to have that desire respected, the State would be able to override the religious objections of the parents.[35]

So far this emerging awareness has only been reflected in minority opinions. There is, however, more scope for protecting the rights of the child by applying the UN Convention. Article 5 places States Parties under a duty to respect the rights of those legally and customarily responsible for the child to provide appropriate direction and guidance "in a manner consistent with the evolving capacities of the child", in the exercise by the child of the rights recognized in the Convention. This provision is reiterated in Article 14(2), specifically in relation to the child's right to freedom of thought, conscience and religion. Both this right and the right to education are enshrined in the Convention. In addition, Article 12(1) of the Convention assures to each child who is capable of forming his or her own views the right to express those views freely in all matters affecting the child and to have those views given due weight in accordance with the age and maturity of the child. Reading Articles 5, 14, 28(1) and 12 together, it is clear that children living in States which are party to the Convention are provided with the right to participate in decisions to help ensure that their education is in conformity with their religious and moral convictions. Further, in contrast with other international treaties, the UN Convention does not contain a provision respecting the parents' right to have their children educated in conformity with the parents' convictions. The majority of States drafting the Convention believed it to be inappropriate for a treaty on the rights of the child to incorporate such a provision, although during the second reading of the Convention, Canada, the Holy See, Ireland, Italy, the Netherlands and the US expressed concern over its absence.

It is now no longer open to a State Party to the Convention to refuse to consider, as a matter of policy, the educational wishes of children. For children who are living in States which are not party to the Convention, it is arguable that the same principle could apply, providing that children are living in States which are parties to treaties guaranteeing the right to freedom of expression and, specifically, to the Convention Against Discrimination in Education. Article 12(1) of the UN Convention on the Rights of the Child only articulates a much overlooked application to children of the general right to freedom of expression which is found in a number of other human rights treaties and which gives to children the right to freedom of expression in all matters involving the State which affect the child, subject to such exceptions as national security and public morality. Article 5(b) of the Convention Against Discrimination in Education provides that "no person or group of persons should be compelled to receive religious instructions inconsistent with his or their conviction". In States which are party to the ECHR, the American Convention, or to the ICCPR and in States which are also party to the Convention Against Discrimination in Education, children as well as adults are entitled to have their religious and philosophical convictions respected by the State educational system.

In addition, apart from instances where children's religious and philosophical convictions depart from their parents, the State will not be under any responsibility to respect the religious or philosophical beliefs of parents where it appears that parental decisions will jeopardize the health or safety of the child. In such instances the rights of the child will be overriding.[36]

There remains one further question. If children have the right at least to participate in ensuring that their education is in conformity with their moral or religious convictions, does this necessarily imply that there is a duty on the State to ensure the existence of non-State funded schools, in particular private schools, to teach in a manner which is in conformity either with the child's or the parent's religious and moral convictions?

International law permits non-State schools to exist but does not place a duty on States to create favourable conditions for their existence. The "liberty of individuals and bodies" to establish and direct educational institutions is included in the UN Convention. Article 29(2) provides that such institutions . can be established, providing that the education of children is directed towards the aims set out in the Convention and that such institutions should conform to such minimum standards as may be laid down by the State Party. This approach is also reflected in the Convention Against Discrimination in Education which excludes from discrimination the establishment or maintenance of private education if

the object of the institutions is not to secure the exclusion of any group but to provide educational facilities in addition to those provided by the public authorities, if the institutions are conducted in accordance with that object, and if the education provided conforms with such standards as may be laid down or approved by the competent authorities in particular for education of the same level.[37]

Specifically, Article 2 of the Convention excludes from its definition of discrimination the establishment or maintenance of separate educational systems or institutions "of the two sexes", if such systems offer equivalent access to education and to courses of study and provide an equal standard in teaching, school premises and equipment.[38] The Convention also allows separate educational institutions and systems for religious or linguistic reasons, in accordance with the wishes of the child's parents or legal guardians.

Although international law would prohibit a State baldly legislating the abolition of non-State schools,[39] there is nothing in international law which places States under a duty to create conditions, such as the creation of tax advantages, in which private schools can flourish. This is also borne out by Article 2 of the First Protocol to the ECHR which was introduced primarily to protect the rights of parents against the use of educational institutions by the State for the ideological indoctrination of children, and not for the retention of private schools *per se.*[40] Therefore, States which seek to abolish private education directly would clearly breach international law but the same goal may be achieved with impunity through indirect methods such as through the fiscal system.

In addition, applying the principles established by the *Belgian Linguistics* case,[41] which reinforce the approach reflected in the *travaux preparatoires* of the Convention, States Parties are not under any duty to subsidize or create favourable conditions for the establishment or continuance of private schools. The European Commission of Human Rights has held that this extends to the provision of textbooks or other educational aids which contribute to particular forms of education, as in the case concerning *Rudolf Steiner Schools.*[42]

The final issue which remains to be resolved in relation to the concept of a child's choice of education is whether this includes the right to educate or be educated at home. According to the European Commission of Human Rights it is clear that Article 2 of the First Protocol:

> implies a right for the State to establish compulsory schooling, be it in State schools or private tuition of a satisfactory standard, and that verification and enforcement of educational standards is an integral part of that right.

Therefore, to require parents who teach their children at home to co-operate with the assessment of their children's educational standards to ensure the required literacy and numeracy levels does not constitute a breach. Children are entitled to be taught at home provided such tuition is in accordance with the national educational standards.[43]

CONCLUSION

The exercise of the right to education is essential for children because it helps realize their potential. Yet an important aspect of education, learning to take responsibility for decisions made, has been overlooked. Children have been excluded from participating in a wide range of educational choices, from government debates over the content of school curricula to the choice of school. International law is only belatedly beginning to acknowledge that the right to education belongs to children as well as to parents.

8.5   Select Bibliography

TEXTS AND MATERIALS

P. Alston et al., eds., *Children, Rights and the Law* (Oxford, 1992).
A. Bainham and D. Pearl, eds., *Frontiers of Family Law* (London, 1983).
T.J. Bernard, *The Cycle of Juvenile Justice* (Oxford, 1993).
H. Burke et al., *Youth and Justice: Young Offenders in Ireland* (Dublin, 1981).
Council for Social Welfare, *The Rights of the Child: Irish Perspectives on the UN Convention* (Dublin, 1991).
Dáil Committee on Crime, *Juvenile Crime: Its Causes and Remedies* (Dublin, 1992).
Defence for Children International, *Protecting Children's Rights in International Adoptions* (Geneva, 1989)
J. Goldstein et al, eds., *Beyond the Best Interests of the Child* (London, 1980).
A. Lester and D. Pannick, *Independent Schools and the European Convention on Human Rights: A Joint Opinion* (London, 1982).
R.B. Lillich, ed., *The Family in International Law: Some Emerging Problems* (London, 1981).
Prison Reform Trust, *Trends in Juvenile Crime and Punishment* (London, 1993).
I. Szabo, *Cultural Rights* (Leiden, 1974).
G. Van Bueren, *International Documents on Children* (London, 1993)
G. Van Bueren, *The Best Interests of the Child—International Co-operation on Child Abduction* (London, 1993)

ARTICLES

M.J. Becker, "The Pressure to Abandon" (1988) 5 *International Child Rights Monitor*.
M. Buquicchio-de Boer, "Children and the European Convention on Human Rights" in F. Matscher and H. Petzold, eds., *Protecting Human Rights—The European Dimension: Essays in Honour of G.J. Wiarda*, 2nd ed. (Köln, 1990) 73.
C. Corrigan, "The Hague and Luxemburg Conventions on Child Abduction" (1992) 10 *ILT* (n.s.) 4.
P.J. Duffy, "The Protection of Privacy, Family Life and Other Rights under Article 8 ECHR" 2 *Ybk Eur L* 191.
W. Duncan, "The Child, the Parent and the State" and "Family Law and Social Policy" in W. Duncan, ed., *Law and Social Policy* (Dublin, 1987) chs. 2 and 9.
W. Duncan, "Regulating Intercountry Adoption—An International Perspective" in A. Bainham and D. Pearl, eds., *Frontiers of Family Law* (London, 1993).
L. Levin, "The Rights of the Child" in P. Davies, ed., *Human Rights* (London, 1988) 40.

D. McGoldrick, "The United Nations Convention on the Rights of the Child" (1991) 5 *Int'l J Law & Fam*. 132.

D. Ngabonzinza, "Moral and Political Issues Facing Relinquishing Countries" (1991) 15 *Adoption & Fostering* 75.

P.H. Pfund, "The Hague Convention on International Child Abduction, the International Child Abduction Act and the Need for Availability of Counsel for All Petitioners" (1990) 24 *Fam LQ* 35.

P. Shanley, "The Formal Cautioning of Juvenile Offenders" (1970) V *Irish Jurist* 262.

G.A. Stewart, "Young Offenders: Children and the Criminal Law" (1976) *ILTSJ* 279.

G.A. Stewart, "Interpreting the Child's Right to Identity in the UN Convention on the Rights of the Child" (1992) 26 *Fam LQ* 221.

H. Storey, "Right to Family Life and Immigration Law in Strasbourg" (1990) 39 *ICLQ* 328.

G. Van Bueren, "The UN Convention on the Rights of the Child" (1991) 3 *J Ch L* 1.

G. Van Bueren, "The United Nations Convention on the Rights of the Child—The Necessity of Incorporation" (1992) 22 *Fam L* 373.

G. Van Bueren, "Child-Oriented Justice—An International challenge for Europe" (1992) 6 *Int'l J Law & Fam* 381.

9 : REFUGEES

9.1 Introduction

Although the plight of the refugee is by no means a new phenomenon in Europe, recent events emanating from within and outside the region have intensified the challenge facing European governments to fashion a humanitarian response to the predicament of displaced groups and individuals. Not least, the emergence of new democracies in Eastern Europe coupled with the devastating impact of war in former Yugoslavia have exacerbated the difficulties facing refugees in the current climate of economic recession and increasingly conservative attitudes to immigration.[1]

In this latter respect, the increased drive towards integration within the European Community carries in its wake some perturbing implications for non-EEC nationals. As Suzanne Egan points out, refugees will not be spared the detrimental effects of a common policy on immigration as among the twelve Member States. Even if one concedes that a tightening of European borders is an inevitable response to an increase in the mobility of persons, worldwide, the crisis facing the individuals fleeing persecution should not be forgotten. The plight of the refugee should not be engulfed in the increasing bureaucracy of European immigration control. Clearly, the momentous challenge facing the world community is to address the root causes of flight; to remove the conditions which create the phenomenon of the refugee. In the more immediate term, however, it is incumbent upon receiving States to ensure that the individual escaping human rights abuse is not forced to return to it, nor subject to further violations of his or her rights by their own hand.[2]

Putting aside, for a moment, the impact of recent developments, it is worth recalling that the status of the refugee in international law has always been a somewhat precarious one.[3] General international law affords the individual no right to asylum, as such; rather, it is the receiving State which enjoys a right, in the form of a discretion, to grant or withhold safe haven. The Universal Declaration of Human Rights, 1948, merely suggests that the individual has the right to "seek" asylum from persecution and, if granted it, to "enjoy" such asylum.[4] Even this limited guarantee has not found its way into substantive human rights treaties such as the European Convention on Human Rights (ECHR) and the International Covenant on Civil and Political Rights (ICCPR).[5]

351

International law does provide a basic guarantee, however, in the form of the principle of *non-refoulement*, that is, the idea that an individual will not be "returned" to a place where he or she will face a substantial risk of persecution.[6] Indeed, this principle also finds expression in Irish constitutional law.[7]

Of course, the State may assume further obligations to recognize and afford protection to refugees, by way of treaty. Ireland is one of a number of States which has done so by ratifying the principal international agreement in this field, the Geneva Convention Relating to the Status of Refugees, 1951, and Optional Protocol thereto, 1967.

Bill Shipsey's discussion of the 1951 Convention and its interaction with Irish law indicates that the guarantees to the refugee are more limited than a first reading of the Convention might suggest. For example, the Convention limits the category of persons who may qualify as refugees to those who are in flight from persecution on the basis of civil or political status. In addition, it places a large measure of discretion in the hands of the Contracting States regarding the implementation of a refugee–determination procedure. In this regard, the Irish arrangements are clearly deficient in a number of respects, not least in the absence of an avenue of appeal, preferably to an independent body. Nevertheless, recent developments in terms of Irish administrative law and practice are an encouraging, albeit indirect, sign of improvement.

Reliance on domestic administrative law, as a vehicle for reform in this area, is but one of the implications of non-incorporation into Irish law of the 1951 Convention. In successive cases, the terms of Article 29.6 of the Constitution have been applied to prevent asylum-seekers from invoking Ireland's obligations under the 1951 Convention, directly before the Irish courts. Moreover, unlike other unincorporated international human rights treaties, such as the ECHR, the 1951 Convention provides no right of petition or complaint to an external court or committee.[8] This fact alone suggests that reform of law and practice in respect of immigration and refugees must be pursued vigorously at domestic level. In addition, as Kevin Costello's discussion indicates, the field of Irish immigration law, generally, is ripe for reform. In this respect, the establishment by the Minister for Justice of an Interdepartmental Committee on Non-Irish Nationals to examine current practice and policy with particular reference to admission, residence, access to the labour market and applications for asylum, may prove a welcome start.[9]

Although the ECHR does not address the rights of refugees specifically in any of its substantive articles, certain of these provisions may apply to the situation of the asylum-seeker. Principal among these is Article 3, the guarantee of freedom from torture and inhuman and degrading treatment or punishment, which has been determined by the European Court of Human Rights to embody the basic concept of *non-refoulement*. Its potential application to the case of the asylum-seeker became apparent following the landmark decision of the Court in an extradition case, *Soering v. United Kingdom.*[10] Here a unanimous Court held that in the event of the applicant being extradited to the US where he might be subjected to "death-row" conditions, the UK would be in breach of the Convention, having exposed him to "a real risk of treatment going beyond the threshold set by Article 3".[11]

In *Cruz Varas v. Sweden,*[12] a Chilean couple and their son sought the protection of the Convention following the expulsion of the husband, and threatened deportation of the wife and son, from Sweden, where they had sought political asylum. Having regard to the principle applied in the *Soering* case, the Court stated:

> Although the present case concerns expulsion as opposed to a decision to extradite, the Court considers that the above principle also applies to expulsion decisions and *a fortiori* to cases of actual expulsion.[13]

In deciding whether substantial grounds had been established for believing that there was a real risk of treatment contrary to Article 3, the Court indicated that its assessment must be made with reference, primarily, to those facts which were known or ought to have been known to the Contracting State at the time of the expulsion.[14] In the Court's view, in light of all available evidence, the Swedish authorities had been entitled to conclude that a real risk of ill-treatment had not been established in the present case. A further argument to the effect that the trauma of expulsion in itself amounted to ill-treatment contrary to Article 3, was similarly rejected:

> It is recalled that ill-treatment must attain a minimum level of severity if it is to fall within the scope of Article 3. The assessment of this minimum is, in the nature of things, relative; it depends on all the circumstances of the case, such as the nature and context of the treat ment, the manner and method of its execution, its duration, its physical or mental effects and, in some instances, the sex, age and state of health of the victim.[15]

The Court found that the circumstances of the *Cruz Varas* case were not such as to justify a determination that the expulsion of the husband constituted a breach under this provision.

That Article 3 protection for asylum-seekers might prove more illusory than real, seem to be confirmed by the subsequent decision of the Court in *Vilvarajah and Others v. United Kingdom.*[16] The applicants were Tamils who had experienced ill-treatment in Sri Lanka and had sought asylum in the UK. Following the rejection of their claims by the UK authorities, they were returned to Sri Lanka where their fears of continued ill-treatment materialized. Although emphasizing that its examination of the existence of a risk of ill-treatment in breach of Article 3 "must be a rigorous one in view of the absolute character of this provision and the fact that it enshrines one of the fundamental values of the democratic societies making up the Council of Europe",[17] the Court found the existence of a substantial risk of ill-treatment, such as to engage Article 3 of the Convention, had not been established.

Given the outcome of these cases, one must conclude that the practical benefit of Article 3 protection for asylum-seekers is limited, not least in light of the problems associated with crossing the evidential threshold of a "substantial risk" of ill-treatment. Moreover, these cases also comprise unsuccessful attempts to invoke other provisions of the Convention to assist the asylum-seeker, such as Article 8 (right to respect for family life) and Article 25 (right of individual petition),[18] as well as Article 13 (availability of national remedy).[19] The matter is further compounded by the inadequacies of the Strasbourg procedures in terms of a response to the urgency of asylum cases.[20] At least for the time being, the concept of legal protection at European level remains a limited one. From the Irish perspective, the possibility of advancing refugee issues via the State reporting mechanism contained in the ICCPR would appear to offer a more practical avenue for change.

LIZ HEFFERNAN

9.2 Some Issues in the Control of Immigration in Irish Law

KEVIN COSTELLO

Two or three years ago the regulation of immigration control ceased to be one of the more inconspicuous areas of Irish administrative practice. From a legal point of view this increased attention has meant that the subject now occupies a remarkably high proportion of cases in the judicial review list, and Ireland has now begun to generate its own indigenous body of immigration case law. Yet, there are a considerable number of issues which remain to be resolved and, here, attention shall be given to examining some of these, using three broad headings: the grounds of inadmissibility; the machinery of immigration control; and the status of refugees in Irish law.

THE RULES GOVERNING INADMISSIBILITY

Under section 5 of the Aliens Act , 1935, anybody is entitled to enter the country save where there is a prohibition on entry laid down in an aliens order; and there are in the Irish immigration code eleven such grounds of inadmissibility[1] laid down in subordinate legislation. Two points will be made about the laws regulating admissibility. First, it is possible that the statutory enactment, section 5, which authorizes this entire body of inadmissible categories of entrant has been definitively constituted; and, secondly, there is also the possibility that the most important grounds of refusal to land (the provisions relating to work-permits[2] and to persons seeking to travel on to the United Kingdom) may be unlawful, on the ground that the Minister for Justice has failed, for various reasons, to discharge fully his duty to legislate in these fields, and has instead unlawfully delegated some of these statutory functions.

The common immigration control provision is one of the most commonly employed grounds of refusal and it is also, perhaps, the one which generated the greatest amount of legal controversy. Article (2)f of the Aliens Order, 1975, permits an Aliens Officer to refuse leave to land if the officer (i) is satisfied that the alien is about to make his way to the United Kingdom and (ii) would be inadmissible in the United Kingdom under the immigration laws of that country. Two issues arise: (a) is the provision unconstitutional for amounting to an abdication of national sovereignty?— and (b) does the provision amount to an unlawful delegation of legislative authority?

The provision appears to have its origins in the concern in the early 1960's about immigration to the United Kingdom which prompted the enactment of the Commonwealth Immigrants Act, 1962. Speaking on the floor of the House of Commons Mr R. A. Butler, the Secretary of State for Home Affairs warned "that if the Government of the Republic of Ireland do not control Commonwealth immigration it will be necessary to adopt the inevitable course, undesirable though the Government regard it, of imposing control at the dock, to control Irish immigrants coming in".[3] The warning had been heeded and on the eve of the Committee Stage of the Bill, and at a time when it looked as if entrants were to be subjected to a work-permit system, Frank Aiken, the Minister for Foreign Affairs, announced the establishment of a new arrangement:[4] for immigrants coming to our ports with an intention of travelling to England, entry to Ireland would be conditional on the right of entry to England. "We are aware", he later stated[5] "that if free movement of persons between here and Britain is to be maintained we shall have to continue to ensure that aliens who are not automatically admitted to Britain cannot land here for the purpose of using this right of free movement to travel to that country."

An obvious preliminary question to be determined, and one which conditions the proper interpretation of the provision, is the issue of whether the
paragraph is, in the first place, constitutional. It is a condition to the constitutionality of every foreign policy and domestic administrative decision that it have
been determined according to what is thought to be the national interest in the
matter or, at least, not according to the interests of a third party.[6] It is one thing,
indeed it is the essence of sovereignty, for the State to enter into a treaty with
obligations the detailed contents of which will have been prescribed by the terms
of the treaty itself; but it is another matter, an abdication of sovereignty, for the
State to enter into a treaty imposing obligations on the State, the detailed content
of which may be determined by another State. In *Crotty v. Ireland*,[7] it was
decided that a treaty which was thought to oblige the executive to align its foreign
policy with that of other states, through the framework of European Political
Co-operation, carried the risk that the State might be obliged to abandon
judgments which reflected its interests and adopt, in its place, foreign policies
which reflected the interests of third parties. Ratification of such a treaty was,
as is well known, accordingly held unconstitutional. Similarly, a provision which
literally, at least, authorizes the executive to turn away, without any investigation
of their desirability in Ireland, aliens who have been declared inadmissible in
the United Kingdom, might appear to contravene the same principle. Inadmissibility to Ireland is, after all, determined not according to the domestic interest
in the matter (which may not even be considered), but according to a statutory
instrument which binds the State to implement the interests of a third party.
Further, for that class of entrant which seeks to travel on to the United Kingdom
the principles regulating entry to Ireland are not pre-determined in Irish law
but may change according as the United Kingdom Immigration Rules are
changed and according as discretion is exercised in individual cases in the United
Kingdom. On a first, literal reading of the provision, therefore, paragraph 5.2(j)
appears unconstitutional for breaching the principle that administrative
decisions should not be taken according to the interests of external bodies.
However, Article 5.2(j) is a discretionary power,[8] and it is an incident of the
presumption of constitutionality that a discretionary power be edited so as to be
given a construction which is consistent with the Constitution. This can be
achieved, not by reading article 5.2(j) literally, but by adding a third condition:
that the applicant is not either so desirable in Ireland as to justify dispensing
with the interests of the United Kingdom authorities. By ensuring that Article
5.2(j) is only exercised when its operation corresponds with the domestic interest
in the matter, the Article is converted into a genuine exercise of the Irish
executive's better judgement, and not a mere cypher for implementing the views
of a third party, and is therefore constitutionally sustainable. In fact, subject only
to the admittedly still quite unresolved question of whether a statutory instrument

is capable of attracting the presumption of constitutionality,[9] Article 5(2)(j) appears relatively secure.

That construction has, then, several consequences: any decision where it could be proven that an immigration officer failed to exercise his discretion to dispense with immigration control before deciding to implement the paragraph would be unlawful; any notice of refusal of leave which simply recited the terms of article would be legally insufficient and bad on its face.[10] Furthermore, there is an argument to be dealt with, that a decision under 5(2)(j) may, even if not unconstitutional, be *ultra vires* where the dominant reason for its exercise is that the applicant has been refused entry in the United Kingdom. One of the conditions of subordinate legislation is that the person designated in the statute himself formulates the legislation, and in the absence of express authority to do so, legislative authority cannot be delegated to any other person. In the context of immigration control that means that the Minister for Justice must himself detail the personal circumstances which render certain categories subject to immigration control, and should not delegate that function to a third party. Has the Minister for Justice, in the case of this special type of applicant for admission, in effect, delegated his legislative function to the United Kingdom authorities?

Where an Aliens Officer refuses leave on the basis that the applicant has been refused entry in the United Kingdom he is, in effect, adopting the implementation of one of the legislative grounds of inadmissibility laid down in the United Kingdom Immigration Rules, a ground which has never been approved or deliberately prescribed by the Minister for Justice, and one of a number of grounds which are liable to fluctuate as the Immigration Rules are amended by the Home Secretary. That that is so, it can be argued, is a consequence of the fact that the Minister has, in the case of one category of entrant, delegated his function of prescribing the grounds of admissibility to an external institution. Of course, it might be possible to argue that the Minister is discharging his duty to regulate the grounds of entry by the simple act of arranging for the competence of a third party to prescribe grounds of refusal. But the established rule is that an institution designated by statute to formulate delegated legislation must itself attend to the substance of those enactments and not just the procedures under which they are taken. *Attorney General of Canada v. Brent*[11] is, in the circumstances at hand, a very convenient illustration of this principle. There the Supreme Court of Canada held that the power of the Governor General to make regulations with respect to immigration restrictions was not validly exercised by making regulations which, in substance, transferred to a local body the competence, in turn, to make those rules. The possibility, therefore, is that even if constitutional, the operation of paragraph 5(2)(j) may perhaps be *ultra vires* on the grounds that it amounts to an unlawful delegation of legislative power.

The delegation question would seem, ultimately, to turn on the neat question of whether it is necessary to the discharge of the Minister's legislative function that he prescribe the personal circumstances of the applicant which make him subject to immigration control; or, whether it is sufficient to describe an intention to enter another country together with the consequences of (an undefined and indeterminate) set of personal circumstances in the law of that country. The position is not clear: on the one hand it may be that the Minister is failing, in the case of one particular category, to regulate sufficiently according to the merits of the claimant for admission; on the other hand, it is, surely, plausible that the proscription of persons, because they are inadmissible in the United Kingdom is, indeed, a precise and intelligent exercise in Ministerial law-making, and not merely a devise for delegating power to another institution

However, the most important threat to the regime governing inadmissibility to Ireland is that the provision in the Aliens Act, 1935, section 5, which gives the Minister competence "when he thinks proper" to make orders prohibiting the entry of aliens into Ireland appears to be unconstitutional. The significant point, and it is an argument which has begun to gain ground over the last three years, is there are no restrictions on the Minister's law-making capacity, or on the contents of his subordinate legislation. He may legislate for what he likes so long as he "thinks it proper". Article 15 of the Constitution, on the other hand, entrusts law-making power to the Oireachtas. The fundamental rule is that to preserve the position of the Oireachtas as the primary legislator, delegations of legislative power to a Minister must not be inordinate.[12] The statute must contain a framework of social policy decisions within which the subordinate legislator then operates; the Minister, in turn, fills in the blanks or applies those standards to particular cases.

It is precisely the abdication of the task of formulating Ireland's immigration policy which, it may be argued, makes the Aliens Act, 1935, so suspect. The Oireachtas could have legislated for a simple quantitative control, simply restricting type numerical size of its intake. More likely, it could have laid down a series of qualitative controls: laying down from what countries immigrants were to be received; confining entry to those who would operate in certain areas of the labour market; laying down what humanitarian concessions it would make. The Oireachtas has done none of these things. The power of classification of desirable and undesirable immigrants has it seems been abandoned by the Oireachtas to a Minister. The constitutional point is, perhaps, even more appealing when it is understood that the "if and when the Minister thinks fit" formula has its origins in the early legislative history of immigration control: in the fact that the 1935 Act virtually re-enacts the original emergency First World War Alien's (Restriction) Act, 1914.[13] Indeed, the point was anticipated by one of the contributors to the debates on the Alien's Bill, 1935, who pointed out, that section 5 was the re-enactment

> of a lot of the powers which were bred entirely in the atmosphere of panic of the war situation in 1914 in Great Britain . . . when there were spies emanating everywhere, and when there was a definite indication on the part of people to hunt up every alien and pursue him. Here we are now putting into the permanent legislation of this country this whole section which gives the Minister, by an Alien's Order, power to do "all or any of the following things".[14]

The formula may, as that contributor points out, have been understandable in its original circumstances; and understandable given the constitutional form of government which originally enacted it. But, if the standards rule prevails there no defence of "necessity" or historical context is available now to protect the constitutionality of Section 5.

Again, however, the matter might not be entirely free from doubt and the doubt relates to the status of the standards rule itself. There is no prohibition on legislation which permits the executive to make subsidiary policy decisions. The restriction is that those policy decisions must be taken within intelligible sufficient legislative standards. In the United States from where the doctrine was patriated into Irish law there is no doubt but that the adequate standards rule has become an increasingly formal and less important condition.[15] There the Supreme Court has held that the fact that delegated legislation was to be exercised in the public interest and in accordance with the broad purposes of the legislation provided a sufficient legislative standard. The result has been that with the possible exception of areas like taxation and personal rights, the policy standards rule has all but disappeared. And, the application of those United States cases could mean that an argument that the Minister for Justice, being limited to those measures necessary to maintain effective immigration control in the public interest, is, in fact, subject to a sufficient legislative standard, might well prevail. The Constitution, it can be argued, does not require the impracticable and it does not in all cases require a detailed determination of the circumstances in which a given statutory power is to be operative; to require a detailed determination of the circumstances in which immigration control is to be applied, would, given the ever-changing profile of those seeking entry and the changing character of the country's absorbitive character, be highly impracticable. Furthermore, those Irish cases which have insisted on detailed legislative standards have all dealt with liability to taxation and can for that reason be distinguished. The specificity of the duty to set standards can expand or contract according to the character of the statutory power in question. In the case of powers which touch on important substantive rights the duty is likely to require greater formulation by the Oireachtas. That may be because the legitimate basis for government interference in private rights like the levying of taxation relies on popular consent, and, under the Constitution, that consent is located in the legislature. Immigration regulation, on the other hand, does not touch on the personal rights of the community and may, it can be argued, fall outside that category of cases requiring stricter parliamentary surveillance.

THE ENFORCEMENT MACHINERY OF IMMIGRATION CONTROL

A second general area of domestic immigration law worth scrutinizing is its enforcement machinery: the power to order the removal of immigrants unlawfully present in the country; and the power to deport immigrant residents whose presence is not "conducive to the public good". Both procedures raise a number of issues. There is the issue, for instance, of whether the power of removal is itself *ultra vires* given that the Alien's Act, 1935, authorizes only one form of expulsion: deportation following an order made by the Minister for Justice; another issue, recently litigated, is the maximum legal period before execution of a removal order;[16] there is also the question of to which categories of immigrant the power of removal applies;[17] and the question of the circumstances in which exercise of the power to remove might be so oppressive as to be legally unreasonable.[18] The deportation power, similarly, raises a number of issues: the question, for instance, whether a Minister must attend personally to the decision to order deportation;[19] the question of what is necessary to show jurisdiction on the face of a deportation order;[20] and most significantly of all: the proper construction of the formula "not conducive to the public good", the finding which is the basis of the authority to deport.

The last mentioned point can be developed in the following way: it is clear that the power to direct removal can be used in the case of a routine immigration infraction; but, can, as has been happening recently, deportation be used in such circumstances? Is rather deportation confined to cases which involve some positive harm to the community? The power to deport is found in Article 13 of the Aliens Order, 1946, which provides that the Minister may if he deems it conducive to the public good make an order requiring an alien to leave and remain thereafter out of the State. It is an elementary rule of construction that the proper objective of a provision of delegated legislation is to be derived from the instrument as a whole.[21] Article 7 of the same instrument constituted, through the power to direct a removal, a comprehensive scheme for dealing with infractions of the immigration code. Thus a person who has entered without leave may be removed; a person refused leave could be removed and a person who overstayed or acted in breach of conditions of entry could be removed.[22] It is difficult, in fact, to find an immigration offence not covered by the removal power. The intention behind the power to direct removal seems, therefore, to have been directed towards those who were not lawfully present in the country; the mischief to which the power to deport on the other hand was directed was the expulsion of immigrants who, though lawfully resident, were regarded as impinging on the public interest in some substantial and immediate way. If that is so, then it might be open to doubt whether it is still legitimate to use the power of deportation in the case for instance of a person who is, or is not, in possession of a valid visa or passport or work permit.[23]

The practice of executing removal or deportation orders without permitting the subject the opportunity of considering the legality of the order, is yet another contentious issue. The practice has resulted in a number of instances recently where lawyers have been forced to seek injunctions at judge's homes late at night or at the weekend.[24] Indeed, concern about incidents where the practice was applied has been raised in the Dáil recently.[25] The principle laid down in the celebrated *State (Quinn) v. Ryan*[26] is that a fixed interval of time must be allowed elapse prior to the execution of a power of removal from the State. In that case the Gardái, frustrated at delays in securing the applicant's removal, had unceremoniously taken the applicant out of the jurisdiction with the intention, it was found, of ensuring that he would not be able to test his extradition by means of a habeas corpus application to the High Court. The Supreme Court declared that the actions of the Gardai amounted to contempt of the Constitution, and Walsh J, with his eye, perhaps, on a new Extradition Bill, 1964, which had just been circulated in replacement of the old procedure under the Petty Sessions Act, 1851, and which omitted such a safeguard, warned that: "any law authorizing the removal of a detained person out of the jurisdiction must to avoid the taint of unconstitutionality, permit the detained person a reasonable opportunity to consider whether to apply to the High Court".[27]

The period subsequently laid down in the Extradition Act, 1965, fifteen days, seems to provide a good analogous guide as to precisely the interval of time required; and, a dramatic remedy for breach of the principle may be available. In *Quinn*, the Court confirmed the principle found in earlier authorities[28] that it might not be good enough for a respondent who previously had custody to justify not producing the applicant on the ground that he had, in the interval, parted with custody. The principle, it was held, is that non-production may be excused only where there is an absolute impossibility of retrieving the applicant and that meant that, in appropriate circumstances, the court could order the authorities to leave the jurisdiction, go abroad, and return with the deportee back to Ireland.[29]

THE CONVENTION ON THE STATUS OF
REFUGEES 1951 IN IRISH LAW

A final issue worth addressing is the unincorporated position in Irish law of the Convention on the Status of Refugees, 1951. Until recently this had looked like becoming an acute problem. Within a year, four injunctions had been taken arising out of cases where it was alleged that the State had breached its international obligations. Furthermore the Irish immigration authorities had taken to defending court proceedings by strongly denying their obligations under the Convention. The virtually unanswerable point made was that by Article 29.6 of the Constitution no treaty can give rise to rights or obligations in Irish law except where it has been passed into legislation; the Convention not having been incorporated into domestic law, the State was free to ignore it. In fact, as a matter of pure administrative practice, such applications were always considered but there had for a long time been concern about the unconsidered and peremptory way in which such applications were being decided.[30]

Some of the disadvantages facing applicants for refugee status were reversed when O'Hanlon J handed down his decision in *Fakih, Hamdan and Slim v. The Minister for Justice*,[31] and decided that an internal administrative arrangement setting out the procedure for the processing of asylum applications was binding against the Government. Two issues arising out of the litigation are of particular importance: the legal source by which this arrangement was made enforceable; and the precise character of the entitlement it generated.

The case involved three members of the Lebanese group who had arrived in Dublin seeking refugee status. They were, it was alleged, declined a full hearing of their asylum request in contravention of procedures which had been agreed (in confidence), in December 1985, between the United Nations High Commissioner for Refugees (UNHCR) and the Assistant Secretary of the Department of Justice. That letter provided for a ten-point procedure whereby a person seeking refugee status was to be provided the right to argue such a claim and procedures regulating such a hearing.[32] This letter, it was argued, generated a legitimate expectation that such procedures would be implemented and reliance was placed on *Attorney General of Hong Kong v. Shiu*.[33] In that case the Secretary for Security in Hong Kong had announced that the Government was to abandon its policy of automatically granting asylum to migrants arriving from China; instead, a new policy was to be inaugurated whereby each case was to be treated on its merits, and a hearing granted before a decision taken to repatriate persons in that category to China. This undertaking, it was held, gave rise to the legitimate expectation of a fair hearing, which, on the facts of the case, had not been fulfilled. O'Hanlon J applied this convenient precedent and concluded that failure to comply with the undertakings given by the Department of Justice to the UNHCR also frustrated a legitimate expectation, and amounted to an abuse of the discretionary power to refuse admission under the Aliens Act. He quoted the Privy Council statement that:

> When a public authority has promised to follow a certain procedure, it is in the interest of good administration that it should act fairly and should implement its promise, so long as the implementation does not interfere with its statutory duty. The principle is also justified by the further consideration that, when the promise was made the authority must have considered that it would be assisted in discharging its functions fairly by any representations from interested parties, and as a general rule that is correct.[34]

Four months later in *Gutrani v. The Minister for Justice*,[35] a Libyan who claimed he was a target of Colonel Gadaffi's regime, alleged a breach of the procedures laid down in the 1985 letter. McCarthy J speaking for the Supreme Court, upheld O'Hanlon J's conclusion that the 1985 letter generated an enforceable right to consultation. McCarthy J, however, explained the basis for the enforceability of the agreement in slightly different terms:

> Having established such a scheme, however informally so, [this Minister for Justice] would appear to be bound to apply it in appropriate cases, and his decision would be subject to judicial review. It does not appear to me to depend upon any principle of legitimate or reasonable expectation; it is simply the procedure which the Minister has undertaken to enforce.[36]

The reason for the distinction would seem to be that, as generally understood, the doctrine of legitimate expectation should not have been applicable. Two conditions in Irish law for enforcing a legitimate expectation are that the expectation be known and that the applicant have acted on foot of that representation.[37] Here the 1985 letter had, until it was discovered in the course of proceedings, remained confidential and was certainly not known to the applicants. The Supreme Court, therefore, distinguished the rules on legitimate expectation and, apparently, based its conclusion on a principle ante-dating, but overlapping with, the doctrine of legitimate expectation, that a government department acts unlawfully and is subject to judicial review merely for failing to observe its own internal regulations,[38] and in arguing in this manner the Supreme Court seems to have confirmed a further ground of judicial review.

The second and more important point is that these cases seem, however, only to recognize a right to have a claim fairly processed; they do not, it appears, recognize a right of *non-refoulement* at the conclusion of a positive finding. In *Fakih*, O'Hanlon J explicitly stated that "the legal status of the applicants, or the question of their legal entitlement is not governed in any way by the terms of the letter and [it] is of benefit to the applicants only in relation to the manner in which their claims to rights of asylum are to be processed".[39] But it is difficult to see how the decision can have done anything other than enforce a right of *non-refoulement*. The courts do not act in vain, and in enforcing a right to a hearing they necessarily enforced a right to a decision. That means that an immigrant with a right to a hearing where he claims that his life or liberty would be endangered were he to be returned to his country of origin, also has a right to a decision as to whether he should be returned. That decision must, according to the principles of administrative law, be correct in law and not fundamentally at variance with the evidence grounding the application. That, at least where there are sufficient grounds, must imply the possibility of a legally enforceable right of *non-refoulement* in accordance with the 1951 Convention on the Status of Refugees.

The constitutional difficulty with that, however, is that it appears logically to result in the incorporation into domestic law, by a back door, of the 1951 Convention. The fundamental constitutional position, after all, is that it is the Oireachtas by statute, and not the Executive by treaty, or otherwise, who make international agreements enforceable by individuals in Irish law. The courts must be alert, as the House of Lords has recently pointed out, not to extend the principles of judicial review where the indirect effect would be to enforce an unincorporated treaty in the absence of parliamentary assent.[40] The Supreme Court decision in *Gutrani* comes very close to affecting such indirect incorporation. Furthermore, it is difficult to see how, on conventional principles, estoppel could, in the circumstances, be enforced. A public authority cannot be estopped by a representation or legitimiate expectation which it has no competence to make.[41] The Department of Justice has, in turn, no competence to give the 1951 Convention the force of an instrument overriding positive statute law. Only the Oireachtas may do that.

However, that constitutional difficulty might be awarded in another way: the principle of *non-refoulement* has an alternative, indigenous basis in Irish law: in the principle propounded in *Finucane v. McMahon*[42] that where there is a real danger, not necessarily a probability, that a person sought to be expelled would be subjected to ill-treatment, the courts must act to prohibit it. That principle appears to offer a sounder justification for the principle of *non-refoulement*. It avoids, at least, the practical difficulty, of the proposition that there is by virtue of the 1985 letter a right to a hearing but not a right to a decision at the conclusion of that hearing; or the constitutional difficulty, on the other hand, of the alternative proposition that the 1985 correspondence indirectly generated a legitimate expectation that the 1951 Convention was to be enforceable in Irish law. The position, therefore, is that there is a right, in certain circumstances, not to be returned, with its origins in the Constitution; and a right to be heard about that matter, with its origins in the 1985 letter. However, whichever option is chosen, the point remains that statements like that carried for so long in Kelly's *The Irish Constitution*, that there is "no 'right of asylum' in Irish law" are now at last due revision.[43]

9.3 Immigration Law and Refugees

BILL SHIPSEY

I propose, in this paper, to concentrate on the legal position affecting refugees who come to Ireland seeking asylum, and a determination of their refugee status.

It is important at the outset to define a "refugee" since not every migrant person who leaves his or her country can be classified as a refugee. The definition of a refugee in international law is to be found in the Geneva Convention Relating to the Status of Refugees, 1951. The Convention, Article 1(a)(2), defines a refugee as a person who:

> As a result of events occurring before 1 January 1951 and owing to a well founded fear of being persecuted for reasons of race, religion, nationality, membership of a particular social group or political opinion is outside the country of his nationality and is unable or, owing to such fear, is unwilling to avail himself of the protection of that country; or, who, not having a nationality and being outside the country of his former habitual residence as a result of such events, is unable or, owing to such fear, is unwilling to return to it.

The 1951 Convention was limited in two respects. In the first place, it applied specifically to events occurring before 1 January 1951, and was confined to refugees within Europe. It was not until more than fifteen years later that the Protocol Relating to the Status of Refugees, which entered into force on 4 October 1967, expanded the scope of the Convention definition to include refugees from all regions of the world. The 1967 Protocol thereby achieved a formal, if not a substantive, universalization of the Convention definition of refugee status.

It is important to remember, however, that only persons whose migration is prompted by a fear of persecution on the ground of civil or political status come within the scope of the Convention-based protection system. In other words those who flee their State as a result of natural disaster, war or broadly-based political and economic turmoil are excluded from the rights regime established by the Convention. The hallmark of a Convention refugee is therefore the inability or unwillingness to return home due to a "well founded fear of being persecuted".

Ireland is a party to both the 1951 Convention and the 1967 Protocol. However, neither the Convention nor the Protocol have been incorporated into the domestic law of Ireland. Indeed one has to search long and hard before one can find any reference whatsoever to the term "refugee" in domestic Irish legislation. There is no reference whatsoever in the Aliens Act, 1935,[1] which pre-dates the 1951 Convention nor in any of the Aliens Orders made by successive Ministers for Justice in exercise of the powers conferred under section 5 of the Aliens Act. To my knowledge the only statutory recognition of the existence of Convention refugees is to be found in section 5 of the Irish Nationality and Citizenship Act, 1986,[2] which allows the Minister for Justice in his or her absolute discretion to grant an application for a Certificate of Naturalization, although the formal conditions for naturalization or any of them are not complied with by, amongst others, a person who is a refugee within the meaning of the 1951 Convention.

There is very often considerable confusion between the term "refugee" and "asylum seeker". States who are party to the 1951 Convention and 1967 Protocol do not in any sense "confer" refugee status upon an individual. A person either is or is not a refugee before approaching the authorities of the relevant State. The role of the State authorities is merely to determine the applicant's status. Once the refugee is recognized as such the obligation upon the Contracting State is to provide protection. This protection is asylum. Unlike refugee status which is determined, asylum is granted and not recognized. There is an obligation in international law to determine refugee status but there is no internationally recognized right to asylum. Having said that, Article 14 of the Universal Declaration of Human Rights provides:

> Everyone has the right to *seek* and to enjoy another country's asylum from persecution (emphasis added).

It is implicit in this article that States have an obligation to consider every application.

The second relevant matter in this context is the principal of "*non-refoulement*" Article 33(1) of the 1951 Refugee Convention provides:

No Contracting State shall expel or return (*refouler*) a refugee in any manner whatsoever to the frontiers of territories where his life or freedom would be threatened on account of his race, religion, nationality, membership of a particular social group or political opinion.

Ireland, for reasons which are part geographic and part economic, does not attract a significant number of refugees and asylum seekers. When one considers that the number of refugees seeking asylum in ten of the largest European countries exceeded 400,000 in 1990, the fifty-plus applicants who apply in Ireland each year is extremely small. However, situations can change rapidly. Norway, the Netherlands and the UK each experienced an almost tenfold increase in the number of applicants in the six-year period from 1984 to 1990.

The principal Order regulating the entry of aliens, including refugees and asylum seekers, to Ireland is the Aliens Order, 1946,[3] as amended by the Aliens (Amendment) Order, 1975.[4] The 1975 Order which amends Article 5 of the principal Order provides that an Immigration Officer may refuse leave to land to an alien coming from a place outside the State, other than Great Britain or Northern Ireland, in circumstances where the Immigration Officer is satisfied that one of eleven conditions set out in the Order applies.

Although it has been represented by the Irish State authorities for many years that no refugee or asylum seeker would be refused leave to land, there were, prior to December 1985, no agreed procedures, whether official or *ad hoc*, for the determination of refugee status. By letter dated 15 December 1985, the then Minister for Justice wrote to the representative of the United Nations High Commissioner for Refugees (UNHCR) accredited to Ireland confirming that procedures which had been proposed by the High Commissioner's representative were acceptable. The letter then went on to set out a ten-point ad hoc determination procedure:

(1) Application for refugee status and asylum may be made by the individual to the Immigration Officer on arrival or directly to the Department of Justice if the individual is already in the country.

(2) Immigration Officers have been provided with written guidelines which indicate clearly that a person should not be returned to a country to which he is unable or unwilling to go owing to a well-founded fear of persecution for reasons of race, religion, nationality, nor should he be returned to a country where his personal safety might be seriously threatened as a result of the political situation prevailing there.

(3)   Whenever it appears to an Immigration Officer as a result of a claim or information given by an individual that he might be an asylum-seeker, his case will be referred immediately to the Department of Justice, Dublin, for decision. Immigration Officers have been instructed that it is not necessary for an individual to use the term "refugee" or "asylum" in order to be an asylum-seeker. Whether or not an individual is an asylum-seeker is a matter of fact to be decided in the light of all circumstances of the particular case as well as guidelines which may be issued from time to time by the Department. In case of doubt, the Immigration Officer shall refer to the Department of Justice.

(4)   Such an individual will not be refused entry or removed until he has been given an opportunity to present his case fully, his application has been properly examined, and a decision reached on it.

(5)   The asylum application will be examined by the Department in accordance with the 1951 Convention and 1967 Protocol on the Status of Refugees. This shall not preclude the taking into account of humanitarian considerations which might justify the grant of leave to remain in the State.

(6)   The applicant will be given the necessary facilities for submitting his case to the Department. If he is not proficient in English, the services of a competent interpreter will be made available when he is interviewed. He will be informed of the procedure to be followed, and will be given the opportunity, of which he will be informed, to contact the UNHCR representative or local representative of his choice. An applicant will be given this information in a language which he understands.

(7)   All applicants will be interviewed in person. Interviews will be conducted, as far as possible, by officials of the Department who understand asylum procedures and the application of refugee criteria, and are informed on human rights situations in the countries of origin. When interviews cannot be undertaken by the Department, for example, because the asylum-seeker is outside Dublin, adequate guidance will be provided by the Department to the local Immigration Officials to ensure that all relevant information has been obtained and forwarded to the Department.

(8)   In line with the supervisory role of UNHCR under the 1951 UN Convention and the 1967 Protocol on the Status of Refugees, the

Department may seek the views of UNHCR on any case prior to reaching a decision, or the UNHCR may make representation on the situation of a specific individual case or group of asylum-seekers.

(9) In any case where refusal of the application is proposed or an immediate positive decision is not possible, the Department of Justice will consult with the UNHCR representative accredited to the Republic of Ireland, before reaching a final decision and before taking steps to remove the applicant from Ireland, provided that the representative is available at the time.

(10) If the applicant is recognized as a refugee, he will be informed accordingly and issued in due course with documentation certifying his refugee status and with a travel document if he needs one. If the applicant is not recognized, he will be informed, in writing, of the negative decision and the reasons for refusal.

There are clearly limitations within the said determination procedures. In the first place, the fact that it is not on a legislative footing is a matter of concern. Secondly, it does not provide for a right of appeal from a negative decision to an independent person or tribunal. Thirdly, there is no automatic right or entitlement to be informed of the right to legal representation. Fourthly, it does not set out what "written guidelines" have been furnished to immigration officers to assist them in the determination procedure.

The above *ad hoc* determination procedures did, however, represent an improvement on the pre-existing situation and whilst there have been individual cases which have caused concern between 1985 and 1990 for the most part the determination procedures have been adhered to.

Over the past two years or so it is my opinion that neither the letter nor the spirit of the determination procedures have been adhered to. This has resulted in the necessity to seek court intervention seeking judicial review of the Minister's decision, either to refuse to consider the application or to refuse the application for determination of refugee status.

There is urgent need for legislative action. It is wholly inappropriate that the determination of refugee status which affects the very life and liberty of the asylum seeker should be regulated by and dependent upon a short ten point *ad hoc* determination procedure.

Until the decisions of Mr Justice O'Hanlon in *Fakih v. The Minister for Justice* and of the Supreme Court in *Gutrani v. Minister for Justice*,[5] the status of this letter was far from clear. Consistently in judicial review proceedings the State authorities had argued that neither the 1951 Convention nor the 1967

Protocol were justiciable in our Courts since they did not form part of the domestic law of the State. Hopefully, however, following these judgments, the State authorities will ensure that the obligations assumed by the State and set out in the December 1985 letter will be adhered to in full. The judgments did not and could not, however, correct the shortcomings in the existing *ad hoc* procedures and the matter is now firmly back in the legislators' court where it rightly belongs.

9.4 European Integration and Refugees

SUZANNE EGAN

It seems appropriate that a few comments should be made concerning the present arrangements being hatched out by European States for the regulation of asylum applications in Western Europe. Geared as they are towards dramatically restricting the number of people seeking asylum in the region, the effect of these arrangements on literally thousands of refugees in desperate need of protection from persecution in their home countries will be devastating in their impact. Since it appears to me that certain fundamental principles of refugee protection are under threat by virtue of these arrangements, the aim of this short paper is to highlight this concern by examining them against the basic backdrop of obligations owed by states to asylum-seekers under international law.

Most discussions regarding the obligations owed by States to asylum seekers under international law usually begin with a few words about the "right of asylum". Though the phraseology "right of asylum" might, at first brush, appear to speak to an individual's legal entitlement to asylum, there is no such thing as an individual right to be granted asylum by any State under international law. On the contrary, the term "right of asylum" in traditional international law is generally recognized as being the sovereign prerogative of the State to grant to the individual at its discretion.[1] In other words, the power of the State to grant asylum to individuals is considered to be an intrinsic aspect of the sovereignty of the State.[2] Although several efforts have indeed been made to coax the international community into recognizing the concept of an *individual's* right to be granted asylum in international instruments relating to refugees, States have consistently proved themselves to be entirely unreceptive to such a notion. The furthest they have come towards recognition of such a concept is the fairly toothless entitlement of individuals to "seek and enjoy" asylum provided for in Article 14 of the Universal Declaration of Human Rights.[3] While the international community has agreed in principle that individuals are free to seek asylum from persecution, there is no correlative duty on States to grant asylum to those in need of protection from persecution.[4]

Nonetheless, while the States which drafted the Geneva Convention Relating to the Status of Refugees, 1951,— commonly referred to as the refugee's "Magna Carta"— refused to accede to the notion of an individual right to be granted asylum, they were prepared to accept one obligation which does approach such a right, *viz.* the principle of *non-refoulement*.[5] The term *"refoulement"* comes from the French verb *refouler* which means to drive back or turn away. The principle of *non-refoulement*, articulated in Article 33 of the 1951 Convention, basically obliges States not to forcibly return a refugee to a country in which he or she fears persecution. The text of Article 33, from which no derogation may be made by signatory states to the Convention, provides as follows:

> (1) No Contracting State shall expel or return a refugee in any manner whatsoever to the frontiers of territories where his life or freedom would be threatened on account of his race, religion, nationality, membership of a particular social group, or political opinion.[6]

This obligation can be distinguished from the grant of asylum insofar as it only obliges a State not to force a refugee to return to a place where he or she fears persecution, as opposed to conferring on him or her positive rights to remain in the asylum State. So important is this principle as a means of filling the gap left by the refusal of States to recognize an individual's right to be granted asylum in international law that it has been referred to as the "key right"[7] of refugees and the "nucleus of international debate on asylum". Although specific loopholes do still exist in its application in particular circumstances, the practical effect of the *non-refoulement* obligation is that once a refugee reaches an asylum country, he or she is at least guaranteed admission to that country, as well as being entitled to stay in the country at least until his or her claim to refugee status is determined.

So how is respect for this fundamental principle of refugee protection being undermined by recent developments in Europe? Certain aspects of the present arrangements which have been set in train in Europe for the harmonization of asylum policy among Member States of the European Community seek to substantially reduce the application of this fundamental guarantee to persons fleeing to Western Europe.[9] Since the early 1980s, European States have joined forces to co-operate in minimizing access to asylum procedures for asylum-seekers in that territory. As these States move closer towards economic and political cooperation, the proverbial doors are being slammed on refugees. This is why slogans like "Fortress Europe" and "Europe 1992: Open for Business, Closed for Refugees" are surfacing with ever-increasing frequency in the current debate on refugee protection in Europe.

What is happening is that European States have begun imposing visa requirements on nationals of certain countries, aimed at impeding access to their territories. Countries targeted for these visa requirements include Iran, Iraq, China and Sri Lanka—countries where serious human rights violations have been consistently documented by non-governmental organizations (NGOs) like Amnesty International.[10] In addition, some EEC Member States have begun to impose sanctions on transport operators and airline companies carrying refugees who do not possess adequate travel documentation to asylum countries. Furthermore, some States have also returned asylum-seekers to other States which they consider to be "first States of asylum" or, in other words, to States through which they have already passed, on the basis that that State owes the primary duty to determine the asylum claim.

Member States of the EEC have now decided to collaborate with each other in the application of these various practices by entering into formal agreements with each other at the inter-governmental level. As such, no supervisory role is conferred on any of the Community institutions to monitor compliance with the provisions of these agreements in practice. The agreements consist of the Schengen Convention, 1990; the Convention Determining the State Responsible for Examining Applications for Asylum Lodged in One of the Member States of the EEC, 1990 (more popularly known and hereinafter referred to as the Dublin Convention); and the Draft Convention on the Crossing of External Borders, 1991. While none of these agreements, which I am about to describe briefly, has yet been fully ratified, there is widespread belief among governments and NGOs alike that their eventual entry into force is but a stone's throw away.

The Schengen Convention puts into effect an initial agreement reached between France, Germany, Belgium, the Netherlands and Luxembourg in 1985, which was originally designed to facilitate the abolition of border controls at their common internal borders. The territory concerned has been pejoratively referred to as "Schengenland".[11] Since the conclusion of the Convention in 1990, its parameters have been aggrandized in scope by the addition of Italy, Spain and Portugal, while Greece was recently granted observer status. The Convention provides for uniform principles to be applied by signatory States in controlling their common borders. These principles include the standardization of visa requirements, whereby Contracting States undertake to pursue by common agreement the harmonization of their policies on visas.[12] No exception in principle is provided for with respect to this common policy in the case of asylum-seekers. Furthermore, Article 26 of the Convention provides for penalties to be imposed by contracting states on carriers ". . . [w]hich transport aliens who do not possess the necessary travel documents by air or sea from a third State to their territories". If an alien is refused entry to the territory of one of those States, responsibility for returning the alien to the third State from whence he or she came, to that which issued him or her her with a travel document, or to one where he or she she may be guaranteed entry falls on the carrier company concerned.[13]

As regards the processing of asylum claims, Article 29 of the Convention provides that while the Contracting States undertake to process any application for asylum lodged in their common territory, this undertaking is subject to the right of any State to refuse entry or expel an applicant to a third State on the basis of its national provisions or international commitments. Moreover, only one Contracting State shall have responsibility for processing each asylum application lodged in their common territory.[14] In this respect, the Convention provides for uniform criteria to be applied in determining which State owes the primary duty to examine the asylum claim.[15] No attempt is made in the Convention, however, to establish uniform criteria to be applied with respect to the determination of the claim itself.

The Dublin Convention, signed by eleven of the Member States in 1990 and by Denmark in 1991, makes similar provision for criteria outlining which State should be responsible for determining an asylum request lodged in any one of the Contracting States. In this respect, Articles 4 to 8 of the Conven- tion set forth the relevant criteria: the State deemed responsible may be the State in which the asylum claim is initially lodged, although other considerations such as family ties in another State or the fact that another State has issued the person with a valid entry visa may be taken into account. Article 3(5) of the Convention contains a provision similar in its effect to Article 29(2) of the Schengen Agreement. It provides that Member States retain the right, pursuant to their national laws, to send an asylum applicant to a third State, in compliance with its obligations under the 1951 Convention.

The Draft Convention on the Crossing of External Borders, 1991, again provides for uniform measures to be applied by Contracting States in controlling their external borders. These include a provision which calls on Member States to incorporate into national legislation, measures obliging airline carriers and shipping companies to ensure that all persons from third States travelling to their territory shall be in possession of adequate travel documentation. Carriers who fail to fulfil this obligation shall be subject to such sanctions as may be appropriate by the Member State concerned. In addition, the carriers shall retain full responsibility for the effective removal of the person to a third State.[16]

The Treaty on European Union, or Maastricht Treaty as it is commonly referred to, also contains provisions which have implications for the determination of asylum applications in Europe.[17] The provisions in the Treaty which deal with asylum policy in Europe basically acknowledge the fact that co-operation in this area thus far amongst Member States has taken place at the inter-governmental level. Although some provision is made in the Treaty for the involvement of Community structures in the asylum process, the framework for action provided for in the Treaty is primarily pitched towards keeping the evolution of asylum policy in Europe at the inter-governmental level. On the issue of visa require-ments, Article 100c of the Treaty itself provides that the Council of Ministers, acting unanimously on a proposal from the European Commission and after consulting the European Parliament, shall determine the third States whose nationals must be in possession of a visa when crossing the external borders of the Member States. It goes on to provide, however, for an emergency procedure in the case of a sudden influx of nationals from that State into the Community, whereby the Council, acting by a qualified majority on a recommendation from the Commission, may impose a visa requirement for nationals coming from the State in question for a period not exceeding six months. The length of time during which the visa requirement may be imposed may be extended by the terms of Article 100c.[18]

Nonetheless, notwithstanding the increased involvement of Community structures in the wake of the ratification of the Maastricht Treaty, as has been mentioned, neither the Schengen Convention, the Dublin Convention nor the Draft Convention on the Crossing of External Borders provides for any mean-ingful independent supervisory body to monitor their implementation in prac-tice. Indeed, the numerous problems with these agreements from a procedural point of view are manifold and are well-documented elsewhere.[19] On a *substan-tive* basis, however, all treaties and particularly the Schengen Convention, seriously threaten potential breaches of the principle of *non-refoulement*. There can be little doubt but that by blocking access to their territory through the imposition of visa requirements, boat interdiction and penalties on airline carriers, there is a clear indication that States are contemplating ways and means of circumventing their obligations under the principle of *non-refoulement* to refugees and asylum-seekers. Direct breaches of the principle may occur where asylum-seekers have reached the territory of a State, but are turned away on the grounds that they lack satisfactory travel documentation. Indirect breaches of the principle will occur, on the other hand, where a refugee is effectively prevented from leaving the territory of his or her State of origin because of the imposition of a visa requirement or sanction on a potential airline carrier. Some commentators have argued further on the latter point that by impeding flight from the country of origin, a potential asylum country acts unlawfully by infringing upon everyone's rights to leave one's country and to seek and enjoy asylum, articulated earlier in the context of Article 14 of the Universal Declaration.[20]

Furthermore, the freedom of States under the Schengen Convention and the Dublin Convention to deny access to their territories and to send asylum seekers to third States is also very problematic. The freedom to take such action is, to a certain extent, left open by the terms of Article 33 of the Refugee Convention itself. The principle of *non-refoulement* articulated in Article 33 only prohibits the return of a refugee to the frontiers of territories where he or she might be subjected to persecution. By inference, therefore, a State of potential refuge might consider itself free to send a refugee to a third country in respect of which there is no immediate or direct threat to his or her life or freedom. The stipulation in the provision, however, that a person should not be returned *in any manner whatsoever* to a country where his or her life or freedom may be threatened imports the suggestion that *refoulement* may occur in circumstances where a refugee is sent to a State, which although not itself imposing a direct threat to his or her life or freedom, would be disposed to sending him or her back to his or her country of origin. While Contracting States to the Schengen Convention and the Dublin Convention expressly reaffirm their obligations under the 1951 Convention in maintaining their freedom of manoeuvre to return asylum-seekers to third countries, neither agreement requires States which resort to such action to ensure that the third country in question will not itself return a refugee to his or her country of origin. The risk of *refoulement* is particularly heightened in these circumstances when determination procedures in the third country in question are so hopelessly inadequate as to make meaningful determination of a refugee's claim to asylum unlikely. The absence of uniform rules for the determination of asylum claims as between the Contracting States themselves gives rise to the same concern when it is remembered that only one State shall be responsible for determining each asylum claim in the common territory of Contracting States. The obligation to examine a request could be transferred under these agreements to a contracting state whose determination system lacks certain essential minimal procedural safeguards.[21]

In conclusion, it should be reiterated that although none of these agreements have yet been ratified, some States have been implementing the principles outlined in them since they were initially ironed out. It appears that if ratification is more or less a *fait accompli* at this stage, provisions for the establishment of uniform substantive and procedural principles for the determination of refugee claims throughout the European Community will simply have to be the next step in the evolution of a common asylum policy in Europe to minimize the increased risk of *refoulement* of refugees from persecution as a result of the three Conventions in question. The cautionary note to be struck in this regard, of course, is whether or not harmonization will be according to the highest or lowest common denominator of asylum procedures.

9.5 Select Bibliography

TEXTS AND MATERIALS

Amnesty International, *Europe: Human Rights and the Need for a Fair Asylum Policy* (AI Index: Eur 01/03/91) (London, 1991).
Centre for Studies and Research in International Law and International Relations, *The Right of Asylum* (Dordrecht, 1989).
Council of Europe Directorate of Human Rights, *Human Rights of Aliens in Europe* (Dordrecht, 1985).
G. Goodwin-Gill, *The Refugee in International Law* (Oxford, 1983).
Irish Commission on Justice and Peace, *Towards a Community Policy on Migrants and Asylum-Seekers in the European Community: Towards a Community Policy in Respect for Human Rights* (Human Rights Note No. 2.) (Dublin, 1992).
R.B. Lillich, *The Human Rights of Aliens in Contemporary International Law* (Manchester, 1984).
D.A. Martin, ed., *The New Asylum-Seekers: Refugee Law in the 1980s* (London, 1988).
A.E. Nash, ed., *Human Rights and the Protection of Refugees in International Law* (Montreal, 1988).
M. Spencer, *1992 And All That: Civil Liberties in the Balance* (London, 1990) ch. 2.

ARTICLES

K. Costello, "The Irish Deportation Power" (1990) 12 *DULJ* (n.s.) 81.
B. Eagar, "Ireland of the Welcomes" (1991) *Irish Reporter* 13.
S. Egan and A. Storey, "European Asylum Policy: A Fortress under Construction" (1992) *Trocaire Dev. Rev.* 49.
G. Goodwin-Gill, "Entry and Exclusion of Refugees: The Obligations of States and the Protective Functions of the Office of the United Nations High Commissioner for Refugees" (1982) *Mich. Ybk. Int'l. L. Stud.* 291.
J.C. Hathaway, "The Evolution of Refugee Status in International Law: 1920–1950" (1984) 33 *ICLQ* 348.
K. Hailbronner, "Harmonisation of the Law of Asylum After Maastricht" (1992) 29 *CMLR* 917.
L. Heffernan, "In Search of a Human Rights Approach to Refugees" in A. Whelan, ed., *Law and Liberty in Ireland* (Dublin, 1993).
O. Kimminich, "The Present Law of Asylum" (1985) 32 *Law and State* 25.
A.H. Leibowitz, "Comparative Analysis of Immigration in Key Developed Countries in Relation to Immigration Reform and Control Legislation in the US" (1986) 7 *HRLJ* 1.
H. Meijers, "Refugees in Western Europe: Schengen Affects the Entire Refugee Law" (1990) 21 *J Refugee L* 428.
F. Morgenstern, "The Right of Asylum" (1949) 26 *BYIL* 327.
M. O'Boyle, "Extradition and Expulsion under the European Convention on Human Rights: Reflections on the *Soering* Case" in J. O'Reilly, ed., *Human Rights and Constitutional Law: Essays in Honour of Brian Walsh* (Dublin, 1992) 93.

R. Plender, "The Legal Protection of Refugees" in R. Blackburn and J. Taylor, eds., *Human Rights for the 1990s: Legal, Political and Ethical Issues* (London, 1991) 49.

R. Sexton, "Political Refugees, Non-Refoulement and State Practice: A Comparative Study" (1985) 18 *Vand J Int'l L* 731.

C. Tomuschat, "A Right to Asylum in Europe" (1992) 13 *HRLJ* 257.

N. Travers, "The Right of Residence of Non-Community Nationals in European Community Law" (1993) 11 *ILT* (n.s.) 152.

P. Weiss, "Territorial Asylum" (1966) *Ind JIL* 173.

NOTES

Chapter 2 : The European Convention on Human Rights

2.1 Introduction

1 Preamble to the European Convention on Human Rights .
2 For a list of the Contracting States, see A. Connelly, "Ireland and the European Convention on Human Rights: An Overview", below.
3 Article 25 provides that the Commission may receive petitions from any person, non-governmental organization or group of individuals claiming to be the victim of a violation by one of the Contracting States of the Convention, provided that the State in question has declared that it recognizes the competence of the Commission to receive such petitions. States which have made such a declaration undertake not to hinder in any way the effective exercise of this right.
4 Contained in the Second, Third, Fifth, Eighth, Ninth and Tenth Protocols.
5 Introduced by the First, Fourth, Sixth and Seventh Protocols.
6 A. Drzemczewski, "The Need for a Radical Overhaul" (1993) January *NLJ* 126.
7 H.G. Schermers, "Has the European Commission of Human Rights Got Bogged Down?" (1988) 9 *HRLJ* 175.
8 See C. Gearty, "The European Court of Human Rights and the Protection of Civil Liberties: An Overview" (1993) 52 *CLJ* 89; M. O'Boyle, "The Reconstruction of the Strasbourg Human Rights System" (1992) 14 *DULJ* (n.s.) 41.
9 C. Tomuschat, "Quo Vadis, Argentoratum? The Success Story of the European Convention on Human Rights and a Few Dark Stains" (1992) 13 *HRLJ* 401 at p. 401.
10 O'Boyle, op.cit., at p. 46.
11 Drzemczewski, op.cit., at p. 134.
12 Entered into force on 1 January 1990.
13 O'Boyle, op.cit.; Drzemczewski, op.cit.
14 A. Drzemczewski, "A Full-Time European Court of Human Rights in Strasbourg" (1993) October *NLJ* 1488.
15 Mary Robinson, President of Ireland, Strasbourg, 30 January 1993.

2.2 Ireland and the ECHR

1 The First Protocol was opened for signature on 20 March 1952 and entered into force on 18 May 1954; both the Second and Third Protocols were opened for signature on 6 May 1963 and entered into force on 21 September 1970; the Fourth Protocol was opened for signature on 16 September 1963 and entered into force on 2 May 1968; the Fifth Protocol was opened for signature on 20 January 1966 and entered into force on 20 December 1971; The Sixth was opened for signature on 28 April 1983 and entered into force on 1 March 1985; the Seventh was opened for signature on 22 November 1984 and entered into force on 1 November 1988; the Eighth was opened for signature on 19 March 1985 and entered into force on 1 January 1990; the Ninth was opened for signature on 6 November 1990 but has not yet entered into force; the Tenth Protocol was opened for signature on 30 March 1992. A separate text, not directly linked to the European Convention on Human Rights, the European Charter for Regional or Minority Languages was opened for signature by Member States of the Council of Europe on 5 November 1992.

2   Article 66(2). Ireland is also Party to the First, Second, Third, Fourth, Fifth and Eighth Protocols.

3   The other States Parties are Austria, Belgium Bulgaria, the Czech Republic, Cyprus, Denmark, Finland, France, Germany, Greece, Hungary, Iceland, Italy, Liechtenstein, Luxembourg, Malta, the Netherlands, Norway, Poland, Portugal, San Marino, Spain, Slovakia, Sweden, Switzerland, Turkey and the United Kingdom.

4   *The Sunday Times Case: European Protection of Human Rights* (Sweet & Maxwell's Lawfilms) (London, 1984).

5   Reference is made in the Preamble to the Convention to the States Parties having "a common heritage of political traditions, ideals, freedom and the rule of law".

6   Article 3 of the First Protocol.

7   The Charter entered into force on 26 January 1965.

8   Application No. 15404, Decision of 16 April 1991; (1991) 12 *HRLJ* 254.

9   This interpretation afforded by RTE to the Ministerial Order as precluding the broadcasting of interviews with members of Sinn Féin irrespective of the subject has since been held by the Supreme Court to be overly broad: see *O'Toole v. Radio Telefís Éireann* (1993) ILRM 458. But cf. the view of the High Court in *Brandon Book Publishers Ltd v. Radio Telefís Éireann* (1993) ILRM 806.

10 *Stoutt v. Ireland*, settled December 1987, 54 D & R 43 at p. 46.

11 Series A, no. 25; (1980) 2 EHRR 25.

12 Para. 205; (1980) 2 EHRR 25 at p. 91.

13 Para. 212; (1980) 2 EHRR 25 at pp. 93–94.

14 Para. 167; (1980) 2 EHRR 25 at p. 80.

15 Id.

16 This term is used in the Preamble to the Convention.

17 Denmark, the Netherlands, Norway and Sweden lodged applications against Greece in 1967. A further joint application against Greece was lodged by Denmark, Norway and Sweden in 1970. In 1982, Denmark, France, the Netherlands, Norway and Sweden lodged applications against Turkey.

18 Judgments of 14 November 1960, 7 April 1961, and 1 July 1961, Series A, no. 3; (1979) 1 EHRR 1, 13 and 15, respectively.

19 Judgment of 1 July 1961; "As to the Law", para. 28; (1979) 1 EHRR 15 at p. 31.

20 Judgment of 9 October 1979, Series A, no. 32; (1980) 2 EHRR 305.

21 Para. 24; (1980) 2 EHRR 305 at p. 314.

22 Para. 24; (1980) 2 EHRR 305 at p. 315.

23 Id.

24 Para. 26; (1980) 2 EHRR 305 at p. 317.

25 Judgment of 18 December 1986, Series A, no. 112; (1987) 9 EHRR 203.

26 Para. 4; (1987) 9 EHRR 203 at p. 225.

27 Judgment of 26 October 1988, Series A, no. 142; (1991) 13 EHRR 186.

28 Para. 46, quoting what it had said in *Dudgeon v. UK*, Judgment of 22 October 1981, Series A, no. 45, para. 52; (1991) 13 EHRR 186 at p. 200.

29 Judgment of 29 November 1991, Series A, no. 222; (1992) 14 EHRR 319.

30 Judgment of 29 October 1992, Series A, no. 246; (1993) 15 EHRR 244.

31 Para. 72; (1993) 15 EHRR 244 at p. 266.

32 Para. 73; (1993) 15 EHRR 244 at p. 266.

33 Id.

34 Para. 66; (1993) 15 EHRR 244 at p. 264.

35 Application No. 16969/90, Report of 17 February 1993.

36 Para. 50; (1991) 13 EHRR 186 at p. 201.

37 See sections 2 and 14 and the Schedule to the Act.

38 On 20 July 1993, the Supreme Court rejected an application by the Dublin Well Woman Centre to have the injunction lifted.

39 *Marckx v. Belgium*, Judgment of 13 June 1979, Series A, no. 31; (1980) 2 EHRR 330.

40 Judgment of 22 October 1981, Series A, no. 45; (1982) 4 EHRR 149.

41 See e.g., *Tyrer v. UK*, Judgment of 25 April 1978, Series A, no. 26, para. 31; (1980) 2 EHRR 1 at p. 10; and *Soering v. UK*, Judgment of 7 July 1989, Series A, no. 161, para. 102; (1989) 11 EHRR 439 at p. 473.

42 See e.g., *Tyrer v. UK*, Judgment of 25 April 1978, Series A, no. 26, para. 31; (1980) 2 EHRR 1 at p. 10; *Rees v. UK*, Judgment of 17 October 1986, Series A, no. 106, paras. 37 and 47; (1987) 9 EHRR 56 at pp. 63–64 and pp. 67–68; *Cossey v. UK*, Judgment of 27 September 1990, Series A no. 184, para. 40; (1991) 13 EHRR 622 at p. 631.

43 See e.g., *Marckx v. Belgium*, Judgment of 13 June 1979, Series A, no. 31; (1980) 2 EHRR 330 at pp. 341–342; and *Winterwerp v. Netherlands*, Judgment of 24 October 1979, Series A no. 33, para. 37; (1980) 2 EHRR 387 at p. 401.

44 Id; *X v. United Kingdom*, Judgment of 5 November 1981, Series A, no. 33; (1982) 4 EHRR 88; *Luberti v. Italy*, Judgment of 23 February 1984, Series A no. 75; (1984) 6 EHRR 440; *Ashingdale v. UK*, Judgment of 28 May 1985, Series A, no. 93; (1985) 7 EHRR 528; *Van der Leer v. Netherlands*, Judgment of 21 February 1990, Series A, no. 170; (1990) 12 EHRR 567; and *Wassink v. Germany*, Judgment of 27 September 1990, Series A, no. 185.

45 *Winterwerp*, para. 39; (1980) 2 EHRR 287 at p. 403.

46 *Klass v. Germany*, Judgment of 6 September, 1978, Series A, no. 28; (1980) 2 EHRR 214. See also *Malone v. UK*, Judgment, 2 August 1984, Series A, no. 82; (1985) 7 EHRR 14; *Huvig and Kruslin v. France*, Judgments of 24 April 1990 Series A, no. 176–B; (1990) 12 EHRR 528 and 547, respectively.

47 *Klass*, para. 50; (1980) 2 EHRR 214 at p. 232.

48 Para. 55; (1980) 2 EHRR 214 at p. 235.

49 Id.

2.3 Individual Remedies and the Strasbourg System in an Irish context

1 Cf. M. O'Boyle, "The Reconstruction of the Strasbourg Human Rights System" (1992) 14 *DULJ* (n.s.) 41; A.R. Mowbray, "Procedural Developments and the ECHR" [1991] *Public Law* 353; S. Trechsel, "Transitional Questions with regard to the Merger of the European Court and Commission of Human Rights" in F. Matscher and J. Petzold, eds., *Protecting Human Rights: the European Dimension—Studies in Honour of G.J. Wiarda*, 2nd ed., (Köln, 1990) 639.

2 Cf. J. Jaconelli, "The European Convention on Human Rights as Irish Municipal Law" (1987) XXII *Irish Jurist* (n.s.) 13; A. Connelly, (1983) XVIII *Irish Jurist* (n.s.) 384 (book review).

3 Cf. A.M. Collins and J. O'Reilly, *Civil Proceedings and the State in Ireland* (Dublin, 1990) Ch. 9 and pp. 100–101; J. Liddy, "Procedures before the European Commission of Human Rights" (unpublished lecture, *ILA* Irish branch, 1992); H.G. Schermers, "Procedure before the European Commission of Human Rights" and M. O'Boyle, "Procedure before the European Court of Human Rights" in E.A. Alkema et. al. (eds.), *The Domestic Implementation of the European Convention on Human Rights in Eastern and Western Europe* (Rhein al Keim, 1992); P. van Dijk and G.J.H. van Hoof, *Theory and Practice of the European Convention on Human Rights*, 2nd ed. (Deventer, 1990) Chs. 2–4. For the Revised Rules of Procedure of the Commission, the Revised Rules of Court and the relevant Rules of the Committee of Ministers, see P. Duffy, *European Human Rights—Collected Texts* (London, 1992).

4 The European Court itself has always emphasised the subsidiary nature of the collective enforcement machinery established by the Convention. See the *Belgian Linguistic* case,

Judgment of 23 July 1968, Series A, no. 6, para. 35; (1979) 1 EHRR 252; *Handyside v. UK*, Judgment of 7 December 1976, Series A, no. 24, para. 48; (1979) 1 EHRR 737.

5 E.g. *Silver v. UK*, Judgment of 25 March 1983, Series A, no. 61, para. 113; (1983) 5 EHRR 347; *Lithgow v. UK*, Judgment of 8 July 1986, Series A, no. 102, para. 205; (1986) 8 EHRR 329.

6 The Convention does not create a "separate legal order" analogous to that created by treaties establishing the European Communities. Indeed, almost any analogy to the respective jurisdictions of the ECJ and national courts in EEC law is inappropriate.

7 *Ireland v. United Kingdom*, Judgment of 18 January 1978, Series A, no. 25, para. 239; (1980) 2 EHRR 25.

8 *State (Jennings) v. Furlong* [1966] IR 183; M. Forde, *Constitutional Law of Ireland* (Dublin, 1987) at pp. 206–9. For an earlier note of optimism in this context, cf. G. Whyte, "The Application of the European Convention on Human Rights before the Irish Courts" (1982) 31 *ICLQ* 856.

9 *Re O Laighleis* [1960] IR 93 at pp. 124–5; *Application of Woods* [1970] IR 154 at pp. 165–66; *Norris v. AG* [1984] IR 36 at pp. 65–67; *O'B v. S* [1984] IR 316 at pp. 325–6 *per* D'Arcy J and at p. 338 *per* Walsh J.

10 Cf. J. Polakiewicz and V. Jacob-Foltzer, "The European Convention on Human Rights in Domestic Law: The Impact of Strasbourg Case Law Where Direct Effect is Given to the Convention" (1991) 12 *HRLJ* 65 and 125; J. Polakiewicz, "The Implementation of the European Convention on Human Rights in Western Europe (Survey and Evaluation)" in Alkema, et al,. op.cit.; A. Drzemczewski, *The European Human Rights Convention in Domestic Law: A Comparative Study* (Oxford, 1983).

11 Cf. *Bourke v. AG* [1972] IR 36; *Boland v. An Taoiseach* [1974] IR 338; *Shannon v. Ireland* [1984] IR 548; *Russell v. Fanning* [1986] ILRM 401; *Crotty v. An Taoiseach* [1987] IR 713; and *In re R Ltd* [1989] ILRM 757.

12 *E v. E* [1982] ILRM 497; *MC v. Legal Aid Board* [1991] 2 IR 43. Cf. R. Byrne and W. Binchy, *Annual Review of Irish Law 1990* (Dublin, 1991) at pp. 144–47.

13 This characterization was adopted by the Commission itself in its admissibility decision in *Chrysostomos and Others v. Turkey*, Decision of 4 April 1991; (1991) 12 *HRLJ* 113 at p. 121; cf. Polakiewicz & Jacob-Foltzer, op.cit. at pp. 141–42.

14 But see O'Hanlon J in *Desmond v. Glackin* [1992] ILRM 490; Costello J in *O'Leary v. AG* [1991] ILRM 454; and *Kearney v. Minister for Justice* [1986] IR 116 at p. 121.

15 *O'Leary v. AG* [1991] ILRM 454 at p. 461 *per* Costello J; *Finucane v. McMahon* [1990] ILRM 505 at p. 522 per Walsh J; *State (C) v. Frawley* [1976] IR 365 at p. 371 and p. 374 *per* Finlay P; *State (Duggan) v. Tapley* [1952] IR 62 at p. 83 *per* Maguire CJ, in a case pre-dating Ireland's ratification.

16 *State (Healy) v. Donoghue* [1976] IR 325 at p. 351 *per* O'Higgins CJ; *Desmond v. Glackin* [1992] ILRM 490 at pp. 510–13; *O'Leary v. AG* [1991] ILRM 454 at pp. 458–9 *per* Costello J. The evidence may equally point to the justifiability of a restriction on the exercise of a right: *Kearney v. Minister for Justice* [1986] IR 116 at p. 121.

17 *Per* Henchy J in *State (DPP) v. Walsh* [1981] IR 412 at p. 440, cited with approval by O'Hanlon J in *Desmond v. Glackin* (1992) ILRM 513.

18 One possible explanation for allowing greater weight to be given to certain provisions of the Convention may be that they are declaratory of customary international law. As a matter of either constitutional or international law, however, it is stretching things, somewhat, to give such an interpretation to the reasoning of the courts in these cases.

19 Forde, op.cit., at p. 209, citing the leading authorities on statutory interpretation, concludes that "the precise extent to which such treaties are relevant to statutory construction remains very much an open question." Apart from cases of extradition, support for the proposition in Irish law may be found in *O'Domhnaill v. Merrick* [1984] IR 151 at p. 159 *per* Henchy J.

However, in *Norris v. AG*, O'Higgins CJ stated, *obiter*, that the Convention could not "affect in any way questions arising" under Irish law: [1984] IR 36 at p. 66.

20 E.g. *Waddington v. Miah* [1974] 2 All ER 377; *R v. Secretary of State for the Home Department, ex parte Phansopkar, ex parte Begum* [1975] 3 All ER 497 at p. 511 *per* Scarman LJ.

21 *Semble, AG v. BBC* [1980] 3 All ER 161 at p. 178 and p. 183 *per* Scarman L J; *In re KD* [1988] 1 All ER 577 at p. 588 *per* Oliver LJ; *Hone v. Maze Prison Board* [1988] 1 All ER 321 at pp. 327–29 *per* Goff LJ; *AG v. Guardian Newspapers Ltd (No.2)* [1988] 3 All ER 545 at pp. 580–82 *per* Scott LJ; *In re W (a minor)* [1992] 1 WLR 100.

22 Supra, note 9. See also *Brind v. Secretary of State for the Home Department* [1991] 1 All ER 720; *Salomon v. Commissioners of Customs and Excise* [1966] All ER 871 at pp. 875 *per* Diplock LJ; *Taylor v. Cooperative Retail Services* [1982] ICR 600 at p. 610 *per* Lord Denning MR.

23 *Malone v. Commissioner of Police of the Metropolis* [1979] 2 All ER 620 at p. 649 *per* Sir Robert Megarry VC; *Brind v. Secretary of State for the Home Department* supra note 22.

24 Cf. P. Duffy, "English Law and the European Convention on Human Rights" (1980) 29 *ICLQ* 585 at pp. 591–93.

25 *Desmond v. Glackin* [1992] ILRM 490 at p. 513. Cf. also *AG v. Guardian Newspapers Ltd (No. 2)*, supra note 21, at p. 581; *R v. Chief Metropolitan Stipendiary Magistrate, ex parte Choudhury* [1991] 1 QB 429; *Derbyshire County Council v. Times Newspapers Ltd* [1992] 3 WLR 28; and, generally, B. Bix and A. Tomkins, "Unconventional Use of the Convention?" (1992) 55 *MLR* 721.

26 (1992) ILRM 490 at pp. 512–13.

27 There is no possibility of a temporal limitation, as at note 23 above; and there is an obvious qualitative difference between the two exercises.

28 Duffy, supra note 24 at pp. 597–99.

29 Once such a duty is recognized, it would appear that there is nothing in principle to prevent it from giving rise to an order of mandamus against the State. The margin of appreciation left to States under the Convention does not affect this conclusion.

30 *Hone v. Maze Prison Board* [1988] 1 All ER 321 at pp. 328–9 *per* Goff LJ; *Raymond v. Honey* [1982] 1 All ER 756 at pp. 759–60 *per* Wilberforce LJ. These dicta in the House of Lords stand in contrast to the consistent rejection of such an argument by the Court of Appeal. Cf. Polakiewicz, "Survey and Evaluation", supra note 10.

31 *R v. Secretary of State, ex parte Brind* [1990] 1 All ER 469 at p. 478 *per* Lord Donaldson MR (CA); *Brind v. Secretary of State for the Home Department* [1991] 1 All ER 720 at pp. 733–35 *per* Ackner LJ. Cf., also, *R v. General Medical Council ex parte Colman* [1990] 1 All ER 489 at p. 505 and p. 509; J. Jowell, "Broadcasting and Terrorism, Human Rights and Proportionality" [1990] *Public Law* 149.

32 See the arguments of Whyte, op.cit., *passim*. Indeed, one English Judge of the House of Lords has argued extra-judicially that *Brind* may be circumvented by established rules of statutory interpretation: Lord Brown-Wilkinson, "The Infiltration of a Bill of Rights" [1992] *Public Law* 397.

33 *Fakih and Others v. Minister for Justice*, (1993) ILRM 274; *Gutrani v. Governor of the Training Unit Mountjoy Prison*, Supreme Court, unreported, 2 July 1992.

34 See Ch. 3 below. Cf., also A.M. Collins, "The Availability of Interim Relief in National Courts to Uphold Community Law Rights" (1992) 1 *EJIL* 60; E. Szyszczak, "EC Law: New Remedies, New Directions?" (1992) 55 *MLR* 690. For a recent heretical view of the ECJ's contribution to the protection of fundamental rights, see J. Coppel and A. O'Neill, "The European Court of Justice: Taking Rights Seriously?" (1992) 29 *CML Rev* 669.

35 Cf. *SPUC v. Grogan* [1992] ILRM 461.

36　*Derbyshire County Council v. Times Newspapers Ltd* [1992] 3 WLR 28 at pp. 42–9 *per* Balcombe LJ. Cf. Bix & Tomkins, op.cit.
37　Supra note 19; Bix & Tomkins, op. cit.
38　*Swedish Engine Drivers Union* case, Judgment of 6 February 1976, Series A, no. 20, para. 50; (1979) 1 EHRR 617; *Ireland v. United Kingdom*, Judgment of 18 January 1978, Series A, no. 25, para. 239; (1980) 2 EHRR 25.
39　Cf. Committee of Experts, infra note 60, para. 3; and the series of Preliminary Reports on State Responsibility undertaken within the International Law Commission, cited in Polakiewicz, "Survey and Evaluation" supra note 10, at note 59.
40　Id. If the violation found in a particular case stems wholly or partially from legislative provisions and not from individual measures of implementation, it follows that only legislative reform can be considered as an effective guarantee against the repetition of that wrongful act.
41　E.g., *Leander v. Sweden*, Judgment of 26 March 1987, Series A, no. 116, para. 77; (1987) 9 EHRR 433; *Boyle and Rice v. UK*, Judgment of 27 April 1988, Series A, no. 131, para. 52 et seq; (1988) 10 EHRR 425; *Plattform "Arzte fur das Leben" v. Austria*, Judgment of 21 June 1988, Series A, no. 139, para. 24 et seq; (1991) 13 EHRR 204.
42　Cf, generally, F. Hampson, "The Concept of the 'Arguable Claim' under Article 13 of the European Convention on Human Rights" (1990) 39 *ICLQ* 891; C.D. Gray, "Remedies for Individuals under the European Convention on Human Rights" (1981) *HRR* 153; W. Strasser, "The Relationship between Substantive Rights and Procedural Rights guaranteed by the European Convention on Human Rights" in Matscher and Petzold, op.cit., 595; van Dijk & van Hoof, op.cit., at pp. 520–32.
43　This is not to deny, as some have suggested, that Article 13 may in the future occupy a central place in the Convention system, operating as the lynchpin of relations between individuals and national courts. This would be a likely consequence of any future reform of the system predicated upon mandatory incorporation.
44　The likely fate of any such complaint, even when linked to a successful plea in respect of another Convention right, is evident in paras. 65–66 of the Court's judgment of 29 November 1991 in *Pine Valley Developments Ltd and Others v. Ireland*, Series A, no. 222; (1992) 14 EHRR 319. See also case of *Vilvarajah and Others v. United Kingdom*, Judgment of 30 October 1991, Series A, no. 215, paras. 117–27; (1992) 14 EHRR 248.
45　Supra, note 41.
46　Case of *Lithgow and Others v. UK*, Judgment of 8 July 1986, Series A, no. 102, para. 206; (1986) 8 EHRR 329. Case of *James and Others v. UK*, Judgment of 21 February 1986, Series A, no. 98, para. 85; (1986) 8 EHRR 123. Nor can such a right be derived from the right of access to a court in Article 6.
47　Contrast the approach of the Court to the absence of such a jurisdiction in the UK courts: case of *Abdulaziz, Cabales and Balkandali v. UK*, Judgment of 28 May 1985, Series A, no. 94, para. 93; (1985) 7 EHRR 471; case of *Campbell and Fell v. UK*, Judgment of 28 June 1984, Series A, no. 80, para. 127; (1985) 7 EHRR 165; case of *Silver and Others v. UK*, Judgment of 25 March 1983, Series A, no. 61, paras 118–19; (1983) 5 EHRR 347.
48　Here in the sense of domestic law.
49　Cf. case of *Van der Sluijs, Zuiderveld and Klappe v. The Netherlands*, Judgment of 22 May 1984, Series A, no. 78 at p. 16; (1991) 13 EHRR 461; *Inze v. Austria*, Judgment of 28 October 1987, Series A, no. 126, at para. 16; (1988) 10 EHRR 394. See, generally, K. Rogge, "The 'victim' requirement in Article 25 of the European Convention on Human Rights" in Matscher and Petzold, op.cit., 539.
50　Id. at pp. 544–45.
51　Id. at pp. 542–43. On the distinction between this and Article 50 awards, see van Dijk & van Hoof, op.cit., at pp. 291–2.
52　The remedy of habeas corpus in Irish law exceeds the minimum protection afforded by the other guarantees of Article 5. Although there is no administrative practice of compensating

persons who successfully invoke the habeas corpus jurisdiction, the possibility of a separate action in damages for false imprisonment will satisfy Article 5(5).

53 Van Dijk & van Hoof, op.cit., at pp. 511–12.

54 See *Irish Times*, 16 September 1992, at p. 1. The provision has no implications for the question of whether the proposed legislation should establish an independent body to inquire into all such allegations.

55 Article 50. For the analogous power of the Committee of Ministers, cf. infra, note 68.

56 E.g., case of *Le compte, Van Leuven and De Meyere v. Belgium*, Judgment of 18 October 1982, Series A, no. 54, para. 13; (1983) 5 EHRR 183; *Pakelli v. Germany*, Judgment of 25 April 1983, Series A, no. 64, para. 45; (1984) 6 EHRR 1; *Belilos v. Switzerland*, Judgment of 29 April 1988, Series A, no. 132, para. 76; (1988) 10 EHRR 466; *F v. Switzerland*, Judgment of 18 December 1987, Series A, no. 128, para. 43; (1988) 10 EHRR 411; *Norris v. Ireland*, Judgment of 26 October 1988, Series A, no. 142, para. 50; (1991) 13 EHRR 186. The views expressed by H. Hannum and K. Boyle, "Ireland in Strasbourg" (1972) VII *Irish Jurist* (n.s.) 329 at p. 341 are mistaken in this respect.

57 Article 53. By virtue of Article 32(4), a respondent State also undertakes to abide by decisions of the Committee of Ministers in the context of Article 32. The difference in wording does not affect the nature of the obligation in international law.

58 Supra, note 12. In countries where direct effect is given to the provisions of the Convention, this will not arise because the conflict may be resolved in favour of the convention, cf. Polakiewicz, "Survey and Evaluation" supra note 10. In the UK, following the decision of the House of Lords in *AG v BBC* [1980] 3 All ER 161, a second confrontation with the European Court was avoided only by the enactment of the Contempt of Court Act, 1981.

59 Application No. 214/56, *De Becker v. Belgium* (1958/59) 2 Ybk ECHR 214; *Vermeire v. Belgium*, Judgment of 29 November 1991, Series A, no. 214–C, para. 26; (1993) 15 EHRR 488.

60 Cf. generally, the Study of the Committee of Experts for the improvement of procedures for the protection of human rights (DH–PR), Institution of Review Proceedings at the National Level to Facilitate Compliance with Strasbourg Decision (1992) 13 *HRLJ* 71.

61 *Piersack v. Belgium*, Judgment (Article 50) of 26 October 1984, Series A, no. 85, para. 11; (1985) 7 EHRR 251.

62 Polakiewicz, "Survey and Evaluation" supra note 10 at note 72.

63 Cf. the survey of national legislation by the Committee of Experts, supra note 60. The logic of a more active domestic jurisdiction in respect of the Convention is that damages and other relief can readily be awarded at the national level in accordance with principles of domestic law.

64 As one illustration of the Court's total dependence on the co operation of respondent States, the Court has amended its own previous Rules to more faithfully reflect the fact that it has no power to compel witnesses.

65 These may include suspension or even expulsion from the Council of Europe in accordance with Article 8 of its Statute.

66 Article 3 of the Statute of the Council of Europe provides that every Member must accept the principles of the rule of law and of the enjoyment by all persons within its jurisdiction of human rights and fundamental freedoms. It is nevertheless open to question whether isolated violations of human rights can give rise to a valid reprisal in international law, cf. T. Meron, *Human Rights and Humanitarian Norms as Customary Law* (Oxford, 1989) at pp. 103–6; T. van Boven (1991) 85 *AJIL* 213 (book review).

67 This role is exercised in practice by the permanent delegates of the respective Member States. ‑

68 Cf. generally, II.J. Bartsch, "The Supervisory Functions of the Committee of Ministers under Article 54" in Matscher and Petzold, op.cit., 47; F. Hondus, "The Other Forum" id., 245; van Dijk & van Hoof, op.cit., at pp. 156–57 and pp. 192–204.

69 For a rare example of non-compliance with such a recommendation and the swift

condemnation of the Committee of Ministers, see Resolutions DH (91) 12 and 13, of 6 June 1991, (1991) 12 *HRLJ* 275.

70 Although Court judgments and Commission reports confine themselves to declaring whether there has or has not been a violation of one or more provisions of the Convention, the inescapable conclusion in many cases is that compliance requires an amendment of the law or practice in question; cf. Polakiewicz, "Survey and Evaluation" supra note 10, at note 93 et seq.

71 Id., at note 100 et seq.

72 Cf. Hondus, op.cit., at pp. 248–49. This results in a certain lapse of time between the vote, at which time the respondent State is put on notice of the need to take remedial steps including any recommendation as to costs and damages, and the subsequent adoption of the Article 32 decision.

73 Bartsch, op.cit.

74 Id. Polakiewicz, op.cit., at note 106 et seq.

75 Although the publication of the Commission's Report might be regarded as a sanction under the terms of Article 32(3) and therefore distinguishable from the automatic publication of the Court's judgments, virtually all such Reports are published as a matter of course and regardless of whether a violation has been found.

76 Hondus, op.cit., at pp. 249–50.

77 The text was adopted on 30 March 1992. It is reprinted together with an explanatory report in (1992) 13 *HRLJ* 182.

78 Council of Europe, *European Court of Human Rights: Survey of Activities 1959–1990* (Strasbourg, 1991) at pp. 43–50.

79 Cf. P. Mahony, "Judicial Activism and Judicial Self-Restraint in the European Court of Human Rights: Two Sides of the Same Coin" (1990) 11 *HRLJ* 57; C. Gearty, "The European Court of Human Rights and the Protection of Civil Liberties: An Overview" (1993) 52 *CLJ* 89.

80 Id. For an incisive analysis of the UK's record of compliance in this regard, cf. F. Hampson, "The United Kingdom before the European Convention on Human Rights" (1989) 9 *YBEL* 121 at pp. 69–73.

81 Judgment of 9 October 1979, Series A, no. 32; (1980) 2 EHRR 305. Cf. FLAC Submission to the Council of Europe (1990) *ILTSJ* 289; G. Whyte, "And Justice for Some" (1984) 6 *DULJ* (n.s.) 88; M. Cousins, "Neither Flesh nor Fowl" (1992) 10 *ILT* (n.s.) 41.

82 Mahony, op.cit., *passim*.

83 See A. Connelly, "Ireland and the European Convention on Human rights: an Overview", above.

84 Judgment of 29 October 1992, Series A, no. 246; (1993) 15 EHRR 244.

85 Cf. van Dijk & van Hoof, op.cit., at p. 178 et seq.

86 Id. at p. 179. One consequence of this is that any sums given by way of legal aid will be deducted from any award of costs made under Article 50.

87 Notably by C.D. Gray, *Judicial remedies in International Law* (Oxford, 1987) at p. 153 et seq. In the *Open Door* case, the separate claim for damages made by one of the applicants made it necessary to abandon the global approach.

88 As is always the case in Ireland because no procedure exists for reopening cases or otherwise reviewing decisions following a ruling in Strasbourg; supra note 58.

89 *Sunday Times* case, Judgment of 6 November 1980, Series A, no. 38, para. 14; (1980) 2 EHRR 245. See O'Boyle, supra note 3, at note 21.

90 Id. The soundness of this rule was questioned at first by some members of the Court, e.g., Ganshof van der Meersch and Evrigenis JJ in the *Engel v. The Netherlands*, Judgment of 23 November 1976, Series A no. 22 at para. 71; (1979) 1 EHRR 706.

91 The particular reasons given by the Court in these cases are noted by van Dijk and van Hoof, op.cit., at p. 184.

92 For an account of these procedures, see Liddy, op.cit., and Schermers, op.cit.

93 Gray, supra note 42 at p. 153.
94 E.g. address by Rolv Ryssdal, President of the Court, to the Conference of Presidents and Attorney Generals of the Supreme Courts of the EEC (Council of Europe, 18 May 1992), paras. 7–8 and 13.
95 Judgment of 29 November 1991, Series A, no. 222; (1992) 14 EHRR 319.
96 In this connection the Court invokes the principle of access to justice: see case of *Young, James & Webster v. UK*, Judgment of 18 October 1982, Series A, no. 55, para. 15; (1982) 4 EHRR 38; Gray, supra, note 42 at pp. 158–9.
97 The Article 50 award in the *Open Door* case, op.cit., provides a good illustration of the way in which the award of costs will usually far exceed the award for damages in the absence of any peculiar special damage.
98 Rules 5 and 9(2), respectively, of the Rules adopted by the Committee of Ministers for the application of Article 32 of the Convention, in Duffy, supra note 3. For the development of this practice, see Hondus, op.cit., at p. 251.
99 Rule 42 of the Rules of Procedure of the Commission and Addendum thereto; Rule 42 of the Rules of Court and Addendum thereto.
100 Addendum to the Rules of Procedure of the Commission, Rule 1.
101 O'Boyle, supra note 3.
102 Supra note 42.
103 Supra note 59.
104 *Soering v. UK*, Judgment of 7 July 1989, Series A, no. 161, para. 90; (1989) 11 EHRR 439.
105 Id. at para. 91; *Cruz Varas v. Sweden*, Judgment of 20 March 1991, Series A, no. 201, para. 69 et seq; (1992) 14 EHRR 1. Cf. O'Boyle, supra note 3, *passim*.
106 Id. paras. 1–10 and 1–11 respectively. In a recent case concerning the liability of the French Government to compensate a person who had been transfused with HIV-contaminated blood, the total length of proceedings was thirteen months: *X v. France*, Judgment of 31 March 1992, Series A, no. 234–C; (1992) 14 EHRR 483.
107 Rule 36 of the Commission's Rules of Procedure and Rule 36 of the Rules of Court.
108 In neither Rule is the request for interim measures limited to urgent situations, but is so applied in practice.
109 Cf. C.A. Norgaard and H.C. Kruger, "Interim and Conservatory Measures under the European System of Human Rights" in *Progress in the Spirit of Human Rights: Festschrift fur Felix Ermacora* (Strasbourg, 1988) 109; M. O'Boyle, "Extradition and Expulsion under the ECHR" in J. O'Reilly, ed., *Human Rights and Constitutional Law: Essays in Honour of Brian Walsh* (Dublin, 1992) 93; C. Van den Wyngaert, "Applying the European Convention on Human Rights to Extradition: Opening Pandora's Box?" (1990) 39 *ICLQ* 757; H. Storey, "The Right to Family Life and Immigration Case Law at Strasbourg" (1990) 39 *ICLQ* 328.
110 Case of *Cruz Varas v. Sweden*, Judgment of 20 March 1991, Series A, no. 201, para. 90 et seq; (1992) 14 EHRR 1.
111 E.g. *Klass v. Germany*, Judgment of 6 September 1978, Series A, no. 28; (1980) 2 EHRR 214; *Soering v. UK*, Judgment of 7 July 1989, Series A, no. 161, para. 87; (1989) 11 EHRR 439. This was the basis of the joint dissenting opinion of 9 judges (reprinted at (1991) 12 *HRLJ* at pp. 155–6).
112 See G. Naldi, "Interim Protection under the European Convention on Human Rights" [1992] 108 *LQR* 43. M. O'Boyle, supra note 1 at p. 44, notes that "with more than five hundred thousand asylum seekers on our doorstep this is not a likely successful candidate for a speedy and effective remedial protocol". Nevertheless, such a power might be modelled on those already conferred on other international tribunals, cf. Statute of the International Court of Justice, Article 41, and American Convention on Human Rights, Article 63.
113 Whereas Article 28(b) of the Convention places a specific duty on the Commission, its general power to facilitate a friendly settlement is, like that of the Court, inherent. Cf. H.C. Kruger and C.A. Norgaard, "Reflections concerning Friendly Settlement under the European Convention on Human Rights" in Matscher and Petzold, op.cit., 329; V. Berger,

"Le Reglement Aimable devant la Cour Europeene des Droits de l'Homme" id. at p. 55. The strict legality of the practice of the Committee in this regard has been questioned by van Dijk and van Hoof, op.cit., at pp. 198–200.

114 It is accepted that the Commission has a more involved role than the Court in friendly settlement negotiations. Its influence may be seen particularly in the indication of its "provisional opinion" to the parties following the oral hearing, in accordance with Rule 47 of its Rules of Procedure.

115 H.C. Kruger and C.A. Norgaard, supra note 113, at pp. 331–32; Berger, op.cit, at pp. 56–8.

116 Id. at p. 58; H.C. Kruger and C.A. Norgaard, supra note 113 at p. 332.

117 Id. at p. 330.

118 Id.

119 But see van Dijk and van Hoof, and supra note 12.

120 The practice of the Committee in adopting a decision only after compliance by the respondent State inevitably distorts this assessment.

121 Cf. Mowbray, op.cit.

122 E.g., *Moreira De Azevedo v. Portugal*, Judgment of 23 October 1990, Series A, no. 189, paras. 73–74; (1991) 13 EHRR 721; *Union Alimentaria v. Spain*, Judgment of 7 July 1989, Series A, no. 157, paras. 40–41; (1990) 12 EHRR 24.

123 Supra note 107.

124 Supra note 3. Cf. also M. O'Boyle, "Practice and Procedure under the European Convention on Human Rights" (1980) 20 *Santa Clara L Rev.* 697; K. Boyle, "Practice and Procedure on Individual Applications under the European Convention on Human Rights" in H. Hannum, ed., *Guide to International Human Rights Practice* (London, 1984) 133.

125 Cf. generally, van Dijk and van Hoof, op.cit., at pp. 78–81.

126 In particular, they cannot look to a reservoir of unenumerated rights to extend the reach of the Convention.

127 Cf. P. van Dijk, "The Interpretation of 'Civil Rights and Obligations' by the European Convention on Human rights—One More Step to Take" in Matscher and Petzold, op.cit., 131.

128 Cf, generally, van Dijk and van Hoof, op.cit., at pp. 15–20; E.A. Alkema, "The Third-Party Applicability or *Drittwirkung* of the European Convention on Human Rights" in Matscher and Petzold, op.cit., 33.

129 Even if successful, the respondent State is under no obligation to provide for the reopening of proceedings, supra notes 59–62.

130 Cf. van Dijk & van Hoof, op. cit., at pp. 19–20.

131 See e.g., the report of the Commission in *Purcell & Others v. Ireland*, Decision of 16 April 1991; (1991) 12 *HRLJ* 254.

132 Cf. Liddy, op.cit., *passim*.

133 Articles 26 and 27(3). Cf. van Dijk and van Hoof, op.cit., at p. 81 et seq.

134 Assuming that there is a corresponding argument. In Ireland, such an argument can always be constructed around Articles 40–44 of the Constitution.

135 But see the indulgence granted to the applicant in *Pine Valley Developments Ltd v. Ireland*, Judgment of 20 November 1991, Series A, no. 222; (1992) 14 EHRR 319; and see generally, van Dijk and van Hoof, op.cit., at pp. 85–86.

136 E.g. *Sigurjonsson v. Iceland*, Decision of 10 July 1991; (1991) 12 *HRLJ* 402. Logically, the rule cannot bar a complaint directed against a State's compliance with Article 13.

137 Application No. 9136/80, *X v. Ireland*, 26 D & R 242 at p. 244.

138 Cf. *Purcell & Others v. Ireland*, Decision of 16 April 1991; (1991) 12 *HRLJ* 254.

139 See *X and Y v. Austria*, Coll. 26 (1968) 46 at pp. 53–4.

140 Van Dijk and van Hoof, op.cit., at p. 98 et seq.

141 Id.

142 E.g. *Sibson v. United Kingdom*, Decision of 9 April 1991; (1991), 12 *HRLJ* 351. Cf. also van Dijk and van Hoof, op.cit., at p. 103.

143 Liddy, op.cit., at p. 5.
144 Articles 28(1) and 31.
145 Cf. O'Boyle, supra note 3, at note 25 et seq.
146 But not fresh arguments, see *Brogan v. UK*, Judgment of 29 November 1988, Series A, no. 92, para. 37; (1989) 11 EHRR 117. The Rules of Procedure of the Commission and the Rules of Court are both very permissive in relation to the admissibility of evidence and they are so interpreted in practice.
147 *B v. France*, Judgment of 26 March 1992, Series A, no. 232–C; (1993) 16 EHRR 1; paras. 34–36; *Drozd and Janousek v. France and Spain*, Judgment of 26 June 1992, Series A, no. 240, para. 100; (1992) 14 EHRR 745.
148 Cf. Martens and Morenilla JJ, dissenting, in *Cardot v. France*, Judgment of 19 March 1991, Series A, no. 200; (1991) 13 EHRR 853.
149 Supra note 3.
150 Opened for signature on 6 November 1990. See Mowbray, op.cit.
151 The Commission Secretariat's functions in this regard are particularly important, cf. E. Fribergh, "The Commission Secretariat's Handling of Provisional Files" in Matscher and Petzold, op.cit., 181.
152 Cf. O'Boyle, supra, note 1; Mowbray, op.cit.; H. Golsong, "On the Reform of the Supervisory System of the European Convention on Human Rights" (1992) 13 *HRLJ* 265.
153 *Ireland v. United Kingdom*, Judgment of 18 January 1978, Series A, no. 25, para. 239 (1980) 2 EHRR 25.
154 Address to the Conference of Presidents and Attorney Generals of the Supreme Courts of the EEC (Council of Europe, 18 May 1992), paras. 11 et seq; address to the International Commission of Jurists (Council of Europe, 23 April 1992) at pp; 3–4.
155 Id. O'Boyle, supra note 1; Mowbray, op.cit.
156 Polakiewicz and Jacob-Foltzer, op.cit.; Committee of Experts, supra note 61.
157 O'Boyle, supra note 1, at p. 50.
158 *Taylor v. Co-operative Retail Services* [1982] ICR 600 at p. 610.

Chapter 3 : The European Community

3.1 Introduction

1 Judgment of 26 October 1988, Series A, no. 142; (1991) 13 EHRR 186.
2 *Norris v. AG* [1984] IR 36
3 This expression is intended to refer to the standards and approaches adopted by the European Court of Human Rights in cases under the European Convention on Human Rights. The basic *prima facie* rights under the Convention are of course similar to those found in the Irish Constitution.
4 Criminal Law (Sexual Offences) Act, 1993.
5 Case 159/90 [1991] ECR 849.
6 *Open Door Counselling and Dublin Well Woman Centre Ltd and Others v. Ireland*, Judgment of 29 October 1992, Series A, no. 246; (1993) 15 EHRR 244.
7 "Fundamental Rights to be Included in a Community Catalogue" (1991) 16 *EL Rev.* 367 at p. 379.
8 Id. at p. 380.
9 *AG v. X* [1992] ILRM 401.

3.2 Human Rights and the Treaty of Rome

1 See case 294/83, *Les Verts v. Parliament* [1986] ECR 1339, at p. 1365, paras. 23. See also Opinion of the Court of 14 December 1991, on the EEA Treaty.

2 Draft treaty of 27 May 1952.
3 Resolution of the *Ad Hoc* Assembly of 9 March 1953.
4 *Les Étapes Européennes* (Doc-Européenne)(Luxembourg, 1987) at p. 13.
5 Case 1/59 [1959] ECR 17, at p. 26, *Stork v. High Authority*. Cases 36, 37, 38 and 40/59, *Geitling a.o. v. High Authority* [1960] ECR 423, at p. 438; Opinion of Advocate General Lagrange of 24 May 1960 [1960] ECR 450; Case 40/64 [1965] ECR 215, at p. 227 *Sgarlata v. Commission*.
6 P. Prescatore, "Les droits de l'homme et l'integration européenne" (1968) *CDE* 629.
7 See M. Dauses, "The Protection of Fundamental Rights in the Community Legal Order" (1989) 14 *EL Rev* 398, especially at pp. 407–410; and D. Edward, "Constitutional rules of Community law in EEC Competition Cases" [1992] *Fordham Proceedings* 383, especially at pp. 384–394.
8 *Internationale Handelsgesellschaft v. Einfuhr und Vorratsstelle fur Getreide und Futtermittel*, case 2 BvL 52/71, 37 BverfGE 271.
9 Judgment No. 183/1973 of 27 December 1973, Giurisprudenza Costituzionale 1973, 2406.
10 Case 29/69, *Stauder v. Ulm* [1969] ECR 419 at p. 425.
11 Case 11/70 [1970] ECR 1125 at p. 1134.
12 Case 4/73, *Nold v. Commission* [1974] ECR 491; Case 36/75, *Rutilli* [1975] ECR 1219.
13 Case 85/87 [1985] ECR at p. 3150 and p. 3156.
14 Case 222/84, *Johnston v. Chief Constable of the Royal Ulster Constabulary* [1986] ECR 1651.
15 *Second German Solange* case, Bundesverfassungsgericht, 22 October 1986, 2 BVerfGE 197/83, 14.
16 *Italian Granitai* case, Corte Costituzionale (No. 170), 8 June 1984, at p. 7.
17 A. Cassese, A. Clapham & J.H.H. Weiler, *1992, What are Our Rights?* (Florence, 1989) at p. 6.
18 See Dauses, op.cit., at pp. 413–16.
19 OJ 1973, C 26/7.
20 OJ 1977, C 103/1, In Case 222/84, *Johnston v. Chief Constable of the Royal Ulster Constabulary* [1986] ECR 1651, at para. 18, the Court refers to this declaration. See J. Forman, "The Joint Declaration on Fundamental Rights" (1977) 2 *EL Rev* 214 for a detailed analysis.
21 OJ 1977, C 299/26.
22 EC Bulletin, supp. 2/79.
23 EC Bulletin, supp. 1/90, p. 40. See H.G. Schermers, "The European Communities bound by Fundamental Human Rights" (1990) 27 *CML Rev* 255.
24 House of Lords Select Committee on the European Communities, Session 1979–80, 71st Report, Human Rights, no. 362.
25 OJ 1979, C 127/69.
26 OJ 1983, C 277/95.
27 OJ 1989, C 120/51.
28 Case 249/86 [1989] ECR 1290.
29 Joined cases 21–24/72 [1972] ECR 1219.
30 See Schermers, op.cit., at pp. 255–259.
31 See Opinion of Advocate General W. Van Gerven of 11 June 1991, in case C 159/90, *SPUC v. Grogan* [1991] ECR 849.
32 Joined cases 60 & 61/84, *Cinéthèque a.o. v. Fédération Nationale des Cinémas Français* [1985] ECR 2605, para. 26.
33 Case 12/86, *Demirel v. Stadt Schwabisch Gmund* [1987] ECR 3719, para. 28.
34 Case 5/88, *Wachauf v. Germany* [1989] ECR 2609, para 19.
35 Case 130/75, *Prais v. Council* [1976] ECR 1589.
36 K Lenaerts, "Fundamental Rights to be Included in a Community Catalogue" (1991) *EL Rev* 367.
37 It has been stated that almost eighty percent of all economic, financial and monetary regulations find their basis in Community legislation.
38 Op.cit.

3.3 Human Rights and the EEC

1   This gap caused problems in the cases brought by German businesses against EEC measures on the basis that these measures infringed provisions on human rights in the German Constitution. See e.g. case 1/59, *Stork v. High Authority* [1959] ECR 17 at p. 26.
2   The main Community institutions are the Commission, the Council of Ministers, the European Parliament and the European Court of Justice.
3   See R.M. Dallen, "An Overview of the European Community Protection of Human Rights with Some Special References to the UK" (1990) 27 *CML Rev.* 761 at p. 762.
4   On the ECJ and human rights, see J. Coppel and A. O'Neill, "The European Court of Justice: Taking Rights Seriously?" (1992) 29 *CML Rev* 669. Judge Mancini of the ECJ wrote in 1989 that "[r]eading an unwritten bill of rights into Community law is indeed the most striking contribution the Court has made to the development of a constitution for Europe. This statement should be qualified in two respects. First, that contribution was forced on the Court from outside, by the German and, later, the Italian Constitutional Courts. Secondly, the Court's effort to safeguard the fundamental rights of the Community citizens stopped at the threshold of national legislation". In Case 11/70, *International Handelsgellschaft*, the ECJ held that "respect for fundamental rights forms an integral part of the general principles of law protected by the Court of Justice".
5   Case 4/73 [1974] ECR 491.
6   Case 26/29 [1979] ECR 419.
7   See H. Rasmussen, *On Law and Policy in the European Court of Justice: A Comparative Study in Judicial Policymaking* (Dordrecht, 1986) at p. 115.
8   Case 1/58, 59 [1959] ECR 17.
9   Cases 36, 37, 38 and 40/59 [1960] ECR 423.
10 Case 40/64 [1965] ECR 215.
11 Dallan, op.cit., at p. 767. There was concern in the 1960's in the German and Italian Courts on whether or not the fundamental rights enshrined in their national constituencies were recognized and protected in EEC law. See K. Brinkhurst and H.G. Schermers, *Judicial Remedies in the European Community*, 4th ed. (Deventer, 1987) at pp. 144–154.
12 Supra note 6.
13 Case 11/70 [1979] ECR 419 at p. 425 where the ECJ stated that "human rights [are] enshrined in the general principles of Community law and protected by the Court."
14 Case 11/70 [1970] ECR 1125 at 1134. The ECJ said (at p. 1134) that "recourse to the legal rules or concepts of national law in order to judge the validity of measures adopted by the institutions of the Community would have an adverse effect on the uniformity and efficacy of Community law. The validity of such measures can only be judged in the light of Community law. In fact, the law stemming from the Treaty, an independent source of law, cannot because of its very nature be overridden by rules of national law, however framed, without being deprived of its character as Community law and without the legal basis of the Community itself being called in question. Therefore the validity of a Community measure or its effect within a Member State cannot be affected by allegations that it runs counter to either fundamental rights as formulated by the constitution . . . or the principles of a national constitutional structure".
15 Case 44/79 [1979] ECR 3727 at p. 3744.
16 Case 234/85 [1986] ECR 897 at p. 2912.
17 In Case 43/75, *Defrenne v. SABENA* [1976] ECR 455.
18 OJ 1989, C 120/51.
19 OJ 1975, L 45/19.
20 OJ 1976, L 39/40.
21 See the Commission's Memorandum of 4 April 1979.
22 This notion of linking aid with human rights was promoted by the Carter Administration in the United States in the 1970s.

23 Bull. EC–3–1978, p. 5. See also A. Clapham, *Human Rights and the European Community: A Critical Overview* (Baden-Baden, 1991) at p. 160, note 1.
24 OJ 1977, C 103/1.
25 See N. Burrows, "The Promotion of Women's Rights by the European Economic Community" (1980) 17 *CML Rev* 191.
26 E.Ellis, *European Community Sex Equality Law* (Oxford, 1991) at p. 1.
27 Id.
28 Id. at p. 3.
29 Id.
30 Article 100 EEC provides: "The Council shall, acting unanimously on a proposal from the Commission, issue directives for the approximation of such provisions laid down by law, regulation or administrative action in Member States as directly affect the establishment or functioning of the common market. The European Parliament and the Economic and Social Committee shall be consulted in the case of directives whose implementation would, in one or more Member States, involve the amendment of legistation".
31 Article 235 EEC provides: "If action by the Community should prove necessary to attain, in the course of the operation of the common market, one of the objectives of the Community and this Treaty has not provided the necessary powers, the Council shall, acting unanimously on a proposal from the Commission and after consulting the European Parliament, take the appropriate measures."
32 OJ 1975, L 45/19.
33 See Ellis, op.cit. at Ch. 3. See also Council Resolution of 21 January 1974, OJ 1974, C 13/1.
34 See the editorial comments in (1974) 1 *CML Rev* at pp. 1–2.
35 In Case 43/75, *Defrenne v. SABENA* [1976] ECR 455. On the implications of this decision, see Case 129/79, *Macarthys Ltd v. Smith* [1980] ECR 1275 [1979]; 3 CMLR 44; Case 69/80, *Worringham v. Lloyds Bank* [1981] ECR 767; Case 96/80, *Jenkins v. Kingsgate (Clothing) Ltd* [1981] ECR 911; Case 12/81, *Garland v. British Rail* [1982] ECR 359; Case 192/85, *Newstead v. Department of Transport* [1987] ECR 4753; Case 19/81, *Burton v. British Railways Board* [1982] ECR 555; and Case 157/86, *Murphy v. Bord Telecom Éireann* [1988] ECR 673.
36 See Case 43/75, *Defrenne v. SABENA* [1976] ECR 455 and Case 96/80, *Jenkins v. Kingsgate (Clothing Productions) Ltd* [1981] ECR 911.
37 OJ 1976, L 39/40.
38 OJ 1979, L6/24.
39 Case 286/85 [1987] ECR 1453.
40 Case C–177/88 [1991] IRLR 27.
41 Case C–179/88 [1991] IRLR 31.
42 See Case 14/83, *Von Colson and Kammen v. Land Nordhein-Westfalen* [1984] ECR 1891.
43 See the *Hertz* Case.
44 J. Shaw "Pregnancy Discrimination in Sex Discrimination" (1991) 16 *EL Rev* 313 at pp. 319–320.
45 As amended by Article 6(20) of the Single European Act.
46 Case 36/74 [1974] ECR 1405; [1975] 1 CMLR 320.
47 See Case 14/68, *Wilhelm v. Bundeskartellamt* [1969] ECR 1; [1969] CMLR 100.
48 Case 13/63, *Italy v. Commission* [1963] ECR 165; [1963] CMLR 289.
49 Case 130/75 [1976] ECR 1589. (See, in particular, at pp. 1598–1599.)
50 Case 136/79 [1980] ECR 2003 at pp. 2056–2057.
51 These five cases were heard by the full Court.
52 EEC Treaty, Article 87.
53 Case 374/87 [1987] ECR 3283.
54 Case 374/87 [1991] ECR 502.
55 Case 374/87.
56 Case 322/82 [1983] ECR 3461 [1985] 1 CMLR 282 at para. 7.

57 [1989] ECR 2859 [1991] 4 CMLR 410 at para. [15].
58 Cases 46/87 and 227/87 [1989] ECR 2859; [1991] 4 CMLR 410.
59 Case 85/87 [1991] 4 CMLR 410.
60 OJ 1977, C 103/1.
61 OJ 1980, C 327/95.
62 Case 379/87. See B.M.E. McMahon (1990) 27 *CML Rev* 129.
63 I.e. not fluency.
64 OJ, Spec. Ed. 1968(II), p. 475. This was the detailed Regulation setting out the terms on free movement of workers
65 Para. 20 of the judgment
66 See e.g., para. 26.
67 Op.cit., at para. 139.
68 See e.g. Resolutions of 17 May 1983 (OJ 1983, C161/58); 22 May 1984 (OJ 1984, C172/36).
69 4 November 1950. See K. Economides and J.H.H. Weiler, "Accession of the Communities to the European Convention on Human rights: Commission Memorandum" (1979) 42 *MLR* 683.
70 Case 4/73. *J Nold, Kohlen-und Baustoffengrosshandlung v. Commission of the European Communities* [1974] ECR 491; [1974] 2 CMLR 338.
71 P. Pescatore, "The Protection of Human Rights in the European Communities" (1972) 9 *CML Rev* 73 at p. 79.
72 Case 63/83 [1984] ECR 2689 at p. 2718.
73 Case 136/79 [1980] ECR 2003 at pp. 2056–2057.
74 Case 130/75 [1976] ECR 1185.
75 On the principle, see P.J.G. Kapteyn and P. Van Themaat, *Introduction to the Law of the European Community* (Deventer, 1989), at para. 3.2.3.
76 See H.G. Schermers and D. Waelbroek, *Judicial Protection in the European Communities,* 5th Ed. (Deventer, 1992), at para. 67.
77 Case 4/73, *Nold* [1974] ECR 491 at p. 507.
78 See Commission, "Memorandum on the Accession of the European Communities to the European Convention on Human Rights and Fundamental Freedoms" (Bull. EC Suppl. 2/79).
79 Joined Cases 60 & 61/84 [1985] ECR 2605 at p. 2618.
80 Case 12/86 [1988] ECR 3754, at para. 28.
81 [1988] IR 593.
82 [1989] IR 753.
83 E.g. *European School in Brussels: D v. Belgium and the EC* [1986] 2 CMLR 57.
84 The negotiations were again suspended in September 1990 following the suspension of the the student protests.
85 OJ 1978, L 264/2.
86 Case 36/75 [1975] ECR 1219.
87 E.A. Alkema, 'The EC and the European Convention of Human Rights: Immunity and Impunity for the Community?' (1979) 16 *CML Rev.* 501.
88 See L. Betten, *The Right to Strike in Community Law: The Incorporation of Fundamental Rights in the Legal Order of the European Communities* (Deventer, 1985).
89 See Kapteyn and Van Theemaat, op.cit.
90 Id.
91 See Case 136/79, *National Panasonic v. Commission* [1980] ECR 2033.
92 Case 374/87 [1987] ECR 3283.
93 Case 230/78, *Eridania* [1979] ECR 2749 at p. 2768.
94 Case 4/73, *Nold v. Commission* [1974] ECR 491. See also Case 44/79, *Hauer* [1979] ECR 3727; Cases 154/78 etc., *Valsabbia v. Commission* [1980] ECR 1979; Case 116/82, *Commission v. Germany* [1986] ECR 2519; and Case 234/85, *Keller* [1986] ECR 2897.

95   R. Addo, "Some Issues in European Community Aid Policy and Human Rights" (1988) 1 *LIEI* 55
96   See T. Van Boven, "Distinguishing Criteria of Human Rights" in K. Vasak, ed., *The International Dimensions of Human Rights* (Westport, Conn., 1982) 43.
97   See "Human Rights in the World for the Year 1985–86 and Community Policy on Human Rights", Resolution of 12 March 1987, at para. 11.

Chapter 4 : Security of the Person

4.1   Introduction

1   Judgment of 29 October 1992, Series A, no. 242; (1993) 15 EHRR 244.
2   Application No 2758/66, *X v. Belgium* (1969) 12 YBK ECHR 174.
3   See A.H. Robertson, *Human Rights in Europe: A Study of the European Convention on Human Rights*, 3rd ed. (Manchester, 1993) at p. 35.
4   Application No 1044/82 (1985) 39 D & R 162. Nevertheless, the application was unsuccessful.
5   See also Application No 9013/80, *Farrell v. United Kingdom*.
6   Applications 6780/74 and 6950/75 (1975) 18 YBK ECHR 82.
7   Judgment of 18 January 1978, Series A, no. 25; (1980) 2 EHRR 25.
8   Entered into force on 1 March 1985.
9   Criminal Justice Act, 1990. Section 1 provides that "[n]o person shall suffer death for any offence". Ireland has ratified the equivalent protocol to the ICCPR.
10   Judgment of 7 July 1989, Series A, no. 161; (1989) 11 EHRR 439.
11   See, e.g. *Ireland v. UK*; *Cyprus v. Turkey*; *Greek Case*, Report of 5 November 1969, Applications 3321/67, 3322/67 and 3344/67; (1969) 22(II) Ybk ECHR; *Tyrer v. UK*, Judgment of 25 April 1978, Series A, no. 26; (1980) 2 EHRR 1; *Tomasi v. France*, Judgment of 27 August 1992, Series A, No. 241–A; (1993) 15 EHRR 1.
12   See, e.g. *Guzzardi v. Italy*, Judgment of 6 November 1980, Series A, no. 39 (1981) 3 EHRR 333; *Campbell and Cosans v. UK*, Judgment of 25 February 1982, Series A, no. 48; (1982) 4 EHRR 293; *Krocher and Moller v. Switzerland*, Report of 16 December 1982, (1983) 34 D & R 24; *Abdulaziz, Cabales and Balkandali v. United Kingdom*, Judgment of 28 May 1985, Series A, no. 94; (1985) 7 EHRR 471.
13   At para 167. The techniques employed were hoodwinking, wallstanding, food and sleep deprivation and sensory disorientation. Amnesty International responded to the judgment thus: "Our organisation must continue to combat torture anywhere in the world and that task makes it impossible for us to follow the restrictive standard set by the Court" (19 January 1978, AI Index NWS 02/04/78). See N. Rodley, *The Treatment of Prisoners in International Law* (Oxford, 1987) at pp. 83–96.
14   Judgment of 27 August 1992, Series A, no. 241–A; (1993) 15 EHRR 1.
15   See, e.g. *Ireland v. UK*; *Vagrancy* Cases, Judgment of 18 June 1971, Series A no. 12; (1979) 1 EHRR 373; *Wemhoff v. Germany*, Judgment of 27 June 1968, Series A, no. 7; (1979) 1 EHRR 55; *Winterwerp v. The Netherlands*, Judgment of 24 October 1979, Series A, no. 33; (1980) 2 EHRR 387; *Bozano v. France*, Judgment of 18 December 1986, Series A, no. 111; (1987) 9 EHRR 297, *Nielsen v. Denmark*, Judgment of 28 November 1988, Series A, no. 144; (1989) 11 EHRR 175; *Brogan v. United Kingdom*, Judgment of 29 November 1988, Series A, no. 145–B; (1989) 11 EHRR 117; *Lamy v. Belgium*, Judgment of 30 March 1989, Series A, no. 151; (1989) 11 EHRR 529;
16   *Airey v. Ireland*, Judgment of 9 October 1979, Series A, no. 32; (1980) 1 EHRR 305. See also *Granger v. United Kingdom*, Judgment of 18 March 1990, Series A, no. 174; (1990) 12 EHRR 469 where the approach adopted in *Airey* was applied in respect of the availability of legal aid to sustain an appeal in the context of an alleged miscarriage of justice.

4.2 The Right to Life and the Abortion Question under the ECHR

1   *Open Door Counselling Ltd and Others v. Ireland*, Judgment of 29 October 1992, Series A, no. 242; (1993) 15 EHRR 244.
2   These principles are already well established. As was said in *Muller v. Switzerland*, Judgment of 24 May 1988 (1991), Series A, no. 133; (1991) 13 EHRR 212: "The view taken of the requirements of morals varies from time to time and from place to place, especially in our era, characterized as it is by a far-reaching evolution of opinions on the subject. By reason of their direct and continuous contact with the vital forces of their countries, State authorities are in principle in a better position than the international judge to give an opinion on the exact content of these requirements as well as on the 'necessity' of a 'restriction' or 'penalty' intended to meet them." On the other hand, as has frequently been observed by the Court in cases such as *Dudgeon v. UK*, Judgment of 22 October 1981, Series A, no. 45; (1982) 4 EHRR 149, and *Norris v. Ireland*, Judgment of 26 October 1988, Series A, no. 142; (1991) 13 EHRR 186, this margin of appreciation is not "unlimited" and the Court must have the right to scrutinize the restriction in question to see whether it is compatible with the Convention.
3   It is reasonably clear that the State has a duty to take adequate steps to protect life (*Association X v. UK*) and that this "may indeed give rise to positive obligations on the part of the State": *X v. UK and Ireland*. As against this, the Commission has ruled that it is not for it to examine the appropriateness and efficiency of the measures taken by the UK to combat terrorism in Northern Ireland: *W v. UK* and *X v. UK and Ireland*.
4   *W v. UK*.
5   Further evidence of this hesitancy is, perhaps, to be found in the fact that nearly all of the decisions are at Commission—as opposed to Court of Human Rights—level. This seems to suggest that the Commission is so aware of the sensitivity of this subject that it is loath to allow the cases to proceed further on to the Court of Human Rights.
6   (1981) 3 EHRR 244. The application was actually decided in 1977.
7   39 BVerfGE 1 (1975).
8   This provides that "Everyone shall have the right to life and to inviolability of his person. The liberty of the person shall be inviolable. These rights may only be encroached upon pursuant to a law". The Court had also invoked Article 1(1) which provides that: "The dignity of man shall be inviolable. To respect and protect it shall be the duty of all State authority".
9   (1981) 3 EHRR 244 at pp. 253–4.
10   (1981) 3 EHRR 408.
11   See *Paton v. British Pregnancy Advisory Service* [1979] QB 276.
12   (1981) 3 EHRR 408 at p. 413.
13   This presumably refers to the situation in Ireland.
14   At p. 415.
15   At p. 416.
16   At p. 417.
17   Judgment of 29 October 1992, Series A, no. 242; (1993) 15 EHRR 244. The decision of the Commission is reported at (1992) 14 EHRR 131.
18   [1988] IR 593.
19   At p. 624.
20   At p. 625.
21   [1989] IR 753.
22   At p. 764. The above observations were made in the context of an application for an interlocutory injunction, but it is, perhaps, significant that when this case reached the European Court of Justice (following an Article 177 reference by Carroll J at the interlocutory hearing in the High Court), that Court proceeded on the assumption in its judgment delivered in October 1991 that Article 40.3.3 of the Constitution imposed an absolute ban

on the supply and distribution of abortion information: see [1992] ILRM 461. The ECJ ruled against the students on the basis that, since there was but a tenuous economic connection between them and the clinics in question, they could not assert a right under Articles 59 and 60 of the Treaty of Rome to provide information about the provisions of medical services which were lawful in another Contracting State. Indeed, the European Commission of Human Rights observed of the *Grogan* case that the Supreme Court had interpreted Article 40.3.3 "to be a total ban on providing any information about such services"; (1992) 14 EHRR at 138. It will be noted that the situation had changed somewhat (in the wake of the judgment of the Supreme Court in *Attorney General v. X* [1992] ILRM 401) by the time the case came on for plenary hearing before Morris J in the High Court in July 1992.

23   (1992) 14 EHRR 131 at p. 137.

24   For example, Mr Schermers observed (at p. 141): "I consider that the emphasis in Irish law on the protection of the right to life of the unborn could reasonably have enabled the individual to conclude that any activity which might at some stage lead to the procurement of an abortion, even abroad, would be condemned". Similar comments were made by Mr Busuttil (at p. 148); Mrs Liddy (at p. 150) and Mr Loucaides (at p. 151).

25   As Costello J remarked in *PH v. John Murphy & Sons Ltd* [1987] IR 621, at p. 626: "Uniquely, the Irish Constitution confers a right of action for breach of constitutionally protected rights against persons other than the State and its officials."

26   At p. 148.

27   At p. 142.

28   [1992] ILRM 401.

29   Costello J said on this point (at 410): "But the risk that the defendant may take her own life if an order is made is much less and is of a different order of magnitude than the certainty that the life of the unborn will be terminated if the order is not made".

30   [1992] ILRM 401, at p. 425, *per* Finlay C J.

31   At p. 263.

32   Id.

33   At p. 266.

34   In this respect, therefore, the approach of Costello J in the *X* case cannot be faulted as far as such a travel injunction merely sustains the strict logic of that which Article 40.3.3 would seem to require. It was at this point, of course, that the public consensus (which had hitherto largely supported or, at least, tolerated, the absolutist approach to Article 40.3.3 in the earlier information cases) began to break down. See generally, P Charleton, "Judicial Discretion in Abortion: The Irish Perspective" (1992) 6 *IntJL & Fam* 349. But, as against this, the comments of Mr Machinez in his dissenting opinion (1992) 14 EHRR 131 (at p. 150) at Commission level (and echoed by the dissenting judgment of Judge Pettiti of the European Court) are also very powerful: "It would be to say the least odd if a state were not allowed to prohibit within its frontiers acts of aid or assistance likely to incite citizens of this State to commit acts disapproved under their criminal law in countries where such acts are not illegal. The fact that such actions are not illegal under other countries' laws does not give citizens of the first country the right to do it. Impunity does not arise because of some subjective right, but from the limited scope of national law".

35   At p. 263.

36   At pp. 266–67.

37   At p. 267.

38   Id.

39   Id.

40   At p. 277.

41   See opinion of Van Gerven in Case C 159/90 [1991] *SPUC (Ireland) Ltd v. Grogan*, ECR 849.

4.3 The European Convention for the Prevention of Torture

1 Article 3. See also Articles 7 and 10(1) of the International Covenant on Civil and Political Rights, Article 5(2) of the American Convention on Human Rights and Article 5 of the African Charter of Human and Peoples' Rights.

2 See, e.g. the UN Declaration on the Protection of all Persons from Being Subjected to Torture and Other Cruel, Inhuman or Degrading Treatment or Punishment, UNGA Res. 3452 (XXX) [9 December 1975].

3 *Filartiga v. Pena-Irala*, 630 F 2d. (1980); (1980) 19 ILM 966.

4 Convention Against Torture and Other Cruel, Inhuman or Degrading Treatment or Punishment, 1984. Entered into force on 26 June 1987. Ireland signed the Convention in September 1992.

5 Entered into force on 1 February 1989.

6 A. Cassese, "The European Convention for the Prevention of Torture and Inhuman or Degrading Treatment of Punishment (CPT)" in A. Cassese, ed., *The International Fight Against Torture* (Baden-Baden, 1991) 135 at p. 135.

7 See generally, id.; A. Cassese, "A New Approach to Human Rights: The European Convention for the Prevention of Torture" (1989) 83 *AJIL* 128; K. Ginther, "The European Convention for the Prevention of Torture and Inhuman or Degrading Treatment or Punishment" (1990) 2 *EJIL* 123; T. O'Malley, "A Ray of Hope for Prisoners—The New European Convention Against Torture" (1990) 8 *ILT* (n.s.) 216; M. Evans and R. Morgan "The European Convention for the Prevention of Torture: Operational Practice" (1992) 41 *ICLQ* 590; Irish Commission for Justice and Peace, *A New Safeguard for People Deprived of Their Liberty: The European Convention for the Prevention of Torture and Inhuman or Degrading Treatment or Punishment* (Human Rights Note No. 5) (Dublin, 1992).

8 Articles 4 and 5.

9 Preamble to the Convention.

10 Reproduced in (1989) 10 *HRLJ* 196 at p. 198.

11 As of 1 January 1994, the Contracting States were: Austria, Belgium, Cyprus, Denmark, Finland, France, Germany, Greece, Iceland, Ireland, Italy, Liechtenstein, Luxembourg, Malta, the Netherlands, Norway, Portugal, San Marino, Slovenia, Spain, Sweden, Switzerland, Turkey and the United Kingdom.

12 Following signature of the Convention on 14th March 1988, it entered into force for Ireland on 1st February 1989.

13 The Conventions and Protocols are reproduced in A. Roberts and R. Guelff, *Documents on the Laws of War*, 2nd ed. (Oxford, 1989) at pp. 169–337 and pp. 387–468.

14 But see para. 29 of the "Explanatory Report on the Convention", reproduced in (1989) 10 *HRLJ* 196 at p. 199.

15 No mention is made of ICRC visits carried out on the basis of *ad hoc* agreements with States.

16 These conditions have also been scrutinized by the UN Committee, operating under the UN Convention Against Torture.

17 Evans and Morgan, op.cit. at p. 592.

18 Judgment of 18 January 1978, Series A, no. 25; (1980) 2 EHRR 25.

19 E.g. in respect of Austria, Denmark and the United Kingdom.

20 Evans and Morgan, op.cit. at p. 592.

21 Para. 28 (1989) 10 *HRLJ* 196 at p. 199.

22 Visits to Malta (1 to 9 July 1990) and Sweden (5 to 14 May 1991).

23 Visit to Sweden (5 to 14 May 1991).

24 Visit to Malta (1 to 9 July 1990).

25 2nd General Report on the CPT's Activities, CPT/Inf (92) 3, at para. 19.

26 Article 8(1).

27 ICJP Information Note, op.cit. at pp. 7–8.

28 Evans and Morgan, op.cit. at p. 603.
29 Rule 30 of the Rules of Procedure. See Cassese, supra note 6, at p. 146.
30 ICJP, Information Note, op.cit. at p. 9.
31 Article 11.
32 Para. 68 of the Explanatory Report to the Convention (1989) 10 *HRLJ* 196 at p. 204.
33 Id. at para. 69. See also Cassese, supra, note 6 at p. 141.
34 2nd General Report, op.cit. at para. 22.
35 2nd General Report, op.cit. at para. 20. A State may advance a case against a visit, either generally or in respect of a particular facility, on one of the specific grounds set out in that Article 9(1): national defence, public safety, serious disorder in places where persons are deprived of their liberty, the medical condition of a person or that an urgent interrogation relating to a serious crime is in progress.
36 Article 10.
37 Para. 73, "Explanatory Report on the Convention" (1989) 10 *HRLJ* 196 at p. 205.
38 Id.
39 Article 8(5).
40 2nd General Report, op.cit. at para. 36.
41 Id. at paras. 37–43.
42 Id. at para. 44.
43 Report of 26 November 1991, CPT/Inf (91) 15.
44 Conducted from 29 July to 10 August 1990.
45 At para. 229 of the Report.
46 Paras. 39–40.
47 Report of 1 October 1992, CPT/Inf (92) 5 at para. 97.
48 Para. 74 of the "Explanatory Report on the Convention" (1989) 10 *HRLJ* 196 at p. 205.
49 Adopted on 15 December 1992. See (1993) 15 EHRR 309; (1993) 14 *HRLJ* 49.
50 Id. at p. 50.
51 Id.
52 Id. at p. 54.
53 But see Cassese, supra note 6 at p. 139.

4.4 Psychiatric Detainees and the Human Rights Challenge to Psychiatry and Law

1 E.B. Brody, MD, "Patients' Rights: A Cultural Challenge to Western Psychiatry" (1985) 142 *Am J Psychiatry* 1.
2 Within the meaning of Sections 45 and 46 of the Health Act, 1970.
3 Section 184 of the 1945 Act as amended by Section 4 of the 1953 Act, Section 16 of the 1961 Act, the Mental Treatment (Adaptation) Order, 1971, and Form 6 of the 1961 Regulations deal with the admission of temporary eligible patients. Section 185 of the 1945 Act, as amended by Section 17 of the 1961 Act, and Form 7 of the 1961 Regulations deal with the admission of temporary private patients.
4 Sections 162, 163, 165 and 166 of the 1945 Act as amended by Sections 6, 7, 9 and 10 respectively, of the 1961 Act, and Form 4 of the 1961 Regulations deal with persons of unsound mind (eligible). Sections 177 and 178 of the 1945 Act, as amended by Section 15 of the 1961 Act, and Form 5 of the 1961 Act deal with persons of unsound mind (private).
5 Amendments to these provisions were effected by the Health Act, 1953, the Mental Treatment Act, 1961, and substituted provisions were inserted as a result of the Mental Treatment Acts (Adaptation) Order, 1971, which was made by the Minister for Health under Section 82 of the Health Act, 1970, to enable the Mental Treatment Acts, 1945 to 1966, have effect in conformity with the changes in the laws on the health services which were made by the Health Act, 1970.
6 On a form similar to Form 8.
7 [1950] IR 235; 85 ILTR 119.

8   Judgment of 24 October 1979, Series A, no. 33; (1980) 2 EHRR 387.
9   See *O'Dowd v. NW Health Board* [1983] IR 186.
10   383 US 107 (1966).
11   See *Winterwerp.*
12   See *Ryan v. AG* [1965] IR 294.

4.5   Access to the Courts: the Limitations of a Human Rights Approach

1   This article concentrates on the civil rather than the criminal courts.
2   There is extensive literature on the questions of access to the courts and access to justice. The following section simply attempts to summarize some of the main issues arising in the context of this article.
3   There are, of course, other factors which are important in determining whether the individual will receive a fair hearing, such as the ability and impartiality of the decision-maker but these relate more to the decision-making process itself and are outside the scope of this article.
4   M. Zander, *A Matter of Justice* (Oxford, 1990) at p. 47.
5   Id. at p. 48.
6   This section concentrates on those barriers specific to the court system. The problem of alienation from the political system generally is not considered.
7   W. Epstein, *Public Services: Working for the Consumer* (Office of the Official Publications of the EC) (Brussels, 1991).
8   A. Van Oorschot, "Non-Take-Up of Social Security Benefits in Europe" (1991) 1 *J Eur Soc Pol* 15.
9   See M. Cousins, "Access to the Courts, The European Convention on Human Rights and European Community Law" (1992) 14 *DULJ* (n.s.) 51.
10   *Golder v. UK*, Judgment of 21 February 1975, Series A, no. 18; (1979) 1 EHRR 524.
11   Judgment of 9 October 1979, Series A, no. 32; (1980) 2 EHRR 305. See G. Whyte, "And Justice for Some" (1984) 6 *DULJ* (n.s.) 88; M. Robinson, "The Strasbourg Connection" in Free Legal Advice Centres and Coolock Community Law Centre, *The Closed Door—A Report on Civil Legal Aid Services in Ireland* (Dublin, 1987).
12   Para. 24.
13   Id.
14   Para. 26.
15   See, e.g. *Zimmerman and Steiner v. Switzerland*, Judgment of 13 July 1983, Series A, no. 66; (1984) 6 EHRR 17.
16   *Feldbrugge v. the Netherlands*, Judgment of 29 May 1986, Series A, no. 99; (1986) 8 EHRR 425.
17   *Eriksson v. Sweden*, Judgment of 22 June 1989, Series A, no. 156; (1990) 12 EHRR 183. See E. Palm, "Access to Court—Strasbourg and Stockholm" in J. O'Reilly, ed. *Human Rights and Constitutional Law: Essays in Honour of Brian Walsh* (Dublin, 1992) 61.
18   *Langborger v. Sweden*, Judgment of 22 June 1989, Series A, no. 155; (1990) 12 EHRR 416.
19   See Ch. 3 above.
20   Articles 8 and 9 of Directive 64/221/EEC. See A. Arnull, *The General Principle of EEC Law and the Individual* (Leicester, 1990).
21   Case 222.84, *Johnston v. Chief Constable of the Royal Ulster Constabulary* [1986] ECR 555.
22   Although the Court decision was not the only relevant factor and there had been an on-going campaign for the establishment of such a service.
23   Supra note 16.
24   Op.cit.
25   Para. 26.
26   *MC v. Legal Aid Board and Others* [1991] 2 IR 43. See Dillon-Malone, "Individual Remedies and the Strasbourg System in an Irish context", Ch. 2 above.
27   *Norris v. Ireland*, Judgment of 26 October 1988, Series A, no. 142; (1991) 13 EHRR 186.

Chapter 5 : Privacy

5.1 Introduction

1   Cf. Article 17 of the CCPR.
2   See *X and Y v. the Netherlands*, Judgment of 26 March 1985, Series A, no. 91; (1986) 8 EHRR 235.
3   *Ludi v. Switzerland* Judgment of 15 June 1992, Series A, no. 238; (1993) 15 EHRR 173.
4   In the context of Article 8 see, *inter alia*, *Silver v. UK*, Judgment of 25 March 1983, Series A, no. 61; (1983) 5 EHRR 347; and *Malone v. UK*, Judgment of 2 August 1984, Series A, no. 82; (1985) 7 EHRR 14. The issue has also arisen in regard to other articles of the Convention; of special interest are the cases of *Sunday Times v. UK*, Judgment of 26 April 1979, Series A, no. 30; (1980) 2 EHRR 245; and *Open Door Counselling and Others v. Ireland*, Report of 7 March 1991; (1991) 12 *HRLJ* 254; Judgment of 29 October 1992, Series A, no. 246 (1993); 15 EHRR 244.
5   This matter is discussed in "Sex and Sexuality" below.
6   In the context of Article 8, see *Golder v. UK*, Judgment of 21 February 1975, Series A, no. 18; (1979) 1 EHRR 524.
7   See. e.g. *Bruggeman and Scheuten v. Germany* (1981) 3 EHRR 244; *Paton v. UK* (1981) 3 EHRR 408. See G. Hogan, "The Right to Life and the Abortion Question under the European Convention on Human Rights", above.
8   See *X v. Germany* (1955–57) YBK ECHR 202.
9   See *Gillow v. UK*, Judgment of 24 November 1986, Series A, no. 109; (1989) 11 EHRR 335 (in relation to property restrictions in Guernsey); and *Chappell v. UK*, Judgment of 30 March 1989, Series A, no. 152; (1990) 12 EHRR 1 (in relation to search of premises).
10 In particular, see *Klass v. Germany*, Judgment of 6 September 1978, Series A, no. 28; (1980) 2 EHRR 214.
11 See, e.g. *Silver v. UK*.
12 See *Chappell*; and *Niemietz v. Germany*, Series A, no. 251–B.
13 See case 227/88, *Hoescht v. EC Commission* [1988] ECR 2859, where the European Court of Justice held that private correspondence and premises were not covered by traditional concepts of privacy, contained in human rights documents, such as the Convention. However, following the decision in *Niemietz*, the ECJ may change its position.
14 For an in-depth analysis of the structure of Article 8, see A. Connelly, "Problems of Interpretation of Article 8 of the European Convention on Human Rights" (1986) 35 *ICLQ* 567.

5.2 Personal Information and Privacy

1   Cmnd. 5012 (1972), at para. 37.
2   *Tolley v. J.S. Fry & Sons* [1931] AC 333.
3   *Kaye v. Robertson* [1991] FSR 62.
4   *Hogan v. Pacific Dunlop* (1989) 12 IPR 225 (parody of scene from plaintiff's film contained in defendant's advertisement appropriated the former's business goodwill). Cf. *McCullock v. Lewis A. May (Produce Distributors) Ltd* [1947] 2 All ER 845.
5   Judgment of 26 March 1987, Series A, no. 116 (1987); 9 EHRR 433.
6   Judgment of 7 July 1989, Series A, no. 160 (1990); 12 EHRR 36.
7   See B. McMahon and W. Binchy, *The Irish Law of Torts*, 2nd ed. (Dublin, 1989), at pp. 691–698; J. Casey, *Constitutional Law in Ireland*, 2nd ed. (London, 1992), at pp. 317–320.
8   B. Walsh, "The Judicial Power and the Protection of the Right of Privacy" [1977] *DULJ* (n.s.) 3 at p. 6.
9   See generally Law Commission Report No. 110, Breach of Confidence, Cmnd. 8388 (1981); F. Gurry, *Breach of Confidence* (Oxford 1984).

10 *Council of the Bar of Ireland v. Sunday Business Post Ltd*, High Court, unreported, 30 March 1993, Costello J.
11 [1969] 1 QB 349 at p. 361. See also *Argyll v. Argyll* [1967] Ch. 302 at p. 322.
12 [1984] IR 611 at p. 663.
13 Id. at p. 709.
14 *Argyll v. Argyll* [1967] Ch. 302 at p. 320.
15 *Saltman Engineering Co Ltd v. Campbell Engineering Co Ltd* (1948) [1963] 3 All ER 413 at p. 415.
16 [1969] RPC 41 at p. 47.
17 *O. Mustad & Son v. S. Allcock & Co Ltd* (1928) [1964] 1 WLR 109; *Printers and Finishers Ltd v. Holloway* [1965] 1 WLR 1. See generally A Coleman, *The Legal Protection of Trade Secrets* (London, 1992).
18 *Faccenda Chicken Ltd v. Fowler* [1987] Ch. 117.
19 [1967] Ch. 302 at p. 329.
20 [1978] FSR 573.
21 R.P. Meagher, W.M.C. Gummow and J.R.F. Lehane, *Equity: Doctrines and Remedies*, 3rd ed. (Sydney, 1992) at p. 864.
22 *Kaye v. Robertson* [1991] FSR 62.
23 R. Keane, *Equity and the Law of Trusts in the Republic of Ireland* (Dublin, 1988) at pp. 349–350; McMahon and Binchy, op.cit., at p. 690.
24 [1987] IR 587.
25 Of course this argument was supported by pronouncements in *McGee v. AG* [1974] IR 284 and *Norris v. AG* [1984] IR 36.
26 [1975] AC 842.
27 Id. at pp. 862–863.
28 (1978) 68 CAR 183.
29 E.g. *Exchange Telegraph Co Ltd v. Howard* (1906) 22 TLR 375.
30 Gurry, op.cit. at pp. 46–57.
31 *AG v. Guardian Newspapers (No.2)* [1990] 1 AC 109 at p. 281 *per* Lord Goff; Meagher, Gummow and Lehane, op.cit., at pp. 877–880.
32 [1979] Ch. 344 at p. 361. See also *Fraser v. Thames Television Ltd* [1984] QB 44 at p. 58 *per* Hirst J; *Oblique Financial Services Ltd v. The Promise Production Co Ltd* [1994] 1 ILRM 74.
33 Id. at p. 376.
34 R. Scott, "Developments in the Law of Confidentiality" [1990] *Denning LJ* 77 at p. 88.
35 [1984] 1 WLR 892 at p. 895 and p. 900, respectively.
36 Unreported, 18 August 1977. See also *Franklin v. Giddins* [1978] QdR 72; Meagher, Gummow and Lehane, op.cit., at pp. 870–872.
37 (1992) 23 IPR 607.
38 Id. at p. 633.
39 Id. at pp. 637–638.
40 Op.cit. at pp. 88–89. See also P.M. North, "Breach of Confidence, Is There a New Tort?" (1972) 12 *JSPTL* 149.
41 [1986] IR 597 at p. 600.
42 [1994] 1 ILRM 74.
43 [1985] QB 526.
44 Id. at p. 536.
45 *Gartside v. Outram* (1856) 26 LJ Ch. 113 at p. 114 *per* Wood VC.
46 See *Khashoggi v. Smith* (1980) 124 SJ 149.
47 [1968] 1 QB 396 at p. 405.
48 Id. at p. 406.
49 [1977] 1 WLR 760.
50 Id. at pp. 763–764.

51 [1985] QB 526.
52 [1981] AC 1096 at p. 1168.
53 [1988] 2 All ER 477.
54 Id. at p. 480–481.
55 Id. at p. 482.
56 [1988] 2 All ER 648.
57 Id. at p. 660.
58 [1972] 2 QB 84.
59 Id. at p. 101.
60 *House of Spring Gardens Ltd v. Point Blank Ltd* [1984] IR 611; *AG v. Guardian Newspapers Ltd (No.2)* [1990] 1 AC 109.
61 *Malone v. Metropolitan Police Commissioner* [1979] Ch. 344 at p. 360 *per* Megarry VC Cf. *Aquaculture Corporation v. New Zealand Green Mussel Co Ltd* [1990] 3 NZLR 299 at p. 301.
62 [1967] 1 WLR 923.
63 In *Seager v. Copydex Ltd (No.2)* [1969] 1 WLR 809, the Court of Appeal set out the criteria for assessing these damages.
64 *English v. Dedham Vale Properties Ltd* [1978] 1 WLR 93 at p. 111 *per* Slade J; *O'Neill v. DHSS* [1986] NIJB 60. The same may be said of other breach of confidence cases where damages have been awarded. See *Nichrotherm Electrical Co Ltd v. Percy* [1956] RPC 272; [1957] RPC 207; *Ackroyds (London) Ltd v. Islington Plastics Ltd* [1962] RPC 97; *Industrial Furnaces Ltd v. Reaves* [1970] RPC 605.
65 Cf. Meagher, Gummow and Lehane, op.cit. at pp. 887–889 where it is argued that equity can award pecuniary relief in the form of a restitutionary remedy so as to put the plaintiff in the position he or she would have been in had the breach of duty not occurred. See also Keane, op.cit. at p. 354.
66 [1986] 5 NIJB 60.
67 See generally R. Clark, *Data Protection Law in Ireland* (Dublin, 1990).
68 In fact the Younger Committee on Privacy could not find any empirical evidence to suggest that computers or databanks had facilitated invasions of privacy: op.cit., App. E, Table H.
69 O. Estadella-Yuste, "The Draft Directive of the European Community Regarding the Protection of Personal Data" (1992) 41 *ICLQ* 170 at p. 175. This approach has also been described as a "stratified model": B.D. Goldstein, "Confidentiality and Dissemination of Personal Information: An Examination of State Laws Governing Data Protection" (1992) 41 *Emory LJ* 1185, at pp. 1191 et seq.
70 *Report of the Committee on Data Protection*, Cmnd. 7341 (1978) at para. 02.
71 Council of Europe Convention No. 108, Strasbourg, 28 January 1981.
72 E/CN.4/1990/72, adopted at the General Assembly on 14 December 1990 (Report A/45/749).
73 Recommendation relating to the Council of Europe Convention for the protection of individuals with regard to automatic processing of personal data: 81/679/EEC, 29 July 1981.
74 "Proposal for a Council Directive concerning the protection of individuals in relation to the processing of personal data", OJ No. C 277 of 5 November 1990, at p. 3. It also produced a draft directive dealing with data protection in the context of telecommunications: "Proposal for a Council Directive concerning the protection of personal data and privacy in the context of public digital telecommunications networks, in particular the integrated services digital network (ISDN) and public digital mobile networks", OJ No. C 277 of 5 November 1990, at p. 12.
75 For example, Articles 6 and 17 of the current draft directive, which relate to data quality and data security, mirror Articles 5 and 7 of the Convention.
76 "Amended proposal for a Council Directive on the protection of individuals with regard to the processing of personal data and on the free movement of such data", OJ No. C 311 of 27 November 1992, at p. 30.

77 Like its predecessor, it has also attracted adverse comment: J. Berkvens and M. Schauss, "The Amended Proposal for an EEC Directive on Data Protection; Progress on the Face of It, Disillusion After Scrutiny" (1993) 8 *JIBFL* 80.

78 See C. Tapper, *Computer Law*, 4th ed. (London, 1989), Ch. 8, for a trenchant critique of popular perceptions of the computer as a threat to privacy.

79 But see McMahon and Binchy, op.cit. at p. 698 where it is suggested that *Kennedy v. Ireland* [1987] IR 587 could support an argument that there is a constitutional right to ensure the accuracy of information regarding an individual irrespective of whether it is held on computer or in manual files.

80 It has been argued that as they do not facilitate processing of large amounts of data at speed, applying the draft directive's provisions to manual files is disproportionate to the aim of securing the free circulation of data within the Community: see Berkvens and Schauss, op cit. at p. 81.

81 Under section 2(2) this obligation also binds a data processor in relation to personal data processed by him or her.

82 Article of the EEC Commission's draft directive lays down specific rules in relation to the processing of such information. Subject to the possibility of legislative exceptions containing appropriate safeguards, data concerning criminal convictions may only be held by judicial and law enforcement authorities or the person to whom the conviction relates.

83 See also Articles 10–13 of the EEC draft directive.

84 Contrast Article 15(3) of the EEC draft directive which obliges the controller to give the data subject the option of having data erased without cost before personal data are disclosed to third parties or used on their behalf for the purposes of marketing by mail. There would seem to be no allowance for the possibility that the data might be held for purposes in addition to marketing by mail: see Berkvens and Schauss, op.cit. at p. 85.

85 See also Article 13(3) of the EEC draft directive obliges the controller to cease processing data where the data subject has made a justified objection.

87 In a Circuit Court decision reported in the *Irish Times* of 8 December 1992, Judge Kelly dismissed a claim by the Revenue Commissioners that the passing of information to the Data Protection Commissioner pursuant to a notice under section 12 would be prejudicial to the collection of taxes. The Data Protection Commissioner had argued that while he required the information in order to fulfil his function of determining whether data should be made available to the data subject, its disclosure to him could have no prejudicial effect as he was not empowered to pass the data to the data subject.

88 Clark, op.cit. at p. 132.

89 [1987] 2 All ER 608.

90 [1993] 2 All ER 273.

91 Clark, op.cit. at pp. 132–136; Tapper, op.cit. at p. 351.

92 D. Korff, "International Data Protection" (1991) 6.4 *Interights Bulletin* 59.

93 These functions are listed in the Data Protection Act, 1988 (s. 5(1)(d)) (Specification) Regulations, 1993 (s.1. no. 95 of 1993)

5.3 Sex and Sexuality under ECHR

1 (1976) 19 YBK ECHR 276.

2 Id. at p. 284.

3 The concept of margin of appreciation relates to the area of discretion given to States when they engage in a balancing act between the rights of the individual and those elements of the public interest recognized by the convention. See further comments of Martens, J in *Cossey v. UK*, Judgment of 27 September 1990, Series A, no. 184; (1991) 13 EHRR 622, infra.

4 See *Dudgeon v. UK*, Judgment of 23 September 1981, Series A, no. 45; (1982) 4 EHRR 149; *X v. UK* (1980) D & R 66.

5   Id.
6   See *Dudgeon v. UK*, supra note 4.; *Norris v. Ireland*, Judgment of 26 October 1988, Series
    A, no. 142; (1991) 13 EHRR 186; *Handyside v. UK*, Judgment of 7 December 1976, Series
    A, no. 24; (1979) 1 EHRR 737.
7   See the remarks of the Commission in *X v. FRG* (1978) 11 D & R 16; (1980) 17 D & R 21.
8   *Per* the Cypriot Embassy in Brussels.
9   With respect to positive obligations, see *Rees v. UK*, Judgment of 17 October 1986, Series
    A, no. 106; (1987) 9 EHRR 56; *X and Y v. Netherlands*, Judgment of 26 March 1985, Series
    A., no. 91 at pp. 11–14; (1986) 8 EHRR 235. See also P. van Dijk and G.J.H van Hoof,
    Theory and Practice of the European Convention on Human Rights, 2nd ed. (Deventer, 1990)
    at p. 372 with respect to the obligations of individuals *inter se*.
10 Supra note 4.
11 See A. Sage, "Gay Men Challenge UK Law in Europe" *The Independent*, 5 April 1993, at
    p. 3.
12 Supra note 7.
13 See also the discussion of the Commission in *Dudgeon* and in *Norris*.
14 Supra note 4.
15 The age being seventeen for heterosexual females and fifteen for male heterosexuals:
    sections 1, 2 and 14 of the Criminal Law (Amendment) Act, 1935. The position of lesbians
    is also apparently covered by the 1935 Act, in that it is unlawful to commit sexual acts with
    persons under the age of fifteen. Heterosexual females may, under the terms of the Act,
    have sexual contact, falling short of penetrative sex, between the ages of fifteen and
    seventeen.
16 *X v. FRG*, supra note 7.
17 *Dudgeon*, supra note 4 and *Norris*, supra, note 6.
18 *Dudgeon*, supra note 4
19 *X v. FRG*, supra note 7.
20 See also *Handyside v. UK*, supra note 6; *Sunday Times v. UK*, Judgment of 26 April 1979,
    Series A, no. 30; (1980) 2 EHRR 245; *Open Door Counselling and Others v. Ireland*, Judgment
    of 29 October 1992, Series A, no. 246; (1993) 15 EHRR 244.
21 *Tyrer v UK*, Judgment of 25 April 1978, Series A, no. 26; (1980) 2 EHRR 1.
22 *Marckx v. Belgium*, Judgment of 13 June 1979, Series A, no. 31; (1980) 2 EHRR 330.
23 As discussed below.
24 As discussed above.
25 See also *Handyside*, supra note 6; *Norris*, supra note 6; *Muller v. Switzerland*, Judgment of
    24 April 1988, Series A, no. 133; (1991) 13 EHRR 212.
26 Supra note 6.
27 The Irish Government made a similar unsuccessful argument in relation to Article 10 in
    Open Door Counselling and Others v. Ireland, supra note 20.
28 See below.
29 The Irish courts had held that *Norris* did not have *locus standi* to challenge the validity of
    the 1861 legislation insofar as his argument related to the right to marital privacy. *Norris v.
    AG* [1984] IR 36.
30 Series A, no. 259; (1993) 16 EHRR 485.
31 Similar factors were held to be relevant in *Dudgeon*, supra note 4 and *Norris* supra note 6.
32 *Costa v. The Republic* (1982) 2 Cyprus LR 120.
33 The case concerned sexual activity between two soldiers, one of whom was nineteen, in the
    presence of a third party.
34 (1983) D & R 34
35 Under pre-1993 Irish military law homosexual activity by members of the armed forces
    was an offence as all civil offences are military offences under the provisions of s. 169 of
    the Defence Act, 1954. The Irish Army does not ask questions relating to sexual orientation
    at recruitment stage. However, the Minister for Defence had stated that when Irish law's

prohibition on male homosexual conduct is amended the Army might draw up a code of conduct in this area. See *Irish Independent*, 29 January 1993. As discussed below, at present Irish law does not criminalize homosexual activity where a member of the Defence Forces is involved.

36 On the subject of permissible differentiation between military and civilian personnel see e.g. *Engels v. The Netherlands*, Judgments of 8 June and 23 November 1976, Series A, no. 22; (1979) 1 EHRR 647 and 706.

37 See the discussion of Matscher J, in *Dudgeon*, supra, note 4.

38 See e.g. the decisions of the Commission in *X v. UK* (1983) 5 EHRR 581 and *X v. UK* (1989) 11 EHRR 49.

39 Van Dijk and van Hoof, op.cit. at p. 532 et seq.

40 See report of the legal committee to the Parliamentary Assembly of the Council of Europe.

41 Van Dijk and van Hoof, op.cit. at p. 532 et seq.

42 The position under the ICCPR has yet to be examined by the UN Human Rights Committee. The Committee did not deal with this issue in its General Comment on Article 17 of the Covenant. However, it will shortly look at the matter in the context of a case brought by an Australian national challenging Tasmania's blanket ban on sexual activity between men. See R. Miliken, "UN Investigates Anti-Gay Island" *The Independent*, 27 December 1992.

43 See *Norris v. AG* [1984] IR.

44 See A. Connelly, "Irish Law and the Judgment of the European Court of Human Rights in the *Dudgeon* case" (1982) 4 *DULJ* (n.s.) 25.

45 *Irish Times*, 11 November 1992.

46 LRC 1990–32, (Dublin, 1990). See also Law Reform Commission, *Consultation Paper on Child Sexual Offences* (Dublin, 1989).

47 The Government, unlike the British Government, legalized anal sex between men and women. However, the ban on bestiality remains.

48 A special provision was recommended dealing with the position of persons in authority.

49 The Act has also been criticized because it deals with prostitution, as well as homosexuality. One of the reasons that prostitution is dealt with is that previous laws dealt solely with women (as all sexual activity between men was illegal anyway, presumably it was felt that any anti-prostitution legislation would be unnecessary). Section 1 of the Act provides that the term "prostitute" applies to both men and women. However, the Act also deals with other aspects of prostitution.

50 This legislation is probably in accordance with the ICCPR, as it contains both freedom of expression (Article 19) and prevention of incitement to hatred (Article 20) clauses. The Convention, however, only contains the former (Article 10); while some limitations on this right are permissible, it is not clear if restrictions as potentially wide ranging as those in the 1989 Act come within the permitted limits.

51 It is argued in this paper that the Commission and the Court have failed to properly address this issue.

52 (1981) 3 EHRR 557. An earlier case, *X v. FRG*, supra note 7, was declared admissible but a friendly settlement was reached following the government's agreement to enter the applicant's change of name and sex in the birth register.

53 In the interim, a number of other cases *X v. Italy* (1979) 17 D & R 21; (1983) 5 EHRR 287 and *Thirty-Eight Transsexuals v. Italy* (1983) 5 EHRR 289 were struck out following changes in the national laws.

54 Supra, note 9.

55 See *Corbett v. Corbett* [1970] 2 All ER 33.

56 See *R v. Tan* [1983] 3 WLR 361.

57 A similar approach was taken in relation to freedom of expression. See *Handyside*, supra, note 6; *Muller*, supra note 25; and *Open Door*, supra note 20.

58 E.g. in relation to the status of non-marital children and their families. See *Marckx v.*

Belgium, supra note 22; *Johnston v. Ireland*, Judgment of 18 December 1986, Series A, no. 112; (1987) 9 EHRR 203.

59 It may be argued that psychological factors are just as relevant, and may even outweigh, biological factors (it has also been argued that psychological factors are biological). If this is the case, then the original entry could be regarded as an error; this argument has not been accepted in Britain or Ireland. See further T. Walton, "A Measure of Appreciation" (1992) 142 *NLJ* 1202; G. Naldi, "No Hope for Transsexuals?" (1987) 137 *NLJ* 129; J. Morton, "The Transexual [sic] and the Law," (1984) 134 *NLJ* 621; R. Omrod, "The Medico-Legal Aspects of Sex Determination" (1972) 40 *Medico-Legal Journal* 78.

60 Bindaschedler-Robert, Russo and Gersing J J.

61 Supra note 3.

62 See also the Court's judgment in *Inze v. Austria*, Judgement of 28 October 1987, Series A, no. 126 at p. 18; (1988) 10 EHRR 394. The Irish Supreme Court, in its judgment in *X v. AG* [1992] ILRM 401, used similar reasoning.

63 At p. 28. See also his separate opinion in *Brozicek v. Italy*, Judgment of 19 December 1989, Series A, no. 167; (1990) 12 EHRR 371.

64 Although, as we have seen in relation to male homosexuality, the Convention organs may be willing to overturn earlier jurisprudence if this is in accordance with changing societal views on moral issues.

65 At p. 21.

66 At p. 23.

67 Judgment of 25 March 1992, Series A, no. 232-C; (1993) 16 EHRR 1.

68 At p. 24.

69 It should be noted that some of the applicant's suffering was caused, in part, by the EEC; traditionally French passports did not disclose the sex of the bearer, but the new EEC passport does.

70 This section is compiled from written and oral information received from a number of government departments and private individuals.

71 But see the Government's proposals on the matter as outlined in the *Irish Times*, 28 July 1992

72 Application 14573/89, unreported decision of the Commission of 9 November 1989.

73 This is despite earlier Convention jurisprudence, including *Rees*, supra note 9, and *Cossey*, supra note 3, holding that Article 12 only envisaged the right to marry of persons of opposite biological sex!

74 See *X v. FRG*, supra note 7.

Chapter 6 : Freedom of Expression

6.1 Introduction

1   403 US 713 (1971)
2   *AG v. Heinemann Publishers Australia Pty Ltd* (1987) 8 NSWLR 341.
3   *AG v. Heinemann Publishers Australia Pty Ltd* (1987) 75 ALR 353.
4   *AG v. Heinemann Publishers Australia Pty Ltd* (1988) 78 ALR 449.
5   [1954] IR 89.
6   *AG v. Newspaper Publishers Plc* [1987] 3 All ER 276.
7   Id. at pp. 289–315.
8   *AG v. Guardian Newspapers Ltd and Others* [1987] 3 All ER 316.
9   Id. at p. 343.
10 Id. at p. 366.
11 Id. at p. 360.
12 *AG v. Guardian Newspapers Ltd and Others (No. 2)* [1990] 1 AC 109.
13 Judgment of 26 November 1991, Series A, no. 217; (1992) 14 EHRR 153 and 229.

6.2 Freedom of Expression

1 *Sunday Times v. UK*, Judgment of 26 April 1979, Series A, no. 30, at pp. 30–31, paras. 47–49; (1980) 2 EHRR 245.
2 *Handyside v. UK*, Judgment of 7 December 1976, Series A, no. 24, at p. 22, para. 48 (1979) 1 EHRR 737.
3 *Muller v. Switzerland*, Judgment of 24 May 1988, Series A, no. 133; (1991) 13 EHRR 212.
4 *Groppera Radio AG v. Switzerland*, Judgment of 20 June 1989, Series A, no. 173, at p. 23, para. 60; (1990) 12 EHRR 321.
5 Id. at p. 24, para. 61.
6 *Lingens v. Austria*, Judgment of 8 July 1986, Series A, no. 103 (1986) 8 EHRR 103.
7 Id. at p. 26, para. 41.
8 Id. at para. 42.
9 See, e.g. Application 7805/77, *X and Church of Scientology v. Sweden*, Decision of 5 May 1979; (1979) 16 D & R 68.
10 *Markt Intern v. Germany*, Judgment of 20 November 1989, Series A, no. 165, at p. 17 para. 26; (1990) 12 EHRR 161.
11 *Young James and Webster v. UK*, Judgment of 13 August 1981, Series A, no. 44, at pp. 21–24; (1982) 4 EHRR 38.
12 *Ezelin v. France*, Judgment of 26 April 1991, Series A, no. 202, at p. 19, para. 33; (1992) 14 EHRR 362,
13 Application 7215/75, Report of 12 October 1978; (1980) 19 D & R.

6.3 Freedom of Expression and Democracy

1 Law Reform Commission, *Report on the Civil Law of Defamation* (LRC 38–1991) (Dublin, 1991).
2 See S. Curry Jensen, *Censorship: The Knot that Binds Power to Knowledge* (Oxford, 1988).
3 Article 40.6.1.
4 *Purcell v. Ireland*, European Commission on Human Rights Decision on Admissibility, 16 April 1991; (1991) 12 *HRLJ*, 255. The Commission rejected as manifestly unfounded a challenge to Section 31 of the Broadcasting Act, 1960, as amended 1976, and its prohibition on the making or broadcasting of interviews with proscribed organizations and with the political party, Sinn Fein. The decision on admissibility seemed effectively to reverse the special status of political speech acknowledged in earlier decisions of the Commission and European Court of Human Rights.
5 For an account of the jurisprudence under the European Convention concerning freedom of expression, see A. Lester, "Freedom of Expression: Relevant International Principles" in London Commonwealth Secretariat, *The Domestic Application of International Human Rights Norms* (London, 1988) 23.
6 *Press Freedom and Libel: A Report Prepared for the national Newspapers of Ireland* (Dublin, 1988). Similar thinking has also come from other academics; see M. McDonald, *Irish Law of Defamation*, 2nd ed. (Dublin, 1989); E. O'Dell "Reflections on a Revolution in Libel" (1991) 10 *ILT* (n.s.) 181.
7 Op.cit.
8 These core characteristics of democracy have been proposed by Professor David Beetham, Professor of Politics, University of Leeds, with whom I am collaborating on a project to conduct a "democratic audit" of the United Kingdom.
9 K. Boyle "What will the New Europe mean for its Citizens?" (1992) 4 *Administration 58*.
10 [1992] ILRM 401.
11 Judgment of 26 April 1979, Series A. no. 24; (1979) 1 EHRR 737.
12 *Open Door Counselling Ltd v. Ireland*, Report of 7 March 1991; (1992) 14 EHRR 131.
13 Id. at pp. 142–3.

14 Judgment of 18 December 1986, Series A, no. 112, at para. 27; (1987) 9 EHRR 203.
15 Id. at p. 37.
16 Cited in K. Boyle, "Law, Pluralism and Community in Contemporary Ireland", in O. Tuathaigh, ed., *Community Culture, and Conflict, Aspects of the Irish Experience* (Galway, 1986) 90.
17 See Council of Europe Committee of Ministers, "Declaration on Freedom of Expression and Information", 1982.
18 See the discussion in the Law Reform Commission, *Consultation Paper on the Civil Law of Defamation* (Dublin, 1991), at pp. 336–343, and its *Report on the Civil Law of Defamation*, op.cit., para. 7. 43–46.
19 See the Report of the 3rd European Ministerial Conference on Mass Media Policy, Nicosia (Cyprus), 9–10 October 1991, "Which Way Forward for Europe's Media in 1990s?", Council of Europe, Strasbourg, 1991.
20 See Law Reform Commission, *Consultation Paper on Contempt of Court* (Dublin, 1991).
21 Law Reform Commission, *Consultation Paper on Defamation*, op.cit., at p. 438 and Appendix A.

6.4   The Contempt Jurisdiction

1   This is Oliver Wendell Holmes' description of the common law.
2   See K. Boyle, "Freedom of Expression and Democracy" above.
3   See *AG v. X and Others* [1992] ILRM 401.
4   The literature has already grown to enormous proportions. For a sample see J. Kingston and A. Whelan "The Protection of the Unborn in Three Legal Orders " (1992) 10 *ILT* (n.s.) 93, 104, 166, and 279, especially parts 1 and 3, with references.
5   *Irish Times*, Friday, 14 February 1992.
6   See H.G. Schermers, "Freedom of Expression" above.
7   250 US 616 (1919).
8   376 US 255 (1964).
9   The analogue is considered in D. Elder, "Freedom of Expression and Defamation" (1986) 35 *ICLQ* 891. Its effect on Irish defamation law is considered in E. O'Dell "Does Defamation Value Free Expression?" (1990) 12 *DULJ* (n.s.) 50; The Law Reform Commission, *Consultation Paper on the Civil Law of Defamation* (Dublin, 1991) p. 285; U. Ní Raifeartaigh, "Defences in Irish Defamation Law" (1992) 13 *DULJ* (n.s.) 76 at p. 83; and G.W. Hogan, "The Federal Republic of Germany, Ireland and the United Kingdom: Three European Approaches to Political Campaign Regulation" (1992) 21 *Capital U L Rev.* 1.
10 Judgment of 8 July 1986, Series A, no. 103; (1986) 8 EHRR 103; cf. *Thorgeirson v. Iceland*, Judgment of 25 June 1992, Series A, no. 239; (1992) 14 EHRR 843; and *Castells v. Spain*, Judgment of 23 April 1992, Series A, no. 236; (1992) 14 EHRR 445.
11 *New York Times v. US* 403 US 713 (1971); (*The Pentagon Papers* case); cf. *Sunday Times v. UK (No.1)*, Judgment of 26 April 1979, Series A, no. 30; (1980) 2 EHRR 245; and *Observer, Guardian* and *Sunday Times (No.2) (Spycatcher)*, Judgment of 26 November 1991, Series A, nos. 216 and 217; (1992) 14 EHRR 153 and 229.
12 See most recently the judgment of the Supreme Court in *AG v. X*, supra note 3, especially *per* McCarthy J at pp. 448 et seq.
13 [1974] AC 273.
14 *New York Times v. United States* 403 US 713 (1971).
15 *Vine Products v. Green* [1966] Ch. 484 at p. 496 *per* Buckley J.
16 [1974] AC 263 at p. 298.
17 [1987] IR 663.
18 High Court, unreported, 30 July 1992, at pp; 12–13. Although Denham J found that there was little chance of influencing the judge sitting alone, the linking of Mr Wong's application for judicial review to the Chinese Triad underworld in Dublin was prejudicial to the

administration of justice "as a result of a litigant in mid-trial being held up to such public obloquy" (at p. 22 of the transcript), and thus constituted a contempt, purged by apology. Contrast *Re Kennedy and McCann* [1976] IR 382.

19 [1984] ILRM 577 at p. 581.

20 Judgment of 26 April 1979, Series A. no. 30; (1980) 2 EHRR 245.

21 [1992] ILRM 490. See D. Conlon, "Contempt of Court—An Issue for Reform?" (1992) 2 *ISLR* 53. The decision of O'Hanlon J was considered by Denham J in *Wong v. Minister for Justice*, High Court, unreported, 30 July 1992.

22 *Desmond v. Glackin* [1992] ILRM 490 at p. 512.

23 Id. at p. 513.

24 Id. at p. 517.

25 Loc. cit. See most graphically, *Open Door and Dublin Well Woman v. Ireland*, Judgment of 29 October 1992, Series A, no. 246, paras. 64–69; (1993) 15 EHRR 244.

26 Judgment of 22 May 1990, Series A, no. 177; (1990) 12 EHRR 508.

27 Judgment of 22 February 1989, Series A, no. 49; (1991) 13 EHRR 493.

28 Series A, no. 204.

29 *Observer, Guardian* and *Sunday Times (No. 2)*, *(Spycatcher)*, Judgment of 26 November 1991, Series A, nos. 216 and 217; (1992) 14 EHRR 153 and 229.

30 Series A, no. 30; (1980) 2 EHRR 245, paras. 65–67.

31 As in *Lingens v. Austria*, supra note 10.

32 As in *Thorgeirson v. Iceland*, supra note 10.

33 As in *Castells v. Spain*, supra note 10.

34 As in *Barfod v. Denmark*, supra note 27.

35 *Hadjianastassiou v. Greece*, Series A, no. 252 (speech *by* a soldier legitimately restricted); Cf. 7050/75, *Arrowsmith v. UK* (1982) 19 D & R 5 (the Commission held that speech *to* soldiers legitimately restricted). Cf. *Spycatcher*, supra note 11.

36 See P. Dillon-Malone, "Individual Remedies and the Strasbourg System in an Irish Context" above.

37 [1960] IR 93.

38 [1981] IR 412.

39 [1992] ILRM 490, 513.

40 Supra, note 3, at p. 414.

41 [1992] 3 All ER 65 (CA); [1993] 1 All ER 1011 (HL).

42 *AG v. Guardian Newspapers (No. 2)* [1990] 1 AC 109 at pp. 283–284.

43 *Brind v. Secretary of State for the Home Office* [1991] 1 AC 696. This is the English "section 31" case, which has also taken the long trek to Strasbourg and is currently pending before the European Commission. Its success must be in doubt now given the failure of the challenge to the more draconian Section 31 of the (Irish) Broadcasting Act, 1961 in *Purcell v. Ireland*, Decision of 16 April 1991 (finding the application "manifestly ill-founded"); (1991) 12 *HRLJ* 254.

44 [1992] 3 All ER 65 at pp. 77–79 *per* Balcombe LJ; cf. at pp. 86–87 *per* Ralph Gibson LJ, and at pp. 92–94 *per* Butler-Sloss LJ.

45 Id. at p. 81 *per* Balcombe LJ.

46 Id. at p. 81 *per* Balcombe LJ; cf. at p. 89 *per* Ralph Gibson LJ, and at 96 *per* Butler-Sloss LJ.

47 [1993] 1 All ER 1011, at p. 1017.

48 *City of Chicago v. Tribune Co* (1923) 307 Ill. 595; *New York Times v. Sullivan*, supra notes 8 and 9.

49 [1993] 1 All ER 1011, at p. 1018.

50 Supra note 42.

51 [1993] 1 All ER 1011, at p. 1021.

6.5 Commercial Speech

1 Three general works on freedom of expression merit particular attention because of their depth and influence over judicial decisions: M. Nimmer, *Nimmer on Freedom of Speech: A*

Treatise on the Theory of the First Amendment (Oakland, 1984) with 1989 Supplement by L.S. Sobel; T. Emerson, *The System of Freedom of Expression* (New York, 1970); and F. Schauer, *Free Speech: A Philosophical Enquiry* (Cambridge, 1981).

2   On liberal theory see C.J. Freiderick, ed., *Nomos IV Liberty* (London, 1962); and A. Pennock and A. Chapman, eds., *Nomos XXV Liberal-Democracy* (London, 1983).

3   See C.E. Baker, "Property and Its Relation to Constitutionally Protected Liberty" (1986) 137 *U Pa L Rev.* 741.

4   See generally K. Greenawalt, "Free Speech Justifications" (1989) 89 *Col L Rev.* 119.

5   This justificatory rationale is attributed to J. Milton, *Areopagitica* (London, 1819) and is critiqued by Greenawalt, op.cit.

6   On this historically myopic focus of rights see M.J. Horan, "Contemporary Constitution-alism and Legal Relations Between Individuals" (1976) 25 *ICLQ* 848.

7   See F. Schauer, "Free Speech And The Argument From Democracy" in Nomos XXV, supra, note 2, at p. 241. See also V. Blasi, "The Checking Value in First Amendment History" (1977) 3 *Am. Bar Foundation Res. J 521*.

8   For a critical overview of the history and basis of the use of the marketplace metaphor in free speech analysis see S. Ingber, "The Marketplace of Ideas: A Legitimising Myth" (1984) *Duke LJ* 1.

9   This is especially pronounced in the writings of Emerson, op.cit.

10 For an overview of the decline of the so-called substantive due process doctrine as applied in the economic sphere see B. Siegan, *Economic Liberties and the Constitution* (Chicago, 1980).

11 *Bigelow v. Virginia* 421 US 809 (1975).

12 *Roe v. Wade* 410 US 113 (1973).

13 *Griswold v. Connecticut* 381 US 479 (1965).

14 *Eisenstadt v. Baird* 405 US 438 (1972).

15 *Carey v. Population Service Int'l* 431 US 678 (1977)

16 *McGee v. Attorney General* [1974] IR 284.

17 *Irish Family Planning Association v. Ryan* [1979] IR 295.

18 *Virginia State Board of Pharmacy v. Virginia Citizens Consumer Council* 425 US 728 (1976).

19 Id.

20 See generally, Symposium, "Commercial Speech and the First Amendment" (1988) 56 *Cinn L Rev* 1181.

21 *Bates v. State Bar of Arizona* 433 US 350 (1977). See generally G. Quinn, "The Right of Lawyers to Advertise in the Market for legal Services: A Comparative Irish, America and European Perspective" (1992) 20 *Anglo-American L Rev*, 1.

22 *In Re: RMJ* 455 US 191 (1982).

23 *Zauderer v. Office of Disciplinary Counsel of the Supreme Court of Ohio* 471 US. 626 (1985).

24 *Ohralik v. Ohio State Bar* 436 US 447 (1978).

25 *In Re: Primus* 436 US 412 (1978).

26 *Central Hudson Elec & Gas Corpn v. Public Service Comm'n* 447 US 557 (1980).

27 *Posadas de Puert Rico Associates v. Tourism Co. of Puerto Rico* 478 US 328 (1986).

28 See *Pittsburgh Press Co v. Human Relations Comm'n* 413 US 376 (1973).

29 *Board of Trustees of State University of New York (SUNY) v. Fox* 492 US (1989).

30 For general works in the field see F.W. Hondius, *Freedom of Commercial Speech in Europe*, VII *Transnational Data Report* (No. 6, 1985), and A. Lester and D. Pannick, *Advertising and Freedom of Expression in Europe* (Paris, 1984).

31 *New York Times v. Sullivan* 376 US 254 (1964); *Lingens v. Austria*, Judgment of 8 July 1986, Series A, no. 103; (1986) 8 EHRR 209. See generally, D. Elder, "Freedom of Expression and the Law of Defamation: The American Approach to Problems Raised by the Lingens Case" (1986) 35 *ICLQ* 891.

32 *X and the Church of Scientology v. Sweden* (1979) 16 D & R 68.

33 *Barthold v. Federal Republic of Germany*, Judgment of 23 March 1985, Series A, no. 90; (1985) 7 EHRR 383.

34 *Muller v. Switzerland*, Judgment of 24 May 1988, Series A, no. 133; (1991) 13 EHRR 212.

35 *Markt Intern v. Germany*, Judgment of 20 November 1989, Series A, no. 164; (1990) 12 EHRR 161.

36 Id. at para. 26.

37 *Open Door Counselling Ltd and Dublin Well Woman Centre Ltd and Others v. Ireland*, Report of 7 March 1991; (1992) 14 EHRR 131.

38 *AG (SPUC) v. Open Door Counselling and the Dublin Well Woman Centre Ltd* (1988) IR 593.

39 The phenomenon of balancing rights against rights, or rights against state powers, is inherently problematic and perhaps nowhere more so than in the context of the Eighth Amendment. For one thing, there is the question of which rights or other considerations should be factored into the equation. There thus arises the standing possibility of gerry-mandering the range of reckonable factors. There is also the question of deciding how to weigh the competing interests or rights. Some supernorm must be operative (e.g. "justice prudence and charity"). But this merely begs another question; viz, how are the super-norms selected or derived and what meaning is to be extracted from them in particular cases? See generally, T. Aleinikoff, "Constitutional Law in the Age of Balancing" (1987) 96 *Yale LJ* 943.

40 The third set of applicants, *X and Y*, were young women of child-bearing age who claimed that the effect of the injunctions was to deny them of the right to receive information and the right to privacy contrary to Articles 10(1) and 8, respectively. Following its own conclusions with respect to the two clinics the Commission held that X and Y's informational rights were "interfered" with and the justifications proffered were not sufficient. As a finding against Ireland was issued under Article 10 the Commission did not proceed to make a finding in relation to the Article 8 arguments of the two women.

41 See paras. 44–47.

42 *Open Door and Dublin Well Women Centre v. Ireland*, Judgment of 29 October 1992, Series A, no. 246; (1993) 15 EHRR 244.

43 Case 362/88, *GB-INNO-BM v. Confederation du Commerce Luxembourgeois (CCL)*, Judgment of 7 March 1990.

44 *SPUC v. Grogan and Others* [1989] IR 753.

45 Case C–159/90, *SPUC v. Grogan and Others*, [1991] ECR 849.

46 See Amended Proposal for a Council Directive on Advertising for Tobacco Products, OJ 1991, (C–167/3).

Chapter 7 : Economic and Social Rights

7.1 Introduction

1 2nd ed., (London, 1945) at pp. 54–57.

2 First published London, 1792. Innumerable editions since then.

3 *Citizens: A Chronicle of the French Revolution* (London, 1989) at p. 680.

4 *The Harvester Judgment, ex parte, H.V. McKay*, 2 *Commonwealth Arbitration Rep.* 2. For an important study of Higgins's career, see J. Richard, H.B. Higgins: *The Rebel as Judge* (Sydney, 1984).

7.2 EEC Social and Employment Law

1 European Commission, *The Social Challenge* (Brussels, 1991) at p. 2.

2 Id. at p. 1.
3 Article 2 of the directive.
4 Council Directive 92/56/EEC.
5 It should however be noted that a Commission recommendation on equal pay was issued in July 1960, and there was also a resolution of Member State governments in December 1961 envisaging the "phased implementation" of equal pay, to be completed by December 1964.
6 *Defrenne v. Sabena*, Case 43/75 [1976] ECR 455.
7 Article 1 of the directive.
8 Article 4; the Article provides that there must be a means of having such discriminatory provisions declared "null and void" or having them amended.
9 Article 2 of the directive.
10 Case 170/84 *Bilka Kaufhaus GmbH v. Weber von Hartz*.
11 Case 262/88 *Barber v. Guardian Royal Exchange Assurance Group*, [1990] 2 CMLR 513.
12 Case 152/84 *Marshall v. Southampton and South-West Hampshire Area Health Authority*, [1986] 1 CMLR 688; and Case C–188/89 *Foster v. British Gas Plc*, [1990] 2 CMLR 833.
13 Case C–6/90 Francovich v. Italy, decided 19 November 1991.
14 A major example is provided by Case 157/86 *Murphy v. Bord Telecom Eirean*, [1988] ECR 673.
15 Articles 1–3.
16 Article 5.
17 Article 7.
18 Articles 11–14.
19 Articles 17–18.
20 Article 19.
21 COM(89) 568, 29 November 1989.
22 Directive 91/533/EEC.
23 Directive 92/85/EEC; this is based on the health and safety provisions of Article 118A of the EEC Treaty.
24 See *Social Europe*, 1/92 at p. 17.
25 Directive 91/383/EEC.
26 Worker Protection (Regular Part-Time Employees) Act, 1991.
27 *Bilka Kaufhaus* case, supra note 10.

7.3 Procedural Aspects of the European Social Charter

1 A. Eide, "Realisation of Social and Economic Rights and the Minimum Threshold Approach" (1989) 10 *HRLJ* 35; P. Alston, "Implementing Economic, Social and Cultural Rights: The Functions of Reporting Obligations" (1990) *Bull HR* 5.
2 See D.J. Harris, *The European Social Charter* (Charlottesville, Va., 1984); A. Jaspers and L. Betten, *25 Years European Social Charter* (Deventer, 1988); O. Kahn-Freund, "The European Social Charter" in F.G. Jacobs, ed., *European Law and the Individual* (Amsterdam, 1976) 181; P. O'Higgins, "The European Social Charter" in R. Blackburn and J. Taylor, eds., *Human Rights in the 1990s: Legal, Political and Ethical Issues* (London, 1991) 121.
3 P. Alston and G. Quinn, "The Nature and Scope of State Parties' Obligations under the International Covenant on Economic, Social and Cultural Rights" (1987) 9 *HRQ* 156.
4 Although, ironically, one of the first organizations operating in the field of international human rights was the International Labour Organization (ILO).
5 *The European Social Charter: Origin, Operation and Results* (Strasbourg, 1991) at p. 5.
6 D.J. Harris, "A Fresh Impetus for the European Social Charter" (1992) 41 *ICLQ* 659 at p. 659.

7   V. Shrubsall, "The Additional Protocol to the European Social Charter—Employment Rights" (1989) 18 *Industrial LJ* 39.
8   E.g. the right to work (Article 1); the right to just conditions of work (Article 2); and the right to social security (Article 12).
9   Or forty-five numbered paragraphs.
10 The right to work (Article 1); the right to organize (Article 5); the right to bargain collectively (Article 6); the right to social security (Article 12); the right to social and medical assistance (Article 13); the right of the family to social, legal and economic protection (Article 16); and the right of migrant workers and their families to protection and assistance (Article 19).
11 See Articles 4(3) and 8(2) of the Charter and Article 1 of the Protocol.
12 Article 2 of Protocol 2.
13 See generally, I. Boerefijn et al., "Towards a New System of Supervision for the European Social Charter" (1991) 46 *ICJ Rev* 42; J.G.C. Schokkenbroek, "The Results of the Ministerial Conference on the European Social Charter" (1992) 13 *HRLJ* 177.
14 As cited in Harris, supra, note 6 at pp. 659–60.
15 The Committee on the European Social Charter.
16 Both Covenants contain certain standard substantive provisions, e.g. a non-discrimination provision, as well as a State reporting procedure.
17 The Charter was opened for signature at Turin on 18 October 1961 and entered into force on 26 February 1965.
18 The other Contracting States are: Austria, Belgium, Cyprus, Denmark, Finland, France, Germany, Greece, Iceland, Italy, Luxembourg, Malta, the Netherlands, Norway, Portugal, Spain, Sweden, Turkey, and the United Kingdom.
19 4 November 1992. The States are Finland, the Netherlands and Sweden.
20 See Harris, supra note 6 at pp. 660–61.
21 Id. at p. 661.
22 Id. at p. 660.
23 Norway, Portugal and Sweden. Nine other States signed the Protocol in Turin on 21 October 1991. Belgium, Cyprus, France, Italy, Luxembourg, Malta, the Netherlands, Spain, and the United Kingdom. It has since been signed by Austria, The Czech Republic, Finland, Greece, Hungary, Norway, Portugal, Slovakia and Sweden.
24 See Harris, supra note 2 at p. 200 et seq.
25 Article 25(1).
26 Article 23 provides that each Contracting State shall communicate copies of its reports to such of its national organizations as are members of the international organizations of employers and trade unions to be invited under Article 27(2) to be represented at meetings of the Sub-Committee of the Governmental Social Committee. This latter provision limits the participation of international NGOs to two employers and two trade union organizations.
27 Article 27.
28 Article 28.
29 Article 29.
30 See Boerefijn et al., op cit. at pp. 43–44; Schokkenbroek, op.cit. at p. 177.
31 Boerefijn et al., op.cit. at p. 44.
32 ILO consultation is based on a tripartite system in which NGOs play a full part.
33 See Schokkenbroek, op.cit. at p. 178; see also Harris, supra note 6 at pp. 663–64.
34 Id.
35 Amended Article 25(1) provides for nine as opposed to the existing seven members and introduces further changes regarding the election of members. Amended Article 25(2) limits the possibility of re-election to one occasion. Finally, Article 25(4) emphasises that the members must exist in their individual capacity and may not perform any function incompatible with the requirements of independence, impartiality and availability inherent in their office.

36   Harris, supra note 6 at p. 644.
37   A proposal for the adoption of a resolution by simple majority of the Committee of Ministers was deferred.
38   Amended Article 22(2).
39   Harris, supra note 6 at p. 370.
40   Schokkenbroek, op.cit., at p. 178.
41   Harris, supra note 6, at p. 675.

7.4   Gender as a Human Rights Issue

1   Article 1.
2   Article 1(a) of the Statute of the Council of Europe.
3   Article 1(b) of the Statute.
4   Article 11 of the Statute.
5   A Protocol Amending the European Social Charter which seeks to improve the effectiveness of this system of international supervision was opened for signature on 21 October 1991. It is not yet in force.
6   See, e.g. Article 26 of the International Covenant on Civil and Political Rights and Article 24 of the American Convention on Human Rights.
7   The Seventh Protocol was adopted on 22 November 1984, and entered into force on 1 November 1988. Ireland is not a party to this Protocol.
8   P. van Dijk and G.J.H. van Hoof, *Theory and Practice of the European Convention on Human Rights*, 2nd ed. (Deventer, 1990) p. 515.
9   Application No. 9250/81, *X v. the Netherlands*, admissibility decision of the European Commission of Human Rights, 3 May 1983, 32 D & R 175.
10   Application No. 8042/77, *Hagmann-Husler v. Switzerland*, admissibility decision of the European Commission of Human Rights, 15 December 1977, 12 D & R 202.
11   Application No. 11418/85, *Jolie and others v. Belgium*, admissibility decision of the European Commission of Human rights, 14 December 1986, 47 D & R 243; Commission Report of a friendly settlement, 8 October 1987, 53 D & R 65. See also Application No. 10961/84, *De Mot and others v. Belgium*, 53 D & R 38.
12   *Rasmussen v. Denmark*, Judgment of the European Court of Human Rights, 28 November 1984, Series A, no. 87, (1985) 7 EHRR 371.
13   Application No. 9639/82, *B, R and J v. Federal Republic of Germany*, admissibility decision of the European Commissions of Human Rights, 15 March 1984, 36 D & R 130.
14   Application No. 11468/85, *K v. United Kingdom*, admissibility decision of the European Commission of Human Rights, 15 October 1986, 50 D & R 199. This case ended in a friendly settlement: see European Commission of Human Rights, *Stock-taking on the European Convention on Human Rights*, Supplement 1988, (Strasbourg, 1989) p. 32.
15   Application No. 16969/90, *Keegan v. Ireland*, Report of the Commission, 17 February 1993. See also Application No. 10148/82, *Garcia v. Switzerland*, admissibility decision of the European Commission of Human Rights, 14 March 1985, 42 D & R 98.
16   *Abdulaziz, Cabales and Balkandali v. UK*, Judgment, 28 May 1985, Series A, no. 94; (1985) 7 EHRR 471.
17   A subsequent case ended in a friendly settlement in the wake of the Court's Judgment. See Application No. 10204/82, *Min and others v. United Kingdom*, Report of the European Commission of Human Rights, 7 October 1986, 48 D & R 58.
18   See, e.g. Application No. 10094/82, *G v. Austria*, admissibility decision of the European Commission of Human Rights, 14 May 1984, 38 D & R 84; Application No. 10503/83, *Kleine Staarman v. The Netherlands*, admissibility decision of the Commission 16 May 1985, 42 D & R 162; and Application No 1 10971/84, *Vos v. The Netherlands*, admissibility decision of the Commission, 10 July 1985, 43 D & R 190.
19   Application No. 13580/88, *Schmidt v. Germany*, Report of the Commission, 14 January 1993.

20 See *Feldbrugge v. The Netherlands*, Judgment of the Court, 29 May 1986, Series A, no. 99; (1986) 8 EHRR 425; and *Deumeland v. Germany*, Judgment of the same date, Series A, no. 120; (1986) 8 EHRR 448.

21 *Schuler-Zgraggen v. Switzerland*, Judgment of 24 June 1993.

22 See Application No. 5935/72, *X v. Federal Republic of Germany*, admissibility decision of the European Commission of Human Rights, 30 September 1975, 3 D & R 46; Application No. 7215/75, *X v. United Kingdom*, admissibility decision of the Commission, 7 July 1977, 11 D & R 36, and Commission Report, 12 December 1978, 19 D & R 66; and Application No. 10389/83, *Johnson v. United Kingdom*, admissibility decision of the Commission, 17 July 1986, 47 D & R 72. In the *Dudgeon* Case, the European Court of Human Rights treated this gender aspect of the applicant's complaints together with his main allegation that the penalization of homosexual acts between consenting adult men in private offended against his right to respect for his private life: Court Judgment, 22 October 1981, 4 EHRR 149.

23 Application No. 6959/75, *Bruggemann and Scheuten v. Federal Republic of Germany*, Commission Report, 12 July 1977, 10 D & R 100; and 3 EHRR 244.

24 Application No. 8416/79, *X v. United Kingdom*, admissibility decision, 13 May 1980, 19 D & R 244.

25 Ibid.

26 *Open Door Counselling Ltd and Dublin Well Woman Centre Ltd and Others v. Ireland*, Judgment of 29 October 1992, Series A, no. 246; (1993) 15 EHRR 244.

27 See, e.g. the Judgments of the European Court of Human Rights in *Marckx v. Belgium*, 13 June 1979, Series A, no. 31; (1980) 2 EHRR 330; *Airey v. Ireland*, 9 October 1979, Series A, no. 32; (1980) 2 EHRR 305; *X and Y v. The Netherlands*, 26 March 1985, Series A, no. 91; (1986) 8 EHRR 235; *Abdulaziz, Cabales and Balkandali v. UK*, 28 May 1985, Series A, no. 94; (1985) 7 EHRR 471; *Johnston and others v. Ireland*, 18 December 1986, Series A, no. 112; (1987) 9 EHRR 203; *Rees v. UK*, 17 October 1986, Series A, no. 106; (1987) 9 EHRR 56; *H v. United Kingdom*, 8 July 1987, Series A, no. 120, (1988) 10 EHRR 95; *Gaskin v. UK*, 7 July 1989, Series A, no. 160; (1990) 12 EHRR 36; *Cossey v. UK* 27 September 1990, Series A, no. 184; (1991) 13 EHRR 622.

28 Application No. 11089/84, *Lindsay v. United Kingdom*, admissibility decision of the European Commission of Human Rights, 11 November 1986, 49 D & R 181.

29 *East African Asians v. United Kingdom*, Commission Report, 14 December 1973, (1981) 3 EHRR 76.

30 *Abdulaziz, Cabales and Balkandali v. UK*, Court Judgment of 28 May 1985, para. 91, Series A, no. 94; (1989) 7 EHRR 76.

31 Article 4(3).

32 Article 10(2).

33 Article 8(1).

34 Article 8(2).

35 Article 8(3).

36 Article 17.

37 Article 19(6), as explained in the Appendix to the Charter.

38 Article 8(4)(a).

39 Article 8(4)(b).

40 See *Conclusions* X–2, Committee of Independent Experts of the European Social Charter (Strasbourg, 1988) p. 97.

41 Id.

42 Id. p. 98.

43 Article 1(1).

44 Article 1(2).

45 Article 1(3).

46 Article 1(4).

47 See, e.g. Article 119 of the EEC Treaty and Council Directives 75/117 of 10 February 1975, 76/207 of 9 February 1976, 79/7 of 19 December 1978, and 86/372 of 24 July 1986. There

is extensive case law on the interpretation of these provisions. For a general review and analysis of the EEC law in this area see E. Ellis, *European Community Sex Equality Law* (Oxford, 1991).

48 See, e.g. the Judgments of the ECJ in Case C–177/88, *Dekker v. Stichting Vormingscentrum voor Jong Volwassenen Plus* [1991], IRLR 27 and Case 179/88, *Handels-og Kontorfunktion-erernes Forbund i Danmark*, 8 November 1990. On indirect discrimination against part-time workers (predominantly women), see the judgment of the ECJ in Case C–184/89, *Helga Nimez v. Freie und Hansestadt Hamburg*, 7 February 1991.

7.5 The Status of Property as a Fundamental Human Right

1 For an interesting discussion of the theory behind anti-trust/competition regulations see D. Fidler, "Competition Law and International Relations" (1992) 41 *ICLQ* 563.

2 Indeed, the legal system in such countries is premised, to a large extent, on the existence of private property.

3 See infra.

4 Article 21 of the American Convention on Human Rights provides for a right to property, and a right to compensation if property is expropriated. Article 14 of the African Charter on Human and Peoples' Rights also incorporates a right to property, but it is regarded as an economic right; it is not thought that a right to compensation is incorporated in this right. See U. Umozurike, "The African Charter on Human and People's Rights " (1983) 77 *AJIL* 902.

5 But see Ch. 1 above.

6 Such as Hobbes, Locke and Paine.

7 While individuals have *locus standi* before quasi-judicial bodies, such as the European Commission of Human Rights and UN Human Rights Committee, they do not, as a general rule, have capacity to bring actions before judicial bodies such as the European Court of Human Rights or the International Court of Justice. See further M Schmidt, "UN Human Rights Complaints Procedures" (1992) 34 *ICLQ* 376. One notable exception is the European Court of Justice, although its human rights jurisdiction is somewhat limited; see also Ch. 2 above and M. Reid, *The Impact of Community Law on the Irish Constitution* (ICEL No. 13) (Dublin, 1990).

8 See generally M. McDougal, "Human Rights and World Public Order: Principles of Content and Procedures for Clarifying Community Policies" (1974) 14 *Virginia JIL* 387; R. Bilder, "Rethinking International Human Rights: Some Basic Questions" (1969) 11 *HRJ* 557; R. Higgins, "Reality and Hope in International Human Rights" (1981) 9 *Hofstra L. Rev* 1485; J. Watson, "Legal theory, Efficacy and Validity in the Development of Human Rights Norms in International Law" [1979] *Illinois L Forum* 609; A. d'Amato, "The Concept of Human Rights in International Law" (1982) 82 *Colombia L Rev* 110; L. Henkin, *The Rights of Man Today* (London, 1979).

9 See T. O'Malley, Ch. 1 above.

10 "The International Protection of the Right to Property" in F. Matscher and H. Petzold, eds., *Protecting Human Rights—the European Dimension: Essays in Honour of G.H. Wiarda*, 2nd ed. (Köln, 1990) 565.

11 This point is also made by R. Higgins in "The Taking of Property by the State" (1982) III *Hague Receuil* 176. She also discusses the scope of the concept of property, its origins as a "right" and its treatment in various idealogies.

12 Id. at p. 569.

13 He also defines a hierarchy of rights, including fundamental human rights and ordinary (legal) rights.

14 See, *inter alia*, the declarations on Permanent Sovereignty over Natural Resources UNGA Res 1803 (XVII); the Establishment of a New International Economic Order, UNGA Res A/Res 3201 (S–VI) and the Charter of Economic Rights and Duties of States, UNGA Res A/Res 3281 (XXIX).

15 Op cit. at Ch. 5.
16 See generally R. Lillich, ed., *The Valuation of Nationalised Property in International Law* (Charlottesville, Va., 1975); M. Sornrajah, "Compensation for Expropriation: The Emergence of New Standards" (1979) 13 *JWTL* 108; R. Higgins, op.cit.; C. Greenwood, "State Control in International Law—The Libyan Oil Arbitrations" (1982) 53 *BYIL* 27; O. Schacter, "Compensation for Expropriation" (1984) 78 *AJIL* 121; S. Chatterjee, "The Charter of Economic Rights and Duties of States: An Evaluation after 15 Years" (1991) 40 *ICLQ* 669; C. Amerasinghe, "Issues of Compensation for the Taking of Alien Property in the Light of Recent Cases and Practice" (1992) 41 *ICLQ* 22.
17 Judgment of 8 July 1986, Series A, no. 102; (1986) 8 EHRR 329.
18 Op.cit. at Ch. 5.
19 Id. at p. 362.
20 Judgment of 23 September 1982, Series A, no. 52; (1983) 5 EHRR 35.
21 *Theory and Practice of the European Convention on Human Rights*, 2nd ed. (Deventer, 1990) at p. 460.
22 *Per* the Commission in *Handyside v. UK*, Judgment of 7 December 1976, Series A, no. 24 (1979) 1 EHRR 737, quoted in van Dijk and van Hoof, op.cit.
23 Judgment of 13 June 1979, Series A, no. 31; (1980) 2 EHRR 330.
24 For a criticism of this reasoning, see Higgins, op.cit. at Chs. 4 and 5.
25 At p. 28.
26 Judgment of 21 February 1986, Series A, no. 98; (1986) 8 EHRR 123.
27 (1990) 12 EHRR 87.
28 Judgment of 23 April 1987, Series A, no. 117; (1987) 9 EHRR 464.
29 Judgment of 23 April 1987, Series A, no. 117; (1988) 10 EHRR 231.
30 Judgment of 23 November 1991, Series A, no. 222; (1992) 14 EHRR 319.
31 See [1982] ILRM 165 (reported *sub nom State (Pine Valley Developments Ltd) v. Dublin County Council*).
32 See [1987] ILRM 753 (reported *sub nom Minister for the Environment v. Pine Valley Developments Ltd*).
33 The Court, in common with the Supreme Court, held that the first named defendant did not have a cause of action on the ground that it had suffered no loss, having sold the lands before the planning permission had been nullified by the Supreme Court.
34 The Court's reasoning regarding Article 14 is not only somewhat peculiar, it is also extremely brief (four short paragraphs). Perhaps a more appropriate means of finding a violation would be to have said that although the Irish Constitution required the discriminatory treatment it was contrary to the Convention. Although the Court may be reluctant to make a finding of conflict between the Convention and domestic constitutions (and it understandably wary of encroaching upon a doctrine as fundamental as the separation of powers) it should be noted that it was willing to find such a conflict between the self-same documents in *Open Door Counselling and Others v. Ireland*. Judgment of 29 October 1992, Series A, no. 246; (1993) 15 EIIRR 244, in the far more controversial area of abortion information. In any event, the Irish Government is still faced with the necessity of breaching its own Constitution in order to fulfil its international obligations.
35 In its Article 50 judgment in this case (Series A, no. 246–B) the Court awarded both pecuniary and non-pecuniary damages (the latter amounting to over £42,000) to the applicants, as well as certain costs incurred during the Irish and Strasbourg proceedings. The non-pecuniary damages were awarded to the third applicant alone.
35a Since this article was written, the Court has handed down a decison in *Papamichalopoulos v. Greece*, Judgment of 24 June 1993; Series A, no. 260–B; (1993) 16 EHRR 440, in which it found a violation of the Article.
36 Cases such as *Sporrong and Lonnroth* where the Court has found a violation of Article 1 on its own involve such seemingly arbitrary interferences with property right as to come within the scope of such a clause. For example, in the Irish context, rent restriction legislation was struck down as being unconstitutional on the grounds that it was too burdensome on property owners. The plaintiffs argued that the measures in question were contrary to both Article 40.3 (property) and Article 40.1 (equality). McWilliam J, in the High Court and

O'Higgins C J, for the Supreme Court, both concentrate on the property aspect of the case, referring only briefly to the plaintiffs' arguments in relation to equality. However, it could be argued that the relevant legislation would have been said to be unconstitutional under the provisions of Article 40.1, standing on its own (see *Blake v. AG* [1982] IR 117).

Chapter 8 :   Children

8.1   Introduction

1   *Airey v. Ireland*, Judgment of 9 October 1979, Series A, no. 32; (1980) 2 EHRR 305.
2   The Commission had ruled that there was a violation of Article 6 of the Convention and that there was no need to consider the application of Article 8. The Court, however, found that there had been a violation of Article 8. A scheme of civil legal aid and advice was subsequently introduced in Ireland.
3   For example *Dudgeon v. UK*, Judgment of 22 October 1981, Series A, no. 45; (1982) 4 EHRR 149; *Modinos v. Cyprus*, Series A, no. 259.
4   *Norris v. Ireland*, Judgment of 26 October 1988, Series A, no. 142; (1991) 13 EHRR 186. See J. Kingston, "Sex and Sexuality under the European Convention on Human Rights", Ch. 5 above.
5   A complaint was made in relation to non-implementation by the Irish Council for Civil Liberties to the Council of Europe: *Irish Times*, 12 March 1990, p. 10.
6   *Van Oosterwijck v. Belgium*, Judgment of 6 November 1980, Series A, no. 40; (1981) 3 EHRR 557. The Commission had determined that there was a breach of Article 8.
7   *Rees v. UK*, Judgment of 17 October 1986, Series A, no. 106; (1987) 9 EHRR 56.
8   *Cossey v. UK*, Judgment of 27 September 1990, Series A, no. 184; (1991) 13 EHRR 622.
9   P. 15 of the judgment of the Court.
10   P. 16 of the judgment of the Court.
11   *B v. France*, Judgment of 25 March 1992, Series A, no. 232–C (1993) 16 EHRR 1.
12   Reports 1980 and 1979, respectively.
13   *Murray and Murray v. Ireland*, Supreme Court, unreported, 27 May 1991.
14   *Pok Sun Shum v. Ireland* [1986] ILRM 593 and *Fajujonu v. Minister for Justice* [1990] 2 IR 151.
15   *Berrehab v. The Netherlands*, Judgment of 21 June 1988, Series A, no. 138; (1989) 11 EHRR 322.
16   *Beldjoudi v. France*, Judgment of 26 March 1992, Series A, no. 234-A; (1992) 14 EHRR 801.
17   Supra note 14, *Fajujonu v. Minister for Justice*.
18   *Johnston v. Ireland*, Judgment of 18 December 1986, Series A, no. 112; (1987) 9 EHRR 203.
19   *F v. Switzerland*, Judgment of 18 December 1987, Series A, no. 128; (1988) 10 EHRR 411.
20   *Keegan v. Ireland*, Application No. 16969/90, Commission Report adopted on 17 February 1993.
21   Status of Children Act, 1987.
22   *O, H, W, R and B v. UK*, Judgments of 8 July 1987, Series A, nos. 120 & 121; (1988) 10 EHRR 82, 95, 29, 74, 87. See also *McMichael v. UK*, Application No. 16424/90.
23   *Olsson v. Sweden*, Judgment of 24 March 1988, Series A, no. 130; (1989) 11 EHRR 259. *Eriksson v. Sweden*, Judgment of 22 June 1989, Series A, no. 156; (1990) 12 EHRR 183.

8.2   Juvenile Justice

1   The Law Reform Commission is the most recent body to express this view: *Consultation Paper on Sentencing* (Dublin, 1993) at p. 45.
2   For an account of this phenomenon, see T.J. Bernard, *The Cycle of Juvenile Justice* (Oxford, 1993) esp. at Ch. 3.
3   *Wild Kids* (Harrisburg, 1967) at p. 31.

4 Quoted in Bernard, op. cit. at p. 31.

5 On the fiftieth anniversary of the Children Act, 1908, Lord Samuel who had introduced it in the House of Commons lamented the current prevalence of "shocking individual crimes of cruelty and violence". "Children and Crime: Fifty years of Juvenile Courts" *Sunday Times*, March 1958).

6 Quoted in L. Radzinowicz and R. Hood, *The Emergence of Penal Policy in Victorian and Edwardian England* (Oxford, 1990) at p. 136.

7 G.F. Vito and D.G. Wilson, *The American Juvenile Justice System* (New York and London, 1985); P. Aries, *Centuries of Childhood* (London, 1962).

8 For a short account of this phenomenon as it related to juvenile crime, see T. Morris, *Crime and Criminal Justice since 1945* (Oxford, 1989) at pp. 93–95. For a more extensive account see D.M. Downes, *The Delinquent Solution* (London, 1966).

9 S. Cohen, *Folk Devils and Moral Panics: the Creation of Mods and Rockers* (Oxford, 1980).

10 Articles 40.3 and 43.

11 D.J. West, *Delinquency* (London, 1982) at p. 142.

12 *Juvenile Crime: Its Causes and Remedies* (Dublin, 1992) at p. 49.

13 Source: Garda Commissioner, *Report on Crime 1989, 1990 and 1991*.

14 This is a remarkable decrease, but there has been a continuing decrease in the number of recorded offences against the person in recent years from 2,035 in 1987 to 1,435 in 1991.

15 In 1989, 35,395 offences against property with violence were recorded compared with 40,676 in 1991. The number of larcenies recorded was 49,223 in 1989 and 51,990 in 1991.

16 P. Parry, "Juveniles" in E. Stockdale and S. Casale, eds., *Justice under Stress* (London, 1992) 210, at p. 211.

17 Prison Reform Trust, *Trends in Juvenile Crime and Punishment* (London, 1993) at p. 1.

18 To these, some writers such as A. Rutherford (*Growing Out of Crime: The New Era*, 2nd ed. (Winchester, 1992)) would add a third, the treatment model, based on the idea of delinquency as an illness. But since the legal and social consequences of this approach are largely the same as the welfare model, it will not be treated separately here.

19 N. Naffine, "Children in the Children's Court: Can there be Rights Without a Remedy" in P. Aston, S. Parker and J.A. Seymour, eds., *Children, Rights and the Law* (Oxford, 1992) 76 at p. 77.

20 S. Fox, "The Reform of Juvenile Justice: The Child's Right to Punishment" (1974) 25 *Juvenile Justice* 2.

21 See Weitsheit and Alexander, "Juvenile Justice Philosophy and the Demise of *Parens Patriae*" (December 1988) *Federal Probation*, 56.

22 G.B. Curtis, "The Checkered Career of *Parens Patriae*: The State as Parent or Tyrant" (1976) 25 *De Paul Law Review* 895.

23 J.W. Mack, "The Juvenile Court" (1909) 23 *Harvard Law Review* 104, at pp. 119–120.

24 B. Hudson, *Justice through Punishment: A Critique of the 'Justice' Model of Corrections* (London, 1987) 134.

25 This is dealt with further under "Decarceration" below.

26 R.J. Harris, "Towards Just Welfare" (1985) 25 *British Journal of Criminology* 31.

27 See below.

28 Status offences may not be, strictly speaking, criminal but they can attract the same consequences as findings of delinquency, including institutional commitment. See S. Fox, Juvenile Courts, 3rd ed. (St Paul, Minn., 1984) at pp. 41–44.

29 *Monagle v. Donegal County Council* [1961] Ir Jur Rep 37; *R v. Coulburn* (1988) 87 Cr App R 309. For a detailed account of the Irish law which has developed mainly in the context of claims for malicious damage, see W.N. Osborough, "Rebutting the Presumption of Doli Incapax" (1975) Ir Jur 48.

30 *Little v. State* 261 Ark 859, 554 SW 2nd 312 at p. 321 (1977).

31 Boys under fourteen could, however, be convicted of aiding and abetting one of these offences or of indecent assault (now sexual assault).

32   A good account of the development of this aspect of law will be found in *State v. Monahan* 15 NJ 34, 104 A 2d 21 (1954).
33   Child and Young Persons Act, 1969, section 16.
34   In Norway, for example, the age was raised from fourteen to fifteen years at the beginning of 1990; see Allen, "Responding to Youth Crime in Norway: Suggestions for England and Wales" (1993) 32 *Howard J Crim Jus* 99 at p. 100.
35   *Report of Committee of Reformatories and Industrial Schools* Prl 1342 (1970).
36   Prl 9345 (1980).
37   *Juvenile Crime: Its Causes and Remedies* (1992) at pp. 40–41.
38   H. Jones, *Crime and the Penal System*, 2nd ed. (London, 1962). It is unlikely, however, that many nowadays would agree with his contention that the rate of maturity may be influenced by climate, leading him to suggest that the Italians mature more quickly than the British. This would leave little hope for the Irish!
39   Section 100. See the comments of Stewart, "Young Offenders: Children and the Criminal Law" (1976) *ILTSJ* 279 at p. 298.
40   Edwin Lemert, a strong proponent of diversion in the United States in the early 1970's described diversion as a "process whereby problems dealt with in a context of delinquency and official action will be defined and handled by other means"—*Instead of Court: Diversion in Juvenile Justice* (Rockville, Maryland, 1971).
41   There is little formal information on the scheme. A brief description of it, with some statistics will be found in the annual *Report on Crime* of the Garda Commissioner. It is also described briefly in the Department of Foreign Affairs, *The International Covenant on Civil and Political Rights: First Report By Ireland*, P.27876/1 (Dublin, 1992) at pp. 53–54. For an older account, see P. Shanley, "The Formal Cautioning of Juvenile Offenders" (1970) *Irish Jurist* (n.s.) 68.
42   Cautioning is also widely used in England. In 1979, fifty percent of juveniles convicted or cautioned for indictable offences were cautioned; by 1990 this figure had increased to seventy-five percent for males and eighty-nine percent for females. A recent Home Office study showed that eighty-five percent of those cautioned do not re-offend within two years. See: Prison Reform Trust, *Trends in Juvenile Crime and Punishment* (London, 1993).
43   For an account of similar English programmes and some criticisms of them see D. Robins, *Sport as Prevention: The Role of Sport in Crime Prevention Programmes Aimed at Young People* (Oxford, 1990) esp. at pp. 43–54.
44   On the concept of net-widening in the context of community-based sentences, see S. Cohen, *Visions of Social Control* (Cambridge, 1985).
45   See J.A. Ditchfield, *Police Cautioning in England and Wales*, Home Office Research Study No. 37 (London, 1976) and Hudson, op.cit. at p. 144–148.
46   Section 4(7)(a) and (b).
47   Pl. 5831 (1988). It stated (at p. 37) that "about one in six of the cases with which the Board dealt during the year involved children or juveniles and it would appear that the standards that should apply in dealing with such cases are not universally appreciated within the Force".
48   [1976] IR 325.
49   *Haley v. Ohio* 332 US 596 at p. 601 (1948).
50   *Gault v. US* 1 at p. 28 (1967).
51   [1966] IR 379.
52   397 US 358 (1970).
53   Id. at p. 367.
54   Criminal Justice (Community Service) Act, 1983.
55   But they are explained with admirable clarity by M. Ring, "Custodial Treatment for Young Offenders" (1991) 1 *Irish Criminal Law Journal* 59.
56   Annual Statistical Report of Department of Education.
57   The distinction between penal servitude and imprisonment is now an anachronism which

the present Government intends, it appears, to abolish. There is, in practice, no difference in custodial regime between the two forms of sentence.

58 *DPP v. X*, Supreme Court, unreported, 18 Nov 1992.
59 [1977] IR 193.
60 [1979] ILRM 109.
61 Id. at p. 112.
62 *Ex tempore* judgment, 11 Feb 1991 (Finlay C J, Johnson and Lavan J J) summarized in R. Byrne and W. Binchy, *Annual Review of Irish Law 1991* (Dublin, 1993) at p. 183.
63 [1991] 1 IR 373.
64 Id. at p. 376.
65 Id. at p. 377.
66 Rules for the Government of Prisons (S R & O No. 320 of 1947).
67 See editor's note attached to judgment [1991] 1 IR 378.
68 It had not, at that time, ratified the Convention on the Rights of the Child, but has since done so.
69 Op. cit. at p. 49.
70 Annexed to Resolution 40/33.
71 Resolution 45/112.
72 Resolution 45/113.
73 A great deal has been written on this Convention. The following are particularly invaluable: D. McGoldrick, "The United Nations Convention on the Rights of the Child" (1991) 5 *Int J Law* 132. *The Rights of the Child: Irish Perspectives on the UN Convention* published by the Council for Social Welfare (Dublin, 1991) contains a series of short essays on aspects of child care in the light of the Convention.
74 A. Cox, *The Constitution and the Court* (Boston, 1987) 331.
75 Proclamation of Easter 1916.
76 *H C Deb* Vol 183, col 1435–6. The other principles were (i) keeping the child offender separate from the adult offender and (ii) abolishing the imprisonment of children.
77 Cmnd 965 (London: HMSO, 1990).
78 John Patten in Home Office Press Notice 30 March 1989. See M. Wasik and R.D. Taylor, *Blackstone's Guide to the Criminal Justice Act 1991* (London, 1991) 81–83.
79 P. Ely and C. Stanley, *The French Alternative: Delinquency Prevention and Child Protection in France*. An occasional paper by NACRO (London, 1990).
80 A. Morris and G. Maxwell, "Youth Justice in New Zealand: A New Paradigm for Making Decisions about Children and Young People who Commit Offences" (December, 1992) 9 *Commonwealth Judicial Journal* 14.
81 Article 41 of the Constitution states that the family is "the natural, primary and fundamental unit group of Society, and as a moral institution, possessing inalienable and imprescriptible rights antecedent and superior to all positive law".
82 See *Some of Our children: A Report on the Residential Care of the Deprived child in Ireland* by London branch of the study group Tuaimim. This was founded in 1954 to provide a forum for the impartial discussion of ideas and policies.
83 Supra, fn. 35.
84 For a vivid account of Artane Industrial School (Dublin) when it contained 900 boys, see P. Touher, *Fear of the Collar* (Dublin, 1991). Patrick Galvin's *Song for a Raggy Boy* (Dublin, 1991) describes life in a reformatory school in the early 1940s.
85 See H. Burke et al., *Youth and Justice; Young Offenders in Ireland* (Dublin, 1981) 89. For an account of the probation service in the mid-1940s, see Fahy, "Probation of Offenders" (November 1943) 62 *Hermathena* 61.
86 Burke, et al., op. cit.
87 Mitchell, *A Report on the Law and Procedures Regarding the Prosecution and Disposal of Young Offenders* (Dublin, 1977).
88 *Tyrer v. UK*, Judgment of 25 April 1978, Series A, no. 26; (1980) 2 EHRR 1.

8.3 Children's Rights Intercountry Adoption

1   Approximately thirty-eight thousand Korean children were adopted by families in the US between 1953 and 1981, and about three thousand Vietnamese children between 1963 and 1976.

2   According to figures supplied by the Romanian Committee for Adoption, there were seven thousand three hundred and eight international adoptions of Romanian children in 1991, two hundred and ninety-four of which were to Ireland. For a description of some of the problems encountered, see Defence for Children International and International Social Service, *Romania, The Adoption of Romanian Children by Foreigners* (Geneva, 1991).

3   Two hundred and seventy nine Albanian children were adopted by foreigners between the beginning of 1991, following the opening of Albania's borders, and March 1992. See UNICEF et al., *Regulating Intercountry Adoption from Albania* (Geneva, 1992).

4   UNICEF estimates that there are about one hundred and fifty-five million children under five in the developing countries living in absolute poverty. UNICEF, *State of the World's Children* (Geneva, 1991). According to D. Ngbonzinza, Secretary General of International Social Service, there exist about one hundred million abandoned children: "Moral and Political Issues facing Relinquishing Countries" (1991) 15 *Adoption and Fostering* 75.

5   See. e.g. M.J. Becker, "The Pressure to Abandon" (1988) 5 *International Child Rights Monitor* (Defence for Children International).

6   The background to the development of this situation of supply and demand is well documented in J.H.A. van Loon, *Report on Intercountry Adoption* (1990), Hague Conference on Private International Law, Part III.

7   See, e.g. Defence for Children International, *Protecting Children's Rights in International Adoptions* (Geneva, 1989), and Van Loon, op. cit. Part III, E. See also the reports concerning Romania and Albania, supra, notes 1 and 2.

8   Adopted by the General Assembly on 20 November 1989.

9   The Preliminary Draft of this Convention was drawn up by the Special Commission on Intercountry Adoption in February 1992.

10   See Van Loon, op. cit. at pp. 174–179.

11   See, in particular, the Inter-American Convention on Conflict of Laws Concerning the Adoption of Minors (La Paz), 1984.

12   All references are to the Preliminary Draft Convention on International Co-Operation and Protection of Children in Respect of Inter-country Adoption, February 1992.

13   See the Report of M.G. Parra Aranguren on the Preliminary Draft Convention, Hague Conference on Private International Law, September 1992.

14   See Memorandum concerning the preparation of a new Convention on international co-operation and protection of children in respect of inter-country adoption, drawn up by the Permanent Bureau in November 1989.

15   Article 1.

16   The responsibilities are placed on "competent authorities" of the respective States, an expression which is nowhere defined.

17   Article 5.

18   Article 6.

19   Article 4.

20   Article 7.

21   Opened for signature on 25 October 1980.

22   Chapter III.

23   Article 10.

24   Article 21. See below.

25   Chapter 4.

26   Article 20.

27   Article 24. See below.

28 Article 23. See below.
29 "Convinced that the family, as the fundamental group of society and the natural environment for the growth and well-being of all its members and particularly children, should be afforded the necessary protection and assistance so that it can fully assume its responsibilities within the community . . . "
30 Article 20, para. 2.
31 Article 20, para. 3.
32 See Becker, op. cit. in which the problems are described in the context of Brazil.
33 Defence for Children International, *Recommendations of a Regional Expert Meeting on Protecting Children's Rights in Intercountry Adoptions and Preventing Trafficking and Sale of Children* (Manila, 1992).
34 W. Duncan, "Regulating Intercountry Adoption—an International Perspective" Ch. 3 in A. Bainham and D. Pearl, eds., *Frontiers of Family Law* (London, 1993).
35 For example the United Kingdom, Ireland and Israel.
36 Nor will the welfare of the child necessarily be the paramount consideration in determining custody of a child where an adoption order is found to be invalid. See, e.g. the judgment of the Supreme Court of Israel in *Re Return of Adopted Child to Brazil*, 16 June 1988, and the Irish case *M v. An Bord Uchtála* [1977] IR 287.
37 Article 5, para. b. The principle is also expressed in the preamble which recognizes the potential benefit of inter-country adoption for a child "who cannot in any suitable manner be cared for in his or her country of origin".
38 A practice of this kind, designed to ensure that placing agencies give adequate consideration to the possibilities of domestic adoption, recently ceased in India.
39 One of the objections to "independent" adoptions (in the sense of not being arranged through an approved agency) is the concern that insufficient attention may be paid to the possible alternatives to adoption.
40 "States Parties shall respect and ensure the rights set forth in the present Convention to each child within their jurisdiction without discrimination of any kind, irrespective of the child's or his or her parent's or legal guardian's race, colour, sex, language, religion, political or other opinion, national, ethnic or social origin, property, disability, birth or other status".
41 The Irish Adoption Act, 1991, which for the first time in Irish law provides for the recognition of foreign adoption orders granted to Irish residents, does not make a probation period a condition of recognition.
42 E.g. Colombia and el Salvador.
43 For the same reason, such countries wish to retain jurisdiction to make the order before the child leaves. This will be possible under the draft Convention, which is neutral on the question of jurisdiction.
44 The basic anomaly is that, pending completion of the probationary period, the child's status is different in the receiving country and the country of origin. Consider the problems arising should the placement come to an end as a result of the deaths of the (prospective?) adopters.
45 It is of note that the simple adoptions appear not to be entitled to recognition under the Irish Adoption Act, 1991. Section 1(b) provides that, in order to qualify under the Act, a foreign adoption must have "essentially the same legal effect as respects the termination and creation of parental rights and duties with respect to the child in the place where it was effected as an adoption . . . [made in Ireland]".
46 Influenced by Article 5 of the European Convention on the Adoption of Children, 1967.
47 E.g. the circumstances in which the consent of the natural father of a child born out of wedlock is required differ between different countries, as do the rules relating to dispensing with consent.
48 At present, before granting an adoption in Ireland, the Adoption Board must apply the Irish requirements to the consents of natural parents obtained abroad. The 1991 Act allows

recognition of a foreign adoption in circumstances where the consent requirements of the foreign country have been met.

49 For further discussion of the matter, see Defence for Children International et al., *Preliminary Findings of a Joint Investigation on Independent Intercountry Adoptions* (1991) and Duncan in Bainham and Pearl, op.cit.

50 Article 21.

51 Islamic countries, it appears, object to the Convention for another reason. Where a Muslim child, who is a national of an Islamic country, is habitually resident in a Contracting State, he or she may be made the subject of an inter-country adoption under the Convention. See Remarks Submitted by the Expert of Egypt to the Special Commission, annexed to the Report of M.G. Parra Aranguren, op. cit.

8.4 Education: Whose Right?

1 Reiterated and codified in binding form in the opening sentence of Article 13(1) of the International Covenant on Economic, Social and Cultural Rights, 1966. The international instruments referred to in this article are found in G. Van Bueren, ed., *Internatonal Documents on Children* (Dordrecht, 1993).

2 See, e.g. *Access to German Minority Schools in Upper Silesia* [1931] PCIJ Rep. Series A, no. 40 at p. 8.

3 Letter from Thomas Jefferson to Joseph Caball, 9 September 1817, in 17 *Writings of Thomas Jefferson* 417.

4 Article 1(a) in Recommendation Concerning Education for International Understanding, Co-operation and Peace and Education Relating to Human Rights and Fundamental Freedoms adopted by the General Conference of the United Nations Educational, Scientific and Cultural Organisation (UNESCO) in 1974. See Van Bueren, supra note 1.

5 I. Szabo, *Cultural Rights* (Leiden, 1974).

6 E.g. most of the provisions in the Convention Against Discrimination in Education are limited to educational institutions and schooling.

7 *Campbell and Cosans v. United Kingdom*, Judgment of 25 February 1982, Series A, no. 48 (1982) 4 EHRR 433.

8 UN Doc E/CN/4/SR 285.

9 Recommendation No. 24 Concerning Education for International Understanding in Human Rights and Fundamental Freedoms.

10 Comments of UNESCO in UN Doc E/CN4/1989/WG1/CRP1.

11 Article 1. The Charter was adopted by the General Conference of UNESCO on 21 November 1978.

12 Articles 13 and 14.

13 Judgment of 23 July 1968, Series A, no. 6; (1979) 1 EHRR 252.

14 *Church of X v. United Kingdom*, Application no. 3798/68. 12 YBK ECHR 306.

15 Id.

16 G. Van Bueren "Child Oriented Justice—An International Challenge for Europe" (1992) 6 *Int'l J Law & Fam* 31.

17 Supra note 2 at p. 19.

18 UN Doc E/CN4/SR227 and see below.

19 UN Doc E/CN4/SR116.

20 UN Doc A/C3/SR1022.

21 UN Doc A/C3/SR1023.

22 UN Doc A/C3/SR1024.

23 UN Doc CCPR/C/40/D 298 (1988).

24 Szabo, op.cit. at p. 8.

25 Consultative Assembly, Preparatory Work on Article 2 of the First Protocol to the Convention.

26 Judgment of 7 December 1976, Series A, no. 23; (1979) 1 EHRR 711.

27 Supra note 7.
28 Supra note 6, at para. 53.
29 R 9/40 HRC 36 at p. 147.
30 Application no. 10491/83; (1988) 10 EHRR 123.
31 *X v. Germany.* Application no. 9411/81.
32 Series B, no. 21, at p. 50.
33 Id.
34 406 US 205.
35 Id. at p. 40.
36 See the approach adopted by the English Courts in cases involving scientology such as *Re B and G* (1977) 7 Fa L 206.
37 Article 2(c).
38 Article 2(a).
39 In July 1981, the United Kingdom Trade Unions Congress and Labour Party issued a plan for private schools which proposed the abolition of private schools, misleadingly called public schools in the UK. Article 5(b) of the Convention Against Discrimination in Education provides: "It is essential to respect the liberty of parents and, where applicable, of legal guardians, firstly to choose for their children institutions other than those maintained by the public authorities and secondly to ensure in a manner consistent with the procedures followed in the State for the application of its legislation, the religious and moral education of the children in conformity with their own convictions; and no persons should be compelled to receive religious instruction inconsistent with his or her conviction". See A. Lester and D. Pannick, *Independent Schools and European Convention on Human Rights— a Joint Opinion* (London, 1982). See also *Pierce v. Society of Sisters* 286 US 510 (1925) where the US Supreme Court upheld a challenge to an Oregon statute requiring all children to attend public (in the true sense) schools.
40 Official report of the 35th Sitting of the Consultative Assembly, 8 December 1951. *Collected Editions,* V at pp. 1229–30.
41 Supra note 13.
42 *Application no. 10476/83 v. Sweden.* Nor does a denial of a place in a single sex selective grammar school, obliging children to attend mixed sex comprehensive schools, amount to a breach. *Applications nos. 10228 and 10229 v. United Kingdom.*
43 *Family H v. United Kingdom* (1984) 37 D & R 105.

Chapter 9 : Refugees

9.1 Introduction

1 R. Plender, "The Legal Protection of Refugees" in R. Blackburn and J. Taylor, eds., *Human Rights for the 1990s: Legal, Political and Ethical Issues* (London, 1991) 49.
2 See L. Heffernan, "In Search of a Human Rights Approach to Refugees" in A. Whelan, ed., *Law and Liberty in Ireland* (Dublin, 1993) 184.
3 See, generally, G. Goodwin-Gill, *The Refugee in International Law* (Oxford, 1985).
4 Article 14(1). In contrast to other provisions in the Declaration, it is doubtful whether these rights have acquired the status of customary international law. See R.B. Lillich, "Civil Rights" in T. Meron, ed., *Human Rights in International Law: Legal and Policy Issues* (Oxford, 1984) 115 at p. 153.
5 But see Article 22(7) of the American Convention on Human Rights, 1969. Articles 12 and 13 of the ICCPR guarantee liberty of movement, freedom of choice of residence and protection from arbitrary expulsion but only in respect of "aliens lawfully within the territory".
6 The principle of *non-refoulement* is embodied in Article 33 of the 1951 Convention which

provides: "No Contracting State shall expel or return a refugee in any manner whatsoever to the frontiers of territories where his life or freedom would be threatened on account of his race, religion, nationality, membership of a particular social group, or political opinion."

7 See *Finucane v. McMahon* [1990] IR 165.
8 Although the UN High Commissioner for Refugees (UNHCR) does have a consultative role in practice, the Convention does not vest the office with a formal function to entertain complaints in individual cases. Nor does UNHCR enjoy the power to make a binding determination as to the State's obligations.
9 *The Irish Times*, 16 June 1993.
10 Judgment of 7 July 1989, Series A, no. 161; (1989) 11 EHRR 439.
11 Id. at p. 478.
12 Judgment of 20 March 1991, Series A, no. 201; (1992) 14 EHRR 1.
13 Para. 70; (1992) 14 EHRR 1 at p. 34.
14 Paras. 74–76; (1992) 14 EHRR 1 at pp. 35–37.
15 Para. 83; (1992) 14 EHRR 1 at p. 37.
16 Judgment of 30 October 1991, Series A, no. 215; (1992) 14 EHRR 248.
17 Para. 108; (1992) 14 EHRR.
18 *Cruz Varas*, supra note 12.
19 *Vilvarajah*, supra note 16. It is certainly feasible that other substantive provisions of the Convention, e.g. Article 5 (liberty) or Article 6 (fair trial) or Articles 2–4 of Protocol 4 (freedom of movement and residence and freedom from expulsion) may be invoked in the future.
20 See P. Dillon-Malone "Individual Remedies and the Strasbourg System in an Irish Context" Ch. 2, above. A more recent application, *Vijayanathan and Pusparajah v. France*, Judgment of 27 August 1992, (75/1991/327/399–400), was declared inadmissible for failure to satisfy the "victim" requirement contained in Article 25.

9.2 Control of Immigration in Irish law

1 The grounds prescribed in Article 5(2) of the Aliens Order, 1946, are (a) that the person is not in a position to support himself; (b) is not in possession of a valid work permit; (c) is suffering from a disease or disability; (d) has been convicted whether in the State or otherwise of an offence punishable by imprisonment for at least one year; (e) is not in possession of a valid Irish visa; (f) is the subject of a deportation order; (g) is subject to a prohibition on entry order; (h) belongs to a class of aliens prohibited from landing by order of the Minister under the Aliens Act, 1935; (i) intends to travel to Great Britain or Northern Ireland while being inadmissible for entry there; (k) having arrived in the State in the course of his employment as a seaman or as a member of the crew of an aircraft has remained in the State without the leave of an immigration officer.
2 Article 4 of the Aliens Order, 1975, provides that an immigrant may be refused leave to land where he is not in possession of a work permit issued to the employer by the Minister for Labour. This provision may be *ultra vires* on two grounds. The proper construction of this Article appears to be that a person arriving with the intention of working may be refused leave to land if the Minister for Labour or one of his subordinates have in their discretion decided that he ought not to be permitted entry for the purposes of working. However, Section 5 provides that the Minister of Justice may "*by order*" prohibit the admission of certain categories of alien. There is a line of Commonwealth authority to the effect that a delegate with a power to enact a prohibition in subordinate legislation must determine the scope of application and substance of the prohibition immediately in the order itself. He may not enact subordinate legislation which makes the determination of the scope of application of the prohibition a matter of discretion. See *Jackson & Co Ltd v. Inspector of Taxes* [1939] NZLR 735. See, also, *Brent Dairy Co v. Milk Cmmr* [1973] SCR 131; see, contra, however, *Ideal Laundry Ltd v. Petone Borough* [1957] NZLR 1038. The effect of the

provision is that entry is determined by the Minister for Labour, not the Minister for Justice. However, legislative power may not be delegated. A further rule is that a Minister may not enact subordinate legislation which leaves the determination of the substantive scope of the prohibition to the discretion of another body. To do that is to pass effective decision-making to another institution and to breach the rule that legislative power may not be delegated. If the legislative instrument is to lawfully permit exercises of discretion by some other institution it must itself prescribe the limits within which that discretion is to be in order to retain the statutory delegate's primary legislative role. See *Hootinas v. Director of Civil Aviation* [1939] NZLR 929; *Geraghty v. Porter* [1917] NZLR 554; and see Aikman (1960) 3 *Vict U Well L Rev* 85. See also *Lavendar v. Minister for Housing and Local Government* [1970] 2 All ER 871.

3 See, Parliamentary debates, 5th series, vol 650, cols 1184, 5 (5 December 1961).
4 See Dáil Debates vol 193, cols 422–23 (21 February 1963).
5 Id.
6 *Crotty v. Ireland* [1987] IR 713; *McGimpsey v. Ireland* [1988] IR 567; [1990] 1 IR 110.
7 Supra note 6.
8 Article 5(2) of the Aliens Order, 1946, as amended in 1975, provides that an immigration officer may refuse an alien leave to land on any one of the prescribed grounds.
9 In *State (Gilliland) v. Governor of Mountjoy Prison* [1987] IR 201, at p. 233, McCarthy J stated " . . . no such [presumption of constitutionality] can apply to a statutory instrument . . . " Compare *H v. Eastern Health Board* [1988] IR 747, and *Osheku v. Ireland* [1986] IR 733.
10 See the notice of refusal framed in precisely those terms reproduced in *Fakih v. Minister for Justice* [1993] ILRM 274.
11 [1956] 2 DLR (2d) 503.
12 *Cityview Press v. An Comhairle Oiliune* [1980] IR 381; *McDaid v. Sheehy* [1991] 1 IR 1.
13 This aspect of the legislative background is discussed in K. Costello, "The Irish Deportation Power" (1990) 12 *DULJ* (n.s.) 81.
14 Dáil Debates, vol 55, cols 109–110 (27 February 1935), Deputy Mcgilligan.
15 See, e.g. *Yakus v. United States* 321 US 414 (1944); *National Cable Television Ass. v. United States* 415 US 336 at p. 341 (1974); *NAACP v. FPC* 425 US 622 at p. 609 (1976). *Mistretta v. United States* 488 US 361 (1989).
16 *Ji Yao Lau v. Minister for Justice*, unreported, High Court, 29 July 1991; *R v. Secretary of State, ex parte Rafiq* [1970] 3 All ER 82.
17 The power to remove following a refusal of leave to land applies only to aliens coming from a place outside the State other than Great Britain or Northern Ireland (Article 5 of the Aliens Order, 1946, as amended). *Fakih v. Minister for Justice*, the High Court, 6 March 1992, involved a removal order which had been made against a group of applicants who were refused leave to land in Hollyhead, had spent several days in detention in the United Kingdom and had then arrived by ferry back in Ireland. They contended that they had come from Great Britain and accordingly were not liable to be subjected to a removal order. O'Hanlon J conceding that he was giving a special meaning to the phrase "coming from a place outside the state other than Great Britian or Northern Ireland" ruled that "the fact that they succeeded in getting foot in the United Kingdom before being refused entry is not, in my opinion, sufficient to convert their status into the status of aliens arriving from Great Britain or Northern Ireland". In effect, the High Court appeared to add to the phrase "coming from a place outside the State other than Great Britain or Northern Ireland", the further phrase, "and not being unlawfully present in Great Britain or Northern Ireland", and in doing so the Court was plugging an obvious loophole. Another loophole in the common travel arrangement which might have been closed as a result of the judgment involves persons arriving from the United Kingdom where they have been lawfully present but who have previously been refused entry to Ireland. The problem here is the issue of the High Court's jurisdiction to add words to a statutory provision, however much such

words might be within the policy of the provision. Compare the very direct statement by Finlay C J in *McGrath v. McDermott* [1988] IR 258 at p. 276: "The function of the courts in interpreting a statute of the Oireachtas is, however, solely confined to ascertaining the true meaning of each statutory provision . . . The courts have not got a function to add or delete from express statutory provisions so as to achieve objectives which to the courts appear desirable"; and see *AG v. Sheehy* [1990] 1 IR 70. These potential abuses in the common travel area agreement were legislatively stemmed in the United Kingdom by the Immigration (Control of Entry through Republic of Ireland) Order, 1972 (SI 1972/161) and the Immigration (Control of Entry through Republic of Ireland (Amendment)) Order, 1979 (SI 1979/730).

18   See *Al-Yatim v. Minister for Justice*, *Irish Times*, 6 December 1990, where a deportation order was prohibited on the grounds of delay and the inability of the authorities to find a place willing to receive the deportee; and *Kajli and Nisli v. Minister for Justice*, unreported, High Court, 21 August 1992, where Barr J found that the Department had acted unreasonably in making a removal order without ascertaining whether there was a place willing to receive the applicants, and on the ground that the voyage might entail unreasonable hardship to the applicants.

19   See *R v. Chiswick Police Station, ex parte Sacksteder* [1918] 1 KB 578; *R v. Secretary of State, ex parte Odalheinde* [1991] AC 254.

20   That doctrine has been applied to deportation orders removal: *R v. Home Secretary, ex parte Bressler* [1924] All ER 668. In *Kajli and Nisli*, supra, the order was held to have failed to display jurisdiction in not specifying the destination to which the applicants were to be removed. And see, analogously, *State (Furlong) v. Kelly* [1971] IR 132 and *State (Holmes) v. Furlong* [1967] IR 210, cases which deal with the requirements of showing jurisdiction on extradition orders.

21   *McEldowney v. Forde* [1971] AC 632 at p. 651.

22   The power to direct the removal of overstayers in Article 5(4) of the Aliens Order, 1946, seems, however, possibly through oversight, to have been deleted by the Aliens Order, 1975.

23   Deportation was the technique used in the case of immigrant overstayers not apparently otherwise non-conducive to the public good in *Fajojuno v. Minister for Justice* [1990] 2 IR 151; *Gutrani v. Minister for Justice*, unreported, Supreme Court, 2 July 1992. See, however, *R v. IAT, ex parte Patel* [1988] AC 910 where the House of Lords decided that immigration offences involving fraud could justify a finding that presence is no longer "conducive to the public good" and, thus, a deportation order. To that extent the two procedures may not be mutually exclusive.

24   See, e.g. *Gutrani v. Minister for Justice*, 2 October 1991, where an interim injunction was granted by Denham J at 11 pm in her own residence; Gutrani's representations then travelled with the order to Dublin airport to interrupt the flight on which Gutrani was to be removed. See also *Boateng v. Minister for Justice*, 15 February 1992, where Blayney J granted an interim injunction and an order for an inquiry under Article 40.4 on a Saturday afternoon at his own home.

25   See Dáil Debates vol 396, col 569 (27 March 1990).

26   [1965] IR 70.

27   At p. 124.

28   In *Re Mathews* [1860] 12 ICLR 233.

29   The High Court was satisfied that it was in fact impossible to produce that applicant who was then on remand in Brixton Prison. However, a majority of the Supreme Court indicated that the Irish authorities might not have exhausted the possibilities of securing Quinn's return. Having regard to the friendly understanding between the two States, it might have been possible to prevail upon the prosecuting authorities in England to suspend the prosecution and release Quinn for his appearance in Dublin. See the remarks of Kingsmill Moore J, Walsh J and Ó Dálaigh C J in the *Irish Times*, 26 June 1964. This point was not, however, pursued in the written judgments.

30 See, e.g. Dáil Debates, vol 72, col 662 (14 January 1959): concern relating to the manner of refusal of a refugee application by a Polish fisherman; Dáil Debates, vol 351, col 386 (2 February 1971): disquiet re refusal of leave to land to a Nigerian with a valid refugee's travel document; and Dáil Debates, vol 193, col 1004 (1 March 1962) and Dáil Debates, vol 338, col 127 (4 November 1982): instances where the Minister for Justice refused to explain the procedures for dealing with asylum requests.

31 [1993] ILRM 274.

32 This ten-point procedure is reproduced in the *Fakih* judgment.

33 [1983] 2 AC 629.

34 [1983] 2 AC at p. 638 [1983] 2 AC 629 at p. 638.

35 Supreme Court, unreported, 2 July 1992.

36 At p. 6 of the unreported judgment.

37 See G.W. Hogan and D.G. Morgan, *Administrative Law in Ireland*, 2nd ed. (London, 1991) at p. 682.

38 See *Latchford v. Minister for Industry and Commerce* [1950] IR 33; *R v. Criminal Injuries Compensation Tribunal, ex parte Lain* [1967] 2 QB 864; Wade "Note" (1967) 83 *LQR 486*; The rule is well established in the United States; see, e.g. *Vitarelli v. Seaton* 359 US 535 (1959); *Sevice v. Dulles* 354 US 303 (1957).

39 At p. 19 of the unreported judgment of 6 March 1992.

40 See *Brind v. Secretary of State for the Home Department* [1991] 1 AC 696.

41 *Dublin Corporation v. McGrath* [1978] ILRM 208; Hogan and Morgan, op. cit. at p. 676.

42 [1990] IR 165.

43 See J.M. Kelly, *The Irish Constitution*, 2nd ed. (Dublin, 1984) at p. 533.

9.3. Immigration Law and Refugees

1 No. 14 of 1935.

2 No. 23 of 1986.

3 SI 395/1946.

4 SI 128/1975.

5 *Fakih v. Minister for Justice* [1993] ILRM 274; *Gutrani v. Minister for Justice*, Supreme Court, unreported, 2 July 1992. See K. Costello, "Some Issues in the Control of Immigration in Irish Law" above.

9.4 European Integration and Refugees

1 "According to traditional international law, the right of asylum is the right of sovereign States to grant asylum within their territory and at their discretion". See P. Weis, "Territorial Asylum" (1966) *Ind JIL* 173 at p. 174.

2 " . . . [t]he power of the state to grant asylum is incidental to the sovereignty of the state": I. de Lupis, *International Law and the Independent State*, 2nd ed. (Aldershot, 1987) at p. 134.

3 Article 14 of the Universal Declaration of Human Rights provides:

  (1) Everyone has the right to seek and enjoy in other countries asylum from persecution.

  (2) This right may not be invoked in the case of persecutions genuinely arising from non-political crimes or from acts contrary to the purposes and principles of the United Nations.

4 "It is accepted without question that the right to enjoy asylum means only that when a State does grant asylum to a refugee—which it is never legally obliged to do—this must be respected by other states. As far as human rights are concerned, therefore, Article 14 does not mark any advance on the previous position": O Kimminich, "The Present International Law of Asylum" (1985) 32 *Law & State* 25 at p. 27.

5 For a thorough examination of the scope and application of the principle of *non-refoulement*

in refugee law, see: G. Goodwin-Gill, *The Refugee in International Law* (Oxford, 1983) at pp. 69–100.

6   Article 33(2) provides: "The benefit of the present provision may not, however, be claimed by a refugee whom there are reasonable grounds for regarding as a danger to the security of the country in which he is residing, or who, having been convicted by a final judgment of a particularly serious crime, constitutes a danger to the community of that country".

7   R. Sexton, "Political Refugees, *Non-Refoulement* and State Practice: A Comparative Study" (1985) 18 *Vand J IL* 731 at p. 739.

8   G. Goodwin-Gill, "Entry and Exclusion of Refugees: The Obligations of States and the Protective Functions of the Office of the United Nations High Commissioner for Refugees" (1982) *Mich YB IL Stud.* 291 at p. 294.

9   See generally: Amnesty International, "Europe: Human Rights and the Need for a Fair Asylum Policy" (AI Index: Eur 01/03/91); S. Egan and A. Storey, "European Asylum Policy: A Fortress Under Construction" (1992) *Trocaire Dev. Rev.* 49; and H. Meijers, "Refugees in Western Europe: Schengen Affects the Entire Refugee Law" (1990) 2 IJRL 428.

10 Amnesty International, op cit. at p. 9.

11 See A. Kuijer, "The Schengen Implementation Agreement: Criticism and Alternatives" (Unpublished lecture, Rotterdam, 29 January 1992); and B. Eagar, "Refugee Issues in Europe: Recent Developments and Ireland's Response" (Unpublished lecture, Irish Refugee Council Meeting, 28 March, 1992).

12 Title 2, Ch. 3 entitled "Visas".

13 Article 26(a).

14 Article 29(3). See also Article 28.

15 Article 30.

16 Article 14.

17 See Egan and Storey, op. cit.

18 This provision leaves open the possibility of an abuse of power on the part of the Council insofar as there is no provision for any element of supervision by the European parliament with respect to the implementation of this provision. Id. at p. 61.

19 Supra, note 11.

20 "Any restriction on entry which obstructs the flight to safety of individuals in need of protection increases the danger that such people will be subjected to human rights violations, undermines the international system for protection of refugees, and prevents effective exercise of the right to seek and enjoy asylum which is guaranteed in Article 14 of the Universal Declaration of Human Rights". See Amnesty International, op. cit. at p. 7 and Meijers, op. cit. at p. 434.

21 Amnesty International, op. cit.

INDEX